# THE FOUNDATIONS OF EUROPEAN COMMUNITY LAW

## AN INTRODUCTION TO THE CONSTITUTIONAL AND ADMINISTRATIVE LAW OF THE EUROPEAN COMMUNITY



by

TC HARTLEY

*Professor of Law Emeritus*

*London School of Economics and Political Science*

*Sixth Edition*

OXFORD
UNIVERSITY PRESS
2007

Great Clarendon Street, Oxford OX2 6DP

Oxford University Press is a department of the University of Oxford.
It furthers the University's objective of excellence in research, scholarship,
and education by publishing worldwide in

Oxford New York

Auckland Cape Town Dar es Salaam Hong Kong Karachi
Kuala Lumpur Madrid Melbourne Mexico City Nairobi
New Delhi Shanghai Taipei Toronto

With offices in

Argentina Austria Brazil Chile Czech Republic France Greece
Guatemala Hungary Italy Japan Poland Portugal Singapore
South Korea Switzerland Thailand Turkey Ukraine Vietnam

Oxford is a registered trade mark of Oxford University Press
in the UK and in certain other countries

Published in the United States
by Oxford University Press Inc., New York



First published 1981



British Library Cataloguing in Publication Data
Data available

Library of Congress Cataloging in Publication Data
Data available

Typeset by Newgen Imaging Systems (P) Ltd, Chennai, India
Printed in Great Britain
on acid-free paper by
Ashford Colour Press Ltd, Gosport, Hampshire

ISBN 978–0–19–929035–2

# PREFACE

My aim in this book is to provide, for the reader with no previous knowledge, a clear and easily understood account of the principles of the constitutional and administrative law of the European Community. The logical place to start is with the institutions: the first Part deals with them and is more descriptive than analytical. The second and third Parts cover the Community legal system and the major constitutional issues: they are analytical, though not excessively technical. The final Part takes us into the realm of administrative law and remedies: it is more legal in character and explains some of the things a lawyer needs to know if he is contemplating litigation in the European Court or the Court of First Instance. My hope is that each Part will prepare the ground for the next so that a balanced understanding of the whole subject will be possible.

There have been a number of developments since the previous edition. The Treaty of Nice has entered into force. The number of Member States has almost doubled, increasing from fifteen to twenty-seven: ten States joined in 2004 and two more in 2007. This has required changes in the institutional structure of the Community.

The most important event turned out to be a non-event: the much-heralded Constitution for Europe was adopted by a Constitutional Convention, but rejected by the voters of France and the Netherlands. It now seems dead. There has been talk of salvaging parts of it; any developments in this regard will be covered in the Online Resource Centre associated with this book.

There have also been important decisions by the European Court on various matters: these are covered in the appropriate places. In order to make room for this new material, I have deleted passages that seem to have outlived their usefulness.

Certain passages in Chapter 3 have been reproduced from my article, 'International Law and the Law of the European Union – A Reassessment' [2002] BYIL 1. I am grateful to Professor James Crawford, the editor of the Yearbook, for granting his permission. Most of the Introduction to Part III is derived from pp. 237–44 of my article, 'The Constitutional Foundations of the European Union' (2001) 117 LQR 225. I would like to thank Professor Francis Reynolds, the editor of the Quarterly, for his permission to re-use it. The section on Denmark in Chapter 8 is taken from pp. 157–9 of my book, *Constitutional Problems of the European Union* (Hart Publishing, Oxford and Portland, Oregon, 1999). I would like to thank Richard Hart for his permission to do so.

Much of the editorial work in preparing this new edition has been done by my wife. To her, as always, I owe my greatest debt.

This edition attempts to state the law as it existed on 1 January 2007.

TCH

16 February 2007

# CONTENTS

## PART I: COMMUNITY INSTITUTIONS



## PART II: THE COMMUNITY LEGAL SYSTEM



## PART III: COMMUNITY LAW AND THE MEMBER STATES



## PART IV: ADMINISTRATIVE LAW

# DETAILED CONTENTS

## PART II: THE COMMUNITY LEGAL SYSTEM

## PART III: COMMUNITY LAW AND THE MEMBER STATES

## PART IV: ADMINISTRATIVE LAW

# NUMBERING OF TREATY ARTICLES

The Articles in the EC Treaty and the Treaty on European Union were renumbered by the Treaty of Amsterdam, 1997. Since cases decided before it came into force still use the old numbering, this will be inserted in square brackets after the new numbering. Thus, for example, a reference to 'Article 94 [100a] EC' is a reference to the provision originally numbered Article 100a and renumbered Article 94. Articles introduced, or substantially modified, by the Treaty of Amsterdam (or subsequently) are referred to by their new numbers only. Articles that have been repealed or substantially modified by the Treaty of Amsterdam or subsequently are referred to by the old numbers (in square brackets) only.

# CITATION AND REPORTING OF EUROPEAN COURT CASES

## CASE NUMBERING

At the beginning of the proceedings, every case is given a number by the Registrar of the European Court or the Registrar of the Court of First Instance. Since the establishment of the Court of First Instance, cases in the European Court have had the prefix 'C', e.g., 'Case C-9/94'. Cases in the Court of First Instance have the prefix 'T' (from the French, *Tribunal*), e.g., 'Case T-9/94'. The figures after the oblique stroke indicate the year when the proceedings began. When a case goes on appeal from the Court of First Instance to the European Court, it is given a new case number by the Registrar of the European Court; thus Case T-120/89 might become Case C-220/91 P, the different figures after the oblique stroke indicating the difference between the date when the proceedings commenced in the Court of First Instance and when the appeal was lodged. 'Opinions' and 'Rulings' of the Court (as distinct from 'Cases') are numbered separately, e.g., Opinion 9/94; Opinions of an advocate general have the number of the case in which they were given.

## CITATION IN THIS BOOK

### IN FOOTNOTES

In footnotes, decisions of the European Court are cited to the European Court Reports. Where a case is not yet reported in the ECR, the date alone is normally given. Since cases are published in chronological order, this will enable the reader to find them without difficulty when the relevant volume is published.

### IN THE TABLE OF CASES

Judgments of the European Court are listed in the Table of Cases in both numerical and alphabetical order. Though the latter may be more convenient to use, the former is more accurate. Cases are cited under their abbreviated name rather than their full name. The abbreviations used are normally those found in the ECR, but since cases are sometimes known under different names, the only sure way of finding a case is to search for it by number.

In the Table of Cases (numerical order), cases are listed first by year (the number after the oblique stroke) and then by the number before it; for each year, 'Opinions' and

'Rulings' are listed before 'Cases', and cases with a C-prefix come before those with a T-prefix.

## INTERNET

Judgments of the European Court (and Opinions of advocates general) may be obtained on the Court's website, http://curia.europa.eu/en/.

# ALPHABETICAL TABLE OF CASES

For "Parliament", see "European Parliament"

# NUMERICAL TABLE OF CASES

* Cases brought before the Court of First Instance (prefix 'T') are listed *after* those brought (in the same year) before the European Court (prefix 'C'). Judgements designated 'Opinion" or 'Ruling' are listed (for convenience) *before* those (in the same year) designated 'Case'.

# TABLE OF ENGLISH, SCOTTISH, AND IRISH CASES

# TABLE OF LEGISLATION

COMMUNITY TREATIES

## UNITED KINGDOM STATUTES

UNITED KINGDOM STATUTORY INSTRUMENTS

# ABBREVIATIONS

| | |
|---|---|
| AG | Advocate General |
| AJDA | L'Actualité Juridique: Droit Aministratif |
| Am. Jo. Comp. L. | American Journal of Comparative Law |
| Am. J. Int. L. | American Journal of International Law |
| BYIL | British Yearbook of International Law |
| CDE | Cahiers de Droit Européen |
| CFSP | Common Foreign and Security Policy |
| CJEL | Columbia Journal of European Law |
| CLP | Current Legal Problems |
| CMLR | Common Market Law Reports |
| CMLRev. | Common Market Law Review |
| COREPER | Committee of Permanent Representatives |
| EAEC | European Atomic Energy Community |
| EC | European Community |
| ECB | European Central Bank |
| EC Bull. | Bulletin of the European Communities |
| ECJ | European Court of Justice |
| ECLR | European Competition Law Review |
| ECOSOC | Economic and Social Committee |
| ECR | European Court Reports (official reports of the judgments of the European Court, English version) |
| ECSC | European Coal and Steel Community |
| EEA | European Economic Area |
| EEC | European Economic Community |
| EFTA | European Free Trade Association |
| ELJ | European Law Journal |
| ELRev. | European Law Review |
| EMI | European Monetary Institute |
| EMS | European Monetary System |
| EMU | Economic and Monetary Union |
| EP | European Parliament |
| EPC | European Political Co-operation |
| ERM | Exchange Rate Mechanism |
| ESCB | European System of Central Banks |
| EU | European Union |
| Euratom | European Atomic Energy Community |
| FIDE | International Federation for European Law |
| GATT | General Agreement on Tariffs and Trade |
| ICJ | International Court of Justice |
| ICLQ | International and Comparative Law Quarterly |

| | |
|---|---|
| JO | Journal officiel (French version of OJ) |
| JCMS | Journal of Common Market Studies |
| LIEI | Legal Issues of European Integration |
| LQR | Law Quarterly Review |
| MCA | Monetary Compensatory Amount |
| MEP | Member of the European Parliament |
| MLR | Modern Law Review |
| MT | Merger Treaty |
| NAFTA | North American Free Trade Agreement |
| OJ | Official Journal (of the European Communities) |
| OJLS | Oxford Journal of Legal Studies |
| RDI | Rivista di Diritto Internazionale |
| Rec. | Recueil de la jurisprudence de la Cour de Justice des Communautés européennes (French version of ECR) |
| RIW | Recht der Internationalen Wirtschaft |
| RMC | Revue du Marché Commun |
| RTDE | Revue Trimestrielle de Droit Européen |
| SEA | Single European Act |
| SEW | Sociaal-Economische Wetgeving |
| TEU | Treaty on European Union (Maastricht Agreement) |
| WEU | Western European Union |
| WTO DSB | World Trade Organization Dispute Settlement Body |
| YEL | Yearbook of European Law |

# PART I

# COMMUNITY INSTITUTIONS

# INTRODUCTION

Although people often think of 'the Community' as a single entity, there are in law two Communities: the most important is the European Community (EC), formerly known as the European Economic Community (EEC); the other is the European Atomic Energy Community (Euratom). Euratom is limited to nuclear energy; the EC covers everything else.

Originally, there were three Communities. The third was the European Coal and Steel Community (ECSC). This was actually the first to be established: the ECSC Treaty was signed on 18 April 1951. The Treaty stated that it was concluded for a period of fifty years.[1] It entered into force on 23 July 1952 and therefore terminated in 2002. When it expired, the ECSC's functions were taken over by the EC.

The signatories to the ECSC Treaty were the six original Member States: Germany, Belgium, France, Italy, Luxembourg, and the Netherlands. The United Kingdom was invited to take part, but declined to do so. The signing took place in Paris – for this reason it is sometimes called the 'Treaty of Paris' – and the French version was the sole authentic text. Four principal institutions were created: the Council (representing the Member States), the Commission (a supranational executive, which was originally called the 'High Authority'), the Assembly, and the Court. Except for the Assembly, which normally met in Strasbourg, they were all located in Luxembourg.

The EC Treaty, then known as the EEC Treaty, and the Euratom Treaty[2] were both signed in Rome on 25 March 1957 and entered into force on 1 January 1958. They were concluded for an unlimited period.[3] The United Kingdom was again invited to participate but dropped out of the preliminary discussions. The signatories were therefore the same six States, but this time the texts in each of their official languages – German, French, Italian, and Dutch – were equally authentic. Separate Commissions and Councils were created for each of the new Communities, but all three shared the same Assembly and Court.[4] The new Councils and Commissions met in Brussels.

The three Treaties contained many common features, but there were also important differences. One difference was that the ECSC Treaty was more specific as regards the policy to be pursued; the EC Treaty, on the other hand, was concerned mainly with creating a framework, and left the creation of policy to the Community institutions. The consequence of this was that the institutions were required to play a more creative role

[1] Art. 97 ECSC.

[2] The reason a separate Treaty was signed governing the non-military use of atomic energy was the fear that the EC Treaty might be rejected by the French Parliament. It was hoped that, in such an eventuality, at least the Euratom Treaty could be saved.

[3] Art. 312 [240] EC; Art. 208 Euratom.

[4] The establishment of a single Assembly and Court for the three Communities was effected by a separate Treaty, the Convention on Certain Institutions Common to the European Communities, which entered into force on the same date as the EC and Euratom Treaties. It was repealed by Art. 9 of the Treaty of Amsterdam, its operative provisions having been moved to the other Treaties.

in the EC. This difference was in turn responsible for another distinction between the ECSC and EC Treaties: under the former, the Commission had much more independent power (and the Council correspondingly less) than under the EC Treaty. In the EC, therefore, the balance of power was more in favour of the Council.

On the purely legal level, the EC and Euratom Treaties are very similar – many provisions concerning legal remedies are identical – while significant differences were to be found in the ECSC Treaty. This can be explained by the fact that the EC and Euratom Treaties were drafted at the same time and the drafters were obviously influenced by the experience gained from the operation of the ECSC Treaty.

It was, of course, illogical and inconvenient for the two most important Community institutions to be triplicated; so a Merger Treaty (officially known as the Treaty Establishing a Single Council and a Single Commission of the European Communities) was signed in Brussels on 8 April 1965 and entered into force on 1 July 1967.[5] This Treaty did not merge the Communities themselves but merged the three Commissions to form a single Commission and merged the three Councils to form a single Council. The new Council and Commission were located in Brussels.[6] In order to compensate Luxembourg for this loss, it was agreed that some Council meetings would be held there. In addition, certain other Community activities are run from Luxembourg, and the European Court still sits there. The European Parliament sits in Strasbourg but holds some sessions, as well as its committee meetings, in Brussels;[7] its secretariat is based in Luxembourg.[8] The end result is highly inconvenient and inefficient and shows that, even in the simplest matters, the common interest has to give way to national interests.

The next step was the widening of Community membership. Britain's original attitude of disdain changed in the early 1960s and in 1961 the Conservative Government of Mr Harold Macmillan took the decision to seek entry. Initially Britain's application was blocked by General De Gaulle; but Britain persevered, and on 22 January 1972 the Final Act was signed which embodied the instruments of accession of the United Kingdom, Ireland, Denmark, and Norway.[9] Norway dropped out when a referendum showed that

[5] It was repealed by Art. 9 of the Treaty of Amsterdam, its operative provisions having been moved to the other Treaties.

[6] For a long time the Community institutions were given only temporary seats and it was not until the 1992 Edinburgh Summit that these were made permanent. See now the Protocol on the Location of the Seats of the Institutions and of Certain Bodies and Departments of the European Communities and of Europol, a Protocol to the Treaty of Amsterdam.

[7] For litigation prior to the Edinburgh decision on the seat of the Parliament, see *Luxembourg v. European Parliament*, Case 230/81, [1983] ECR 255 and *France v. European Parliament*, Cases 358/85, 51/86, [1988] ECR 4821. For litigation subsequent to the Edinburgh decision, see *France v. European Parliament*, Case C-345/95, 1 October 1997.

[8] Attempts by the Parliament itself to rationalize the situation by moving its staff to its places of work were declared illegal by the European Court at the suit of Luxembourg: *Luxembourg v. European Parliament*, Case 108/83, [1984] ECR 1945. See also *Luxembourg v. European Parliament*, Cases C-213/88, C-39/89, [1991] ECR I-5643.

[9] The new Member States actually joined the EC and Euratom through ratification of the Treaty of Accession and the ECSC by depositing an instrument of accession on the basis of the Decision of Accession. The latter was a decision of the Council of the European Communities under Art. 98 ECSC. The terms of admission are laid down in the Act of Accession which is an integral part of both the Treaty of Accession and the Decision of Accession.

a majority of the Norwegian electorate opposed entry; but the other three new Member States joined the Community on 1 January 1973. English, Danish, and Irish became official Community languages and the translations into these languages of the EC and Euratom Treaties were declared to be authentic texts.

Greece was the next country to join. On 28 May 1979 the Treaty of Accession and other relevant instruments were signed in Athens, and Greece became the tenth Member State on 1 January 1981. Spain and Portugal followed. The relevant instruments were signed on 12 June 1985 and membership came into effect on 1 January 1986. The Community then had twelve Member States, and the official languages included Greek, Portuguese, and Spanish.

In 1991, negotiations were concluded with the members of the European Free Trade Area (EFTA) – Norway, Sweden, Finland, Iceland, Switzerland, Liechtenstein,[10] and Austria – for an agreement to establish the European Economic Area (EEA).[11] This agreement, which some saw originally as a substitute for membership, was intended to integrate the EFTA countries economically into the Community without giving them a role in its institutions. In the relevant areas,[12] Community law from all sources – treaty provisions, legislation, and rules laid down by the European Court – was made applicable to them.[13] This covered not only the law as it existed when the agreement was concluded, but also new legislation which might be adopted in the future, as well as future decisions of the European Court. Under the terms of the agreement, if the EFTA countries refused to accept these new rules, they risked losing their rights in the sector in question. This scheme had great attractions – it created the world's largest trading area[14] – but it also had serious drawbacks. In particular, it meant that the EFTA countries would have to apply rules of law in the making of which they would have had virtually no say.[15]

In 1991 the EEA Agreement was declared by the European Court to be incompatible with the EC Treaty.[16] The reasons for this were complex, but they centred around the European Court's objection to the creation of a rival court, the proposed EEA court. Since this would have had jurisdiction to interpret EEA law, it would have had great influence on the development of Community law. The European Court's objections were not assuaged by the fact that the majority of judges on the EEA court would have been judges from the European Court; indeed, this was an added grievance.[17]

[10] At the time, Liechtenstein was not a member of EFTA but had applied to join.

[11] On the Community side, the parties were the EC (then known as the EEC) and the ECSC as legal entities and the twelve individual Member States; on the EFTA side they were the states listed above.

[12] These include free movement of goods (but only regarding products originating in the Contracting States), persons, services, and capital. Agriculture is excluded.

[13] In some cases modifications were made.

[14] Though smaller in area than the territory covered by the North American Free Trade Agreement (NAFTA), it had more consumers and a greater gross domestic product.

[15] For details, see Reymond, 'Institutions, Decision-Making Procedure and Settlement of Disputes in the European Economic Area' (1993) 30 CMLRev. 449; Cremona, 'The "Dynamic and Homogeneous" EEA: Byzantine Structures and Variable Geometry' (1994) 19 ELRev. 508; Christiansen, 'The EFTA Court' (1997) 22 ELRev. 539.

[16] *First EEA Case*, Opinion 1/91, [1991] ECR I-6079.

[17] See, further, Hartley, 'The European Court and the EEA' (1992) 41 ICLQ 841.

The agreement was then amended to meet the European Court's objections and the new version was approved by the Court in 1992.[18] A further setback occurred when the agreement was rejected by the Swiss voters in a referendum, which meant that Switzerland had to drop out.[19] However, it eventually came into force on 1 January 1994 between the Community countries and Norway, Sweden, Finland, Iceland, and Austria. Liechtenstein joined later, after a referendum in 1995.

Even before the EEA Agreement had come into force, most of the EFTA countries had applied to join the Community. The Swiss dropped out of these negotiations when their electorate rejected the EEA,[20] but Austria, Finland, Norway, and Sweden persevered. The Accession Treaty for these countries was signed on 24 June 1994. Referendums in Austria, Finland, and Sweden approved membership; but the Norwegian electorate again rejected it. On 1 January 1995, Austria, Finland, and Sweden became Member States of the Community; only Iceland, Liechtenstein, and Norway remained in EFTA. The Community then had fifteen members; Finnish and Swedish are official Community languages.[21]

The next group of new members consisted of eight former Communist countries in Eastern Europe (Lithuania, Latvia, Estonia, Poland, the Czech Republic, Slovakia, Hungary, and Slovenia) and two Mediterranean islands (Malta and Cyprus). They joined on 1 May 2004. The Community then had twenty-five members; Lithuanian, Latvian, Estonian, Polish, Czech, Slovak, Hungarian, Slovenian, and Maltese became official languages. Bulgaria and Romania joined on 1 January 2007, adding their languages to the total. There are now twenty-seven Member States and twenty-two official languages. The translation difficulties are immense.

In 1985 Greenland left the Community following a referendum held in 1982 in which there was a narrow majority in favour of withdrawal. Greenland was not a Member State but, being associated with Denmark (though with internal self-government), was part of the Community.[22]

The structure of the Community has already undergone considerable change in the course of its development. In addition to the treaties previously mentioned, amendments have been made by the first and second Budgetary Treaties, 1970 and 1975, and by the Single European Act of 1986, which came into force on 1 July 1987. Other changes have resulted from the establishment of political (constitutional) conventions and practices which have developed without any formal legal foundation.

Further changes resulted from the Maastricht Agreement, officially known as the Treaty on European Union (TEU). This was signed in Maastricht, a provincial town in

[18] *Second EEA Case*, Opinion 1/92, 10 April 1992. The Agreement was finally signed in Oporto, Portugal, on 2 May 1992.

[19] As a result, the Agreement had to be amended by a Protocol signed in Brussels on 17 March 1993.

[20] In 2001, a referendum was held in Switzerland on a proposal that the Government should commence negotiations for membership of the EU. It was rejected by a majority of approximately 3:1.

[21] For further details, see Goebel, 'The European Union Grows: The Constitutional Impact of the Accession of Austria, Finland and Sweden' (1995) 18 Fordham International Law Journal 1092; Lee Miles (ed.), *The European Union and the Nordic Countries* (1996).

[22] It is now associated with the Community. For further details, see Weiss, 'Greenland's Withdrawal from the European Communities' (1985) 10 ELRev. 173.

the Netherlands, on 7 February 1992 and came into force on 1 November 1993. Of all the amending treaties, this had the most difficult birth. It was rejected by a referendum in Denmark (though this was reversed in a later referendum, held after a Community summit in Edinburgh had produced a gloss on the Treaty provisions of most concern to Denmark)[23] and almost rejected by a referendum in France. Opinion polls in both Germany and Britain showed considerable opposition.

In the United Kingdom, the necessary legislation[24] was passed only after great turmoil; indeed, it could have brought the Government down.[25] The anti-Maastricht forces then resorted to the courts: an action was brought by a well-known journalist, Lord Rees-Mogg, for a declaration that the United Kingdom could not lawfully ratify the Treaty.[26] Only when this had failed, was the way open for British ratification.

In the end, Britain was not the last country to ratify. Germany's ratification was delayed even longer by legal proceedings in the Constitutional Court and, though ratification was eventually permitted, the judgment makes clear that the German Constitution (*Grundgesetz*) imposes definite limits on Germany's participation in a federal Europe.[27]

The Treaty on European Union brought about important changes of a conceptual kind. The European Economic Community (EEC) was renamed the European Community (EC) and a new entity was created, the European Union. This is 'founded on the European Communities, supplemented by the policies and forms of co-operation' established by the Treaty on European Union.[28] The latter are two in number: a 'common foreign and security policy'[29] and 'co-operation in the fields of justice and home affairs'.[30] The European Union (EU) has its own citizenship: Article 17(1) [8(1)] EC declares that every person holding the nationality of a Member State is a citizen of the Union.[31]

The most important achievement of the Treaty on European Union was the establishment of a common currency for the Community – the euro. However, the United

[23] The meeting was held on 12 December 1992 and resulted in a Decision and a Declaration by all the Member States, and a Declaration by Denmark alone. For the contents and legal effect of these instruments, see Hartley, 'Constitutional and Institutional Aspects of the Maastricht Agreement' (1993) 42 ICLQ 213 at 234–7; Howarth, 'The Compromise on Denmark and the Treaty on European Union: A Legal and Political Analysis' (1994) 31 CMLRev. 765.

[24] The European Communities (Amendment) Act 1993.

[25] This was not due to any widespread anti-European sentiment among British MPs: officially at least, the Treaty enjoyed overwhelming support. However, the die-hard anti-Community faction in the parliamentary Conservative Party, though small, was greater than the Conservative majority. This was exploited by the Labour Party, which voted for motions that, though not ostensibly anti-Maastricht, would have had the practical effect of killing the Bill. In this way, Labour could embarrass the Government without compromising their official support for the Bill. It was finally passed in the Commons only when the Prime Minister stated that he would call a general election if the Government lost the vote. Since the Conservative Party would almost certainly have lost the election and many Conservative rebels would have lost their seats, this threat of self-destruction proved effective. For a full discussion, see Rawlings, 'Legal Politics: The United Kingdom and the Ratification of the Treaty on European Union' [1994] PL 254.

[26] *R v. Secretary of State for Foreign and Commonwealth Affairs, ex parte Lord Rees-Mogg* [1993] 3 CMLR 101; [1994] 2 WLR 115 (DC).

[27] *Bundesverfassungsgericht*, 12 October 1993, [1993] NJW 3047; [1994] 1 CMLR 57. For constitutional proceedings in France, see *Conseil Constitutionnel*, 9 April 1992, [1993] 3 CMLR 345; see also Oliver, 'The French Constitution and the Treaty of Maastricht' (1994) 43 ICLQ 1.

[28] Art. 1 [A] TEU.

[29] See Title V [V] TEU.

[30] See Title VI [VI] TEU.

[31] See Shaw, 'The Many Pasts and Futures of Citizenship in the European Union' (1997) 22 ELRev. 554.

Kingdom,[32] Denmark,[33] and Sweden[34] have rejected it and the new Member States are not yet ready for it; so at present it applies in only twelve of the twenty-seven Community countries.

Another feature of the Treaty on European Union was the so-called 'Social Chapter', which was intended to develop the social dimension of the Community. It was originally drafted as a chapter of the EC Treaty, but the United Kingdom refused to accept it; so it had to be adopted in the form of a separate treaty, the Agreement on Social Policy, to which the United Kingdom was not a party. When the Labour Party won the election in 1997, they decided to opt in. Effect was given to this by the Treaty of Amsterdam 1997, which re-inserted the Social Chapter into the body of the EC Treaty.

The Treaty of Amsterdam was signed in 1997, and came into force on 1 May 1999. Although it ended Britain's opt-out on social policy, it established a new one on passport controls. It makes provision for the abolition of entry controls on persons travelling from one Member State to another.[35] The scheme started with two agreements, signed in Schengen, Luxembourg, in 1985 and 1990 between France, Germany, and the Benelux countries, under which it was agreed that controls would be gradually lifted. Subsequently, all the other Member States except Britain and Ireland also joined. Two non-member States, Iceland and Norway, became associated with the scheme. These agreements were brought into the main body of Community law though a Protocol annexed to the Treaty on European Union and the EC Treaty by the Treaty of Amsterdam.[36] Two further Protocols allow Britain and Ireland a permanent opt-out.[37] A fourth Protocol gives a more limited opt-out to Denmark.

The Treaty of Amsterdam also saw the insertion into the Treaty on European Union of a new Title[38] on what was then known as 'closer co-operation' (further developed and renamed 'enhanced co-operation' in the Treaty of Nice). Once called 'variable geometry', this means allowing some Member States to go ahead with further integration while others opt out.

The next major development was the Treaty of Nice,[39] which was signed on 26 February 2001 and entered into force on 1 February 2003. Although originally

[32] The United Kingdom is not obliged to adopt the common currency unless the British Government and Parliament so decide: see the Protocol on certain provisions relating to the United Kingdom of Great Britain and Northern Ireland.

[33] See the Protocol on certain provisions relating to Denmark; see also the Decision of the Heads of State and Government, section B, adopted at the Edinburgh Summit on 12 December 1992. Denmark held a referendum in September 2000, in which adoption of the euro was rejected.

[34] Since the Treaty gives it no opt-out and it meets the criteria for adoption of the euro, Sweden's refusal to join is actually illegal, but no one wants to make an issue of this.

[35] Arts 61–69 [73i-q] EC, introduced by the Treaty of Amsterdam.

[36] Protocol Integrating the Schengen *Acquis* into the Framework of the European Union.

[37] Protocol on the Application of Certain Aspects of Article 14 [7a] of the Treaty Establishing the European Community to the United Kingdom and Ireland; Protocol on the Position of the United Kingdom and Ireland (see Art. 69 [73q] EC). An interesting feature of the first of these Protocols is that it expressly provides that Art. 14 [7a] EC, which in some quarters is viewed as already requiring the abolition of controls, will not preclude these two countries from continuing to operate passport controls on persons entering their territory, even if they come from another Member State.

[38] Title VII [VIa]. See also Art. 11 [5a] EC.

[39] Published in OJ 2001, C 80. For a summary of its provisions, see Bradley, 'Institutional Design in the Treaty of Nice' (2001) 38 CMLRev. 1095.

rejected by the voters of Ireland, it was accepted in a second referendum held in October 2002. Its main purpose was to reform the institutions of the Community in preparation for further enlargement.

A Charter of Fundamental Rights was adopted by proclamation of the Commission, Council, and Parliament in December 2000.[40] It has as yet no binding force.

The most ambitious project in recent times has been the attempt to give the Community a Constitution. A body known as the 'European Convention' or the 'Convention on the Future of Europe' was set up for the purpose. It consisted of representatives of:

- the existing Member States and the applicant Member States;
- the national parliaments of the existing and applicant Member States;
- the European Parliament; and
- the Commission.

It was chaired by a former President of France, Mr Valéry Giscard d'Estaing.

In due course it produced a Constitution, contained in a draft treaty, the Treaty Establishing a Constitution for Europe. After a setback at a meeting of the Heads of State or Government in Brussels on 12 and 13 December 2003, it was finally agreed by the national Governments in October 2004. It then had to be ratified by each Member State according to its constitutional requirements. In many Member States, this required a referendum. Although the approval of the voters was obtained in several states, the process ground to a halt when the Constitution was rejected, first by the people of France and then by the people of the Netherlands.[41] Since France had initiated the process of European integration and the Netherlands is its most enthusiastic supporter, this was a serious blow. It was therefore decided to suspend the ratification process in order to consider what to do next. At the time of writing (1 January 2007), no further steps have yet been taken.

In law there are still two Communities, though there is only one set of institutions. The powers of the institutions vary, depending on the Treaty under which they are acting. The best analogy is that of two commercial companies with the same shareholders and the same board of directors: in law there are two legal persons; in reality there is only one. The European Union may be regarded as the legal and political concept which gives expression to this underlying unity.

It is not easy to compare the Community with other political entities: it contains some of the features of a traditional international organization and, less prominently, some features of a federation.[42] Perhaps it is best regarded as the forerunner of a new

[40] OJ 2000, C 364/8.

[41] This must have come as a relief to the British Government, since it was politically committed to a referendum in the United Kingdom, a referendum in which the Constitution would almost certainly have been rejected.

[42] Interestingly, the federal elements are strongest with regard to the judicial and legal system of the Community; they are weakest in the political area, including such vital matters as legislative and executive powers, taxation, and defence: see Hartley, 'Federalism, Courts and Legal Systems: The Emerging Constitution of the European Community' (1986) 34 Am. Jo. Comp. L. 229. For a full and detailed study of this question, see M. Cappelletti, M. Seccombe, and J. Weiler (eds), *Integration Through Law* (1986) (3 vols).

breed of enhanced international organizations which have real power over their Member States. Though less advanced, the WTO and the Council of Europe (European Convention on Human Rights) are other examples. The term 'supranational' is often used to refer to the features which distinguish such organizations.

The hybrid nature of the Community must constantly be borne in mind when considering its structure. The three political organs – the Council, the Commission, and the Parliament – each contain both inter-governmental and supranational elements, though the former are more noticeable in the case of the Council and the latter in the case of the Commission.

The most important characteristic of a traditional international organization is that it is basically only a form of institutionalized inter-governmental co-operation. It is based on the principle that no Member State may be bound without its consent. If the decisions of the organization are taken by majority vote, they are no more than mere declarations; if, on the other hand, they are to have any real 'bite', they must be approved by each Member State.

In contrast to this, the organs of the Community have a significant measure of autonomy, and unanimity is required only in special cases. Nor can it be doubted that the Community has real teeth: Community law is binding on Member States and (in many cases) on individuals; it is frequently applied by national courts. Moreover, in certain cases fines can be levied on companies, individuals, and even Member States for breach of Community law. The decisions of the Community derive their binding force from the fact that they are taken by organs endowed with the appropriate power by the Treaties – the constitution of the Community – and not because each decision has been individually agreed to by the Member States. These features give the Community its supranational character.

## FURTHER READING

John Gillingham, *European Integration, 1950–2003* (2003).

Walter van Gerven, *The European Union, A Polity of States and Peoples* (2005).

Jean-Claude Piris, *The Constitution for Europe: A Legal Analysis* (2006).

# 1

# THE POLITICAL INSTITUTIONS

According to the Treaties,[1] the Community has five institutions – the Commission, the Council, the European Parliament, the Court of Justice, and the Court of Auditors.[2] The first three are political institutions; they will be dealt with in this chapter. The Court of Justice and the Court of Auditors will be considered in Chapter 2.

## THE COMMISSION

The Commission is intended to give expression to the Community interest. Its most important activities are formulating proposals for new Community policies, mediating between the Member States to secure the adoption of these proposals, co-ordinating national policies, and overseeing the execution of existing Community policies.

### COMPOSITION

Each Member State is at present entitled to one Commissioner.[3]

The procedure for appointing Commissioners is as follows.[4] The first step is for the Council, meeting in the composition of Heads of State or Government (European Council) and acting by a qualified majority, to nominate the person it intends to appoint as President of the Commission. The nomination then has to be approved by

[1] See Arts 7 [4] EC and 3 Euratom.

[2] Though founded earlier, the Court of Auditors attained institutional status only as a result of the Treaty on European Union. Other important organs, which do not have the status of institutions, include the Economic and Social Committee, the Committee of the Regions (both of which assist the Council and Commission), the European System of Central Banks (ESCB), the European Central Bank (ECB), and the European Investment Bank. The Treaty on European Union made provision for the establishment of the Committee of the Regions, the ESCB, and the ECB; the others were established earlier.

[3] Art. 45(2) of the 2003 Act of Accession (for the ten new Member States) and Art. 45 of the 2005 Act of Accession (Bulgaria and Romania). There was a plan to reduce the size of the Commission by ending the right of each Member State to have a Commissioner: Art. 4(1) of the Protocol to the Treaty of Nice on the Enlargement of the European Union. This should have gone into operation once the number of Member States reached twenty-seven, something that happened when Bulgaria and Romania joined in 2007; however, the Acts of Accession cited above made provision for the right to continue at least until 31 October 2009.

[4] Arts 214 [158] EC and 127 Euratom (as amended by the Treaty of Nice).

the European Parliament. Next, the Council draws up a list of the other persons it intends to appoint as members of the Commission. In doing so, it acts by a qualified majority and in agreement with the President-elect. In addition, the list of nominees must be in accordance with the proposals made by each Member State. The last requirement seems to mean that a Commissioner from a given Member State cannot be anyone other than the person nominated by that state.

The entire Commission – President and other members – must be approved 'as a body'[5] by the European Parliament, after which the Commission is formally appointed by the Council, acting by a qualified majority. The appointments are for a (renewable) period of five years.

Members of the Commission cannot be dismissed during their term of office by the national governments or by the Council, but the whole Commission must resign *en bloc* if a vote of no confidence is passed by the European Parliament.[6] Commissioners cannot be dismissed individually in this way; but the European Court can compel a Commissioner to retire on grounds of serious misconduct or because he no longer fulfils the conditions required for the performance of his duties.[7] Moreover, under an amendment brought in by the Treaty of Nice, a Commissioner must resign if the President of the Commission so requests, provided the Commission as a whole agrees.[8] This could be used to get rid of a Commissioner who was incompetent or whose activities were politically objectionable.

According to the Treaties, Commissioners are supposed to be above national loyalties. It is provided by Articles 213(2) [157(2)] EC and 126(2) Euratom:

> The members of the Commission shall, in the general interest of the Community, be completely independent in the performance of their duties.
>
> In the performance of these duties, they shall neither seek nor take instructions from any government or from any other body. They shall refrain from any action incompatible with their duties. Each Member State undertakes to respect this principle and not to seek to influence the members of the Commission in the performance of their tasks.

Any overt breach of these principles could lead to the compulsory retirement of the Commissioner concerned.[9]

[5] This means that the Parliament must approve or reject all of them together: it cannot reject one and approve the rest. It can, however, threaten to reject the whole Commission unless the unacceptable Commissioner stands down. Prospective candidates must appear before the Parliament to answer questions, a procedure which seems to be modelled on American confirmation hearings.

[6] Arts 201 [144 EC] and 114 Euratom.

[7] Arts 216 [160] EC and 129 Euratom. The procedure is set in motion by an application by the Council or Commission.

[8] Art. 217(4) EC, as amended by the Treaty of Nice. This means that there will be six different ways in which a Commissioner may cease to hold office: (1) death; (2) expiry of his term of office; (3) individual (voluntary) resignation; (4) collective (compulsory) resignation (following a motion of no confidence in the European Parliament); (5) compulsory retirement by the Court; (6) compulsory resignation at the request of the President. Except in the first and fifth of these cases, he remains in office until his successor has been appointed. See Arts 215 [159] EC and 128 Euratom.

[9] It is further stated that a Commissioner must not engage in any other occupation, whether gainful or not, during his term of office (though in practice certain academic activities are allowed). After he has ceased to hold office, he must behave with integrity and discretion as regards the acceptance of appointments and benefits.

These provisions do not, however, prevent governments (or private interests) from lobbying individual Commissioners or the Commission as a whole. The balance of power in the Community is such that, though the Commission is an independent force in its own right, it cannot fulfil its functions without the co-operation of national governments. Consequently, it is very much concerned with national interests, and one of its most important tasks is the reconciliation of national policies with Community objectives. Therefore, even in those cases where the Commission is legally empowered to take action independently of the Council, it will still pay careful attention to national susceptibilities.

Portfolios are allocated to Commissioners so that each is responsible for one or more subjects. At one time, this was done by agreement among the Commissioners themselves, with the President playing a pivotal role. However, a Declaration attached to the Treaty of Amsterdam stated that the Inter-Governmental Conference which adopted the Treaty considered that the President should enjoy broad discretion in the allocation of tasks.[10] The Treaty of Nice now states explicitly that the President allocates responsibilities among the members of the Commission. He may also reshuffle portfolios during the Commission's term of office.[11] These developments suggest that his role will come to resemble that of a British Prime Minister. No doubt the lobbying by Member States to get their Commissioners the best jobs will continue as before.

The Commission works under the political guidance of its President.[12] It is divided into departments known as Directorates General. Not all of these are of equal importance or prestige; hence the scramble for portfolios. Each Directorate General is headed by a Director General, who is responsible to the relevant Commissioner. Directorates General are subdivided into Directorates (headed by a Director) and these in turn are made up of Divisions (each under a Head of Division). There are also a number of specialized services. One of these is the Legal Service, which gives legal advice to all Directorates General and represents the Commission in legal proceedings. Appointments to the higher posts are subject to intense national rivalry. The decision is taken by the Commissioners themselves and depends in part on ensuring that each country maintains its share of posts. This means that the best person will not always get the job, a fact which is damaging to morale.

Disregard of these obligations could lead to compulsory retirement (if he is still in office) or loss of pension. Proceedings under this provision were brought for the first time in 1999, when the Council applied to the Court for an order depriving Mr Bangemann of his pension rights because he accepted a position with a Spanish telecommunications company. Mr Bangemann was the outgoing Commissioner responsible for telecommunications in the disgraced Santer Commission. The proceedings were withdrawn when he agreed not to take up the position for a year, and not to engage in negotiations with Community institutions for two years. Deprivation of pension rights can also be used to punish misbehaviour in office that does not come to light until afterwards. This happened to Ms Cresson, who was also a member of the Santer Commission. She had given her dentist a scientific appointment with the Commission, even though he was clearly unqualified. The Court found that she had committed a breach of the obligations arising from her office, but decided not to deprive her of her pension. This was in *Commission v. Edith Cresson*, Case C-432/04, 11 July 2006, a case suggesting that the Court takes a fairly relaxed attitude towards nepotism.

[10] Declaration 32 adopted by the Conference. [11] Art. 217(2) EC, as amended by the Treaty of Nice.

[12] Prior to the Treaty of Nice, this was laid down by Art. 219 [163] EC. Now, the relevant provision is Art. 217(1) EC.

Each Commissioner is assisted by his *Cabinet*, a group of officials personally appointed by him and directly responsible to him, who are not necessarily on the permanent staff of the Commission. The head of the *Cabinet* (*Chef de Cabinet*) plays an important role as his Commissioner's right-hand man. The *Chefs de Cabinet* of all the Commissioners meet regularly to co-ordinate activities and prepare the ground for Commission meetings. If the *Chefs de Cabinet* reach unanimous agreement on a question, their decision is normally adopted by the Commission without debate.[13]

Officials of the Commission (and the other Community institutions) enjoy various privileges and immunities under Community law,[14] the most important of which are immunity from legal proceedings in national courts in respect of acts performed by them in their official capacity[15] and immunity from national income tax on their Community salary.[16] They are, however, subject to a special Community income tax, though the rate of taxation is low. All the privileges and immunities enjoyed by Community officials are granted to them solely in the interests of the Community, and the institution concerned is obliged to waive the immunity whenever such waiver is not contrary to the interests of the Community.[17]

## LEGISLATIVE POWERS

Under the ECSC Treaty, the Commission was the main legislative authority, though sometimes it had to obtain the approval of the Council. Under the EC and Euratom Treaties, on the other hand, it has legislative powers in only a few cases, though, where granted, these powers enable the Commission to enact legislation in the true sense.[18] Moreover, the European Court has held that, whenever the EC Treaty confers a specific task on the Commission, it impliedly grants the Commission the powers (including legislative powers) that are indispensable in order to carry out that task.[19] In a much wider range of cases, the Commission enjoys powers delegated to it by the Council. Here the basic principles must be laid down in the Council measure which delegates the power: the Commission can then adopt measures that fill in the details.[20]

13 Compare the role played by COREPER with regard to the Council (discussed below).

14 See the Protocol on the Privileges and Immunities of the European Communities, Arts 12–16. These privileges and immunities also apply to members of the Commission.

15 As to the meaning of this, see *Sayag v. Leduc (No. 1)*, Case 5/68, [1968] ECR 395.

16 Member States are also prohibited from taking an official's salary into account for the purpose of determining the tax payable by the official's spouse: *Humblet v. Belgium*, Case 6/60, [1960] ECR 559.

17 Protocol on the Privileges and Immunities of the European Communities, Art. 18. See *Weddel & Co. BV v. Commission*, Case C-54/90, 1992 [ECR] I-829.

18 *France, Italy and United Kingdom v. Commission*, Cases 188–190/80, [1982] ECR 2545 (paras 4–7 of the judgment). See, further, *France v. Commission*, Case C-202/88, [1991] ECR I-1223; *Spain v. Commission*, Cases C-271, 281, 289/90, [1992] ECR I-5833.

19 *Germany v. Commission*, Cases 281, 283–5, 287/85, [1987] ECR 3203 (para. 28 of the judgment). See Hartley, 'The Commission as Legislator under the EEC Treaty' (1988) 13 ELRev. 122. However, the Commission has no implied power under the EC Treaty to conclude international agreements, even on a subject matter (such as competition) with regard to which it has internal executive power: *France v. Commission*, Case C-327/91, [1994] ECR I-3641.

20 See Chap. 4.

## DECISION-MAKING PROCEDURE

The Commission takes decisions by a simple majority vote.[21] Frequently, however, use is made of the so-called 'written procedure' under which draft decisions are circulated among the Commissioners and, if no objections are made within a given period, the proposal is regarded as adopted.

Special procedures are followed where powers are delegated by the Council to the Commission. In order to retain some measure of control, the Council usually provides for the establishment of a committee to which the Commission must submit drafts of measures it intends to adopt under the delegated power. These committees are composed of representatives of the national governments under the chairmanship of a Commission official.

The Single European Act attempted to put this system on a more regular footing by making provision for a framework-decision establishing the principles and rules to be followed.[22] The first such decision was adopted by the Council in 1987.[23] It has now been replaced by a decision adopted in 1999.[24] This decision sets out a number of procedures which may be required in any given case by the instrument delegating the power.

Under the first, known as the advisory procedure, the committee's functions are purely advisory. The Commission must put a draft of the measure before the committee,[25] but an unfavourable opinion does not affect the Commission's powers.[26]

Under the second, known as the management procedure, the Commission must put the draft before the committee, and the chairman sets a time-limit within which it must give its opinion. The committee votes according to the same system of weighted voting as the Council itself (explained below) and a decision can be adopted only if a 'qualified majority' of votes is obtained. The chairman has no vote. If the Commission follows the committee's opinion (or if the committee gives no opinion within the time-limit), the Commission may adopt the draft and this will be definitive. Even if the Commission does not follow the committee's opinion, it may still adopt the measure, but in this case it must

[21] Arts 219 [163] EC and 132 Euratom.

[22] Art. 10 SEA, amending Art. 202 [145] EC.

[23] Decision 87/373, OJ 1987, L197/33. This decision differed considerably from the Commission proposal: see OJ 1986, C70/6. It was subject to criticism by the Commission (see Press Release IP (89) 803 of 31 October 1989; see also the declarations in the Council minutes for the proceedings in which the decision was adopted, published by the news agency 'Europe', 28 October 1987: Docs. No. 1477) and was challenged by the European Parliament in the European Court, although the action was dismissed as inadmissible: *European Parliament v. Council*, Case 302/87, [1988] ECR 5615. The Declaration Relating to the Council Decision of 13 July 1987, adopted by the Amsterdam Inter-Governmental Conference (Declaration 31 annexed to the Treaty of Amsterdam), called for the amendment of Decision 87/373 by the end of 1998. The new decision was in fact adopted on 28 June 1999.

[24] Council Decision 99/468/EC, OJ 1999 L184/23, amended by Council Decision 2006/512/EC, OJ 2006 L200/11.

[25] Failure to do so would probably constitute an infringement of an essential procedural requirement, leading to the annulment of the measure under Art. 230 [173] EC.

[26] The chairman of the committee (who is a Commission appointee) fixes the time-limit within which the committee must give its opinion, and if no opinion is given within this time, the Commission can go ahead without it. Presumably the time-limit would have to be reasonable.

immediately communicate it to the Council. The Commission may defer the application of the measure for a limited period[27] and the Council may then adopt a different measure (which replaces the Commission measure) provided it acts within this period.[28]

The third system, which is the least favourable to the Commission, is known as the regulatory procedure. Under it, the committee gives its opinion in the same way as under the management procedure. However, the Commission may proceed immediately to adopt the measure only if it follows the committee's opinion. If it does not, or if no opinion is given, the Commission must put a draft measure before the Council.[29] If the Council does not act within the period specified by the instrument under which the power was originally delegated,[30] the Commission may adopt its draft. If, on the other hand, the Council rejects the draft, the Commission cannot adopt it.[31] The Commission may submit an amended proposal to the Council. It may also resubmit its original proposal, if it believes that the Council will drop its opposition. Alternatively, it may submit a proposal for an original (non-delegated) legislative act under an appropriate provision of the Treaty.

A special procedure[32] may be applied where the original instrument gives the Commission the power to take safeguard measures (measures designed to deal with emergencies). The Commission takes the decision (without reference to any committee) and notifies the Council and the Member States. The Council, acting by a qualified majority, may then take a different decision. If it does not act within a time-limit laid down in the original instrument, the Commission's decision stands. However, the original instrument may lay down a variant, under which the Commission decision is revoked, unless the Council confirms (or amends) it within the time-limit.

An amendment to Decision 99/468 was adopted in 2006 to meet the European Parliament's objection that its interests were insufficiently protected under the existing procedure.[33] The amendment applies only where the original instrument was adopted under the 'co-decision' procedure (discussed below), a procedure under which the Council shares legislative power with the Parliament. The amendment requires a special procedure, known as the 'regulatory procedure with scrutiny', to be followed where the proposed delegated legislation seeks to amend the original instrument by either deleting provisions from it or by adding new provisions to it.[34] Where this occurs, a draft of the

[27] It may not be greater than three months: Art. 4(3) of Decision 99/468.

[28] The Council acts by a qualified majority.

[29] The Commission must also inform the European Parliament. If the instrument which originally conferred the delegated power was adopted under the co-decision procedure (explained below), and the Parliament considers that the draft measure exceeds the implementing powers provided for in the original instrument, it will inform the Council of its position. The Council must take this into account when it exercises its powers. The Parliament also has a general power under Art. 8 of Decision 99/468 to consider whether draft implementing measures which have been submitted to a committee would exceed the implementing powers provided for in the instrument under which the power was originally delegated. If it decides that this is the case, it will inform the Commission, which must take the Parliament's opinion into account.

[30] The period may not be longer than three months: Art. 5(6) of Decision 99/468.

[31] The Council again acts by a qualified majority.

[32] Art. 6 of Decision 99/468.

[33] Council Decision 2006/512/EC, OJ 2006 L200/11.

[34] It applies only to amendments of non-essential elements in the original instrument. However, amendments to essential elements cannot be made by delegated legislation: see *Einfuhr- und Vorratsstelle v. Köster*,

delegated measure must be sent to the Council and the Parliament for scrutiny. Either of these two institutions may object to it on one of the following grounds:

- it goes beyond the implementing power conferred by the original instrument;
- it is incompatible with the aim or content of the original instrument; or
- it violates the principles of 'subsidiarity' or 'proportionality' (discussed in later chapters).[35]

Where such an objection is made, the measure cannot be adopted by the Commission. In such a case, the Commission would have to amend it to meet the objection, or the measure would have to be adopted by the Council and Parliament under the co-decision procedure.[36]

### ASSESSMENT

In the early days of the Community, Commission officials were often idealists. Today, they are more concerned with furthering their careers. Although few are actually corrupt, there seems to exist a widespread culture of looking after one's own interests and ignoring those of the Community. This came most glaringly to light in the scandal surrounding the Santer Commission (discussed below), in which the whole Commission resigned after a report by a committee of independent experts set up by the European Parliament said that it was increasingly difficult to find anyone in the Commission with 'even the slightest sense of responsibility'.[37] Despite these shortcomings, the Commission enjoys a powerful position in the Community, mainly because it is seen as being above national rivalries. This raises the question whether it is right for a bureaucracy that is subject to little political control to determine policy in the Community.

## THE COUNCIL

The Council is the body where the interests of the Member States find direct expression. It takes the final decision on most EC legislation (often acting jointly with the Parliament), concludes agreements with foreign countries, and, together with the Parliament, decides on the Community budget. It consists of the delegates of the Member States, each state being represented by a government minister who is authorized to commit his government.[38] When general matters are discussed, Member States will normally be

Case 25/70, [1970] ECR 1161, discussed in Chap. 4. It also applies only if the proposed delegated legislation is of general scope, but this will almost always be the case.

[35] Subsidiarity is discussed in Chap. 4 and proportionality in Chap. 5.

[36] For further discussion, see 'Editorial Comment' (2006) 43 CMLRev.1243 at pp. 1245–9.

[37] Committee of Independent Experts, *First Report on Allegations of Fraud, Mismanagement and Nepotism in the European Commission* (15 March 1999). See Tomkins (1999) 62 MLR 744.

[38] Arts 203 [146] EC and 116 Euratom.

represented by their foreign ministers; but other ministers will attend for specialist discussions: for example, ministers of agriculture for meetings dealing with agriculture and ministers of finance for financial meetings. Meetings of foreign ministers are often called the 'general Council' and meetings of other ministers are referred to, collectively, as 'sectoral', 'specialized', or 'technical' Councils and, individually, as the 'agricultural Council', 'financial Council', etc.[39] Ministers attending Council meetings are usually accompanied by officials. A representative of the Commission also takes part in the proceedings.

The Presidency of the Council rotates among the Member States at six-monthly intervals.[40] While it holds the Presidency, a Member State will provide the President (chairman) for all meetings of the Council and other Community bodies on which the Member States are represented.[41] The functions of the President are to call meetings, to preside at them, to call for a vote, and to sign acts adopted at the meeting. The Presidency also involves a general responsibility to ensure the smooth running of the Council. The Member State holding the Presidency has the role of mediator between the Member States in the search for agreement. In matters coming within the common foreign and security policy, it represents the European Union *vis-à-vis* the outside world.[42] In recent years, the Presidency has become increasingly important, and the Member States vie with each other to achieve maximum progress during their term of office.

The Council has its own General Secretariat staffed by permanent officials.[43] It is similar to, but much smaller than, the Commission staff. It is divided into Directorates General and headed by a Secretary General. It has its own Legal Service.

## COREPER

The ministers are able to be in Brussels only for short periods. In order to provide continuity, a Committee of the Permanent Representatives of the Member States, usually known by its French acronym, 'COREPER', was set up to prepare the work of the Council.[44] The Permanent Representatives are the ambassadors of the Member States to the Community and the Committee represents the Member States at a lower level than the ministers. COREPER itself meets on two levels: deputy Permanent Representatives (COREPER I) for more technical questions; and the Permanent Representatives themselves (COREPER II) for the more important political questions. At a lower level still, there are many committees and Council working groups, staffed by national officials based in Brussels or in their home countries.

COREPER plays an important role in the Council mechanism. Matters to be decided by the Council come to it first. If unanimous agreement is reached in COREPER, the item will be listed under Part A of the Council agenda; it will then be adopted without

[39] For further details on the various Council 'formations', see the Communication from the Council of 23 June 2000, OJ 2000 C174.

[40] Arts 203 [146] EC and 116 Euratom.

[41] These bodies include the European Council, COREPER, committees and working groups of COREPER, and meetings of the Representatives of the Governments of the Member States.

[42] Art. 18 [J.5] TEU.

[43] Arts 207(2) [151(2)] EC and 121(2) Euratom.

[44] Arts 207(1) [151(1)] EC, and 121(1) Euratom.

discussion. Negotiations with the Commission take place in COREPER: if a Commission proposal is unacceptable, attempts will be made to induce the Commission to amend it in order to secure agreement. The result of this is that in fact, though not in law, COREPER is an integral part of the Council decision-making process and could be regarded as an extension of the Council itself.[45]

## VOTING

Since the most important decisions are taken by the Council, the question of voting is crucial. At first sight, the Treaties[46] give the impression that the supranational element is strong. Thus Article 205(1) [148(1)] EC states:

> Save as otherwise provided in this Treaty, the Council shall act by a majority of its members.[47]

In fact, however, the specific provisions dealing with almost every matter of importance *do* provide otherwise: only matters of minor significance are decided by this system.[48] There are some matters (for example, the admission of new members)[49] which must be decided unanimously.[50] Most matters, however, are decided by what is called a 'qualified majority'.

The qualified-majority voting system is an attempt to solve one of the most intractable problems facing supranational organizations. Once you get away from the idea that nothing can be done without unanimity, it is necessary to decide how voting is to be conducted. If each state were given equal voting power, it would mean that Luxembourg would be on the same footing as the United States or China. This would be absurd. However, to base voting power solely on population would be unacceptable to most states. In the UN Security Council, the problem is solved by giving each state one vote, but, in addition, giving a veto to what were originally regarded as the most important states.

In the EU, a different solution has been adopted. When qualified-majority voting takes place in the Council, the votes of the Member States are weighted. The votes given to each state are in essence a compromise between the principle of equality and the principle that votes should reflect population.

Certain additional factors also play a role, in particular, the idea of grouping states together. This latter idea produces anomalies. In the past, Germany, France, Italy, and

[45] In *Commission v. Council* (*FAO* case), Case C-25/94, [1996] ECR I-1469, the European Court held that, not being an institution of the Community, COREPER has no power to take decisions in its own name. However, an amendment to Arts 207(1) [151(1)] EC and 121(1) Euratom brought about by the Treaty of Amsterdam allows it to adopt procedural decisions in cases provided for in the Council's Rules of Procedure.

[46] The position is the same under the Euratom Treaty (see Art. 118).

[47] Note that this is a majority of members (absolute majority), not a majority of votes: abstentions count as votes against the proposal.

[48] For example, Art. 209 [153] EC.

[49] Art. 49 [O] TEU.

[50] However, an abstention by one or more members of the Council does not prevent such a decision from being adopted, provided that the members in question were 'present in person or represented' at the meeting: Art. 205(3) [148(3)] EC. Such decisions can be blocked if one member boycotts the meetings, as France did during the crisis of 1965–6.

the United Kingdom were all approximately the same size; so it made sense to give them the same voting power. This changed with German reunification. However, France was unwilling to allow Germany to have more votes than it had; so Germany remains grouped with the other members of the 'Big Four'.

The allocation of votes has been subject to frequent changes. At present, it is as follows:[51]

| | |
|---|---|
| Germany, France, Italy, United Kingdom | 29 votes each |
| Spain, Poland | 27 votes each |
| Romania | 14 votes |
| Netherlands | 13 votes |
| Belgium, Czech Republic, Greece, Hungary, Portugal | 12 votes each |
| Bulgaria, Austria, Sweden | 10 votes each |
| Denmark, Ireland, Lithuania, Slovakia, Finland | 7 votes each |
| Estonia, Cyprus, Latvia, Luxembourg, Malta, Slovenia | 4 votes each |

The total number of votes is 346. A qualified majority is 255. This is approximately 74 per cent of the total number of votes.

In addition, there is a second rule that a majority of Member States must vote in favour of the act when it is adopted on a proposal from the Commission; when it is not adopted on a proposal from the Commission, a two-thirds majority of Member States must vote for it.[52] This second rule benefits the smaller states. However, there is a third rule, which benefits the larger states. This is the rule that when a decision is adopted by a qualified majority, any Member State may request verification that the states making up the qualified majority represent at least 62 per cent of the total population of the Community. This will prevent a coalition of small states outvoting the larger states.[53]

In every constitution, the provisions of strict law are supplemented, and sometimes modified, by convention. Constitutional conventions are rules of political practice based on the realities of political life. They reflect political power and do not normally endure for long, once the assumptions on which they are based have disappeared. Conventions operate in the Community as they do in national constitutions.

International bodies usually work on a system of give and take. States try to achieve what they want by influencing other Member States, either by offering something in return – 'We will vote for you on issue X if you support us on issue Y' – or by threatening to cause trouble. In the latter category, three tactics (in order of increasing stringency) are: threatening to block progress on other, unrelated issues; threatening to boycott future meetings; and threatening to withdraw. Negative tactics of this kind can, if the threats are credible, be very effective, but there is a price to be paid. Bad feeling is created and other states will be less co-operative. Moreover, boycott or withdrawal will

[51] Act of Accession (Bulgaria and Romania) 2005, Art. 10(1), OJ 2000 L157, p. 203 (replacing Arts 205(2) EC and 118(2) Euratom). For decision-making under the Common Foreign and Security Policy and under Police and Judicial Co-operation in Criminal Matters, see Arts 10(2) and 10(3) of the Act of Accession (replacing Art. 23(2), third paragraph, TEU and Art. 34(3) TEU).

[52] *Ibid.*

[53] Arts 205(4) EC and 118 Euratom (inserted by Art. 3(1)(a)(ii) of the Protocol to the Treaty of Nice on the Enlargement of the European Union).

hurt the state concerned more than the others. For these reasons manœuvres of this kind will be used only if a country feels that its vital interests are at stake (though a relatively powerful country will feel able to take tougher measures than a weaker one).

In view of this, it would be surprising if a 'constitutional convention' had not sprung up in the Community to the effect that majority voting should not be used to push through a measure regarded by one Member State as harming its vital interests. Such a convention did indeed come into existence, though today it has to some extent withered away. Its history is instructive. The EC Treaty envisaged the establishment of the Common Market in three stages. In many instances, it provided that the Council would take decisions unanimously during the first two stages and by a qualified majority thereafter. The third stage began on 1 January 1966 and should have marked the transition to qualified majority voting. However, General de Gaulle was not prepared to accept this. From the middle of 1965 France boycotted the Community institutions (the so-called 'empty chair' policy) in protest against various developments, including the imminent onset of qualified-majority voting.[54] This precipitated a crisis in the Community which was settled only when France agreed to a meeting with the other five Member Sates. It was held in Luxembourg in January 1966 and resulted in a press release containing the famous 'Luxembourg Accords'.

The main provisions of the Luxembourg Accords dealing with majority voting are as follows:

> I. Where, in the case of decisions which may be taken by majority vote on a proposal of the Commission, very important interests of one or more partners are at stake, the Members of the Council will endeavour, within a reasonable time, to reach solutions which can be adopted by all the Members of the Council while respecting their mutual interests and those of the Community, in accordance with Article 2 [2] of the Treaty.
>
> II. With regard to the preceding paragraph, the French delegation considers that where very important interests are at stake the discussion must be continued until unanimous agreement is reached.
>
> III. The six delegations note that there is a divergence of views on what should be done in the event of a failure to reach complete agreement.

There is also a fourth paragraph under which the Six agreed that five specified matters, all concerned with agriculture, should be decided by common consent.

It should be noted that this is in part an agreement between the Member States (of which the legal effect is uncertain) and in part an agreement to disagree; nevertheless, for a long time afterwards the French view prevailed in practice, and when the United Kingdom joined the Community it was confidently asserted by the British Government that each Member State enjoyed a veto.[55] Even at that time, however, qualified-majority voting was practised in one special case, the Community budget.[56] The next development

54 Initially the French were more concerned with agricultural markets, Community financing, and the budgetary powers of the European Parliament, but they subsequently broadened their demands to include the suppression of qualified majority voting.

55 See *The UK and the European Communities*, Cmnd. 4715 (1971), para. 29 and *Membership of the European Community – Report on Renegotiation*, Cmnd. 6003 (1975), para. 124.

56 It was also used for staff matters.

occurred in 1982 when the Council adopted an agricultural price increase despite an attempted British veto. In what appears to have been a pre-planned move, the Belgian President of the Council called for a vote, ignoring the British representative's claim that very important interests of the United Kingdom were at stake. The United Kingdom, Denmark, and Greece refused to vote;[57] the others voted in favour, thus ensuring the qualified majority required by the relevant Treaty provision. The United Kingdom was outraged, but a month later, after a meeting of the General Council called specially to discuss the matter, Mr Francis Pym, the British Foreign Secretary at the time, expressed the view that the veto remained intact.

How is one to explain this? It is not known what was said in that meeting, but one explanation is that the events of the previous month did not constitute a violation of the convention, because the United Kingdom's attempt to use the veto was improper. Britain admitted that the price increases were not unacceptable in themselves: they were being blocked in order to force the other Member States to make concessions on Britain's budgetary contribution. Therefore, if one takes the view that the right to veto a measure exists only when *that* measure is contrary to the vital interest of the state concerned, the other Member States were fully entitled to press the matter to a vote.[58]

However this may be, the principle of unanimity had obviously been weakened.[59] Moreover, in the years that followed, it became increasingly clear that greater use of majority voting would be essential if reasonable progress was to be made towards the attainment of the objectives of the Community. How this might be brought about was considered in the discussions leading up to the Single European Act and, though the latter did not directly refer to it, there was an understanding that more votes would take place, at least with regard to the completion of the single European market.[60] Since then, voting has become increasingly common[61] and now takes place quite often; nevertheless, one cannot say that the convention is dead, since many decisions are still taken without a vote and considerable efforts are made to reach a consensus.[62]

[57] Denmark and Greece both supported the measure but regarded the principle of the veto as sacrosanct.

[58] See the statement in the House of Commons by Sir Geoffrey Howe (Foreign Secretary at the time), on 23 April 1986, H C Deb., 96, cols 320–1.

[59] See Nicoll, 'The Luxembourg Compromise' (1984) 23 JCMS 35 at 40–1, where it is said that further votes took place in 1984.

[60] However, in his statement in the House of Commons on 23 April 1986, the British Foreign Secretary said that the Luxembourg Accords were 'in no way affected one way or the other by the Single European Act'. See H C Deb., 96, cols 320–1.

[61] It is interesting to note that on 20 July 1987 the Council amended its Rules of Procedure so that a vote can now be taken not only on the initiative of the President, but also on the initiative of any member of the Council (or on the initiative of the Commission), provided that a (simple) majority of the members of the Council is in favour. This means there are two votes: a procedural vote (on whether the substantive question should be put to the vote) and, if the procedural motion is supported by a majority of Member States, a substantive vote. Previously a vote on a substantive question would be taken only if the President so decided. See OJ 1987, L291/27. For the current Rules, see Decision 2006/683/EC, OJ 2006 L285/47, Art. 11(1).

[62] According to one study, only one decision in four is contested; a negative vote (as distinct from an abstention) is cast against only one in seven; and there is more than marginal opposition to only one in sixteen. The topics are usually highly technical. The most frequent 'no-sayers' are (in order) Denmark, the Netherlands, Germany, and the United Kingdom. See Fiona Hayes-Renshaw and Helen Wallace, *The Council of Ministers* (1997), p.53.

### THE EUROPEAN COUNCIL

In 1974 it was agreed that the Heads of State or of Government[63] of the Member States, together with their foreign ministers, would hold summit conferences at regular intervals. In time these meetings became formalized and were known as 'the European Council', a term now used in the Treaties. (This must not to be confused with the regular Council, referred to simply as 'the Council', nor with the Council of Europe, which is an entirely different organization.) In 1986 the European Council was given legal recognition by Article 2 SEA.[64]

Today the governing provision is Article 4 [D] TEU, which states that the European Council will provide the European Union with the necessary impetus for its development and will define its general political guidelines. Article 4 [D] also confirms the right of the President of the Commission and one other Commissioner to attend. The meetings, which take place at least twice a year, are chaired by the representative of the Member State holding the Presidency. Discussions cover both Community matters and matters outside the jurisdiction of the Community (but within that of the Union).[65] When it discusses Community matters it could act as the Council of the European Communities: there is nothing in Community law preventing Member States from being represented at Council meetings by their Heads of State or of Government.[66] In practice, however, the European Council usually takes only general political decisions; these are then translated into legal form at meetings of the Council held at ministerial level. The appointment of members of the Commission is an exception. As we saw above, the Treaty of Nice provides that this will be done by the Council, meeting in the composition of Heads of State or Government.

## COMMON FOREIGN AND SECURITY POLICY

As far back as the early 1950s, attempts were made to promote European integration in the fields of defence and foreign policy, but these collapsed in 1954 when the French National Assembly rejected the European Defence Treaty. It was another fifteen years before a new effort was made.[67] This deliberately avoided any element of supranationalism and concentrated instead on establishing an inter-governmental framework for political co-operation, mainly in the field of foreign policy. The Member States agreed to regular consultations and exchanges of information in the hope that this would lead to common positions and joint action in international affairs.

63 This means the British Prime Minister, the German Chancellor, the French President, etc.

64 Now repealed.

65 The Common Foreign and Security Policy, and Police and Judicial Co-operation in Criminal Matters (explained below). See Art. 1 [A] TEU.

66 Solemn Declaration on European Union 1983, Point 2.1.3, EC Bull. 6 – 1983, p. 5.

67 The origin of European Political Co-operation is usually traced to the Hague Summit of December 1969 and the Luxembourg Report of October 1970.

A striking feature of the system in its initial stage was that it operated almost entirely outside the institutional structure of the Community. There was a rigid division between the European Community and European Political Co-operation (EPC), as it was then called: the Commission was largely excluded from EPC meetings, which took place in the capital of the Member State holding the Presidency, rather than in Brussels. The argument was that the subject matter of EPC was outside the scope of the Treaties; therefore, it was outside the jurisdiction of the Community institutions. It soon became apparent, however, that this distinction could not be fully maintained. For example, if it were wished to adopt economic sanctions against a third country, would this be a matter for EPC (because it concerned foreign policy) or a matter for the Community (because it concerned commercial policy, a subject covered by Articles 131–135 [110–116] of the EC Treaty)? In fact, when the Falklands War broke out, sanctions against Argentina were adopted by the Community after 'discussions in the context of European political co-operation', but 'in accordance with the relevant provisions of the Community Treaties'.[68] Thus both systems came together to produce the desired result.

As time went on, therefore, the dividing line between the Community and EPC became blurred and Title III of the Single European Act, which gave legal recognition to EPC, provided that the Commission would be 'fully associated with the proceedings of Political Co-operation'[69] and that the European Parliament would be 'closely associated' with it.[70] Title III SEA also made provision for the establishment of a political and administrative structure for EPC.

Title III SEA was replaced by Title V of the Treaty on European Union, which was amended and restructured by the Treaty of Amsterdam. These provisions establish a common foreign and security policy (CFSP), which Member States are obliged to support 'actively and unreservedly in a spirit of loyalty and mutual solidarity'.[71] The Treaty provides that the CFSP includes all questions relating to the security of the Union, including the progressive framing of a common defence policy. This may lead to a common defence, should the European Council so decide, though such a decision must be adopted by each Member State in accordance with its constitutional requirements.[72]

The European Union pursues the CFSP by various means: defining the principles and general guidelines on which it is to be based; deciding on common strategies; adopting joint actions; adopting common positions; and strengthening co-operation between the Member States.[73] The European Council decides on principles and general guidelines; it also decides on common strategies.[74] The Council takes decisions on joint actions and common positions. Joint actions address specific situations where operational action by the Union is required; they commit the Member States in their foreign-policy activities.[75] Common positions lay down the approach of the Union to problems relating to a particular geographical area or theme.[76]

[68] See the preamble to Council Regulation 877/82, OJ 1982, L102/1.
[69] Art. 30(3)(b) SEA. See now Art. 27 [J.17] TEU.
[70] Art. 30(4) SEA. See now Art. 21 [J.11] TEU.
[71] Art. 11(2) [J.1(2)] TEU.
[72] Art. 17(1) [J.7(1)] TEU, as amended by the Treaty of Nice.
[73] Art. 12 [J.2] TEU.
[74] Art. 13(1) and (2) [J.3(1) and (2)] TEU.
[75] Art. 14 [J.4] TEU.
[76] Art. 15 [J.5] TEU.

When operating within the scope of the CFSP, the Council must normally be unanimous; nevertheless, abstentions by members present in person (or represented) do not prevent the adoption of decisions.[77] If, when abstaining, a member makes a formal declaration invoking Article 23 TEU, it is not obliged to apply the decision, though it must accept that it commits to the Union. In these circumstances, the Member State in question must refrain from any action likely to conflict with action taken by the Union. If, however, the number of members making such a declaration command more than a third of the total votes in the Council (as weighted under the qualified-majority voting system), the decision cannot be adopted.[78]

The unanimity rule does not apply in all cases: the Council acts by a qualified majority when adopting joint actions, common positions, or other decisions on the basis of a common strategy, or when adopting a decision implementing a joint action or common position. In such cases, however, any Member State may declare that, for important and stated reasons of national policy, it intends to oppose the decision. If it does this, no vote may be taken; the Council may, however, vote (by a qualified majority) to refer the matter to the European Council for decision by unanimity.[79]

The Presidency (Member State holding the Presidency of the Council) represents the Union in matters coming within the CFSP; it is also responsible for the implementation of decisions and for speaking on behalf of the Union in international organizations and conferences.[80] The Presidency is assisted by the Secretary General of the Council, clearly destined to be a key figure. With regard to the CFSP, he has the title 'High Representative'.[81]

The most striking feature about the CFSP is that the supranational element is almost entirely lacking. All power is concentrated in the hands of the Council, which does not have to act on a proposal from the Commission, though the Commission has the power to make proposals;[82] no Member State can be forced to accept a decision against its will; and the jurisdiction of the Court is largely excluded.[83]

## POLICE AND JUDICIAL CO-OPERATION IN CRIMINAL MATTERS

A similar system has been set up by Title VI of the Treaty on European Union (as amended and restructured by the Treaty of Amsterdam) for police and judicial co-operation in criminal matters.[84] This system is intended to combat crime in general, though particular attention is paid to terrorism, trafficking in persons, offences against children, drug trafficking, arms trafficking, corruption, and fraud.

To achieve these objectives, the Council, acting unanimously on the initiative of a Member State or of the Commission, may adopt common positions defining the approach of the Union to a particular matter; adopt framework decisions to harmonize

[77] Art. 23(1) [J.13(1)] TEU. [78] *Ibid.*

[79] Art. 23(2) [J.13(2)] TEU. The provisions of this paragraph do not apply to decisions having military or defence implications: Art. 23(1) [J.13(1)] TEU. For procedural questions, the Council acts by a majority of its members: Art. 23(3) [J.13(3)] TEU. [80] Art. 18 [J.8] TEU.

[81] *Ibid.*, para. 3. The Secretary General also assists the Council: Art. 26 [J.16] TEU.

[82] Art. 22 [J.12] TEU. Member States may also make proposals.

[83] Art. 46 [L] TEU, as amended by the Treaty of Nice.

[84] The discussion that follows is based on Title VI as amended by the Treaty of Amsterdam.

national legislation;[85] adopt decisions for other purposes;[86] and establish conventions.[87] Conventions must be adopted by the Member States in accordance with their constitutional requirements; measures to implement them may be adopted within the Council by a majority of two-thirds of the Contracting Parties.[88]

As in the case of the CFSP, supranational elements are largely lacking; nevertheless, the European Court has jurisdiction to give preliminary rulings on the validity and interpretation of framework decisions and other decisions; on the interpretation of conventions; and on the validity and interpretation of measures implementing conventions.[89] However, the European Court's jurisdiction in this regard applies only to those Member States which declare that they are willing to accept it.[90] The Court also has jurisdiction to review the legality of framework decisions and other decisions in actions brought by Member States or the Commission.[91]

## THE EUROPEAN PARLIAMENT

### COMPOSITION

The European Parliament[92] is intended to represent the peoples of the Community. This is made clear by Article 189 [137] EC,[93] which states that it consists of 'representatives of the peoples of the States brought together in the Community'. In spite of this, however, the Members of the European Parliament were for a long time selected by the national legislatures and it was only in 1976 that agreement was reached on direct elections.[94] The Treaties provided that the Parliament would draw up proposals for direct elections and that the Council, acting unanimously, would 'lay down the appropriate provisions', which it would recommend to Member States for adoption in accordance with their

85 Framework decisions are similar to directives but are expressly stated to have no direct effect: Art. 34(2)(b) [K.6(2)(b)] TEU. On the concept of direct effect, see Chap. 7.

86 These also have no direct effect: Art. 34(2)(c) [K.6(2)(c)] TEU. The Council may adopt measures to implement these decisions; when doing so, it acts by a qualified majority: *ibid.*

87 These powers are all conferred on the Council by Art. 34(2) TEU.

88 Art. 34(2)(d) [K.6(2)(d)] TEU.

89 Art. 35(1) [K.7(1)] TEU.

90 Art. 35(2) [K.7(2)] TEU. However, the Court may in no circumstances review police action in the Member States, nor may it review the actions of Member States regarding the maintenance of law and order and the safeguarding of national security: Art. 35(5) [K.7(5)] TEU.

91 Art. 35(6) [K.7(6)] TEU. For a general discussion of proceedings of this kind, see Chaps 11, 12, 15, and 16. The Court also has jurisdiction to rule on disputes between Member States on the interpretation or application of acts adopted under Art. 34(2) [K.6(2)] TEU and on disputes between Member States and the Commission regarding the interpretation or application of conventions established under Art. 34(2)(d) [K.6(2)(d)] TEU: see Art. 36(7) [K.8(7)] TEU.

92 Referred to in the original Treaties as the 'Assembly', the European Parliament adopted its present name in 1962 (EP Resolution of 30 March 1962, JO 1962, p.1045). This was recognized by the Member States in the Single European Act: see Art. 3(1) SEA. See now Art. 7 [4] EC.

93 See also Art. 107 Euratom.

94 Council Decision 76/787, and the annexed Act concerning the election of the representatives of the Assembly by direct universal suffrage, OJ 1976, L278/1. See, further, Forman, (1977) 2 ELRev. 35.

respective constitutional requirements.[95] The Parliament first drew up proposals as long ago as 1960, but it took the intervening sixteen years for the Council to reach a decision. Thereafter, the provisions had to be adopted at national level and this involved further difficulties and delays, not least in the United Kingdom; so the first elections were not held until 1979. Thereafter they have been, and will be, held every five years.[96]

The instrument providing for elections took an unusual form, since all its substantive provisions are in an Act annexed to the Council Decision. The legal nature of this Act is controversial. Does it take effect as an international agreement between the Member States based on a draft recommended by the Council? Or does it take effect as a decision of the Council to which the Member States have agreed? Perhaps the best view is that Articles 190(4) [138(3)] EC and 108(3) Euratom lay down a special procedure for amending these Treaties which derogates from the normal procedure.[97] If this view is correct, the Act takes effect as an agreement between the Member States but forms part of the three Treaties.[98] The importance of this question is that the jurisdiction of the European Court to annul,[99] interpret,[100] or enforce[101] the Act depends on the Act's legal status.[102]

Prior to 1994, the four largest Member States (Germany, France, Italy, and the United Kingdom) all had the same number of seats (eighty-one). After the unification of Germany, however, the German electorate became so much greater that parity with the other three could no longer be maintained; so Germany was given ninety-nine seats. When further states joined, there was a danger of the Parliament getting too large. The Treaty of Nice therefore made provision for a reduction in the number of seats allocated to all the existing Member States except Germany (the largest) and Luxembourg (then the smallest).

At present, the total number of seats is 736. They are allocated as follows:[103]

| | |
|---|---|
| Germany | 99 |
| France, Italy, United Kingdom | 72 (each) |
| Spain, Poland | 50 (each) |
| Romania | 33 |
| Netherlands | 25 |
| Belgium, Czech Republic, Greece, Hungary, Portugal | 22 (each) |
| Sweden | 18 |
| Bulgaria, Austria | 17 (each) |

[95] Arts 190(4) [138(3)] EC and 108(3) Euratom. Amendments brought in by the Treaty on European Union provide that the Council must obtain the consent of the European Parliament (which acts by a majority of its members) before adopting the provisions to be recommended to the Member States.

[96] See Art. 3 of the Act providing for direct elections (above).

[97] This was previously set out in Arts 236 EC and 204 Euratom; see now Art. 48 [N] TEU.

[98] See Joliet, *Institutions*, pp. 75–7, where the problem is fully discussed.

[99] See Arts 230 [173] EC and 146 Euratom (direct actions); and 234 [177] EC and 150 Euratom (preliminary rulings on validity).

[100] See Arts 234 [177] EC and 150 Euratom.

[101] See Arts 226–228 [169–171] EC and 141–143 Euratom.

[102] If the third view is correct, the European Court cannot annul the Act, even if it infringes the Treaties, but it can interpret or enforce it where the Treaties so provide.

[103] Act of Accession (Bulgaria and Romania) 2005, Art. 9, replacing Art. 189(2) EC and Art. 107(2) Euratom.

| | |
|---|---|
| Denmark, Slovakia, Finland | 13 (each) |
| Ireland, Lithuania | 12 (each) |
| Latvia | 8 |
| Slovenia | 7 |
| Estonia, Cyprus, Luxembourg | 6 (each) |
| Malta | 5 |
| TOTAL | 736 |

It will be noticed that these allocations are not proportional to population: the smaller Member States are over-represented compared with the larger ones. For example, the population of the United Kingdom is more than 130 times that of Luxembourg. If it is right for Luxembourg to have six seats, the United Kingdom should have something like 780 seats, instead of seventy-two. To put it another way: the vote of one Luxembourger is worth more than those of ten British citizens. This is not exactly consistent with the principle of 'one person – one vote – one value', which shows that democratic principles must give way before the national interests of the smaller states.[104]

The Act providing for direct elections states that, until a uniform electoral procedure has been adopted, each Member State is free to choose its own electoral system.[105] So far no agreement has been reached on a fully uniform system; therefore, the question still depends on national law[106] and the electoral system differs from country to country. For many years, the United Kingdom used its normal 'first past the post' system (except in Northern Ireland).[107] When Labour came to power, however, there was a change of policy, and the 1999 elections were held on the basis of proportional representation in all parts of the United Kingdom.[108] Now, some form of proportional representation is used in every Member State.[109]

[104] It is sometimes said that this unequal allocation of seats is necessary in order to ensure that all parties in the smaller countries can gain representation. Such an argument cannot, however, justify a departure from the basic principle of equality of voting rights, nor can it explain why Northern Ireland, with its distinctive and diverse political scene, should have only half as many seats as Luxembourg, even though it has more than four times as many voters. The fact that Northern Ireland is not an independent state is irrelevant, since the European Parliament is not intended to provide a forum to represent states, a function fulfilled by the Council. Similar arguments may be made with regard to Scotland and Wales, as well as with regard to culturally distinct regions in other Member States.

[105] Art. 7(2). This is subject to the other provisions of the Act; as to these, see Joliet, *Institutions*, pp. 77–82. It might originally have been argued that Art. 7(2) was invalid, since the Treaty provisions (Arts 190(3) [138(3))] EC, 21(3) ECSC, and 108(3) Euratom) required the procedure to be uniform in all Member States. The counter-argument was that this requirement applied only to the Parliament's proposals, not to the final measure: see Joliet, *Institutions*, p. 77. In any event, the Treaty of Amsterdam amended these provisions to state that the Parliament's proposal must be for elections according to a uniform procedure in all Member States *or in accordance with principles common to all Member States.*

[106] For this reason, a grant by the European Parliament to the political parties to cover election expenses was held invalid by the European Court: *Parti Ecologiste – 'Les Verts' v. European Parliament*, Case 294/83, [1986] ECR 1339. (The Ecologist Party (the Greens) had challenged the grant on the ground that it was distributed in a way that was unfair to the newer parties.) See, further, Joliet and Keeling, 'The Reimbursement of Election Expenses: A Forgotten Dispute' (1994) 19 ELRev. 243.

[107] European Parliamentary Elections Act 1978, s. 3.

[108] European Parliamentary Elections Act 1999.

[109] On the citizenship requirement for voting, and the right of persons in Gibraltar to vote, see *Spain v. United Kingdom*, Case C-145/04, 12 September 2006.

Members of the European Parliament (MEPs) are permitted also to be members of their national parliaments,[110] but Article 6(1) of the Act annexed to Council Decision 76/787 specifies a number of offices with which the office of MEP is incompatible. The most important are: member of the Government of a Member State; member of the Commission; Judge, Advocate General, or Registrar of the European Court; or active official of a Community institution. Article 6(2) permits Member States to lay down additional incompatibilities at national level, and in the United Kingdom most of the disqualifications for membership of the House of Commons apply also to membership of the European Parliament.[111]

## PAY OF MEPS

At present, MEPs are paid the same salaries as their national counterparts, which means there are large differences between the pay of MEPs from different countries. These salaries are subject to income tax in the MEP's home country. They also receive substantial allowances (often greater than their salaries), which are not (at least in principle) subject to national tax.[112]

There have been persistent allegations in the past that some MEPs have obtained allowances fraudulently – for example, by claiming expenses for travel not actually undertaken. It has also been said that the Parliament shows little inclination to investigate.[113] After much discussion, a reformed system was finally adopted. In exchange for a uniform level of basic pay that would constitute an increase for most MEPs, it was agreed to clean up the allowance system. However, the new regime will only come fully into force in 2009.[114]

## PRIVILEGES AND IMMUNITIES

MEPs are entitled to various privileges and immunities[115] of which the most important are, first, freedom of movement to and from the meeting place of the Parliament; secondly, immunity from legal proceedings in respect of opinions expressed, or votes cast, in the performance of their duties; and thirdly, in their own Member State, the same immunities as are enjoyed by members of their national parliament and, in other Member States, freedom from detention and immunity from legal proceedings. Immunities in the third category apply only during parliamentary sessions but, as these last virtually all the year,[116] this

110 Art. 5 of the Act annexed to Council Decision 76/787.

111 European Parliamentary Elections Act 1978, Sched. 1, para. 5.

112 *Lord Bruce v. Aspden*, Case 208/80, [1981] ECR 2205.

113 See, for example, Special Report 10/98 of the Court of Auditors, OJ 1998 C243/1.

114 See OJ 2005 L262/1; OJ 2006 C133/48.

115 See the Protocol on the Privileges and Immunities of the European Communities, Arts 8–10.

116 The length of the sessions is a matter for the Parliament itself to decide. Although it does not actually sit throughout the year, it holds various ancillary activities, such as committee meetings, during most of the year and for the purpose of Parliamentary immunity is regarded as in session until the formal closing of the session, which takes place immediately before the opening of the new session. See *Wybot v. Faure*, Case 149/85, [1986] ECR 2391.

limitation is of little importance.[117] Immunities in this category may be waived by the Parliament itself.

## POLITICAL PARTIES[118]

Members of the European Parliament sit according to their party, not their country. The Rules of Procedure provide for the official recognition of 'political groups'[119] and there are various advantages, both procedural and administrative, in being so recognized. To gain recognition, a group must have a certain minimum number of MEPs. Most of the groups are coalitions of national parties, though in some cases one national party is dominant. Thus, for example, the European Socialists include Labour MEPs from Britain and social democrats from other Member States; and the Green Group is made up of environmentalists from various countries. As might be expected, the cohesiveness of these groups varies, and on some issues national allegiances are more important than loyalty to one's political group.[120]

## COMMITTEES

A characteristic feature of the European Parliament is the role of committees. There are a number of standing committees, and much of the work of the Parliament is done in these committees. When matters come before the Parliament for discussion, they are usually considered first in the appropriate committee and the subsequent debate on the floor of the House is based on the Committee's report.

## PARLIAMENTARY QUESTIONS

Parliamentary questions have become an important part of the Parliament's proceedings. Article 197 [140] EC[121] requires the Commission to reply orally or in writing to questions put to it by the Parliament or by its members. The Council replies to questions on a voluntary basis. Article 21 [J.7] TEU requires the Member State holding the Presidency to keep the Parliament informed of developments regarding the common foreign and security policy; it also states that the Parliament may ask questions of the Council. Similar provisions concerning co-operation in the fields of justice and home affairs are to be found in Article 39 [K.6] TEU.

117 As to whether a former MEP may be prosecuted in England for dishonestly obtaining money for expenses from the European Parliament, see *R v. Manchester Crown Court, ex parte DPP* [1993] 1 WLR 693, QBD, reversed on other grounds [1993] 1 WLR 1524, HL. According to the House of Lords (*ibid.* at 1530–1), the decision of the Divisional Court in this case, having been made without jurisdiction, will not be binding on any other court.

118 Art. 191 [138a] EC, a provision inserted by the Treaty on European Union, declares that political parties at European level are important as a factor for integration within the Union. They are also stated to contribute to forming a 'European awareness' and to expressing the political will of the citizens of the Union.

119 These are not political parties in the normal sense. They exist simply for the purpose of the internal functioning of the Parliament, not for fighting elections.

120 For litigation on the formation of political groups, see *Front national v. Parliament*, Case C-486/01 P, [2004] ECR I-6289.

121 See also Art. 110 Euratom.

The answers to Parliamentary questions are published in the Official Journal and are an important means of gaining information on Community affairs. It is sometimes noticeable, however, that the replies are uninformative to a degree that would hardly be acceptable in the House of Commons.

## PROPOSALS, INQUIRIES, AND PETITIONS

Three amendments to the Community Treaties brought into force by the Treaty on European Union may conveniently be mentioned at this point: the right of the Parliament to request proposals, its right to set up inquiries, and the right of citizens (and others) to petition the Parliament.

The second paragraph of Article 192 [138b] EC[122] gives the Parliament the right, acting by a majority of its members, to request the Commission to submit any 'appropriate proposal' on matters on which it considers that a Community act is required for the purpose of implementing the Treaty. There is no obligation on the Commission to comply.

Article 193 [138c] EC[123] gives the Parliament the right to set up (temporary) committees of inquiry, at the request of a quarter of its members, to investigate alleged contraventions or maladministration in the implementation of Community law (except where the matter is pending before a court).

Article 194 [138d] EC[124] gives any citizen of the European Union, acting individually or in association with others, the right to petition the European Parliament on a matter within the Community's fields of activity which affects him directly.[125] This gave legal recognition to a practice which had existed for some time and can be a valuable means of putting pressure on the Community.[126]

## THE OMBUDSMAN

Article 195 [138e] EC[127] gives the Parliament the power to appoint an Ombudsman,[128] who can receive complaints from any citizen of the Union[129] concerning maladministration in the activities of any Community institution or body except the Court of Justice and the Court of First Instance acting in their judicial roles. The appointment is made after each Parliamentary election and the Ombudsman holds office until the next election. He is eligible for reappointment. His status is in some ways similar to that of a member

[122] See also Art. 107a Euratom. [123] See also Art. 107b Euratom.

[124] See also Art. 107c Euratom.

[125] The right also extends to non-citizens residing in a Member State (as well as to companies having their registered office there).

[126] For further details, see Marias, 'The Right to Petition the European Parliament after Maastricht' (1994) 19 ELRev. 169; Pliakos, 'Les conditions d'exercise du droit de pétition' [1993] CDE 317.

[127] See also Art. 107d Euratom.

[128] The office of Ombudsman originated in Scandinavia (the Parliamentary Commissioner for Administration in Britain is based on the Scandinavian model). The first Ombudsman was a Finn, Jacob Soderman, appointed in 1995.

[129] This right, too, extends to non-citizens residing in a Member State, and to companies having their registered office there.

of the Commission: he is completely independent in the performance of his duties and can be dismissed only if the European Court, at the request of the Parliament, finds that he no longer fulfils the conditions required for the performance of his duties or is guilty of serious misconduct.

Where the Ombudsman establishes an instance of maladministration, he must refer the matter to the institution concerned, which has three months to inform him of its views. The Ombudsman then forwards a report to the Parliament and the institution concerned. The person lodging the complaint must be informed of the outcome. The Parliament does not, however, have power to provide redress in the event that the complaint is upheld. Perhaps it is hoped that the institution or body concerned will do this.[130]

## CONSULTATION

The legislative procedure in the Community, and the Parliament's role in it, are discussed below. It will be seen from this that the Parliament's rights vary, depending on the provision under which the measure is being adopted: in some cases the Parliament has fairly extensive rights; in others it has the right merely to be consulted.[131] Here the procedure will be discussed where the latter is the case.

Under this procedure, the Commission sends a proposal to the Council, which in turn forwards it to the Parliament for its opinion. The proposal is first considered by one of the Parliament's committees, which produces a report and a draft resolution. These go to the full Parliament, which will give its opinion (either positive or negative) and may suggest amendments to the proposal. The Commission may modify its proposal on the basis of the Parliament's opinion but there is no obligation on either it or the Council to follow the opinion or even to give reasons for rejecting it.

Although this procedure gives the Parliament no power to affect the content of legislation, its right to be consulted must be respected. If it is not, the European Court will declare the measure invalid. This happened in *Roquette v. Council*,[132] where the Council sent a proposal for legislation to the Parliament in March 1979. As the measure was to enter into force on 1 July of that year, the Council asked that the opinion be given during the April session. This proved impossible because the draft resolution proposed by the Parliamentary Committee on Agriculture, to which the proposal had been sent, was rejected by the Parliament in plenary session. This meant that the matter had to go back to the Committee for reconsideration and the resulting delay made it impossible to complete the procedure during the April session. The Parliament was willing to convene an extraordinary session should the Council or Commission so desire, but the Council made no such request. Instead it adopted the measure on 25 June 1979, referring in the

[130] For further details, see Pliakos, 'Le Médiateur de l'Union européenne' [1994] CDE 563; Magliveras, 'Best Intentions but Empty Words: The European Ombudsman' (1995) 20 ELRev. 401.

[131] Where the relevant Treaty provision does not give the Parliament the right to be consulted, it is consulted by virtue of an inter-institutional agreement between the Parliament and the Council: see EP Resolution 65 of 27 November 1959, JO 1959, p.1267. It is uncertain what the legal effect of failure to consult in such a case would be.

[132] Case 138/79, [1980] ECR 3333. See also *Maizena v. Council*, Case 139/79, [1980] ECR 3393.

preamble to the fact that the Parliament had been 'consulted', rather than (as is normal) referring to its opinion.

Is it sufficient that the Parliament has been *asked* for its opinion or must it actually *give* its opinion? If the latter were the case, the Parliament could delay legislation indefinitely by the simple expedient of not giving an opinion. If such stonewalling were possible, the right to be consulted would turn into a veto power.

In its judgment, the Court said that observance of the requirement of consultation 'implies that the Parliament has expressed its opinion. It is impossible to take the view that the requirement is satisfied by the Council's simply asking for the opinion.'[133] The Council had argued that the Parliament, by its own conduct, had made observance of the requirement impossible. The Court, however, pointed out that the Council had not exhausted all the possibilities of obtaining an opinion; in particular it had not asked for an extraordinary session. The Council had not, therefore, proved its allegations; and the Court declared the measure void. It was, however, careful to leave open the questions of principle raised by the Council.

In 1995, the question again came before the Court. This time, however, the fault lay with the Parliament: it had not done everything possible to give an opinion in sufficient time; so the Court held that it could not complain that the Council had gone ahead and adopted the measure without waiting for its opinion. The measure was, therefore, valid.[134]

What is the position where, after the Parliament has given its opinion, the proposal is amended? If it was always necessary to ask the Parliament for a new opinion on the amended proposal, the procedure would become very cumbersome, since amendments often have to be made in order to secure the assent of the Member States in the Council. In view of this, the Court has held that, if the provisions of the final text of the measure are 'substantially identical' to those in the version submitted to the Parliament, or if any amendment is substantially in accordance with the Parliament's own proposal, there is no need for a second consultation.[135] Where, however, the amended text differs in substance from the one on which the Parliament was consulted, the Parliament must be consulted again. If this is not done, the measure will be annulled.[136]

International agreements between the Community and non-Member States are another area where the Parliament has the right to be consulted. The procedure for the

133 Para. 34 of the judgment.

134 *European Parliament v. Council*, Case C-65/93, [1995] ECR I-643. See also *European Parliament v. Council*, Case C-417/93, [1995] ECR I-1185, where the Court ruled that the Council is entitled to take a preliminary decision on the measure in question before obtaining the Parliament's opinion, provided that such a decision is not definitive. For a comment on both cases, see Boyron, 'The Consultation Procedure: Has the Court of Justice Turned against the European Parliament?' (1996) 21 ELRev. 145.

135 *Chemiefarma v. Commission*, Case 41/69, [1970] ECR 661 (paras 68 and 69 of the judgment). *Buyl v. Commission*, Case 817/79, [1982] ECR 245 (paras 23 and 24 of the judgment). The Court has also held that where power to implement a measure is delegated by the Council either to the Commission or to itself, it is not necessary to consult the Parliament on the implementing measures, provided the Parliament was consulted on the original measure: *Einfuhr- und Vorratsstelle v. Köster*, Case 25/70, [1970] ECR 1161; *European Parliament v. Council*, Case C-417/93, [1995] ECR I-1185. For a discussion of delegation, see Chap. 4.

136 *European Parliament* v. *Council*, Case C-65/90, [1992] ECR I-4593; *European Parliament* v. *Council*, Case C-388/92, [1994] ECR I-2067; *European Parliament v. Council*, Case C-21/94, [1995] ECR 1827; *European Parliament* v. *Council*, Case C-392/95, [1997] ECR I-3213.

conclusion of international agreements under the EC Treaty is laid down in Article 300 [228] EC. In some cases (discussed below) the Parliament has a right of veto; in all other cases under the EC Treaty, except tariff and trade agreements under Article 133(3) [113(3)], the Parliament has the right to be consulted.[137] It is expressly provided, however, that when it consults the Parliament, the Council can lay down a time-limit for the Parliament to deliver its opinion and, if no opinion is given by the due date, act without it.[138]

Although not previously laid down in the Treaties, the right of the Parliament to be consulted with regard to international agreements was recognized as early as 1983 in the Solemn Declaration on European Union,[139] and in one respect the new provisions could be regarded as a setback for the Parliament since the Solemn Declaration appears to cover all 'significant agreements', including – apparently – tariff and trade agreements, which are now expressly excluded by Article 300(3) [228(3)].

It should finally be mentioned that Article 21 [J.7] TEU states that the Member State holding the Presidency must consult the Parliament on 'the main aspects and the basic choices of the common foreign and security policy' and must ensure that the views of the Parliament are 'duly taken into consideration'. However, since the jurisdiction of the European Court does not extend to this area,[140] there is no legal sanction if this is not done.

## VETO RIGHTS

There are a number of circumstances in which the Parliament must give its assent to action taken by the Council. In such cases the Parliament has a right of veto. With regard to legislation and treaties, there are six instances.

The first concerns sanctions imposed on a Member State under Article 7 [4] TEU for a serious and persistent breach of fundamental rights. The second concerns international agreements and arises under the second paragraph of Article 300(3) [228(3)] EC, under which the assent of the Parliament must be obtained in the case of association agreements under Article 310 [238] EC, agreements which establish a specific institutional framework by organizing co-operation procedures, agreements having important budgetary implications for the Community, and agreements entailing amendment of an act adopted under the co-decision procedure.[141] The third arises under Article 49 [O] TEU, which provides that the Parliament, acting by a majority of its members (absolute majority, not a majority of votes) must give its assent to the admission of new Member States to the Community. The procedure is discussed in Chapter 3. The fourth concerns Council measures under Article 161 [130d] EC regarding the structural and cohesion funds. The fifth relates to Council decisions on the procedure for elections to the European Parliament (discussed above). The sixth concerns amendments to the ECB Statute (Article 107(5) [106(5)] EC).

[137] See the first para. of Art. 300(3) [228(3)] EC. [138] *Ibid.*

[139] See Point 2.3.7 of the Solemn Declaration, EC Bull. 6 – 1983, pp. 26–7. [140] Art. 46 [L] TEU.

[141] Discussed below.

### APPROVAL OF THE COMMISSION

Here, the Parliament has two powers: first, it must approve the nomination of the President of the Commission; secondly, the President and the other members of the Commission nominated by the Member States are subject 'as a body' to a vote of approval by the Parliament.[142] Before it grants its approval, the Parliament requires the President-elect and the would-be Commissioners to appear before it to answer questions. Some nominees are said to find these sessions gruelling.

The power to approve Commissioners other than the President is weakened by the fact that the Parliament must approve the nominations *en bloc*; so it cannot veto individual nominations. However, if it objects strongly enough to a particular appointment, it can threaten to reject the whole Commission unless the offending nominee is replaced.

### CENSURE OF THE COMMISSION

The Parliament also has the power to obtain the resignation of the Commission by passing a vote of censure. This is laid down by Articles 201 [144] EC and 114 Euratom, which provide that the Commission must resign *en bloc* if such a motion is passed by a two-thirds majority of votes cast representing a majority of all members. However, these provisions also state that the resignation takes effect only after the new Commission has been appointed; so if the Parliament did not approve the new nominees put forward by the Council – who could in fact be the same individuals – the existing Commissioners would remain in office indefinitely.

The most important occasion on which resort was had to this procedure was in January 1999, when there was a motion of censure against the Commission headed by Mr Santer. This failed to achieve a two-thirds majority;[143] but the Commission had to accept the establishment of a committee of independent experts to investigate allegations against it of fraud, mismanagement, and nepotism. When the experts produced a damning report, the whole Commission resigned on 15 March 1999. However, the Member States failed to appoint a new Commission and, in accordance with the rule mentioned above, the existing Commissioners continued to carry out their duties – and draw their salaries – until their terms of office expired in January of the following year.[144]

### CONCLUSIONS

It will be clear from what has been said that the powers of the European Parliament fall short of those normally enjoyed by the legislature of a modern state. Nevertheless, they are gradually increasing and the days are long past when it could be dismissed as no more than a 'talking shop'. Moreover, its most important powers, those concerning legislation and the budget, have yet to be considered.

[142] Arts 214 [158] EC and 127 Euratom.
[143] There were 292 votes in favour and 232 against.
[144] See Tomkins (1999) 62 MLR 744.

## THE ECONOMIC AND SOCIAL COMMITTEE

Article 7(2) [4(2)] EC provides that the Council and Commission are to be assisted by an Economic and Social Committee (often called ECOSOC). This is an advisory body intended to represent various sectional interests. According to Article 257 [193] EC, it consists of representatives of, among others, producers, farmers, carriers, workers, dealers, craftsmen, the professions, and the general public. In practice it consists of three groups: employers, workers (largely represented by trade unionists), and others (the last group includes spokesmen for farmers, consumers, and the professions). Its members are appointed by the Council for renewable four-year terms on the basis of national allocations:[145] the largest (for the United Kingdom and the other large countries) is twenty-four; the smallest (Luxembourg) is six.[146] The members, though intended to represent particular groups, may not be bound by any 'mandatory instructions'.[147] In certain cases the Committee has the right to be consulted by the Council or Commission;[148] where this is done, however, the Council or Commission may set it a time-limit (of at least one month), and, if no opinion is given within this period, go ahead without it.

## THE COMMITTEE OF THE REGIONS

The Committee of the Regions, which was established by the Treaty on European Union and operates only under the EC Treaty, represents regional and local bodies within the Community.[149] Like the Economic and Social Committee, its role is to advise the Council and Commission.[150] Its membership is divided among the Member States in the same way as that of the Economic and Social Committee.[151]

## THE LEGISLATIVE PROCESS

The legislative process in the Community is complex. It depends both on the Treaty under which the measure is adopted and on the provision of that Treaty applicable to the case in question. Legislation on atomic energy comes under the Euratom Treaty and

[145] Prior to the Treaty of Nice, the Council acted unanimously: Art. 258 [194] EC. Under the Treaty of Nice, it acts by a qualified majority 'in accordance with the proposals made by each Member State': Art. 259(1) EC, as amended by the Treaty of Nice. This latter provision uses the same formula as that for the appointment of members of the Commission. It is ambiguous, but presumably means that the representatives of each Member State must be the persons nominated by that state.

[146] The number of persons from each Member State remains unaffected by the Treaty of Nice. For the proposed allocations for the new Member States, see Declaration 20 to the Treaty of Nice.

[147] Arts 258 [194] EC and 166 Euratom.

[148] Arts 262 [198] EC and 170 Euratom. The Committee may also be consulted by the Parliament, but there is no obligation to do so: *ibid.*

[149] See Arts 263–265 [198a–c] EC.

[150] Art. 7(2) [4(2)] EC.

[151] For a discussion of the Committee's role and objectives, see Jones, 'The Committee of the Regions, Subsidiarity and a Warning' (1997) 22 ELRev. 312.

legislation on other matters under the EC Treaty. In this section, we will confine our attention to the latter.

Depending on the subject matter, legislation under the EC Treaty may be adopted by three authorities: the European Parliament acting jointly with the Council, the Council acting alone, and the Commission.[152] The EC Treaty confers legislative power on the Commission only in very limited cases,[153] though the Council frequently delegates powers to it. The procedures adopted for the enactment of delegated legislation, as well as the general decision-making procedure in the Commission, have already been discussed. Here we will consider only legislation adopted jointly by the Parliament and Council or by the Council alone.

We will first consider the procedure where the Council, acting alone, adopts the measure and the Parliament has no role other than a consultative one.

## THE BASIC PROCEDURE

Under the basic procedure (sometimes called the 'consultation procedure'), the Commission makes a proposal and, after the Parliament has been consulted, the Council takes the final decision. Here the Council is in the strongest position; but no decision can be taken unless the Commission initiates the process and, since the Commission can amend the proposal at any time until a final decision has been taken but the Council cannot do so unless it is unanimous,[154] the Commission is not without tactical advantages. In theory, complete deadlock could be reached if the Commission (supported by at least one Member State) insisted on a particular provision and the majority of Member States wanted something different. In practice, however, the Commission will usually amend its proposals in order to secure the agreement of the Council.

Diagram 1.1 represents the basic decision-making process.[155] The first stage is the formulation of the Commission proposal. A working group is established, made up of persons nominated by the national governments, who are usually civil servants but are sometimes academics or other independent experts. The powers of the group are only advisory: at this stage the final decision rests with the Commission; but the views of the national experts are listened to carefully, since the consent of the national governments will have to be obtained at a later stage. After the working group has held a number of meetings and consideration has been given to the opinions of the national governments and appropriate non-governmental interest groups (for example, the relevant trade associations), the Commission will draft its proposal.

The proposal is sent to the Council, which in turn sends it to the Parliament (and sometimes also the Economic and Social Committee or the Committee of the Regions or both) for their opinions. After these opinions have been received, the proposal (which may have been amended by the Commission in the light of these consultations) is sent to the Committee of Permanent Representatives (COREPER). A working group

[152] Art. 249 [189] EC. [153] See above. [154] Art. 250 [189a] EC.

[155] Where the co-decision procedure applies, it comes into operation after Point 15 on the chart. In such a case, Diagram 1.2 may be regarded as beginning where Diagram 1.1 ends.

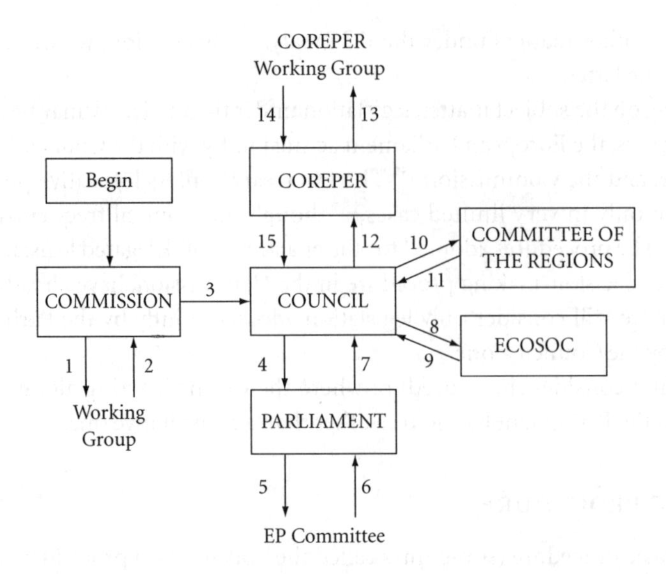


**Diagram 1.1** The EC Decision-Making Process (Basic Procedure)

of national officials is set up within COREPER to prepare a report for the Council. Commission representatives attend the meetings of these groups. Amendments are usually put forward by the national representatives and these may, or may not, be accepted by the Commission.

Finally, the proposal, together with the report of the COREPER working group, goes to the Council. The Commission is also represented at the Council meetings in which it is considered. If full agreement was reached in COREPER, the proposal will be adopted by the Council without debate, unless a last-minute objection is made. If no agreement was reached in COREPER, the matter will be thrashed out in the Council. Sometimes this takes a long time, and in important matters hard bargaining may take place. In the end, agreement may be reached on the basis of a package deal in which several decisions are combined, so that concessions made by a state on one issue are balanced by gains on another. In such a situation the Commission plays a crucial role in suggesting possible compromises. If no agreement can be reached in the appropriate technical Council, the matter may go up to the general Council, or even to the European Council. This will almost always be necessary where a package deal contains elements from different policy areas.

## THE CO-OPERATION PROCEDURE

The powers of the European Parliament in the legislative process were increased in 1986 by Articles 6 and 7 of the Single European Act, which provided for a 'co-operation procedure' applicable in certain instances under the EC Treaty. This procedure, which is now governed by Article 252 [189c] EC, has, however, been almost entirely eliminated under the Treaty of Amsterdam. For this reason, no attempt will be made to describe it in detail.[156] Even when first established, the co-operation procedure was subject to criticism on the ground that it granted the Parliament very little.[157] Its main innovation was that, if the Parliament was opposed to a measure, it could be passed only if the members of the Council were unanimous. This was a real, though small, increase in the powers of the Parliament. With regard to amendments, on the other hand, the Parliament's powers were not significantly increased. If the Parliament's proposed amendment was adopted by the Commission, the Council could reject it only on a unanimous vote. This, however, has always been the case, since the Council has never been able to amend a Commission proposal except by unanimity, and the Commission has always had the power to amend its proposal so as to give effect to amendments proposed by the Parliament.[158]

### THE CO-DECISION PROCEDURE

The procedure for legislation adopted jointly by the Parliament and the Council, usually called the 'co-decision procedure' or 'joint legislative procedure', is laid down in Article 251 [189b] EC, a provision inserted into the EC Treaty by the Treaty on European Union and modified by the Treaty of Amsterdam. It is depicted in Diagram 1.2. When the co-decision procedure applies, the process described previously (the 'basic procedure'), including the consultation of the Parliament, goes ahead in the usual way until the point is reached at which the Council would normally be ready to adopt the act. At this point, if the Council (acting by a qualified majority) is able to adopt the act as amended by the Parliament (or if the Parliament has not proposed any amendments), it will adopt it.

If it is not able to adopt it – this will normally be because it cannot accept the Parliament's amendments – it will instead adopt what is called a 'common position'. A common position (which must be adopted by a qualified majority) is a statement by the Council of the version of the act that it favours. Under Article 250 [189a] EC, a Commission proposal can be amended only if the Council is unanimous; consequently, the common position will correspond to the Commission proposal (including any of the Parliament's amendments adopted by the Commission) unless the Council is unanimous.

The common position is then sent to the Parliament together with a statement of the reasons which led the Council to adopt it and a statement of the Commission's position. This will be the second occasion on which the Parliament has considered the matter, the first having been under the normal consultation (basic) procedure. At this point, the Parliament has three months in which to act. If it approves the common position, or if it has taken no decision within the three-month period, the act is deemed to have been adopted in accordance with the common position. If, on the other hand, the

[156] A full description, together with a chart, may be found in the third edition of this book, at pp. 41–4.

[157] Nevertheless, the European Court went to some lengths to ensure that what rights the Parliament did have were protected: *Commission v. Council*, Case C-300/89, [1991] ECR I-2867.

[158] See the second para. of Art. [149] EEC, as it existed before the Single European Act.

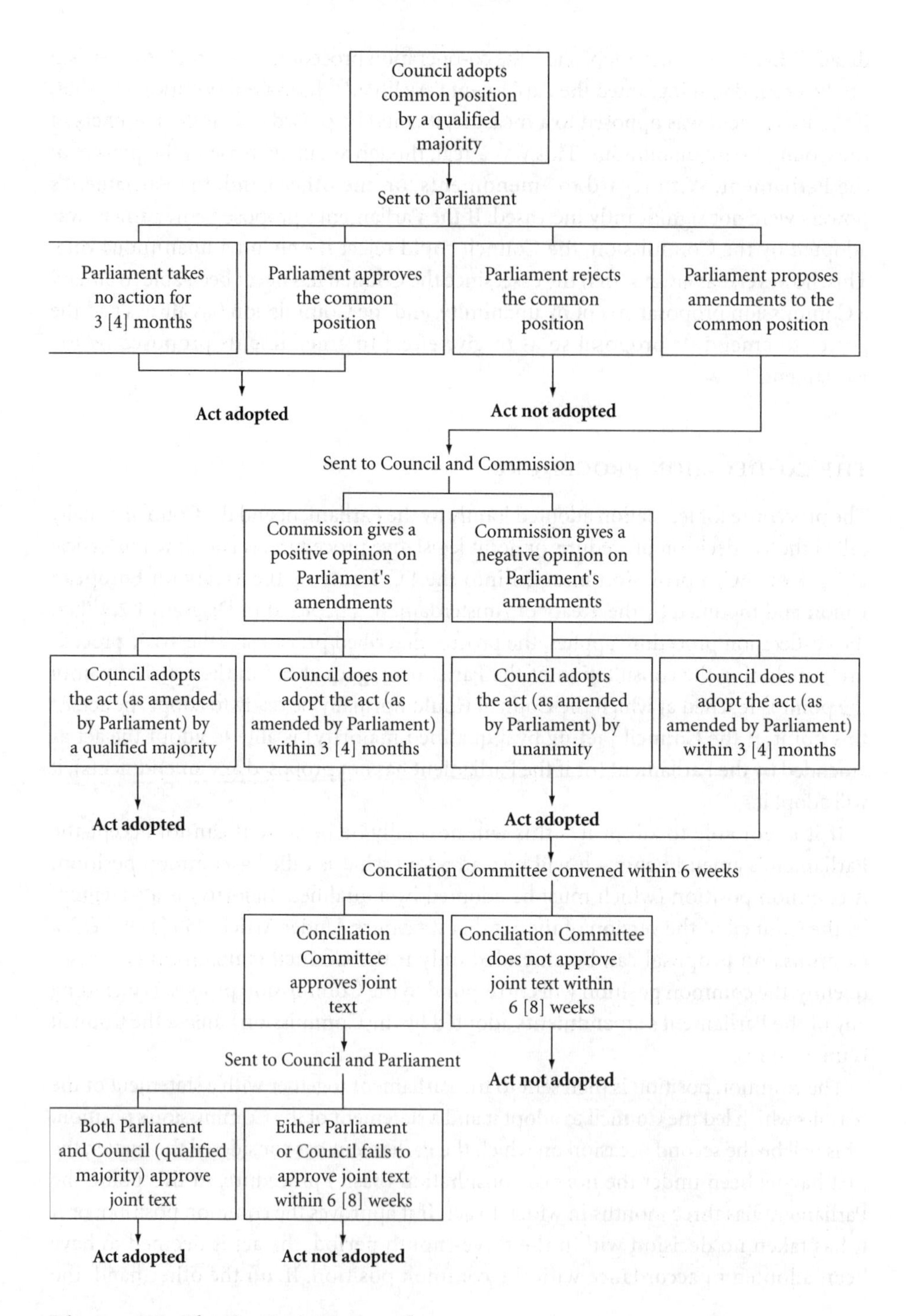


**Diagram 1.2** The Co-Decision Procedure

Parliament, acting by an absolute majority of its members, rejects the common position, the proposed act is deemed not to have been adopted: there is no way in which the Council can override the rejection.

The Parliament can also propose amendments to the common position. These must be adopted by an absolute majority of members. If this occurs, the amended text is forwarded to the Council and Commission, and the latter delivers an opinion on the amendments. The Council then has three months to act. If it approves all the amendments, the act is deemed to have been adopted in the form of the common position thus amended. (In doing this, it acts by a qualified majority, unless the Commission gave a negative opinion on the amendments, in which case the Council must be unanimous.) If, on the other hand, the Council does not approve the act as amended, a meeting of the Conciliation Committee must be convened within six weeks by the President of the Council in agreement with the President of the Parliament.[159]

The Conciliation Committee has an equal number of members from the Council and the Parliament. On the Council's side, it may consist of all the members of the Council or their representatives. The two sides of the Committee vote separately and it cannot take a decision unless both sides agree. Consequently, there must be both a qualified majority of the representatives of the Council, on the one side, and a majority of the representatives of the Parliament, on the other. The Commission takes part in the proceedings and attempts to reconcile the positions of the two sides.[160] The Conciliation Committee has six weeks to act. If it approves a joint text, the Parliament, acting by a majority of votes, and the Council, acting by a qualified majority, have a further six weeks in which to adopt the act in accordance with the joint text.[161] If one of the two institutions fails to adopt it, the act is deemed not to have been adopted. If the Conciliation Committee fails to agree on a joint text, the act is also deemed not to have been adopted.[162]

It is interesting to analyse the voting majorities needed under the co-decision procedure. The Council votes by a qualified majority[163] (except where it wishes to approve an amendment to which the Commission objects). The Parliament normally acts by an absolute majority of its members, but this does not apply where it approves the common position of the Council: in such a case no specified majority is mentioned, which means that it acts by an absolute majority of votes cast.[164] Moreover, no more than an absolute majority of votes is required for approving a joint text agreed by the Conciliation

[159] This will not occur if the Parliament and the Council are able to settle their differences without it.

[160] The last sentence of Art. 251(4) [189b(4)] EC, which was added by the Treaty of Amsterdam, reads, 'In fulfilling this task, the Conciliation Committee shall address the common position on the basis of the amendments proposed by the European Parliament.' This appears to exclude the possibility of any new amendments being put forward by the representatives of the Parliament, though no doubt it would permit a compromise between the amendments proposed by the Parliament and the common position.

[161] The period of six weeks begins from the date of the approval of the joint text.

[162] The periods of three months and six weeks which apply at various points in the co-decision procedure may be extended by a maximum of one month and two weeks respectively at the initiative of the Parliament or the Council: Art. 251(7) [189b(7)] EC. However, a Declaration (No. 34) adopted by the Conference at which the Treaty of Amsterdam was agreed, the Declaration on Respect for Time Limits under the Co-Decision Procedure, states that such extensions should be considered only when strictly necessary.

[163] In a Conciliation Committee this may be a qualified majority of the representatives of the Council.

[164] Art. 198 [141] EC.

Committee. In other words, a majority of members is required where the Parliament wishes to block the Council's proposals, but a majority of votes is sufficient if it approves the Council's proposals.

It is a truism that the Community is not really democratic. Rectifying this, however, is not easy. There are two difficulties, one well known and the other less so. The well-known difficulty is that any increase in the powers of the European Parliament must entail a diminution in the powers of the Member States, something which many national governments are reluctant to approve. The less well-known difficulty is that any increase in the powers of the Parliament must probably also entail a diminution in the powers of the Commission.

How do the Commission's powers apply under the co-decision procedure? In general, the foundation of the Commission's power is its right to make proposals. It retains this right under the co-decision procedure. However, the right to make proposals is of little value if those proposals can be easily amended. Consequently, the Commission gains considerable bargaining power from the rule that the Council must be unanimous in order to amend the Commission's proposals.[165] It is true that the Council can refuse to adopt a measure unless the Commission agrees to amend it, but if the Commission is determined, it may well be able to force the Council to accept a compromise.

Under the co-operation procedure, the Commission's prerogatives were fully respected: amendments proposed by the Parliament which were not accepted by the Commission could be adopted by the Council only if it was unanimous. Prior to the convening of the Conciliation Committee, the same is true under the co-decision procedure. Once the Conciliation Committee has been convened, however, the position is different: a text accepted by the Conciliation Committee may be adopted by the Council by a qualified majority even if the Commission objects.[166] Once the conciliation procedure comes into operation, therefore, it is possible for the Commission's proposal to be amended by a qualified majority in the Council even if the Commission objects. This is a significant weakening of the Commission's power: the Commission's loss is the Parliament's gain.

The Conciliation Committee is convened whenever the Council does not approve the Parliament's amendments within three months. Consequently, if the Council wishes to approve an amendment proposed by the Parliament which the Commission rejects, but the Council cannot muster a unanimous vote, it merely has to wait for three months and convene the Conciliation Committee, which may adopt the amendment by a qualified majority on the Council side. The amendment may then be approved by the Council, acting by a qualified majority. In other words, the only effect of a Commission veto is to delay adoption of the measure. The result is that, while the Council still cannot itself amend the Commission's proposals unless it is unanimous, it may adopt the Parliament's amendments by a qualified majority even if the Commission objects.

165 Art. 250 [189a] EC.

166 The rule that the Council must be unanimous to amend a Commission proposal does not apply in this case (or in the Conciliation Committee itself): Art. 250(1) [189a(1)] EC, read with Art. 251(4) and (5) [189b(4) and (5)] EC.

## THE BUDGETARY PROCEDURE[167]

The budgetary procedure is illustrated in Diagram 1.3.[168] The first step is for each institution to draw up its estimates of expenditure. These are sent to the Commission, which consolidates them into a 'preliminary draft budget' (there is a common budget for the three Communities). This preliminary draft budget, which must also contain an estimate of revenue, is then sent to the Council. The next step is the establishment of the 'draft budget' by the Council. In doing this, the Council acts by a qualified majority.[169] It is not bound by the proposals of the Commission: the normal rules which prevent the Council from making amendments to Commission proposals except by unanimity do not apply here, though the Council is obliged to consult the Commission when it intends to depart from the Commission's proposals. In all cases the Council will also consider the views of the Parliament.

The third stage takes place in the Parliament. The Parliament has the power to accept the budget, to amend it, or to reject it. If it accepts it, the budget is thereby adopted; in addition, if the Parliament takes no action at all during the following forty-five days, it is deemed to have adopted it.

The Parliament's right to make changes in the budget depends on the distinction between expenditure necessarily resulting from Treaty provisions or Community legislation (known as compulsory expenditure) and other expenditure (non-compulsory expenditure).[170] In the case of non-compulsory expenditure the Parliament may make amendments; in the case of compulsory expenditure, on the other hand, it may only propose 'modifications'. The significance of this distinction is that the Parliament has the last word in the case of amendments to provisions regarding non-compulsory expenditure; but the Council has the last word as regards proposed modifications to compulsory expenditure. Since amendments carry more weight, it is not surprising that they have to be passed by a majority of *Members* of Parliament (absolute majority); in the case of proposed modifications, on the other hand, only a majority of *votes cast* is required.

If amendments are made, or modifications proposed, the draft budget is sent back to the Council. The procedure in the Council depends on whether an amendment or modification is involved and, in the case of a modification, on whether or not the effect of the proposed modification is to increase the total expenditure of the institution in

[167] The main provisions on Community finance are Arts 268–280 [199–209a] EC and 171–183a Euratom. The main provisions on budgetary procedure are Arts 272 [203] EC and 177 Euratom. For litigation between the institutions on the budget, see *Council v. European Parliament*, Case 34/86, [1986] ECR 2155; *European Parliament v. Council (Draft Budget)*, Case 377/87, [1988] ECR 4017; *Commission v. Council*, Case 383/87, [1988] ECR 4051; *Council v. European Parliament*, Case C-284/90, [1992] ECR I-2277; *European Parliament v. Council*, Cases C-181, 248/91, [1993] ECR I-3685; *Council v. European Parliament*, Case C-41/95, [1995] ECR I-4411.

[168] The main sources of Community revenue ('own resources') are agricultural levies, customs duties on imports from outside the Community, a slice of the proceeds of the value added tax (VAT) imposed by the Member States on the basis of EC rules, and revenue based on the GNP of the Member States.

[169] As previously mentioned, this is one occasion on which majority voting has always been practised in the Council.

[170] See Arts 272(4) [203(4)] EC and 177(4) Euratom.

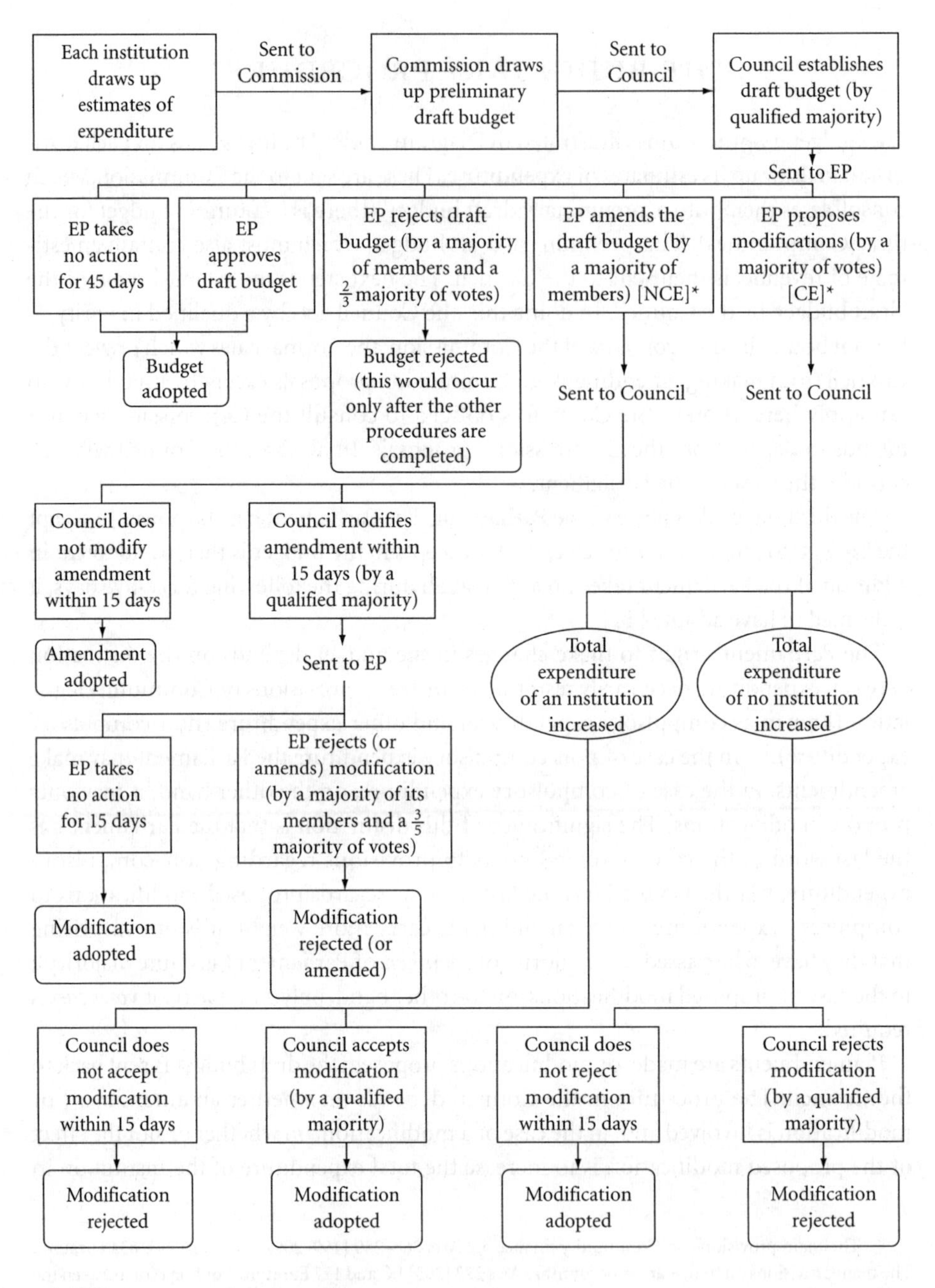


**Diagram 1.3** The Budgetary Procedure

question. (This, in turn, depends on whether increases in particular items of expenditure are balanced by cuts in other items for the same institution.)

The procedure is as follows:

1. *Amendments:* amendments passed by the Parliament may be modified by the Council provided there is a qualified majority in favour.[171] If no such motion is passed within fifteen days, the amendment is deemed to have been accepted.

2. *Modifications which do not increase total expenditure of an institution:* these modifications may be rejected by the Council if a motion to this effect is passed by a qualified majority; if no such motion is passed, the modifications are deemed to have been accepted.

3. *Modifications increasing total expenditure of an institution:* in this case the modification is deemed to have been rejected unless it is accepted. A motion accepting it must be passed by a qualified majority.

If, within fifteen days, the Council has not modified any of the Parliament's amendments, and has accepted its modifications, the budget is deemed to have been finally adopted. If this is not the case, it goes back again to the Parliament.

When the budget comes back to it, the Parliament no longer has power to change provisions dealing with compulsory expenditure: if its modifications to these provisions have not been accepted by the Council, there is nothing it can do unless it decides to reject the budget as a whole. In the case of non-compulsory expenditure, on the other hand, the Parliament has the right to reject the Council's modifications to its amendments and such a rejection is definitive. A motion to this effect must, however, be passed by a majority of the *Members* of the Parliament; in addition, three-fifths of the *votes* must be in favour. If, however, no such action is taken within fifteen days, the budget is deemed to have been adopted.

The Parliament also has the power to reject the budget *in toto* if there are 'important reasons' for doing so.[172] Such a motion must be passed by a majority of all the members of the Parliament and also by two-thirds of the votes cast. This happened for the first time in December 1979. When this occurs, a new budget must be drawn up by the Council and put before the Parliament. If no budget has been passed at the beginning of a financial year, a sum equal to one-twelfth of the previous year's budget may be spent each month, provided that the Commission may not be granted more than one-twelfth of the appropriation in the draft budget under consideration.[173] The monthly sums available may be increased by the Council, provided the consent of the Parliament is obtained with regard to non-compulsory expenditure.

It will be seen from this that the Parliament has substantial powers with regard to non-compulsory expenditure. These are, however, restricted by a rule that the annual growth of expenditure of this kind is subject to a limit (known as a 'maximum rate'),

171 It should be noted that, since such a decision is not taken on the basis of a Commission proposal, there must be at least eight Member States in favour: see Arts 205(2) [148(2)] EC and 118(2) Euratom.

172 Arts 272(8) [203(8)] EC and 177(8) Euratom.

173 Arts 273 [204] EC and 178 Euratom.

based on the increase in GNP, national budgets, and inflation within the Community.[174] This limit may, however, be increased by agreement between the Council (acting by a qualified majority) and the Parliament (acting by a majority of members and a three-fifths majority of votes cast).[175] The greatest weakness of the system from the point of view of the Parliament is that the latter has only limited powers over compulsory expenditure. This deficiency has been somewhat alleviated, however, by a Joint Declaration of 4 March 1975 and an Interinstitutional Agreement of 6 May 1999.

The Joint Declaration of the Parliament, the Council, and the Commission of 4 March 1975[176] establishes a conciliation procedure intended to reconcile the views of the Parliament and the Council regarding Community legislation with 'appreciable financial implications', the adoption of which is not required by pre-existing legislation. This is intended to give the Parliament a say in the enactment of legislation giving rise to compulsory expenditure. The procedure is initiated, at the request of either the Parliament or the Council, when the Council does not intend to follow the Parliament's opinion on the legislation. A Conciliation Committee is convened, consisting of the Council and representatives of the Parliament, with the participation of the Commission. Its object is to seek agreement on the legislation between the Parliament and the Council. The procedure does not normally continue for more than three months and, where necessary, the Council may set a deadline. The Joint Declaration concludes by saying, 'When the positions of the two institutions are sufficiently close, the European Parliament may give a new Opinion, after which the Council shall take definitive action.' In such a case, the Council will presumably be able to follow the Parliament's opinion. The Joint Declaration is, however, silent as to what will occur where this is not possible. The Council apparently takes the view that it can then go ahead and adopt the measure without following the Parliament's opinion, but the Parliament is reluctant to accept this.[177]

The Interinstitutional Agreement of 6 May 1999 between the European Parliament, the Council, and the Commission on Budgetary Discipline and the Improvement of Budgetary Procedure[178] provides that all budgetary items must be initially classified by the Commission as compulsory or non-compulsory. If either the Council or the Parliament cannot accept the classification of any item, the matter is referred to a meeting of the Presidents of the Parliament, the Council, and the Commission (under the chairmanship of the Commission), where an attempt is made to reach agreement.[179]

[174] It is fixed by the Commission. When the Parliament refused to abide by this limit in 1985, the European Court declared the budget invalid: *Council v. European Parliament*, Case 34/86, [1986] ECR 2155.

[175] Art. 272(9) [203(9)] EC. For litigation on this, see *Council v. European Parliament*, Case C-41/95, [1995] ECR I-4411. There is also a rule that, if the draft budget established by the Council provides for increases in non-compulsory expenditure which are greater than half the maximum rate laid down by the Commission, the Parliament is nevertheless entitled to make further increases amounting to not more than half the maximum rate, even though the end result will be that the total increases will then be over the maximum: *ibid.* The idea of this rule is to prevent the Council from pre-empting the Parliament's right to make increases by taking up the whole of the permitted amount. The amount by which the Parliament is entitled to increase the non-compulsory expenditure is known as its 'margin of manœuvre'.

[176] OJ 1975, C89/1.

[177] See Joliet, *Institutions*, p. 107, where it is said that the Parliament takes the view that, in such a case, the Council may adopt the measure only by unanimity.

[178] OJ 1999 C172/1.

[179] See *Greece v. Council*, Case 204/86, [1988] ECR 5323.

The budget is implemented by the Commission.[180] At the end of the financial year, the Parliament, acting on a recommendation from the Council (which itself acts by a qualified majority), gives a discharge to the Commission after considering the accounts and financial statement submitted by the Commission and the annual report of the Court of Auditors.[181]

## CONCLUSIONS

Two facts will by now have become apparent: first, the supranational element in the Community, though real, is limited; secondly, the democratic element, though also real, is even more restricted. It seems probable that a link exists between these two facts: the supranational element is unlikely to grow much stronger unless the democratic element is greatly strengthened. Significantly increased powers are not going to be given to a bureaucracy.

In the years since the beginning of the Community, various changes have taken place in the distribution of powers among the political institutions. The European Parliament, being directly elected for the first time in 1979, has significantly increased its powers, mainly in the field of the budget[182] but also in other fields, especially legislation.[183] The balance of power between the Commission and the Council has shifted in various ways. The power of the Commission relative to the other institutions was at its height in the days when only the ECSC existed, since under that Treaty it was intended to be the dominant authority. (It is interesting that the original draft of the ECSC Treaty contained no mention of the Council: it was included only to allay the fears of the smaller countries that the Commission would be dominated by the big countries.) The EC and Euratom Treaties show a diminution in the Commission's role and an enhanced position for the Council. Perhaps this was only to be expected in view of the fact that, unlike the ECSC Treaty, the EC Treaty sets out only the basic, initial policies to be pursued; beyond this, everything is left to the discretion of the institutions. In such circumstances, it is hardly surprising that the Member States insisted that the Council should have the dominant position.

A further shift in power, probably not intended by the authors of the EC Treaty, took place after that Treaty entered into force. The refusal for many years to apply majority voting meant that the adoption of legislation depended on negotiations carried on in COREPER and the Council, a development which lessened the importance of the Commission's power to make proposals; the increased prestige and effectiveness of the Presidency diluted the role of the Commission as mediator, and the establishment of the European Council (itself in part a response to the paralysis of the Council under the unanimity system) involved a move back to traditional inter-governmental procedures.

180 Arts 274 [205] EC and 179 Euratom.

181 Arts 276 [206] EC and 180b Euratom.

182 Budgetary Treaties of 1970 and 1975.

183 This took place under the Single European Act 1986 and the Treaty on European Union 1992.

In the 1980s, however, the Commission began to strengthen its position, and, since the coming into force of the Single European Act, majority voting has begun to take place regularly in the Council. Important changes have also taken place in the legal sphere: in a series of key judgments, the European Court has enhanced the status of Community law to the point where, as far as its legal system is concerned, the Community now possesses most of the characteristics of a federation.[184] The most noticeable feature of this process has been the development, beginning in 1963 with the *Van Gend en Loos* case,[185] of the doctrine of direct effect (the principle that Community law must be applied by national courts as the law of the land) and the establishment of the supremacy of Community law over national law.[186] Another feature has been the widening of Community jurisdiction, especially in the international sphere.[187] As a consequence, the Community has become more supranational in the legal sphere than in the political.[188]

## FURTHER READING

R JOLIET, *Institutions*, 1–109.

WEILER, 'The Community System: The Dual Character of Supranationalism' (1981) 1 YEL 267.

KRANZ, 'Le vote dans la pratique du Conseil des ministres des Communautés européennes' (1982) RTDE 403.

NICOLL, 'The Luxembourg Compromise' (1984) 23 JCMS 35.

WEILER, 'The Evolution of Mechanisms and Institutions for a European Foreign Policy: Reflections on the Interaction of Law and Politics', European University Institute, Working Paper No. 85/202.

KOLTE, 'The Community Budget: New Principles for Finance, Expenditure Planning and Budget Discipline' (1988) 25 CMLRev. 487.

ZANGL, 'The Interinstitutional Agreement on Budgetary Discipline and Improvement of the Budgetary Procedure' (1989) 26 CMLRev. 675.

BRADLEY, 'Comitology and the Law: Through a Glass Darkly' (1992) 29 CMLRev. 693.

HARLOW, 'A Community of Interests? Making the Most of European Law' (1992) 55 MLR 331.

LENAERTS, 'Regulating the Regulatory Process: "Delegation of Powers" in the European Community' (1993) 18 ELRev. 23.

TEASDALE, 'The Life and Death of the Luxembourg Compromise' (1993) 31 JCMS 567.

BONO, 'Co-Decision: An Appraisal of the Experience of the European Parliament as Co-legislator' (1994) 14 YEL 21.

BOVIS, 'Legal Aspects of the European Union's Public Finances: The Budget and

[184] See Hartley, 'Federalism, Courts and Legal Systems: The Emerging Constitution of the European Community' (1986) 34 Am. Jo. Comp. L. 229.

[185] Case 26/62, [1963] ECR 1.

[186] See Chap. 7, below.

[187] See Chap. 6, below.

[188] For a full discussion, see Weiler, 'The Community System: The Dual Character of Supranationalism' (1981) 1 YEL 267.

the Communities' Own Resources System' (1994) 28 Int. Lawyer 743.

DASHWOOD, 'Community Legislative Procedures in the Era of the Treaty on European Union' (1994) 19 ELRev. 343.

FOSTER, 'The New Conciliation Committee under Article 198b EC' (1994) 19 ELRev. 185.

MARIAS, 'The Right to Petition the European Parliament after Maastricht' (1994) 19 ELRev. 169.

MULLER-GRAFF, 'The Legal Bases of the Third Pillar' (1994) 31 CMLRev. 493.

FIONA HAYES-RENSHAW AND HELEN WALLACE, *The Council of Ministers* (1996).

JONES, 'The Committee of the Regions, Subsidiarity and a Warning' (1997) 22 ELRev. 312.

BRIGID LAFFAN, *The Finances of the European Union* (1997).

HARDEN, 'When Europeans Complain – The Work of the European Ombudsman' (2000) 2 *Cambridge Yearbook of European Studies* 199.

BRADLEY, 'Institutional Design in the Treaty of Nice' (2001) 38 CMLRev. 1095.

DASHWOOD, 'The Constitution of the European Union after Nice: Law-Making Procedures' (2001) 26 ELRev. 215.

E DENZA, *The Intergovernmental Pillars of the European Union* (2002).

JOHN PETERSON AND MICHAEL SHACKLETON (EDS), *The Institutions of the European Union* (2002).

SIMON HIX, *The Political System of the European Union* (2003).

JACQUÉ, 'The Principle of Institutional Balance' (2004) 41 CMLRev. 383.

VON ARNIM, ' "Fraudulent and Unacceptable"? The Uncontrolled Growth in Allowances in the European Parliament' (2004) 29 ELRev. 698.

RICHARD CORBETT, FRANCIS JACOBS, AND MICHAEL SHACKLETON, *The European Parliament*, 6th edn (2005).

WALTER VAN GERVEN, *The European Union, A Polity of States and Peoples* (2005).

LEFEVRE, 'Rules of Procedure Do Matter: The Legal Status of the Institutions' Power of Self-Organization' (2005) 30 ELRev. 802.

PAUL CRAIG, *EU Administrative Law* (2006).

STEVE PEERS, *EU Justice and Home Affairs Law*, 2nd edn (2006).

# 2

# THE EUROPEAN COURT AND THE COURT OF AUDITORS

This chapter is concerned with the non-political institutions of the Community, the European Court – officially known as the 'Court of Justice' – and the Court of Auditors. We will also deal with the Court of First Instance and the Civil Service Tribunal, which exercise the jurisdiction conferred on them by the Treaty, but are not institutions in their own right.

The most important of these is the European Court.[1] Its main functions are to ensure that the law is enforced (especially against Member States); to act as referee between the Member States and the Community as well as between the Community institutions *inter se*; and to ensure the uniform interpretation and application of Community law throughout the Community.

The powers of the Court and the law which it administers are considered in detail in the following chapters of this book. Here the stage will be set by discussing the Court as an institution.

## THE EUROPEAN COURT

### JUDGES

There are twenty-seven judges in the Court, appointed by the common accord of the Member States. Prior to the Treaty of Nice, there was no express rule that there had to

[1] The treaty provisions on the European Court are Arts 220–223 EC and 136–139 Euratom. Further provisions are contained in the Statute of the Court of Justice (since the Treaty of Nice, there is one Statute for both the EC and Euratom), which is an annex to the EC Treaty, the Euratom Treaty, and the Treaty on European Union (see Art. 7 of, and Protocol B to, the Treaty of Nice). There are separate Rules of Procedure for the European Court and the Court of First Instance. Until the entry into force of the rules of procedure of the Civil Service Tribunal, the Rules of the Court of First Instance will apply to the Civil Service Tribunal: Council Decision 2004/752, Art. 3(4). Current versions of all the provisions mentioned in this footnote may be found on the European Court's website, http://curia.europa.eu. The best general accounts of the Court are L Neville Brown and Tom Kennedy, *The Court of Justice of the European Communities* (5th edn, 2000) and Anthony Arnull, *The European Union and its Court of Justice* (2nd edn, 2006).

be one from each Member State, but an amendment brought in by the Treaty of Nice says this explicitly.[2] It is stated in the Treaties[3] that judges must be 'persons whose independence is beyond doubt and who possess the qualifications required for appointment to the highest judicial offices in their respective countries or who are jurisconsults of recognized competence'. The latter provision permits academic lawyers to be appointed, even if they are not eligible for appointment to the judiciary in their own countries.

Judges are appointed for staggered terms of six years, so that every three years either fourteen or thirteen of the posts fall vacant. They are eligible for re-appointment and this frequently occurs; there is no retirement age. The Member States cannot remove a judge during his term of office, but he may be dismissed if, in the unanimous opinion of the other judges and advocates general, 'he no longer fulfils the requisite conditions or meets the obligations arising from his office'.[4] So far this procedure has never been put into operation.

The President of the Court is elected by his brother judges for a renewable term of three years. The election is by secret ballot.[5] The President's function is to direct the judicial and administrative business of the Court and to preside at sessions of the full Court. The Court is divided into Chambers and the President of each Chamber is also elected by the judges.[6]

On taking office, a judge swears to perform his duties impartially and conscientiously and to preserve the secrecy of the Court's deliberations. During office, he is not permitted to hold any political or administrative (governmental) office; nor may he engage in any occupation, whether gainful or not, unless exemption is granted by the Council.[7] Several judges have in fact been permitted to undertake academic functions. Even after they have ceased to hold office, judges must behave with integrity and discretion as regards the acceptance of appointments or benefits.[8]

As the Court reaches decisions by a majority, and the President has no casting vote, there must always be an uneven number of judges deciding a case. If one judge has to withdraw – for example, through illness – the most junior remaining judge will abstain from taking part in the deliberations.[9]

The Court normally sits in Chambers; it sits as a full Court only in exceptional cases.[10] In addition to Chambers of three or five judges, there is provision for a Grand Chamber, consisting of at least thirteen judges. It is presided over by the President of the Court. The Court will sit as a Grand Chamber where a Member State or a Community institution which is a party to the proceedings so requests.[11] The Court will normally sit in plenary formation (full Court) only in the special cases laid down in the Statute – for

[2] Arts 221 EC and 137 Euratom, as amended by the Treaty of Nice.

[3] Arts 223 [167] EC and 139 Euratom.

[4] See Art. 6 of the Statute of the Court.

[5] Art. 7(3) of the Rules of Procedure.

[6] Art. 10(1) of the Rules of Procedure. The presidents of five-judge Chambers are elected for a term of five years and the president of one-judge Chambers for a term of one year.

[7] Art. 4 of the Statute of the Court.

[8] *Ibid.*

[9] Rules of Procedure, Art. 26(1). If the most junior judge is the judge-rapporteur, the next most junior judge stands down.

[10] Arts 221 EC and 137 Euratom.

[11] Art. 16, third para., of the Statute.

example, dismissal of a member of the Commission for misconduct.[12] However, a Chamber will be able to refer a case of exceptional importance to the full Court.[13]

It might be thought that the comparatively short terms of office, as well as the appointment procedure, would lessen the independence of the judges. This is not, however, the case. No one who has any acquaintance with the Court can doubt the complete independence of its members from their national governments. A judge does not, just because he is British, consider himself to be 'the British judge' on the Court: he is a Community judge who happens to come from Britain. There is in fact a remarkable sense of corporate identity and solidarity among the judges and advocates general and, though they may be influenced by the different traditions of their respective legal systems, they have never been accused of taking national advantage into account; on the contrary, the Court is generally regarded as one of the most 'European-minded' institutions in the Community.

The most important protection the judges have against national pressure is the fact that there is always just one 'judgment of the Court' without any separate concurring or dissenting judgments. Since, moreover, the judges swear to uphold the secrecy of their deliberations, it is never known how individual judges voted. Therefore it is impossible to accuse a judge of being insufficiently sensitive to national interests or of having 'let his government down'; no one outside the Court can ever know whether he vigorously defended the position adopted by his own country or was in the forefront of those advocating a 'Community solution'.

The background of the judges is varied: some previously held political or administrative offices; some were in private practice or were members of the national judiciary; others had academic appointments.

## ADVOCATES GENERAL

In addition to the judges, there are also eight advocates general. Although not required by law, this normally includes one from each of the big countries. They have the same status as judges: the same provisions regarding appointment, qualifications, tenure, and removal apply to them as to judges; they receive the same salary, and they rank equally in precedence with the judges according to seniority in office. One advocate general is appointed First Advocate General.[14] When administrative matters concerning the functioning of the Court are being discussed, the advocates general sit with the judges; but they play no part in the Court's deliberations regarding cases.

Their function has no parallel in the English legal system, though it is similar to that of a *commissaire du gouvernement* in the French *Conseil d'Etat*. In the words of the Treaty,[15] 'It shall be the duty of the Advocate-General, acting with complete impartiality and independence, to make, in open court, reasoned submissions on cases brought

[12] Art. 16, fourth para., of the Statute. [13] Art. 16, last para., of the Statute.

[14] Art. 10(1) of the Rules of Procedure. The appointment is for a one-year term. The Rules of Procedure provide for a secret ballot (*ibid.*); in practice, the position seems to rotate.

[15] Arts 222 [166] EC and 138 Euratom.

before the Court of Justice, in order to assist the Court . . .'. When each new case comes to the Court, it is assigned by the First Advocate General to one of the advocates general. The advocate general to whom the case is assigned, together with his legal secretary (discussed below), will study the issues involved and undertake any legal research they think necessary. After the parties have concluded their submissions to the Court, the advocate general will give his opinion. This opinion is not binding on the Court, but will be considered with great care by the judges when they make their decision. It is printed, together with the judgment, in the law reports.

Impartiality and independence are important characteristics of the advocate general's office. He represents neither the Community nor any Member State: he speaks only for the public interest. He works quite separately and independently from the judges; one could say that he gives a 'second opinion' which is in fact delivered first. This opinion shows the judges what a trained legal mind, equal in quality to their own, has concluded on the matter before them. It could be regarded as a point of reference, or starting point, from which they can begin their deliberations. In many cases they follow the advocate general fully; in others they deviate from his opinion either wholly or in part. But always his views will be of great value.

An advocate general's job must in many ways be more satisfying than that of a judge. A judge works as a member of a committee: any proposal he puts forward regarding a judgment must be agreed to by at least a majority of his colleagues. He cannot, therefore, put his personal stamp upon a judgment in the same way that an English judge can; and even if he succeeds in winning over his brother judges to his way of thinking on a particular issue, the result is always anonymous: no one outside the closed circle of the Court will ever know that it was his work. The advocate general, on the other hand, is on his own: his opinion is his own work (though he may receive assistance from his legal secretary) and he alone is responsible for it. He will receive praise or blame according to his deserts.

One feature of the European Court which has sometimes given rise to comment is that there is no appeal from its judgments.[16] In most cases it may be regarded as a court of first and last resort. This puts a heavy burden on the judges, a burden not made any lighter by the uneven quality of the lawyers who appear before it. The Court cannot always draw the same assistance from counsel as an English court would. In these circumstances, the role of the advocate general is especially important. His opinion could in fact be regarded as a judgment of first instance which is subject to instant and invariable appeal. It is, however, an appeal of a special nature, since the parties normally have no opportunity to comment on the opinion before the Court begins its deliberations.[17]

The advocate general's opinion is usually much easier to read than the Court's judgment. The latter, being the work of a committee, is often lacking in logical rigour; its

[16] However, the European Court itself hears appeals from the Court of First Instance.

[17] It could be argued that the absence of such an opportunity is an infringement of Art. 6 of the European Convention on Human Rights. The Court has rejected this view: *Emesa Sugar (Free Zone) NV v. Aruba*, Case C-17/98, [2000] ECR I-665 (Order of 4 February 2000). However, the European Court of Human Rights may take a different view: see *Vermeulen v. Belgium* [1996] I *Reports of Judgments and Decisions* 224 (distinguished by the ECJ in the *Emesa Sugar* case).

terse and formal style is unattractive – at least to those brought up in the common law tradition – while the need to achieve consensus may produce obscurities and inconsistencies. The advocate general's opinion, on the other hand, is closer in style to an English judgment, this similarity being especially marked – as one would expect – in the case of an English or Irish advocate general. In it one normally finds a discussion of the facts, reference to (and quotation from) the relevant legislative provisions, and a full consideration of previous decisions of the Court. In some cases, the advocate general will provide a short comparative survey, prepared with the assistance of the Court 'Documentation Service', of the way the point at issue would be dealt with in the legal systems of the Member States. He will also analyse the arguments put forward by the parties and finally give his own views on the issues before the Court.

In reaching his conclusions, the advocate general is not restricted to the arguments advanced by the parties. A good example of a case in which the advocate general put forward an original solution, which had not occurred to the parties, was *Transocean Marine Paint Association v. Commission.*[18] This case will be considered in detail below;[19] here all that need be said of the facts is that it was an attempt to set aside a decision of the Commission which was unfavourable to the interests of the applicants. They advanced various grounds for their contention; but it was Advocate General Warner, drawing on the law of the Member States – and particularly on that of England – who proposed that it should be annulled for failure to comply with natural justice. This was accepted by the Court and the rule *audi alteram partem* was incorporated into the Community legal system as a general principle of law.

## THE REGISTRAR

The Registrar of the European Court plays a more important role than his equivalent in most national systems. He is appointed by the Court for a term of six years and is eligible for reappointment.[20] His functions are twofold. The Registry is responsible for all procedural matters; documents filed with the Court are the responsibility of the Registry, which distributes them to the members of the Court and serves them on the parties. Secondly, the Registrar is in charge of the administration of the Court and is present when the Court holds an administrative meeting, though he does not have a vote. In all these activities, he is responsible to the President of the Court.

## LEGAL SECRETARIES

Each judge and advocate general has a number of assistants, officially known as 'legal secretaries' (*référendaires* in French). They usually belong to a younger generation than the judges and advocates general; they may be lecturers or practising lawyers, and they usually spend a few years at the Court before returning to their careers in their own countries. Their main task is to carry out legal research and to assist in the preparation

[18] Case 17/74, [1974] ECR 1063. [19] See Chap. 5.

[20] Rules of Procedure, Art. 12. A secret ballot is held: *ibid.*

of opinions or other legal writing. They are chosen by the judge or advocate general for whom they work.

### SPECIALIZED SERVICES

The Court has an excellent library with materials covering the legal systems of the Member States as well as that of the Community. There is at least one lawyer on the staff from each Member State, and the Research and Documentation Division provides the judges and advocates general with background papers on Community law and comparative surveys of national law.

There is a Translation Directorate which translates legal documents, including the judgments of the Court and the opinions of the advocates general, into the various languages of the Court. There is also an Information Office, which provides lawyers (and others) with information on recent cases and other aspects of the Court's work.

## THE COURT OF FIRST INSTANCE[21]

The Court of First Instance was established in 1989, following amendments contained in the Single European Act.[22] The idea was to lessen the workload of the European Court by relieving it of some of the cases with no political or constitutional importance, especially those involving complex facts. The European Court could then concentrate on the task of deciding the more important cases and maintaining the unity of Community law. A right of appeal to the European Court on points of law would ensure that the new court stayed in line. It was hoped that the establishment of the Court of First Instance would reduce the backlog of cases pending before the European Court. The Court of First Instance has indeed relieved the European Court of a significant number of cases, but the unremitting build-up of new cases has meant that delays in getting cases heard (and decided) by the European Court have not been significantly shortened.[23]

The Court of First Instance has twenty-seven judges.[24] The provisions regarding their appointment, and terms of office are the same as those for the European Court, but the provision concerning their qualifications is slightly different: they must possess the 'ability required for appointment to high judicial office'.[25] They elect one of their

[21] The treaty provisions on the Court of First Instance are Arts 224 and 225 EC and 140 and 140a Euratom. In addition, the Court of First Instance is dealt with in Title IV of the Statute of the Court. The Court of First Instance has separate Rules of Procedure: see OJ 1991, L136/1. These rules have been frequently amended. A current version may be found on the European Court's website, *http://curia.europa.eu*. The Rules are very similar to those of the European Court.

[22] For the background, see Kennedy, 'The Essential Minimum: The Establishment of the Court of First Instance' (1989) 14 ELRev. 7; see also 'Reflections on the Future Development of the Community Judicial System' (a discussion paper issued by the Court of First Instance in 1990) (1991) 16 ELRev. 175.

[23] See Vesterdorf, 'The Court of First Instance of the European Communities After Two Full Years in Operation' (1992) 29 CMLRev. 897.

[24] Arts 224 EC and 140 Euratom; Art. 48 of the Statute of the Court (as amended by the Act of Accession for Bulgaria and Romania).

[25] Arts 224 EC and 140 Euratom.

number as President for a renewable term of three years.[26] There are no advocates general as such, but one of the judges acts as advocate general in those cases where there is felt to be a special need.[27] In practice this is rare.

The Court of First Instance usually sits in Chambers of three or five judges or in a Grand Chamber of thirteen judges.[28] It may also be constituted by a single judge.[29] It sits in plenary session in certain special instances – for example, if the Chamber hearing the case refers it to the full Court because of the difficulty or importance of the case.[30]

## CIVIL SERVICE TRIBUNAL

The Treaty of Nice made provision for the creation of 'judicial panels',[31] which were intended to lessen the workload of the Court of First Instance by relieving it of some of the less important cases. Acting under this provision, the Council established a judicial panel known as the 'European Civil Service Tribunal',[32] which hears disputes involving the European Union Civil Service. At present, it consists of seven judges, appointed by the Council acting unanimously. They are appointed for a renewable period of six years[33] and are chosen from among persons who 'possess the ability required for appointment to judicial office.'[34] An appeal from their decisions (on points of law only) lies to the Court of First Instance.[35]

## JURISDICTION

This section is concerned with the jurisdiction of the European Court, the Court of First Instance, and the Civil Service Tribunal. Initially, no distinction will be made between them and, for ease of explanation, they will all be referred to as 'the European Court'.

[26] Arts 224 EC and 140 Euratom.

[27] See the Rules of Procedure of the Court of First Instance, Arts 17–19; see also Art. 49 of the Statute of the Court. Where the Court of First Instance sits in plenary session, there is always an advocate general; in other cases, the decision to designate an advocate general is taken by the Court of First Instance sitting in plenary session at the request of the Chamber concerned. The Rules of Procedure do not provide for the parties to have any say in the matter. Amendments brought in by the Treaty of Nice make it possible for advocates general to be appointed for the Court of First Instance, but so far this has not occurred. See Arts 224 EC and 140 Euratom (as amended by the Treaty of Nice).

[28] Rules of Procedure of the Court of First Instance, Art. 10. The criteria by which cases are allocated among the Chambers are laid down in decisions of the Court of First Instance published in the *Official Journal*: Art. 12 of the Rules of Procedure of the Court of First Instance.

[29] Art. 50 of the Statute. See also Art. 14 of the Rules of Procedure of the Court of First Instance. For the cases that may be heard by a single judge, see *ibid.*, Art. 14(2).

[30] *Ibid.*, Art. 11(1) and the provisions referred to therein, including Art. 14(1).

[31] Arts 225a EC and 140b Euratom.

[32] Council Decision 2004/752, OJ 2004 L333/7. See also Art. 62a of the Statute and Annex I to the Statute, both the latter being added by Decision 2004/752.

[33] Art. 2 of Annex I to the Statute.

[34] Art. 225a (fourth paragraph) EC and Art. 140b (fourth paragraph) Euratom. The Council is advised by a committee chosen from among former members of the European Court and the Court of First Instance and lawyers of recognized competence: Art. 3(3) of Annex I to the Statute.

[35] Art. 225a (third paragraph) EC and Art. 140b (third paragraph) Euratom; Art. 11 of Annex I to the Statute.

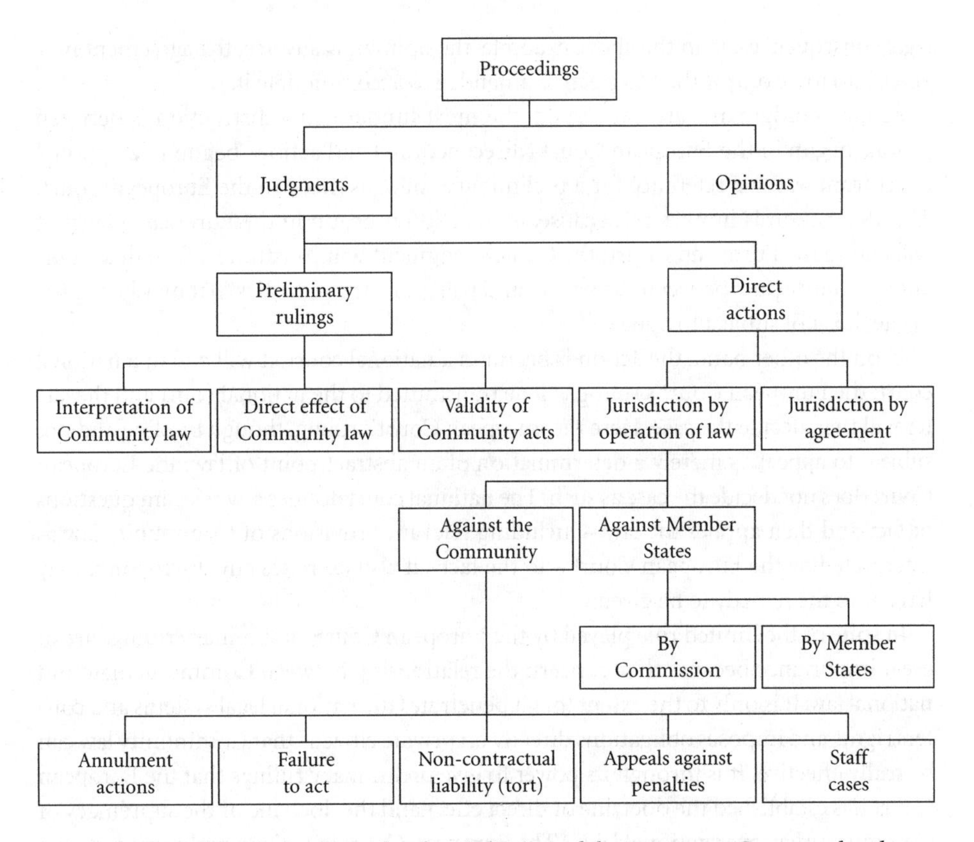


**Diagram 2.1** The Principal Heads of Jurisdiction of the European Court under the EC Treaty

The Treaties give the European Court only limited jurisdiction.[36] There are a number of specific heads of jurisdiction and a case must be brought within one of them if the Court is to hear it. The various kinds of actions will be analysed in detail in the chapters that follow; here it is enough to give an overall picture. (For a diagrammatic representation of the principal heads of jurisdiction under the EC Treaty, see Diagram 2.1.)

There are several criteria according to which the Court's jurisdiction may be classified. The most basic distinction is between judgments and opinions or rulings. The latter are very much rarer than the former, but they occur in a number of situations, for example where the Council, the Commission, or a Member State requests an opinion on whether an international agreement which the Community intends to conclude with a non-Member State is compatible with the EC Treaty. Though advisory, these opinions have

[36] As an institution of the Community, the European Court must 'act within the limits of the powers conferred on it by this Treaty': Arts 7 [4] EC and 3 Euratom. In spite of this, the Court interprets its jurisdiction generously and in some cases clearly goes beyond the limits set by the Treaties (see, e.g., *Zwartveld*, Case C-2/88, [1990] ECR I-4405). It may even consider that it has the power to confer jurisdiction on itself, though it has not said so expressly. For a general discussion of the question, see Arnull, 'Does the Court of Justice Have Inherent Jurisdiction?' (1990) 27 CMLRev. 683; Usher, 'How Limited is the Jurisdiction of the European Court?' in Dine, Douglas-Scott, and Persaud, *Procedure and the European Court* (1991) at 72 *et seq.*

legal consequences: if, in the above example, the opinion is adverse, the agreement may enter into force only if the EC Treaty is amended to accommodate it.

As far as judgments are concerned, the most fundamental distinction is between actions begun in the European Court (direct actions) and actions begun in a national court from which a reference for a preliminary ruling is made to the European Court. This distinction is important because, if an action is begun in the European Court, it will end in the European Court: the Court's judgment will constitute a final determination of the dispute between the parties and will grant any remedies that may be appropriate; it is not subject to appeal.[37]

If, on the other hand, the action is begun in a national court, it will end in a national court: the European Court's ruling will be transmitted to the national court and the latter will then decide the case. Here the European Court's ruling, though binding and not subject to appeal, is merely a determination of an abstract point of law: the European Court does not decide the case as such. The national court decides any relevant questions of fact and then applies the law – including relevant provisions of Community law as interpreted by the European Court – to the facts; it also exercises any discretion it may have as to the remedy to be given.

In spite of the limited role played by the European Court, preliminary rulings are of great importance because they concern the relationship between Community law and national law. It is only to the extent that it penetrates the national legal systems and confers rights and imposes obligations directly on private citizens that Community law can be really effective. It is through its power to give preliminary rulings that the European Court has established the doctrine of direct effect and the doctrine of the supremacy of Community law over national law.[38] The European Court will give a preliminary ruling only when requested to do so by a national court which considers that a question of Community law is relevant to its decision: any court or tribunal *may* make such a request; a court or tribunal from which there is no appeal *must* do so. The issues which may be referred to the European Court are of three kinds: the interpretation of a provision of Community law, the effect of such a provision in the national legal system (which, in theory, is also a question of interpretation), and, in the case of a measure passed by the Community itself, the validity of such a provision.

Direct actions may be divided into two categories: those over which the Court has jurisdiction by virtue of an agreement between the parties and those where the Court's jurisdiction is conferred by direct operation of the law. The former are not very important in practice; the main example is actions arising out of a contract concluded by the Community which contains a clause giving jurisdiction to the European Court.

Direct actions where the Court's jurisdiction does not depend on consent may be classified according to whether the defendant is the Community or a Member State. A number of different kinds of action may be brought against the Community. The two most important are actions for judicial review and actions for damages for non-contractual liability (tort). Actions for judicial review may be brought either to annul a

[37] There are, however, appeals (on points of law) from the Court of First Instance to the European Court and from the Civil Service Tribunal to the Court of First Instance.

[38] See Chaps 7 and 9.

Community measure or to oblige a Community institution to pass a measure which it had previously refused to pass. Such proceedings are brought against the relevant Community institution; they may be brought by a Member State, another Community institution, or – in certain special cases – by a private individual.

Actions for damages for non-contractual liability may be brought against the Community by either a Member State or a private individual. The applicant must prove that he has suffered loss as a result of Community action (or inaction).

Other proceedings in which a Community institution is the defendant include appeals against penalties imposed under Community regulations (if the regulation in question so provides), and employment disputes between the Community and its staff.

Actions against a Member State are called enforcement actions. They may be brought against a Member State alleged to have violated Community law. The applicant may be either the Commission or another Member State; in practice it is almost always the Commission. There is a preliminary procedure in which an opinion is given by the Commission after the Member State has explained its position: if the Member State refuses to abide by this opinion, the Commission (or the other Member State) brings the action before the Court.

## JURISDICTION OF THE COURT OF FIRST INSTANCE

The European Court (Court of Justice) has jurisdiction in all the above instances, except where jurisdiction has been conferred on the Court of First Instance or the Civil Service Tribunal.

The rules governing the jurisdiction of the Court of First Instance are to be found in Article 225 EC, Article 140a Euratom, and Article 51 of the Statute. They are rather complex. The Treaty Articles confer jurisdiction on the Court of First Instance in a fairly wide range of cases (annulment actions,[39] actions for failure to act,[40] tort actions,[41] staff actions,[42] and contract cases where the contract so provides[43]); however, they also provide, first, that the Statute may reserve some of these cases for the European Court and, secondly, that it may give the Court of First Instance jurisdiction in other cases. Article 51 of the Statute does not give the Court of First Instance any additional jurisdiction; however, it reserves a number of cases for the European Court. These cover a wide range of proceedings brought by Member States or Community institutions. The result is that cases before the Court of First Instance consist mainly, though not entirely, of cases brought by private persons (usually companies) against the Community (usually the Commission). Competition cases, anti-dumping cases, and trade mark cases are the most important. The full list is as follows:

- annulment actions, or actions for failure to act, by private persons against Community institutions;
- actions by Member States against the Commission;

[39] Arts 230 [173] EC and 146 Euratom.
[40] Arts 232 [175] EC and 148 Euratom.
[41] Arts 235 [178] EC and 151 Euratom.
[42] Arts 236 [179] EC and 152 Euratom.
[43] Arts 238 [181] EC and 153 Euratom.

- actions by Member States against the Council, though only regarding acts adopted in the fields of state aids and dumping, and acts by which the Council exercises implementing powers;
- actions in tort against the Community;
- actions in contract where the contract expressly confers jurisdiction on the Court of First Instance; and
- actions relating to Community trade marks.

The Treaty of Nice opens up the possibility of the Court of First Instance being given jurisdiction to hear references from national courts for preliminary rulings under Articles 234 EC and 150 Euratom in specific areas laid down in the Statute.[44] So far, however, the Statute has not provided for this.

## APPEALS FROM THE COURT OF FIRST INSTANCE[45]

There is a right of appeal, on points of law only, from the Court of First Instance to the European Court. The grounds of appeal are lack of competence (equivalent to *ultra vires*); a breach of procedure (which must adversely affect the interests of the appellant); or any other infringement of Community law.[46]

Appeals may be brought by a party or intervener; however, a Member State or Community institution may appeal even if it is not a party or intervener. Interveners other than Community institutions or Member States may appeal only where the decision of the Court of First Instance directly affects them.

If the Court of First Instance annuls a Community regulation, the annulment does not take effect until the time for bringing an appeal has expired; if an appeal is brought, the annulment does not take effect unless and until the appeal is dismissed.

If the European Court allows the appeal, it quashes the judgment of the Court of First Instance. It may then either give final judgment itself, or it may refer the case back to the Court of First Instance for final judgment.[47]

## JURISDICTION OF THE CIVIL SERVICE TRIBUNAL AND APPEALS FROM IT

The jurisdiction of the Civil Service Tribunal is limited to disputes between the Community and its staff.[48] There is a right of appeal on points of law from its decisions

[44] Arts 225(3) EC and 140a(3) Euratom.

[45] Arts 225(1), second para. EC and 140a(1), second para. Euratom, together with Arts 56–61 of the Statute.

[46] An appeal may not be taken only on the amount of costs or the party ordered to pay them.

[47] For statistics on appeals from the Court of First Instance up to the end of 1994, see Brown, 'The First Five Years of the Court of First Instance and Appeals to the Court of Justice: Assessment and Statistics' (1995) 32 CMLRev. 743. On the basis of these statistics, Professor Brown concludes (at 757) that, of the cases decided by the Court of First Instance, only about one in ten is appealed and, of these appeals, only one in ten is wholly successful; consequently, only one decision in a hundred is completely overturned on appeal.

[48] Arts 236 [179] EC and 152 Euratom.

to the Court of First Instance.[49] Most of what was said above regarding appeals from the Court of First Instance also applies to appeals from the Civil Service Tribunal.

## PROCEDURE

This section focuses on the European Court, but most of what is said applies to the other courts as well. The procedure in the European Court is laid down partly in the Statute(s) of the Court and partly in the Rules of Procedure. There is one set of Rules for the EC and Euratom, but there is a separate set for the Court of First Instance.[50] They were originally modelled on those of the International Court of Justice.

The two most important ways in which the procedure in the European Court differs from that in an English court are the greater importance of written documents (and the consequent downgrading of oral proceedings) and the more active role played by the Court. Both these features are generally characteristic of Continental courts. The normal procedure in a direct action may be divided into four stages: the written proceedings, the preparatory inquiry, the oral hearing, and the judgment.

### THE WRITTEN PROCEEDINGS

Direct actions in the European Court are begun with a document called an application, in which the applicant (claimant) sets out the basis of his claim. This is not served on the defendant but lodged with the Court;[51] the Registrar will serve it on the defendant, who then has one month to lodge his defence. The applicant is entitled to reply to the defence by means of a document called a reply, and the defendant may answer this in a rejoinder. Then the pleadings are closed.

### ADMISSIBILITY

At this point the defendant may make a preliminary objection regarding admissibility. This concerns the question whether the Court is able to hear the case, in particular whether the subject matter is within the Court's jurisdiction, whether the applicant has *locus standi*, and whether the proceedings were brought within the relevant time-limit. A preliminary objection to admissibility is made in a separate document, to which the applicant is entitled to reply. There is a special hearing on the point and the advocate general gives an opinion. The Court will then give judgment: it may uphold the objection

[49] Art. 225a (third para.) EC and Art. 140b (third para.) Euratom; Arts 9–13 of Annex I to the Statute.

[50] See n. 1.

[51] The case officially begins at this moment and this is the cut-off date for time-limits for the commencement of proceedings: Rules of Procedure, Art. 37(3). On receipt of the application, the Registrar gives the case its number.

(in which case the action will be at an end) or dismiss it (in which case the proceedings will continue from the point where they were broken off) or the Court may decide to reserve its decision until the final judgment: in this case the main action will continue, but in the end the Court may decide that it was inadmissible and reject it without going into the merits.

### PREPARATORY INQUIRY

The second stage is the preparatory inquiry. This is concerned with the determination of questions of fact. Unlike the English procedure, however, it is the Court which decides what evidence is needed. As soon as the application has been lodged, the President of the Court will assign the case to one of the Chambers and designate a judge from that Chamber as 'judge-rapporteur'; the First Advocate General will then decide which advocate general will take the case. After the close of pleadings, the judge-rapporteur will prepare a preliminary report dealing with the issues of fact arising in the case. The Court will then decide, at a so-called general meeting (formerly 'administrative meeting'), what issues of fact (if any) need to be proved and what evidence is necessary for this purpose. In practice, questions of fact are not often in dispute and the Court will usually content itself with requiring the production of documents, and, possibly, putting questions to the parties. Where witnesses are called, the procedure is rather different from that in an English court. The witnesses are always witnesses of the Court, not the parties. (If a party wishes a certain witness to be called, he must make a request to the Court.) A witness is summoned by an order of the Court which will indicate the facts on which he is to be examined. The witness is heard before a Chamber of the Court in the presence of the parties or their representatives; the presiding judge will examine the witness, but the parties – as well as the other judges and the advocate general – may put questions as well. The testimony is put into writing and signed by the witness after being read back to him.

### ORAL PROCEDURE

This corresponds to the 'day in court' in English procedure. However, since the evidence has already been taken at an earlier stage, it is much less important to the outcome of the case. A few weeks beforehand, the judge-rapporteur issues his report for the hearing, which is distributed to the parties so that they can comment on it at the hearing. The report sets out the facts of the case and contains a summary of the arguments put forward by the parties.

At the hearing, counsel will address the Court and expound their contentions. After the main speeches, each side is allowed a brief reply. The judges and the advocate general may address questions to counsel. The Court then usually adjourns and the advocate general prepares his opinion; the hearing resumes at a later date for him to deliver it. The parties have no right to comment on it: the hearing is now over and the Court must consider its judgment.

## JUDGMENT

The Court always reserves judgment. The judges meet in a special deliberation room to decide on their judgment; no one other than the judges themselves may be present, not even secretaries or interpreters. The judge-rapporteur has the task of preparing a draft of the judgment which is then put before the other judges; if necessary a vote is taken. The procedure is that each judge gives his opinion in turn, starting with the most junior.[52] When a decision is finally reached, the judgment is signed by all the judges sitting and is delivered in open court. It is also published: the operative part (formal ruling) in the Official Journal and the whole judgment, together with advocate general's opinion, in the official law reports.

## EXECUTION

In most cases the defendant is either the Community (or an institution thereof) or a Member State; in neither of these cases is it possible to obtain execution of the judgment. The judgment is binding, and it is assumed that it will be obeyed. The question of execution only arises, therefore, in those rare cases where the defendant is a private individual and damages are awarded against him, or where the applicant is a private person and costs are awarded against him. In these cases the judgment creditor must go to the appropriate national court to obtain enforcement according to national procedure; enforcement is, however, automatic and the national court has no right to question the judgment.[53]

## SPECIAL PROCEDURES AFTER JUDGMENT

There is no appeal from judgments of the European Court; there are, however, three special procedures which, to a very limited extent, might be said to serve a similar function. These are third-party proceedings, revision, and interpretation. The first two allow a request to be made to the European Court to review a judgment previously given by it; under the third, the Court may be asked to clarify the meaning of its judgment.[54] Though of theoretical interest, these proceedings are rare in practice.

Third-party proceedings provide a means whereby a person who was not a party to the original action may contest a judgment which is prejudicial to his rights.[55] The proceedings are begun by an application to which similar rules apply as in the case of an

[52] In cases which strongly affect the national interests of a particular Member State, it is apparently the custom for the judge from that state to express no view on the merits of the case until all the other judges have done so.

[53] Arts 244 [187] and 256 [192] EC, 159 and 164 Euratom. For the procedure in the United Kingdom, see Chap. 8.

[54] Clerical mistakes, errors in calculation, and obvious slips in the judgment may also be corrected by the Court of its own motion, or on application of a party within two weeks after the delivery of the judgment; see Art. 66 of the Rules of Procedure. A party may apply within one month for the Court to make good any omission in its judgment: Art. 67 of the Rules of Procedure.

[55] Art. 42 of the Statute. See also Art. 97 of the Rules of Procedure.

ordinary action, and which is lodged with the Court and served by the Registrar on all the parties to the original proceedings. The third party must show that the judgment is prejudicial to his rights and give good reasons why he was unable to take part in the original action (normally this would be because it was not brought to his notice). The proceedings must be brought within two months of the publication of the judgment in the Official Journal.

When a new fact comes to light after the judgment which would have had a decisive impact on it, a party to the original proceedings may apply for revision.[56] The fact must not have been before the Court when it gave judgment and must also have been unknown to the party making the application. The proceedings must be brought within three months of the discovery of the new fact and also within ten years of the original judgment. When an application is made, the Court first decides whether the new fact is of sufficient importance to warrant the re-opening of the case; if it decides that this is so, it will then reconsider the previous judgment in the light of the new fact. The other party is, of course, allowed to contest the application, both at the stage of admissibility and when the judgment is reviewed.

An application for the interpretation of a judgment may be brought by a party to the previous case, or by a Community institution even if it was not a party.[57] The request may be directed only to the actual ruling or the reasoning on which it was based; the clarification of *obiter dicta* may not be requested.

## PRELIMINARY RULINGS

The procedure is different where the European Court is asked by a national court to give a preliminary ruling. Here there are, strictly speaking, no parties; the proceedings are not regarded as contentious: the European Court views its function simply as assisting the national court. The parties to the national proceedings cannot, therefore, take the initiative: the national court sets the procedure in motion by making an order for reference, and the judgment of the European Court is sent back to the national court where the case will continue on its course. The events in the European Court are only an episode in the national proceedings.

When an order for reference reaches the European Court, the Registrar will transmit copies to the parties in the national proceedings and also to the Member States, the Commission, and, where a measure of the Council is in issue, to the Council. These persons and bodies may submit written observations to the Court and they may also attend the oral hearing. At the hearing, submissions are made by those attending; then the advocate general presents his opinion, and judgment is given in the normal way. The parties to the national proceedings may not request revision or interpretation of the judgment; but the national court may, if it wishes, make a second reference in order to deal with a new issue or to clarify the original ruling.

[56] Art. 44 of the Statute. See also Arts 98–100 of the Rules of Procedure.

[57] Art. 43 of the Statute. See also Art. 102 of the Rules of Procedure.

## LAWYERS

The rules regarding legal representation differ according to whether the party is, on the one hand, a private person or company or, on the other hand, a Member State or Community institution.[58] In the former case, representation by a lawyer is obligatory; the only exception is that in references for preliminary rulings the national rules apply: therefore, if a party is permitted to appear in person in the court from which the reference was made, he will be allowed to do so in the European Court.

Member States and Community institutions are represented by an agent appointed for the particular case; he may be assisted by an adviser or lawyer. National governments often choose a civil servant (normally with legal qualifications) as their agent; alternatively they may brief a barrister. The Council, Commission, and Parliament are normally represented by a member of their legal services; sometimes outside lawyers may be briefed.

The right of a lawyer to appear before the European Court depends on national law. In direct actions, any lawyer entitled to practise before a court of any Member State may appear before the European Court; in preliminary references, anyone (even if not legally qualified) entitled to represent a party before the court or tribunal which made the reference may do so before the European Court. Agents and advisers of Member States and Community institutions may appear even if not entitled to plead in national courts.

The position regarding English lawyers is more complicated. The English texts of the Statutes and Rules of Procedure use the word 'lawyer',[59] and this is wide enough to cover both barristers and solicitors. An agreement to regulate the matter was entered into between the two professions in 1971 in anticipation of Britain's entry into the Community. Under this agreement, barristers could appear in any case, but the right of audience of solicitors was subject to restrictions. However, the Council of the Law Society rescinded the agreement on 19 June 1981 and the position now is that solicitors can appear in any direct action;[60] on a preliminary reference, they can appear if they have a right of audience before the court which made the reference. In practice, however, almost all English lawyers appearing before the European Court are barristers.

In direct actions the general rule is that costs are awarded to the successful party if he has asked for them. (There is an exception regarding staff cases: here the employing institution pays its own costs even if it wins.) Where costs are granted, the unsuccessful party must not only pay his own costs (e.g., lawyers' fees, travelling expenses, etc.) but also those of the successful party. In the event of a dispute, either party may apply for costs to be taxed by the Court. In preliminary rulings, on the other hand, the European Court does not award costs: they are regarded as costs in the case before the national court and any ruling made by it applies to them as well.

[58] For the position prior to the Treaty of Nice, see Art. 17 of the Statute of the Court (EC and Euratom); for the position after the Treaty of Nice, see Art. 19 of the Statute. See also Arts 32–36, 37(1), 38(3), and 104(2) of the Rules of Procedure.

[59] In other languages the provision seems more restrictive: the French text, for example, refers to '*un avocat inscrit à un barreau de l'un des Etats membres*'.

[60] The first case in which this occurred was *Tither v. Commission*, Case 175/80, [1981] ECR 2345.

A person who is wholly or partly unable to meet the costs of proceedings in the European Court may apply for legal aid.[61] The application is made to the Court itself and is heard by a Chamber. Legal representation is not necessary for such an application. If legal aid is granted, the cashier of the Court pays out the sum allowed; it is, however, provided in the Rules of Procedure that the Court may order the repayment of this sum in a subsequent decision regarding costs.

## MULTILINGUALISM

One of the characteristics of the Community is that it is multilingual. Between them, the Member States have twenty-three official languages – Bulgarian, Czech, Danish, Dutch, English, Estonian, Finnish, French, German, Greek, Hungarian, Irish, Italian, Latvian, Lithuanian, Maltese, Polish, Portuguese, Romanian, Slovak, Slovene, Spanish, and Swedish. The principle of linguistic equality was not fully accepted in the beginning. When the ECSC Treaty was signed in 1951, Germany (and, to some extent, Italy) were in a weak political position as a consequence of the war; Britain had chosen to stand aloof from Europe. Therefore it was hardly surprising that France played the leading role and that the French language enjoyed a special position. The result was that the Treaty was drawn up in a single text in French.[62] There was no express statement that only the French text was authentic, but this was generally regarded as following from the fact that it was the original.[63] Official translations were, however, made into Dutch, German, and Italian and, subsequently, into the official languages of the new Member States.

The EC and Euratom Treaties, on the other hand, are authentic in the official languages of all the Member States: they were originally drawn up in the four official languages of the original Member States and it was provided that all versions would be equally authentic.[64] When Denmark, Ireland, and the United Kingdom joined the Community, it was laid down that the official translations into Danish, Irish, and English would have the same status as the original versions.[65] The same steps were taken when the other Member States joined the Community.

All the official languages except Irish are working languages of the institutions.[66] Community legislation is published in all the working languages, and it is generally

[61] Art. 76 of the Rules of Procedure. See Kennedy, 'Paying the Piper: Legal Aid in Proceedings before the Court of Justice' (1988) 27 CMLRev. 559. For references for a preliminary ruling, see Art. 104(6) of the Rules of Procedure.

[62] See Art. 100 ECSC.

[63] Thus, while Art. 160 of the Act of Accession 1972 provides for authentic versions of the EC and Euratom Treaties in the Danish, English, and Irish language, there is no equivalent provision in the case of the ECSC Treaty: see Art. 159.

[64] See Arts 314 [248] EC and 225 Euratom.

[65] See Art. 160 of the Act of Accession.

[66] See Arts 290 [217] EC and 190 Euratom, together with Regulation 1 (EC), JO 1958, p. 385 and Regulation 1 (Euratom), JO 1958, p. 401, as amended on the accession of new Member States. As far as the ECSC was concerned, see P. Reuter, *La Communauté Européenne du Charbon et de l'Acier* (1953) at 81–2, referring to an unpublished decision of the foreign ministers of the original Six, taken at a meeting in Paris on 23 and 24 July 1952, that Dutch, French, German, and Italian would be the working languages.

accepted that all versions are equally authentic.[67] When Denmark, Ireland, and the United Kingdom joined, pre-accession Community measures still in force were translated into Danish and English, and Article 155 of the Act of Accession stated that they would have the same authenticity as the versions in the other languages. This was also done when other Member States joined later.

The interpretation of multilingual texts poses particular problems. In public international law, various theories on the interpretation of multilingual treaties have been put forward. They include the following: that the least onerous version should be preferred (theory of minimum obligation); that each Contracting State should be bound only by the version in its own language; and that the text in the original language should prevail.[68] However, theories which might be appropriate for international law are not necessarily appropriate for Community law. In particular, it would be unthinkable for the obligations of Member States to vary because of differences in the texts: the unity of the Community is paramount.[69]

In practice, the European Court does not appear to have been troubled by linguistic differences in the texts. The reason is simple: even when there are no linguistic problems, the Court does not put a great deal of weight on the literal meaning of the words. Policy considerations play a particularly important role and sometimes prevail over the literal meaning even when it is clear.[70] Linguistic discrepancies are, therefore, treated in the same way as other obscurities in the text: the Court adopts the meaning which, in its view, best accords with the purpose of the provision and the policy objectives pursued by the Court.[71] This applies both in those cases where the same term is used in all the versions but its meaning differs in the various national systems and also in those cases where different terms are used.

The chapters that follow contain many examples of the Court's practice of choosing between the various versions on the basis of policy objectives. Here it is sufficient to mention one: *Stauder v. City of Ulm*.[72] This case, which is considered further in Chapter 5, concerned a Community scheme under which persons in receipt of welfare benefits could obtain butter at a reduced price on presentation of a coupon. The scheme had been established by a Commission decision addressed to all the Member States, and the German version stated that the coupon had to contain the beneficiary's name; the Dutch version was similar, but the French and Italian texts stated merely that the coupon had to be 'individualized'.

The German authorities charged with implementing the scheme had looked only to the German version and had issued vouchers which had to contain the name and

67 See H. Kutscher, 'Methods of Interpretation as Seen by a Judge at the Court of Justice', p. 17 (paper delivered at the Judicial and Academic Conference held at the European Court in 1976).

68 See Dickschat, 'Problèmes d'interprétation des traités européens résultant de leur plurilinguisme' [1968] Revue Belge de Droit International 40 at 43–4.

69 See the quotation from *Stauder v. City of Ulm* given below.

70 See below.

71 See *Mij PPW Internationaal*, Case 61/72, [1973] ECR 301 (para. 14 of the judgment) and *Moulijn v. Commission*, Case 6/74, [1974] ECR 1287 (paras 10 and 11 of the judgment); see further Kutscher, 'Methods of Interpretation' (above), p. 20.

72 Case 29/69, [1969] ECR 419. See also *Moksel v. BALM*, Case 55/87, [1988] ECR 3845 (paras 14–19 of the judgment).

address of the beneficiary. The plaintiff in the case maintained that it was a humiliation to have to reveal his identity to the shopkeeper when he bought the butter; he even went so far as to argue that this constituted a violation of his human rights. He therefore brought legal proceedings in the German courts and the case came before the European Court on a reference for a preliminary ruling on the interpretation and validity of the Commission decision. The Court held that it should be interpreted so as not to require the recipient's name to be revealed. The relevant passage of the judgment reads as follows:[73]

> When a single decision is addressed to all the Member States the necessity for uniform application and accordingly for uniform interpretation makes it impossible to consider one version of the text in isolation but requires that it be interpreted on the basis of both the real intention of its author and the aim he seeks to achieve, in the light in particular of the versions in all four languages.
>
> In a case like the present one, the most liberal interpretation must prevail, provided that it is sufficient to achieve the objectives pursued by the decision in question. It cannot, moreover, be accepted that the authors of the decision intended to impose stricter obligations in some Member States than in others.

The consequence of this judgment is that, even when a Community decision is addressed to a Member State, that State must be prepared to consider all the linguistic versions if it wants to be sure of the correct interpretation.[74]

## COURT PROCEDURE

What languages may be used in Court proceedings? The question depends on what is known as the 'language of the case'.[75] Any one of the official languages of the Member States (including Irish) may be chosen, and the theory behind the rules governing the choice of language is that the Community is regarded as multilingual and consequently able to operate in any official language. Community institutions are therefore required to accommodate themselves to the needs of the other party.

In direct actions the basic rule is that the applicant has the choice of language. However, where the defendant is a Member State, or an individual or corporation having the nationality of a Member State, the language of the case is the official language of that State. (Where the Member State has more than one official language – as, for example, is the case with Belgium – the applicant may choose between them.) Except in the rare cases where a Member State brings enforcement proceedings against another Member State, the Community will always be a party to a direct action; the effect of these rules, therefore, is to benefit the other party. The Court may depart from the rules at the request of the parties; however, where the request is not made jointly by the parties, the advocate general and the other party must be heard.

[73] [1969] ECR at 424–5 (paras 3 and 4 of the judgment).

[74] See Kutscher, 'Methods of Interpretation' (above), pp. 18–19.

[75] See Art. 29 of the Rules of Procedure.

In the case of a preliminary ruling, the language of the case is that of the national court or tribunal which made the reference,[76] though other Member States may submit observations in their own languages.

In general, the language of the case is used for all purposes in the proceedings, and documents in other languages must be translated into it. Members of the Court, however, may use any official language of their choice. This applies to comments and questions during the hearing, to the judge-rapporteur's report, and to the advocate general's opinion. There is simultaneous translation at the oral hearing. Court publications, including law reports, are published in the working languages of the Community (i.e., in all the official languages except Irish).

It will readily be appreciated that litigants in the European Court face linguistic problems not encountered in domestic courts. The private litigant normally has the choice of language; however, a litigant who chooses, for example, Finnish must be aware of the fact that most judges cannot understand this language. The precision of the pleadings may suffer on translation, and at the hearing the eloquence of counsel may have little effect when it is heard through the earphones of the simultaneous translation apparatus. Clearly, a French-speaking lawyer – or an English-speaking one – will find it easier to present his case.

## DRAFTING THE JUDGMENT

In order to maintain the secrecy of their discussions, the judges do not allow any interpreters into the deliberation room. In these circumstances multilingualism is impossible and the Court has informally adopted French as its working language. This choice was made when the Court was first set up and is another example of the special position enjoyed by the French in those days. Indeed the choice of French was almost inevitable in view of the fact that it was an official language of three of the six original Member States (France, Belgium, and Luxembourg). Today, English is more widely spoken in the majority of Community countries, but it is unlikely, for a considerable time at least, to replace the French as the working language of the Court: once made, a choice of language is hard to change, since appointments to the Court are made with this in mind.

The choice of French as the working language of the Court means that the judges speak French when they discuss their judgment. All drafting is done in French and the final version approved by the Court is in French, even if this is not the language of the case. The French text of the judgment is then translated into the language of the case and this text is signed by the judges and delivered in open court. The result is that the text signed by the judges may be in a language which many of them do not understand. This throws a great deal of responsibility on those judges who are fluent in the language of the case to ensure that the translation truly reflects what was agreed on.

One drawback of the unilingual code of operation of the Court is that it puts judges whose mother tongue is not French at a disadvantage. Most people feel less confident

[76] Provided it is one of the official languages: it would seem that some other language – such as Welsh – would not be acceptable.

about giving their opinions in a group discussion if they are not fully at home in the language spoken. French-speaking judges must therefore enjoy a subtle psychological advantage over their colleagues. The use of French in the deliberation room must, moreover, work to some extent in favour of French legal thinking: it is hard to draft a judgment in French without using French legal terminology, while concepts peculiar to other systems might be ignored simply because they cannot easily be expressed in French.

Another difficulty is that, although the official version of the judgment is in the language of the case, the French-language version is the one actually agreed on by the Court and therefore might be said to represent the opinion of the Court more accurately than the former. One can imagine that, if there is a discussion in the deliberation room as to exactly what was decided in a previous case, it is the French text which will be examined. Consequently, a lawyer trying to convince the Court that it ought to follow its previous decision would be well advised to study the French text as well as that in his own language, even if the latter is the authentic version; where this is not the case, it is especially important not to rely exclusively on the one version.

It is almost impossible for even the best translator to find a form of words with exactly the same meaning as the original; translations, therefore, can never be exact. Sometimes there is simply no equivalent word in the other language. For example, Article 40 ECSC used the phrase '*faute de service*' in the French version; this is a French legal term which cannot be translated directly into English: the translators of the Treaty therefore had to make do with the circumlocution 'wrongful act or omission [on the part of the Community] in the performance of its functions', a phrase which entirely lacks the precise connotations of the French. (One can imagine that if the English word 'trust' were translated into French, the translators might well come up with something equivalent to 'legal relationship in which one person has a beneficial interest in property nominally owned by another', a phrase which can have little meaning for someone ignorant of English law.)

In addition to the inaccuracies which inevitably result from translation, actual mistakes sometimes occur. For example, in the English version of the judgment in *Royer*,[77] the word 'save' was omitted from the following passage: 'the procedure of appeal to a competent authority must precede the decision ordering expulsion [save] in cases of emergency'. This was a simple slip; a less obvious, and thus more insidious, error occurred in the *Bonsignore* case.[78] Here the phrase '*Gefährdungen der öffentlichen Ordnung*' in the authentic German version of the judgment – '*des menaces à l'ordre public*' in the French version – was mistranslated into English as 'breaches of the peace', a mistake which caused difficulties in a later case when an English court made a reference for a preliminary ruling on the same issue.[79]

[77] Case 48/75, [1976] ECR 497 at para. 59 of the judgment. The authentic version of this judgment was in French.

[78] Case 67/74, [1975] ECR 297 at 307.

[79] *R v. Bouchereau*, Case 30/77, [1977] ECR 1999; see *per* Advocate General Warner at 2024. 'Threats to public policy' would be a literal translation of the German and French texts.

## THE FORM OF JUDGMENT

Judgments of the European Court consist of three main parts. The first[80] is based on the report of the judge-rapporteur and contains a statement of the facts and a summary of the arguments of the parties; the second part,[81] which is usually drawn up in numbered paragraphs and may be set in larger print in the official version of the law reports, contains the reasoning of the judgment; the final part is the actual ruling.[82]

For lawyers, the second part is the important one, since this gives the Court's reasons for its decision. After a certain amount of experimentation in the early days, the Court adopted a style based on that of the French courts. This is formal, terse, and abstract. For some time, the French version was written in the form of one long sentence, each paragraph beginning with the words '*Attendu que*...' ('Whereas...') or simply '*que*' ('that') and ending with a semicolon. These subordinate clauses would all lead up to the final ruling that, for example, the application was dismissed. This was broken up into separate sentences in the English version (a style now adopted in French as well) but it still reads as a series of *ex cathedra* statements, completely lacking the close reasoning of an English or American judgment.

This style was probably necessitated by the decision-making procedure adopted by the Court. For the reasons discussed above, the Court gives a single judgment: concurring or dissenting judgments are not permitted. However, it is the policy of the Court to involve all the judges in the drafting of the judgment in an attempt to attain the maximum consensus. Though the judge-rapporteur might be expected to play a special role, the judgment is the collective work of the whole Court, and it is apparently not uncommon for each sentence to be subject to lengthy discussion. Committee procedure of this kind does not lend itself to the production of a discursive judgment of the English sort.

This does not, of course, mean that a court which gives a single judgment must inevitably adopt the French style. The judgments of the Privy Council in the days before it allowed dissenting and concurring judgments are evidence of this. However, if it were desired to produce a judgment in the English style, it would be necessary to sacrifice any attempt to gain a consensus: the drafting of the judgment would have to be entrusted to a single judge – who would no doubt be the member of the Court whose views most clearly represented those of the majority – and the role of the others would be limited to the suggesting of minor alterations.

Two further consequences of the attempt to attain consensus are evident in the Court's judgments. In some cases there appear to be two separate lines of reasoning, both leading to the same conclusion. Since these may be quite different, the result is disconcerting for the lawyer trying to extract the *ratio decidendi*. The reason for this

[80] It is now headed 'Report for the Hearing', but previously such headings as 'Issues of Fact and Law', 'Facts', or 'Facts and Issues' have been used. Since the beginning of 1994, it has been omitted from the European Court Reports.

[81] It is now headed 'Judgment', but previously headings such as 'Grounds of Judgment', 'Law', or 'Decision' have been used.

[82] This is usually set in bold type in the official reports.

appears to be that, though there was a majority in favour of the result, there were two different schools of thought as to the reasons. The inclusion of both sets of reasons appears to be an attempt to satisfy both groups.

The second expedient adopted in the case of dissension among the judges is to take the opposite course: instead of putting in something to please both groups, the Court deletes anything which might displease either. The result is that no reasons of substance are given at all. Examples of both these methods of arriving at a consensus may be found below.[83]

## PRECEDENT[84]

Does the doctrine of precedent apply in the European Court?[85] The answer is that there is no legal doctrine of *stare decisis*, but the Court does follow its previous decisions in almost all cases. The case law of the European Court is just as important for the development of Community law as that of English courts is for modern English law: the following chapters contain ample proof of this. However, though lawyers and advocates general have always cited copious precedents, the Court itself used to refer to its previous decisions only in rare instances. One almost got the impression that it was trying to disguise the extent to which it followed precedent:[86] sometimes it would reproduce sentences, or even whole paragraphs, from previous judgments, without quotation marks or any acknowledgement of source. Today the position has changed, though the Court usually cites precedents only when they support its reasoning: it does not normally cite them in order to distinguish them.[87]

There are a number of important instances where the Court has not followed precedent.[88] These are the result of changing circumstances or a change of opinion among the judges, possibly following criticism by advocates general or academic writers. Where this happens, the Court does not normally overrule the earlier case as an English

[83] See *Compagnie Française v. Commission*, Case 64/69, [1970] ECR 221, where two lines of reasoning were given, and *International Fruit Company v. Commission*, Cases 41–4/70, [1971] ECR 411, where virtually no reasons at all were given.

[84] See Arnull, 'Owning Up to Fallibility: Precedent and the Court of Justice' (1993) 30 CMLRev. 247.

[85] For the position in the Court of First Instance, see Arnull, 'Owning Up to Fallibility: Precedent and the Court of Justice' (1993) 30 CMLRev. 247 at 262–4, where it is suggested that the Court of First Instance is not bound either by its own previous decisions or even by those of the European Court. There is an exception to the latter proposition where the European Court allows an appeal from the Court of First Instance and refers the case back to the latter for a final judgment: here the Court of First Instance is bound by the decision of the European Court on points of law (Statute of the Court of Justice (EC), Art. 54, second para.). A second exception arises where the European Court rules that the Court of First Instance, not it, has jurisdiction in a case: the Court of First Instance cannot then decide that it lacks jurisdiction (Statute of the Court of Justice (EC), Art. 47, second para.).

[86] The Court may have been under the influence of the Continental theory that precedents cannot constitute a formal source of law.

[87] There are some exceptions: see, for example, *TWD*, Case C-188/92, [1994] ECR I-833 (paras 19–24 of the judgment). See also Arnull, above, (1993) 30 CMLRev. 247 at 253–60.

[88] For examples, see the Opinion of Advocate General Jacobs in the *HAG GF* case (below) at I-3747–50.

court would: it simply ignores it. The most prominent exception to this,[89] and indeed the most famous example of a *volte face* by the European Court, is its decision in *HAG GF*.[90] The striking feature of this case is that it arose on largely the same facts as a previous case decided some sixteen years earlier, *Van Zuylen v. HAG*.[91] The issue was the right of the holder of a trade mark to block the importation from another Member State of goods bearing that mark. Both the earlier and the later case involved the same mark, 'HAG', the well-known brand of decaffeinated coffee. In the later case, the Court confronted the issue directly and said that it had decided to reconsider its previous judgment. After considering the policy factors involved, it reversed it.[92] The following passage from the Opinion of Advocate General Jacobs is of interest:[93]

> The Court has consistently recognised its power to depart from previous decisions... That the Court should in an appropriate case expressly overrule an earlier decision is I think an inescapable duty, even if the Court has never before expressly done so.

That the Court did so in *HAG GF* was probably due to the close factual links between the two cases, though the persuasiveness of the Advocate General no doubt played its part.

The opinions of advocates general are frequently cited by lawyers (and advocates general) in cases before the Court. Do they have any weight as precedents? Obviously a great deal depends on whether the Court itself has pronounced on the issue. The first possibility is that the Court did not consider the point in the previous case. Here, the advocate general's opinion has a value somewhat similar to that of a judgment at first instance which is upheld (or reversed) on appeal on different grounds without the appellate court expressing any opinion on the ground on which the case was originally decided. The second possibility is that the advocate general's opinion was rejected by the Court in the previous case. Even here, it will be cited by counsel, but they will have to show that the advocate general was right and the Court wrong. The third possibility is that the Court followed the advocate general. Here the main value of his opinion will be to explain and clarify the judgment, something which is often necessary in view of the brevity of the Court's reasoning.

## INTERPRETATION

The interpretation of the Treaties and Community legislation is one of the principal tasks of the Court. To some extent the Court's approach to this is the same as that of an English court: it looks at the words used and considers their meaning in the context of the instrument as a whole. In doing this, it tries to give the provision an interpretation which fits in with the general scheme of the instrument, though it is much more willing than an English court to depart from the literal meaning of the words to achieve this.

89 *European Parliament v. Council (Chernobyl)*, Case C-70/88, [1990] ECR I-2041, is another exception.

90 Case C-10/89, [1990] ECR I-3711.

91 Case 192/73, [1974] ECR 731.

92 It seems that the Court felt that the rather drastic solution adopted in the earlier case was not after all needed in order to protect the functioning of the Common Market.

93 At I-3749–50.

Beyond this, the Court makes little attempt to establish the actual subjective intention of the authors of the text. The preparatory documents (*travaux préparatoires*) for the Treaties have never been published; there are certain national materials, such as official statements by the national governments to their parliaments during ratification debates, but these are little used. As far as Community legislation is concerned, Commission proposals (including an explanatory memorandum) and the opinions of the European Parliament and the Economic and Social Committee (where these bodies have been consulted) are available, but not often considered by the Court.

One reason for disregarding the subjective intention of the authors of the text is that, in the case of an agreement reached after hard bargaining, there may be no common intention – only an agreement on a form of words. A more important reason is that the Court prefers to interpret texts on the basis of what it thinks they should be trying to achieve; it moulds the law according to what it regards as the needs of the Community.[94] This is sometimes called the 'teleological method of interpretation', but it really goes beyond interpretation properly so called: it is decision-making on the basis of judicial policy.

## POLICY

One of the distinctive characteristics of the European Court is the extent to which its decision-making is based on policy. By policy is meant the values and attitudes of the judges – the objectives they wish to promote. The policies of the European Court are basically the following:

1. strengthening the Community (and especially the federal elements in it);
2. increasing the scope and effectiveness of Community law;
3. enlarging the powers of Community institutions.[95]

They may be summed up in one phrase: the promotion of European integration.

All courts are of course influenced by policy, but in the European Court policy plays a particularly important role: occasionally the Court will ignore the clear words of the Treaty in order to attain a policy objective. An example of this is *Parti Ecologiste – 'Les Verts' v. European Parliament*,[96] which concerned a decision of the European Parliament authorizing the payment of grants from the Community budget to political parties,

[94] Thus Judge Kutscher (a former President of the European Court) has said extrajudicially, 'Interpretations based on the original situation would in no way be in keeping with a Community law orientated towards the future' (H. Kutscher, 'Methods of Interpretation', (above), p.22).

[95] But see the *Tobacco Advertising* case, *Germany v. European Parliament and Council*, Case C-376/98, [2000] ECR I-8419, where the Court held that the Community lacked the power to adopt a general ban on tobacco advertising. Only the Member States could do so. This case is discussed below in Chap. 4.

[96] Case 294/83, [1986] ECR 1339. Other examples are mentioned elsewhere in this book: they include *Sevince*, Case C-192/89, [1990] ECR I-3461; *Busseni*, Case C-221/88, [1990] ECR I-495 and *SPI*, Cases 267–9/81, [1983] ECR 801.

ostensibly to cover an information campaign to explain the work of the Parliament to the electors at the time of the 1984 elections, but in reality to contribute towards the parties' election expenses. The formula adopted for the distribution of the money was strongly biased in favour of those parties represented in the Parliament before the elections and discriminated against those parties seeking representation for the first time. One party in the latter category, the French Ecologists, brought proceedings in the European Court to annul the decision.

The proceedings were brought under Article 230 [173] EC which, as it stood at the time of the case, provided: 'The Court of Justice shall review the legality of acts of the Commission and the Council.' This provision was perfectly clear and did not mention acts of the Parliament; nevertheless, the Court held that acts of the Parliament were covered. It reached this conclusion in four steps. The first step was to state that the Community is based on the rule of law, and acts of both the Member States and the Community institutions are subject to judicial review to ensure that they conform to the Treaty. The second step was to explain that no power had been given in the EC Treaty to review the acts of the Parliament because, at the time when the Treaty was drawn up, the Parliament did not possess the power to pass measures which could affect the rights of third parties.[97] The third step was to point out that it subsequently obtained such powers, notably in the Budgetary Treaties and the Decision and Act on direct elections. The fourth step was to conclude that it would be contrary to the spirit and system of the Treaty if the acts of the Parliament were not now subject to review. Therefore, the Court decided, Article 230 [173] covered acts of the Parliament.

The logic of this ruling should be fully understood: what the Court did was to say that the acts of the Parliament *ought* to be reviewable; therefore, they *were* reviewable. This logic, which also formed the basis of the decision in the *SPI* case (discussed below),[98] ignores the distinction between what the law ought to be and what it is, a distinction which is fundamental to the Western concept of law.

An equally striking example is provided by the *Chernobyl* case,[99] which also concerned the European Parliament. This case was in some ways the reverse of the *Parti Ecologiste* case: the issue was whether the Parliament could bring proceedings under Article 146 Euratom[100] to annul an act of the Council. As it stood at the time, this provision did not cover the Parliament. The Court recognized this,[101] but nevertheless held that the Parliament *could* bring proceedings (though only for a limited purpose). It said:[102]

> The absence in the Treaties of any provision giving the Parliament the right to bring an action for annulment may constitute a procedural gap, but it cannot prevail over the fundamental interest in the maintenance and observance of the institutional balance laid down in the Treaties establishing the European Communities.

[97] The Court pointed out that under the ECSC Treaty, where the Parliament does have such powers (see Art. 95, fourth para.), its acts are reviewable: see Art. 38.

[98] See Chap. 9.

[99] *European Parliament v. Council*, Case C-70/88, [1990] ECR I-2041. For the background to the case, see Chap. 12.

[100] At the time, this was identical to Art. 230 [173] EC.

[101] In a previous case, *European Parliament v. Council* (*Comitology*), Case 302/87, [1988] ECR 5615, it had in fact given an express ruling to this effect.

[102] Paras 26 and 27 of the judgment.

> Consequently, an action for annulment brought by the Parliament against an act of the Council or the Commission is admissible.

It is hard to imagine a clearer example of changing the law while supposedly interpreting it.

The Court's decisions in these cases did not represent a challenge to the interests of the national governments.[103] Where this is the case, the Court moves more carefully. A common tactic is to introduce a new doctrine gradually: in the first case that comes before it, the Court will establish the doctrine as a general principle, but suggest that it is subject to various qualifications; the Court may even find some reason why it should not be applied to the particular facts of the case. The principle, however, is now established. If there are not too many protests, it will be re-affirmed in later cases; the qualifications can then be whittled away and the full extent of the doctrine revealed.

This process is well illustrated by the lines of cases concerning the treaty-making power of the Community and the doctrine of direct effect. These are both discussed below;[104] here a case will be considered which reveals in a particularly stark form the interplay between law and policy, principle and expediency: the second *Defrenne* case.[105] This concerned Article 141 [119] EC, which, as it stood at the time, provided: 'Each Member State shall during the first stage ensure and subsequently maintain the application of the principle that men and women should receive equal pay for equal work.'

The first stage for bringing the Treaty into operation ended on 31 December 1961, but the Member States felt that they were not in a position to implement Article 141 [119] by this date. They therefore held a conference which laid down a fresh timetable: the new date was 31 December 1964. This deadline was not, however, met by all the Member States, and the Commission then convened various meetings and drew up a series of reports in an attempt to bring the recalcitrant governments into line. Finally, the Commission announced that it would take enforcement proceedings against those Member States which had not complied by 18 July 1973, but this threat was not carried out. Then, on 10 February 1975, the Council issued a directive on equal pay which had to be implemented within one year.

In 1970, however, Gabrielle Defrenne, an air hostess who had worked for the Belgian airline Sabena, brought proceedings against it in the Belgian courts because it had paid her less than male cabin crew doing the same work. She claimed that it had no right to do this and demanded back-payment of the difference. The Belgian courts referred various questions of Community law to the European Court for a preliminary ruling; in particular, they wished to know whether Article 141 [119] conferred rights directly on individuals, even though it had not been implemented, and, if so, from what date it did this.

These questions raised highly delicate issues. In particular, if back-pay could be claimed by all women who had suffered discrimination, the economic consequences would be serious: according to the United Kingdom Government, many British firms

[103] This is shown by the fact that the Treaty on European Union amended the Treaties to make them accord with both rulings.

[104] In Chaps 6 and 7, respectively.

[105] *Defrenne v. Sabena*, Case 43/75, [1976] ECR 455.

would be driven into bankruptcy if the right to equal pay were backdated to Britain's entry into the Community.[106] As far as the law was concerned, the principal issue was whether Article 141 [119] was directly effective. There were quite strong reasons for believing that it was not,[107] but such a ruling would have conflicted with the Court's policy of enhancing the scope and effectiveness of Community law. On this point, policy triumphed: the Court ruled that Article 141 [119] conferred rights directly on individuals in the Member States and that the various resolutions putting off the date for implementation were of no effect. This meant that there had been a right to equal pay in the original Member States since 1 January 1962 and in the United Kingdom, Ireland, and Denmark since 1 January 1973.

However, the Court felt it expedient to sweeten the pill by ruling that only those workers who had instituted legal proceedings (or made equivalent claims) before the date of the judgment could rely on the direct effect of Article 141 [119] in order to claim back-pay for periods prior to that date. Thus Ms Defrenne won her case but the Member States were shielded from an avalanche of similar claims.[108]

This ruling neatly reconciled the Court's policy with the interests of the Member States. But it did so at the expense of legal principle: there was no possible ground in law for limiting the effect of the judgment in this way: if Article 141 [119] was directly effective for Ms Defrenne, it must have been directly effective for all other workers; claims for back-pay might be affected by national statutes of limitation, but there was no legal ground for making the date of the judgment in the *Defrenne* case decisive.[109]

These cases are extreme examples; nevertheless, they prompt the question whether it is right to allow policy to play so dominant a role. In this connection it is desirable to draw a distinction between those cases where the Court makes a choice on policy grounds between two or more legally tenable solutions, and those cases where it allows policy considerations to dictate a solution that conflicts with generally accepted legal principles. The former is perfectly proper, but the latter may be criticized as going beyond the proper function of a court.[110] It might be argued that in the case of the

106 The Equal Pay Act 1970 only came into force on 29 December 1975; consequently, the Court's decision could have made employers liable for claims going back three years.

107 Art. 141 [119] was far from clear and it envisaged action by the Member States to bring it into force: see Chap. 7.

108 The principle has also been applied in *Pinna*, Case 41/84, [1986] ECR 1; *Barra v. Belgium*, Case 309/85, [1988] ECR 355; *Blaizot v. University of Liège*, Case 24/86, [1988] ECR 379; *Barber v. Guardian Royal Exchange Assurance Group*, Case C-262/88, [1990] ECR I-1889 (on this see the Protocol Concerning Article 141 [119] EC, a Protocol to the Treaty on European Union); *Union Royale Belge v. Bosman*, Case C-415/93, [1995] ECR I-4921; *Sürül*, Case C-262/96, [1999] ECR I-2685.

109 The reasons given by the Court in its judgment were: first, the economic difficulties feared by the British and Irish Governments (it said that these could not affect the *future* application of the law, thereby implying that they could affect its application as regards the past); secondly, the fact that the conduct of the Member States and the views adopted by the Commission had led employers to continue their violation of the principle of equal pay; and thirdly, that the general level at which pay would have been fixed could not be known (a rather doubtful proposition). These latter arguments, however, apply just as much to workers who made claims before the *Defrenne* judgment as to those who began proceedings after it. They therefore provide no justification for the Court's ruling.

110 For evidence that the Court may have changed its attitude in recent years, see *Unión de Pequeños Agricultores v. Council*, Case C-50/00 P, [2002] ECR I-6677 (para. 44 of the judgment).

Community this activist approach is necessary because of the lack of a proper legislature; however, if the Community is to fulfil the expectations of its founders, it must be firmly based on the rule of law: this could be jeopardized if policy is allowed to override clear provisions of law.[111]

## THE COURT OF AUDITORS[112]

Though established some time previously, the Court of Auditors attained institutional status only when the Treaty on European Union came into force. It sits in Luxembourg, and its structure and status are in many ways similar to those of the European Court.

It consists of one national from each Member State. They are chosen from among persons who belong, or have belonged, in their respective countries to external audit bodies or who are specially qualified for such an office. Their independence must be beyond doubt. They are appointed for a term of six years by the Council, acting by a qualified majority on the basis of proposals made by each Member State. The members of the Court of Auditors are eligible for re-appointment.

The President of the Court of Auditors is elected by the Court from among its own members for a period of three years. He may be re-elected. The members of the Court must be completely independent in the performance of their duties, and they may neither seek nor take instructions from any government or other body. They must refrain from any action incompatible with their duties.

A member of the Court of Auditors may be deprived of his office (or his right to a pension or other benefits) only if the European Court, at the request of the Court of Auditors, finds that he no longer fulfils the requisite conditions or meets the obligations arising from his office. The provisions of the Protocol on the Privileges and Immunities of the European Communities applicable to the judges of the European Court also apply to the members of the Court of Auditors.

The function of the Court of Auditors is to examine the accounts of revenue and expenditure of the Community. It provides the European Parliament and the Council with a statement assuring them of the reliability of the accounts, and of the legality and regularity of the underlying transactions. It examines whether revenue has been received and expenditure incurred in a lawful and regular manner, and decides whether financial management has been sound. It draws up an annual report after the close of each financial year, which is forwarded to the other institutions of the Community and

[111] This theme is explored more fully in Trevor C Hartley, *Constitutional Problems of the European Union* (1999), Chaps 2 and 3; see also Hartley, 'The European Court, Judicial Objectivity and the Constitution of the European Union' (1996) 112 LQR 95. For a critique of this latter article, see Arnull, 'The European Court and Judicial Objectivity: A Reply to Professor Hartley' (1996) 112 LQR 411. See also Tridimas, 'The Court of Justice and Judicial Activism' (1996) 21 ELRev. 187.

[112] The relevant provisions are Arts 246–248 [188a–188c] EC and 160a–c Euratom. They have been amended by the Treaty of Nice. See also Kok, 'The Court of Auditors of the European Communities: "The Other European Court in Luxembourg"' (1989) 26 CMLRev. 345, an article written before the Court of Auditors became an institution of the Community.

is published, together with the replies of these institutions to the observations of the Court of Auditors, in the Official Journal. It acts by a majority of its members.

Fraud and financial mismanagement are serious problems in the Community. The importance of these problems was recognized by the Member States when they gave the Court of Auditors the status of a Community institution.

## FURTHER READING


Stevens, 'The Principle of Linguistic Equality in Judicial Proceedings and in the Interpretation of Plurilingual Legal Instruments: The *Régime Linguistique* in the Court of Justice of the European Communities' (1967) 62 Northwestern University Law Review 701.

Dickschat, 'Problèmes d'interprétation des traités européens résultant de leur plurilinguisme' [1968] Revue Belge de Droit International 40.

Brown, 'The Linguistic Regime of the European Communities: Some Problems of Law and Language' (1981) 15 Valparaiso University Law Review 319.

Hjalte Rasmussen, *On Law and Policy in the European Court of Justice* (1986).

Borgsmidt, 'The Advocate General at the European Court of Justice: A Comparative Study' (1988) 13 ELRev. 106.

Kennedy, 'Paying the Piper: Legal Aid in Proceedings before the Court of Justice' (1988) 27 CMLRev. 559.

Rasmussen, 'Between Self-Restraint and Activism: A Judicial Policy for the European Court' (1988) 13 ELRev. 28.

Kok, 'The Court of Auditors of the European Communities: "The Other European Court in Luxembourg" ' (1989) 26 CMLRev. 345.

Arnull, 'Does the Court of Justice Have Inherent Jurisdiction?' (1990) 27 CMLRev. 683.

T Millett, *The Court of First Instance of the European Communities* (1990).

Court of First Instance, 'Reflections on the Future Development of the Community Judicial System' (a discussion paper issued in 1990) (1991) 16 ELRev. 175.

Usher, 'How Limited is the Jurisdiction of the European Court of Justice?' in Janet Dine, Sionaidh Douglas-Scott, and Ingrid Persaud, *Procedure and the European Court* (1991), p. 72.

Vesterdorf, 'The Court of First Instance of the European Communities After Two Full Years in Operation' (1992) 29 CMLRev. 897.

Arnull, 'Owning Up to Fallibility: Precedent and the Court of Justice' (1993) 30 CMLRev. 247.

KPE Lasok, *The European Court of Justice: Practice and Procedure*, 2nd edn (1994).

Arnull, 'The Community Judicature and the 1996 IGC' (1995) 20 ELRev. 599.

Brown, 'The First Five Years of the Court of First Instance and Appeals to the Court of Justice: Assessment and Statistics' (1995) 32 CMLRev. 743.

Edward, 'How the Court of Justice Works' (1995) 20 ELRev. 539.

Mancini and Keeling, 'Language, Culture and Politics in the Life of the European Court of Justice' (1995) Columbia J. Euro. Law 397.

Van Gerven, 'The Role and Structure of the European Judiciary Now and in the Future' (1996) 21 ELRev. 211.

Neville March Hunnings, *The European Courts* (1996).

Scorey, 'A New Model for the Communities' Judicial Architecture in the New Union' (1996) 21 ELRev. 224.

Tridimas, 'The Court of Justice and Judicial Activism' (1996) 21 ELRev. 199.

Hjalte Rasmussen, *European Court of Justice* (Copenhagen, 1998).

Kenney, 'The Members of the Court of Justice of the European Communities' (1998/99) 5 CJEL 101.

Trevor C Hartley, *Constitutional Problems of the European Union* (1999), Chaps 2 and 3.

L Neville Brown and Tom Kennedy, *The Court of Justice of the European Communities*, 5th edn (2000).

Forwood, 'The Evolving Role of the Court of First Instance of the European Communities – Some Comments on the Changes Agreed at Nice as They Affect the Judicial Architecture of the Community Court' (2000) 3 *Cambridge Yearbook of European Studies* 139.

Alec Stone Sweet, *Governing with Judges: Constitutional Politics in the European Union* (2000).

Karen J Alter, *Establishing the Supremacy of European Law* (2001).

Alan Dashwood and Angus Johnston (eds), *The Future of the European Judicial System* (2001).

Johnston, 'Judicial Reform and the Treaty of Nice' (2001) 38 CMLRev. 499.

T Koopmans, *Courts and Political Institutions – A Comparative View* (2003).

Schønberg and Frick, 'Finishing, Refining, Polishing: The Use of *travaux préparatoires* as an Aid to the Interpretation of Community Legislation' (2003) 28 ELRev. 149.

Vesterdorf, 'The Community Court System Ten Years from Now' (2003) 28 ELRev. 303.

Jacobs, 'Recent and Ongoing Measures to Improve the Efficiency of the European Court of Justice' (2004) 29 ELRev. 823.

KPE Lasok, T Millet, and A Howard, *Judicial Control in the EU: Procedures and Principles* (2004).

R Creech, *Law and Language in the European Union: The Paradox of a Babel 'United in Diversity'* (2005).

Hans-W Micklitz, *The Politics of Judicial Co-Operation in the EU* (2005).

Anthony Arnull, *The European Union and its Court of Justice*, 2nd edn (2006).

Noreen Burrows, *The Advocate General and EC Law* (2007).

# PART II

# THE COMMUNITY LEGAL SYSTEM

# INTRODUCTION

The Community legal system was created by a set of treaties. It depends for its validity on those treaties; and the treaties depend for their validity on international law. Ultimately, therefore, Community law is a sub-system of international law. However, if a group of states conclude a set of treaties to govern their relations with each other in a given area, international law permits them to create a new system of law that is self-contained and separate from international law.[1] The normal rules of international law will not necessarily apply within that system. (Peremptory norms of international law, also known as *jus cogens*,[2] constitute an exception, though these will not often be relevant in Community law.) Consequently, the Community Treaties will not necessarily be interpreted in the same way as ordinary treaties, a point much emphasized by the European Court.[3]

Though the Community Treaties are treaties under international law, they are treaties of a special character. They are treaties that create a new international organization of the supranational kind. They also create a new legal system. For this reason, they may be regarded as a kind of constitution, though that term should not be regarded as calling into question their status as treaties.[4]

Although Community law forms a coherent system, there are various purposes for which it is necessary to make distinctions, on the basis of their origin, between different provisions of Community law. Thus proceedings for judicial review may be brought only with respect to legally binding acts of the Community institutions; in determining the validity of such acts, the Court may have regard to the relevant Treaty and 'any rule of law relating to its application'; enforcement actions may be brought against Member States for a failure to fulfil an obligation 'under' the relevant Treaty. There are also special problems as to which questions of Community law may be referred by a national court to the European Court for interpretation in a preliminary ruling; and the

[1] *Van Gend en Loos*, Case 26/62, [1963] ECR 1 at 12. See also *Costa v. ENEL*, Case 6/64, [1964] ECR 585 at 593, where the European Court said that, unlike ordinary treaties, the EC Treaty has created its own legal system; and *per* Advocate General Lagrange in *Fédération Charbonnière de Belgique v. High Authority*, Case 8/55, [1956] ECR 245 at 277, where it is said that the rules of law derived from the Treaties constitute the internal law of the Community.

[2] A peremptory norm of international law is defined in Art. 53 of the 1969 Vienna Convention on the Law of Treaties as 'a norm accepted and recognized by the international community of States as a whole as a norm from which no derogation is permitted and which can be modified only by a subsequent norm of general international law having the same character.'

[3] This is vividly illustrated by cases such as *Polydor*, Case 270/80, [1982] ECR 329, in which a provision in an agreement between the Community and a non-member state was given a different interpretation by the European Court from a similar provision in the EC Treaty. See also *Kupferberg*, Case 104/81, [1982] ECR 3641 (paras 28–31 of the judgment); *First EEA Case*, Op. 1/91, [1991] ECR I-6079 (para. 14 of the judgment).

[4] See *Les Verts – Parti Ecologiste v. European Parliament*, Case 294/83, [1986] ECR 1339, where the European Court said that the Community Treaties constituted the 'constitutional charter' of the Community (para. 23 of the judgment).

doctrine of direct effect depends in part on the nature of the provision in question. For all these reasons, but above all in order to delimit the extent of the system as a whole, it is necessary to analyse the sources of Community law.

In the analysis of Community law according to its sources, the most important distinction is between enacted and non-enacted law. Enacted law is law created by some authority; non-enacted law is not so created. It is, of course, true that the existence of non-enacted law is not certain unless it has been recognized by a court; and it could be argued that it, too, is created – by the courts. There are, however, important differences between judge-made law and enacted law, and it is therefore reasonable to use this distinction as the basis for the classification of Community law.

Enacted Community law may be created either by a Community institution or by the Member States. The second distinction, therefore, is between acts of Community institutions (Community acts) and acts of the Member States. In this context it is important to stress that, though the most important Community institution, the Council, is composed of representatives of the Member States, its acts are Community acts, not acts of the Member States. If, on the other hand, the representatives of the Member States meet when they are *not* acting in their capacity as members of the Council, their decisions will be acts of the Member States. Such meetings may take place in the Council: the important question is not the *place* where they meet, but the *capacity* in which they meet.

Non-enacted Community law consists of the so-called 'general principles of law' – the 'common law' of the Community – which have been adopted by the European Court. They are an important source of Community law and have a significant role to play in the Community legal system.

International agreements with non-Member States constitute another source of Community law. They may be concluded either by the Community alone, by the Community acting jointly with the Member States or, in certain special cases, by the Member States alone. These agreements are thus either acts of the Member States or Community acts; because of their special nature, however, it is desirable to consider them separately.

It is possible, therefore, to establish the following four major sources of Community law:

1. acts of the Member States;
2. Community acts;
3. general principles of Community law;
4. international agreements with non-Member States.

These will be considered in turn in the chapters in this Part of the book.

Finally, it should be said that it is not always easy to discern exactly where a legal system begins and ends: the Community legal system, like most other legal systems, has fuzzy edges. A legal system is made up of legal rules; a legal rule is a rule that has legal effects; a legal effect involves a change in the legal position of some person: all this is easy to say, but sometimes difficult to apply in practice. In the Community context, there is a range of instruments – Resolutions, Statements in Minutes, Joint Declarations,

Interinstitutional Agreements, Codes of Conduct, Recommendations, and many more – that are often on the edge of the Community legal system, sometimes falling on the one side and sometimes on the other. Moreover, legal effect is not an all-or-nothing characteristic: an instrument may have some legal effects but not others – for example, an instrument may not have direct legal consequences in its own right, but may affect the interpretation of another instrument and thus have indirect legal consequences. The phrase 'soft law' is sometimes used to designate instruments with doubtful, or only partial, legal effects.[5] Some such instruments have already been mentioned;[6] others will be discussed in the appropriate places.

## FURTHER READING

PIERRE PESCATORE, *L'ordre juridique des Communautés européennes* (1975).

WYATT, 'New Legal Order, or Old?' (1982) 7 ELRev. 147.

FRANCIS G JACOBS, *European Community Law and Public International Law – Two Different Legal Orders?* (Institut für Internationales Recht an der Universität Kiel, 1983).

SØRENSEN, 'Autonomous Legal Orders' (1983) 32 ICLQ 559.

DOWRICK, 'A Model of the European Communities' Legal System' (1983) 3 YEL 169.

WELLENS AND BORCHARDT, 'Soft Law in European Community Law' (1989) 14 ELRev. 267.

BIEBER AND SALOMÉ, 'Hierarchy of Norms in European Law' (1996) 33 CMLRev. 907.

PELLET, 'Les fondements juridiques internationaux du droit communautaire' (1997) 5 Collected Courses of the Academy of European Law, Book 2, 193.

HARTLEY, 'International Law and the Law of the European Union – A Reassessment' [2002] BYIL 1.

[5] For a fuller discussion, see Klabbers, 'Informal Instruments before the European Court of Justice' (1994) 31 CMLRev. 997; Wellens and Borchardt, 'Soft Law in European Community Law' (1989) 14 ELRev. 267.

[6] Two examples are the Luxembourg Accords and the Ioannina Compromise (Council Decision of 29 March 1994), both of which were discussed in Chap. 1, in the context of voting in the Council.

# 3

# ACTS OF THE MEMBER STATES

For purposes of discussion, acts of the Member States may be divided into three major categories: the constitutive Treaties, subsidiary conventions, and acts of the representatives of the Member States.

## THE CONSTITUTIVE TREATIES

The constitutive Treaties lay the foundations of the Community. They may be regarded as the constitution of the Community: they set up the various organs of the Community and grant them their powers.[1] They also contain many provisions of a non-institutional nature which would not normally be found in a constitution. These are mainly concerned with economic and social law, and are evidence of the hybrid nature of the Treaties, and, indeed, of the Community itself.

Which are the constitutive Treaties? They may be defined as the Treaties which created the two Communities – the EC and Euratom Treaties – together with the Treaties which amend or supplement them. The principal Treaties falling within this category are as follows:[2]

1. ECSC Treaty (expired);
2. EC Treaty;
3. Euratom Treaty;
4. Convention on Certain Institutions Common to the European Communities (repealed);
5. Merger Treaty (Convention Establishing a Single Council and a Single Commission of the European Communities) (largely repealed);

[1] Certain Council decisions are also of a constitutional nature, for example the decision providing for direct elections to the European Parliament, discussed in Chap. 1.

[2] There is no official list of these Treaties, but see the European Communities Act 1972, s. 1(1) (as amended) and Sch. 1, Part I. For the Second Budgetary Treaty, see the European Communities (Definition of Treaties) Order 1976 (SI 1976/217). Certain other instruments are also listed in s. 1(1) – for example, certain Decisions of the Council on the Communities' system of 'own resources'.

6. First Budgetary Treaty;
7. First Treaty of Accession (Denmark, Ireland, and the United Kingdom);
8. Second Budgetary Treaty;
9. Second Treaty of Accession (Greece);
10. Third Treaty of Accession (Spain and Portugal);
11. Single European Act;
12. Treaty on European Union (Maastricht Agreement);
13. Fourth Treaty of Accession (Austria, Finland, and Sweden);
14. Treaty of Amsterdam;
15. Treaty of Nice.[3]

The history and objectives of these Treaties were outlined briefly in Chapter 1; here certain legal points of a general nature will be considered.

Appended to many of the Treaties there are certain supplementary instruments. Annexes and Protocols are an integral part of the Treaty to which they relate.[4] The status of the declarations annexed to the Treaties – some of which are joint declarations on the part of all the Contracting States and some of which are unilateral declarations by one Contracting State only – is not entirely clear. Many of them were apparently intended to be only of political significance; others have an indirect legal effect. For example, certain provisions in the EC Treaty grant rights to nationals of the Member States. The Treaty contains no definition of who is a national, and it may be assumed that the intention was that each Member State should decide who its own nationals are (subject to any relevant provisions of Community law). When the United Kingdom acceded to the Community, the Government of the United Kingdom made a Declaration regarding the definition of a United Kingdom national for Community purposes.[5] This Declaration would therefore have effect in Community law to the extent that Community law refers to national law on this matter.

The amendment of these Treaties, formerly regulated by provisions contained in each Treaty,[6] is now governed by Article 48 [N(1)] of the Treaty on European Union. Under this provision, the initiative may come from a Member State or from the Commission. In either case, a proposal for an amendment is submitted to the Council, which must then decide whether to call a conference of the national governments.[7] Before deciding, the Council must consult the Parliament and – where the initiative came from a Member State – the Commission.[8] The conference is convened by the

[3] Decisions of the Council and agreements of the representatives of the Governments of the Member States have not been listed, even though they may amend the constitutive Treaties.

[4] See, e.g., Art. 311 [239] EC, and Art. 207 Euratom.

[5] This was made necessary by the complicated and confusing state of British nationality law. In 1982 it was replaced by a new Declaration, following the enactment of the British Nationality Act 1981.

[6] Arts 309 [236] EC and 204 Euratom.

[7] Art. 48 [N(1)] does not specify any majority by which the Council must act; consequently, an absolute majority (majority of members) is sufficient: see Arts 205(1) [148(1)] EC, and 118(1) Euratom.

[8] The European Central Bank must also be consulted in the case of changes in the monetary area.

President of the Council and must act by common accord. If it decides to make amendments, these must go to the Member States for ratification in accordance with their respective constitutional requirements.[9]

This procedure, which accords greater respect to national sovereignty than those laid down in some other multilateral treaties,[10] largely follows the rules of international law that would be applicable in the absence of any provision in the Treaties. The main exception is the requirement to consult the European Parliament and, where appropriate, the Commission. Since neither of these bodies has a veto over the proceedings, this is not an onerous limitation; nevertheless, the question arises whether the Treaties could be validly amended if it was not satisfied.

Most EC lawyers who have considered the issue take the view that the Treaties may be amended only by the procedure laid down in them,[11] and there is an *obiter dictum* of the European Court to the same effect.[12] However, the European Court, and most of the writers, have considered the question only from within the system. Any investigation based on this premise must inevitably reach such a conclusion. But is this the right way to go about it? Is this an issue to be decided by the EU legal system, or is it a question to be determined by international law?

We have also seen that the validity of the Community Treaties (like that of the whole EU legal system) depends on international law. It follows from this that any question which affects their validity, including the question whether a purported amendment is valid, must fall to be determined by international law. Such a question is logically prior to the EU system and cannot be determined by it alone.

What is the position under international law? If the treaty setting up an international organization specifies a given procedure for its amendment, and – let us assume – states that it may be amended in no other way, may the Member States nevertheless amend it[13] by a new treaty to which they all agree? The matter is somewhat controversial; nevertheless, it is suggested that the amending treaty would be valid.[14] Although Article 48

[9] In addition, certain specific provisions in the Treaties may be amended by the Council under procedures laid down in the provisions in question. See Arts 190(4) [138(4)] and 269 [201] EC, and 76, 85, 90, 92, 108, 173, 197, and 215 Euratom. Ratification by the Member States is usually necessary.

[10] For example, the United Nations Charter may be amended (for all members) if the amendment is adopted by a two-thirds majority in the General Assembly and ratified by two-thirds of the members, including all the permanent members of the Security Council: see Art.108 of the Charter. See De Witte, 'Rules of Change in International Law: How Special is the European Community?' (1994) 25 Netherlands Yearbook of International Law 299 at pp. 331–2.

[11] See the citations in De Witte (above) at p. 315, n. 54.

[12] *Defrenne v. Sabena*, Case 43/75, [1976] ECR 455 (para. 58 of the judgment).

[13] It is assumed that their intention to amend it is clear. A mere conflict of treaties without any express intention to amend the earlier one would be a different matter. On this, see below.

[14] Deliège-Sequaris, 'Révision des traités européens en dehors des procédures prévues' [1980] CDE 539 at pp. 542–8 (where the competing arguments and the views of other writers are carefully analysed); Weiler and Haltern, 'Response: The Autonomy of the Community Legal Order – Through the Looking Glass' (1996) 37 Harvard Journal of International Law 411 at p. 418, n. 26. For the opposite view, see Pellet 'Les fondements juridiques internationaux du droit communautaire' (1997) 5 Collected Courses of the Academy of European Law, Book 2, 193 at pp. 214–17. Pellet bases his view on Art. 5 of the 1969 Vienna Convention on the Law of Treaties, but this cannot give the rules of an international organization any greater force and effect than they would have had apart from the Vienna Convention; it therefore leaves open the position under customary

[N] imposes an obligation on the Member States to consult the Parliament and (where appropriate) the Commission, an obligation that might well produce legal consequences within the Community system,[15] it does not divest them of the *capacity* to enter into a new treaty: the conclusion of the new treaty may be a violation of Community law (as laid down in the existing treaties), but this does not make it invalid. The position then is that there is a conflict of treaties, a conflict between the earlier treaty, which says that it cannot be amended (except under a procedure which, we assume, has not been followed) and the later treaty, which nevertheless amends it. The solution to such a conflict is to be found in Article 30(3) of the 1969 Vienna Convention on the Law of Treaties.[16] This states that where all the parties to the earlier treaty are also parties to the later treaty (and the latter does not provide that it is subject to the former),[17] the earlier treaty applies only to the extent that its provisions are compatible with those of the later treaty. It follows from this that, in the situation we are considering, the amendments would be valid. This conclusion makes sense, since the purpose of a treaty must, first and foremost, be to serve the interests of the states that are parties to it. If they all want to amend it, they should not be barred from doing so by what they previously agreed.[18] Moreover, since the parties to a treaty are free to terminate it at any time by mutual consent, irrespective of its terms,[19] it would be strange if its terms could restrict their power to amend it. It should also be said that on two occasions in the past the ECSC Treaty has been amended without complying with the procedures laid down in it. No one has ever questioned the validity of these amendments.[20]

international law. It should be noted that Weiler and Haltern do not consider that international law is applicable; however, they believe that, if it were applicable, it would permit the Community Treaties to be amended without following Art. 48 [N]. Pellet, on the other hand, considers that international law *is* applicable, but that it requires the parties to respect Art. 48 [N]; nevertheless, he admits that if they did not do so, the European Court could not (and probably should not) do anything about it.

[15] The Commission might bring proceedings under Art. 226 [169] EC to prevent the Member States from concluding the new treaty, though the prospect of such an action against *all* the Member States is somewhat bizarre. If the Member States refused to obey any judgment given by the European Court, the Commission could bring further proceedings for the Court to impose a fine on them. If they refused to pay the fine, there would be no way in which it could be enforced.

[16] Strictly speaking, the Vienna Convention does not apply to the EC and Euratom Treaties because they were concluded before it entered into force: see Art. 4 of the Vienna Convention. However, the Vienna Convention is regarded in general as declaratory of customary international law: see Sir Ian Sinclair, *The Vienna Convention on the Law of Treaties* (2nd edn, 1984), pp. 10–21; Anthony Aust, *Modern Treaty Law and Practice* (2000), pp. 10–11. There can be little doubt that Art. 30 represents customary international law: Mus, 'Conflicts Between Treaties in International Law' (1998) 45 Netherlands International Law Journal 208 at p. 213.

[17] See Art. 30(2) of the Vienna Convention.

[18] It might be argued that the interests of the peoples of Europe should also be considered, but these can be better protected through the national ratification processes than through consulting the European Parliament.

[19] Art. 54(b) of the 1969 Vienna Convention.

[20] The first was the Treaty of 27 October 1956, which brought about certain amendments consequent on the return of the Saar to Germany, and the second was the Convention on Certain Institutions Common to the European Communities, which was signed at the same time as the EEC and Euratom Treaties: see Pierre Pescatore, *L'ordre juridique des Communautés européennes* (1975), pp. 62–3.

A special form of amendment procedure applies when new Member States join the Community.[21] Any European state may apply for admission, provided it respects the principles of liberty, democracy, respect for human rights and fundamental freedoms, and the rule of law.[22] The application is addressed to the Council, which must act unanimously, after consulting the Commission and obtaining the assent of the European Parliament (which acts by an absolute majority of its members). The conditions of admission and the resulting adjustments to the Community Treaties are laid down in a treaty between the applicant state and the existing Member States; this treaty must be ratified by the Contracting States in accordance with their constitutional requirements.[23] When it joins the Community, the new Member State must also accept all existing Community law, the *acquis communautaire*.[24]

There is no provision for expelling a Member State, but amendments introduced by the Treaty of Amsterdam and modified by the Treaty of Nice[25] provide that the rights of a Member State under the Treaties may be suspended for a serious and persistent breach of the principles of liberty, democracy, respect for human rights and fundamental freedoms, and the rule of law.

Prior to the Treaty of Nice there was a two-stage procedure. This has been retained under the Treaty of Nice, but a preliminary procedure has been introduced under which the Council may decide that there is a clear risk of a serious breach of these principles and address appropriate recommendations to the Member State in question.[26]

The two stages already in existence before the Treaty of Nice are as follows. The first stage is a determination that the Member State in question is guilty of such a breach. This is done by the European Council (the Council meeting in the composition of the Heads of State or Government), which acts by unanimity – though the vote of the representative of the accused Member State is disregarded.[27] The proposal for such a decision must be made jointly by a third of the Member States or by the Commission; the assent of the European Parliament must also be obtained.[28]

Once this is done, the Council may proceed to the second stage. This is the determination of the rights that will be suspended. For this purpose, the Council does not have

[21] Art. 49 [O] TEU (Maastricht Agreement). Previously, there were separate procedures under each of the three Treaties: see Arts 237 EC, 205 Euratom, and 98 ECSC (now repealed). It is doubtful whether an applicant could accede to one Treaty without also acceding to the others: see Joliet, *Institutions*, 131.

[22] The proviso is the result of amendments introduced by the Treaty of Amsterdam to Arts 49 [O] and 6(1) [F(1)] TEU. Previously, there was a generally accepted understanding that applicants must be democratic and respect human rights: see the Declaration on Democracy issued at the meeting of the European Council in Copenhagen on 7 and 8 April 1978 (EC Bull. 3–1978, pp. 5–6).

[23] Art. 49 [O], second para., TEU. Previously, accession to the ECSC was brought about by a decision of the Council (acting unanimously), which also set out the terms of accession and the necessary amendments to the Treaty: see Art. 98 ECSC (now repealed).

[24] See, e.g., Arts 2–4 of the first Act of Accession, which cover acts of the Member States, Community acts, and international agreements.

[25] Arts 7 TEU, 309 EC, and 204 Euratom.

[26] The Council acts by a four-fifths majority of its members after obtaining the assent of the European Parliament. The Council may call on independent persons to submit a report on the situation in the Member State.

[27] As regards other Member States, the abstention of a member of the Council who is present in person or is represented does not prevent the adoption of the decision.

[28] The Parliament must act by a two-thirds majority of votes cast, representing a majority of its members.

to be composed of the Heads of State or Government; it does not have to be unanimous (it acts by a qualified majority, though again the vote of the accused Member State is disregarded);[29] and the assent of the Parliament is not required. The Treaty expressly provides that one of the rights of the accused Member State that may be suspended is the right to vote in the Council. A decision to suspend the rights of a Member State may subsequently be varied or revoked.

## SUBSIDIARY CONVENTIONS

In addition to the constitutive Treaties, there are certain other international agreements between the Member States. Where these deal with matters within the scope of the Community and were drawn up within the Community context, they may in some cases be regarded as part of Community law.[30] In certain cases the constitutive Treaties themselves make provision for such conventions. Article 34(2)(d) TEU, for example, provides for the Council to establish conventions on police and judicial co-operation in criminal matters, which it will recommend to the Member States for adoption in accordance with their respective constitutional requirements. Measures to implement such conventions may be adopted by the Council by a majority of two-thirds of the Member States that are parties to the convention. Such conventions are clearly part of the legal system of the European Union.

Article 293 [220] EC provides that Member States 'shall, so far as is necessary, enter into negotiations with each other with a view to securing for the benefit of their nationals' various rights, including the recognition and enforcement of judgments. The Convention on Jurisdiction and the Enforcement of Judgments in Civil and Commercial Matters of 27 September 1968[31] was concluded to attain this latter objective.

Since Article 293 [220] imposes an obligation on the Member States rather than on the Community, one may reasonably assume that the authors of the EC Treaty intended the Member States to enter into conventions to attain its objectives. There can be no doubt that these objectives are highly relevant to the establishment of a Common Market and consequently fall within the scope of the Community. For these reasons, it is generally thought that conventions under Article 293 [220] form part of the Community legal system.

[29] The number of votes required to adopt the measure is adjusted so that the proportion remains the same.

[30] The precise limits of Community law in this regard have never been clarified. It is uncertain, for example, whether treaties such as the Schengen Agreements of 1985 and 1990 on frontier controls (to which some Member States (including the United Kingdom) are not parties) could, before the coming into force of the Treaty of Amsterdam, be regarded as part of the Community legal system. See O'Keeffe, 'The Schengen Convention: A Suitable Model for European Integration?' (1991) 11 YEL 185.

[31] OJ 1972, L299/32. It came into force between the original six Member States on 1 February 1973. The Convention of Accession by which Denmark, Ireland, and the United Kingdom became parties to it was signed on 9 October 1978 (see OJ 1978, L304) and came into force, as far as the United Kingdom was concerned, on 1 January 1987 (Civil Jurisdiction and Judgments Act 1982). The Convention has now been terminated and its provisions incorporated in Reg. 44/2001, OJ 2001 L12/1.

This is confirmed by the fact that when new Member States join the EC, they are obliged to accede to conventions under Article 293 [220], subject to any necessary adjustments.[32] Moreover, the Commission played an active role in the elaboration of the 1968 Convention and it was concluded by the representatives of the Member States meeting in the Council; there is also a Protocol granting jurisdiction to the European Court to interpret it under a procedure analogous to that under Article 234 [177] EC.[33]

However, even conventions which are not envisaged by any of the constituent Treaties may form part of the Community legal system. A good example is the Convention on the Law Applicable to Contractual Obligations, opened for signature in Rome on 19 June 1980.[34] The parties to it are described as 'The High Contracting Parties to the Treaty establishing the European Economic Community'; its objective – the establishment of uniform rules throughout the Community on the law applicable to contractual obligations under private international law – is relevant to the creation of a Common Market and the Commission was closely associated with the work involved in drawing it up.[35] When new Member States join the Community, they are expected to become parties to it.[36]

What would the position be if there were a conflict between a subsidiary convention and one of the constitutive Treaties or a legislative act under such a Treaty? This must be determined by international law. As stated above, the relevant principles are laid down by Article 30 of the 1969 Vienna Convention on the Law of Treaties.[37] It will be remembered that the rule is that if the parties to the two treaties are the same, the later one prevails unless it provides that the earlier one takes priority. Many subsidiary conventions contain a provision of this kind.[38]

What is the position where there is no such provision? It is suggested that where the parties to a treaty create a new legal system, and a later treaty is adopted within the context of that legal system and is intended to form part of it, the parties may, in the absence of evidence to the contrary, be regarded as having intended that it should be subject to the treaties that created the system. The reasonableness of such a rule is supported by Article 5 of the Vienna Convention, which states that the Vienna Convention applies to a treaty which is the constituent instrument of an international organization, and to any treaty adopted within an international organization, without prejudice to the relevant rules of the organization. Admittedly, this provision cannot affect a rule of

[32] See, e.g., Art. 3(2) of the first Act of Accession. [33] OJ 1975, L204/28.

[34] OJ 1980, L266/1. The Convention was signed by the United Kingdom on 7 December 1981 and came into force in the United Kingdom on 1 April 1991 under the Contracts (Applicable Law) Act 1990. It is set out in Schedule 1 to the Act. There are plans to replace it with a regulation, the so-called 'Rome I' Regulation.

[35] Two Protocols to the Convention, which were signed in Brussels on 19 December 1988, give the European Court jurisdiction to interpret it. The first of these Protocols is set out in Schedule 3 to the Contracts (Applicable Law) Act 1990.

[36] See, e.g., the Convention on the Accession of the Hellenic Republic to the Rome Convention, signed by the United Kingdom in Luxembourg on 10 April 1984. It is set out in Schedule 2 to the Contracts (Applicable Law) Act 1990. [37] On the applicability of the Vienna Convention to the Community Treaties, see n. 16.

[38] For example, Art. 20 of the Rome Convention of 1980 states that Community acts which 'in relation to particular matters' lay down choice of law rules regarding contractual obligations will prevail over the Convention, whether they are adopted before or after the latter.

customary international law that would have applied independently of the Vienna Convention. Nevertheless, it is consistent with the idea that the principle in Article 30 should be applied flexibly in such a situation.[39]

A similar argument applies where there is a conflict between a subsidiary convention and a Community act such as a regulation or directive. Community acts are adopted by the Community institutions under powers granted by the constitutive Treaties. If the subsidiary convention does not override the Treaties, it cannot affect the legislative powers conferred by them; consequently, acts adopted under those powers also cannot be affected.[40] It follows from this that, even in the absence of an express provision in the convention, the Community act will prevail.

It has been argued that resort to subsidiary conventions is excluded whenever the Community could itself have attained the objective by means of legislation, even where the Community's power rests on Article 308 [235] EC, a catch-all provision which applies where no other Treaty provision gives the Community power to act.[41] This, however, is going too far. Moreover, the principle of subsidiarity, established by Article 5 [3b] (second paragraph) EC, would seem to preclude resort to Community action under Article 308 [235] if the objective could be sufficiently achieved by means of a convention between the Member States.[42]

## ACTS OF THE REPRESENTATIVES OF THE MEMBER STATES

This is a somewhat anomalous group of acts adopted by the representatives of the Governments of the Member States, meeting in the Council. The representatives here are the delegates sent to the Council by the Member States, i.e., ministers in their respective Governments; but, since they do not act in their capacity as members of the Council when they adopt these acts, the acts are not acts of the Council but are acts of the Member States.

These acts are usually designated either 'Decision of the Representatives of the Governments of the Member States, meeting in the Council' or 'Agreement between the Representatives'. They are usually published in the Official Journal and are often signed

[39] For further arguments, see Pescatore, *L'ordre juridique des Communautés européennes* (1975), pp. 143–4.

[40] See the opinion to this effect of the legal service of the Council, Document R/697/78 of 28 March 1978. It is also of interest to note that the legal service opinion states that a provision of national legislation enacted in implementation of a directive will also prevail over a conflicting provision in a subsidiary convention: *ibid.*, 5.

[41] Schwartz, 'Art. 235 and Law-Making Powers in the European Community' (1978) 27 ICLQ 614. Art. 308 [235] is discussed in Chap. 4.

[42] Subsidiarity is discussed in Chap. 4. It does not apply to matters within the exclusive jurisdiction of the Community. What these matters are is far from certain, but it is hard to imagine that a matter not covered by an express power (and therefore within the potential scope of Art. 308 [235]) could be within the exclusive jurisdiction of the Community.

by the President of the Council. They are an established feature of the Community – they were first used as long ago as 1954 – and they deal with a wide variety of subjects. Where they are referred to as 'agreements' they are often subject to ratification; but this is not the case where they carry the designation 'decision'. The subjects they deal with are relevant to the functioning of the Community, though they do not normally fall within any specific power to adopt a Community act.[43] The Commission often plays a part in their preparation.

What is the status of these acts? They probably all fall into one of three categories. Some of them are international agreements concluded in simplified form. In this case, they have the same status as the subsidiary conventions discussed above, and, for the reasons mentioned there,[44] are part of the Community legal system.[45] Others, however, are not intended to be legally binding at all: their consequences are merely political. The 'Luxembourg Accords' are probably an example. Acts falling into this category have no legal effects and are not part of any legal system, including the Community legal system. Finally, some acts of the representatives of the Member States constitute the exercise of a power conferred jointly on the Member States. For example, Article 223 [167] EC provides that judges and advocates general on the European Court are appointed 'by common accord of the Governments of the Member States': such appointments are made by acts of the representatives of the Member States. Acts falling into this category – though they must be adopted by unanimous agreement of all the Member States – take effect, not as international agreements, but by virtue of the Treaty provision in question. They plainly fall within the Community legal system.

## CONFLICTING TREATIES

Since the Community Treaties (like all treaties) are based on international law, international law should determine whether their validity is affected by reason of a conflict with another treaty.[46] The rules applicable under international law are complex,[47] but Article 30 of the 1969 Vienna Convention on the Law of Treaties is generally regarded as setting them out.[48] According to Article 30(2) of the Vienna Convention, if one of the

[43] They may, however, fall within the scope of the general power contained in Art. 308 [235] EC.

[44] However, they do not usually contain provisions giving jurisdiction to the European Court. (For exceptions to this, see Bebr [1966] SEW at 538–9.)

[45] What was said above concerning a conflict with a Treaty provision applies also to acts in this category.

[46] *Italy v. Commission*, Case 10/61, [1962] ECR 1, at p. 10. This case concerned a conflict between the EC Treaty and a GATT agreement signed in Geneva. The Commission based its argument on 'the principles of international law' and the Court held that its interpretation was 'well founded'. See also *Levy*, Case C-158/91, [1993] ECR I-4287 (para. 12 of the judgment).

[47] Jenks, 'The Conflict of Law-Making Treaties' (1953) 30 BYIL 401; Sir Ian Sinclair, *The Vienna Convention on the Law of Treaties* (2nd edn, 1984), pp. 93–8; Mus, 'Conflicts Between Treaties in International Law' (1998) 45 NILJ 208.

[48] The Constitutive Treaties were originally concluded before the Vienna Convention entered into force (for the original parties) on 27 January 1980. Since Art. 4 of the Vienna Convention provides that it applies only to

conflicting treaties provides that the other one prevails, that other treaty will prevail. If neither treaty contains such a rule, paragraphs 3 and 4(a) of Article 30 apply. They may be summarized as follows:

1. If the parties to the two treaties are the same, the second one prevails.
2. Even if the parties are not the same, the second one prevails if all the parties to the first treaty are also parties to the second.
3. If only some of the parties to the first treaty are also parties to the second, the latter prevails as between those states that are parties to both treaties.

These rules solve only some of the possible problems. If none of them applies, Article 30(4)(b) of the Convention comes into operation. It provides:

> as between a State party to both treaties and a State party to only one of the treaties, the treaty to which both States are parties governs their mutual rights and obligations.

This means that if State X concludes a treaty with State Y and a second treaty with State Z, the first treaty governs its relations with State Y and the second with State Z. This is clearly correct, but is unhelpful if the two treaties contain inconsistent provisions. If the treaties are of a contractual nature, State X could no doubt carry out its obligations under one of them, and pay compensation to the state with which it concluded the other treaty. However, if the treaties are of a legislative nature, Article 30(4)(b) is of no assistance to a court which needs to know which to apply.

## CONFLICTS BETWEEN COMMUNITY TREATIES

Since Article 305 [232] EC states that the EC Treaty is subject to the Euratom Treaty, the latter will prevail in the event of a conflict. Article 305 [232] is, of course, concerned only with a conflict between the two Treaties. It does not prevent the application of provisions of the EC Treaty in fields covered by the Euratom Treaty if there is no contrary provision in the latter.[49] Subsidiary Conventions and other acts of the Member States were intended to be subordinate to the Constitutive Treaties and often have a provision to this effect.[50] Even in the absence of such a provision, the European Court would probably interpret them as being subject to the Constitutive Treaties.[51]

treaties concluded after it entered into force, it cannot as such apply to the original Community Treaties; nevertheless, it may be regarded as stating the customary international law previously applicable. It should also be said that Art. 5 of the Vienna Convention states that the Convention applies to a treaty which is the constituent instrument of an international organization, and to any treaty adopted within an international organization, 'without prejudice to any relevant rules of the organization'. This means that a principle laid down in the Convention cannot apply if it conflicts with such a rule, unless that principle would have applied under customary international law if the Convention had not been adopted.

49 *WTO* case, Opinion 1/94, [1994] ECR I-5267 (para. 24 of the Opinion).

50 See, for example, Art. 20 of the Rome Convention on the Law Applicable to Contractual Obligations, 1980.

51 This would probably be justifiable under Art. 5 of the Vienna Convention: see n. 48, above.

## CONFLICTS WITH NON-COMMUNITY TREATIES

More difficult questions are raised where one of the Community Treaties conflicts with a non-Community treaty to which some or all of the Member States are parties. The EC Treaty also contains a provision on this. The first paragraph of Article 307 [234] EC[52] provides:

> The rights and obligations arising from agreements concluded before 1 January 1958 or, for acceding States, before the date of their accession,[53] between one or more Member States on the one hand, and one or more third countries on the other, shall not be affected by the provisions of this Treaty.[54]

According to the European Court, the purpose of this provision is to make clear, in accordance with the principles of international law, that the application of the EC Treaty does not affect the commitment of the Member State concerned to respect the rights of non-Member States under an earlier agreement.[55] As was pointed out by the European Court in *Italy v. Commission*,[56] the word 'rights' in Article 307 [234] refers to the rights of the non-Member State and the word 'obligations' refers to the obligations of the Member State. Thus the obligations of the EC State towards the non-Member State are not affected: the *rights* of the EC State may very well be affected.[57]

Article 307 [234] was probably adopted because some States might have been reluctant to conclude the EC Treaty if it could have given rise to obligations inconsistent with those arising out of earlier treaties. There is no equivalent provision in the Euratom Treaty, probably because it was thought unlikely that it would conflict with any other treaty.

[52] In subsequent paras, Art. 307 [234] requires the Member State in question to take all appropriate steps to eliminate the incompatibilities.

[53] The original text of the EC Treaty spoke simply of 'agreements concluded before the entry into force of this Treaty'. This was amended by the Treaty of Amsterdam 1997, Art. 6 (heading I, point 78), by deleting the words 'before the entry into force of this Treaty' and replacing them with 'before 1 January 1958 or, for acceding States, before the date of their accession'. Since the relevant date for the EC Treaty is that of entry into force, not that on which the text was adopted, it might be argued that the relevant date for the other agreement (the date on which it was 'concluded') should also be that on which it entered into force. Under Art. 30 of the 1969 Vienna Convention, however, the relevant date appears to be that on which the text is adopted, not that on which the treaty enters into force: Sir Ian Sinclair, *The Vienna Convention on the Law of Treaties* (2nd edn, 1984), p. 98; Anthony Aust, *Modern Treaty Law and Practice* (2000), p. 183; Mus, 'Conflicts Between Treaties in International Law' (1998) 45 NILJ 208 at pp. 220–2. A different view is advanced in Vierdag, 'The Time of the "Conclusion" of a Multilateral Treaty: Art. 30 of the Vienna Convention on the Law of Treaties and Related Provisions' (1988) 59 BYIL 75, but this seems to be incorrect for the reasons given in Mus, above. According to the European Court, Art. 307 [234] was intended to reflect the principles of international law: *Commission v. Italy*, Case 10/61, [1962] ECR 1 at p. 10. In view of this, it would make sense to interpret it (in this respect) in the same way as Art. 30 of the Vienna Convention. Moreover, if the purpose of Art. 307 [234] is to protect Member States from the embarrassment of conflicting obligations, the relevant date should be that on which the text of the other agreement was adopted, rather than that on which it entered into force.

[54] On the effect of Art. 307 [234] in international law, see Art. 30(2) of the 1969 Vienna Convention.

[55] *Levy*, Case C-158/91, [1993] ECR I-4287 (para. 12 of the judgment).

[56] Case 10/61, [1962] ECR 1, at p. 10. See also *Evans Medical and Macfarlan Smith*, Case C-324/93, [1995] ECR I-563, para. 27 of the judgment; and *Centro-Com*, Case C-124/95, [1997] ECR I-81, para. 56 of the judgment.

[57] Thus in *Italy v. Commission*, Italy's right under the GATT agreement to charge the higher rate of duty was affected in so far as it conflicted with the rights of other EC countries under the EC Treaty.

The *Levy* case[58] is an illustration of the operation of Article 307 [234]. Prior to the conclusion of the EC Treaty, France had concluded an ILO agreement which provided that women would not be permitted to work at night. France gave effect to this agreement by passing appropriate legislation. Subsequently, the EC adopted a directive on sex equality in employment, [59] which gave women the same rights as men to work at night.[60] There was thus a conflict between, on the one hand, the ILO agreement and the French legislation and, on the other hand, the directive. Levy, an employer who had infringed the French legislation, was prosecuted. Normally, the directive would have given him a good defence,[61] but because the French legislation was adopted to give effect to France's obligations under the ILO agreement, the European Court ruled that the directive would not take effect in France to the extent to which it prevented France from complying with its obligations under the ILO agreement. It made clear, however, that this would be the case only if the performance of the agreement could still be required by States that were parties to it and were not parties to the EC Treaties.[62]

## THE EUROPEAN CONVENTION ON HUMAN RIGHTS

The most noteworthy instance in which these problems have arisen is where the Community Treaties have been in conflict with the European Convention on Human Rights. The leading case concerns the right of persons resident in Gibraltar to vote in elections to the European Parliament. Originally, the Community Treaties provided that the European Parliament (then called the 'Assembly') would consist of delegates designated by Member-State parliaments from among their own number.[63] The Treaties went on to state, however, that the European Parliament would draw up proposals for direct elections. These had to be agreed by the Council and adopted by the Member States 'in accordance with their respective constitutional requirements'.[64] After a long delay, the Council adopted a decision to which was annexed an 'Act' providing for direct elections.[65] The Act was ratified as a treaty by the Member States, and, though there is some controversy surrounding its legal status, it is best regarded as a treaty amending the relevant Community Treaties.[66] The Act specifies how many representatives will be elected in each Member State; it also states in Annex II that the United Kingdom will apply the provisions of the Act only in respect of the United Kingdom itself. Article 15 of the Act states that the Annexes form an integral part of the Act. Since Gibraltar, though a British dependency, is not constitutionally part of the United

[58] Case C-158/91, [1993] ECR I-4287.

[59] The Equal Treatment Directive, 76/207, OJ 1976, L39/40.

[60] *Stoeckl*, Case C-345/89, [1991] ECR I-4047.

[61] See *Stoeckl* (above). This would have been a case of 'vertical' direct effect, since the other party was the State, the prosecutor in the criminal proceedings. On the meaning of 'vertical' direct effect, see Chap. 7, section entitled 'Directives'.

[62] There was some doubt whether the ILO agreement had been terminated or suspended under international law by virtue of later agreements, a question which the European Court held was for the French court to decide.

[63] Arts [138(1)] EEC and 108(1) Euratom.

[64] Arts [138(3)] EEC and 108(3) Euratom.

[65] Decision 76/787, OJ 1976, L278/1.

[66] See above, Chap. 1, section entitled 'The European Parliament', subsection entitled 'Composition'.

Kingdom, this had the effect of excluding Gibraltarians from participating in elections to the European Parliament, even though the Community Treaties apply, in part, to Gibraltar and, to that extent, the European Parliament has jurisdiction over Gibraltar.[67]

In *Matthews v. United Kingdom*,[68] Ms Matthews, a resident of Gibraltar, brought proceedings before the European Court of Human Rights, claiming that the denial of her right to vote in European elections constituted a violation of Article 3 of Protocol 1 to the Convention, a provision which guarantees the right to free elections.[69] The United Kingdom argued that the Act constituted a treaty which was binding on it, and that it could not be liable for any infringement of the Convention that resulted from the Act. The Court rejected this argument: even though the Act was a treaty, the United Kingdom had chosen to conclude it, and it was, therefore, liable for any resulting infringement.[70] It ruled that Article 3 of Protocol No. 1 does not apply only to the legislature of a State, but can also apply to that of an international organization. It then held that, as a result of increases in the powers of the European Parliament as a result of amendments brought in by the Treaty on European Union,[71] the Parliament now constitutes a 'legislature' for the purpose of Article 3. It concluded, therefore, that the United Kingdom had violated the Convention.[72]

As a result of this decision, there was a conflict between two treaties binding on the United Kingdom, the European Convention on Human Rights, which required voting rights to be given to Gibraltarians, and the EC Treaty, which forbade it. This put the United Kingdom in a difficult position. It had no objection to allowing Gibraltarians to vote in European elections,[73] and the obvious course was to ask the other EC States to amend the Act. However, Spain did not agree, since it was campaigning for the return of Gibraltar.

The United Kingdom then decided to carry out its obligations under the European Convention on Human Rights by giving Gibraltarians the right to vote in elections to the European Parliament as part of one of the electoral regions in England and

[67] The Treaties apply to Gibraltar by virtue of Art. 299(4) [227(4)] EC. However, the Treaty of Accession by which the United Kingdom joined the Community provides that many parts of the Community Treaties, including those dealing with such important matters as the free movement of goods and the Common Agricultural Policy, will not apply to Gibraltar.

[68] (1999) 28 EHRR 361.

[69] She also invoked Art. 14 of the Convention, which provides that the enjoyment of the rights laid down in the Convention must be secured without discrimination. The Convention applies to Gibraltar by virtue of a declaration made by the United Kingdom on 23 October 1953 under what was then Art. 63 of the Convention; Protocol No. 1 applies by virtue of a declaration made on 25 February 1988 under Art. 4 of Protocol No. 1.

[70] For the case law of the European Court of Human Rights on this issue (both before and after the *Matthews* case), see below, Chap. 5, section entitled 'Fundamental Human Rights', sub-section entitled, 'The European Convention on Human Rights'.

[71] The Treaty on European Union provided that, in certain cases, legislation would be enacted jointly by the European Parliament and the Council: see Art. 251 [189b] EC, as amended by the TEU.

[72] The judgment was largely declaratory, but the applicant was awarded £45,000 for costs and expenses.

[73] The reason Gibraltarians were originally excluded was that there were too few of them to make up a constituency (electoral district) on their own, and they were too remote from the United Kingdom to be joined to any constituency there. The United Kingdom had, however, decided that future elections in the United Kingdom to the European Parliament would be held under a system of proportional representation; so the reason no longer existed.

Wales.[74] Spain objected, and brought proceedings against the United Kingdom under Article 227 [170] EC.[75]

The position under both Article 30 of the Vienna Convention and under Article 307 [234] EC is complicated; nevertheless, it is arguable that the European Convention on Human Rights enjoyed priority by virtue of Article 307 [234] EC.[76] The European Court did not, however, decide the case on this basis. In a judgment that carefully avoided the issue of conflicting treaties, it simply held that, since the United Kingdom had done no more than was necessary to comply with the judgment in the *Matthews* case, Spain's application should be dismissed.

The issue of conflicting treaties was clouded because Spain and the United Kingdom had concluded an informal agreement in 2002, under which the United Kingdom could take the steps necessary to comply with the judgment in the *Matthews* case, provided it did so in accordance with Community law. This agreement was reflected in a Declaration made by the United Kingdom on 18 February 2002, which was recorded in the minutes of the EC Council.[77] In the proceedings before the Court, Spain was, therefore, unable to argue that Gibraltarians could not be allowed to vote at all. It did, however, argue that the United Kingdom had infringed the EC Treaty by allowing them to cast their votes in Gibraltar: they should have been required to travel to the United Kingdom to vote or to vote by post.[78] None of this, however, was relevant to whether the United Kingdom had infringed the EC Treaty. An agreement between two Member States (even if noted by the others) cannot amend the Treaty; nor can it absolve one Member State from its obligation to comply with the Treaty.

As we shall see in Chapter 5, human rights constitute a 'general principle of law' in the Community system and, as such, override Community legislation. However, they cannot on this basis override a Treaty provision. The judgment in *Spain v. United Kingdom* must, therefore, be regarded as laying down a tacit rule that the European Convention on Human Rights (and possibly other human rights conventions) override the constitutive Treaties in the event of a conflict,[79] something that was hinted at by the Court in two earlier cases.[80] This is based on the 'privileged position accorded to the protection of fundamental rights by the Community legal order'.[81] The position may, therefore, be different where the conflict is with a treaty that is not concerned with human rights.

[74] European Parliament (Representation) Act 2003, Part 2; European Parliamentary Elections (Combined Region and Campaign Expenditure) (United Kingdom and Gibraltar) Order 2004, SI 2004/366.

[75] *Spain v. United Kingdom*, Case C-145/04, 12 September 2006. The Commission had refused to bring proceedings against the United Kingdom under Art. 226 [169] EC, and even went so far as to appear in the proceedings in support of the United Kingdom.

[76] See Hartley, 'International Law and the Law of the European Union – A Reassessment' (2001) 72 BYIL 1 at pp. 32–5.

[77] This should have settled the matter; however, there was a change of Government in Spain and the new Government was less sympathetic to the British position.

[78] It also objected to the fact that electoral challenges could be brought before the courts of Gibraltar and that certain administrative activities took place there.

[79] See *per* Advocate General Tizzano at paras 118–121 of his Opinion in *Spain v. United Kingdom*.

[80] *Schmidberger*, Case C-112/00, [2003] ECR I-5659, para. 74 of the judgment; *Omega*, Case C-36/02, [2004] ECR I-9609, para. 35 of the judgment.

[81] Advocate General Tizzano at para. 118 of his Opinion in *Spain v. United Kingdom*.

## UNITED NATIONS LAW

Recently the question has arisen regarding a conflict between Community law and a resolution of the UN Security Council. This was in *Ahmed Ali Yusuf and Al Barakaat International Foundation v. Council and Commission*, a case decided by the Court of First Instance, but going on appeal to the European Court.[82] The Security Council had adopted several resolutions under Chapter VII of the UN Charter freezing the assets of certain named individuals and organizations on the ground that they were associated with the Taliban and Osama Bin Laden. The EC then adopted regulations to give effect to the resolutions. The applicants, Somali individuals resident in Sweden and a Swedish organization giving assistance to Somali refugees, had been named in a Security Council resolution and in an EC regulation. Sweden had been obliged to give effect to the regulation. The applicants brought annulment proceedings against the EC regulation under Article 230 [173] EC. Since the applicants' property had been seized without any judicial proceedings or hearing or other right of redress and without their even being told what they were supposed to have done wrong, their human rights had been violated. Without the Security Council resolution, the regulation would have been annulled on this ground. However, the Court of First Instance held it valid.

Its reasoning was as follows.[83] Under international law, the Security Council resolution was binding on all members of the UN,[84] and prevailed over all treaties, whether prior or subsequent;[85] therefore, it was binding on the Member States of the Community and had to be carried out even if it conflicted with the EC Treaties. Since the Member States of the EC became parties to the UN Charter before the EC Treaty,[86] the first paragraph of Article 307 [234] EC (discussed above) required the Community not to prevent the Member States from fulfilling their obligations under the resolution; consequently, under EC law the resolution prevailed over Community law. Although the Community was not bound by the resolution under international law, it was bound under Community law: this followed from a principle originally laid down by the European Court in the third *International Fruit Company* case,[87] a principle under which the Community will, in certain cases, become bound by obligations entered into by the Member States (discussed in Chapter 6).[88] As a consequence, the Community

[82] Case T-306/01, 21 September 2005 (going on appeal as case C-415/05). See also *Yassin Abdullah Kadi v. Council and Commission*, Case T-315/01, Court of First Instance, 21 September 2005 (going on appeal to the ECJ as case C-402/05).

[83] See paras 233–259 of the judgment.

[84] Art. 25 of the UN Charter.

[85] Art. 103 of the UN Charter. Art. 30(1) of the Vienna Convention on the Law of Treaties 1969 expressly provides that the rules it lays down are subject to Art. 103.

[86] Germany was an exception, but its duty to carry out its obligations under the Charter followed from certain other international agreements that predated the EC Treaty.

[87] Cases 21–4/72, [1972] ECR 1219. See also *Schlüter*, Case 9/73, [1973] ECR 1135 and *Nederlandse Spoorwegen*, Case 38/75, [1975] ECR 1439.

[88] See the section entitled 'International Agreements and the Community Legal System' and the sub-section entitled 'Binding the Community'.

was obliged to adopt the regulation, an obligation that overrode the requirement to respect human rights.[89]

It is interesting to contrast this with a later case before the Court of First Instance, *Organisation des Modjahedines du peuple d'Iran (OMPI) v. Council*,[90] which also concerned the freezing of the assets of an organization accused of being associated with terrorism. Although the freezing of OMPI's assets was part of the same programme as that in the earlier cases, there was one important difference: it was the EC Council, not the Security Council, that had designated OMPI as being associated with terrorism. The Court of First Instance held, therefore, that the Community had had a choice in the matter: it was not just following instructions from the Security Council. For this reason, it was obliged to observe the Community law requirement of a fair hearing. Since it had not done so, the decision designating OMPI was annulled.

### CONCLUSIONS

It has not been possible to discuss all the possible circumstances in which there might be a conflict between Community law and another international instrument. It will be seen from what has been said, however, that the position is complex and that the outcome may depend on the particular circumstances.[91]

## FURTHER READING

R Joliet, *Institutions*, 127–38.

Bebr, 'Acts of Representatives of the Governments of the Member States' [1966] SEW 529.

Pescatore, 'Remarques sur la nature juridique des "décisions des représentants des Etats Membres réunis au sein du Conseil" ', *ibid.*, 579.

Hauschild, 'L'importance des conventions communautaires pour la création d'un droit communautaire' [1975] RTDE 4.

Rasmussen, 'A New Generation of Community Law?' (1978) 15 CMLRev. 249.

Weiler and Modrall, 'Institutional Reform: Consensus or Majority?' (1985) 10 ELRev. 316.

Klabbers, 'Informal Instruments before the European Court of Justice' (1994) 31 CMLRev. 997.

Hartley, 'International Law and the Law of the European Union – A Reassessment' (2001) 72 BYIL 1.

Douglas-Scott, 'A Tale of Two Courts: Luxembourg, Strasbourg and the Growing European Human Rights *Acquis*' (2006) 43 CMLRev. 629.

[89] The only exception existed under the international law doctrine of *jus cogens* (on which see Art. 53 of the 1969 Vienna Convention on the Law of Treaties). However, the Court found that the violation of the applicants' rights was not sufficiently serious to bring this principle into operation.

[90] Case T-228/02, 12 December 2006.

[91] See, further, *Commission v. Ireland*, Case C-459/03, 30 May 2006.

# 4

# COMMUNITY ACTS

Community legislation is produced in considerable volume and can directly affect the everyday lives of ordinary citizens. This chapter is concerned with the legislative powers of the Community and the procedure to be followed.

## CLASSIFICATION

Article 249 [189] EC lists five different kinds of act that may (if other provisions confer the power) be adopted by the European Parliament and the Council acting jointly, by the Council, or by the Commission.[1] These are:

1. Regulations;
2. Directives;
3. Decisions;
4. Recommendations;
5. Opinions.

Article 249 [189] also contains a short statement of the characteristics each kind of act is supposed to have. Thus a regulation is essentially legislative (normative): it lays down general rules which are binding both at the Community level and at the national level. Directives and decisions differ from regulations, in that they are not binding generally: they are binding only on the person (or persons) to whom they are addressed. Directives may be addressed only to Member States, but decisions may also be addressed to private citizens. According to Article 249 [189], another characteristic of directives is that they are binding only 'as to the result to be achieved' and leave to the national authorities 'the choice of form and methods'. This suggests that directives lay down an objective and allow each national government to achieve it by the means it regards as most suitable. A decision, on the other hand, is binding in its entirety. Recommendations and opinions are not binding at all.[2]

[1] An identical classification is provided in Art. 161 Euratom.

[2] They cannot, therefore, create rights upon which individuals may rely before a national court: *Grimaldi*, Case C-322/88, [1989] ECR 4407 (para. 16 of the judgment); nevertheless, the European Court has said that a measure in the form of a recommendation may have to be examined to see whether it is a 'true'.

These provisions appear to form a neat and tidy system in which formal designations correspond to differences in function. The differences suggest a hierarchy. Regulations appear to be at the top, since they are both wide in scope, being binding on everybody, and lay down directly applicable rules. One might think that EC decisions came next: although they bind only a limited category of persons, their obligatory quality is just as intense as that of a regulation. Directives, on the other hand, appear to be the weakest form: they are limited in scope and are binding only as to their objective.

Unfortunately, things are not as simple as this. The first complication is that the formal designation of an act – the label given to it by its author – is not always a reliable guide to its contents. An act may be called a regulation but bear all the characteristics of a decision; or it may be called a directive but leave very little choice as to form and methods. Faced with this situation, the European Court has sometimes rejected the formal designation and looked instead at the substance of the act. If an act in the form of a regulation does not lay down general rules but is concerned with deciding a particular case, the Court may call it a 'disguised decision' and treat it for certain purposes as a decision. It is not, however, clear how far the Court will go in this 'relabelling' process: so far it has done so only for the purpose of deciding questions of *locus standi* in judicial review.[3]

A second complication is that in practice the difference between the various kinds of act are not as great as might appear from the Treaty provisions. In particular, judgments of the European Court have had the effect of upgrading directives so that they are now much closer to regulations: even if they have not been implemented by the Member State to which they are addressed, they can directly confer rights on private citizens which may be invoked against public authorities.

A third complication is that the European Court has ruled that the list in Article 249 [189] EC is not exhaustive: it is possible to have a legally binding act which does not fall into any of the categories enumerated in the Treaty. Acts falling into this residual category are usually called, for want of a better name, acts *sui generis*. The case in which the European Court gave this ruling was the *ERTA* case,[4] which concerned the negotiations leading to the European Road Transport Agreement (ERTA) and in particular a Council 'resolution' – to use a neutral term – in which it was settled what negotiating procedure would be adopted at the conference. The Commission disagreed with the content of this 'resolution' and wished to obtain a ruling from the Court on whether the negotiating procedure laid down in it was in accord with Community law. The only means available of bringing this issue before the Court was an action for the annulment of the 'resolution'.

One question which the Court had to decide was whether the 'resolution' could in fact form the subject of annulment proceedings.[5] If the Court had decided this in the negative, it would have been obliged to declare the proceedings inadmissible and would thus have been deprived of the opportunity to rule on the substantive issues involved, principally the capacity of the Community to conclude international agreements. The Court was, however, faced with a problem: if it decided that the 'resolution', which was

[3] See Chap. 12. [4] *Commission v. Council*, Case 22/70, [1971] ECR 263; discussed further in Chap. 6.

[5] For a general discussion of which measures are subject to annulment by the Court, see Chap. 11.

not in the form of any legal act listed in Article 249 [189] EC, was in fact a regulation, directive, or decision, it would have been obliged to annul it for lack of reasons, since there is a rule, laid down in Article 253 [190] EC, that regulations, directives, and decisions must state the reasons on which they are based.[6]

The Court was clearly reluctant to annul the 'resolution', since this might have meant that the negotiations for the ERTA, which had been concluded by the time the judgment was given, would have had to begin all over again. Since the Agreement had already been signed by at least some Member States, this would have been most undesirable and might have made non-Member States reluctant to enter into similar negotiations in the future. In view of this, one can see the attractiveness, from a policy point of view, of declaring the 'resolution' to be a legal act *sui generis*: by holding it to be a legal act, the Court was able to declare the proceedings admissible and could therefore rule on the substantive issues; and by declaring that it was not a regulation, a decision, or a directive, it could hold that Article 253 [190] did not apply to it and it need not be annulled for lack of reasons. The Court was thus able to give a judgment in which the substantive issues were decided in principle in favour of the Commission – which was all the Commission wanted – and at the same time avoid upsetting the Agreement. There were, therefore, strong policy reasons why the Court classified the 'resolution' as an act *sui generis*; had it not been for these considerations, the Court would probably have declared it to be a decision in terms of Article 249 [189].[7]

## LEGISLATIVE POWERS OF THE COMMUNITY

It is often said that the Community is based on the principle of limited powers (sometimes referred to as the principle of 'conferred powers' – in French, '*compétences d'attribution*'). By this is meant that the Community institutions have no inherent powers – they possess only those powers conferred on them – and that they must not go outside the limits of those powers.[8] Thus Article 5 [3b] EC provides: 'The Community shall act within the limits of the powers conferred upon it by this Treaty and of the objectives assigned to it therein.'[9] However, while it is undoubtedly true that the Community has no inherent powers[10] and must keep within the powers conferred

[6] This rule is discussed below.

[7] This was the solution adopted in another case in which the act carried no formal designation, the *Noordwijks Cement Accoord* case, discussed in Chap. 11.

[8] It should be noted that Art. 249 [189] EC and the corresponding provisions in the other Treaties do not confer powers; they merely enumerate and define the kinds of acts that may be adopted under powers granted by other provisions.

[9] This provision was inserted by the Maastricht Agreement (TEU); however, a similar provision has existed all along in Art. 7 [4] EC.

[10] The European Court has, however, come very close to claiming inherent powers for itself: see Arnull, 'Does the Court of Justice Have Inherent Jurisdiction?' (1990) 27 CMLRev. 683; Usher, 'How Limited is the Jurisdiction of the European Court of Justice?' in Dine, Douglas-Scott, and Persaud, *Procedure and the European Court* (1991), p. 72.

on it by the Treaties, the practical significance of this is diminished by two factors: first, the European Court interprets the empowering provisions of the Treaties in a wide manner, partly on the basis of the theory of implied powers; secondly, some Treaty provisions, notably Article 308 [235] EC, confer on the Community what can only be described as an open-ended power.

### THE THEORY OF IMPLIED POWERS

This theory, which was originally developed in the constitutional and administrative law of such countries as the United States and England, and which has been recognized as a principle of international law,[11] may be expressed in both a narrow and a wide formulation. According to the narrow formulation, the existence of a given power implies also the existence of any other power which is reasonably necessary for the exercise of the former; according to the wide formulation, the existence of a given *objective* or *function* implies the existence of any power reasonably necessary to attain it.

The narrow formulation was adopted by the European Court as long ago as 1956;[12] the wide formulation was applied (with regard to the Commission) in 1987. This was in *Germany v. Commission*,[13] a case arising out of Article 137 [118] EC. As it existed at the time, Article 137 [118] provided: 'the Commission shall have the task of promoting close co-operation between Member States in the social field, particularly in matters relating to . . . '. This provision gave the Commission a task, but nowhere did it confer on the Commission any legislative power. The authors of the Treaty probably thought that it was not necessary. However, in 1985 the Commission, acting under Article 137 [118], adopted a decision which obliged the Member States to consult with the Commission regarding certain matters, and to inform it of draft measures and agreements concerning the topic in question. This decision was challenged by some of the Member States, but it was upheld by the Court (except for certain provisions). The Court held that, whenever a provision of the EC Treaty confers a specific task on the Commission, that provision must also be regarded as impliedly conferring on the Commission 'the powers which are indispensable in order to carry out that task'.[14] Since the EC Treaty confers many tasks on the Commission, including such wide-ranging functions as that of ensuring that the provisions of the Treaty are applied,[15] this judgment is potentially significant, though so far it has not been widely applied.[16]

[11] See International Court of Justice, Advisory Opinion on Reparation for Injuries Suffered in the Service of the United Nations [1949] ICJ 174 at 182. See further Lauwaars, pp. 94–8.

[12] *Fédération Charbonnière de Belgique v. High Authority*, Case 8/55, [1956] ECR 245 at 280. For a more recent example, see *Commission v. Council*, Case 165/87, [1988] ECR 5545 at para. 8 of the judgment.

[13] Cases 281, 283–5, 287/85, [1987] ECR 3203.

[14] Para. 28 of the judgment. The Court immediately went on to use the word 'necessary' instead of 'indispensable', and then applied the new doctrine in a way which suggests that it will adopt a generous view of what is 'necessary': see Hartley, 'The Commission as Legislator under the EC Treaty' (1988) 13 ELRev. 122.

[15] Art. 211 [155] EC.

[16] For a case in which the Court might have applied it but did not, see *France v. Commission*, Case C-327/91, [1994] ECR I-3641.

## OPEN-ENDED POWERS: ARTICLE 308 [235] EC

A second, and more severe, objection to the view that the Community is based on the principle of limited powers is that not all Treaty provisions are of the nature described above. A wider provision is contained in Article 94 [100] EC, which empowers the Council to issue directives for the 'approximation' of such laws or other provisions of the Member States as 'directly affect the establishment or functioning of the common market'.[17] Directives have been issued under this power to unify the laws of the Member States on a wide variety of subjects.

Article 94 [100] might still be regarded as granting a specific power; but another provision clearly goes beyond this. Article 308 [235] EC provides:

> If action by the Community should prove necessary to attain, in the course of the operation of the common market, one of the objectives of the Community and this Treaty has not provided the necessary powers, the Council shall, acting unanimously on a proposal from the Commission and after consulting the Assembly, take the appropriate measures.

Similar powers are granted by Article 203 Euratom. These may be regarded as an express adoption (with regard to the Council) of the wide formulation of the doctrine of implied powers; broadly speaking, it grants power to take whatever measures are necessary to attain the objectives of the Community.

In order to appreciate the precise extent of this power, the conditions prescribed for its exercise must be analysed. These may be divided into procedural and substantive requirements. The former follow the standard pattern – proposal from the Commission and consultation with the European Parliament – except that Council must be unanimous. The substantive requirements are as follows:

1. the power must be used in order to attain one of the objectives of the Community;
2. action by the Community must be necessary for this purpose;
3. the attainment of the objective must take place in the course of the operation of the Common Market;
4. the Treaty must not have provided the necessary powers;
5. the measure must be appropriate for the attaining of the objective.

Each of these will be considered in turn.

The objectives of the EC are set out in Articles 2 [2] and 3 [3] of the Treaty; they include, in addition to more specific goals, such matters as economic growth and the raising of the standard of living. These objectives are broad; moreover, since Article 308 [235] EC does not refer expressly to Articles 2 [2] and 3 [3], it may be legitimate to infer additional objectives from other provisions of the Treaty.

[17] Under Art. 94 [100], the Council must be unanimous, but Art. 95 [100a] makes provision for qualified majority voting for the purpose of establishing the internal market, though Art. 95(4) [100a(4)] gives Member States a limited right to opt out.

The second requirement is that action by the Community must be necessary to attain the objective. Although a determination that a Community act is necessary may seem to be a pure decision of fact, it actually involves a large measure of discretion; in the first instance at least, it will be made by the Commission and the Council. It is unlikely, except in extreme cases, that the Court will substitute its own judgment for that of the institutions to which the power to act is given by the Treaty.[18]

The third requirement is that the objective must be attained in the 'course of the operation of the common market'.[19] The equivalent phrases in the French and Italian texts ('*dans le fonctionnement du marché commun*' and '*nel funzionamento del mercato comune*') mean literally 'in the functioning of the Common Market'. The German and Dutch texts, on the other hand, mean 'within the framework (or scope) of the common market' ('*im Rahmen des Gemeinsamen Marktes*' and '*in het kader van de gemeenschappelijke markt*'). The latter seem slightly wider; they also make clear that the phrase cannot be given a purely temporal interpretation,[20] which might have seemed possible on the basis of the English text alone.

What exactly is the effect of this phrase? Article 2 [2] EC appears to draw a distinction between establishing the Common Market and carrying out certain common policies; so it might be thought that the effect of the phrase is to limit the use of Article 308 [235] to the former. Some writers, however, reject this view;[21] if they are correct, the phrase seems to mean no more than that the action must fall within the context of the Treaty.[22]

The fourth requirement is that a specific provision of the Treaty should not have provided the necessary powers. This seems straightforward enough, but in fact more problems are created by this requirement than by any other. For instance, what is the position where the Treaty expressly covers the matter in issue but grants powers which are regarded as insufficient? This question arose in *Hauptzollamt Bremerhaven v. Massey-Ferguson*,[23] which concerned a regulation on the valuation of goods for customs purposes. The object of this regulation, which had been enacted under Article 308 [235], was to ensure that uniform rules were applied throughout the Community: this was clearly necessary to ensure the proper functioning of the customs union. However, Article 27 EC (now repealed) was concerned with just this question, though it granted only the power to make recommendations. Since recommendations are not legally binding, it could be argued that Article 27 did not grant the necessary powers. On the other hand, it could be maintained that, since the authors of the Treaty had expressly dealt with the matter and had seen fit to give the power only to make recommendations, they must be regarded as having impliedly excluded the use of greater powers. The Advocate General, however, preferred the former argument and this was implicitly accepted by the European Court, which upheld the validity of the regulation. One can conclude, therefore, that the express grant of a power considered insufficient does not preclude resort to Article 308 [235].

[18] But see Dashwood, 'The Limits of European Community Powers' (1996) 21 ELRev. 113 at 123.
[19] This phrase does not occur in Art. 203 Euratom.
[20] By this is meant interpreting the phrase to mean 'during the time when the Common Market is in operation'.
[21] Marenco, 'Les conditions d'application de l'article 235 du traité CEE' [1970] RMC 147 at 150.
[22] But see Dashwood, 'The Limits of European Community Powers' (1996) 21 ELRev. 113 at 123.
[23] Case 8/73, [1973] ECR 897.

A second objection to the validity of the regulation in the *Massey-Ferguson* case was that the necessary power *was* in fact granted by certain other provisions in the Treaty, provided these were given a sufficiently broad interpretation in line with the doctrine of implied powers (narrow formulation).[24] Advocate General Trabucchi took the view, however, that the interpretation of these other powers was subject to doubt; therefore, even if they were sufficiently wide, recourse to Article 308 [235] was legitimate. He expressed his opinion as follows:[25]

> Even supposing that this Regulation could have been adopted by a simpler procedure under a different rule or by implication on the basis of a number of specific rules and powers provided by the Treaty, one cannot see what damage to the public interest has been caused by the adoption of such a measure on the basis and under the procedure of Article 308 [235]. It would certainly be against the spirit of the system created by the Treaty if the Commission or the Council were to consider it necessary to act on the basis of Article 308 [235] in a case where other provisions of the Treaty already clearly provide suitable powers of action. But we do not have to consider what legal consequences could result on such a hypothesis. In the present case, in the absence of an express and clear provision of the Treaty specifically empowering the enactment of this Regulation, one must dismiss the idea that because this provision was prudently based on the general authorizing rule of Article 308 [235], such fact could possibly constitute an irregularity liable to render it invalid.

This was accepted by the Court; the relevant passage reads as follows:[26]

> If it is true that the proper functioning of the customs union justifies a wide interpretation of Articles 9, 27, 28, 111 and 113 of the Treaty and of the powers which these provisions confer on the institutions to allow them thoroughly to control external trade by measures taken both independently and by agreement, there is no reason why the Council could not legitimately consider that recourse to the procedure of Article 308 [235] was justified in the interest of legal certainty. This is the more so as the Regulation in question was adopted during the transitional period.
>
> By reason of the specific requirements of Article 308 [235] this course of action cannot be criticized since, under the circumstances, the rules of the Treaty on the forming of the Council's decisions or on the division of powers between the institutions are not to be disregarded.

Recourse to Article 308 [235] is, however, impermissible where the power to act is clearly given by another provision of the Treaty.[27]

The fifth requirement for the exercise of the power granted by Article 308 [235] is that the act must be appropriate. This means that it must be reasonably suitable for achieving the objective in question. It probably also means that any hardship caused must not be disproportionate to the benefits accruing from the attainment of the

[24] See *per* Advocate General Trabucchi, [1973] ECR at 913–14.

[25] See *per* Advocate General Trabucchi, [1973] ECR at 914.

[26] *Ibid.* at 908 (para. 4). The phrase at the very end of this passage, 'are not to be disregarded', appears in the French text as '*ne se trouvent pas déjouées*'. In the context, a better translation would have been 'have not been prejudiced'.

[27] See the cases discussed below in the section on 'Legal Basis'.

objective: this follows from the doctrine of 'proportionality', which has been adopted by the European Court as a general principle of law.[28]

Finally, it should be said that there is a general requirement, which applies to all Community legislation but which applies with particular force to measures adopted under Article 308 [235]. This is the requirement of subsidiarity. It will be discussed in a separate section below.

It is now possible to review the effect of Article 308 [235] as a whole. It will be seen that it confers a wide and ill-defined power, a power that was previously described as open-ended. This prompts the question whether there are any significant limits to its use. One obvious limit is that measures taken under Article 308 [235] must not be contrary to an express prohibition contained in the Treaty.[29]

Secondly, Article 308 [235] should not be used to adopt measures which would constitute an amendment of the Treaty: Treaty amendments are expressly dealt with by Article 48 [N] TEU, which, as will be remembered,[30] provides for the calling of a conference of Member States; it also lays down that any amendments must be ratified by each Member State according to its constitutional provisions. It is suggested that this procedure must be used, not only where a provision of the Treaty is expressly amended, but also where the basic constitutional structure set up by the Treaty is modified. These limitations are quite reasonable when one remembers that, even in a fully fledged federation, the federal organs do not normally have power to make constitutional amendments without going through special procedures, usually involving either a referendum or the agreement of the constituent States.

This limitation on the use of Article 308 [235] was affirmed by the European Court in its Opinion on the accession of the Community to the European Convention on Human Rights.[31] The background to this case is explained in Chapter 6; here, all we will do is to quote two paragraphs from the judgment:[32]

> Article 308 [235] is designed to fill the gap where no specific provisions of the Treaty confer on the Community institutions express or implied powers to act, if such powers appear none the less to be necessary to enable the Community to carry out its functions with a view to attaining one of the objectives laid down by the Treaty.
>
> That provision, being an integral part of an institutional system based on the principle of conferred [limited] powers, cannot serve as a basis for widening the scope of Community powers beyond the general framework created by the provisions of the Treaty as a whole and, in particular, by those that define the tasks and the activities of the Community. On any view, Article 308 [235] cannot be used as a basis for the adoption of provisions whose effect would, in substance, be to amend the Treaty without following the procedure which it provides for that purpose.

[28] This is discussed in Chap. 5.

[29] See, e.g., the new version of Art. 149 [126] EC, which, while giving the Community a certain role in education, makes it clear that the Member States are responsible for the content of teaching and the organization of education systems; consequently, any attempt to use Art. 308 [235] with regard to these matters would be wrong.

[30] See Chap. 3.

[31] *ECHR* case, Opinion 2/94, [1996] ECR I-1759. This Opinion (in effect, a binding judgment) was given under Art. 300(6) [228(6)] EC, a provision discussed in Chap. 6, under the heading 'Legal Proceedings'.

[32] Paras 29 and 30.

The Court concluded that the suggested use of Article 308 [235] would involve a modification of the Community system that would be 'of constitutional significance'; consequently, the Court ruled, it would go beyond the scope of Article 308 [235].[33] It could be brought about only by an amendment to the Treaty.

The extensive scope of Article 308 [235] might appear of little significance in view of the rule that measures passed under it must be agreed to by all the members of the Council. This means that any Member State can veto a proposal (though an abstention will not stop the passage of the measure).[34] However, if Article 308 [235] did not exist, the Member States would be obliged to enter into a convention or treaty and this would be subject to ratification, which normally entails the approval of the national parliaments. The importance of Article 308 [235], therefore, is that it allows governments to bypass this procedure.

## LEGAL BASIS

It was said above that a measure cannot be adopted under Article 308 [235] if another provision of the Treaty clearly gives the power to act. Where the Community indisputably has the power to adopt the measure under one provision or another of the Treaty, arguments about its correct legal basis[35] might appear sterile. However, there are circumstances, alluded to in the second paragraph of the passage quoted above from the Court's judgment in the *Massey-Ferguson* case, in which the provision under which a measure is adopted could have significant constitutional consequences. These are where it affects 'the rules of the Treaty on the forming of the Council's decisions' or 'the division of powers between the institutions'. The former concerns the procedure under which the measure is adopted in the Council, in particular whether unanimity or qualified majority voting applies;[36] the latter could cover the use of Article 308 [235] where it would allow the Council to take over powers granted to the Commission or Parliament (an unlikely event), or where it would deprive the Commission or Parliament of its proper role in the legislative process (a distinct possibility).

The former situation is illustrated by the *Tariff Preferences* case,[37] which concerned Council regulations giving tariff preferences to imports from developing countries. As the regulations dealt with tariffs and trade, the Commission considered that they were covered by Article 133 [113] EC. The Council, on the other hand, took the view that, since their purpose was developmental (aid), they could be adopted only under Article

[33] Para. 35. [34] See Art. 205(3) [148(3)] EC.

[35] The phrase 'legal basis' is used in Community law to indicate the Treaty provision (or other source of legal authority) under which a Community institution adopts a measure. Some writers use 'legal base', a term closer to the French equivalent, '*base juridique*', from which the English phrase is probably derived, but the Court prefers 'legal basis'.

[36] The significance of the statement in the Court's judgment that the regulation was adopted during the transitional period is that Art. 133 [113], which requires unanimity during that period, provides for qualified majority voting thereafter.

[37] *Commission v. Council*, Case 45/86, [1987] ECR 1493.

308 [235]. The significance of this dispute was that Article 133 [113] allowed for qualified majority voting,[38] while Article 308 [235] required unanimity. The Council tried to avoid the issue by not specifying any particular Treaty Article as the legal basis of the measure: the reference in the Commission proposal to Article 133 [113] was deleted and the preamble simply referred to the EC Treaty as a whole.

In annulment proceedings brought by the Commission, the Court held that the regulations could have been adopted under Article 133 [113] and declared them void on two separate grounds: first, that the failure to specify the precise legal basis was an infringement of an essential procedural requirement;[39] and, secondly, that, as the regulations could have been adopted under Article 133 [113], the Council was not justified in adopting them under Article 308 [235]. The Court expressly mentioned that the two Articles 'entail different rules regarding the manner in which the Council may arrive at its decision'.[40]

What is the position where a measure comes partly within the area covered by one Article and partly within that covered by another? According to the *Commodity Coding*[41] case, the procedural requirements of both Articles must be satisfied.[42] This case again concerned a measure which, in the view of the Commission, could have been adopted under Article 133 [113]. The Council, however, amended the Preamble to give Articles 26 [28] and 308 [235] (in addition to Article 133 [113]) as its legal basis. In annulment proceedings brought by the Commission, the Court held that Articles 26 [28] and 133 [113] together constituted the appropriate legal basis for the measure. The requirements of both these provisions had to be fulfilled, but recourse to Article 308 [235] was impermissible. However, at the time in question, Article 26 [28] (like Article 308 [235]) required unanimity; so the addition of Article 308 [235] as a legal basis did not affect the voting procedure in the Council. Consequently, the Court did not annul the measure.[43]

It is interesting to note that in another respect there *was* a significant difference between Article 308 [235] and Article 26 [28]: the former, but not the latter, required the Parliament to be consulted. This had taken place, but the Court held that, while wrongful failure to consult the Parliament leads to nullity, legally unnecessary consultation does not do so, since the Council is always entitled to ask the Parliament for its opinion.[44]

[38] By this time, the transitional period was over.

[39] This is one of the recognized grounds for the annulment of a measure: see Art. 230 [173] EC. The Court stated that failure to refer to a precise provision of the Treaty does not necessarily constitute an infringement of an essential procedural requirement when the legal basis of the measure may be determined from other parts of the measure, but it held that explicit reference is indispensable where the parties and the Court would otherwise be left uncertain as to the precise legal basis: see para. 9 of the judgment.

[40] Para. 12 of the judgment.

[41] *Commission v. Council*, Case 165/87, [1988] ECR 5545.

[42] Para. 11 of the judgment.

[43] See para. 19 of the judgment, where the Court said that the illegality which resulted from using the wrong legal basis was 'only a purely formal defect which cannot make the measure void'.

[44] Para. 20 of the judgment. In a later case, *European Parliament v. Council*, Case C-316/91, [1994] ECR I-625, the Parliament considered that the measure should have been adopted under a provision that would have given it the right to be consulted. The Council argued that, since the Parliament had in any event been consulted (on a voluntary basis), the application for annulment should be declared inadmissible. This argument was rejected by the Court, which held that the application was admissible (though in the end it was dismissed on the merits).

A further twist was given to the law by the *Titanium Dioxide* case,[45] which concerned a Council measure intended to lay down uniform environmental-protection standards for the titanium dioxide industry. This measure, the Court held, had two purposes: to protect the environment and (because it laid down uniform standards in all Member States) to promote fair competition. The former was covered by Article 175 [130s] EC (which required unanimity in the Council and the consultation of the Parliament) and the latter fell within the scope of Article 95 [100a] (which envisaged qualified majority voting and the co-operation procedure).

On the basis of the Court's judgment in the *Commodity Coding* case,[46] one would have thought that the correct procedure would have been to follow the requirements of both provisions. This would have entailed applying the more onerous requirement with regard to each aspect of the procedure, in other words, applying the unanimity rule as far as voting in the Council was concerned, and following the co-operation procedure as far as the role of the Parliament was concerned.

This, however, created a problem. It will be remembered that the main difference between the co-operation procedure and simple consultation is that, under the former, the Council can override a negative opinion on the part of the Parliament only if it is unanimous. However, if the Council has to be unanimous in any event, the opinion loses its sting: it makes no difference what the Parliament says. In view of this, the Court held that its ruling in the *Commodity Coding* case could not be applied: one or other of the two Treaty provisions had to be chosen as the sole legal basis. After some discussion, the Court selected Article 95 [100a]. The Commission had proposed this provision as the legal basis for the measure, but the Council had substituted Article 175 [130s]. As a result, the Court annulled the measure.

This series of cases provides an insight into the policies pursued by the European Court. Where a measure is adopted by a public authority under the wrong enabling provision, most courts would be concerned to ensure only that the substantive and procedural requirements of the correct provision had been satisfied. Where the correct provision provides for majority voting, but the authority acted by unanimity because this was required by the provision under which the measure was adopted, most courts would take the view that, since a unanimous vote necessarily constitutes a majority, the requirements of both provisions had been met. In such a case, there would seem little point in annulling the measure. The fact that the European Court follows a different policy shows that it is not concerned simply with ensuring respect for the law, but has a more political objective: that of pushing the Community in the direction of greater integration. It is also noticeable that, where the Court has to decide which of two provisions constitutes the correct legal basis for a measure, it more often than not comes down in favour of the one providing for qualified majority voting, rather than unanimity.

[45] *Commission v. Council*, Case C-300/89, [1991] ECR I-2867. See also *European Parliament v. Council*, Case C-295/90, [1992] ECR I-4193, where the Treaty provision under which the measure should have been adopted involved the co-operation procedure, as distinct from the Parliament's merely giving its opinion.

[46] Above.

## SUBSIDIARITY[47]

The principle of subsidiarity is defined and established[48] by the second paragraph of Article 5 [3b] EC,[49] inserted into the Treaty by the Maastricht Agreement (Treaty on European Union), where it is stated:[50]

> In areas which do not fall within its exclusive competence, the Community shall take action, in accordance with the principle of subsidiarity, only if and in so far as the objectives of the proposed action cannot be sufficiently achieved by the Member States and can therefore, by reason of the scale or effects of the proposed action, be better achieved by the Community.

The Treaty of Amsterdam added a Protocol to the EC Treaty, the Protocol on the Application of the Principles of Subsidiarity and Proportionality, which states that both these requirements must be met: for Community action to be justified, it must be established *both* that the objectives of the proposed action cannot be sufficiently achieved by the Member States *and* that they can be better achieved by action on the part of the Community.[51] The Protocol also lays down guidelines for determining whether these conditions are fulfilled.[52] These read:

- the issue under consideration has transnational aspects which cannot be satisfactorily regulated by action by Member States;
- actions by Member States alone or lack of Community action would conflict with the requirements of the Treaty (such as the need to correct distortion of competition or avoid disguised restrictions on trade or strengthen economic and social cohesion) or would otherwise significantly damage Member States' interests;
- action at Community level would produce clear benefits by reason of its scale or effects compared with action at the level of the Member States.

These developments are to be welcomed, but it should be noted that, under the Treaties, the principle of subsidiarity applies only in areas which do not fall within the exclusive

[47] See the Commission document entitled 'The Principle of Subsidiarity', Com. Doc. SEC(92) 1990, 27 October 1992; 'Overall Approach to the Application by the Council of the Subsidiarity Principle and Article 3b of the Treaty on European Union', Annex 1 to Part A of the *Conclusions of the Presidency*, European Council in Edinburgh, 11–12 December 1992.

[48] It was previously applied in a limited area, the environment, by the Single European Act (see Art. 174(4) [130r(4)] EC as inserted by the Single European Act); see also Art. 5 ECSC. Its genealogy may be traced back through the Preamble (last recital) and Art. 12 of the draft Treaty establishing the European Union adopted by the European Parliament on 14 February 1984 (OJ 1984, C77/33) and the Commission's *Report on European Union*, 1975 (EC Bull., Supplement 5/75) to German constitutional law. On the latter, see Emiliou, 'Subsidiarity: An Effective Barrier against "the Enterprises of Ambition"?' (1992) 17 ELRev. 383 at 388–91. Its origin seems to lie in Catholic doctrine.

[49] There is no comparable provision in the Euratom Treaty.

[50] In the Preamble to the Treaty on European Union (Maastricht Agreement), it is declared that, in the process of creating an ever closer union among the peoples of Europe, decisions will be taken 'as closely as possible to the citizen in accordance with the principle of subsidiarity'. See, further, Art. 1 [A] (second paragraph) TEU. It is also stated, in the final paragraph of Article 2 [B] TEU, that, in achieving the objectives of the Union, the principle of subsidiarity (as defined in Art. 5 [3b] EC) will be respected.

[51] Art. 5 of the Protocol.

[52] *Ibid.*

jurisdiction of the Community, and it is far from clear which areas should be so regarded.[53] The Commission takes the view that an area falls within the exclusive jurisdiction of the Community if the Treaties impose an obligation to act on the Community because it is regarded as having sole responsibility for the performance of a particular task.[54] The Commission has identified the following areas as satisfying this criterion: the removal of barriers to the free movement of goods, persons, services, and capital; the common commercial policy; the general rules on competition; the common organization of agricultural markets; the conservation of fisheries resources; and the essential elements of transport policy.[55] This is a large area, but the Commission has made clear that it will expand as integration progresses.[56]

Moreover, if one looks at the decisions of the European Court on the implied treaty-making powers of the Community, it seems that whenever the EC Treaty gives the Community an internal power to take binding measures, and the Community exercises that power either by adopting legislation or by entering into an international agreement, the Member States are no longer permitted to make treaties that would affect what the Community has done. In other words, the relevant area is thenceforth regarded as falling, to that extent, within the exclusive jurisdiction of the Community as far as international agreements are concerned.[57] It is uncertain whether the European Court will apply a similar principle with regard to Article 5 [3b], but if it does, an area could be regarded as falling within the exclusive jurisdiction of the Community once the Community has adopted measures within it; consequently, subsidiarity would be applicable only when the Community legislated for the first time.

The effectiveness of these provisions may be considered from both a political and a legal point of view. From a political point of view, they may make the Commission more restrained in the measures it proposes and the Council more cautious in the measures it accepts.[58] From a legal point of view, the question to be considered is the extent to which the European Court would be prepared to declare measures invalid for infringement of the principle of subsidiarity.[59] Clearly, the political effectiveness of subsidiarity depends

[53] Commentators have expressed divergent views on this issue. Toth considers that *all* the areas of power granted to the Community under the EEC Treaty as originally concluded are exclusive: Toth, 'The Principle of Subsidiarity in the Maastricht Treaty' (1992) 29 CMLRev. 1079 at 1080–6 (the author admits of an exception in the case of implied treaty-making powers); Steiner, on the other hand, suggests that the only areas in which the Community has exclusive competence for the purpose of Article 5 [3b] are those in which it has *already legislated*: Steiner, 'Subsidiarity under the Maastricht Treaty', in David O'Keeffe and Patrick M Twomey, *Legal Issues of the Maastricht Treaty* (1994), p. 49 at pp. 55–8; see, further, Emiliou, 'Subsidiarity: Panacea or Fig Leaf?', *ibid.*, p. 65 at pp. 74–5; Schilling, 'A New Dimension of Subsidiarity: Subsidiarity as a Rule and a Principle' (1994) 14 YEL 203 at pp. 217 *et seq.*

[54] See 'The Principle of Subsidiarity', Com. Doc. SEC(92) 1990, 27 October 1992, 5.

[55] *Ibid.*, 7.

[56] *Ibid.*, 8.

[57] See Chap. 6.

[58] The *Conclusions of the Presidency*, European Council in Edinburgh (11–12 December 1992), sets out practices and procedures intended to ensure that subsidiarity is taken into account at every stage of the legislative process (see 10–12 of Annex 1 to Part A). Effect was given to this by the Inter-Institutional Agreement of 25 October 1993 between the European Parliament, the Council and the Commission, OJ 1993, C329/135.

[59] Article 1 of the Protocol added by the Treaty of Amsterdam provides that, in exercising the powers conferred on it, each institution 'shall ensure that the principle of subsidiarity is complied with'. Since the European Court is an institution, this appears to require it to use its judicial powers to ensure that the other institutions

to a considerable extent on its legal effectiveness: the Commission and the Council will not adopt a measure if it is likely to be declared invalid by the Court.

In order to challenge a Community measure on the basis of Article 5 [3b], an applicant must establish the objectives of the measure and show that those objectives could be sufficiently (or equally well) attained through action by the Member States. Both of these requirements present difficulties. Most measures adopted by the Community have a number of objectives, some general and some specific. If any one of the objectives could be better attained by Community action, the European Court would probably regard that as sufficient to justify the measure (though it might be prepared to strike down clearly severable parts which did not fulfil the requirements of Article 5 [3b]).

In practice, it will almost always be possible to formulate the objectives of the measure in different ways. In defending the measure, the Commission or the Council will argue for a formulation which requires Community action. One can even expect that the preamble and wording of the measure might be drafted so as to facilitate this.

In such a situation, everything will depend on the European Court. It will decide whether the measure falls within an area in which the Community has exclusive jurisdiction; it will formulate the objectives of the measure; and it will decide whether they can be better achieved by Community action. All these questions involve so many imponderables that it will almost always be possible for the Court, if it wishes, to find grounds for upholding the measure. As a result, the effectiveness of subsidiarity will depend, to a considerable extent, on the attitude and policy of the European Court.

So far the European Court has not struck down legislation on the ground of subsidiarity. There is, however, a case which is of interest in this regard. This is the *Tobacco Advertising* case,[60] in which Germany brought proceedings before the European Court to annul a directive that imposed a general ban on the advertising or sponsorship of tobacco products in the EU. Germany put forward various grounds, including subsidiarity, for its claim, but the only ground considered by the Court was that the directive was outside the powers of the Community (lack of competence, or *ultra vires* in English legal terminology). The directive was declared invalid on this ground.

Since the Community is bound by the principle of limited powers, it was not enough to prove that the ban was beneficial. It had to be shown that it was within the powers of the Community. The Community has no general power to legislate in the area of public health. It can adopt incentive measures, but the relevant provision, Article 152(4)(c) [129(4)(c)] EC, expressly excludes the harmonization of Member-State law. The directive was, therefore, based on Articles 95 [100a], 47(2) [57(2)], and 55 [66] EC. For these provisions to apply, the ban on tobacco advertising had to be necessary to promote the free movement of goods or services, freedom of establishment, or free competition.

The Court agreed that these provisions could justify a ban on tobacco advertising in certain cases. For example, if there were different rules in different Member States on

respect the principle, if necessary by annulling legislation that conflicts with it. The *Conclusions of the Presidency* (above) also envisages that the European Court will ensure compliance by the Community institutions in so far as the issues in question fall within the scope of the EC Treaty: see Annex 1 to Part A, 4.

60 *Germany v. European Parliament and Council*, Case C-376/98, [2000] ECR I-8419.

tobacco advertising in magazines and newspapers, the free movement of these items could be impeded. Consequently, Article 95 [100a] EC could be used to lay down a uniform rule. However, such an argument could not be used with regard to advertising on, for example, billboards. So it did not justify a *general* ban. In any event, the directive in question did not ensure that the rules were uniform, since it expressly said that Member States were not prevented from imposing stricter requirements.

It could also be argued that a ban in one Member State on tobacco sponsorship for sporting events might result in such events being moved to another Member State where sponsorship was allowed, thus distorting competition. Again, however, while this might justify a ban on tobacco sponsorship for such events, it could not justify a general ban.

What is interesting about this case is that the kind of analysis adopted by the Court, though directed at the question whether the directive came within the competence of the Community, was equally pertinent with regard to subsidiarity. The Court was not concerned with the question whether a general ban on tobacco advertising was a good thing, but with the question whether it should be imposed by the Community, rather than by the Member States. This is the essence of subsidiarity.

This does not, however, mean that such an analysis will be appropriate in all cases in which measures are alleged to be beyond the powers of the Community. It was applied in the *Tobacco Advertising* case because of the nature of the Treaty provisions on the basis of which the measure had been enacted. It should also be said that it is rare for the European Court to rule that a measure is invalid on the ground of lack of competence. More usual grounds are that it was adopted under the wrong procedure or on the wrong legal basis, or that it violated some higher rule of law.

## DELEGATION OF POWERS

So far we have been considering the powers granted to the Community institutions by the Treaties; the next question is the extent to which these powers may be delegated either to other Community institutions or to outside bodies.[61]

From a formal point of view, a delegation takes place whenever the authority granted a power by the Treaty conveys it to some other body. This definition is not, however, wholly satisfactory, since the formal position may not always correspond with the real situation: a formal delegation may be made without any real transfer of responsibility; or, conversely, formal power may remain with the delegating authority but real power may pass out of its hands.

In order to decide whether a real delegation has taken place, one must consider a number of questions. First, is the delegate granted a wide discretion or is the exercise of the power made subject to rules laid down by the delegating authority which are so restrictive that the delegate's role is merely executive? In this case the 'delegation' will be of little practical significance, since the way the power is exercised will not be affected.

[61] For a discussion of delegation to international organizations, see Chap. 6.

Secondly, can the delegating authority exercise effective control over the delegate? This may be done in various ways. For example, it may be provided that the decision of the delegate will not come into force until it has been confirmed by the delegating authority; or the latter may be given the power to rescind it, provided it acts within a given period. This power might be exercisable by the delegating authority on its own initiative or on an appeal to it by some person or body affected by the decision. In Community law, controls of this nature are applicable when powers are delegated by the Council to the Commission.[62]

Thirdly, one must consider whether the powers granted to a body are actually exercised by that body or whether the real decision is taken elsewhere. For example, the formal decision may be taken by the delegating authority and the role of the delegate may be confined to making proposals; but if the delegating authority never questions these proposals and merely rubber-stamps them, a *de facto* delegation will have taken place. Likewise, powers of control that are not in practice exercised are of little real significance.

Any effective system of administrative law must take all these factors into account in deciding whether a delegation has taken place. It must also be understood that a delegation is not a question of all or nothing: it is often a matter of degree. The practical significance of the delegation will depend on the extent to which real power has been transferred.

## DELEGATION TO THE COMMISSION

At one time, the only provisions in the Treaties expressly concerned with delegation were Articles 211 [155] EC and 124 Euratom. Article 211 [155][63] reads:

> In order to ensure the proper functioning and development of the common market, the Commission shall . . . exercise the powers conferred on it by the Council for the implementation of the rules laid down by the latter.

This merely requires the Commission to exercise the powers delegated to it by the Council; it contains no express authorization for such delegation. However, express authority has since been provided by Article 202 [145] EC, as amended by Article 10 SEA, which authorizes the Council to delegate powers to the Commission to implement provisions laid down by the Council. As previously explained, such delegations are often subject to special procedures involving advisory committees; these procedures are now regulated by a framework decision adopted by the Council under Article 202 [145].[64]

The validity of these procedures has been considered by the European Court in a number of cases. Though these cases were decided before the Single European Act came into force in 1987, the principles laid down in them still stand. The first was the *Köster* case,[65] which arose as follows. Acting under Article 37(2) [43(2)] EC (which empowers the Council to legislate in the field of agriculture), the Council passed a regulation

[62] See Chap. 1 ('The Commission', 'Decision-Making Procedure').

[63] Art. 124 Euratom is virtually identical.

[64] See Chap. 1.

[65] *Einfuhr- und Vorratsstelle v. Köster*, Case 25/70, [1970] ECR 1161.

setting out the general principles for the organization of a common market in cereals. This regulation also made provision for the detailed rules to be laid down in measures to be adopted by the Commission under the management committee procedure.

Two objections to this were raised. First, it was pointed out that where measures are enacted by the Council under Article 37(2) [43(2)], the opinion of the European Parliament must be obtained; but when the power was delegated to the Commission, no provision for this was made. Thus the effect of the delegation was to deprive the Parliament of its right to be consulted. The Court, however, ruled that it is not necessary for all the details of regulations concerning agriculture to be enacted according to the procedure laid down in Article 37(2) [43(2)]. It is sufficient if the general principles governing the question are set out in a measure adopted under this procedure: the details may then be laid down under a different procedure, either by the Council itself or by the Commission.

The second objection was against the management committee procedure itself. It was argued that this constituted an unwarranted restriction of the decision-making power of the Commission and jeopardized its independence. The Court, however, pointed out that the management committee could not itself take decisions; if it disapproved of a proposed measure, the only consequence was that the Commission was obliged to communicate the measure to the Council, which could then substitute its own measure for that of the Commission. The Court therefore ruled that this procedure was not contrary to the Treaty.

It will be seen from this case that the important distinction is between laying down general principles and detailed implementation; only the latter function may be delegated. However, the Court is prepared to give a wide interpretation to this concept. For example, in the *Chemiefarma* case,[66] the Council adopted a regulation under Article 83 [87] EC which provided for fines to be levied by the Commission on firms guilty of a violation of the Community competition provisions. Article 19 of this regulation stated that firms accused of such a violation should be granted a hearing before the Commission. Article 24 delegated to the Commission the power to make detailed rules governing the procedure at such a hearing. In the case, it was objected that this entailed the power to legislate and went beyond the concept of 'implementation'. The Court held, however, that the concept of implementation includes the adoption of regulations (provisions of a legislative character). This was confirmed in a case decided after the amendment to Article 202 [145], *Commission v. Council*,[67] in which the European Court stated that, for the purposes of Article 202 [145], the concept of implementation comprises 'both the drawing up of implementing rules and the application of those rules to specific cases by means of acts of individual application'. Moreover, in an earlier case, *Rey Soda*,[68] the European Court said that the concept of implementation must be given a wide interpretation and in the sphere of agriculture the Council may confer on the Commission 'wide powers of discretion and action'.[69]

[66] *Chemiefarma v. Commission*, Case 41/69, [1970] ECR 661.

[67] Case 16/88, [1989] ECR 3457 (para. 11 of the judgment).

[68] *Rey Soda v. Cassa Conguaglio Zucchero*, Case 23/75, [1975] ECR 1279.

[69] See paras 10 and 11 of the judgment.

It is possible to conclude, therefore, that extensive discretionary powers may be delegated to the Commission, provided the empowering provision lays down the basic principles governing the matter in question.

## DELEGATION BY AN INSTITUTION TO ITSELF

The same principles apply where a Community institution delegates power to itself.[70] The significance of this is that the delegated power may be exercised by a simpler procedure than that applicable under the Treaty. For example, if the Treaty grants power to the Council to adopt regulations on a proposal from the Commission after consulting the European Parliament, the Council may – provided it lays down the general principles by means of a regulation passed under this procedure – delegate power to itself to enact implementing provisions without the involvement of the Commission or Parliament. The instrument delegating the power must, of course, be adopted under the original procedure.[71]

Article 202 [145] EC (as amended by the Single European Act) states, 'The Council may also reserve the right, in specific cases, to exercise directly implementing powers itself'. This of course gives express authority for the Council to delegate implementing powers to itself.[72] The phrase 'in specific cases' has been taken by the Commission to mean that such delegation is permitted only in exceptional cases where there are special reasons for doing so,[73] and the European Court has said that the Council must 'state in detail' the grounds for such a decision.[74] In a later case, however, the Court allowed the Council to delegate power to itself to amend the original Regulation in a specified way in the light of experience gained;[75] amending measures had to be adopted on a proposal from the Commission but there was no obligation to consult the Parliament.

## DELEGATION TO OUTSIDE BODIES

The leading case on delegation to bodies other than Community institutions is the *Meroni* case.[76] This concerned the scrap iron equalization fund which had been set up by the High Authority (Commission) in an attempt to deal with the scrap shortage in the 1950s. The idea was to subsidize imported scrap in order to bring its price down to the level of Community scrap; the subsidies were to be paid for by a levy on all scrap users. Two bodies were set up to run the scheme, the *Office Commun des Consommateurs de Ferrailles*, which arranged the imports, and the *Caisse de Péréquation des Ferrailles Importées*, which imposed the levy and distributed the subsidies. Both bodies were incorporated as co-operatives under Belgian law.

[70] See *Einfuhr- und Vorratsstelle v. Köster*, Case 25/70, [1970] ECR 1161 at para. 6 of the judgment.

[71] On the delegation of powers by the Commission to one of its members, see *AKZO Chemie v. Commission*, Case 5/85, [1986] ECR 2585 (paras 28–40).

[72] *European Parliament v. Council*, Case 417/93, [1995] ECR I-1185, at 1208–9, *per* Advocate General Léger (para. 109 of his Opinion).

[73] See the answer given by the Commission to Written Parliamentary Question No. 1058/88: OJ 1989, C121/21–2.

[74] *Commission v. Council*, Case 16/88, [1989] ECR 3457 (para. 10 of the judgment).

[75] *European Parliament v. Council*, Case 417/93, [1995] ECR I-1185.

[76] *Meroni v. High Authority*, Case 9/56, [1958] ECR 133. The relevant part of the judgment is section III.

The scheme was set up by a general decision of the High Authority which granted the two organizations their powers. There were, however, a number of ways in which the High Authority could control their activities. First, though the *Caisse* had the power to assess levy payments due from a particular firm and to issue a demand for the sum in question, it could not enforce its claims directly: if the firm failed to pay, the *Caisse* had to request the High Authority to take a decision having executive force. Secondly, both organizations had the power to take decisions only if the members of their governing bodies were unanimous; failing this, the matter would be decided by the High Authority itself. Thirdly, all meetings of the two organizations were attended by a representative of the High Authority and he had the power to declare that any decision taken by them would be conditional on the High Authority's approval. The High Authority also had the power to call a meeting of either organization and lay proposals before it; if the proposals were not accepted within ten days, the High Authority could itself put the proposals into effect.

On paper, these powers of control appear extensive; however, according to evidence given by the High Authority in the case, they were rarely exercised. In practice the organizations had a large measure of independence.

The way the case arose was as follows. The *Caisse* had asked Meroni, an Italian steel manufacturer, to inform it of the quantity of scrap it had used, so that the *Caisse* could assess the levy payments due. Meroni failed to do this and the *Caisse* therefore told Meroni that it would make estimates of the relevant figures and assess the levy on that basis. Meroni still refused to co-operate; so the *Caisse* sent a demand for payment on the basis of the estimates. When Meroni failed to pay, the High Authority, at the request of the *Caisse*, took a decision demanding payment. Under Article 92 ECSC this decision would be enforceable against Meroni through the Italian courts; Meroni therefore brought proceedings in the European Court to have it set aside. One of the arguments put forward was that the whole scrap equalization scheme involved an unlawful delegation of powers and was consequently invalid.

The first question the Court had to consider was whether there really had been a delegation of power to collect the levy, since the decision subject to challenge was that of the High Authority. It was, however, admitted by the High Authority that it never questioned assessments made by the *Caisse*: all it did was to rubber-stamp the *Caisse*'s decision. The Court therefore held that effective decision-making power had been delegated. The next question was whether the delegation was lawful. The Court held, on three separate grounds, that it was not. First, the Court held that the High Authority had attempted to transfer wider powers than it possessed itself. By this it meant that certain obligations and restrictions which apply when the High Authority itself acts were not applicable to the *Caisse* and *Office Commun*: for example, the High Authority is obliged by the Treaty to give reasons for its decisions[77] but this obligation was not imposed on the two organizations.[78]

[77] See below.

[78] The Court also felt that decisions made by the two organizations would be immune from judicial review, but a later case established that this is not so: see *SNUPAT v. High Authority*, Cases 32–3/58, [1959] ECR 127 (discussed in Chap. 11).

The second ground given by the Court was that the High Authority decision delegating powers to the two organizations did not expressly give them the power to assess the levy on the basis of an estimate of scrap used. One might have thought that this would have been covered by the doctrine of implied powers (narrow formulation),[79] but the Court ruled that a delegation of powers can never be implied. Even if the High Authority had been entitled to delegate this power, an express decision would have been necessary.

The third ground given by the Court was by far the most important: it concerned the question whether the High Authority has any power to delegate at all. The Court ruled that the High Authority possesses only very limited power to delegate to outside bodies: clearly defined executive powers may be delegated, provided their exercise is subject to strict rules based on objective criteria; but discretionary powers involving extensive freedom of judgment may not be delegated. This distinction between discretionary and non-discretionary (ministerial) powers is, of course, known to English administrative law and its adoption here may be justified on the ground that the authors of the Treaties were prepared to grant extensive discretionary powers to the Commission because they had confidence in it; they might not have been prepared to see these same powers exercised by an outside body not subject to the safeguards applicable to the Commission itself.

The outcome of all this was that the High Authority decision addressed to Meroni demanding payment of the levy was quashed because it was based on a decision of the *Caisse* made under an illegal delegation of powers.[80] In view of the Court's ruling on this point, the scrap equalization scheme had to be extensively restructured.

One may conclude from this case that there is an important difference between a delegation to the Commission and a delegation to an outside body: wide discretionary powers may be delegated in the former case but not in the latter.

## DELEGATION TO MEMBER STATES

In view of the special position of national governments in the Community structure, it is desirable to give separate treatment to the question of delegation to Member States. At the outset it is necessary to emphasize the distinction between a delegation of powers and a direction to a Member State to exercise its own powers in a particular way. The latter is very common: one form of Community act – the directive – was designed for just this purpose. Delegation of powers, on the other hand, is comparatively rare. The reason is that it is not generally necessary for powers to be transferred to Member States: they normally possess sufficient powers in their own right. If, however, Member States have given up their powers in a particular area in favour of the Community, it will be possible for powers to be transferred back to them by means of a delegation.

The leading case on the topic is *Rey Soda*.[81] This was concerned with the common organization of the market in sugar, which had been brought about by Council

[79] See above.

[80] The Court also gave other grounds for its decision which were not concerned with the question of delegation.

[81] *Rey Soda v. Cassa Conguaglio Zucchero*, Case 23/75, [1975] ECR 1279.

Regulation 1009/67. In previous cases the European Court had laid down the principle that when the market in a particular product is brought under a common organization, the Member States lose their powers to regulate it, except as regards the implementation of Community rules.[82] Under Regulation 1009/67 the Commission was given power to take measures to prevent disturbances in the market as a result of alterations in the price level. These powers were to be exercised under the management committee procedure. Acting under this provision, the Commission passed a regulation delegating to Italy the power to take measures to prevent disturbances on the Italian market as a result of the increase on 1 July 1974 in the price of sugar expressed in Italian lire. The Italian Government exercised this power by passing a decree imposing a levy on sugar stockholders. The validity of this measure was challenged in the Italian courts and the European Court had to decide on the validity of the sub-delegation to the Italian Government.

The European Court ruled that the delegation by the Council to the Commission was valid, but the sub-delegation to the Italian Government was not. This ruling illustrates vividly the difference in the legal principles governing a delegation within the Community and a delegation to an outside body. The Court upheld the delegation to the Commission on the ground that, since the general principles had been laid down by Council Regulation 1009/67, it was legitimate to entrust the Commission with the task of implementation, even though this involved conferring wide discretionary powers on it. But the Commission had no power to delegate these discretionary powers to the Italian Government: only strictly defined powers of execution could be sub-delegated. Thus the same principle applies in the case of a delegation to a Member State as in the case of a delegation to a body such as the *Caisse*. In the *Rey Soda* case the Court seemed to have been influenced by the fact that one effect of the sub-delegation was to remove the exercise of the power from the supervision of the management committee; but there nevertheless seems no reason to believe that the Court would apply different principles where the management committee procedure was not applicable.

## CONCLUSIONS

The most important feature of the law in this area is the distinction between delegation to the Commission, which may involve wide discretionary power, and delegation to outside bodies (including Member States), which may be only of a very limited nature. Why has the European Court made this distinction? Perhaps it can be explained on the basis of the Court's underlying policy of strengthening the Community, and particularly the more federal elements in it. If this is correct, one would expect the Court to be just as favourable in its attitude towards delegation to the European Parliament. So far the Court has not had occasion to rule on this.

[82] See *per* Advocate General Mayras, *ibid.* at 1317–18.

## FORM

The main requirements of form laid down by the Treaties regarding legal acts of the Council and Commission are a reference to proposals and opinions and a statement of reasons.

### PROPOSALS AND OPINIONS

Article 253 [190] EC provides (in part) as follows:

> Regulations, directives and decisions adopted jointly by the European Parliament and the Council, and such acts adopted by the Council or the Commission, ... shall refer to any proposals or opinions which were required to be obtained pursuant to this Treaty.[83]

Three points should be made about this provision. The first concerns the word 'required'. This is qualified by the phrase 'pursuant to this Treaty', which suggests that requirements in measures made under the Treaty, as well as those in the Treaty itself, are covered.[84] Delegated legislation will therefore have to refer to proposals or opinions required by the empowering measure. Secondly, it should be noted that the obligation applies only to the kinds of measures specified: legal acts *sui generis*[85] are not covered.[86] Thirdly, it has been held by the European Court that it is sufficient if reference is made to the fact that the opinion has been obtained: it is not necessary to specify the contents of the opinion or to attempt to refute any objections raised.[87]

The main cases where the obligation will apply are proposals from the Commission and consultations with the European Parliament,[88] the Economic and Social Committee, and the Committee of the Regions. In the case of delegated legislation, reference should be made to consultations with the management committee where this procedure applies.

### REASONS

The most important formal requirement is the obligation to give reasons. This is laid down in the same provisions. Article 253 [190] EC states:

> Regulations, directives and decisions adopted jointly by the European Parliament and the Council, and such acts adopted by the Council or the Commission, shall state the reasons on which they are based . . .[89]

[83] Art. 162 Euratom is the same except that there is no reference to acts adopted jointly by the Parliament and the Council.

[84] Lauwaars, p. 150.

[85] Legal acts *sui generis* are discussed above.

[86] See *Commission v. Council (ERTA)*, Case 22/70, [1971] ECR 263 (para. 98 of the judgment). It is possible, however, that in certain cases an obligation of this kind might apply by virtue of some other provision.

[87] See *ISA v. High Authority*, Case 4/54, [1955] ECR 91 at 100. See also Lauwaars, p. 151.

[88] It is interesting to note that the Council has, since 1969, adopted the practice of referring to consultations with the European Parliament even where these are *not* required: see Parliamentary Question No. 316 of 1971, JO 1972, C18/3 at 18/4. There is of course no obligation to do this.

[89] Art. 162 Euratom is the same, except that there is no reference to acts adopted jointly by the Parliament and the Council. There are also a number of provisions applying in specific circumstances: see Arts 85(2) [89(2)], 226 [169], and 227 [170] EC.

It is interesting to note that there is no *general* obligation to give reasons in the law of most Member States (e.g., England, France, Italy, and Belgium), though in all these countries reasons must be given in certain cases. (In Germany and the Netherlands, on the other hand, there *is* a general obligation to give reasons for administrative acts.) The Community provision is therefore different from (some would say, in advance of) the law of many Member States. It is particularly remarkable that the requirement of reasons applies not only to administrative acts, but also to legislation. Even in Germany and the Netherlands, the requirement of reasons does not extend this far.[90]

The purpose of the requirement has been explained by the European Court in the *Brennwein* case (*Germany v. Commission*):[91]

> In imposing upon the Commission the obligation to state reasons for its decisions, Article 253 [190] is not taking mere formal considerations into account but seeks to give an opportunity to the parties of defending their rights, to the Court of exercising its supervisory functions and to Member States and to all interested nationals of ascertaining the circumstances in which the Commission has applied the Treaty.

What the Court meant by this is as follows. As regards the parties, reasons will help them in two ways: if they know why the enacting authority[92] adopted the act in question, they will be able to address representations to it to persuade it to change its mind; they will also be in a better position to decide whether to bring legal proceedings to have it set aside. As regards the Court, a statement of reasons will be of assistance in deciding on the validity of the act; while third parties (including Member States) will find it useful to know the policies followed by the enacting authority so that they can appreciate the way the power is likely to be exercised in the future.

Two further purposes that will be served by the requirement of reasoning are that the European Parliament will be able to give a better-informed opinion when the draft comes before it; and the enacting institution will itself be forced to consider exactly why it is adopting the act, and this might induce it to make modifications.[93]

In discussing the effect of the requirement of reasoning, two questions must be considered: the scope of the provision (to which acts does it apply?), and its content (what constitutes sufficient reasoning?). As far as the scope is concerned, the answer is given in Article 253 [190] EC itself. It applies to regulations, directives, and decisions adopted by the Council or Commission, and to such acts adopted by the Parliament and Council jointly.[94] It makes no difference whether the institution in question is acting under a power conferred by the Treaties or a power delegated to it by another institution.[95]

In the *ERTA* case,[96] the European Court held that the requirement of reasoning did not apply to the act *sui generis* in issue there.[97] However, such acts may be adopted in

[90] See Hen, 'La motivation des actes des institutions communautaires' (1977) 13 CDE 49.

[91] Case 24/62, [1963] ECR 63 at 69. For a more recent formulation of the same idea, see *REWEHandelsgesellschaft Nord v. Haupzollamt Kiel*, Case 158/80, [1981] ECR 1805 at para. 25 of the judgment.

[92] In *Germany v. Commission* the enacting authority was the Commission, but the Court's statement would apply equally where it was the Council.

[93] See Lauwaars, p. 153.

[94] In the special cases covered by Arts 226 [169] and 227 [170] EC, the requirement of reasoning applies also to an opinion.

[95] *Schwarze*, Case 16/65, [1965] ECR 877 at 887.

[96] *Commission v. Council*, Case 22/70, [1971] ECR 263 (paras 97 and 98 of the judgment).

[97] It is possible that in some cases acts *sui generis* will have to be reasoned, perhaps on the basis of a general principle of law. See Lauwaars, p. 152 and n. 227.

special circumstances only: even if the empowering provision does not specify the nature of the measure to be adopted, it is reasonable to assume that the authors of the Treaties intended that the powers conferred on the Community institutions should, in the absence of special considerations, be exercised in the form of one of the acts listed in Articles 249 [189] EC or 161 Euratom, as the case may be. In support of this, it should be mentioned that the act in question in the *ERTA* case was not adopted in terms of any provision in the Treaty: it was a resolution[98] of the Council setting out the procedure to be followed in international negotiations with non-Member States. In the *ERTA* case itself, the Court referred to it as 'an act of a private nature'.[99]

Finally, if the Council or Commission delegates a power which it may exercise only in the form of one of the named acts, the delegate must also exercise it in such a form or, at least, must be made subject to the same requirement of reasoning as the delegating authority. This follows from the decision in the *Meroni* case,[100] where the Court said that a Community institution cannot delegate a greater power than it possesses itself and that consequently any requirements or restrictions that apply when the delegating authority exercises the power must also be imposed on the delegate. Failure to do this renders the delegation invalid. It will be remembered that in the *Meroni* case the Court specifically mentioned the requirement of reasoning.[101]

One may conclude from the above that the requirement applies to almost all acts having legal effects. Only in exceptional cases will the Council or Commission be absolved from it.

The next question is what constitutes sufficient reasons. The objectives which the requirement of reasoning is intended to serve were set out above. It would seem clear, as a matter of general principle, that the test for the sufficiency of the reasons given in a particular case should be derived from these objectives: the reasons given for an act are sufficient if, but only if, they permit the attainment of these objectives.[102] To do this, they must at the very least set out the factual background which the author of the act regards as relevant; they must specify the Treaty provision (or other source of legal authority) under which the act was adopted (its legal basis);[103] they must state the objectives which the act is designed to attain; and they should state why, in the opinion of the enacting authority, it is desirable to attain these objectives.

An important rule laid down by the European Court is that the degree of specificity required depends on the nature of the act in question: in the case of an act of a truly legislative nature, affecting general categories of persons (the normal type of regulation), it is sufficient if the reasoning is limited to broad outlines; in the case of an individual act, affecting only a specific person (the normal type of decision), on the other hand, more detail is required. The reason for this distinction is that a legislative act, by its very nature, is of general application. The circumstances in which it might possibly apply

[98] The Court itself called it a 'discussion', though this term seems inappropriate in English. (The French term was *délibération*.)

[99] At para. 98 of the judgment.

[100] *Meroni v. High Authority*, Case 9/56, [1958] ECR 133 (discussed above).

[101] See [1958] ECR at 171.

[102] See Lauwaars, p. 156.

[103] *Commission v. Council (Tariff Preferences)*, Case 45/86, [1987] ECR 1493. However, failure to refer to a precise provision will not result in the nullity of the act if other parts of the act make clear what its legal basis was: see para. 12 of the judgment.

can never be fully known in advance; consequently, it would be impractical to expect a high degree of specificity. An individual act, however, applies only to a particular case. All the relevant facts are known and it is therefore possible to give much fuller reasons.

An indication of what is required in the case of a legislative act was given by the judgment of the European Court in the *Beus* case:[104]

> The extent of the requirement laid down by Article 253 [190] of the Treaty to state the reasons on which measures are based, depends on the nature of the measure in question.
>
> It is a question in the present case of a regulation, that is to say, a measure intended to have general application, the preamble to which may be confined to indicating the general situation which led to its adoption, on the one hand, and the general objectives which it is intended to achieve on the other.
>
> Consequently, it is not possible to require that it should set out the various facts, which are often very numerous and complex, on the basis of which the regulation was adopted, or *a fortiori* that it should provide a more or less complete evaluation of those facts.

An example of what the Court expects in the case of an individual act is provided by the *Brennwein* case (*Germany v. Commission*).[105] Brennwein is an alcoholic drink distilled from wine. Large quantities were produced in Germany and most of the wine was imported from outside the Community. When the common external tariff came into operation there was a substantial increase in the duty on this wine and the German Government took the view that this posed a threat to the industry. They therefore asked the Commission for a quota of 450,000 hectolitres to be imported at the old rate of duty. The Commission took a decision granting only 100,000 hectolitres. The key passage in its reasoning was as follows:[106]

> On the basis of the existing information it has been possible to ascertain that the production of the wines in question within the Community is amply sufficient. The grant of a tariff quota of the volume requested might therefore lead to serious disturbances of the market in the products in question...

The Court held that this was insufficient. Instead of referring merely to 'the existing information', the Commission should have been more specific and given an indication of the evolution and size of the surpluses within the Community; secondly, it should have specified what the 'serious disturbances' were and shown why they would have resulted from the granting of the request. The decision was therefore quashed.

May the enacting authority incorporate by reference reasons given in another instrument? This happens quite often, especially in the case of agricultural measures fixing the levels of levies and refunds. These are usually changed at short notice and it is common for the measure fixing the new rate to refer back to a previous measure in which the full criteria are set out. The practice of incorporating reasons by reference has been accepted by the European Court in a number of cases.[107] In the *Schwarze* case,[108] for

[104] Case 5/67, [1968] ECR 83 at 95; see also *Barge v. High Authority*, Case 18/62, [1963] ECR 259 at 280.

[105] Case 24/62, [1963] ECR 63.

[106] Taken from the opinion of Advocate General Roemer, at p. 72.

[107] See Lauwaars, pp. 161–2 for a summary of the cases; note that incorporation by reference was rejected in *Dalmas v. High Authority*, Case 1/63, [1963] ECR 303 (discussed by Lauwaars at p.161) but accepted again in later cases.

[108] Case 16/65, [1965] ECR 877.

example, the Court upheld a Commission decision fixing the free-at-frontier price of barley, even though it contained very little reasoning, because it included a reference to a previous decision which set out the general considerations applicable to the fixing of these prices. The Court stated that less strict criteria should be applied in cases of this kind in view of the short period of time within which the Commission must act, the confidentiality of the data on which their decisions are based, and the administrative difficulties which would result if detailed reasoning were required in every case.

In *Papiers Peints de Belgique v. Commission*,[109] on the other hand, the Commission had taken a decision imposing fines on a number of companies for breach of Article 81(1) [85(1)] EC. The reasoning referred to a judgment of the European Court in a previous case. The Court held that this was insufficient: a decision under Article 81 [85] which merely follows established policy may refer to the reasons given in a previous case, but a decision which breaks new ground – as was the case here – must be fully reasoned.

This shows that incorporation by reference is permissible only in certain cases. It is suggested that, where it is allowed, the reference should always be to a published document, or, where the measure itself need not be published, to a document available to all interested parties.[110] In deciding who are to be regarded as interested parties, one should remember the Court's statement that one of the purposes of the requirement of reasoning is to enable third parties to know the policies which the Community institutions pursue and the way in which they interpret their powers.[111]

Should insufficient reasoning be excused if interested parties are subsequently informed what the enacting authority's reasons were? Against such a principle one could argue that Article 253 [190] EC clearly provides that measures 'shall state the reasons on which they are based': allowing incorporation by reference is stretching Article 253 [190] to its limit; an *ex post facto* statement can in no sense be regarded as compliance. On the other hand, however, it might be said that to insist on the letter of Article 253 [190], when the reasons are in fact known, would serve no purpose.

In the *Brennwein* case[112] the Court appeared not to regard it as sufficient that the Commission provided the relevant data in Court; however, in the *Schwarze* case[113] the Court accepted that, in certain circumstances, the requirement of reasoning will be satisfied if the parties are supplied with the information once judicial proceedings have been commenced. Although the kind of decision in issue justified a relaxation of the requirement, it is hard to accept that Article 253 [190] has been satisfied when the party must wait not only until after the promulgation of the measure before being given the reasons, but must first commence legal proceedings. According to the Court,[114] one of the purposes of the requirement of reasoning is to enable the parties to defend their rights; but they will frequently not be in a position to know whether they ought to take legal action until they have seen the reasons. Moreover, the requirement is also supposed to protect third parties: they cannot be expected to commence proceedings just in order to see the reasons.[115]

[109] Case 73/74, [1975] ECR 1491. [110] Lauwaars, p. 163. [111] See above. [112] Above.
[113] Above. [114] See the quotation from the *Brennwein* case, set out above.
[115] Other cases in which information given privately to a party has been taken into account by the Court are *Netherlands v. Commission*, Case 13/72, [1973] ECR 27 and *De Wendel v. Commission*, Case 29/67, [1968] ECR 263.

A more acceptable compromise between administrative and legal requirements is to be found in *Michel v. European Parliament*,[116] a case concerning the rejection of an application to take part in the selection procedure for appointment to the staff of the Parliament. Here the Court annulled the decision, though the applicant had been informed of the reasons during the court proceedings. The Court stated that the reasons must in principle be given at the same time as the decision, but relaxed this requirement in view of the large number of applications (1,455 out of 1,740 were rejected). It held that the selection board was obliged in the letter of rejection to set out only the general criteria applied, but if the candidate asked for the particular reasons that led to his rejection, these must be supplied within the time-limit for commencing legal proceedings.

It will be evident from what has been said that the degree of detail required depends to a large extent on the circumstances of the case. Consequently, it is impossible to lay down precise rules as to what constitutes sufficient reasoning. It is, however, worth asking whether the rather ambitious objectives set out by the European Court in the *Brennwein* case are normally attained. As has been seen, the normal standards are of necessity relaxed in certain cases: in these circumstances the interests of third parties, and sometimes even of those directly involved, are liable to suffer. But are the objectives met even where these special circumstances do not exist?

The most serious problem is that the objectives set out by the Court will not be achieved unless the reasons given are the real ones. It has, however, been said that in the everyday practice of the Commission the substantive provisions of measures are drawn up first and the reasons are added afterwards by the legal service.[117] (In one case, the Secretariat of the Council even went so far as to change the statement of reasons after the measure had been adopted, but the Court regarded this as overstepping the mark and declared the measure invalid.)[118] In these circumstances there is a danger that the real reasons will not always be given: the legal service may be tempted to 'dress up' the measure by giving more acceptable reasons than those which the Commission actually had in mind. In this situation the requirement of reasons would degenerate into an empty formality.

One can conclude that, while the requirement of reasoning undoubtedly serves a useful purpose, the objectives set out in the *Brennwein* case are not fully attained.

## PUBLICATION AND NOTIFICATION

At one time, Article 254 [191] EC required only regulations to be published in the Official Journal.[119] Directives and decisions did not have to be published (though in practice they often were), but had to be notified to the persons to whom they were

[116] Case 195/80, [1981] ECR 2861. See also *Bonu v. Council*, Case 89/79, [1980] ECR 553 at para. 6 of the judgment; and *European Parliament v. Innamorati*, Case C-254/95 P, [1996] ECR I-3423 at paras 21–34, where the European Court held that, while reasons must be given for a decision rejecting an application to take part in a selection test, reasons need not be given for the marks awarded to a candidate in such a test, nor are the examiners required to inform candidates of the criteria used in marking such tests.

[117] Hen, 'La motivation des actes des institutions communautaires' (1977) 13 CDE 49 at 54 and 90.

[118] *United Kingdom v. Council*, Case 131/86, [1988] ECR 905 (paras 31–9 of the judgment).

[119] Previously known as the 'Official Journal of the European Communities', it was renamed 'Official Journal of the European Union' by the Treaty of Nice. It is published in each of the official languages.

addressed.[120] One of the changes brought about by the Treaty on European Union was that directives of the Council or Commission must now also be published in the Official Journal if they are addressed to all Member States. Moreover, all regulations, directives, and decisions adopted jointly by the Parliament and the Council must be published in the Official Journal.[121] Under the Rules of Procedure of the Council, all other directives and decisions (as well as recommendations and opinions) are published in the Official Journal, unless the Council or COREPER decides otherwise.[122]

Instruments which have to be published in the Official Journal enter into force on the date specified in them or, in the absence thereof, on the twentieth day following that of their publication. Instruments which have to be notified to the person to whom they are addressed take effect upon notification.[123] Publication and notification are not, however, constitutive requirements: an act which has not been published or notified is nevertheless an act. Failure to publish or notify does not affect its existence, but only its legal consequences. This was decided by the European Court in a number of cases concerning a provision under which the High Authority was empowered to make decisions only up to a certain date. The decisions in question had been made before this date, but had been notified to the addressees only afterwards. The Court held they were valid.[124] In a similar case concerning a regulation, it was held that the validity of the measure was not affected by the fact that publication took place only after the date in question.[125]

## FURTHER READING

RH Lauwaars, Chapters II and III.

Le Tallec and Ehlermann, 'La motivation des actes des Communautés européennes' [1966] RMC 179.

Marenco, 'Les conditions d'application de l'article 235 du traité CEE' [1970] RMC 147.

Lesguillons, 'L'extension des compétences de la CEE par l'article 235 du traité de Rome' [1974] Annuaire Français de Droit International 886.

Hen, 'La motivation des actes des institutions communautaires' (1977) 13 CDE 49.

Bradley, 'The European Court and the Legal Basis of Community Legislation' (1988) 13 ELRev. 379.

Bradley, 'Comitology and the Law: Through a Glass Darkly' (1992) 29 CMLRev. 693.

Emiliou, 'Subsidiarity: An Effective Barrier against "the Enterprises of Ambition"?' (1992) 17 ELRev. 383.

120 Similar provisions were found in Art. 163 Euratom; they still stand.

121 They also have to be signed by the Presidents of both institutions.

122 Council Decision 2006/683, OJ 2006 L285/47, Art. 17(2)(d).

123 It might be thought that this would mean that such acts could never be retroactive. However, this is possible at least in those cases where the effect of the act is beneficial to the addressee: see *Rewe-Zentrale des Lebensmittel-Großhandels*, Case 37/70, [1971] ECR 23. This question is discussed further in Chap. 5.

124 See Lauwaars, pp. 166–7 and the cases cited there.

125 *Hauptzollamt Bielefeld v. König*, Case 185/73, [1974] ECR 607 (paras 5–8 of the judgment). It has also been held that irregularities in the procedure for notification of a decision do not constitute a ground for its annulment: *ICI v. Commission*, Case 48/69, [1972] ECR 619 at 652 (paras 39–44 of the judgment).

Toth, 'The Principle of Subsidiarity in the Maastricht Treaty' (1992) 29 CMLRev. 1079.

Lenaerts, 'Regulating the Regulatory Process: "Delegation of Powers" in the European Community' (1993) 18 ELRev. 23.

Monar, 'Interinstitutional Agreements: The Phenomenon and its Dynamics after Maastricht' (1994) 31 CMLRev. 693.

Bermann, 'Taking Subsidiarity Seriously: Federalism in the European Community and the United States' (1994) 94 Columbia Law Rev. 331.

Emiliou, 'Opening Pandora's Box: The Legal Basis of Community Measures before the Court of Justice' (1994) 19 ELRev. 488.

Emiliou, 'Subsidiarity: Panacea or Fig Leaf?', in David O'Keeffe and Patrick M. Twomey, *Legal Issues of the Maastricht Treaty* (1994), p. 65.

Schilling, 'A New Dimension of Subsidiarity: Subsidiarity as a Rule and a Principle' (1994) 14 YEL 203.

Steiner, 'Subsidiarity under the Maastricht Treaty' in David O' Keeffe and Patrick M. Twomey, *Legal Issues of the Maastricht Treaty* (1994), p. 49.

Toth, 'A Legal Analysis of Subsidiarity' in David O'Keeffe and Patrick M. Twomey, *Legal Issues of the Maastricht Treaty* (1994), p. 37.

Toth, 'Is Subsidiarity Justiciable?' (1994) 14 ELRev. 268.

Dashwood, 'The Limits of European Community Powers' (1996) 21 ELRev. 113.

Dashwood, 'The Constitution of the European Union after Nice: Law-Making Procedures' (2001) 26 ELRev. 215.

A Estella, *The Principle of Subsidiarity and its Critique* (2002).

Von Bogdany, Arndt and Blast, 'Legal Instruments in European Union Law and their Reform: A Systematic Approach on an Empirical Basis' (2004) 23 YEL 91.

Weatherill, 'Competence Creep and Competence Control' (2004) 23 YEL 1.

Sacha Precha, *Directives in EC Law*, 2nd edn (2006).

# 5

# GENERAL PRINCIPLES OF LAW

In what way are 'general principles' a source of law? In answering this question, it is desirable to look for a moment at a problem of judicial psychology. In no legal system is it possible for legislation or other written sources of law to provide an answer to every question which comes before the courts. The judges are therefore obliged to create rules of law to decide the issues before them; but if their law-creating role becomes too apparent, they may be accused of going beyond their proper function and trespassing on the domain of the legislature. How are they to resolve this dilemma? In England the courts have traditionally resorted to the myth of the common law, the age-old tradition of customary law which, by a fiction, was regarded as being both immemorial and within the special cognizance of the judges. The European Court, on the other hand, has utilized general principles of law to cloak the nakedness of judicial law-making: the idea is that, if a ruling can be shown to be derived from a principle of sufficient generality as to command common assent, a firm legal foundation for the judgment will be provided. For this reason, the European Court has developed a doctrine that rules of Community law may be derived, not only from treaties and legislation, but also from the general principles of law.[1]

What is the origin of these general principles? They are derived from various sources, but the most important are the Community Treaties and the legal systems of the Member States. In the former case, the Court declares that a specific provision in one of the Treaties is an application of some more general principle which is not itself laid down in the Treaty. This is then applied in its own right as a general principle of law. An example of this is Article 12 [6] EC which prohibits all discrimination based on nationality between Community citizens as regards matters within the scope of the Treaty. This, together with other texts, has been used by the Court as the foundation for a general doctrine of equality which forbids arbitrary discrimination on any ground (discussed below). Another example is Article 36 ECSC[2] which provided that, in an

[1] It must not be forgotten that 'general principles of law' are also one of the sources of international law, recognized in Article 38(1)(c) of the Statute of the International Court of Justice. Unlike the Statute of the International Court, however, the Community Treaties contain no reference to general principles of law as a general source of Community law. Their adoption by the European Court as such a source may, therefore, have been inspired by the role they play in international law. See, further, Akehurst, 'The Application of General Principles of Law by the Court of Justice of the European Communities' [1981] BYIL 29.

[2] The ECSC Treaty has now expired.

appeal against a fine or penalty, the applicant could claim that the measure which he had contravened was invalid. In *Meroni v. High Authority*[3] the applicant wished to invoke this plea in a case involving not a fine, but a levy (tax). Article 36 could not apply, but the Court held that this provision was a particular application of the general principle that all legislative measures may be challenged indirectly. This general principle was then applied to the case at hand so as to allow the applicant to challenge the measure. It will be noticed that this reasoning involves two stages: the first is inductive, in which the Court derives a general principle from specific provisions in the Treaty; the second stage is deductive – here the Court arrives at a solution to the particular issue before it by applying the general principle. It should be stressed that when the Court acts in this way, the legal source of its decision is not the Treaty but the general principle.

When the Court looks to national law for inspiration, it is not necessary that the principle should be accepted by the legal systems of all the Member States. It would be sufficient if the principle were generally accepted by the legal systems of most Member States, or if it was in conformity with a trend in the Member States, so that one could say that the national legal systems were developing towards it.[4] It must again be emphasized, however, that whatever the factual origin of the principle, it is applied by the European Court as a principle of Community law, not national law.

It should also be mentioned that the Treaties themselves provide some justification for recourse to general principles as a source of law. First, there is Article 220 [164] EC,[5] the first paragraph of which states: 'The Court of Justice shall ensure that in the interpretation and application of this Treaty the law is observed.' It is usually thought that here the word 'law' must refer to something over and above the Treaty itself; if correct, this means that Article 220 [164] not only entitles, but also obliges, the Court to take general principles into account.

There is a more specific provision in Article 230 [173] EC. This Article lays down (among other things) the grounds on which a Community act may be annulled by the Court.[6] One of these grounds is 'infringement of this Treaty, or of any rule of law relating to its application'. The phrase 'any rule of law relating to its application' must refer to something other than the Treaty itself and it has been used by the Court as the basis for the doctrine that a Community act may be quashed for infringement of a general principle of law.

The third Treaty provision is Article 288 [215] (second paragraph) EC.[7] This is concerned with non-contractual liability (tort) and it expressly provides that the liability of the Community is based on 'the general principles common to the laws of the Member States'. This is discussed in detail in Chapter 16, below; all that need be said here is that, in spite of the wording of the provision, the Court is prepared to apply principles of law

[3] Case 9/56, [1958] ECR 133.

[4] See *Hoogovens v. High Authority*, Case 14/61, [1962] ECR 253 at 283–4, where Advocate General Lagrange said that the Court is not content to adopt the common denominator between the different systems but 'chooses from each of the Member States those solutions which, having regard to the objects of the Treaty, appear to it to be the best'.

[5] Art. 136 Euratom contains similar provisions.

[6] There is an identical provision in Art. 146 Euratom.

[7] There is an identical provision in Art. 188 Euratom.

even if they are not found in the legal system of every Member State. In other words, it adopts the same free and independent approach to the elaboration of its case law as in those areas where there is no express Treaty obligation to apply general principles of law.

The general principles of law are, therefore, an independent source of law and there can be little doubt that the Court would have applied them even if none of the Treaty provisions mentioned above had existed. It should not, however, be thought that the Court always makes express reference to general principles whenever it propounds new rules of law. Sometimes it simply states a rule without any express indication of its source; or it may give a justification based on policy or the general requirements of the Community legal system. However, if a formal source for such rules were required, it could always be found either on the basis of a wide interpretation of a written text or on the basis of the general principles.

What general principles has the Court so far adopted? It is impossible to enumerate them all, but some of the more important will now be discussed.

## FUNDAMENTAL HUMAN RIGHTS

In spite of their importance in the world today, fundamental human rights were not mentioned in the original Treaties and it was only later that they came to play a significant role in Community law. Moreover, it is probably fair to say that the conversion of the European Court to a specific doctrine of human rights has been more a matter of expediency than conviction. How this came about is as follows.

One of the most strongly pursued objectives of the European Court has always been to ensure the effectiveness of Community law and this in turn has led to the doctrine of the supremacy of Community law over national law, a doctrine which the European Court has upheld with the greatest vigour. By and large, this doctrine has been accepted by the national courts; however, since the early days of the Community, German lawyers have had doubts whether Community law should prevail over the provisions of the German Constitution (*Grundgesetz*), especially those concerning fundamental human rights. There has been no difficulty in Germany regarding the supremacy of Community law over ordinary German law, including statutes of the Federal Parliament. However, all German laws, including federal statutes, are subordinate to the Constitution; and there is a special Federal Constitutional Court (*Bundesverfassungsgericht*) which has power to determine the constitutionality of legislation. Since their own national legislation had to comply with the principles of the Constitution, it was hardly surprising that some German lawyers took the view that Community law could not apply in Germany if it violated the fundamental human rights provisions of the *Grundgesetz*. The strong attachment of German lawyers to the concept of fundamental law, and especially fundamental human rights, is, of course, understandable in the light of German history.

In the 1960s, the argument that Community law should comply with the fundamental human rights provisions of the *Grundgesetz* was frequently put forward by German litigants both in German courts[8] and in the European Court. At first the European Court was unsympathetic.[9] However, it was soon apparent that the German courts found the doctrine very persuasive, and it became imperative for the European Court to take action to head off a possible 'rebellion'. The solution it adopted was to proclaim a Community concept of human rights and to make clear that it would itself annul any provision of Community law contrary to human rights.

The case in which the European Court announced the new doctrine was *Stauder v. City of Ulm*.[10] This concerned a Community scheme to provide cheap butter for recipients of welfare benefits. The applicant received war victims' welfare benefits in Germany and was therefore entitled to the cheap butter; however, he objected to the fact that he was obliged to present a coupon bearing his name and address in order to obtain the butter: he maintained that it was a humiliation to have to reveal his identity, and argued that this constituted a violation of his fundamental human rights. He therefore claimed that the Community decision in question was invalid in so far as it contained this requirement. The action was originally brought before the German courts and a reference was made to the European Court.

The European Court held that on a proper interpretation the Community measure did not require the recipient's name to appear on the coupon.[11] It then continued:[12] 'Interpreted in this way the provision at issue contains nothing capable of prejudicing the fundamental human rights enshrined in the general principles of Community law and protected by the Court.' This recognized that fundamental human rights are a general principle of Community law.

Next came the *Internationale Handelsgesellschaft* case,[13] which concerned the Common Agricultural Policy. In order to control the market in certain agricultural products, a system had been introduced under which exports were permitted only if the exporter first obtained an export licence. When application was made for the licence, the exporter had to deposit a sum of money which would be forfeit if he failed to make the export during the period of validity of the licence. The applicants in this case, however, claimed that the whole system was invalid as being contrary to fundamental human rights. One principle invoked was that of proportionality. This is a doctrine of German constitutional law under which public authorities may impose on the citizen only those obligations which are necessary for attaining the public objective in question.[14] It was argued in the German *Verwaltungsgericht* (administrative court) where the proceedings commenced that the relevant Community measure was invalid for violating the German Constitution, and the question of its validity was referred to the European Court.

[8] For summaries of the German cases, see Brinkhorst and Schermers, *Judicial Remedies in the European Communities*, pp. 143–54 and *Supplement*, pp. 72–7.

[9] See *Stork v. High Authority*, Case 1/58, [1959] ECR 17 at 26; and *Geitling v. High Authority*, Cases 36–8, 40/59, [1960] ECR 423 at 438.

[10] Case 29/69, [1969] ECR 419.

[11] This aspect of the case was discussed in Chap. 2.

[12] Para. 7 of the judgment.

[13] Case 11/70, [1970] ECR 1125. See also *EVGF v. Köster*, Case 25/70, [1970] ECR 1161 at para. 22 of the judgment.

[14] This doctrine has actually been adopted by the European Court as a general principle in its own right: see below.

The European Court first stated that the validity of Community measures cannot be judged according to the rules or concepts of national law: only Community criteria may be applied. Consequently, even a violation of the fundamental human rights provisions of a Member State's constitution could not impair the validity of a Community provision. Having said this, however, the Court then sweetened the pill by adding:[15]

> However, an examination should be made as to whether or not any analogous guarantee inherent in Community law has been disregarded. In fact, respect for fundamental rights forms an integral part of the general principles of law protected by the Court of Justice. The protection of such rights, whilst inspired by the constitutional traditions common to the Member States, must be ensured within the framework of the structure and objectives of the Community. It must therefore be ascertained, in the light of the doubts expressed by the Verwaltungsgericht, whether the system of deposits has infringed rights of a fundamental nature, respect for which must be ensured in the Community legal system.

The Court then examined the system in detail but concluded that no fundamental right had been violated by it.

It will be noticed that the *dictum* quoted above goes beyond that in the *Stauder* case in one important respect: it states that the concept of human rights applied by the Court, while deriving its validity solely from Community law, is nevertheless 'inspired' by national constitutional traditions.

A further step was taken in *Nold v. Commission.*[16] This case concerned a Commission decision under the ECSC Treaty which provided that coal wholesalers could not buy Ruhr coal direct from the selling agency unless they agreed to purchase a certain minimum quantity. Nold was a Ruhr wholesaler who was not in a position to meet this requirement and consequently had to deal with an intermediary. He claimed that the decision was a violation of his fundamental human rights, partly because it deprived him of a property right and partly because it infringed his right to the free pursuit of an economic activity. He therefore brought proceedings before the European Court under Article 33 ECSC for the annulment of the decision.

The Court appeared to recognize the two rights as principles of Community law, but held that they must not be regarded as absolute and unqualified: they are subject to limitations 'justified by the overall objectives pursued by the Community', and 'mere commercial interests or opportunities' are outside their scope. No infringement had therefore taken place.

In the course of its judgment, the European Court made the following statement:[17]

> As the Court has already stated, fundamental rights form an integral part of the general principles of law, the observance of which it ensures. In safeguarding these rights, the Court is bound to draw inspiration from constitutional traditions common to the Member States, and it cannot therefore uphold measures which are incompatible with fundamental rights recognised and protected by the constitutions of those States.

[15] At 1134. [16] Case 4/73, [1974] ECR 491. [17] At 507.

> Similarly, international Treaties for the protection of human rights on which the Member States have collaborated or of which they are signatories, can supply guidelines which should be followed within the framework of Community law.

This goes beyond the statement in the *Handelsgesellschaft* case in two respects: first, it makes clear that a Community measure in conflict with fundamental rights will be annulled; secondly, it reveals a new source of 'inspiration' for these rights – international treaties.

A detailed discussion of human rights is to be found in *Hauer v. Land Rheinland-Pfaltz*,[18] a case concerning a Community regulation which imposed a temporary ban on all new planting of vines. Hauer owned land in Germany which she wanted to plant as a vineyard and was prevented from doing so by the regulation. She began proceedings before the German courts and a reference was made to the European Court, which accepted as principles of Community law the right to property and the freedom to pursue a trade or profession but, after pointing out that these rights are not absolute, found that the Community measure was justified in the general interest and thus fell within an exception to the rights. The judgment is of particular interest because the European Court not only referred to particular provisions in the constitutions of three Member States (Germany, Italy, and Ireland) in order to establish that the right to property is subject to restrictions, but also analysed in some detail the relevant provisions of the European Convention on Human Rights.

The cases discussed show that the Court's approach to fundamental rights is a little different from its approach to other general principles of law. The reason is that the acceptance of an express doctrine of fundamental rights was prompted by the desire to persuade the German courts to accept the supremacy of Community law even in the case of an alleged conflict with the fundamental rights provisions of the *Grundgesetz*. In view of this, national provisions are likely to be much more influential than in the case of other general principles. However, the European Court will never admit to applying national law as such; this is why it puts forward the notion that the Community concept of fundamental rights is merely 'inspired' by the philosophical concepts underlying the national provisions. It follows that there is no rule of law that a particular right will be accepted as fundamental by the European Court if it is protected in the constitutions of some of the Member States, or even a majority of them.[19] As was said extra-judicially by a member of the European Court, Judge Mancini:

> [T]he Court does not have to go looking for maximum, minimum or average standards. The yardstick by which it measures the approaches adopted by the various legal systems

[18] Case 44/79, [1979] ECR 3727.

[19] Some authorities take a different view. They argue that any right constitutionally protected in even one Member State must, as a matter of law, be accepted as a fundamental right at the Community level. See *per* Advocate General Warner, *IRCA*, Case 7/76, [1976] ECR 1213 at 1237, who reasoned as follows: Community law owes its existence to a partial transfer of sovereignty by the Member States to the Community; but since a Member State cannot be regarded as having included in that transfer the power to legislate contrary to rights protected by its constitution, it must be assumed that the Community has no power to infringe rights embodied in the constitution of *any* Member State. A similar view has been expressed by Schermers, 'The European Communities Bound by Fundamental Human Rights' (1990) 27 CMLRev. 249 at 253–5. The European Court has not, however, accepted this argument.

derives from the spirit of the Treaty and from the requirements of a Community which is in the process of being built up.[20]

In other words, it all depends on the policy of the European Court. If the right in question were generally accepted throughout the Community and did not prejudice fundamental Community aims, it is probable that the Court would, as a matter of policy, accept it as a fundamental right under Community law, even if it was constitutionally protected in only one Member State. The position would be different, however, if it was controversial.

Abortion is the best example of a controversial right. The right to life of the unborn is constitutionally protected in Ireland[21] and, as a result, abortion is prohibited there.[22] The right enjoys more limited constitutional protection in Germany.[23] In many other Member States, however, the right of a pregnant woman to choose whether to give birth or have an abortion, though not constitutionally protected,[24] is strongly supported by public opinion. In these circumstances, for the European Court to accept either the right to life of the unborn or the right to choose as a fundamental right would cause intense hostility in one part of the Community or another. The appropriate course, therefore, is to let each Member State decide for itself.

The issue came before the European Court in *SPUC v. Grogan*,[25] a case in which a private organization, the Society for the Protection of Unborn Children, brought legal proceedings before the Irish courts to prevent student unions in Ireland from publicizing the addresses of British abortion clinics. The Society based its case on the provision of the Irish Constitution upholding the right to life of the unborn.[26] The students raised a defence under Community law: they argued that abortion was a service within the terms of Article 49 [59] EC and that Community law therefore prohibited Ireland from placing restrictions on the right of Irish residents to have abortions in another Member State. The European Court accepted that abortion clinics perform a service for the purpose of Article 49 [59] if their activities are legal in the Member State where they are located. Subject to certain exceptions, this would normally mean that they could publicize their activities in other Member States.[27] However, the Court held that the defendants could not benefit from this right because they were not acting on behalf of the abortion clinics: they were simply trying to help their fellow students.

[20] Mancini, 'Safeguarding Human Rights: The Role of the Court of Justice of the European Communities' (Johns Hopkins University, Bologna, Occasional Paper 62, March 1990), quoted in Phelan, 'Right to Life of the Unborn *v.* Promotion of Trade in Services: The European Court of Justice and the Normative Shaping of the European Union' (1992) 55 MLR 670 at 674.

[21] See Art. 40.3.3 of the Constitution of Ireland.

[22] There is an exception where there is a real and substantial risk to the life, as distinct from the health, of the mother.

[23] See the decision of the *Bundesverfassungsgericht* of 28 May 1993, Entscheidungen des Bundesverfassungsgerichts 39, 1 [44]; see Forder, 'Abortion: A Constitutional Problem in European Perspective' (1994) 1 Maastricht J. of European and Comparative Law 56.

[24] The only Western country in which abortion rights are constitutionally protected appears to be the United States: see *Roe v. Wade*, 410 US 113 (1973), a case somewhat battered in recent times, but still good law.

[25] Case C-159/90, [1991] ECR I-4685.

[26] Art. 40.3.3.

[27] See *GB-INNO-BM*, Case C-362/88, [1990] ECR I-667. This case concerned free movement of goods, but the same principle probably applies to services: see para. 25 of the judgment in *SPUC v. Grogan* (above).

It was argued by the Society that abortion cannot be regarded as a service for Community purposes because it is immoral. The Court refused to accept this. It said that it could not substitute its judgment for that of the Member State in which the abortion clinics were situated. It has been criticized for this;[28] but if it had accepted the argument, it would have meant that Ireland's anti-abortion views would have been forced on other Member States: British abortion clinics would not have been entitled to benefit from Community law even when receiving patients from Member States where abortion is legal.

On the other hand, it would be equally wrong if Community law had the effect of undermining the Irish Constitution in so far as it operates in Ireland. Even if one ignores developments which took place subsequent to the judgment,[29] however, it is doubtful whether it could have this effect. If British abortion clinics had sought to advertise in Ireland in contravention of Irish law, they could have been prevented from doing so under the public policy proviso contained in Article 46(1) [56(1)] EC.[30] Resort to the proviso would have been precluded only if the right to an abortion had been held by the European Court to constitute a fundamental human right, an unlikely eventuality.

International treaties constitute the second source of 'inspiration' for the Community concept of fundamental human rights. If a Community measure were contrary to a human right embodied in a treaty to which a Member State was a party, the Member State might be unwilling to apply it on its territory for fear of breaching the treaty.[31] For this reason, what was said previously regarding constitutionally protected rights applies also to rights protected by treaties.

[28] See, e.g., Phelan, 'Right to Life of the Unborn *v.* Promotion of Trade in Services: The European Court of Justice and the Normative Shaping of the European Union' (1992) 55 MLR 670.

[29] A Protocol attached to the Treaty on European Union (Maastricht Agreement) and to the Treaties establishing the European Communities now provides that nothing in any of the Community Treaties affects the application in Ireland of Art. 40.3.3 of the Irish Constitution (the provision on the right to life of the unborn); however, a subsequent Declaration adopted on 1 May 1992 at a meeting in Guimares, Portugal, states, as a 'legal interpretation', that it was the intention of the Member States that this Protocol should not limit freedom to travel between Member States or, in accordance with conditions which may be laid down, in conformity with Community law, by Irish legislation, freedom to obtain or make available in Ireland information relating to services lawfully available in other Member States. Following a referendum held on 25 November 1992, the Irish Constitution was amended by the addition of provisions specifying that Art. 40.3.3 does not limit freedom to travel to another state or freedom to obtain or make available (subject to such conditions as may be laid down by law) information relating to services available in other states. As a result of these developments, there is probably no longer any conflict between the Irish Constitution and Community law in this regard, provided Irish legislation concerning information on abortion services available in other Member States does not infringe Community law. This is unlikely to be the case in view of the public policy proviso in Art. 46(1) [56(1)] EC.

[30] This applies to services by virtue of Art. 55 [66]. It allows Member States to make exceptions to Community rights on grounds of public policy. Each Member State decides its public policy for itself: *Adoui and Cornuaille*, Cases 115–16/81, [1982] ECR 1665 (para. 8 of the judgment).

[31] If the Member State became a party to the human rights treaty before it joined the Community, it would not be obliged to apply Community law to the extent that it conflicted with the previous treaty: see Art. 307 [234] EC, which provides that rights and obligations arising from such treaties 'shall not be affected by the provisions of this Treaty'. This provision, which does not apply where all the other parties to the treaty are EC Member States, does not, however, require the Community to uphold the right: it merely requires the Community not to prevent the Member State from upholding it.

It will be remembered that in the *Nold* case the European Court spoke of treaties on which Member States have 'collaborated' or to which they are signatories. This suggests that it is not necessary for the Member State actually to be a party to the treaty: it is sufficient if it took part in the negotiations leading to its conclusion; likewise signature of the treaty need not necessarily be followed by ratification.[32] This gives the Court considerable latitude in its search for guidelines.

The most important treaty in this respect is the European Convention for the Protection of Human Rights and Fundamental Freedoms. All the Member States are parties to it and there is no doubt that the rights protected by it are Community human rights. The European Court has made express reference to it on a number of occasions.[33] Other treaties to which it has referred include the European Social Charter of 18 November 1961 and Convention 111 of the International Labour Organization (25 June 1958).[34]

In spite of all its efforts, the European Court's attempt to head off a revolt by the German courts was not immediately successful. In the *Internationale Handelsgesellschaft* case, the German *Verwaltungsgericht* was not satisfied with the European Court's ruling and it proceeded to request a ruling from the German Constitutional Court. The Constitutional Court stated that, in the absence of a codified catalogue of human rights in Community law, it was impossible to decide whether the Community standard of human rights was adequate in terms of that laid down by the *Grundgesetz*; consequently, it was not prepared to accept the European Court's ruling as conclusive. It then examined the question itself and concluded that the Community measure in question did not violate the fundamental rights provisions of the *Grundgesetz*. However, it affirmed the supremacy of the latter and alluded to the possibility that Community measures might be declared inapplicable in Germany if they violated these provisions. It was only in 1986, in the *Wünsche Handelsgesellschaft* case, that the Constitutional Court announced that it would no longer review Community measures to ensure that they did not infringe human rights. It was content to leave this to the European Court.[35]

[32] The reason why the European Court said this may have been because France did not ratify the European Convention on Human Rights for a long time after the other Member States. By the time the judgment in *Nold* was given, France had in fact ratified it; however, the European Court might not have been aware of this when the judgment was drawn up, which took place some time before it was delivered (to allow for translation).

[33] See, for example, *Rutili*, Case 36/75, [1975] ECR 1219 (what restrictions may be placed on human rights); *Hauer v. Rheinland-Pfaltz*, Case 44/79, [1979] ECR 3727 (First Protocol: right to property); *Pecastaing v. Belgium*, Case 98/79, [1980] ECR 691 (Art. 6: right to a fair hearing); *Valsabbia v. Commission*, Case 154/78, [1980] ECR 907 (First Protocol); *National Panasonic v. Commission*, Case 136/79, [1980] ECR 2033 (Art. 8: privacy – respect for home and correspondence); *Musique Diffusion Française v. Commission*, Cases 100–3/80, [1983] ECR 1825 (Art. 6: right to a fair hearing); *R. v. Kirk*, Case 63/83, [1984] ECR 2689 (Art. 7: non-retroactivity of penal provisions); *Johnston v. Chief Constable of the RUC*, Case 222/84, [1986] ECR 1651 (Arts 6 and 13: right to a legal remedy); *Hoechst v. Commission*, Cases 46/87, 227/88, [1989] ECR 2859; *Dow Benelux v. Commission*, Case 85/87, [1989] ECR 3137, and *Dow Chemical Ibérica v. Commission*, Cases 97–9/87, [1989] ECR 3165 (Art. 8(1): inviolability of the home); *ERT*, Case C-260/89, [1991] ECR I-2925 (Art. 10(1): freedom of expression); *SPUC v. Grogan*, Case C-159/90, [1991] ECR I-4685 (Art. 10(1): freedom of expression); *X v. Commission*, Case C-404/92 P, [1994] ECR I-4737 (Art. 8: respect for private life – testing for AIDS).

[34] *Defrenne v. Sabena*, Case 149/77, [1978] ECR 1365 at para. 28 of the judgment.

[35] During this period the Constitutional Court never actually found any provision of Community law to be contrary to the *Grundgesetz*. For a fuller discussion of these cases, see Chap. 8.

Attempts to enhance the protection of human rights have also been made by the political institutions of the Community.[36] In 1976 the Commission submitted a report[37] to the European Parliament in which it expressed the belief that the best level of protection would be provided by the European Court through its doctrine of general principles of law, the flexibility of which would ensure that the law kept pace with changing needs. The Commission also called for a Joint Declaration by the three political institutions affirming their commitment to fundamental rights; this was made in 1977.[38] In it, the three institutions stressed the importance they attached to fundamental rights, as derived in particular from the constitutions of the Member States and the European Convention on Human Rights, and pledged to respect them in the exercise of their powers. No attempt was made to specify the rights in question. In 1986, there was a Joint Declaration against Racism and Xenophobia[39] by the same three institutions, and in 1989 the European Parliament adopted its own Declaration of Fundamental Rights and Freedoms, which spelt out in detail the rights which the Parliament thinks should be protected.[40] None of these instruments has the force of law, though it is possible that the European Court may 'draw inspiration' from them.

More recently, provisions on human rights have been embodied in the Treaties themselves. In addition to general references to fundamental rights in the Preambles to the Single European Act and the Treaty on European Union,[41] Article 6(2) [F(2)] of the Treaty on European Union provides:

> The Union shall respect fundamental rights, as guaranteed by the European Convention for the Protection of Human Rights and Fundamental Freedoms signed in Rome on 4 November 1950 and as they result from the constitutional traditions common to the Member States, as general principles of Community law.

This merely restates what the European Court has decided; nevertheless, it indicates the Member States' approval and support.[42] In addition, amendments brought in by the Treaty of Amsterdam now specify that respect for human rights is a precondition for

[36] For a full list of statements, declarations, and other political instruments adopted by the Community institutions and the Member States, see the European Court's Opinion in the *ECHR* case, Opinion 2/94, [1996] ECR I-1759 at 1768–9.

[37] 'The Protection of Fundamental Rights in the European Community', EC Bull., Supp. 5/76.

[38] Joint Declaration by the European Parliament, the Council and the Commission, 5 April 1977, OJ 1977, C103/1.

[39] Joint Declaration of the European Parliament, the Council and the Commission against Racism and Xenophobia, 11 June 1986, OJ 1986, C158/1.

[40] Declaration of Fundamental Rights and Freedoms of 1989, OJ 1989, C120/51; EC Bull. 4/1989. It is not clear from the text of the Declaration, which was adopted 'in the name of the peoples of Europe', whether the European Parliament intended that it should apply only to the Community or whether it was also addressed to the Member States. Art. 25 provides that it applies 'in the field of application of Community law'. This suggests that it might apply to Member States, but only when they are acting within this field. If this is the case, some of its provisions – for example, Art. 23, which abolishes the death penalty – seem hardly relevant. As regards the rights covered, in addition to those usually found in such instruments, there are some of a less traditional nature – for example, the right to social welfare (Art. 15); there is also a statement (Art. 24) that consumer protection and the protection of the environment 'shall form an integral part of Community policy'.

[41] An amendment to the latter under the Treaty of Amsterdam adds a reference to fundamental social rights.

[42] There is a further reference to human rights in the provisions on a Common Foreign and Security Policy (Art. 11(1) [J.1(1)] TEU); and the Provisions on Police and Judicial Co-operation in Criminal Matters state that

joining the Community[43] and that a Member State which persistently disregards them may have some of its rights under the Treaties suspended.[44]

## THE EUROPEAN CONVENTION ON HUMAN RIGHTS

In a report published in 1979, the Commission proposed that the Community should formally adhere to the European Convention on Human Rights.[45] This proposal was renewed in 1990: the Commission thought it was anomalous that, while acts of the Member States are subject to scrutiny by the organs set up under the Convention, the acts of the Community are not. Although it recognized the value of the European Court's work in developing a Community doctrine of human rights and acknowledged that the European Court draws inspiration from the Convention, it nevertheless felt that a danger existed that Community acts could infringe the rights protected under the Convention, or that those rights might be interpreted in different ways by the European Court and the European Court of Human Rights (the court set up under the Convention).[46] In response to this, the Council decided to ascertain from the European Court whether it was legally possible for the Community to become a party to the Convention. An Opinion was sought under a procedure laid down in Article 300 [228] EC, a procedure which will be explained in Chapter 6.[47]

In its Opinion, the Court ruled that the Community had no power to accede to the Convention without an amendment to the Community Treaties.[48] The grounds of the decision will be discussed in Chapter 6, below; all that need be said here is that the Court's ruling, while not unjustifiable, was remarkable for its detached and sober analysis of the law: the Court's normal enthusiasm for expanding the powers of the Community was conspicuous by its absence. It seems that it did not relish the prospect of a rival court – the European Court of Human Rights – having the final word on human rights in the Community.[49]

This decision constituted a setback for those who wanted the Community to join the Human Rights Convention. For some time thereafter, no progress was made. However, when the proposed Constitution of the EU was drawn up, it contained the necessary

one of the objectives of the European Union is the combating of racism and xenophobia (Art. 29 [K.1] TEU). There are also various other provisions which could be regarded as relating to human rights – for example, Art. 286 [213b] EC (data processing) and the following Declarations annexed to the Treaty of Amsterdam: Declaration 1 (abolition of the death penalty); Declaration 11 (status of churches and non-confessional organizations); and Declaration 22 (needs of disabled persons).

43 Arts 49 [O] and 6(1) [F(1)] TEU.

44 Arts 7 TEU, 309 EC, and 204 Euratom. These provisions, and those referred to in the previous footnote, are all discussed in Chap. 3.

45 'Accession of the Communities to the European Convention on Human Rights', EC Bull., Supp. 2/79.

46 See Press Release IP (90) 892, 31 October 1990.

47 On the difficulties that would arise if the Community were to adhere to the European Convention, see the House of Lords Select Committee on the European Communities, 71st Report, *Human Rights* (HL 362, 1979/80); for a full discussion, see McBride and Brown, 'The United Kingdom, the European Community and the European Convention on Human Rights' (1981) 1 YEL 167.

48 Opinion 2/94, [1996] ECR I-1759.

49 For a discussion of possible ways forward after this decision, see Toth, 'The European Union and Human Rights: The Way Forward' (1997) 34 CMLRev. 491.

provisions. If the Constitution were ever to be ratified, the Community could be expected to become a party to the Convention.

In recent years, the problem of a conflict between Community law and the Convention has become more pressing. As the Community is not a party to the Convention, it cannot itself incur responsibility for its infringement;[50] but could not the Member States (which are all parties to the Convention) incur responsibility if some act they were required by Community law to perform constituted a violation of the Convention? At first, the European Commission of Human Rights (now abolished) took a sympathetic view. It accepted that a party to the Convention cannot escape responsibility for the protection of human rights within its jurisdiction simply because its actions are required by an international agreement. It also accepted that it cannot escape liability simply by joining an international organization and conferring powers on it. However, it ruled that it could do so if the organization itself had an adequate system for the protection of human rights. Since it considered that the protection of human rights by the European Court was adequate, the Member States were protected from liability.[51]

Subsequently, the European Court of Human Rights seemed to take a different view. In *Matthews v. United Kingdom*[52] (discussed in Chapter 3), it held that the United Kingdom had infringed the Convention by not permitting residents of Gibraltar to vote in elections to the European Parliament. These elections are governed by an 'Act' under Articles [138] EC and 108 Euratom (discussed in Chapter 1).[53] The Member States ratified the Act as a treaty, and, though there is some controversy surrounding its legal status, it is best regarded as a treaty amending the relevant Community treaties.[54] This Act provides that it will apply only in respect of the United Kingdom itself, thus excluding Gibraltar.[55] The consequence was that Community law in the form of a treaty obligation precluded the United Kingdom from extending the franchise to Gibraltarians. The Human Rights Court, however, held that this was no defence.[56]

The decision could be reconciled with that of the Human Rights Commission on the ground that, since the Act has treaty status, the European Court cannot annul it for infringement of human rights. In this particular case, therefore, the European Court cannot provide an adequate system for the protection of human rights. However, in the *Matthews* case, the European Court of Human Rights made no attempt to reconcile it on this ground.

In a later case, however, the Human Rights Court reaffirmed the position adopted by the Human Rights Commission. This was in *Bosphorus Hava Yollari Turizm Ve Ticaret Anonim Sirketi v. Ireland*,[57] in which, sitting as a Grand Chamber, it had to decide

[50] *CFDT* (*Confédération Française Démocratique du Travail*) case, Application No. 8030/77, Decision of 10 July 1978, 13 Decisions and Reports 213 (European Commission of Human Rights).

[51] *M & Co.*, Application No. 13258/87, Decision of 2 February 1990, 64 Decisions and Reports 138.

[52] (1999) 28 EHRR 361.

[53] The Act was annexed to Council Decision 76/787, OJ 1976, L278/1.

[54] See Chap. 1.

[55] See Annex II.

[56] For further discussion, see Hartley, 'International Law and the Law of the European Union – A Reassessment' [2002] BYIL 1.

[57] [2006] 42 EHRR 1 (30 June 2005). The key reasoning is in paras 149–58.

whether Ireland had violated the human rights of a Turkish company by impounding an aircraft which it had leased from a Yugoslav (Serbian) airline.[58] The Irish Government had been required to impound the aircraft under an EC regulation adopted to impose sanctions on Serbia.[59] It claimed that since it had no option but to act as it did, it could not incur responsibility under the Human Rights Convention.

The Human Rights Court first held that the Convention does not prohibit a Contracting Party from transferring sovereign rights to an international organization, such as the European Community. However, such a Party remains responsible for acts and omissions of state organs even if they are taken in order to comply with an obligation under the law of the international organization. Nevertheless, government action to comply with an obligation under the law of the organization is justified as long as the organization itself protects fundamental rights – both as regards substantive guarantees and methods of redress – in a manner at least equivalent to that provided under the Convention.[60] If this is the case, the presumption will be that the State in question has not departed from the requirements of the Convention when it has done no more than carry out obligations flowing from its membership of the organization.[61] However, such a presumption may be rebutted if, in a particular case, the protection of Convention rights is manifestly deficient.[62]

Applying these principles to the case before it, the Human Rights Court decided, after a careful review of EC law, that the Community system provided a level of protection that was equivalent to that under the Convention.[63] There was, therefore, a presumption that Ireland had not infringed the Convention. The Court then looked at the protection afforded in the case in question and ruled that this was not manifestly deficient. So it gave judgment for Ireland. This case means that it will be rare (though not impossible) for Member States of the Community to be held to have infringed the Human Rights Convention where they are simply carrying out obligations under Community law.

## THE CHARTER OF FUNDAMENTAL RIGHTS

On 7 December 2000, the European Parliament, the Council, and the Commission 'solemnly proclaimed' the Charter of Fundamental Rights of the European Union, a text broadly similar to the European Convention on Human Rights.[64] The Charter has

[58] The relevant right was contained in Art. 1 of Protocol No. 1 to the Human Rights Convention (protection of property).

[59] The regulation was itself the consequence of a UN Security Council resolution.

[60] 'Equivalent' means comparable, not identical.

[61] The State in question remains responsible for acts falling outside its strict legal obligations.

[62] The Court distinguished the *Matthews* case on the ground that the infringement of human rights for which the United Kingdom was responsible followed directly from a treaty voluntarily concluded by the United Kingdom.

[63] Prior to the case before the Human Rights Court, there had been proceedings in the European Court of Justice (ECJ), in which it was held that the negative consequences of the regulation for the Turkish airline were justified by the importance of the aims pursued by the sanctions (putting an end to the war in Yugoslavia and the large-scale violations of human rights that took place there): *Bosphorus*, Case C-84/95, [1996] ECR I-3953.

[64] OJ 2000, C364.

no legal force, though this would be changed under the proposed EC Constitution if it were ever to go into effect.

## DO COMMUNITY HUMAN RIGHTS BIND THE MEMBER STATES?

In all the cases considered so far, human rights have been applied by the European Court against the Community, either to interpret or strike down Community measures. To what extent is the Community concept of human rights binding on the Member States? For a long time, the answer appeared to be that it had no direct application at all.[65] It has now become clear, however, that there are a number of situations in which Community law requires Member States to respect human rights (and possibly other general principles of Community law).

First, and most obviously, Member States will be indirectly bound by the Community concept of human rights whenever that concept is used to interpret provisions in the Treaties or Community legislation. This has always been the case. Secondly, where such a provision grants rights to individuals, but those rights are subject to a proviso allowing derogations on grounds such as public policy,[66] any derogations thus made by the national governments must not violate the Community concept of human rights.[67] Thirdly, when Member States implement Community rules – for example, by passing legislation – they are bound by human rights as understood in Community law.[68]

In addition to these rules, there are *dicta* by the European Court that Member States are also bound by the Community concept of human rights whenever they act within the scope of Community law. The Court has said that, when national legislation enters the field of application of Community law, the European Court must provide the national court with all the elements of interpretation necessary to enable the latter to assess the compatibility of the legislation with fundamental rights.[69] The implication is that the national court will be obliged to strike down, or not to apply, the national

[65] See *Defrenne v. Sabena*, Case 149/77, [1978] ECR 1365. For unsuccessful attempts to invoke the European Convention on Human Rights in the British courts on the ground that it is part of Community law, see *Allgemeine Gold und Silberscheideanstalt v. Commissioners of Customs and Excise* [1978] 2 CMLR 292, aff'd [1980] QB 390, CA; *Surjit Kaur v. Lord Advocate* [1980] 3 CMLR 79 (Court of Session). See further Drzemczewski, 'The Domestic Application of the European Human Rights Convention as European Community Law' (1981) 30 ICLQ 118.

[66] Such provisos are numerous in the Treaties.

[67] *ERT*, Case C-260/89, [1991] ECR I-2925 (para. 43 of the judgment); see also *Rutili v. Minister of the Interior*, Case 36/75, [1975] ECR 1219 (paras 31 and 32 of the judgment). The European Court has no power to strike down national legislation, but if it ruled that such legislation was contrary to Community law, the national court would be bound by such a ruling.

[68] *Wachauf*, Case 5/88, [1989] ECR 2609 (para. 19 of the judgment). It is not clear whether national implementing legislation must be struck down by the national courts if it infringes human rights, or merely that it must, if possible, be interpreted so as not to infringe human rights. The European Court said in the *Wachauf* case that Member States must 'as far as possible' apply Community rules in accordance with the requirements of human rights, a formulation repeated in *Bostock*, Case C-2/92, [1994] ECR I-955 (para. 16 of the judgment). This might suggest that the second alternative is correct. Of course, if the national implementing legislation was based on an incorrect interpretation of the Community rule, it might be invalid as a matter of national law.

[69] *ERT* (above) (at para. 42 of the judgment); *SPUC v. Grogan*, Case C-159/90, [1991] ECR I-4685 (at para. 31 of the judgment).

legislation if it fails the test. This could occur in those areas where national legislation is permitted only if justified under principles laid down by Community law.[70] In areas outside the scope of Community law, on the other hand, Member States are not bound by the Community concept of human rights.[71]

## HUMAN RIGHTS AS A JUSTIFICATION FOR RESTRICTING COMMUNITY LAW

Can human rights constitute a justification for what would otherwise be an infringement of Community law? This question first arose in *Schmidberger v. Austria*,[72] in which environmentalists had blocked a vital motorway through the Austrian Alps as part of a protest against pollution caused by the heavy trucks moving along it. The organizers gave the Austrian authorities advance notice of the demonstration, which lasted approximately thirty hours. The authorities decided not to ban the demonstration. They considered that it constituted a legitimate exercise of the rights of free expression and free assembly as guaranteed by the European Convention on Human Rights and the Austrian Constitution.

Schmidberger, a German company that carried goods between Germany and Italy on the motorway, claimed that the demonstration infringed its rights under Community law. It sued the Austrian Government for damages in an Austrian court, arguing that the Government was responsible. On a reference to the European Court, the latter held that free movement of goods is a basic Community right that must be protected by Member States. This meant that the Austrian Government would incur liability for its failure to keep the motorway open, unless it could show that its decision was justified. The right of free movement of goods is not absolute under Community law, but must be balanced against other considerations. The right of free expression must also be balanced against other interests. The Court held that, in balancing the two rights, the national Government has a wide measure of discretion. Since the Austrian Government had taken all reasonable steps to minimize disruption – the closure was widely publicized in advance and alternative routes designated – the Court held that no infringement of Community law had occurred.

The important point to note is the wide measure of discretion enjoyed by national governments. The Court did not say that it considered the closure of the motorway to be justified, but rather that the decision of the national government fell within the latter's area of discretion.

[70] In *Konstantinidis*, Case C-168/91, [1993] ECR I-1191 at 1211–13, it was argued by Advocate General Jacobs that, where the victim is an immigrant from another Community country, *any* infringement of human rights is a matter for Community law: his reason was that Community citizens would be less willing to move to another Member State if their human rights might be infringed there. The Court did not, however, accept this argument.

[71] This was expressly stated in the *dicta* in *ERT* (above) and *SPUC v. Grogan* (above). See also *Demirel*, Case 12/86, [1987] ECR 3719 (para. 28 of the judgment); *Kremzow*, Case C-299/95, [1997] ECR I-2629. However, a Member State which persistently disregards human rights may have some of its rights under the Treaties suspended: Arts 7 TEU, 309 EC and 204 Euratom (discussed above).

[72] Case C-112/00, [2003] ECR I-5659.

This was made even clearer in a later case. In *Omega*,[73] the German authorities had prohibited a German company from operating an establishment, known as a 'laserdrome', in which participants played at killing other participants by shooting them with lasers. The lasers were supplied by a British company, with which the German company had concluded a franchise agreement, thus raising issues of Community law. The German authorities had closed the 'laserdrome' on human rights grounds: they considered simulated killing an affront to human dignity, a principle enshrined in the German Constitution. The European Court accepted this justification, even though similar establishments operate freely in other Member States.

### INTERNATIONAL LAW AS A JUSTIFICATION FOR RESTRICTING HUMAN RIGHTS

Although international instruments, in particular the European Convention on Human Rights, can enhance the protection of human rights in the Community, they can also impose restrictions on them. The leading cases were discussed in Chapter 3.[74] Thus, if a UN Security Council resolution so requires, property can be seized without any judicial proceedings or hearing or other right of redress and without the owners even being told what they are supposed to have done wrong. The Community must carry out such resolutions, and Community concepts of human rights are ousted.[75] This shows that human rights in Europe rest on a less secure foundation than might have been supposed.[76]

## LEGAL CERTAINTY

Legal certainty – sometimes referred to as 'legal security' (*sécurité juridique*, in French) – is one of the most important general principles recognized by the European Court. It is a wide concept which cannot easily be explained in a few words, though predictability is probably the core aspect of it. The general idea of legal certainty is of course recognized by most legal systems; however, in Community law it plays a much more concrete role in the form of various sub-concepts which are regarded as applications of it. The most important of these are non-retroactivity, vested rights, and legitimate expectations.

### RETROACTIVITY AND VESTED RIGHTS

'Retroactivity' is a term often used by lawyers but rarely defined. On analysis it soon becomes apparent, moreover, that it is used to cover at least two distinct concepts. The

[73] Case C-36/02, [2004] ECR I-9609.

[74] See the section entitled 'Conflicting Treaties' and the sub-section entitled 'United Nations Law'.

[75] The one exception seems to be the international law doctrine of *jus cogens*, which might apply in the case of a very severe infringement of human rights – for example, torture or assassination.

[76] See, further, *European Parliament v. Council*, Cases C-317/04 and C-318/04, 30 May 2006.

first, which may be called 'true retroactivity', consists in the application of a new rule of law to an act or transaction which was completed before the rule came into force. The second concept, which will be referred to as 'quasi-retroactivity', occurs when a new rule of law is applied to an act or transaction in the process of completion.[77] Since the foundation of these concepts is the distinction between completed and pending transactions, it will be useful to give examples of each.

As the first example one may take a law imposing a customs duty on imported goods. Let us assume that the obligation to pay arises when the goods cross the frontier. Now, if a law is passed increasing the duty and it is provided that the new duty will apply to goods which crossed the frontier before the new law came into force, this will be a case of true retroactivity. Assume, however, that the new duty applies only to goods crossing the frontier after the law comes into force but it applies even if the importer was legally committed to import them before it came into force, for example by virtue of a contract. This will be a case of quasi-retroactivity.

As a second example one may take the granting of a licence by a public authority to a private citizen. If, after it has been granted, the authority withdraws it in circumstances such that the licensee is deemed never to have had a licence, one would have a case of true retroactivity. However, if it is withdrawn only for the future, but the withdrawal takes place before the expiration of its period of validity, one could say that this was a case of quasi-retroactivity.

These examples will make clear that true retroactivity can often cause severe injustice to the individual. In both examples given, one would say that the action of the public authority was unacceptable in the absence of special circumstances. In the case of quasi-retroactivity, the injustice is much less; but nevertheless it could be quite considerable in some circumstances. The importer might have calculated his profit margins on the assumption that the rate of duty would remain constant and he might face a loss if he is obliged to absorb the new duty. Likewise, the licensee might have committed himself to a capital outlay on the assumption that the licence would remain in force for its stated period of validity. In both cases of quasi-retroactivity, however, the injustice lies not so much in the fact of retroactivity as in the fact that the legitimate expectations of the person concerned have been upset. This will occur if he had reasonable grounds for assuming that the legal position would remain unchanged and he acted to his detriment on that assumption.

The concept of vested rights is normally no more than another aspect of retroactivity. Normally, a provision which destroys vested rights will be retroactive in the strict sense: in fact, one could say that one test whether a law is truly retroactive is whether it affects vested rights. The problem with this formulation, however, is that it raises two very difficult questions: what constitutes a right for this purpose, and when such a right should be regarded as vested.[78]

[77] See *per* Advocate General Roemer in *Westzucker*, Case 1/73, [1973] ECR 723 at 739. See also *Gardner & Co v. Cone* [1928] Ch. 995, *per* Maugham J. at 966. See further Letemendia, 'La rétroactivité en droit communautaire' (1977) 13 CDE 518 at 518–19.

[78] See, e.g., in *Westzucker*, Case 1/73, [1973] ECR 723, where it could be argued that, when Westzucker obtained an advance fixing certificate subject to the condition that the amount of the export refund would

In Community law, there are two rules on true retroactivity: first, there is a rule of interpretation that, in the absence of a clear provision, legislation is presumed not to be retroactive;[79] secondly, there is a substantive rule that prohibits retroactivity in general, but allows exceptions where the purpose of the measure could not otherwise be achieved, provided the legitimate expectations of those concerned are respected.[80]

An example of the first rule is provided by *Société pour l'Exportation des Sucres v. Commission*,[81] where the Commission had passed a regulation taking away the right of exporters to obtain cancellation of their export licences. The regulation was made on 30 June 1976 and was published in an issue of the Official Journal which was dated 1 July 1976 and which should have been published on that date. However, it was delayed by a strike and appeared only on 2 July. On 1 July the applicant applied for cancellation of certain licences but this was refused on the basis of the regulation. The Court, however, interpreted the regulation as coming into force only on the date of actual publication (2 July), so that it did not apply to the applicant. This ruling was given in spite of the fact that the regulation expressly stated that it would enter into force on 1 July: the Court presumably considered that the Commission would not have included this provision if it had known that publication would be delayed; in other words, there was no intention to apply the regulation retroactively.

*Amylum v. Council*[82] is an example of the second rule. Here, a regulation imposing a system of quotas and levies on producers of isoglucose (a kind of sugar) had been annulled in previous proceedings because the European Parliament had not been consulted. The Council then passed another regulation (after consulting the Parliament) which reimposed the system with retroactive effect. Proceedings were brought to annul the new regulation, but the Court held that the requirements for retroactivity had been met: the purpose of the regulation was to ensure that isoglucose producers were subject to the same production system as other sugar producers and this would not be the case if the regulation were not backdated; the legitimate expectations of the isoglucose producers had been respected since, in the circumstances of the case, they had good reason to expect the retrospective reimposition of the system. The regulation was therefore upheld.[83]

automatically be adjusted if the intervention price changed, he obtained a vested right to an increased refund in the event of an increase in the intervention price; the better view, however, is that the right was not vested until either the intervention price was increased or he actually exported the sugar.

[79] See *Kalsbeek v. Sociale Verzekeringsbank*, Case 100/63, [1964] ECR 565 at 575; *per* Advocate General Mayras in *Commission v. Germany*, Case 70/72, [1973] ECR 813 at 844; and *per* Advocate General Warner in *IRCA*, Case 7/76, [1976] ECR 1213 at 1237–9. This principle does not apply to procedural provisions: *Salumi*, Cases 212–17/80, [1981] ECR 2735.

[80] *Amylum v. Council*, Case 108/81, [1982] ECR 3107 at paras 4–17 of the judgment; *Racke*, Case 98/78, [1979] ECR 69 at para. 20; *Rewe-Zentrale des Lebensmittel-Großhandels*, Case 37/70, [1971] ECR 23, paras 17–19. See also *per* Advocate General Roemer in *Westzucker*, Case 1/73, [1973] ECR 723 at 739; *IRCA*, Case 7/76, [1976] ECR 1213, where the Court held that true retroactivity was not involved at all, but the Advocate General considered that it was.

[81] Case 88/76, [1977] ECR 709.

[82] Case 108/81, [1982] ECR 3107.

[83] This decision is not without disquieting implications, not least because it established the validity of a regulation which entirely nullified the effect of the Court's judgment in the earlier case.

## LEGITIMATE EXPECTATIONS

The principle of legitimate expectations is a concept derived from German law, where it is known as *Vertrauensschutz*. This was originally translated into English as 'protection of legitimate confidence', a phrase which corresponds more closely to the original German and to the French '*protection de la confiance légitime*'. It was, however, thought that this might be misleading in English; so 'legitimate expectations' is now generally used.[84] According to this principle, Community measures must not (in the absence of an overriding matter of public interest) violate the legitimate expectations of those concerned. It is the foundation of a rule of interpretation[85] as well as a ground for annulment of a Community measure;[86] most often, however, it is used as the basis for an action for damages for non-contractual liability (tort).

What constitutes a legitimate expectation? In answering this, a number of points must be considered. First of all, an expectation is not legitimate unless it is reasonable: the question here is whether a prudent man would have had the expectation. In deciding this, one must take all the circumstances into account: for example, in the case of a measure affecting grain dealers, one must ask whether a prudent dealer of reasonable knowledge and experience would have relied on the expectation; if he would not, the expectation is not legitimate.[87]

There is also a rule that if the person concerned was not acting in the normal course of business but was trying to take advantage of a weakness in the Community system to make a speculative profit, his expectations cannot be regarded as legitimate: he should realize that the authorities will take the swiftest possible action to plug the loophole. This is well illustrated by *EVGF v. Mackprang*,[88] a case concerned with the intervention system for grain, under which the intervention agencies were obliged to buy grain at the intervention price. Grain could be offered to the intervention agencies in different places and there was usually no advantage to the seller in choosing one rather than another. Normally the product would be offered at the marketing centre nearest to where it was produced. However, in early 1969 there was a fall in the forward rate for the French franc in anticipation of its devaluation, and it became profitable for German grain dealers to buy grain in France in order to resell it to the German intervention agency, the EVGF. This threatened to exhaust the agency's storage capacity and bring about a collapse of the intervention system in Germany. To meet this threat, the Commission adopted a decision authorizing the German Government to confine intervention purchases of wheat and barley to German-grown products. The decision

[84] See Usher, 'The Influence of National Concepts on Decisions of the European Court' (1976) 1 ELRev. 359 at 363.

[85] *Deuka v. EVGF*, Case 78/74, [1975] ECR 421, a case where, as in *Société pour l'Exportation des Sucres v. Commission* (above), the Court adopted a strained interpretation of the provision in order to protect the rights of the persons concerned without having to annul the measure.

[86] See *Töpfer v. Commission*, Case 112/77, [1978] ECR 1019.

[87] See, e.g., *Union Nationale des Coopératives Agricoles de Céréales*, Cases 95–8/74, 15, 100/75, [1975] ECR 1615; *Union Malt*, Cases 44–51/77, [1978] ECR 57; and *Lührs*, Case 78/77, [1978] ECR 169.

[88] Case 2/75, [1975] ECR 607.

was made on 8 May and came into force on the same day; it expressly stated that it would not apply to cereals offered to the agency before it came into force.

Mackprang was a German grain dealer who had bought wheat in France with the object of importing it into Germany and selling it to the German agency. On 8 May most of the wheat was aboard ships and barges in transit to Germany and Mackprang could not make a valid offer of this wheat because there was a rule that grain could not validly be offered while it was still in transit. When it did arrive, the agency refused to buy it and Mackprang brought proceedings in the German courts claiming that he had had a legitimate expectation, when he bought the grain and arranged for shipment, that he would be able to sell it to the agency.

It was, however, pointed out by Advocate General Warner, when a reference to the European Court was made, that the importation of the wheat was not part of normal Community trade but was a speculative transaction of a kind which the Community provisions setting up the system had not been designed to assist. It was possible to profit from transactions of this kind only in an abnormal situation such as that resulting from the fall of the French franc. Advocate General Warner then continued:[89]

> No trader who was exploiting that situation in order to make out of the system profits that the system was never designed to bestow on him could legitimately rely on the persistence of the situation. On the contrary, the only reasonable expectation that such a trader could have was that the competent authorities would act as swiftly as possible to bring the situation to an end.

This view was accepted by the Court, which stated that the application of the Commission decision to cereals in transit to Germany was not an infringement of the principle of legitimate expectations but 'a justified precaution against purely speculative activities'.[90]

Where the principle of protection of legitimate expectations is used as the foundation for an action for damages, the applicant must prove not only that he had an expectation which was legitimate in the above sense, but also that he acted in reliance on it and suffered loss as a result of the Community measure. He will then be able to obtain damages under Article 288(2) [215(2)] EC or Article 188(2) Euratom, unless the Community measure is justifiable by reason of an overriding matter of public interest. The leading case on this is *CNTA v. Commission*,[91] which is considered in detail in Chapter 16, below.

One of the best-known cases on the protection of legitimate expectations is one which at first sight appears not to involve retroactivity at all. This is *Commission v. Council* (first *Staff Salaries* case),[92] where the Commission brought proceedings against the Council because it felt that the latter had not given Community staff a sufficient increase in pay. Staff pay was governed by Article 65 of the Staff Regulations which provided for an annual review of staff salaries by the Council in the light of a report prepared by the Commission. In determining the level of pay, the Council was required to take a number of factors into account, including inflation and salary increases in the

[89] [1975] ECR at 623. [90] At para. 4 of the judgment. [91] Case 74/74, [1975] ECR 533.
[92] Case 81/72, [1973] ECR 575.

public services of the Member States. In the past, serious friction had arisen as a result of disagreement as to how these factors should be measured. Protracted negotiations then took place between the Council, the Commission, and the staff associations, and a formula was eventually devised to settle the matter. This formula was embodied in a Council decision made in March 1972 and was stated to be applicable for a period of three years. When the next salary increase took place, however, the Council laid down new scales which the Commission regarded as being in breach of the formula.

The Court had to decide whether the decision containing the pay formula was legally binding on the Council. The Advocate General took the view that it was not, since a similar decision would not, in his opinion, be binding in the national legal systems. The Court, however, decided that the decision was binding. It held that, in view of the employer–employee relationship between the Council and the staff, the latter had a reasonable expectation that the Council would abide by its undertaking regarding the formula. The new pay scales were, therefore, invalid in so far as they conflicted with it.

### REVOCATION OF DECISIONS

The principle of legal certainty also imposes limits on the extent to which an individual legal act (decision) may be withdrawn. If it is lawful and valid, it may never be withdrawn retroactively, and may not be withdrawn prospectively if it provides otherwise (for example, a decision appointing a person to a post until retirement age).[93] If it is unlawful, it may always be revoked prospectively;[94] whether it may be revoked retrospectively depends on various considerations which involve balancing the public interest in legality against the private interest in legal certainty;[95] unreasonable delay on the part of the Community authority may also be a factor.[96]

## PROPORTIONALITY

Proportionality is another principle derived from German law. In Germany it is called *Verhältnismässigkeit* and it is regarded as underlying certain provisions of the German Constitution. Its constitutional aspect has already been mentioned in connection with fundamental human rights and it was in the *Internationale Handelsgesellschaft* case (discussed above) that it first made an impact on Community law, though some earlier cases could be said to have applied it in a somewhat broader sense.[97]

According to the principle of proportionality, a public authority may not impose obligations on a citizen except to the extent to which they are strictly necessary in the



[93] *Algera v. Common Assembly*, Cases 7/56, 3–7/57, [1957] ECR 39.

[94] See *Algera* (above); see also *Simon v. Court of Justice*, Case 15/60, [1961] ECR 115; *Elz v. Commission*, Case 56/75, [1976] ECR 1097; and *Herpels v. Commission*, Case 54/77, [1978] ECR 585 (at para. 38 of the judgment).

[95] *SNUPAT v. High Authority*, Cases 42, 49/59, [1961] ECR 53; *Hoogovens v. High Authority*, Case 14/61, [1962] ECR 253; *Lemmerz-Werke v. High Authority*, Case 111/63, [1965] ECR 677.

[96] *Consorzio Cooperative d'Abruzzo v. Commission*, Case 15/85, [1987] ECR 1005.

[97] See, e.g., *Fédéchar v. High Authority*, Case 8/55, [1956] ECR 292 at 299.

public interest to attain the purpose of the measure.[98] If the burdens imposed are clearly out of proportion to the object in view, the measure will be annulled.[99] This requires that there exist a reasonable relationship between the end and the means. It implies both that the means must be reasonably likely to bring about the objective, and that the detriment to those adversely affected must not be disproportionate to the benefit to the public. It is to some extent analogous to the English concept of reasonableness.

Although first incorporated into Community law by the European Court, the principle of proportionality has now been embodied in the Treaties. Under the Treaty on European Union, a new provision, Article 5 [3b], was inserted into the EC Treaty. The third paragraph of this reads: 'Any action by the Community shall not go beyond what is necessary to achieve the objectives of this Treaty.' While this does not go any further than the previous case law of the Court, it emphasizes the importance attached to the principle by the Member States.

Proportionality is particularly important in the sphere of economic law, since this frequently involves imposing taxes, levies, charges, or duties on businessmen in the hope of achieving economic objectives. The application of proportionality in such a situation as this is well illustrated by the *Skimmed-Milk Powder* case[100] where the Council had sought to reduce the surplus of skimmed-milk powder in the Community by forcing animal feed producers to incorporate it in their product in place of the normal protein element, soya. The drawback of this scheme was that skimmed-milk powder was approximately three times more expensive than soya. In consequence, the European Court held that the regulation embodying the scheme was invalid, partly because it was discriminatory, and partly because it offended against the principle of proportionality: the imposition of the obligation to purchase skimmed-milk powder was not necessary in order to diminish the surplus.[101]

The most striking point about the doctrine of proportionality is that it leaves a great deal to the judgment of the Court. Is the measure reasonably likely to attain its objective? Does it impose disproportionate burdens on those concerned? These are clearly questions on which opinions may frequently differ. The Court will not, of course, interfere unless there is a clear and obvious infringement of the principle; nevertheless, it is not always easy to predict when the Court will consider that that point has been reached.

## EQUALITY

The principle of equality finds expression in a number of provisions in the Treaties: Article 12 [6] EC, as has already been mentioned, prohibits discrimination on grounds of nationality; Article 34(2) [40(3)] EC prohibits discrimination between producers

[98] See *per* Advocate General Dutheillet de Lamothe in *Internationale Handelsgesellschaft*, Case 11/70, [1970] ECR 1125 at 1146.

[99] See *Balkan-Import-Export*, Case 5/73, [1973] ECR 1091 at 1112, in which the Court stated that it was not satisfied the measure in question imposed burdens which were 'manifestly out of proportion to the object in view'. See also the German decision, *Re Export of Oat Flakes* [1969] CMLR 85 at 91.

[100] *Bela-Mühle Josef Bergman v. Grows-Farm*, Case 114/76, [1977] ECR 1211; see also Case 116/76 and Cases 119, 120/76 at 1247 and 1269 respectively.

[101] Case 114/76 at para. 7 of the judgment; Case 116/76 at para. 24; and Cases 119, 120/76 at para. 7.

and consumers in connection with agriculture; and Article 141[119] EC establishes the principle of equal pay for equal work irrespective of sex. The European Court has, however, gone beyond these specific provisions by holding that there is a general principle of non-discrimination in Community law.[102] This does not mean that Community institutions must treat everyone alike, but that there must be no arbitrary distinctions between different groups within the Community.[103]

The *Skimmed-Milk Powder* case (discussed above) was partly decided on the basis of this principle, especially as formulated in Article 34(2) [40(3)] EC: the effect of making animal feed producers use skimmed-milk powder was to increase the price of animal feed, and this harmed all livestock breeders; the benefits of the policy were, on the other hand, felt only by dairy farmers. Thus the policy worked in a discriminatory fashion between different categories of farmers.

In *Sabbatini v. European Parliament*,[104] the Court established sex equality as a general principle of law. This case concerned a female Community official who was denied a certain allowance because she was not the 'head of the family'. The relevant provision defined this concept in such a way as to make it possible for a woman to be regarded as head of the family only in very exceptional circumstances, for example if her husband was incapacitated by illness. The provision was, therefore, discriminatory and, despite the prompting of the Advocate General, the Court held that it could not stand.

The Court went a step further in *Airola v. Commission*,[105] where the discriminatory provision was part of national law. Here, the applicant had lost her allowance because she had acquired Italian nationality on marriage to an Italian. Under Italian law, a foreign woman who married an Italian man automatically acquired Italian nationality, even if this was not her wish; but this rule did not apply to a foreign man marrying an Italian woman. Community law had simply given effect to Italian law for the purpose of a rule which provided that an expatriation allowance would not be paid if the official acquired the nationality of the country where she worked. But the European Court ruled that Community law could not take account of nationality acquired involuntarily under a discriminatory provision of national law.[106]

The question of religious discrimination came before the Court in *Prais v. Council*.[107] This concerned a woman of Jewish faith who wished to obtain a post as a Community official. In her application she did not mention her religion. However, when she was informed that she would have to sit a competitive examination on a particular day, she told the Council that the day in question was a Jewish festival and she would be unable to attend. She asked the Council to allow her to sit on an alternative date, but this was

[102] See *Frilli v. Belgium*, Case 1/72, [1972] ECR 457 (para. 19 of the judgment) and *Sotgiu v. Deutsche Bundespost*, Case 152/73, [1974] ECR 153 (para. 11 of the judgment); see also *ECSC v. Ferriere Sant'Anna*, Case 168/82, [1983] ECR 1681.

[103] See *Hauts Fourneaux et Aciéries Belges v. High Authority*, Case 8/57, [1958] ECR 245 at 256–7; and *Union des Minotiers de la Champagne v. France*, Case 11/74, [1974] ECR 877 (para. 22 of the judgment).

[104] Case 20/71, [1972] ECR 345.

[105] Case 21/74, [1975] ECR 221. For a somewhat different situation, see *Van den Broeck v. Commission*, Case 37/74, [1975] ECR 235; see also *Devred v. Commission*, Case 257/78, [1979] ECR 3767.

[106] For a case involving discrimination against men, see *Razzouk and Beydoun v. Commission*, Cases 75, 117/82, [1984] ECR 1509 (pension rights for husbands of deceased Community officials).

[107] Case 130/75, [1976] ECR 1589.

refused on the ground that it was essential for all candidates to sit the examination on the same date. It was too late to change the date of the examination as the arrangements had been completed. The examination was duly held and Mrs Prais did not attend. Another candidate was appointed.

She then brought proceedings in the European Court to annul the decision to hold the examination on a Jewish festival and to annul the result of the competition; she also asked for damages. She based her case partly on Article 27 of the Staff Regulations, which provided that officials must be selected without reference to race, creed, or sex, and partly on what she claimed was a general principle of Community law prohibiting religious discrimination. The defendant accepted that freedom of religion was a general principle of Community law but maintained that its action did not constitute a violation of it.

It should be noted that the appointing authority had not been guilty of religious discrimination in the ordinary meaning of the term: there was no evidence that it knew the date in question was a Jewish festival when it originally scheduled the examination and it had certainly had no wish to create difficulties for the applicant. She, however, argued that subjective intention was not the only matter: if procedures were in fact adopted which put any candidate at a disadvantage by reason of her religion, her religious freedom had been violated.

The Court held that the appointing authority was not under an obligation to avoid holding an examination on a religious holiday if it had not been informed of the fact before the date was fixed. For this reason, Mrs Prais lost her case. However, it went on to state that if the appointing authority is informed in advance, it should take the religious difficulties of candidates into account and endeavour to avoid holding the examination on that date. This means that, even if informed in advance, the authority is not absolutely barred from choosing such a date: but it must give reasonable weight to the desirability of not doing so and should avoid it if reasonably practicable.[108]

## THE RIGHT TO A HEARING

This principle is of interest because it was the first example of the European Court drawing on English law in the elaboration of its general principles. The case in which this occurred was *Transocean Marine Paint Association v. Commission*,[109] which concerned Community competition law. Article 81 [85] EC prohibits agreements which restrict competition but provision is made in Article 81(3) [85(3)] for the Commission to grant exemptions in particular cases. The agreement establishing the Transocean Marine Paint Association was *prima facie* contrary to Article 81 [85], so an application was made to the Commission for exemption. This was initially granted, subject to

[108] For a similar decision in the English courts, see *Ostreicher v. Secretary of State* [1978] 1 WLR 810; [1978] 3 All ER 82, CA; see also *Ahmad v. ILEA* [1977] 3 WLR 396; [1978] 1 All ER 574, CA.

[109] Case 17/74, [1974] ECR 1063.

conditions, for a period of ten years. When the Association applied for renewal, it was told by the Commission of certain new conditions that the Commission had in mind and was given the opportunity to make representations. It was not, however, adequately informed of one condition which was in fact imposed. For various reasons the Association objected to this condition and it brought proceedings to quash the decision granting the exemption, in so far as it imposed the condition. It put forward various grounds of invalidity but a breach of the principle of *audi alteram partem* was not one of them. It was Advocate General Warner who proposed that the case should be decided on this basis. He argued that the right to a hearing was a general principle of Community law and that it was binding on the Commission even in the absence of a specific legislative provision. He reached this conclusion after a survey of the national legal systems, in which he pointed out the important role that natural justice plays in England and was able to show that it also applies in most other Member States, though often in a less developed form.

This view was accepted by the Court, which held that there is a general rule of Community law that 'a person whose interests are perceptibly affected by a decision taken by a public authority must be given the opportunity to make his point of view known'.[110] The Court said that this rule requires that the persons concerned be clearly informed in advance of the essential features of any conditions the Commission intends to impose. Because this had not been done in the case, the condition was annulled.

Since this case, the European Court has developed a general doctrine of what it calls 'the rights of the defence',[111] a rather unhappy term for what English lawyers know as the principles of natural justice and what American lawyers call due process.[112] Besides the right to a fair hearing,[113] this also covers such rights as that of legal representation, the privileged nature of communications between lawyer and client (discussed below), and non-self-incrimination.[114]

[110] At para. 15 of the judgment. It is interesting to note that in the later case of *Mollet v. Commission*, Case 75/77, [1978] ECR 897, the Court spoke of a 'measure which is liable gravely to prejudice the interests of an individual' (para. 21), a narrower formulation than that in the *Transocean* case.

[111] This is a literal translation of the French expression, '*les droits de la défense*'. There is, however, no reason to believe that it is limited to the defendant: it could apply equally to the applicant (plaintiff).

[112] *Michelin v. Commission*, Case 322/81, [1983] ECR 3461 (para. 7 of the judgment); *Hoechst v. Commission*, Cases 46/87, 227/88, [1989] ECR 2859.

[113] For later developments, see *Oslizlok v. Commission*, Case 34/77, [1978] ECR 1099; *Hoffmann-La Roche v. Commission*, Case 85/76, [1979] ECR 461; and *Musique Diffusion Française v. Commission*, Cases 100–3/80, [1983] ECR 1825 (paras 6–36 of the judgment); *Fiskano v. Commission*, Case C-135/92, [1994] ECR I-2885; see also, Ehlermann and Oldekop, 'Due Process in Administrative Procedure' in FIDE, Reports of the 8th Congress, 1978, vol. III, 11–1 at 11–3 to 11–17; and Korah, 'The Rights of the Defence in Administrative Proceedings under Community Law' [1980] CLP 73. In *Al-Jubail Fertilizer v. Council*, Case C-49/88, [1991] ECR I-3187, the principle was applied to anti-dumping proceedings and in *Belgium v. Commission*, Case C-142/87, [1990] ECR I-959, to state aids. In the latter case, the European Court ruled that an infringement of the right to a hearing will not result in an annulment unless it is established that, had it not been for the infringement, the outcome of the procedure might have been different (para. 48 of the judgment).

[114] *Orkem v. Commission*, Case 374/87, [1989] ECR 3283.

## LEGAL PROFESSIONAL PRIVILEGE

The privileged nature of communications between lawyer and client was first recognized as a general principle in *A. M. & S. v. Commission.*[115] The issue arose when Commission inspectors arrived one day at the office of a British company and demanded to see its business records. This inspection was part of a general investigation into alleged anti-competitive practices in the zinc industry. It was carried out under a Community measure, Article 14 of Regulation 17, which made no mention of legal privilege. The company nevertheless refused to hand over certain documents on the ground that they were privileged. The Commission took a decision requiring the production of the documents and the company brought proceedings before the European Court to annul it.

The Court held that the confidentiality of written communications between lawyer and client, which was generally recognized in the legal systems of the Member States, would be upheld in Community law subject to two conditions: the communication must be for the purpose of the client's 'rights of defence'[116] and the lawyer[117] must be in private practice, not an employee of the client. This latter rule has been criticized as unfair to companies employing in-house lawyers.

The procedure laid down by the European Court is as follows. If a client wishes to claim privilege, he must – without revealing the contents of the document – give the Commission sufficient information to demonstrate that the conditions have been satisfied. If the Commission does not accept this, it will take a decision requiring production of the document and, if necessary, impose a penalty for failure to comply, normally a periodic fine of a given amount for each day that the client fails to hand over the document. The client can then challenge this decision before the Court, which will decide the issue, if necessary after inspecting the document. The mere initiation of annulment proceedings will not suspend the decision but the Court may, if it thinks fit, make an interlocutory order to this effect.

In the case before the Court, the documents were legal opinions, given shortly before, and immediately after, the United Kingdom joined the Community, concerning possible conflicts with Community law – especially in the field of competition – and ways in which these could be avoided. The Court held that they were entitled to protection.

[115] Case 155/79, [1982] ECR 1575.

[116] See para. 21 of the judgment. This phrase appears to be the best the translator could come up with for the French '*[le] droit de la défense du client*', which shows that, though the English version of the judgment was supposed to be the authentic one, English having been the language of the case, in reality it was no more than a translation from the French.

[117] The Court adopted the definition of 'lawyer' contained in Directive 77/249, OJ 1977, L78/17, which covers lawyers admitted in other Member States, but not non-Community lawyers, a fact which has been criticized by American lawyers in view of the fact that American courts have extended the attorney-client privilege to non-American lawyers: see Barsade, 'The Effect of EC Regulations upon the Ability of US Lawyers to Establish a Pan-European Practice' (1994) 28 International Lawyer 313 at 323–4.

## FURTHER READING


Usher, 'The Influence of National Concepts on Decisions of the European Court' (1976) 1 ELRev. 359.

Korah, 'The Rights of the Defence in Administrative Proceedings under Community Law' [1980] CLP 73.

Akehurst, 'The Application of General Principles of Law by the Court of Justice of the European Communities' [1981] BYIL 29.

McBride and Brown, 'The United Kingdom, the European Community and the European Convention on Human Rights' (1981) 1 YEL 167.

Mendelson, 'The European Court of Justice and Human Rights' (1981) 1 YEL 126.

Lamoureux, 'The Retroactivity of Community Acts in the Case Law of the Court of Justice' (1983) 20 CMLRev. 269.

Dauses, 'The Protection of Fundamental Rights in the Community Legal Order' (1985) 10 ELRev. 398.

Weiler, 'Eurocracy and Distrust: Some Questions Concerning the Role of the European Court of Justice in the Protection of Fundamental Human Rights within the Legal Order of the European Communities' (1986) 61 Washington Law Rev. 1103.

Schermers, 'The European Communities Bound by Fundamental Human Rights' (1990) 27 CMLRev. 249.

Lenaerts, 'Fundamental Rights to be Included in a Community Catalogue' (1991) 16 ELRev. 367.

De Búrca, 'The Principle of Proportionality and its Application in EC Law' (1993) 13 YEL 105.

Brown, 'Is There a General Principle of Abuse of Rights in European Community Law?' in Curtin and Heukels (eds), *Institutional Dynamics of European Integration* (Essays in Honour of Henry G. Schermers) (1994), vol. II, p. 511.

Rodríguez Iglesias, 'The Protection of Fundamental Rights in the Case Law of the Court of Justice of the European Communities' (1995) 1 Columbia Journal of European Law 169.

Toth, 'The European Union and Human Rights: The Way Forward' (1997) 34 CMLRev. 491.

John A Usher, *General Principles of EC Law* (1998).

Lenaerts, 'Fundamental Rights in the European Union' (2000) 25 ELRev. 575.

De Búrca, 'The Drafting of the European Charter of Fundamental Rights' (2001) 26 ELRev. 126.

Douglas-Scott, 'A Tale of Two Courts: Luxembourg, Strasbourg and the Growing European Human Rights *Acquis*' (2006) 43 CMLRev. 629.

Takis Tridimas, *The General Principles of EC Law*, 2nd edn (2006).

# 6

# AGREEMENTS WITH THIRD COUNTRIES

In some ways international agreements are an anomalous source of Community law. The constitutive Treaties are acts of the Member States; regulations, decisions, etc., are acts of the Community itself; general principles of law are the creation of the European Court; but international agreements have their origin outside the Community legal order and are, in part, the acts of non-Member States. However, they have effects in Community law and are applied by the European Court, which has declared them to be 'an integral part of Community law'.[1] In spite of their origin, therefore, they may be regarded as a true source of Community law.

International agreements forming part of Community law may be divided into three categories. The first consists of agreements between the Community (acting alone) and one or more non-Member States.[2] This method is used where the subject matter of the agreement falls wholly within the treaty-making competence of the Community. The second category consists of 'mixed' agreements, that is, agreements between, on the one side, the Community and the Member States acting jointly and, on the other side, the non-Member States. It is used when the subject matter falls partly within the competence of the Community and partly within that of the Member States, or when there is concurrent competence. The third category consists of agreements between the Member States (acting alone) and non-Member States. The European Court has accepted such agreements as forming part of Community law, and being binding on the Community, only in special circumstances.

An international organization cannot conclude international agreements unless it has legal personality under international law. The EC Treaty expressly confers legal personality on the EC, and the Euratom Treaty expressly confers it on Euratom.[3] There is no provision expressly conferring legal personality on the EU; nevertheless, in 2001 it concluded an international agreement with the Federal Republic of Yugoslavia.[4] It did this under Article 24 [J.14] TEU, a provision which lays down the procedure for the conclusion of agreements in connection with the common foreign and security policy (CFSP). Article 24 [J.14] does not expressly confer legal personality on the Union, but the Council and the Member States must have regarded it as doing so by implication.

[1] *Haegeman v. Belgium*, Case 181/73, [1974] ECR 449 (para. 5 of the judgment).

[2] They may also be concluded with other international organizations.

[3] For the EC, see Art. 281 [210] EC. For Euratom, see Art. 184 Euratom.

[4] Council Decision 2001/352/CFSP of 9 April 2001, OJ 2001, L125, p. 1.

# THE TREATY-MAKING POWER OF THE EC

## EXPRESS POWERS

Express treaty-making power is granted by the EC Treaty in a number of cases, of which commercial agreements under Article 133 [113] and association agreements under Article 310 [238] are the most important.[5] Article 300 [228] lays down general rules regarding the procedure to be followed where the treaty-making power is exercised, but does not itself confer such power.

Commercial agreements are negotiated by the Commission. Article 133(3) [113(3)] provides that the Commission must obtain the authorization of the Council to open negotiations; these are conducted in consultation with a special committee appointed by the Council. The Council also has the power to issue directives to the Commission. If the negotiations are successful, the agreement is concluded by the Council, acting by a qualified majority. There is no requirement to consult the European Parliament.[6]

The power granted by Article 133 [113] is not limited to tariff and trade agreements but covers all aspects of the Community's common commercial policy, including export aids, credit, and finance, as well as the matters normally forming part of multilateral commodity agreements. It also covers development policy (aid to Third World countries).[7] This power is exclusive: the Member States are precluded from entering into such agreements.

Association agreements can operate either as a preliminary to, or as a substitute for, membership of the Community. They are governed by Article 310 [238] EC, which provides for association agreements with non-Member States or international organizations. They are concluded by the Council, acting unanimously,[8] after receiving the assent of the European Parliament.[9]

The provisions on relations with international organizations (Articles 302–304 [229–231] EC) require the Commission to maintain appropriate relations with international organizations in general, and the Community to establish 'all appropriate forms of co-operation' with the Council of Europe and 'close co-operation' with the

[5] See also Arts 111(3) [109(3)] (monetary matters); 170 [130m] (research and technological development); 174(4) [130r(4)] (environment); and 181 [130y] (development co-operation). There is something approaching an express power in the provisions concerning co-operation with international organizations: see Arts 302–304 [229–231]. There is in addition a power of minor importance to enter into agreements with third countries for the recognition of travel documents issued by the Community to the members and staff of Community institutions: see Art. 7(1) of the Protocol on the Privileges and Immunities of the European Communities. This is a Protocol to the Merger Treaty (see Art. 28 of the latter); the Merger Treaty was repealed by the Treaty of Amsterdam, but it was expressly provided that the Protocol will remain in force: see Art. 9(1) of the Treaty of Amsterdam.

[6] Art. 300(3) [228(3)] EC.

[7] *Commission v. Council*, Case 45/86, [1987] ECR 1493.

[8] Art. 300(2) [228(2)] EC (last sentence).

[9] Art. 300(2) and (3) [228(2) and (3)] EC. *Demirel*, Case 12/86, [1987] ECR 3719, a case concerning immigration from a non-member state associated with the Community, shows that in the context of an association agreement the Community's treaty-making power may be wider than its internal legislative competence. In such a situation, the Community may have to rely on the Member States to pass measures to give effect to the agreement.

OECD. In the latter case, Article 304 [231] states that the details of this will be determined 'by common accord'. The Community (together with the Member States) is in fact a member of several international organizations.[10]

## TREATY-MAKING PROCEDURE

General provisions regarding the procedure to be adopted for international agreements under the EC Treaty are laid down by Article 300 [228] EC.[11] The Commission conducts the negotiations, after it has obtained authorization from the Council, in consultation with special committees appointed by the Council and is subject to any directives the Council may adopt.[12]

The decision to sign the agreement (which may involve its provisional application before entry into force) and to conclude it is taken by the Council. In doing so, the Council normally acts by a qualified majority on a proposal from the Commission: it must, however, act by unanimity where the agreement covers a field for which unanimity is required for the adoption of internal rules or in the case of association agreements. Save in the case of agreements under Article 133(3) [113(3)] EC (commercial policy), the European Parliament must be consulted before the agreement is concluded.[13] The Council can set a time-limit within which the opinion must be delivered: if no opinion is given by this deadline, the Council may conclude the agreement without it. The only exceptions concern association agreements (Article 310 [238] EC), other agreements establishing a specific institutional framework, agreements having important budgetary implications, and agreements entailing amendment to an act adopted under the co-decision procedure (Article 251 [189b]). In these cases, the assent of the Parliament must be obtained.

Although Article 300 [228] gives the impression that the Parliament enters the picture only after the agreement has been negotiated, it is normal practice for it to be briefed throughout the procedure. The relevant committee will usually be informed that the Council proposes to open negotiations and the Parliament may hold a debate on the issue. During the course of the negotiations, confidential briefings will be given to the committee by the Commission. The Parliament is thus able to exert influence on the course of the negotiations. This influence will be especially strong in those cases where the agreement cannot be concluded without the assent of the Parliament, since it can threaten to veto the agreement if its wishes are not taken into account.

[10] On the division of voting rights between the Community and the Member States in such cases, see *Commission v. Council* (*FAO* case), Case C-25/94, [1996] ECR I-1469.

[11] Special rules are applicable in certain cases. For the procedure regarding agreements on foreign-exchange and monetary matters, see Art. 111[109] EC. For the procedure where the agreement is concluded in the context of the common foreign and security policy, or police and judicial co-operation in criminal matters, see Art. 24 [J.14] TEU.

[12] In exercising the powers referred to in this paragraph, the Council acts by a qualified majority except in those cases where the Council may conclude the agreement, if successfully negotiated, only by unanimity.

[13] Even in cases where the joint legislative procedure or the co-operation procedure applies to internal legislation (Arts 251 and 252 [189b and 189c]), the Parliament's rights are no more than consultation. The only exceptions are those expressly mentioned.

## IMPLIED POWERS

International relations are an area which is traditionally regarded as touching the very heart of state sovereignty and it is hardly surprising, therefore, that the Member States have always viewed the treaty-making power of the Community with a degree of suspicion. Almost from the beginning, the Member States and the organ which represents their collective opinion – the Council – have tried to limit the powers of the Community.

For a long time there were two rival theories regarding the Community's power to conclude treaties. On the one hand, it was argued that the treaty-making power of the Community – its external competence – should reflect its internal competence. According to this doctrine of 'parallelism', as it is sometimes called, it would be illogical for the Community to have internal law-making power with regard to a certain topic and yet be unable to conclude international agreements in that field. Therefore, argued the proponents of this doctrine, the Community must be regarded as having not only those treaty-making powers expressly granted to it in the Treaty, but must also have such powers with regard to any topic which falls within its internal competence. This may be justified on the basis of the theory of implied powers.[14]

In the beginning, the Member States rejected this doctrine: they took the view that the EC possesses only such external powers as are expressly granted to it by the Treaty. This standpoint may be supported by comparing the EC Treaty with the Euratom Treaty: Article 300 [228] EC, the general provision covering all treaty-making by the EC, begins with the words: 'Where *this Treaty provides* for the conclusion of agreements . . . ',[15] thus suggesting that it is only in the case of an express provision that the Community may conclude international agreements. Article 101 Euratom, on the other hand, states: 'The Community may, within the limits of its powers and jurisdiction, enter into obligations by concluding agreements or contracts with a third State.' This implies that wherever the Community has internal competence with regard to a given question, it will also have power to enter into international agreements. The contrast between these two provisions is all the more significant in view of the fact that the two Treaties were drafted at the same time and in many instances contain identical provisions. It is hard, therefore, to avoid the conclusion that the authors of the Treaties intended the EC to have considerably more restricted treaty-making powers than Euratom.

The Member States also favoured a narrow interpretation of the provisions which expressly grant treaty-making powers. In particular, they appear to have taken the view that the provisions concerning association agreements – especially Article 310 [238] – do not themselves confer any distinct treaty-making power: they merely regulate the way in which the power to conclude commercial agreements is exercised in a particular context.[16]

As a consequence of this, they took the position that association agreements entered into by the Community alone could deal only with tariffs and trade (Article 133 [113]).

[14] Discussed in Chap. 4. [15] Emphasis added.

[16] See Leopold, 'External Relations Power of EEC in Theory and in Practice' (1977) 26 ICLQ 54 at 62; Costonis, 'The Treaty-Making Power of the European Economic Community' (1968) 5 CMLRev. 421 at 444. There is no doubt that this view was wrong: see Costonis, 444–9.

Where, as was frequently the case, it was desirable to include other provisions – for example, concerning development aid[17] – resort had to be had, in the view of the Council, to a 'mixed agreement', i.e., one concluded jointly by the Member States and the Community. Though referred to in Article 102 of the Euratom Treaty,[18] this joint procedure is not mentioned in the EC Treaty, which appears to have envisaged a different solution to the problem: an amendment of the EC Treaty so that the Community could conclude the agreement by itself. In their original form, both Article 310 [238] and Article 300 [228] envisaged the possibility of a Treaty amendment, though neither of them expressly excluded the mixed procedure.[19]

Since association agreements have almost always been more than mere commercial agreements, the mixed procedure has been frequently used, and many of the most important agreements have been concluded under it. Such agreements are first ratified by the Member States according to their respective constitutional requirements and then approved by the Council on behalf of the Community.

This difference of opinion between the Council and the Commission led to several clashes. In 1968, for example, there was a dispute as to which would conduct the negotiations for an additional Protocol to the association agreement with Turkey.[20] The Commission proposed a compromise: it would act as spokesman for the Community with regard to those matters within the general competence of the Community, and the Member State holding the presidency of the Council would speak on matters within the competence of the Member States. This was rejected by the Council, which insisted that the Member State holding the presidency should speak for the Community on all matters; the Commission would be limited to explaining and supplementing the Community's position. The Commission disagreed fundamentally with this, but took no action.

A similar dispute occurred shortly afterwards regarding the Second Yaoundé Convention. Here, too, the Council was determined that the leading role in the negotiations should be played by the Member States. This issue gave rise to strong feelings, and at one point the President of the Commission threatened to bring proceedings against the Council in the European Court. Eventually, however, the Commission accepted a compromise proposal, which was nevertheless regarded by most observers as a defeat for its position.[21]

These events provide the background to the first legal action between the Council and the Commission, the *ERTA* case.[22] The history of this dispute goes back to 1962 when five of the six Member States, together with some other European countries, signed an agreement to harmonize certain social provisions relating to road transport. This agreement, normally known as the first ERTA (European Road Transport

[17] It was originally thought that development aid was not covered at all by Art. 133 [113]. The Court has now ruled it is covered where it takes the form of tariff reductions for developing countries: *Commission v. Council*, Case 45/86, [1987] ECR 1493.

[18] See below.

[19] The use of the mixed procedure under the EC Treaty was, however, approved by the European Court in the *Natural Rubber Agreement* case, Opinion 1/78, [1979] ECR 2871.

[20] See Bot, 'Negotiating Community Agreements: Procedure and Practice' (1970) 7 CMLRev. 286 at 296–301.

[21] See Bot, *ibid.*, 301–6.

[22] *Commission v. Council* (*ERTA* case), Case 22/70, [1971] ECR 263.

Agreement), never came into force, since it was not ratified by a sufficient number of contracting states. In 1967, negotiations started for a second ERTA and these were also conducted by the Member States. In 1969, however, the Council enacted a regulation covering much the same ground within the internal competence of the Community. The Member States were nevertheless still anxious to regulate the matter on a wider basis and they decided to continue the negotiations for a second ERTA.

On 20 March 1970, the Council met to discuss the matter and decided that the negotiations would be carried on by the six Member States, which would become parties to the new ERTA. It was agreed that the Member States would co-ordinate their positions and the Member State holding the presidency of the Council would act as spokesman. The Commission objected to this: it felt that it should have a role to play in view of the fact that the subject matter of the negotiations had already been regulated internally on a Community basis by the 1969 regulation. In May 1970, it therefore brought legal action against the Council in the European Court to annul the Council resolution entrusting the conduct of the negotiations entirely to the Member States. On 1 July 1970, agreement on the new ERTA was reached and the text was declared open for signature; before the Court gave judgment, at least some of the Member States had signed it.

The jurisdictional aspects of this case have already been considered: it will be remembered that the Court eventually decided that the application was admissible since the Council resolution constituted a legal act *sui generis*.[23] As far as the substance was concerned, the main point was whether the Member States or the Community had power to enter into the agreement. This in turn depended on whether the Community has any treaty-making powers beyond those expressly granted by the EC Treaty.

In its judgment, the Court first drew an implicit distinction between *capacity* to enter into an agreement and *authority* to do so. Capacity appears to relate to the Community's legal power to enter into an agreement; authority to the legality of its exercise of that power. For present purposes the important concept is that of authority. As regards this, the Court said that it is necessary to consider the 'whole scheme of the Treaty' as well as its substantive provisions. It then went on to say, in paragraphs 16 to 19 of its judgment:

> Such authority arises not only from an express conferment by the Treaty – as is the case with Articles 133 [113] and [114] for tariff and trade agreements and with Article 310 [238] for association agreements – but may equally flow from other provisions of the Treaty and from measures adopted, within the framework of those provisions, by the Community institutions.
>
> In particular, each time the Community, with a view to implementing a common policy envisaged by the Treaty, adopts provisions laying down common rules, whatever form these may take, the Member States no longer have the right, acting individually or even collectively, to undertake obligations with third countries which affect those rules.
>
> As and when such common rules come into being, the Community alone is in a position to assume and carry out contractual obligations towards third countries affecting the whole sphere of application of the Community legal system.

[23] See Chap. 4.

> With regard to the implementation of the provisions of the Treaty the system of internal Community measures may not therefore be separated from that of external relations.

This, of course, constitutes approval of the doctrine of 'parallelism'; it is, however, expressed in a particular form. The vital element bringing about a transfer of treaty-making power from the Member States to the Community is the adoption by the Community of provisions laying down rules which might be affected if the Member States entered into treaties with regard to the subject matter in question.[24]

Having enunciated this new principle, the Court then applied it to the facts of the case. It noted that the adoption of a common transport policy is one of the objectives laid down in Part One of the Treaty and that common rules for the attainment of this objective had been laid down in the 1969 regulation. It followed from this that the Community obtained treaty-making power in the area covered by the regulation when the latter came into force on 1 October 1969. This automatically entailed the loss of such power on the part of the Member States.

One might have thought that the consequence of this would have been that the Commission should have negotiated the agreement on behalf of the Community. It must not be forgotten, however, that the negotiations for the second ERTA were based on the first ERTA: the idea was merely to make such modifications as were necessary to secure its acceptance. The negotiations taken up again in 1967 were, therefore, a continuation of those which resulted in the first ERTA in 1962. Consequently, a considerable part of the negotiations had been carried out before the transfer of treaty-making power in 1969. In the circumstances, it would not have been fair to third countries if the negotiating procedure, and indeed the parties to the negotiations, had been changed at that point. In such a situation, said the Court, the Council and Commission should have agreed between themselves on appropriate methods of co-operation to ensure the most effective way of defending the Community's interests. Clearly, no such agreement was reached. The Court therefore concluded that the Council had not violated the Treaty in deciding that the negotiations would continue to be conducted by the Member States. Technically, therefore, the Commission lost the case: in reality, of course, it won a great victory.

[24] See also paras 66, 82, and, above all, 84 of the judgment. In para. 84 the Court expressly said that power was conferred on the Community as a result of the 1969 regulation. There is also, however, a different (and somewhat inconsistent) strand of reasoning. Article 71(1)(a) [75(1)(a)] EC gives the Council the power to lay down common rules applicable to international transport to or from the territory of a Member State or passing across the territory of one or more Member States. The Court said that this provision is equally concerned with transport to or from non-member states, and thus assumes that the powers of the Community involve the need for international agreements: see paras 23–27 of the judgment. This could be interpreted as meaning (though it does not expressly say) that Article 71(1)(a) [75(1)(a)] gives the Community an implied treaty-making power which exists irrespective of internal measures, a view which the Court seems to have adopted in later cases: see the *WTO* case, Op. 1/94, [1994] ECR I-5267 at para. 76 of the judgment. This power seems to be concurrent with that of the Member States until such time as internal measures are adopted: see the *WTO* case at para. 77 of the judgment, where the Court said, 'Only in so far as common rules have been established at internal level does the external competence of the Community become exclusive.' See, further, Dashwood and Heliskoski, 'The Classic Authorities Revisited' in Alan Dashwood and Christophe Hillion (eds), *The General Law of EC External Relations* (2000), 3 at pp. 7–9 *et seq.* If this interpretation of the *ERTA* case is correct, it means that subsequent developments were foreshadowed in it.

The Court's ruling in the *ERTA* case can be fully understood only if one analyses it from a policy point of view. What the Court was intent on doing was enhancing the Community's powers and thus reversing the trend away from Commission involvement in international negotiations. It did not, however, wish to jeopardize the agreement which had been reached on the second ERTA by ruling that it had to be renegotiated by the Commission: this would have upset the other parties and damaged the international reputation of the Community. Moreover, the Eastern Bloc was reluctant to accept the Community as a party to the agreement. The Court therefore had to find a way of upholding the Commission's contention in principle, without applying it to the facts of the case. As already mentioned, this was done by holding that a transfer of treaty-making power occurred in 1969 when the internal measure came into effect.

The same result could, however, have been achieved by ruling that the enactment of the regulation did not *confer* power on the Community but merely *deprived* the Member States of power. This could be justified by the adoption of the doctrine of parallelism in its strong form by saying that the existence of an internal power automatically implies an external power, but this power does not become exclusive until it is exercised either internally or externally. Before this, the Member States would have concurrent powers. The outcome of the *ERTA* case would have been the same, but the Commission's position in future cases would have been stronger. However, it is far from clear that this is what the Court said in the *ERTA* case.

The next step came in the *North-East Atlantic Fisheries Convention (Kramer)* case.[25] The Convention was an international agreement entered into by seven of the nine Member States and several non-Member States for the purpose of ensuring the conservation of fish stocks in the North-East Atlantic. A Fisheries Commission was set up under it, and this had the power to make recommendations for conservation measures if there was a two-thirds majority in favour. These were binding on each party to the Convention unless it rejected the recommendation within a given period. Such a recommendation had been made concerning sole and plaice, and this became binding under the terms of the Convention. The Netherlands, which was a party to the Convention, then enacted national measures to implement the recommendation, and these included criminal provisions. The case arose when certain Dutch fishermen were prosecuted in a Dutch court for breach of these provisions. They argued that the Member States had no power to enter into the Convention and the Dutch legislation was therefore contrary to Community law. This raised the question whether the Convention fell within the exclusive competence of the Community.

The position regarding fisheries was that the Community had internal power but at the relevant time had not exercised that power for the purpose of conservation. However, conservation of fish in international waters is rather a special case, since it is normally feasible to proceed only by way of international measures: there is no point in imposing quotas on Community fishermen if non-Community fishermen are subject to no restrictions. It is hardly surprising, therefore, that the European Court held that

[25] Cases 3, 4, 6/76, [1976] ECR 1279. This case was preceded by the *Local Cost Standard* case, Opinion 1/75, [1975] ECR 1355, which did not, however, significantly develop the law on the point under consideration.

the Community had treaty-making power in the area. However, it went on to rule that until the Community exercised its powers – one assumes either internally or externally – the Member States had concurrent powers. Consequently, the Dutch measure was not contrary to Community law.

In the *North-East Atlantic Fisheries Convention* case, the European Court appears to have taken the position that the mere existence of an internal power can give rise to an external power, even if no internal measures have in fact been adopted; nevertheless, this could be regarded as applying only in the special case of fisheries conservation. In the *Inland Waterway Vessels*[26] case, however, the Court made clear that it was laying down a general principle. After stating that the grant of internal power to attain a specific objective implies the authority to enter into international agreements where these are necessary for the attainment of that objective, it continued: 'This is particularly so in all cases in which internal power has already been used . . . it is, however, not limited to that eventuality.'[27] It went on to say:[28]

> [T]he power to bind the Community *vis-à-vis* third countries nevertheless flows by implication from the provisions of the Treaty creating the internal power and in so far as the participation of the Community in the international agreement is, as here, necessary for the attainment of one of the objectives of the Community.

This new principle, which has been called the principle of 'complementarity',[29] seems to be that an implied external power may result from an express internal power where the purpose for which the latter was given cannot be fully attained without the former.

The *Inland Waterway Vessels* case is also interesting because it throws light on two other matters. The case concerned an international agreement for the regulation of vessels on the Rhine–Moselle waterway system. The Community had internal competence in the area and could have dealt with the problem by means of a regulation. However, the Swiss were major users of the waterway and, as they had to be included in the scheme, action on the international level was necessary.

The solution chosen was a mixed agreement to which the parties were the Community, Switzerland, and six of the Member States. The six contracting Member States were the three Benelux countries, Germany, France, and the United Kingdom. The reason these Member States participated in their individual capacities was that the waterways in question were already subject to two international conventions, the Mannheim Convention of 1868 and the Luxembourg Convention of 1956, and there was a potential conflict between certain provisions of the new agreement and the two earlier Conventions. The six participating Member States were all parties to one or other of the earlier Conventions and they undertook in the agreement to make the necessary amendments to those Conventions.

On the basis of the Court's earlier decisions, one might have thought that there would have been no problem regarding the participation of the Member States. These

[26] Opinion 1/76 on *The Laying-Up Fund for Inland Waterway Vessels*, [1977] ECR 741.

[27] Paras 3 and 4 of the Court's reasoning.

[28] Para. 4.

[29] Dashwood and Heliskoski, 'The Classic Authorities Revisited' in Alan Dashwood and Christophe Hillion (eds), *The General Law of EC External Relations* (2000), 3 at pp. 9 *et seq.*

cases hold that the implied powers of the Community are not exclusive until they have been exercised. In the *Inland Waterway Vessels* case the Court did indeed accept the participation of the Member States; however, there is a suggestion that this was only because their intervention was necessary to secure the required amendments to the earlier Conventions. After referring to the necessity of amending the Conventions, the Court said: 'The participation of these States in the Agreement must be considered as being solely for this purpose and not as necessary for the attainment of other features of the system.'[30] It was for this reason, said the Court, that the participation of the six Member States 'is not such as to encroach on the external power of the Community'.[31] This suggests that the Court might not have accepted the participation of the Member States if these special circumstances had not been present.

The main question in the case was something much more fundamental than either of the issues already discussed. The agreement set up an organization called the 'Laying-Up Fund for Inland Waterway Vessels', which was modelled on the Community itself. According to the Statute of the Fund, it was an international public institution with legal personality. Its organs were a Supervisory Board (analogous to the Council), a Board of Management (analogous to the Commission), and a court, the Fund Tribunal. The Supervisory Board was to consist of one representative of each Member State except Ireland (which did not want to be represented) and one representative of Switzerland; the (non-voting) chairman was to be a representative of the Commission. Voting was normally to be by a simple majority, but there was a provision that the majority had to contain the votes of at least three of the states with the greatest interest in the Fund (Belgium, Germany, France, the Netherlands, and Switzerland). The Board of Management was to consist of persons appointed by the same five states together with Luxembourg; but representation was not to be equal: Germany and the Netherlands were to have four members each, Luxembourg one, and the others two each. Decisions were to be taken by a two-thirds majority.

It was provided that the Fund was to have the power, within the very narrow limits of its competence, to enact measures having direct effect in all Member States of the Community as well as in Switzerland.

The Fund Tribunal was to consist of one judge from each of the six Member States that were parties to the agreement and one from Switzerland. The intention was that the six Community judges would be appointed by the European Court from among its own members. The jurisdiction of the Tribunal was to be similar to that of the European Court and it was to have the power to give preliminary rulings on references from national courts in the Community or Switzerland.

It will be seen from this that the Fund was a supranational organization like the Community itself. Could the Community join another Community? In its Opinion, the European Court held that it was possible for the Community to set up a public international institution of this kind, but it found the structure of the Fund unacceptable. In particular, it considered that the Member States played too great a role – it felt that the Community institutions should have been given a greater say in the running of

[30] At para. 7. [31] *Ibid.*

the Fund – and it thought that it was wrong for some Member States to be given powers which were not given to others. It also took objection to the fact that the Community judges on the Tribunal were to be appointed from among the judges of the European Court. The reason for this latter objection was that the agreement setting up the Fund was itself part of Community law and might have had to be interpreted by the European Court: if some judges of the European Court had already given a ruling on it in their capacity as members of the Fund Tribunal, they would be precluded from sitting when the issue came before the European Court. This might make it impossible for the European Court to find a quorum.

The interesting point about this opinion is that none of the points to which the European Court objected were essential characteristics of a supranational organization. It follows from this that, if the right structure were chosen, the Community might be able to become a member of such a body.[32]

In the cases discussed so far, the European Court has followed a consistent policy of enhancing the powers of the Community and restricting those of the Member States. Recent judgments, however, show a more balanced attitude.

The first of these is the *WTO* case.[33] It concerned a group of agreements resulting from the Uruguay Round of multilateral trade negotiations launched by the Punta del Este Ministerial Declaration of 20 September 1986. These were the Multilateral Agreements on Trade in Goods, the General Agreement on Trade in Services ('GATS'), and the Agreement on Trade-Related Aspects of Intellectual Property Rights ('TRIPs'). These agreements are annexed to the Agreement Establishing the World Trade Organization ('WTO Agreement').

Right from the outset, there was controversy in the Community as to where competence lay to negotiate and conclude these agreements, the Commission considering that sole competence lay with the Community and the Member States taking the view that it was a matter of joint competence. The Council decided that the Commission would act as 'sole negotiator on behalf of the Community and the Member States', but it was stated in the minutes of the Council meeting that this did not prejudge 'the question of the competence of the Community or the Member States on particular issues'. Subsequently, the Commission authorized the President of the Council and the commissioner involved in the negotiations, Sir Leon Brittan, to sign on behalf of the Council. Representatives of the Member States also signed.

The Commission then brought proceedings before the Court under Article 300(6) [228(6)] EC for an opinion as to whether sole competence rested with the Community, in which case the signatures of the individual Member States would have been otiose. The Commission's prime argument was that all the agreements fell within the scope of Article 133 [113] EC; alternatively, it contended that various versions of the doctrine of parallelism were applicable.

The Court started by considering to what extent the agreements fell within Article 133 [113]. It dealt first with the Multilateral Agreements on Trade in Goods. These were

[32] For a fuller discussion of the case, see Hartley (1977) 2 ELRev. 275.

[33] Opinion 1/94, [1994] ECR I-5267.

in issue only in so far as they applied to products covered by the Euratom and ECSC Treaties. Euratom was not very controversial. Article 305(2) [232(2)] EC provides that the EC Treaty does not derogate from the Euratom Treaty. From this the Court apparently concluded that, where the Euratom Treaty is silent, the EC Treaty applies. Since the Euratom Treaty contains no provisions on international trade, the Court held that agreements concluded pursuant to Article 133 [113] EC could also apply to trade in Euratom products.

The ECSC Treaty was more problematic. Article 71 ECSC provided that the powers of the Member States in matters of commercial policy were not affected by the Treaty.[34] Moreover, Article 305(1) [232(1)] EC expressly states that the EC Treaty does not affect the ECSC Treaty as regards the rights and obligations of the Member States. These provisions together could be read as preventing the EC Treaty – and especially Article 133 [113] – from taking powers away from the Member States in so far as ECSC products were concerned. The Court, however, held that Article 133 [113] EC could apply to agreements of a general nature, even if they covered ECSC products. Since none of the Multilateral Agreements on Trade in Goods related specifically to ECSC products, the Court held that the Community's exclusive competence under Article 133 [113] was not affected by the fact that the Agreements also applied to ECSC products.

The next issue was agricultural products: it was argued by the Council that Article 37 [43] EC (the provision which governs legislation on agriculture) should apply to certain annexes to the WTO Agreement which concerned international trade in agricultural products. The Court, however, ruled that Article 133 [113] nevertheless applied: the fact that internal measures would have to be adopted under Article 37 [43] in order to implement the agreement did not prevent the agreement itself from being covered by Article 133 [113].

So far everything had been decided in favour of the Commission. The next issues concerned GATS and TRIPs. The Court first considered services other than transport. Article I(2) of GATS refers to four modes of supplying services internationally:

1. cross-frontier supplies of services not involving any movement of persons;
2. consumption abroad (where the consumer goes to the country in which the supplier is established);
3. commercial presence (where the supplier sets up a subsidiary or branch in the consumer's country); and
4. where the supplier sends a person to the consumer's country to supply the service.

Of these, the Court ruled that the first was covered by Article 133 [113], since it envisages a situation similar to that where goods are traded. The Court held, however, that the other three cases were different: since they involve the movement of persons or corporations (topics dealt with in separate sections of the EC Treaty), they could not fall under Article 133 [113].

[34] This is subject to any contrary provisions in the ECSC Treaty itself, but no relevant provisions exist.

Transport is also covered by separate provisions in the EC Treaty; consequently, GATS also fell outside Article 133 [113] in so far as it applied to transport.

The Court then considered TRIPs. One provision of this agreement prohibited the release into free circulation of counterfeit goods: this was so closely related to trade in goods that, the Court ruled, it was covered by Article 133 [113]. The other aspects of TRIPs, however, were not covered. Although intellectual property rights can affect international trade, they do not relate specifically to it and they can affect internal trade just as much or even more.

The Court also pointed out that, if intellectual property rights were regarded as covered by Article 133 [113], the Community's decision-making procedure would be distorted. Internal legislation in this field can be adopted under Articles 94 [100], 95 [100a], or 308 [235] EC. Under the first and last of these, the Council must be unanimous and the Parliament must be consulted; under Article 95 [100a], the co-decision procedure applies. Under Article 133 [113], on the other hand, the Council acts on the basis of qualified-majority voting and there is no requirement to consult the Parliament. Consequently, if Article 133 [113] were held to apply to international agreements on intellectual property, the Community could enter into such agreements on the basis of no more than a qualified-majority vote in the Council. These could affect the law internally, even though internal legislation would require a more onerous procedure.[35]

The result so far was that the Multilateral Agreements on Trade in Goods were fully covered by Article 133 [113] and therefore within the exclusive competence of the Community; GATS and TRIPs, on the other hand, were covered only to a limited extent.

This was not, however, the end of the matter, since the Commission had a second set of arguments based on the doctrine of parallelism. An important difference between these two sets of arguments is, however, that an agreement covered by Article 133 [113] is *automatically* within the exclusive competence of the Community; the doctrine of parallelism, on the other hand, does not necessarily give the Community exclusive competence. It was for this reason that the Commission preferred to base its case on Article 133 [113].

In order to succeed under the doctrine of parallelism, the Commission had to do two things. First, it had to establish that the Community had implied treaty-making powers in the areas in question. To do this, it had to show that the Community had internal power to legislate with regard to the subject matter of the agreement. Secondly, the Commission had to establish that the resulting treaty-making power was exclusive: only then could it obtain a ruling that the Member States should not be parties to the agreements.

The Commission put forward various grounds for its contention that these requirements were satisfied, but the Court rejected all of them. It ruled that, with regard to GATS and TRIPs, the Community and the Member States were jointly competent.[36]

[35] Paras 58–60 of the judgment. The Treaty of Amsterdam has now added a new paragraph (para. 5) to Art. 133 [113], which provides that the Council may extend Art. 133 [113] to cover international agreements on services and intellectual property. To do this, however, the Council must be unanimous and the Parliament must be consulted.

[36] The concept of joint competence or shared competence – the Court uses both terms in the *WTO* case – is ambiguous. Does it mean that *either* the Community *or* the Member States may act alone, or that *neither* may

In the case of the Multilateral Agreements on Trade in Goods, on the other hand, the Community had exclusive competence.

The *WTO* case, and the Court's later opinion in the *OECD* case,[37] have clarified the law as to when the Community's implied treaty-making powers (under the doctrine of parallelism) are exclusive. It is now settled that the mere existence of an internal power in the relevant area does not automatically result in exclusivity.[38] There are, however, two cases in which the Community's power *is* exclusive.[39] The first is where the Community has adopted internal legislation in the relevant area which could be affected by the agreement. This would be the case where, for example, the agreement would require the internal rules to be amended. It seems that exclusivity may also result where the Community adopts internal legislation which purports to effect a complete harmonization of the area – thus indicating an intention to take it over – even if there would be no direct clash with the agreement. The second case is where internal legislation expressly empowers the Community to negotiate with non-Member States.

In the *WTO* case, the Commission argued that the power is also exclusive where this is necessary for the attainment of one of the objectives of the Community. As was pointed out above in connection with the *North-East Atlantic Fisheries Convention* case, there are some instances where it is not possible for the Community to act first on the internal level: it is only through international action that the objective can be achieved. It could be argued that in such instances, even before the Community has acted, the Member States should be precluded from entering into international agreements if these would prejudice future Community action. The Court, however, made conflicting statements on this point: in paragraph 85 of the judgment it said (with reference to the *Inland Waterway Vessels* case and the *North-East Atlantic Fisheries Convention* case) that, where it is not possible to act first on the internal level, 'external powers may be exercised, and thus *become* exclusive, without any internal legislation having first been adopted',[40] a statement which suggests that the power is not exclusive until exercised; in paragraph 89, on the other hand, it said, 'Save where internal powers can only be effectively exercised at the same time as external powers (see Opinion 1/76 and paragraph 85 above), internal competence can give rise to exclusive external competence only if it is exercised', a statement implying that, in such cases, it is exclusive *before* being exercised. Perhaps the judges were themselves divided on the issue. However, the first of the above statements was repeated in the *OECD* case,[41] while the second was not. Since the Court held in the *North-East Atlantic Fisheries Convention* case that, even where it is not possible to act first on the internal level, external competence remains concurrent until exercised, this must still be regarded as the law, though the conflicting dicta in the *WTO* case serve as a warning that the Court may change its mind.

act alone? These are clearly two different concepts. In the *North-East Atlantic Fisheries Convention* case, it seems that *either* the Member States *or* the Community could have acted alone to conclude the agreement; in the *WTO* case, on the other hand, it seems clear that the Member States could not have acted on their own. It also seems that the Community could not have done so.

[37] Opinion 2/92, [1995] ECR I-521.

[38] See paras 77, 88, and 89 of the judgment in the *WTO* case, and para. 31 of the judgment in the *OECD* case.

[39] See paras 95 and 96 of the judgment in the *WTO* case and paras 31–3 of the judgment in the *OECD* case.

[40] Italics added. [41] At para. 32 of the judgment.

Another case in which the Court displayed its new-found restraint was *France v. Commission.*[42] Here the Commission had both negotiated and *concluded* an agreement with the United States on co-operation in the enforcement of competition (antitrust) law. As was explained above, Article 300 [228] EC provides that the Commission negotiates international agreements, but they are concluded by the Council. France brought proceedings under Article 230 [173] EC to annul the agreement (or the Commission decision to conclude it) on the ground that the procedure violated Article 300 [228] EC. In its defence, the Commission advanced an interesting variant of the doctrine of parallelism: it argued that, since it had internal competence to enforce EC competition law, it should have external competence to conclude agreements in this area. It also claimed that, since the main provisions of the agreement required it to do no more than keep the American authorities informed of its activities, it could carry out the agreement without the assistance of the Council.

The Court refused to accept this argument. It first held that only the Community, and not an institution of the Community such as the Commission, could be a party to an international agreement. It then rejected the parallelism argument:[43]

> Even though the Commission has the power, internally, to take individual decisions applying the rules of competition, a field covered by the Agreement, that internal power is not such as to alter the allocation of powers between the Community institutions with regard to the conclusion of international agreements, which is determined by Article 228 of the Treaty.

In other words, the doctrine of parallelism applies only between the Community and the Member States, not between the Council and the Commission.

The Court continued with its conservative approach in the *ECHR* case,[44] a case in which it was asked to decide whether the Community could accede to the European Convention on Human Rights, an international treaty to which all the Member States and a number of non-Member States are parties. The Community Treaties give no express competence to the Community regarding human rights, but the Commission argued that implied competence resulted from Article 308 [235] EC. Since this provision empowers the Council to 'take the appropriate measures' even if the EC Treaty has *not* provided the necessary powers, it might be thought that it gives the Community almost unlimited power to conclude international treaties where these are necessary to attain one of the objectives of the Community: not only could it be argued that Article 308 [235] gives an internal power which, under the doctrine of parallelism, automatically results in an external power, but it could also be argued that since it speaks of 'measures' – a term which could include treaties – it directly confers an external power.[45]

As explained in Chapter 4, however, the Court ruled that Article 308 [235] cannot be used for the adoption of a measure that would have constitutional significance.

42 Case C-327/91, [1994] ECR I-3641.

43 Para. 41 of the judgment.

44 Opinion 2/94, [1996] ECR I-1759.

45 In fact, the Community has already concluded a number of agreements under Article 308 [235] – for example, the Convention for the Prevention of Marine Pollution from Land-Based Sources, signed in Paris on 4 June 1974, OJ 1975, L194/6.

Adherence to the European Convention on Human Rights would have such significance, not least because it would place the European Court of Human Rights above the European Court of Justice (EC) in matters of human rights. The European Court, therefore, held that the Community lacked competence to adhere to the Convention, unless the EC Treaty was first amended.[46]

## LEGAL PROCEEDINGS

A special legal procedure is laid down by Article 300(6) [228(6)] EC, which provides:

> The Council, the Commission or a Member State may obtain the opinion of the Court of Justice as to whether an agreement envisaged is compatible with the provisions of this Treaty. Where the opinion of the Court of Justice is adverse, the agreement may enter into force only in accordance with Article 48 [N] of the Treaty on European Union.[47]

This provision applies to all agreements to which the EC is to be a party. In essence, it provides a power of judicial review, but this takes place before the conclusion of the agreement[48] and is given in the form of an opinion.[49] This opinion, despite its name, has legal consequences: if it is adverse, the agreement cannot enter into force unless the EC Treaty is amended to permit the Community to conclude the agreement.[50] Since the procedure under Article 48 [N] TEU for amending the Treaty is cumbersome[51] – the amendments have to be ratified by each Member State according to the requirements of its constitution – an adverse opinion will normally prevent the conclusion of the agreement. If the Court's objections are comparatively minor, however, it may be possible – if the other parties are willing – to revise the agreement in accordance with the Court's judgment.

There can be no doubt that the object of this procedure as envisaged by the authors of the Treaty was to prevent the Community from entering into agreements which are incompatible with the Treaty. The Court, however, has allowed the Commission to use it for quite a different purpose: to prevent the Member States from encroaching on the competence of the Community. The *Natural Rubber Agreement* case[52] is a good

[46] For later cases in which the Court reverted to its previous policy of expanding Community competence and restricting that of the Member States, see the '*Open Skies*' cases, for example *Commission v. United Kingdom*, Case C-466/98, [2002] ECR I-9427; *Lugano Convention Case*, Opinion 1/03, 7 February 2006.

[47] Art. 48 [N] TEU lays down the procedure for amending the Community Treaties.

[48] Normally the agreement will have been negotiated, but not concluded. If the agreement is concluded by the time it comes to give its opinion, the Court will not give a ruling: Opinion 3/94 (*Bananas* case) [1995] ECR I-4577. In such a case, the appropriate remedy for a Member State or Community institution that wished to contest the agreement would be to bring proceedings under Art. 230 [173] EC to annul the decision of the Council to conclude it: *ibid.*, para. 22 of the judgment. In the *ECHR* case, Opinion 2/94, [1996] ECR I-1759, the Court was willing to give a ruling on whether the Community had *competence* to accede to the European Convention on Human Rights, even though negotiations had not been commenced; it was not, however, willing to give a ruling on whether accession would be *compatible* with the Community Treaties. This was because, though the provisions of the Convention were known, there was no indication of the terms on which the Community would adhere to it.

[49] For this reason, an application under this provision will not be called, for example, 'Case 1/76', but 'Opinion 1/76'.

[50] This procedure is similar to that under Art. 54 of the French Constitution.

[51] For a discussion of this procedure, see Chap. 3.

[52] Opinion 1/78, [1979] ECR 2871.

example. The International Agreement on Natural Rubber was a draft agreement drawn up within the framework of UNCTAD. On the Community side, the negotiations had initially been conducted jointly by the Commission and the national governments, and it was intended by the latter that both the Community and the Member States should be parties. The Commission, however, felt that the matter came within the exclusive competence of the Community – it maintained that it was covered by the express treaty-making power in Article 133 [113] – and considered that the Member States should not participate in the negotiations.

In some ways the situation was similar to that in the *ERTA* case,[53] but here the Commission decided to use a different legal remedy: it brought an application under Article 300 [228] and asked the Court for an opinion whether it would be compatible with the Treaty for the proposed agreement to be concluded in the mixed form. Since it was not disputed that the Community would be a party to the agreement, the issue before the Court was the participation of the Member States. The Member States protested at the use of the procedure for this purpose, but the Court held the application admissible, though it eventually gave an opinion which was not wholly in favour of the Commission. It held that the Member States could be parties if, but only if, it was eventually agreed that the scheme would be financed out of national funds. Until this question was decided, the Member States could continue to participate in the negotiations.

The *ILO Convention 170* case[54] is an even more striking example. This concerned a convention on safety in the use of chemicals at work, which had been drawn up under the auspices of the International Labour Organization. The Commission claimed that it fell under the exclusive competence of the Community; several Member States disputed this.

The Commission brought the matter before the Court under the procedure laid down by Article 300 [228]. The striking fact about the case was that, as the Community was not a member of the ILO,[55] it was not in a position to conclude the Convention: only the Member States could have done so. Since Article 300 [228] applies only where the agreement is to be concluded by the Community, the German and Dutch Governments challenged the jurisdiction of the Court.

The Court solved the problem by ignoring it. It stated that its opinion was concerned only with the question whether the Community had exclusive competence under Community law, not whether the ILO rules permitted the Community to conclude the Convention.[56] This was a fair point, but it was not the point made by the German and Dutch Governments: they had argued that the procedure under Article 300 [228] can be used only where the agreement is to be concluded by the Community, something

[53] The procedural aspects of this case were discussed in Chap. 4. In the *ERTA* case the Commission could not have invoked Art. 300 [228] since that provision applies only where the Community is to be a party to the agreement.

[54] Opinion 2/91, [1993] ECR I-1061.

[55] It only had observer status.

[56] It suggested that, if necessary, the Community's external competence could be exercised through the medium of the Member States acting jointly in the Community's interest.

which would admittedly not have occurred in the case before the Court. Nevertheless, the Court held that the jurisdictional requirements of Article 300 [228] were satisfied.[57]

Certain features of the procedure under Article 300 [228] are rather unusual.[58] The Council, the Commission, and the Member States may submit written observations, but there is no public hearing. All the advocates general give opinions in a closed session; these are not published. The Court then gives judgment in the normal way; this is published.

### CONCLUSIONS

The authors of the EC Treaty probably intended the EC to have relatively limited treaty-making power (in contrast to Euratom which was intended all along to have wide powers). The Member States originally adopted a restrictive interpretation of these powers and even tried to deny the Community some of the powers which it undoubtedly possessed. In the 1970s, however, the Commission staged a counterattack by resorting to legal action, knowing that it could count on the Court for support. The result is that the powers of the Community have been extended, and those of the Member States have been reduced.

The series of cases by which this has been achieved is also of interest as an example of the law-making strategy of the Court. This can best be characterized as a 'step-by-step' approach: the first step, taken in the *ERTA* case, was regarded at the time as very bold – *Le Monde* published an article on 27 April 1971 asking whether the Court had exceeded its jurisdiction – but the Court nevertheless went ahead with the second step – hesitantly in the *North-East Atlantic Fisheries Convention* case and firmly in the *Inland Waterway Vessels* case: what seemed bold in 1971 had been discarded as insufficient by 1977.

## THE TREATY-MAKING POWER OF EURATOM

The Euratom Treaty gives the Community wide treaty-making powers within the atomic energy field. This was probably necessitated by the circumstances: at the time when the Treaty was concluded, the Community countries were much less advanced in nuclear technology than the United States or Britain, and the authors of the Treaty probably thought that international agreements would be required to obtain technology and materials; they may also have thought that the Community would have to enter into international agreements concerned with the security aspects of atomic energy.

The Euratom Treaty contains a special chapter on External Relations (Chapter X of Title Two). This is concerned with the treaty-making power of both the Community and the Member States; it also covers international agreements entered into by individuals or undertakings in Member States.

[57] In the end, the Court ruled that the subject matter of the Convention did not fall within exclusive Community competence.

[58] See the Rules of Procedure, Arts 107 and 108, OJ 1991, L176/7.

The treaty-making power of the Community is laid down in Article 101.[59] This gives the Community power to conclude international agreements 'within the limits of its powers and jurisdiction': in other words, the Euratom Treaty expressly applies the doctrine of parallelism. As in the case of the EC, such agreements are negotiated by the Commission in accordance with the directives of the Council; but unlike in the case of the EC, they are *concluded* by the Commission, though the approval of the Council must be obtained. It is, moreover, provided in the third paragraph of Article 101 that agreements may be negotiated and concluded solely by the Commission if their implementation does not require action by the Council and can be effected within the limits of the relevant budget.

The Euratom Treaty does not contain provision for a reference to the European Court to determine whether proposed Community agreements are compatible with the Treaty. It does, however, provide for an analogous procedure to test the compatibility of agreements which the *Member States* propose to conclude. This is Article 103, under which Member States are required to communicate to the Commission any agreements they propose to enter into which concern matters within the purview of the Treaty. This enables the Commission to ascertain whether the proposed agreement could impede the application of the Treaty. The Commission has one month to scrutinize the draft and make its comments known to the Member State concerned. If the Commission raises objections, the agreement may not be concluded until the Commission's objections have been satisfied. The Member State may, however, apply to the European Court for a ruling (not an opinion, as under the EC Treaty) as to the compatibility of the proposed agreement with the Treaty. If the Court's ruling is favourable, the Member State may go ahead with the agreement.

The procedure for an application under Article 103 Euratom is similar to that under Article 300 [228] EC, though there are significant differences.[60] The application may be made only by a Member State; it is served on the Commission, which may submit observations (analogous to a defence under the ordinary procedure) and these are served on the applicant. Only one advocate general is heard and, as under Article 300 [228] EC, the hearing takes place in private in the deliberation room. The applicant and the Commission have the right to make oral submissions.

This procedure was used for the first time in 1978 with regard to the draft Convention on the Physical Protection of Nuclear Materials, Facilities, and Transports.[61] This agreement, which was drawn up under the ægis of the International Atomic Energy Agency, was to be concluded by the Member States without the participation of the Community. The object of the agreement was to ensure that nuclear materials were protected from theft and possible misuse. Many of the provisions of the agreement were clearly within the competence of the Member States – for example, those relating to criminal offences and extradition of offenders – but, in the opinion of the Commission, others impinged on areas in which the Community had direct responsibility. In particular, the Commission took the view that provisions concerning the export and import of

[59] See also Arts 2(h), 10, 29, 46(2)(e), and 52. Art. 206 gives a power to conclude association agreements.

[60] See Art. 105 of the Rules of Procedure, OJ 1991, L176/7.

[61] Ruling 1/78, [1978] ECR 2151.

nuclear materials could not be agreed to by the Member States acting alone. Therefore, when the text was communicated to it under Article 103 Euratom, the Commission stated in its comments that it was necessary for the Community to become a party to the agreement in addition to the Member States: such mixed agreements are expressly envisaged by Article 102 Euratom. The Belgian Government then referred the matter to the Court in order to clarify the legal position.

After a careful analysis of the terms of the draft agreement, the Court concluded that it fell partly within the competence of the Member States and partly within that of the Community. It therefore ruled that the participation of the Community in the agreement was essential: the conclusion of the agreement by the Member States would be compatible with the Treaty only if the Community were also a party. The Court also stated that it would not be necessary for the other parties to the agreement to be told which parts of the agreement were within the competence of the Community and which parts within the competence of the Member States: this, they should be told, was a domestic matter for the Community.

## ACTS OF INSTITUTIONS ESTABLISHED BY AGREEMENTS WITH THIRD COUNTRIES

International agreements entered into by the Community sometimes set up institutional structures. Association councils under association agreements are an example. If these organs have power under the agreement to adopt legally binding acts, can those acts constitute part of the Community legal system? According to the European Court, they can: decisions of the Association Council under the Association Agreement between Turkey and the EC have been held to constitute 'an integral part of the Community legal system'.[62] It seems that such decisions are regarded as in some sense partaking of the legal nature of the agreement under which the organ which adopted them was set up.

## INTERNATIONAL AGREEMENTS AND THE COMMUNITY LEGAL SYSTEM

The legal effect of international agreements with non-member states must be looked at on three levels: the international level, the Community level, and the national level. The effect of an agreement on the international level depends on whether there is a binding obligation between the Community (or the Member States), on the one hand, and the non-Member State, on the other hand. This is decided by international law. At this level,

[62] *Greece v. Commission*, Case 30/88, [1989] ECR 3711 (para. 13 of the judgment). See also *Sevince*, Case C-192/89, [1990] ECR I-3461; *Deutsche Shell*, Case C-188/91, [1993] ECR I-363.

the only way in which Community law could come into play would be if international law referred a particular issue to it.

The effect of an international agreement within the Community legal system, however, is for Community law to decide. It must determine whether international agreements are a source of law within the Community legal order, and it can lay down the terms and conditions of that recognition.

The effect of an international agreement at the national level depends on national law. However, when the Member States concluded the EC and Euratom treaties, they gave the European Court jurisdiction to interpret them.[63] Acting under this jurisdiction, the European Court has ruled that the Community treaties require the Member States to give effect to many provisions of Community law in their legal systems. The courts of the Member States accept that the Member States are under an international obligation to give such effect to Community law. Subject to certain limitations, the national legal systems give to provisions of Community law the effect that Community law requires. In this indirect way, therefore, Community law has a large role to play in determining the effect in the national legal systems of those provisions of treaties with non-Member States that form part of the Community legal system.

The effect of a treaty obviously depends in part on its validity: a treaty can have no legal effects if it is invalid. A ruling by the European Court that an international agreement with a non-Member State is invalid under international law would not be binding on non-Member States. Nevertheless, the European Court can decide whether the agreement should be *recognized* and *applied* within the Community legal system. This could, of course, involve considering whether the agreement was valid – a question which should be decided according to international law – but no determination made by the Court would be binding on the international level.[64]

Even if the agreement is valid under international law, the European Court may still refuse to apply it, either because it is not the kind of agreement which it is prepared to enforce, or because it violates a principle of Community law. It is these questions that will now be considered; in doing so, a distinction will sometimes have to be drawn between the three kinds of international agreement – those concluded by the Community, those concluded by the Member States within the general scope of the Community Treaties, and those concluded jointly by the Community and the Member States (mixed agreements).

## BINDING THE COMMUNITY

Article 300(7) [228(7)] EC provides that international agreements concluded by the Community are binding on the Community. This is, of course, obvious and would be the case even if it were not expressly so provided by the Treaty. The European Court has,

[63] Arts 234 [177] EC and 150 Euratom.

[64] See Pescatore, 'Les relations extérieures des Communautés européennes' (1961) (II) 103 Recueil des cours de l'Académie de Droit International de la Haye 1 at 127–8; and *per* Advocate General Mayras in the third *International Fruit Company* case, Cases 21–4/72, [1972] ECR 1219 at 1234.

however, gone further and laid down that international agreements entered into by the Member States can also bind the Community. The leading case on this is the third *International Fruit Company* case,[65] in which the question arose whether the Community was bound by the General Agreement on Tariffs and Trade (GATT). This was the original GATT, which was concluded before the establishment of the Community. All the Member States were parties to it. It was concerned, as its name suggests, with tariffs and trade, and thus fell within the area in which the Community had express treaty-making power. For these reasons the European Court held that the Community was bound by it. The key paragraph of its judgment reads as follows:[66] '... in so far as under the EEC Treaty the Community has assumed the powers previously exercised by Member States in the area governed by the General Agreement, the provisions of that agreement have the effect of binding the Community'. In a later case,[67] the Court said that, as regards the fulfilment of commitments under GATT, the Community had 'replaced' the Member States.[68]

It is not yet clear in what circumstances the Community will become bound by agreements entered into by the Member States alone but, according to Advocate General Capotorti, four conditions are necessary: first, the agreement must have been concluded prior to the EC Treaty and all the Member States must have been parties to it when the EC Treaty was concluded; secondly, it must have been the wish of the Member States to pledge the Community to observe the agreement, the aims of which must be shared by the Community; thirdly, action must have been taken by the Community institutions within the framework of the agreement; and fourthly, the other parties to the agreement must have recognized that powers had been transferred to the Community with regard to the subject matter of the agreement.[69] It remains to be seen whether the Court will adopt these principles.[70]

Difficult problems can arise where the Community does not take over the rights and obligations of Member States towards third countries. Where the agreement has been concluded prior to the EC Treaty (or, in the case of an agreement concluded by a new Member State, prior to its accession), the Community, though not bound by the agreement, is nevertheless under an obligation not to impede the fulfilment by the Member States which are parties to it of their obligations under the agreement.[71] This rule, which applies even if only one Member State is a party, follows from Article 307 [234]

[65] Cases 21–4/72, [1972] ECR 1219. See also *Schlüter*, Case 9/73, [1973] ECR 1135 and *Nederlandse Spoorwegen*, Case 38/75, [1975] ECR 1439. In the latter case, it was held that the Community was bound by two Conventions of 15 December 1950 on customs tariffs. See, further, the decision of the Court of First Instance in *Ahmed Ali Yusuf and Al Barakaat International Foundation v. Council and Commission*, Case T-306/01, 21 September 2005 (going on appeal as case C-415/05), discussed in Chap. 3, section entitled 'Conflicting Treaties', sub-section entitled 'United Nations Law'.

[66] Para. 18 of the judgment.

[67] *Nederlandse Spoorwegen*, Case 38/75, [1975] ECR 1439 (paras 16 and 21 of the judgment). See also *SPI*, Cases 267–9/81, [1983] ECR 801 (paras 17–19 of the judgment).

[68] When the original GATT was superseded by the WTO Agreement (and its associated instruments) the Community became a party, along with the Member States.

[69] *Procureur Général v. Arbelaiz-Emazabel*, Case 181/80, [1981] ECR 2961 at 2987; see also *Attorney General v. Burgoa*, Case 812/79, [1980] ECR 2787 at 2815–16.

[70] If it does, the results could be strange. For example, the Community would not be bound by the European Road Transport Agreement.

[71] *Attorney General v. Burgoa*, Case 812/79, [1980] ECR 2961 (para. 10 of the judgment).

EC (discussed above in Chapter 3).[72] Article 307 [234] does not, however, give the earlier treaty any greater effect than it would have had if the Community Treaties had not been concluded; in particular, it does not require Member States to give direct effect to it,[73] though it does not prevent them from doing so.

The position of the Community with regard to agreements covered by Article 307 [234] must be distinguished from its position under agreements to which it becomes a party by succession. In the latter case the Community is bound by the agreement and is responsible to the non-Member States for its fulfilment. The agreement is part of the Community legal system. In the former case, on the other hand, the Community is not bound by the agreement and is not responsible to the non-Member States for its fulfilment. This is the responsibility of the Member States which are parties to it. The agreement is not part of the Community legal system, though the powers of the Community are restricted by it.[74]

The law is less clear with regard to agreements concluded after the EC Treaty. In principle, the position should be analogous to that under Article 307 [234], provided the subject matter of the agreement was not, under Community law, within the exclusive competence of the Community. If the subject matter *was* within the Community's exclusive competence at the time of the conclusion of the agreement, the European Court would probably consider that the Community's powers were not restricted by the agreement. Whether the agreement was valid at the international level would be a matter for international law.

Mixed agreements raise particular difficulties. Such agreements are concluded where the subject matter is regarded as falling partly within the competence of the Community and partly within that of the Member States. However, in the case of some mixed agreements, part or all of the agreement may be subject to concurrent competence, by which is meant that either the Community or the Member States could have concluded the agreement independently of the other.

It is clear that the Community is bound by all parts of a mixed agreement that fall within its competence, whether or not those parts also fall within the competence of the Member States.[75] A more difficult question is whether the Community is bound by those parts of the agreement that are outside its competence. It is suggested that it should not be; otherwise, the conclusion of the agreement would constitute an amendment to the EC Treaty, which is surely not what would have been intended.[76] If this is correct, those parts of the agreement within the exclusive competence of the Member States would not form part of the Community legal system.

[72] See the section entitled 'Conflicting Treaties' and the sub-section entitled 'Conflicts with Non-Community Treaties'.

[73] *Attorney General v. Burgoa*, Case 812/79, [1980] ECR 2787 (para. 10 of the judgment and para. 2 of the ruling). On the meaning of 'direct effect', see Chap. 7, below.

[74] Such an agreement would not be covered by Art. 234 [177] EC.

[75] *Commission v. France*, Case C-239/03, 7 October 2004, para. 23–25 of the judgment; *Commission v. Ireland*, C-13/00, [2002] ECR I-2943, para. 14 of the judgment; *Demirel*, Case 12/86, [1987] ECR 3719, para. 9 of the judgment.

[76] Pietri, 'La valeur juridique des accords liant la CEE' (1976) 12 RTDE 50 at 75. See also Ehlermann in O'Keeffe and Schermers (eds), *Mixed Agreements* (1983), 18.

This reasoning seems to be in accord with that of the European Court. In *Hermès v. FHT*,[77] the Court had to decide whether it had jurisdiction to interpret Article 50 of TRIPs, a mixed agreement concluded jointly by the Community and the Member States as part of the WTO Agreement. Article 50 is concerned with provisional measures for the protection of intellectual property rights. The Court held that it did have jurisdiction. The reason was that a Community measure, Regulation 40/94,[78] entered into force shortly before TRIPs was signed. Article 99 of this Regulation is concerned with provisional measures for the protection of Community trade marks. It provides that an application may be made to the courts of a Member State for such provisional measures as are available under the law of that Member State for the protection of national trade marks. Since Article 50 of TRIPs affects the national measures available for the protection of trade marks, it has an indirect effect on the protection of Community trade marks. On these flimsy and insubstantial grounds the Court held that it had jurisdiction to interpret Article 50 of TRIPs when a Community trade mark was in issue.[79] The *Hermès* case concerned a trade mark, though not a Community trade mark. However, the Court thought that it would be undesirable if Article 50 were interpreted in one way when a Community trade mark was in issue and in another way when a non-Community trade mark was in issue. So it held that it had jurisdiction in the latter case as well.

Article 50 of TRIPs was again before the Court in *Dior v. Tuk Consultancy*.[80] This time the Court had to decide whether it had jurisdiction to interpret it when the right in issue was not a trade mark, but an industrial design. It applied the same reasoning: it held that it would be undesirable if Article 50 was interpreted differently depending on whether it was being applied to a trade mark or to some other right.

The Court was also asked to decide on the effect of Article 50. Was the national court obliged to apply it to the case before it? On this, the Court gave a ruling[81] with regard to the field within the competence of the Community,[82] but refused to do so in so far as Article 50 applied outside that field. This was a matter to be decided by the national courts under national law.

One can conclude from this that provisions of mixed agreements that fall within the exclusive competence of the Member States do not form part of the Community legal system. It seems that the European Court has jurisdiction to interpret them only if there is some special reason.

[77] Case C-53/96, [1998] ECR I-3603. The Court's reasoning in this case is not very clear, but it is clarified in the *Dior* case (below).

[78] OJ 1994 L11, p. 1.

[79] If the European Court's argument were valid, it would have had jurisdiction to interpret national law on provisional measures to protect trade marks, which it clearly does not. A stronger argument in favour of the Court's position would be to regard Reg. 40/94 as conferring international competence on the Community under the *ERTA* doctrine (discussed above) though this argument is not very satisfactory in view of the limited scope of Art. 99.

[80] Cases C-300, 392/98, 14 December 2000.

[81] It held that it was not directly effective, but it should, as far as possible, be taken into account by national courts when interpreting national law ('indirect effect', explained in Chap. 7).

[82] The test is whether the Community has already legislated in the field in question, which appears to refer to the *ERTA* doctrine on the international competence of the Community. Para. 47 of the judgment suggests that this field might be trade marks in general, rather than just Community trade marks.

## BINDING THE MEMBER STATES

Article 300(7) [228(7)] EC provides that agreements concluded by the Community are binding on the Member States. Agreements concluded by the Member States which subsequently became binding on the Community would, of course, continue to bind the Member States as well. All agreements binding on the Community are consequently binding on the Member States.

## EFFECT

When might the European Court refuse to give effect to an international agreement on the ground that it was contrary to Community law? At the present time, one cannot lay down any hard and fast rules, but a few general observations may be made. In the *ERTA* case, the Court drew a distinction between the capacity of the Community to enter into international agreements and its authority to do so. If the agreement was outside the authority of the Community, its conclusion would be contrary to Community law, and a ruling on this point could be obtained under Article 300 [228] EC. This procedure, however, can be used only before the conclusion of the agreement. If no application is made under Article 300 [228] and the question arises after it is concluded, the Court would not necessarily apply the same test. In particular, it is unlikely that the agreement would be held invalid or inapplicable on the ground that the wrong negotiating procedure was used.

The Court has said that the Community has the capacity to enter into international agreements 'over the whole field of objectives defined in Part One of the Treaty'.[83] If the agreement was outside the capacity of the Community it might be of no effect in the Community legal system. Even if it came within this area, however, it is hard to see how it could be applied in the Community legal system if it directly conflicted with a provision in one of the constitutive Treaties: the powers of the Community come from the Treaties and they must be subject to the provisions of the Treaties.[84] The position would probably be the same if the international agreement was contrary to a general principle of law. If it conflicted with a Community act, on the other hand, the agreement would be valid: in the third *International Fruit Company* case, this was expressly stated by Advocate General Mayras[85] and is implicit in the judgment of the Court. One may therefore conclude – tentatively – that an international agreement entered into by the Community will be of no effect within the Community legal system if it is outside the capacity of the Community or if it conflicts with one of the constituent Treaties or (possibly) with a general principle of law.[86] It must again be stressed, however, that this

[83] *ERTA*, Case 22/70, [1971] ECR 263 (para. 14 of the judgment).

[84] See Pescatore, 'Les relations extérieures des Communautés européennes' (1961) (II) 103 Recueil des cours de l'Académie de Droit International de la Haye 1 at 127.

[85] [1972] ECR 1219 at 1233–4. Where a directly effective agreement conflicts with a Community act, the act will be invalid if it was subsequent to the agreement, and would probably be regarded as suspended if it was prior to it.

[86] Such a question might come before the Court on a preliminary reference from a national court or in an enforcement action against a Member State (if the Member State is accused of violating the agreement). See also

relates solely to the effect of the agreement in the Community legal system, not under international law.

As we shall see in the next chapter, international agreements which are binding on the Community, and therefore part of the Community legal system, have to be applied by national courts if they are directly effective. In such a case, they will override inconsistent provisions of national law. In the third *International Fruit Company* case,[87] the European Court held that a Community act may be challenged in a national court on the ground that it is contrary to an international agreement which is binding on the Community. However, this applies only if the agreement is directly effective.[88]

In *Germany v. Council* (*Bananas* case),[89] the Court held that the same rule applies if the challenge originates in the European Court (for example, in an annulment action under Article 230 [173] EC): a conflict between a Community act and an international agreement affects the validity of the former only if the latter is directly effective.[90] The only exceptions are where the Community act was intended to give effect to an obligation under the international agreement[91] or where the Community act expressly refers to the agreement.[92]

## FURTHER READING

SCHERMERS, 'Community Law and International Law' (1975) 12 CMLRev. 77.

MEESSEN, 'The Application of Rules of Public International Law within Community Law' (1976) 13 CMLRev. 485.

CWA TIMMERMANS AND ELM VÖLKER, *Division of Powers between the European Communities and their Member States in the Field of External Relations* (1981).

DAVID O'KEEFFE AND HENRY G SCHERMERS (eds), *Mixed Agreements* (1983).

House of Lords Select Committee on the European Communities, *External Competence of the European Communities* (H.L. 236, 1984/85).

JEAN GROUX AND PHILIPPE MANIN, *The European Communities in the International Order* (1985).

CHURCHILL AND FOSTER, 'European Community Law and Prior Treaty Obligations of Member States: The Spanish Fishermen's Cases' (1987) 36 ICLQ 504.

RIDEAU, 'Les Accords Internationaux dans la Jurisprudence de la Cour de Justice des Communautés Européennes: Réflexions sur les Relations entre les Ordres Juridiques International, Communautaire et Nationaux' [1990] Révue Générale de Droit International Public 289.

Pietri, 'La valeur juridique des accords liant la Communauté économique européenne' (1976) 12 RTDE 50 and 194 at 207–14.

[87] Cases 21–4/72, [1972] ECR 1219. [88] *Van Parys*, Case C-377/02, 1 March 2005.

[89] Case C-280/93, [1994] ECR I-4973; see also *Portugal v. Council*, Case C-149/96, [1999] ECR I-8395.

[90] If the international agreement is not directly effective, its violation cannot give rise to an action in tort against the Community: Case C-93/02 P, *Biret International v. Council*, [2003] ECR I-10497. In view of the *Van Parys* case (n. 88, above), it is unlikely that there is an exception where the WTO DSB has given a ruling.

[91] *Nakajima v. Council*, Case C-69/89, [1991] ECR I-2069.

[92] *FEDIOL v. Commission*, Case 70/87, [1989] ECR 1781.

CHEYNE, 'International Agreements and the European Community Legal System' (1994) 19 ELRev. 581.

TRIDIMAS AND EECKHOUT, 'The External Competence of the Community and the Case-Law of the Court of Justice: Principle versus Pragmatism' (1994) 14 YEL 143.

WEISS, 'Succession of States in Respect of Treaties Concluded by the European Communities' (1994) 10 SEW 661.

BOURGEOIS, 'The EC in the WTO and Advisory Opinion 1/94: An Echternacht Procession' (1995) 32 CMLRev. 763.

SACK, 'The European Community's Membership of International Organizations' (1995) 32 CMLRev. 1227.

I MACLEOD, ID HENDRY, AND STEPHEN HYETT, *The External Relations of the European Community* (1996).

NEUWAHL, 'Shared Powers or Shared Incompetence? More on Mixity' (1996) 33 CMLRev. 667.

ALAN DASHWOOD AND CHRISTOPHE HILLION, *The General Law of EC External Relations* (2000).

SCHÜTZE, 'Parallel External Powers in the European Community: From "Cubist" Perspectives Towards "Naturalist" Constitutional Principles?' (2004) 23 YEL 225.

KUIJPER AND BRONCKERS, 'WTO Law in the European Court of Justice' (2005) 42 CMLRev. 1313.

# PART III

# COMMUNITY LAW AND THE MEMBER STATES

# INTRODUCTION

This Part is concerned with the relationship between Community law and national law, in particular with the extent to which provisions of Community law must be applied by national courts.

In what circumstances is a provision of one legal system applicable in another? This depends on the relationship between the two systems. If one is dependent on the other (in the sense that it derives its validity from it), the question of transfer must be determined by the primary system. It can decide whether provisions of the one system can apply in the other and, if they do, in what circumstances this will occur. If, on the other hand, neither system is dependent on the other, each system decides for itself whether provisions of the other can be transferred to it.

This will be clear from two examples. Assume, first, that the United Kingdom decides to give home rule to a territory under its jurisdiction. It sets up a regional assembly with law-making powers and creates a system of courts for that territory. Clearly, United Kingdom law determines whether, and in what circumstances, provisions of United Kingdom law apply in the dependent legal system. It also decides whether, and in what circumstances, provisions of the dependent system apply in the United Kingdom system. This is because United Kingdom law is the primary system: it created the regional system and gave it its validity.

Now contrast the position where each system is independent of the other. Let us take the relationship between English and French law. The question whether a provision of French law should be applied in the English legal system depends on English law. It is the English rules of conflict of laws that determine whether a rule of French law will be applied by an English court to determine, for example, the validity of a marriage celebrated in France. French law cannot decide whether a rule of French law is part of the English legal system and must be applied by the English courts. Likewise, English law cannot decide whether a rule of English law is part of the French legal system. This is because each system is autonomous.

These principles also govern the relationship between international law and national law. Since these two systems are independent of each other,[1] the question whether a provision of international law applies in national law must depend on the latter. This is indeed the case. The law of each country decides to what extent international law has effect as part of the legal system of that country.[2]

Since Community law is based on a set of treaties, the important issue for our purposes is the application of a treaty in the domestic law of the States that are parties

[1] This may be rejected by theorists who follow the monist view of international law, but it accords with the actual, real-life relationship between the two systems.

[2] See Francis G Jacobs and Shelly Roberts (eds), *The Effect of Treaties in Domestic Law* (1987), at p. xxiv (introduction by Jacobs, based on studies of individual countries in later parts of the book).

to it. If a treaty (or a provision in it) applies in the legal system of such a State without that State having to adopt any legislation specifically providing for the application of that treaty, the treaty is said to be 'directly effective' or to have 'direct effect'. A treaty that is directly effective is automatically part of the legal system of the State in question. If, on the other hand, it is not directly effective, it cannot be applied in the domestic law of that State without the adoption of legislation to make provision for this.

When States sign a treaty, they normally agree to achieve a certain result, but reserve to themselves the right to determine the means by which this will be brought about. If the desired result involves an alteration of their law, their law decides whether this will follow automatically from the treaty (direct effect) or whether legislation will be necessary. In certain States (sometimes called 'monist'), direct effect is possible;[3] in others (sometimes called 'dualist') it is not.[4] In both cases, however, it is by virtue of the law of the State in question that the treaty is applied: in a 'monist' country, it is the rule permitting the direct application of treaties (a rule that may be anything from a judge-made principle to a constitutional provision); in a 'dualist' country, it is the legislation passed to give effect to the particular treaty in question. In this latter case, the legislation may take various forms. At one end of the spectrum, it may simply amend national law to bring it into line with the treaty, possibly without even referring to it. At the other end, it may provide that the treaty (contained in a Schedule to the legislation) will have the force of law in the country concerned.[5] In this last situation, the only real difference between a 'dualist' and a 'monist' country is that in the former there is a separate legislative measure each time a treaty has to be applied in the domestic legal system, while in the latter there is one measure providing for the application of all future treaties.[6]

Since Member State law is not dependent on Community law – it does not derive its validity from it – Community law cannot apply in the legal systems of the Member States unless Member State law says so: no rule of Community law can itself bring this

[3] This does not mean that every treaty will be directly effective: the law of the State in question specifies the requirements for direct effect. Frequently, it must be shown that the treaty is self-executing. This concept was explained as long ago as 1829 by the United States Supreme Court in *Foster and Elam v. Neilson* 2 Pet. 253 at p. 314, where it distinguished a treaty provision which 'operates of itself, without the aid of any legislative provision' from a provision in which one of the parties 'engages to perform a particular act'. In the former case, the treaty provision is self-executing; in the latter, it is not.

[4] The distinction between the 'monist' and 'dualist' approaches is actually more complex and far-reaching than this, since it concerns the overall relationship between international and domestic law: see Ian Brownlie, *Principles of Public International Law* (5th edn, 1998), p. 31 *et seq.* In adopting these terms, we are not, however, raising these wider questions: we are simply using the terms as handy tags to denote the two approaches set out in the text above. Even if the terms are used in this limited sense, however, the statements in the text are still something of an over-simplification: see Jacobs in Jacobs and Roberts (n. 2, above), at pp. xxiv–xxvi.

[5] For an example of this latter method, see s. 2(1) of the Carriage of Goods by Sea Act 1971, which provides that the Hague-Visby Rules (an international agreement) will have the force of law in the United Kingdom. For a more detailed discussion of the position in the United Kingdom, see Higgins in Jacobs and Roberts (n. 2, above), at pp. 126–9.

[6] Even though the United Kingdom is a 'dualist' country, legislation adopted to give effect to a treaty will, if possible, be interpreted in such a way as to conform to the treaty: *James Buchanan & Co. Ltd v. Babco Forwarding and Shipping (UK) Ltd* [1978] AC 141; *Fothergill v. Monarch Airlines Ltd* [1981] AC 251. This rule can apply even if the United Kingdom legislation does not refer to the treaty, provided it is shown that the legislation was passed to give effect to it.

about.[7] However, as we shall see in Chapter 7, some provisions of the Treaties provide, and others have been interpreted by the European Court as providing, that Community law must in certain cases have direct application in the legal systems of the Member States. This means that, unlike the position in most treaties, the parties to the EC Treaty agreed not only to achieve a certain result, but also agreed on the means by which this would be brought about (direct effect). In other words, all the Member States undertook to adopt the 'monist' position in certain cases. Though unusual, such a provision is in no any way contrary to international law.[8]

Having undertaken this, the Member States then had to carry it out. In the case of the 'monist' countries, the rule of national law making general provision for direct effect – the rule making that country 'monist' – was sufficient; in the case of 'dualist' countries, on the other hand, a special rule had to be adopted for the purpose. In the United Kingdom, this was section 2(1) of the European Communities Act 1972, which states that all provisions of Community law (including those to be adopted in the future) that under Community law are to be given direct effect will be directly effective in the United Kingdom. It is only by virtue of this provision that Community law is directly effective in the United Kingdom. Thus, while the obligation to give direct effect to certain provisions of Community law stems from the treaties, the *carrying out* of that obligation is a matter for national law. A detailed discussion of the way in which these obligations have been carried out in various Member States is provided in Chapter 8.

If a provision of one legal system is applied in another, it may conflict with a provision of the latter. When this occurs, the principles discussed above must determine which prevails. Thus, where an international treaty is applied in the legal system of one of the parties to it, the question whether the treaty overrides national law must be determined by the law of that State. In the case of a 'monist' country, the rule providing for the direct effect of treaties may also indicate their position in the legal hierarchy; otherwise, there will usually be a judge-made rule. In the United States, for example, a treaty that is directly effective[9] has the same position in the legal hierarchy as a federal statute: it prevails over earlier federal statutes but is subordinate to later ones.[10] This is a judge-made rule, though it is partly derived from Article VI, section 2, of the United States Constitution. In the Netherlands, on the other hand, the Constitution provides that directly effective treaties prevail over both prior and subsequent legislation.[11]

[7] Thus in *Thoburn v. Sunderland District Council* [2002] 3 WLR 247, Laws LJ said that the relationship between the United Kingdom and the European Union depends on United Kingdom law, not European Union law (para. 69, proposition 4). See also *Brunner v. European Union Treaty, Bundesverfassungsgericht*, decision of 12 October 1993, [1994] 1 CMLR 57; (1994) 33 ILM 388; 89 BVerfGE 155, in which the German Constitutional Court stated that Community law applies in Germany only because the German laws ratifying the Community Treaties said that it would (paragraph [55] in the CMLR text). There was a similar ruling by the Danish Supreme Court in *Carlsen v. Rasmussen* [1999] 3 CMLR 854.

[8] See Jackson in Jacobs and Roberts (n. 2, above), at p. 154; see also Plender, 'The European Court as an International Tribunal' [1983] CLJ 279 at 287–8; cf. the Advisory Opinion of the Permanent Court of International Justice in the *Danzig Railway Officials* case (1928) PCIJ Ser. B No. 15.

[9] Not all international agreements count as 'treaties' in the United States, and not all 'treaties' are directly effective. For the details, see Jackson in Jacobs and Roberts (n. 2, above), pp. 142–59.

[10] Jackson, *ibid.*, p. 162. For further details, see *ibid.*, pp. 159–64.

[11] See Schermers in Jacobs and Roberts (n. 2, above), at pp. 112–14.

In the case of a 'dualist' country (such as the United Kingdom), the status of a treaty depends on the instrument by which it was given legal effect. If words from a treaty are incorporated into a statute (either with, or without, a reference to the treaty), they take effect as part of that statute: it is the statute, not the treaty, that is applied. If there is a conflict with another legal provision, the conflict is not between the treaty and the other provision, but between the statute and the other provision. The normal rules determine which prevails. If, on the other hand, the statute says that the treaty has the force of law, it makes sense to say that the treaty itself is being applied. Nevertheless, it is applied only because the statute says so; consequently, the status of the treaty is the same as that of the statute. In both cases, therefore, the position of the treaty in the legal hierarchy depends on that of the legislation by which it was given effect. If this was a statute, it will prevail over earlier statutes, but not over later ones. If it was subordinate legislation, it will have the same status as that legislation.[12] These rules can, however, be changed if the legislation which gave effect to the treaty so provides. The Human Rights Act 1998 is an example: though it gives (limited) effect to the European Convention on Human Rights in the domestic law of the United Kingdom, it provides that the Convention does not prevail over *any* United Kingdom legislation, either subsequent or prior.[13]

These rules do not normally prevent States from carrying out their treaty obligations. Since most treaties merely require the parties to achieve a given result, the status of the treaty in their domestic law does not matter as long as the result is achieved. The fact that the treaty could be overridden by later legislation is not a breach of the obligations under it, if this does not in fact occur. If it occurs inadvertently, the matter can be put right as soon as the conflict is evident. For example, the United Kingdom was a party to the European Convention on Human Rights for many years before the Human Rights Act 1998 came into force. Whenever it appeared, perhaps in a judgment of the European Court of Human Rights, that United Kingdom law conflicted with a provision of the Convention, the position was rectified by the amendment of the offending legislation.[14]

There is no provision in the Community Treaties stating that Community law prevails over Member State law. It could, however, be argued that Article 249 [189] EC, which provides that regulations are directly applicable, implies that they should be given at least a certain degree of supremacy.[15] The numerous statements by the European Court that directly effective Community law prevails over Member State law, both prior and subsequent, are based on the proposition that this is what the Member States (implicitly) agreed when they signed the Treaties.[16]

Have the Member States carried out this agreement? Here we have a problem. As we have seen, Community provisions can have effect in Member States only by virtue of Member State law, and the extent to which they prevail over domestic law also depends on a rule of Member State law. However, all rules of Member State law derive their validity from the national constitution: consequently, they cannot be valid if the

[12] The status of subordinate legislation normally depends on that of the statute under which it was adopted.

[13] See sections 3 and 4.

[14] In this respect, the position will not be greatly changed by the Human Rights Act, though amendments are now more likely to be made as a result of a ruling by a United Kingdom court.

[15] *Costa v. ENEL*, Case 6/64, [1963] ECR 585 at 594.

[16] See *Costa v. ENEL*, above.

constitution declares them invalid. Since the rule providing for the supremacy of Community law is itself a rule of Member State law, its validity too depends on the national constitution. This means that the supremacy of Community law in a country always depends, in the last analysis, on the constitution of that country. If the constitution imposes limits on such supremacy, there is no way those limits can be avoided – unless the constitution itself is amended.

This is most obvious in those countries with written constitutions. In Germany, for example, the Constitutional Court has stated expressly that Community law applies in Germany only because the Treaties were approved by the German Parliament. Since the German Parliament is subject to the Constitution, it could not grant the Community any powers that conflicted with the Constitution. Although the Constitution permits Germany to confer powers on an international organization like the Community, those powers must not be open-ended: they have to be defined in advance. This means that the Community cannot be given the power to extend its powers, what the Germans call *Kompetenz-Kompetenz*. The German Constitutional Court has, therefore, ruled that any Community measure that contravenes this principle would be inapplicable in Germany.[17] The Danish Supreme Court has reached a similar conclusion.[18] Section 20 of the Danish Constitution permits the delegation of powers to an international organization, but this too requires that they be defined in advance. The Supreme Court, therefore, held that if a Community measure went beyond the powers conferred on the Community, the Danish courts would declare it inapplicable in Denmark. In both Germany and Denmark, the national courts would be the ones to decide.

Similar views have been expressed by courts in other Member States (though they have not always been so clearly formulated). So far, it has always been possible to solve the problems that have arisen. Sometimes a constitutional amendment or new legislation is required. If this is not possible,[19] the Member States would have to work together to find a solution, possibly by amending Community law. The adoption of human rights as a general principle of Community law, as explained in Chapter 5, shows that the European Court is prepared to play its part.

## FURTHER READING

JOHN USHER, *European Community Law and National Law. The Irreversible Transfer?* (1981).

PELLET, '*Les Fondements Juridiques Internationaux du Droit Communautaire*' (1997) V(2) *Collected Courses of the Academy of European Law* 193.

HARTLEY, 'The Constitutional Foundations of the European Union' (2001) 117 LQR 225.

[17] *Brunner v. European Union Treaty*, Federal Constitutional Court *(Bundesverfassungsgericht)*, decision of 12 October 1993, [1994] 1 CMLR 57.

[18] *Carlsen v. Rasmussen*, Danish Supreme Court (*Højesteret*), judgment of 6 April 1998, [1999] 3 CMLR 854.

[19] Certain provisions of the German Constitution cannot be amended: *Grundgesetz*, Art. 79(3); moreover, in both Germany and in other Member States, it might be politically impossible to obtain the necessary majority to amend the Constitution.

# 7

# DIRECT EFFECT AND NATIONAL REMEDIES

The purpose of this chapter is to consider the rules laid down by the European Court on the obligations of the Member States under Community law to give direct effect to provisions of Community law. The way in which, and the extent to which, these obligations are carried out in different Member States is considered in Chapter 8.

## THE PRINCIPLE OF DIRECT EFFECT

Direct effect was explained in the Introduction to this Part. If direct effect is given to a provision of Community law, that provision is applied by the national court as part of the law of the land. No rule of national law *specifically* referring to it is necessary. As we saw in the Introduction, however, a rule of national law making general provision for direct effect *is* necessary.

The *Van Gend en Loos*[1] case was the first decision by the European Court on direct effect; it is also one of the most important judgments ever handed down by the Court. The case arose when a private firm sought to invoke Community law against the Dutch customs authorities in proceedings in a Dutch tribunal. The tribunal made a reference to the European Court. The main issue was whether Article 12 of the EC Treaty was directly effective. As it stood at the time,[2] it read:

> Member States shall refrain from introducing between themselves any new customs duties on imports or exports or any charges having equivalent effect, and from increasing those which they already apply in their trade with each other.

It will be noticed that this provision was addressed to Member States: it imposed an obligation on them but did not expressly grant any corresponding right to individuals to import goods free from any duty imposed after the establishment of the EC; nor did it state explicitly that any such duty would be invalid. For these reasons, one might have thought that it was not directly effective. The European Court, however, took the view that a provision is not prevented from being directly effective merely

[1] Case 26/62, [1963] ECR 1.

[2] In the Treaty of Amsterdam, it is replaced by a new provision.

because it is addressed to Member States and does not expressly confer rights on private individuals.[3]

The Court instead laid down a different test:[4]

> The wording of Article 12 contains a clear and unconditional prohibition which is not a positive but a negative obligation. This obligation, moreover, is not qualified by any reservation on the part of states which would make its implementation conditional upon a positive legislative measure enacted under national law. The very nature of this prohibition makes it ideally adapted to produce direct effects in the legal relationship between Member States and their subjects.

In later cases, this test has been modified and refined. The suggestion that only negative obligations (prohibitions) may be directly effective has been dropped and the test may now be stated succinctly as follows:[5]

1. the provision must be clear and unambiguous;
2. it must be unconditional;
3. its operation must not be dependent on further action being taken by Community or national authorities.

## CLEAR AND UNAMBIGUOUS

Clarity and unambiguity are striven for by every legal draftsman; frequently, however, they are not attained. This is particularly true in the case of instruments which have to be agreed to by a number of different parties with conflicting interests, as is the case both with the constitutive Treaties and Community legislation. Like many provisions of national law, Community law is often unclear and ambiguous. This does not in itself, however, prevent its being directly effective: the European Court is there to interpret it and once this has been done the ambiguities will be resolved.

The difficulty, therefore, is not so much ambiguity, as generality and lack of precision. If the provision merely lays down a general objective or policy to be pursued, without specifying the appropriate means to attain it, it can hardly be regarded as a legal rule suitable for application by a court of law. In such cases, further legislation is necessary before it can become operative.

A good example of such a provision is Article 10 [5], which states:

> Member States shall take all appropriate measures, whether general or particular, to ensure fulfilment of the obligations arising out of this Treaty or resulting from action taken by the institutions of the Community. They shall facilitate the achievement of the Community's tasks.

[3] For an affirmation of this, see *Defrenne v. Sabena*, Case 43/75, [1976] ECR 455 at para. 31 of the judgment.

[4] At 13.

[5] See Dashwood, 'The Principle of Direct Effect in European Community Law' (1978) 16 JCMS 229, at 231 *et seq.*

> They shall abstain from any measure which could jeopardize the attainment of the objectives of this Treaty.

This is far too general to be directly effective by itself, though it might be suitable for application in conjunction with some other provision which spelled out more clearly what Member States were required to do, or not to do.[6]

The degree of precision that is necessary will of course vary according to the situation. A provision imposing obligations on private citizens should attain a higher degree of precision than a measure granting rights to individuals against national authorities. In the case of criminal law, a particularly high degree of precision is essential. Thus, for example, if a Community regulation required Member States to enact measures imposing criminal penalties for breach of Community law, one could hardly imagine the European Court holding that a new crime had been established by virtue of the direct effect of the regulation if a Member State had failed to enact the required measures.

## UNCONDITIONAL

A Community provision will not be prevented from being directly effective merely because the rights it grants are dependent on some objective factor or event: once the condition is satisfied, there is no reason why the provision should not be enforced by the national courts. What is meant by the requirement of unconditionality is rather that the right must not be dependent on something within the control of some independent authority, such as a Community institution, or the Member State itself. In particular, it must not be dependent on the judgment or discretion of any such body.

An example of a situation where the judgment or discretion of a Community institution is involved is furnished by Articles 87–89 [92–94] EC. These concern state aid which distorts competition by favouring certain enterprises or products at the expense of others. This is stated by Article 87(1) [92(1)] to be 'incompatible with the common market' where it affects trade between Member States; certain exceptions are provided by Article 87(2) and (3) [92(2) and (3)]. It might be thought that this was sufficiently definite to be directly effective; however, Article 88(2) [93(2)] makes provision for the Commission to decide whether any such aid infringes the provisions of Article 87 [92] and to order the offending Member State to terminate it within a period of time laid down by the Commission. Moreover, Article 88(2) [93(2)] allows the Council to authorize any aid which might otherwise be regarded as contrary to the Treaty and, where an application is made to the Council for this purpose, any Commission proceedings must be suspended. In view of this, it is clear that Article 87(1) [92(1)] cannot have been intended to be directly effective: the prohibition it contains is conditional on the decisions of the Council and Commission.[7]

[6] However, in *Schlüter*, Case 9/73, [1973] ECR 1135 at para. 39 of its judgment, the European Court held that Art. 10 [5] was not directly effective, even when combined with Art. 108 [107]. See also *Hurd v. Jones (Inspector of Taxes)*, Case 44/84, [1986] ECR 29 at paras 47 and 48 of the judgment.

[7] See *Capolongo*, Case 77/72, [1973] ECR 611 at paras 4–6, where the Court held that, at least as regards systems of aid in operation at the time when the Treaty went into effect, Art. 87(1) [92(1)] is not directly effective

An extreme example of a right dependent on the discretion of a Member State would be a provision stating: 'Each Member State shall, in so far as it considers it desirable . . .'. This obviously could not be directly effective: if the Member State failed to take the action in question, it could always argue that it did not consider it desirable to do so.

A more limited, but still significant, discretion is that which exists where Community law requires the attainment of an objective but allows the Member States to choose the means. If there are a number of quite different ways in which the objective could be attained, the discretion given to the Member States may prevent the provision from being directly effective.[8]

An example is a Community provision[9] which requires Member States to give effect to the principle of equal treatment for men and women as regards access to employment, a provision going beyond the requirement of equal pay contained in Article 141 [119] EC. Among other things, this provision obliges Member States to provide a legal remedy for the victims of discrimination. In the *Von Colson* case[10] a woman who had been refused a job because of her sex argued that Community law gave her a directly effective right to demand that the court order the employer to appoint her to the post. The European Court, however, held that there were several ways in which Member States could fulfil the obligation to provide a legal remedy: for example, the victim of discrimination could be given the right to demand appointment or she could be given the right to claim damages. Any effective remedy would constitute compliance with the obligation. The discretion given to the Member States consequently prevented the obligation from being directly effective.[11]

A different kind of discretion is given in the so-called 'safeguard' clauses which occur quite frequently in different parts of the Treaty. The normal pattern is for the Treaty to grant rights, but allow the Member States to restrict these rights in special cases, it being understood that it is for the Member State concerned to decide whether the situation justifies recourse to the safeguard clause.

One example of this is Article 39(3) [48(3)] EC, which grants workers the right of free movement between Member States but provides that this right is 'subject to limitations justified on grounds of public policy, public security, or public health'. Since it is the national authorities who decide what the requirements of public policy are, it will be appreciated that this provision makes the right to immigrate subject to a condition dependent on the judgment of the Member State. For example, if a government decides that the activities of a certain organization are against public policy, it will be entitled

in the absence of a decision under Art. 88(2) [93(2)]. As regards the ECSC Treaty, see *Banks*, Case C-128/92, [1994] ECR I-1209 (paras 15–19 of the judgment).

[8] However, if the individual would be entitled to certain minimum rights whichever way the Member State exercised its discretion, the provision might be directly effective to that extent: *Francovich v. Italy*, Cases C-6, 9/90, [1991] ECR I-5357 (paras 15–21 of the judgment).

[9] The provision is contained in a directive, Directive 76/207, OJ 1976, L39/40. As will be seen below, directives can be directly effective only where they are invoked against the State, as was the case in *Von Colson* (below).

[10] *Von Colson and Kamann v. Land Nordrhein-Westfalen*, Case 14/83, [1984] ECR 1891.

[11] This does not mean that other provisions in the Directive are not directly effective: see *Marshall v. Southampton and South West Hampshire Area Health Authority (Teaching)*, Case 152/84, [1986] ECR 723.

to invoke the proviso so as to prevent members of that organization from entering the country.

In view of this, one would have thought that the right of free movement granted by Article 39 [48] was conditional and that, as a discretionary element is present, it could not be directly effective. In *Van Duyn v. Home Office*,[12] however, the European Court rejected this argument. The case concerned a Dutchwoman who wanted to enter the United Kingdom to take up a post with the Church of Scientology. Scientology might, perhaps, be described as a 'fringe religion': it is strongly supported by its adherents but disapproved of by the more established religious bodies. Some years previously, the British Government had reached the conclusion that Scientology was harmful to the mental health of those involved and adopted a policy of discouraging it, though it was not made illegal. One consequence of this was that immigration permission was normally refused to known Scientologists.

When Miss Van Duyn arrived in England, she was refused permission to enter, and this was justified on the basis of the public policy proviso. She then brought legal proceedings in the English courts to challenge this decision, and one question which arose was whether Article 39(3) [48(3)] was directly effective. A reference was made to the European Court for a ruling on the issue and it was argued that the discretionary element eliminated the possibility of direct effect. The Court rejected this on the ground that the application of the proviso is 'subject to judicial control'. By this it seemed to be referring to the fact that decisions of the national authorities based on the proviso are subject to judicial review in the courts of the Member States.[13]

The difference between the situation in the *Von Colson* case and that in the *Van Duyn* case seems to be that in the former the Member States had a discretion as to how they would give effect to the right, while in the latter the right was provided by Community law and the Member States were merely given a limited power to restrict it in certain circumstances. In the former case the right was incomplete until the Member State had acted; in the latter case it was not.

## NOT DEPENDENT ON FURTHER ACTION

If the Community provision states that the rights it grants will come into effect when further action of a legislative or executive nature has been taken by the Community or the Member States, it would seem reasonable to hold that it cannot have direct effect until that action is taken. In accordance with its general policy, however, the European Court has sought to whittle this requirement down to its very minimum. It has done this by laying down a rule that if the Community provision gives a time-limit for its implementation, it can become directly effective if not implemented by the deadline.

Article 141 [119] EC provides an example. In its original form,[14] it stated: 'Each Member State shall during the first stage ensure and subsequently maintain the application of the

[12] Case 41/74, [1974] ECR 1337 at para. 7 of the judgment.

[13] This was required by Art. 8 of Directive 64/221, OJ (Spec.Ed.) 1963/64, p. 117.

[14] It was amended by the Treaty of Amsterdam.

principle that men and women should receive equal pay for equal work.' This clearly envisaged action by the Member States to bring the principle into operation, but it laid down a deadline: the end of the first stage. The Court therefore held in the second *Defrenne* case[15] that the requirement of further action did not prevent Article 141 [119] from being directly effective thereafter.

In practice, this modification of the original rule to a large extent nullifies it, since almost all Community provisions requiring further action contain a time-limit. In such cases, the only consequence of the requirement is that direct effect is postponed until the deadline has passed.

### CONCLUSIONS

The rulings of the European Court on direct effect are a good example of the Court's strategy in introducing new legal principles: in the first case in which this question arose – the *Van Gend en Loos* case – it used language which suggested that there was a fairly stringent test and that direct effect, at least in the case of Treaty provisions, was a rather rare phenomenon. Once the principle was accepted, however, the requirements were cut down: the rule regarding negative obligations was dropped and the requirements that the obligations must be unconditional and not dependent on further action were considerably qualified. The result is that direct effect may now be regarded as the norm rather than the exception.

One can, in fact, say that the test is of an essentially practical nature: it lays down the minimum conditions for the application of almost any legal rule. In other words, the test is really one of feasibility: if the provision lends itself to judicial application, it will almost certainly be declared directly effective; only where direct effect would create serious practical problems is it likely that the provision will be held not to be directly effective.[16]

The above comments concern direct effect in general. It is now desirable to change the focus of the discussion and give separate consideration to provisions derived from each of the various sources of Community law.

## TREATY PROVISIONS

There is no statement in any of the Treaties as to whether Treaty provisions are directly effective. It is in fact probable that the authors of the Treaties assumed that the question of direct effect would be decided by national courts according to the criteria of national law. If this is correct, the European Court's assumption of jurisdiction in this matter, as well as the liberal criteria it has adopted, constitutes a development of the greatest importance.

[15] *Defrenne v. Sabena*, Case 43/75, [1976] ECR 455.

[16] *Banks*, Case C-128/92, [1994] ECR I-1209 at 1237 (*per* Advocate General van Gerven). See also Pescatore, 'The Doctrine of "Direct Effect": An Infant Disease of Community Law' (1983) 8 ELRev. 155, especially at 174–7.

## REGULATIONS

Articles 249 [189] EC and 161 Euratom state that a regulation is 'directly applicable in all Member States'. The authors of the Treaties probably intended 'directly applicable' to mean the same thing as 'directly effective'. Since there is no similar statement regarding other kinds of Community legislation, or regarding the Treaties themselves, it seems likely that they intended that regulations, and only regulations, would be directly effective. The Court has ruled, however, that other Community instruments are also capable of having direct effect. This has given rise to the problem of reconciling the Court's ruling with the wording of the Treaties, a problem which has caused much concern to legal writers,[17] though not (apparently) to the Court itself. The dilemma is as follows: if one interprets 'directly applicable' to mean the same thing as 'directly effective',[18] it would seem to follow that only regulations can be directly effective. If, on the other hand, one treats the two terms as meaning something different, one has to find a suitable meaning for 'directly applicable', a meaning that refers to some quality possessed by regulations but not by other instruments of Community law.[19] This in turn causes other problems because, though such features undoubtedly exist, they are neither clear-cut nor important enough to warrant a special provision in the Treaty, especially when the Treaty does not (it is assumed) make express provision for direct effect. In fact, the whole debate is sterile since the sole purpose of drawing a distinction between the two terms is to rebut the accusation that the Court is acting contrary to the Treaties: it does not lead to any better understanding of the law.[20] The best solution, therefore, is to bypass these semantic issues and proceed directly to the concrete features of the different instruments. This will now be done.

In view of Article 249 [189] EC, it might be thought that regulations were always directly effective. Very frequently this is the case – but it is not always so.[21] Take, for example, Regulation 1463/70[22] (now repealed). This was concerned with the introduction of recording equipment (tachographs) in commercial vehicles, and Article 4 stated

[17] For a summary of the different views, see Steiner, 'Direct Applicability in EEC Law – A Chameleon Concept' (1982) 98 LQR 229.

[18] See Bebr, 'Directly Applicable Provisions of Community Law: The Development of a Community Concept' (1970) 19 ICLQ 257, *passim* and especially at 266–7; and Toth, I, p. 119, n. 1.

[19] This theory was first put forward by JA Winter in an article entitled 'Direct Applicability and Direct Effect: Two Distinct and Different Concepts in Community Law' (1972) 9 CMLRev. 425. He makes the distinction between the two terms clear at 425–6 and again at 435–6, though paradoxically he himself sometimes uses 'direct applicability' as if it meant 'direct effect': see, e.g., 427 *et seq.* Other authors who regard the two terms as having different meanings include Dashwood, 'The Principle of Direct Effect in European Community Law' (1978) 16 JCMS 229 at 230, and LJ Brinkhorst (1971) 8 CMLRev. 380 at 390–1.

[20] At the time when these developments were taking place, the Court seemed to use the two terms as meaning the same thing: see Pescatore, 'The Doctrine of "Direct Effect": An Infant Disease of Community Law' (1983) 8 ELRev. 155, n. 2. Pescatore was one of the leading judges on the European Court at the time in question.

[21] See *per* Advocate General Warner in *Galli*, Case 31/74, [1975] ECR 47 at 70 and in *Steinike und Weinlig v. Germany*, Case 78/76, [1977] ECR 595 at 583; and *per* Advocate General Reischl in *Ratti*, Case 148/78, [1979] ECR 1629 *passim*.

[22] OJ 1970 (Spec.Ed.) 482.

that the use of this equipment would be compulsory from a given date. Article 21(1)[23] then provided:

> Member States shall, in good time and after consulting the Commission, adopt such laws, regulations or administrative provisions as may be necessary for the implementation of this Regulation.
>
> Such measures shall cover, *inter alia*, the reorganization of, procedure for, and means of carrying out, checks on compliance and the penalties to be imposed in case of breach.

This provision clearly could not have been directly effective; in particular, it could not have created a new criminal offence – that of driving a commercial vehicle without a tachograph. It was far too vague: it did not state exactly what would constitute the offence, who would be regarded as responsible (owner or driver), what the penalties would be, or what defences would be available.

Since regulations are normally directly effective, there is usually no need for the enactment of national legislation to give effect to them. The European Court has moreover laid down a general rule that, except where they are necessary, national implementing measures are improper.[24] The reason for this is that the Court does not want the Community nature of the provision to be obscured: it must be clearly applied as a provision of Community law, not of national law. In particular, the Court seems concerned about three matters. First, if the provisions of the regulation were enacted as part of a national measure, it might be thought that they took effect from the date of the national measure, rather than that of the Community measure: this could mean that the provisions would not come into force on the same date in all the Member States. Secondly, there is a danger that when the Community provisions are transformed into national law, subtle changes will be made in their content to suit national interests: in this way the uniformity of Community law would be jeopardized. Thirdly, national implementation could prejudice the European Court's jurisdiction to give a ruling on the interpretation and validity of the measure under the procedure for a preliminary reference.[25] It is true that the Court has expressly stated that its jurisdiction cannot be affected by national implementation measures;[26] nevertheless, it is conceivable that some national courts might be less ready to make a reference to the European Court if the Community provisions were incorporated in a national measure.

The doctrine that national measures are improper was first laid down in 1973 in *Commission v. Italy*.[27] This case concerned a Community plan to counter the chronic

[23] Art. 21 was renumbered Art. 23 with effect from 1 January 1978 by Art. II of Regulation 2828/77, OJ 1977, L334/5.

[24] This rule is often justified on the ground that, under Art. 249 [189] EC, regulations are directly applicable. This could, therefore, indicate an appropriate meaning to give to 'directly applicable' if one wanted to distinguish it from 'directly effective', but this would then mean that not all regulations were directly applicable, which would conflict not only with Art. 249 [189] EC, but also with the opinion of Advocate General Warner in *R v. Secretary of State for Home Affairs, ex parte Santillo*, Case 131/79, [1980] ECR 1585 at 1608. Moreover, the European Court has said that the fact that regulations are directly applicable does not mean that they cannot contain provisions empowering Member States to pass implementing measures: *Eridania*, Case 230/78, [1979] ECR 2749 at para. 34 of the judgment.

[25] See *Variola*, Case 34/73, [1973] ECR 981 at para. 11 of the judgment.

[26] *Ibid.*

[27] Case 39/72, [1973] ECR 101.

over-production of dairy products by the introduction of a premium for the slaughter of cows. The Italian Government had passed a decree which stated that the provisions of the relevant regulations were 'deemed to be included' in it and then proceeded to reproduce them together with certain procedural provisions of a national character.

Enforcement proceedings were taken against Italy, both because it had failed to bring the scheme into operation on time, and because certain aspects of it had not been put into effect at all. In the course of its judgment, the Court made the following comments concerning the enactment of the national decree:[28]

> By following this procedure, the Italian Government has brought into doubt both the legal nature of the applicable provisions and the date of their coming into force.
>
> According to the terms of Articles 249 [189] and 254 [191] of the Treaty, Regulations are, as such, directly applicable in all Member States and come into force solely by virtue of their publication in the *Official Journal* of the Communities, as from the date specified in them, or in the absence thereof, as from the date provided in the Treaty.
>
> Consequently, all methods of implementation are contrary to the Treaty which would have the result of creating an obstacle to the direct effect of Community Regulations and of jeopardizing their simultaneous and uniform application in the whole of the Community.

The Court went on to point out that in one respect the Italian decree had departed from the terms of Community law in that it had failed to take into account an extension of the time allowed for slaughter under a later regulation. It then concluded:[29] 'The default of the Italian Republic has thus been established by reason not only of the delay in putting the system into effect but also of the manner of giving effect to it provided by the decree.'

The rule that national measures are improper is subject to exceptions in a number of situations. The first and most obvious exception is where the regulation itself expressly requires the Member States to take action to implement it: this was the case with Article 21 of the tachograph regulation discussed previously. Here, implementing measures are not only permitted, they are obligatory: when the United Kingdom failed to implement Article 21, it was ordered to do so by the European Court.[30]

Secondly, there may be cases in which, though the regulation does not expressly require implementation, it may impliedly permit it. This would be the case where the terms of the regulation are rather vague and provision for its detailed application is desirable. It appears that in such a case national measures will be permissible, provided they are not incompatible with the provisions of the regulation.[31]

Whether national measures are permissible in other circumstances is uncertain. One situation in which they would serve a useful function is where national provisions purport to codify the law in a particular area and thus give a complete statement of all the relevant legal rules. If a regulation impinges on that area, so that in certain cases rights may be derived from it, it might be desirable in the interests of clarity, certainty, and legislative 'tidiness' for those aspects of the issue governed by the regulation to be repeated in the national provision.

[28] Para. 17. [29] Para. 18. [30] *Commission v. United Kingdom*, Case 128/78, [1979] ECR 419.
[31] See *Bussone*, Case 31/78, [1978] ECR 2429 at para. 32 of the judgment.

## DIRECTIVES

Whatever the position may be regarding other Community measures, there is little doubt that the authors of the Treaties did not intend directives to be directly effective. This view, which was generally accepted in the early days of the EC, follows from the concept of a directive as laid down in the EC and Euratom Treaties: Articles 249 [189] EC and 161 Euratom pointedly refrain from declaring directives directly applicable. Moreover, they state that a directive is binding only 'as to the result to be achieved' but leaves 'the choice of form and methods' to the national authorities. In other words, the directive lays down an objective and leaves it to the Member States to achieve that objective according to such means as they might think fit. This clearly implies that legislative measures will be taken by the national authorities and that, though the result must be the same in all Member States, the details of the legislation may vary: this is the essence of the distinction between regulations and directives. In these circumstances, one might have thought, there could be no possibility of directives having direct effect.

### THE FIRST STEP

The European Court, however, has decided otherwise. The first tentative step was taken in two cases decided within a couple of months of each other in 1970, *Grad*[32] and *SACE*.[33] In both these cases, the role of the directive was limited to setting the date when a provision in another instrument would come into force.[34] The European Court held that this fact did not prevent the provision in the other instrument from being directly effective. It was only in a limited sense, therefore, that the directives in these cases were themselves directly effective.

### THE NEW PRINCIPLE

This reasoning might have suggested that these were special cases; any such illusions were, however, dispelled when the Court decided the *Van Duyn* case in 1974.[35] The facts have already been outlined above, where it was mentioned that the Court held Article 39 [48] EC to be directly effective. This, however, was only one issue in the case; the Court was also asked whether Article 3(1) of Directive 64/221[36] was directly effective. The purpose of this Directive is to limit the discretion of Member States when they invoke the public policy proviso under Article 39 [48] EC, and Article 3(1) lays down that such measures must be 'based exclusively on the personal conduct of the individual concerned'. It was argued on behalf of Miss Van Duyn that this provision was

[32] Case 9/70, [1970] ECR 825. [33] Case 33/70, [1970] ECR 1213.

[34] In *SACE* the provision was contained in the EC Treaty; in *Grad* it was in a decision. The ruling in the latter case that a decision can be directly effective may be thought of as foreshadowing that in the *Van Duyn* case (below). [35] Case 41/74, [1974] ECR 1337.

[36] OJ 1963/64 (Spec. Ed.) 117.

directly effective and that she could therefore rely on it before the English court: she maintained that the only ground the Home Office had for refusing her admission to the United Kingdom was her membership of the Church of Scientology, and she contended that this did not constitute 'personal conduct' in terms of Article 3(1).

This was, of course, a different situation from that in the previous cases: here the very essence of the right was laid down in the Directive. There could be no question of a 'special case': the Court was obliged to decide, as a matter of general principle, whether a directive could have direct effect. The United Kingdom Government argued that it could not, basing its argument on the provisions of Article 249 [189] mentioned above. The European Court, however, held that directives can be directly effective.

The Court gave three arguments in support of this conclusion. The first was that it would be incompatible with the binding effect attributed to a directive in Article 249 [189] to exclude in principle the possibility of direct effect. This argument is unsound: it is quite possible for a measure to be fully binding at the international level without its being enforceable in national courts by private individuals. In such a case it could be enforced by means of an action brought in the European Court by the Commission, or by another Member State, under Articles 226–228 [169–171] EC.

The second argument was much stronger. This, however, was a policy argument, not a legal one. It was that the *effectiveness* (*'effet utile'*, in French) of the measure would be greater if individuals were entitled to invoke it before the national courts. This will be considered further below.

The third argument was based on Article 234 [177] EC. This is the provision which governs references from national courts to the European Court. It grants the Court jurisdiction to give preliminary rulings on, among other things, the validity and interpretation of 'acts of the institutions of the Community'. The exact meaning of this phrase will be considered in Chapter 9; there can, however, be no doubt that it includes decisions and directives as well as regulations. The Court argued that this implies that all such acts can be directly effective.

The Court's argument, however, assumes that a national court might require a preliminary ruling only in the case of a directly effective provision. This is not so: if a Community provision which is not directly effective is implemented by a national measure, the validity and interpretation of the latter might – under *national* law – depend on the validity and interpretation of the former. As will be shown below, this is the case in the United Kingdom. Consequently, a national court might very well require a preliminary ruling on the validity and interpretation of a Community provision which was not directly effective: the European Court has itself said that this is permissible.[37] It may also be required as a matter of Community law by virtue of the doctrine of 'indirect effect' (discussed below). Consequently, no inference can be drawn from the terms of Article 234 [177].[38]

The strongest argument of a legal, or quasi-legal, nature is in fact one that was not even mentioned in the *Van Duyn* case. This is an argument derived from the English

[37] *Mazzalai*, Case 111/75, [1976] ECR 657 at 665.

[38] It is interesting to note that this argument has been abandoned in subsequent cases: see, e.g., *Verbond van Nederlandse Ondernemingen*, Case 51/76, [1977] ECR 113 at paras 20–4 of the judgment.

doctrine of equity and similar principles in civil law systems.[39] The problem in the *Van Duyn* case was that the United Kingdom Government had done nothing to implement Article 3(1) of the Directive: there was no British provision stating that entry could be refused only on the basis of the personal conduct of the would-be immigrant. If the Directive had been implemented, there would have been no difficulty: Miss Van Duyn could have relied on the British provision. In effect, therefore, the United Kingdom Government was seeking to deny her a right on the ground of its own failure to implement the Directive. This could bring into play the principle that no one should profit from his own wrongdoing. In other words, Miss Van Duyn's rights should have been regarded as being no less than they would have been if the United Kingdom Government had fulfilled its obligation to implement the Directive. This would have entailed allowing her to invoke the provisions of the Directive in the English courts.

The idea that the direct effect of directives can be justified on the ground that it prevents a Member State from taking advantage of its own wrongdoing was first put to the Court by an Englishman, Advocate General Warner, in 1977, three years after the *Van Duyn* case was decided.[40] It was adopted by the Court in 1979.[41] Today, the other arguments have been quietly dropped and the 'equity' argument is now routinely put forward by the Court as the official justification.[42]

Whatever one may think about these arguments, there can be no doubt that it was on policy grounds that the Court decided to proclaim the new doctrine: the argument of *effectiveness* was what really won the day. The fact of the matter is that Member States were (and still are) remiss in implementing directives,[43] and it was this that persuaded the Court to act. Without direct effect, a directive can be enforced only by means of an action brought in the European Court by the Commission (or by another Member State) under Articles 226–228 [169–171] EC. The difficulty is that – for reasons of manpower, if for no others – the Commission is able to handle only a small number of such cases each year: it would be quite impossible for them to bring proceedings with regard to every directive which had not been fully implemented. In some cases, moreover, pressure may be brought against the Commission to dissuade it from taking action. By declaring a directive directly effective, on the other hand, the Court can open the way for individuals to enforce it in the national courts. This has the added advantage both of shielding the Commission from political pressure and of casting on the national courts the burden of ensuring compliance.

[39] See *per* Advocate General van Gerven in *Barber*, Case C-262/88, [1990] ECR I-1889, n. 34, where the civil law principle of *nemo auditur propriam turpitudinem allegans* is contrasted with the common law doctrine of estoppel.

[40] *Enka*, Case 38/77, [1977] ECR 2203 at 2226.

[41] *Ratti*, Case 148/78, [1979] ECR 1629 at para. 22 of the judgment.

[42] See, for example, *Faccini Dori v. Recreb*, Case C-91/92, [1994] ECR I-3325 at para. 22 of the judgment; *Arcaro*, Case C-168/95, [1996] ECR I-4705 at para. 36 of the judgment.

[43] The Netherlands is generally regarded as one of the most conscientious of the Member States, yet a study by two Dutch authors at roughly the same time as the *Van Duyn* decision shows that even the Dutch had a bad record in this regard. Of the ninety-four directives chosen for examination, almost two-thirds (sixty) were not implemented on time: Maas and Bentvelsen, 'De tijdige uitvoering van EEG-richtlijnen in Nederland' [1978] Bestuurswetenschappen 443 at 446. If this was the state of affairs in the Netherlands, things were probably even worse in some other countries.

## THE IMPORTANCE OF THE DEADLINE

In the *Van Duyn* case the time-limit for the implementation of the directive had long since passed; the significance of this date was not therefore given much emphasis. The *Ratti* case,[44] however, shows that it is in fact crucial. This concerned two directives dealing with the packaging and labelling of solvents and varnishes respectively. The first, Directive 73/173,[45] was adopted on 4 June 1973 and required Member States to implement its provisions by 8 December 1974; the second, Directive 77/728,[46] was adopted on 7 November 1977 and laid down a deadline of 9 November 1979.

Mr Ratti was an Italian who ran a firm selling both solvents and varnishes in Italy. The firm decided that it would package and label its products so as to comply with the two directives, even though neither had been implemented in Italy. The matter was, however, covered by an Italian law passed in 1963 which applied to both products and was in some ways more lenient than the directives, but in other ways stricter. When the firm put its products on the market, Ratti was prosecuted for failure to comply with the provisions of the Italian law. At the relevant time, the deadline for implementation of the first directive had expired but that for the second had not. Ratti admitted that he had not complied with the Italian law but argued that compliance with the directives was sufficient.

The court in Milan, before which the prosecution had been brought, made a reference to the European Court for a ruling on whether the directives were directly effective. The European Court held that a directive can become directly effective only when the deadline for implementation has expired; therefore, the first directive was directly effective, but the second was not. The Court held that this result was not affected by the fact that some of the varnishes had been imported from Germany, which had already implemented the second directive, and were therefore packaged and labelled in accordance with it. The result was that Community law afforded Ratti a defence to the charges relating to the solvents, but not those concerning the varnishes.

This case shows that a directive which has not been implemented cannot become directly effective before the expiry of the time-limit,[47] but this does not mean that it has no effects at all. In *Inter-Environnement Wallonie v. Région Wallonne*,[48] the European Court held that, in the period between the adoption of the directive and the expiry of the deadline, Member States must not enact any legislation that could seriously compromise the attainment of the result required by the directive. A recent case, *Mangold*,[49] could be interpreted as extending this principle. The case is discussed in some detail below,[50] and all that needs to be said at this point is that it could be interpreted as prohibiting any retrograde legislation during the period for implementation: even

[44] Case 148/78, [1979] ECR 1629. For an illuminating comment, see Usher (1979) 4 ELRev. 268.

[45] OJ 1973, L189/7. [46] OJ 1977, L303/23.

[47] For the position where, after it has expired, the deadline is postponed, see *Kloppenburg*, Case 70/83, [1984] ECR 1075. [48] Case C-129/96, [1997] ECR I-7411.

[49] Case C-144/04, 25 November 2005 (Grand Chamber).

[50] See the section of this chapter entitled 'Vertical and Horizontal Direct Effect'.

though a State is not required to implement a directive before the deadline, it must not move further away from the result to be achieved. Such an interpretation would give a directive the effect of a standstill provision during this period. This was the view put forward by Advocate General Sharpston in a recent case,[51] but the Court did not accept it;[52] so perhaps *Mangold* should be regarded as confined to its own rather special facts.[53]

## DIFFERENCES BETWEEN DIRECTIVES AND REGULATIONS

The granting of direct effect to directives has probably done more than any other initiative by the European Court to enhance the effectiveness of Community law. Yet there has been a price to pay: the distinction between regulations and directives has been blurred and the structure of the Treaty deformed. This, in turn, has provoked a reaction at the national level.[54] The question must therefore be asked to what extent significant differences between directives and regulations still remain.

Some differences have already been mentioned. First of all, there is the date on which direct effect comes into operation: a regulation can be directly effective as soon as it comes into force, but a directive cannot be directly effective before the expiry of the time-limit for implementation.

A second difference is that Member States are not normally either required or permitted to pass national legislation giving effect to the provisions of a regulation; in the case of a directive, on the other hand, there is the much-vaunted right to choose the 'form and methods' by which the objective of the directive will be attained.[55] There is no doubt that this applies even where the directive is directly effective; however, in such a case the discretion enjoyed by Member States could be severely restricted.

There are two reasons for this. First, the Community institutions long ago adopted the habit of enacting directives with provisions every bit as detailed and precise as those to be found in a regulation.[56] Moreover, the Court has developed a doctrine that the area of choice left to the Member States regarding the 'form and methods' of implementation depends on the objective to be achieved: in some cases, the objective will be such that this diminishes to vanishing point. For example, in *Enka v. Inspecteur der Invoerrechten en Accijnzen*[57] the Court stated that in the case of customs legislation absolute uniformity may be necessary. It therefore held that the relevant provision of the directive in issue had to be reproduced in exactly the same way in the implementing

[51] *Stichting Zuid-Hollandse Mileufederatie*, Case C-138/05, 14 September 2006, at para. 86 of the Opinion.

[52] *Ibid.* at paras 39–48 of the judgment.

[53] These facts are explained below (see the section of this chapter entitled 'Vertical and Horizontal Direct Effect'). They were the fact that Germany had to report annually to the Commission; the fact that employees caught by the 52-year rule might subsequently be caught by the 58-year rule; and the fact that a general principle of law was said to be involved. It is interesting to note that in *Adeneler*, Case C-212/04, 4 July 2006, also a decision of a Grand Chamber, the Court cited *Mangold* simply as authority for the principle in *Inter-Environnement Wallonie v. Région Wallonne*: see para. 121 of the judgment in *Adeneler*.

[54] See Chap. 8. [55] Arts 189 EC and 161 Euratom.

[56] Compare, e.g., Directive 75/34, OJ 1975, L 14/10, with Regulation 1251/70, OJ (Spec. Ed.) 1970 (II), p. 402.

[57] Case 38/77, [1977] ECR 2203 at paras 11–18.

legislation of each Member State.[58] In such a situation, implementation is, from the Member State's point of view, an empty exercise.[59]

It is, of course, true that there are many cases in which a real discretion will exist. It must not be forgotten, however, that some regulations have to be implemented and sometimes Member States will enjoy a significant discretion in this case as well. The tachograph regulation (discussed above) was a case in point: the powers of inspection, the details of criminal procedure and the maximum penalty were all matters which, within certain limits, could be determined by the Member States.

Another possible difference which has sometimes been suggested is that, while direct effect is the normal characteristic of a regulation, it is exceptional in the case of a directive.[60] From a purely theoretical point of view, this is obviously true: if the Member States carry out their obligations under Community law, there will never be occasion for a directive to have direct effect. In practice, of course, Member States do not always implement directives as they should: from the practical point of view, therefore, the important question is whether a provision is less likely to be declared directly effective simply because it is contained in a directive, rather than in a regulation.

In the *Van Duyn* case[61] the European Court said that, while regulations 'may by their very nature have direct effects', directives 'have no automatic direct effect'.[62] This suggests that such a difference does indeed exist. However, the test applied to directives is exactly the same as that adopted in the case of Treaty provisions and, though the Court gave very careful scrutiny to the provision in issue in the *Van Duyn* case, it has subsequently shown itself prepared to declare whole groups of directives directly effective *en bloc*, without even listing them individually, much less attempting to examine their provisions in order to see whether they comply with the requirements for direct effect.[63] It is, therefore, hard to discern any practical difference between regulations and directives on this point.

The differences discussed so far have shown themselves to be rather insubstantial; there is, however, one difference which is of great significance. This is that, according to the Court, directives are not capable of imposing *obligations* on individuals.

## VERTICAL AND HORIZONTAL DIRECT EFFECT

There is no doubt that both regulations and Treaty provisions are able not only to confer rights on private individuals, but also to impose obligations on them.[64] However, the European Court has stated, many times over, that directives can only confer rights on

[58] For a less strict attitude, see *Commission v. Italy*, Case 363/85, [1987] ECR 1733.

[59] It is an exercise which must nevertheless be gone through. The Member State cannot rely on the direct effect of the directive to excuse its failure to implement it: see *Commission v. Belgium*, Case 102/79, [1980] ECR 1473 at para. 12 of the judgment.

[60] See Brinkhorst (1971) 8 CMLRev. 380 at 390; Dashwood, 'The Principle of Direct Effect in European Community Law' (1978) 16 JCMS 229 at 241; and *per* Advocate General Reischl in *Ratti*, Case 148/78, [1979] ECR 1629 at 1650 and 1653–4.

[61] Case 41/74, [1974] ECR 1337.

[62] At paras 12 and 13 of the judgment.

[63] In *Watson and Belmann*, Case 118/75, [1976] ECR 1185, the Court said that all measures adopted by the Community in application of Arts 39–55 [48–66] of the EC Treaty are directly effective: see the first paragraph of its formal ruling.

[64] As far as regulations are concerned, this follows from the terms of Arts 249 [189] EC and 161 Euratom, which state that regulations have general application. In the second *Defrenne* case, Case 43/75, [1976]

individuals (against the State); they cannot impose obligations on individuals (in favour of the State or other individuals). Put another way, directives are capable of only 'vertical' direct effect; unlike regulations and Treaty provisions, they are not capable of 'horizontal' direct effect.

The question whether it is possible for directives to have horizontal direct effect was controversial for many years. The writers were divided on the question;[65] two advocates general came out against the possibility;[66] the Court gave hints that it shared this view;[67] finally, in *Marshall v. Southampton and South West Hampshire Area Health Authority (Teaching)*,[68] the Court stated explicitly that a directive 'may not of itself impose obligations on an individual' and that 'a provision of a directive may not be relied on as such against such a person'.[69]

This was not, however, the end of the matter: some time later, a campaign appears to have been mounted by a group of advocates general to have the decision in *Marshall* reversed. Two of them argued, in cases in which the point was not actually in issue, that directives *should* be capable of horizontal direct effect.[70] When the point finally arose for decision in *Faccini Dori v. Recreb*,[71] a third advocate general[72] took the same view; the Court, however, reaffirmed its earlier position. Since this was a Full Court, consisting of thirteen judges, it should have been possible to regard the matter as settled.[73]

This has not, however, been the case. Although the Court continues to pay lip service to the principle that directives are incapable of horizontal direct effect, and indeed actually applies it in some cases, there are other cases in which it is not applied. Unfortunately, it is not easy to find any feature that distinguishes the two sets of cases.

The first case to consider is *CIA Security v. Signalson and Securitel*.[74] It concerned a Belgian law passed in 1990, which provided that security firms had to obtain authorization from the Government. A decree adopted in 1991 stated that alarm systems could not be sold unless approved by a government committee. An EC directive (Directive 83/189[75]), however, provided that all 'technical regulations' had to be notified to the Commission and, in certain circumstances, could not come into force for specified periods. Neither the law nor the decree had been notified.

CIA Security, Signalson, and Securitel were all security firms. The latter two claimed that CIA Security's alarm systems did not meet Belgian requirements. CIA Security

ECR 455, the Court held that Treaty provisions can also have this effect. This has since been confirmed in numerous cases.

[65] See the list in Easson, 'Can Directives Impose Obligations on Individuals?' (1979) 4 ELRev. 67 at 70, n. 24.

[66] Advocate General Reischl in *Ratti*, Case 148/78, [1979] ECR 1629 at 1650; and (more clearly) Advocate General Slynn in *Becker*, Case 8/81, [1982] ECR 53 at 81.

[67] See, e.g., *Becker*, (above) at paras 17–26 of the judgment.

[68] Case 152/84, [1986] ECR 723.

[69] Para. 48 of the judgment. See also *Kolpinghuis Nijmegen*, Case 80/86, [1987] ECR 3969, in which the European Court held that a Member State cannot rely on the direct effect of a (non-implemented) directive in criminal proceedings against an individual; see, further, *Pretore di Salò v. X.*, Case 14/86, [1987] ECR 2545.

[70] Advocate General van Gerven in the second *Marshall* case, *Marshall v. Southampton and South West Hampshire Area Health Authority (Teaching) (No. 2)*, Case C-271/91, [1993] ECR I-4367; and Advocate General Jacobs in *Vaneetveld*, Case C-316/93, [1994] ECR I-763.

[71] Case C-91/92, [1994] ECR I-3325.

[72] Advocate General Lenz.

[73] For a possible exception with regard to remedies, see *Draehmpaehl v. Urania Immobilienservice*, Case C-180/95, [1997] ECR I-2195.

[74] Case C-194/94, [1996] ECR I-2201.

[75] OJ 1983 L109/8, subsequently replaced by Directive 98/34, OJ 1998 L204/37.

brought proceedings in Belgium for an order preventing them from making such statements. The defendants tried to justify their statement by claiming that CIA Security had not been authorized under the law of 1990 and that its alarm systems had not been approved under the decree of 1991; they counterclaimed for an order that CIA Security cease trading. CIA Security responded by arguing that since the two measures had not been notified as required by the directive, the court could not apply them.

A reference was made to the European Court, which ruled that the law of 1990 was not a technical regulation and did not, therefore, have to be notified. The 1991 decree should, however, have been notified. The European Court ruled that, as a result, the Belgian court could not apply the decree.

Since all the companies concerned were private parties, it could be argued that this constituted horizontal direct effect. The decree imposed an obligation on an individual: it precluded him from selling an alarm system that had not been approved. However, if a public authority had sought to enforce the decree, CIA Security could have invoked the directive as a defence. This would have been a case of vertical direct effect, since CIA Security would have been claiming a right against the State. Did it make a difference if a private party was trying to enforce the decree? Views may differ on this. However, the decree was a measure intended to benefit the public, and it would normally be enforced by a public authority. If a private party seeks to enforce such a measure, it could be argued that the defendant should not be in a weaker position than he would be if the measure were enforced by a public authority.

Directive 83/189 was again before the Court in *Unilever Italia v. Central Food.*[76] The parties were two Italian companies. Unilever Italia had sold a consignment of olive oil to Central Food. The latter refused to pay on the ground that the oil did not comply with Italian legislation. The legislation constituted a 'technical regulation' in terms of the directive. It had been notified, but its promulgation was an infringement of a provision in the directive, under which such legislation could not be brought into force for a specified period. For this reason, Unilever Italia, which had brought proceedings before an Italian court, claimed that the court could not apply the legislation in deciding whether the olive oil complied with Italian law.

The European Court agreed. It held that the principle laid down in *Faccini Dori* does not apply to technical regulations brought into force contrary to Directive 83/189. The reason it gave was that Directive 83/189 lays down a procedural bar to the adoption of national legislation, while the directive in *Faccini Dori* required Member States to adopt positive rules granting rights to, and imposing obligations on, individuals.[77]

In *Lemmens,*[78] a case decided after *CIA Security* but before *Unilever Italia,* a motorist convicted of drunken driving sought to have his conviction overturned on the ground that the breathalyser on which he had been tested was based on national regulations which should have, but had not, been notified under Directive 83/189. The Court, however, rejected his argument: it restricted the *CIA Security* principle to cases where the

[76] Case C-443/98, 26 September 2000.

[77] Paras 50 and 51 of the judgment.

[78] Case C-226/97, [1998] ECR I-3711.

application of the national regulations would hinder the use or marketing of a product not in conformity with them.

*Unilever Italia* was of course such a case; nevertheless, it could be criticized on the ground that it introduces uncertainty into the law: private parties might not know whether the requirements of Directive 83/189 had been satisfied.[79] This point was strongly made by the Advocate General in the case (Advocate General Jacobs), who said:[80]

> 111. In my view, a failure to notify (which may happen very frequently, given the vast range of measures potentially within the scope of the directive, and which may of course be inadvertent) cannot be treated as having far-reaching effects on contractual relations between individuals. In substance the effect would be that, solely on the basis of such failures by Member States, courts would be obliged to find a breach of contract.
>
> 112. Such consequences would be contrary to principles fundamental to our legal systems, and contrary in particular to fundamental requirements of legal certainty. There may be uncertainty as to whether the measure is a technical regulation and whether it required notification; uncertainty, in the absence of any provisions laying down a transparent procedure, as to whether it has in fact been notified; uncertainty, where a national regulation or parts of it are disapplied, as to what legal regime is to replace the disapplied measures; uncertainty as to the appropriate remedies for the breach of contract, in the absence of fault in either party. Moreover, such consequences would follow whether or not the technical regulation was an obstacle to the free movement of goods, and even where it facilitated such freedom of movement. I can see no basis for giving such consequences to a failure to notify.

This is a powerful criticism of the judgment the Court was about to deliver.

Subsequent cases have further muddied the waters, causing problems for those trying to make sense of the law. One theory is that of 'triangular' relationships.[81] It is said that an exception exists where there is a relationship between an individual and the State which also affects a second individual. In such a case, the first individual may rely on the direct effect of a directive against the State, even though this might have adverse repercussions on the other individual.

*Wells* provides an example.[82] In this case, the owners of a quarry in England applied for development consent. The matter went to the Secretary of State. A neighbouring landowner brought proceedings (in England) against the Secretary of State, claiming that he should apply the provisions of an EC directive, something that would have been detrimental to the interests of the quarry owners. On a reference to the European Court, the United Kingdom argued that acceptance of the neighbouring landowner's claim would allow one individual to use a directive to deprive other individuals (the quarry owners) of their rights. After restating the principle that directives cannot have horizontal direct effect, the Court said, 'On the other hand, mere adverse repercussions on the

[79] See Weatherill, 'Breach of Directives and Breach of Contract' (2001) 26 ELRev. 177. For further cases and further analysis, see the articles by Lackhoff, Hilson, Lenz, and Dougan in 'Further Reading', below.

[80] Paras 111 and 112 of the Opinion.

[81] Lackhoff and Nyssens, 'Direct Effect of Directives in Triangular Situations' (1998) 23 ELRev. 397.

[82] Case C-201/02, [2004] ECR I-723.

rights of third parties, even if the repercussions are certain, do not justify preventing an individual from invoking the provisions of a directive against the Member State concerned.'[83] So it ruled that the directive could be invoked by the claimant.

This accords with the theory of 'triangular situations', but it involves an extension of the concept of vertical direct effect. In the classic cases, an individual was invoking a directive to claim a freedom or immunity against the State: he wanted to defend himself against a criminal charge, to avoid paying tax, or to enter the country. In a case such as *Wells*, on the other hand, the individual was using a directive to require the State to deprive another individual of the freedom to develop his land. Moreover, such a 'repercussion' was not incidental or unintended: it was the whole purpose of the exercise.

A second theory is based on the distinction between an 'exclusionary effect' and a 'substitution effect'.[84] The former occurs when a directive has the negative effect of eliminating national legislation – for example, because it was not notified to the Commission; the latter has the positive effect of imposing rules laid down in the directive. According to the theory, the inapplicability of the national legislation may be relied on by one individual against another, while the positive effect of the new rules cannot. Both *CIA Security* and *Unilever Italia* could be regarded as examples of a purely 'exclusionary' effect.

Though both useful, these theories[85] do not fully explain all the cases. *Pfeiffer*[86] is an example. This was a case concerning maximum permitted hours of work. The Community had adopted a directive (the Working Time Directive),[87] Article 6 of which established the principle that no one may be required to work more than forty-eight hours per week (on average), though there were certain exceptions. Paragraph 3 of the German legislation transposing this Directive, the *Arbeitsgesetz*, established maximum working hours, but provided (in paragraph 7) for an exception in the case of emergency workers (such as ambulance crews) who spend significant periods of time on standby, waiting for a call.

Pfeiffer and his colleagues worked for the German Red Cross as emergency workers, operating ambulances and similar vehicles. The contract under which they were employed required them to work more than forty-eight hours a week. The Red Cross considered that this was justified under paragraph 7 of the *Arbeitsgesetz*. Pfeiffer objected and sued the Red Cross in a German court. He argued that paragraph 7 was contrary to the Directive. Since the Red Cross is not a State organization, this meant that he was claiming that the relevant provisions of the directive had horizontal direct effect.

The German court referred the issue to the European Court, which ruled that paragraph 7 of the *Arbeitsgesetz* was indeed contrary to the Directive. The relevant provision of the Directive (Article 6) fulfilled the requirements for direct effect. The

[83] Paras 55–57 of the judgment.

[84] See *per* Advocate General Saggio in *Oceano Grupo Editorial v. Rocio Murciano Quintero*, Cases C-240–44/98, [2000] ECR 1–4941, at paras 37–9 of the Opinion.

[85] Both theories must be applied, since cases like *Wells* involve a 'substitution effect' and are not, therefore, covered by the second theory.

[86] Cases C-397–403/01, 5 October 2004. For a comment, see Prechal (2005) 42 CMLRev. 1445.

[87] Directive 93/104, OJ 1993 L307, p. 18.

Court, therefore, ruled that it had vertical direct effect. It did not, however, have horizontal direct effect; consequently, it could not be invoked by Pfeiffer against the Red Cross.[88]

This seems to conflict with the second theory. All Pfeiffer wanted was for paragraph 7 of the *Arbeitsgesetz* to be ruled inapplicable. Then, paragraph 3 of the *Arbeitsgesetz* would apply to his case. This was all he needed to win his case. In other words, his claim involved only an 'exclusionary effect', not a 'substitution effect'.[89]

In its judgment, the Court did not mention *CIA Security* or *Unilever Italia.* The ruling could, however, be reconciled with these cases on the basis that, in them, the directive imposed a procedural bar to the application of the national legislation, while in *Pfeiffer* the national legislation conflicted with a substantive provision in the directive.[90] The Court did not, however, justify its decision on this basis; it simply referred to the classic cases on horizontal direct effect.[91]

*Pfeiffer* was a judgment of a Grand Chamber of the Court and might, therefore, be regarded as having special authority. A year later, however, another Grand Chamber (with a somewhat different composition) reached a different conclusion. This was in *Mangold*,[92] which concerned the interaction of two other aspects of employment law: fixed-term employment contracts and discrimination on grounds of age. The former are regarded as undesirable on the ground that they create insecurity, and an EC Framework Agreement, put into effect by Council Directive 1999/70,[93] imposed restrictions on them. However, older workers who lose their job often find it difficult to get another one. One possible solution is to make an exception in their case with regard to fixed-term contracts: if fixed-term contracts are made lawful for older workers, employers might be more willing to give them work. However, this could be regarded as condoning discrimination on grounds of age, something that was contrary to another EC directive, Directive 2000/78.[94] It was these difficult problems that constituted the background to the *Mangold* case.

German law had a general rule prohibiting fixed-term employment contracts unless there was 'objective justification', a concept explained in the legislation.[95] However, the Law of 23 December 2002, which came into force on 1 January 2003, provided that objective justification was not necessary if the worker was aged fifty-eight or over; moreover, it went on to say that, up until 31 December 2006, fixed-term contracts without objective justification would be permitted for workers aged fifty-two or over when the contract began. This was intended to combat the unemployment crisis in Germany by making it easier for older workers to find a job.

The case concerned an employment contract between an employer, Mr Helm, and an employee, Mr Mangold. The contract was for a fixed term: it began on 1 July 2003 and ended on 28 February 2004. When it commenced, Mr Mangold was fifty-six years of

[88] Paras 107–10 of the judgment.

[89] For another case that seems to conflict with the theory, see *Berlusconi*, Cases C-387/02, 391/02 and 403/02, 3 May 2005.

[90] This was the ground on which the Court based its judgment in *Unilever Italia.*

[91] *Marshall* and *Faccini Dori*, though it also cited *Wells.*

[92] Case C-144/04, 25 November 2005.

[93] OJ 1999 L175, p. 34.

[94] OJ 2000 L303, p. 16.

[95] The legislation was extremely complicated: what follows is intended to convey the gist of it.

age. The contract (rather surprisingly)[96] stated that there was no objective justification for it other than the employee's age. Mangold then sued Helm in a German court, claiming that the provision limiting the term of the contract was contrary to Directive 2000/78. The German court referred the matter to the European Court.

Now, there was one obvious and easy answer to the question. In the case of Germany, the deadline for implementing Directive 2000/78 was 2 December 2006. The contract began and ended before that date. As we saw above, the European Court held in the *Ratti* case that direct effect cannot arise until after the deadline; so the Directive should have been irrelevant to the proceedings in the case. Admittedly, the European Court qualified this in the *Inter-Environnement Wallonie* case[97] by saying that, during the period before the deadline, a Member State must not adopt measures that seriously compromise the attainment of the result prescribed by the directive. However, it is hard to see how a national provision that is due to expire twenty-nine days after the deadline could be said to 'seriously compromise' the attainment of the result to be achieved. Nevertheless, this is exactly what the European Court did say.[98]

It advanced two strands of reasoning. The first[99] concerned the direct effect of the Directive. (The second,[100] which concerned general principles of law, will be considered below.)[101] The Court pointed out that the deadline for implementation was originally 2 December 2003. Member States were, however, entitled to an additional three years if they so requested. Germany had made such a request; so its deadline was 2 December 2006. However, the Directive contained a provision that where a Member State availed itself of this right, it had to report annually to the Commission on the progress it had made. This, the Court said, implied that it could not adopt legislation that constituted a retrograde step. It also said that some workers, including Mangold himself, would be over fifty-eight by the time the deadline expired and would, therefore, be caught by the general rule that fixed-term contracts were permitted without objective justification if the worker was aged fifty-eight or above.

For these reasons, the Court concluded that the fact that the deadline had not expired was irrelevant. This, however, still left the question we are concerned with. Since Mangold and Helm were both private parties, the case involved horizontal direct effect. The Advocate General held that the Directive could not have direct effect for this reason.[102] The Court, however, ignored the issue: it simply ruled that the Directive had to be applied by the German court. No mention was made of *Pfeiffer*.[103]

The judgment gives one the feeling that the European Court has got out of its depth in this area. Indeed, the *Common Market Law Review* ran an editorial on the *Mangold*

[96] The contract was fairly obviously contrived to provide a test case. As we shall see in Chap. 9 (section entitled 'Hypothetical Questions and Contrived Proceedings'), there have been occasions in the past (most notably the two *Foglia v. Novello* cases) in which the European Court has held that it has no jurisdiction to decide references in such circumstances. In *Mangold*, however, it refused to be deterred by these considerations.

[97] Case C-129/96, [1997] ECR I-7411.

[98] Para. 70 of the judgment.

[99] Paras 68–73 of the judgment.

[100] Paras 74–77 of the judgment.

[101] See the section of this chapter entitled 'General Principles of Law'.

[102] Paras 116–11 of the Opinion.

[103] *Mangold* was also a case of 'exclusionary effect': if the special provision in the law of 23 December 2002 was rendered inapplicable, the general rule would apply under which the age limit was 58. However, the Court made no attempt to explain its ruling on this ground.

case under the heading 'Horizontal direct effect – A law of diminishing coherence?'[104] This contained scathing criticism of the Court's reasoning.[105]

Where does this leave the law? The distinction between 'exclusionary effect' and 'substitution effect' has never been adopted by the Court; moreover, it does not explain *Pfeiffer*. It would be rash, therefore, to assume that it represents the law, though one could perhaps say that a *procedural* rule in a directive can have horizontal direct effect to the extent that it renders a national provision inapplicable. The theory of 'triangular' relationships may also have some validity. However, no theory provides a full explanation of the twists and turns of the Court's case law. Perhaps it will be possible to provide such an explanation in the next edition of this book.

## THE 'STATE'

Since, in at least some situations, directives can be directly effective only against the State, we must next consider what exactly constitutes the 'State'. The first question is whether it matters in what capacity the State is acting. In the *Marshall* case the European Court held that it does not: it is not necessary that it should be exercising governmental powers (for example, collecting taxes); vertical direct effect applies even if it is entering into an ordinary private-law transaction, such as a contract of employment. In both cases 'it is necessary to prevent the State from taking advantage of its own failure to comply with Community law'.[106]

The second question is exactly what bodies are regarded as being part of the State. In the *Marshall* case, Advocate General Slynn said that 'State' must be taken broadly, as including all organs of the State. In matters of employment, it covers the employees of such organs and not just the central civil service.[107] The Court itself seemed to use the terms 'State' and 'public authority' interchangeably. In the *Marshall* case the claimant was an employee of an Area Health Authority, which the Court of Appeal had described as 'an emanation of the State'. It was clearly covered. Nevertheless, other bodies could present more difficult problems.

In later cases, the European Court has tried to clarify matters. In *Johnston v. Chief Constable of the RUC*,[108] it held that the chief constable of a United Kingdom police force is, when acting in his official capacity, an emanation of the State.[109] He cannot take advantage of the failure of the State to comply with Community law. In *Fratelli Costanzo v. Comune di Milano*,[110] it held that a local authority is also part of the State for this purpose.[111] In neither case, it should be noted, could the body in question be

[104] (2006) 43 CMLRev. 1.

[105] It said the Court's inapt citation of authority would have provoked thick red underlining if it had occurred in a student essay. The compatibility of *Mangold* with established case law of the Court also seems to have worried other members of the Court: see *per* Advocate General Kokott in *Commission v. Ireland*, Case C-418/04, 14 September 2006, at para. 89, n. 58 of his Opinion.

[106] At para. 49 of the judgment.

[107] Case 152/84, [1986] ECR 723.

[108] Case 222/84, [1986] ECR 1651.

[109] Para. 56 of the judgment.

[110] Case 103/88, [1989] ECR 1839.

[111] In *Rienks*, Case 5/83, [1983] ECR 4233, a case decided before *Marshall*, the European Court appeared to hold that a directive can be directly effective against the governing body of a profession insofar as the latter is 'entrusted with a public duty' (para. 10 of the judgment). The facts were, however, rather special: the public duty

regarded as in any way responsible for the Government's failure to implement the directive;[112] nevertheless, both are clearly public authorities.

In *Foster v. British Gas*,[113] the European Court was faced with a more difficult question: was British Gas part of the State before it was privatized? This question was referred to the European Court by the House of Lords in a case in which the facts were similar to those in the *Marshall* case.

The first ruling made by the Court concerned the division of jurisdiction between it and the national courts: it held that it had jurisdiction to determine the categories of persons against whom a directive may be directly effective; the national courts, on the other hand, decide whether a particular body falls into one of those categories. In other words, the European Court lays down the rules and the national courts apply them to the facts of the case.

Next came the question of substance. In keeping with its ruling on the jurisdictional point, the Court did not decide directly whether a nationalized industry is to be regarded as part of the State. Instead, it laid down a general formula:

> [A] body, whatever its legal form, which has been made responsible, pursuant to a measure adopted by the State, for providing a public service under the control of the State and has for that purpose special powers beyond those which result from the normal rules applicable in relations between individuals is included in any event among the bodies against which the provisions of a directive capable of having direct effect may be relied upon.

This test consists of four elements. First, the body must provide a public service; secondly, it must do so pursuant to a measure adopted by the State; thirdly; it must do so under the control of the State; and fourthly, it must possess special powers beyond those normally applicable in relations between individuals. Each of these is important.

The first element would seem to exclude a government-owned industry that carries on normal commercial activities, for example an engineering company. The second would seem to rule out a charity created by some private act like a will or trust deed, even if it provides a public service (unless it is part of the State system).[114] The third element might seem to exclude privatized industries, but the English High Court has held otherwise: in *Griffin v. South West Water Services*[115] it ruled that a privatized water company was part of the State for the purpose of direct effect;[116] the third element might also be thought to exclude the holder of an independent public office, such as the chief constable of a police force, but, as we have seen, this is also not the case.[117] The fourth element requires that the body should possess special powers of a governmental nature. This, too, would normally exclude private charities (unless they were given special powers),

was the enrolment of a practitioner on a professional register, and the case was a criminal prosecution for illegal practice. *Cf. R v. Royal Pharmaceutical Society*, Cases 266–7/87, [1989] ECR 1295.

[112] See *per* Advocate General van Gerven in *Foster v. British Gas* (below) at I-3330.

[113] Case C-188/89, [1990] ECR I-3313.

[114] As to which see *NUT v. St Mary's School* [1997] 3 CMLR 630; [1997] ICR 334, CA.

[115] [1995] IRLR 15.

[116] The court held that the test is not whether the body providing the service (the privatized water company) is subject to the control of the State, but whether the *public service* is under the control of the State.

[117] *Johnston v. Chief Constable of the RUC*, Case 222/84, [1986] ECR 1651.

as well as commercial companies even if government-owned. It must, however, be kept in mind that the European Court has a history of whittling down requirements for the application of Community law – the general rules for the direct effect of directives are an example in point – and one should not be surprised if it did so here too. In any event, it seems that the Court does not necessarily regard the *Foster* formula as being the exclusive test: bodies not covered may be included on some other basis.[118]

When the *Foster* case came back to the House of Lords, the test was applied to the facts of the case.[119] The first and second elements were present, since British Gas was given the duty by statute of maintaining an efficient system of gas supply for Great Britain.[120] The element of State control was also present, since the minister had statutory authority to give directions to British Gas.[121] The fourth element was held to be present since British Gas was given a monopoly in the supply of gas.[122] As a result, the House of Lords held that British Gas, when a nationalized industry, was an emanation of the State for the purpose in question.

*Foster v. British Gas* is so far the last word of the European Court on the subject. However, in *Doughty v. Rolls-Royce*,[123] the Court of Appeal had to determine whether Rolls-Royce PLC was an emanation of the State. The facts were similar to those in *Foster*, except that Rolls-Royce PLC was a commercial company, though all its shares were held by nominees of the Crown. Was this sufficient to make it part of the State? The Court of Appeal held that it was not. It was prepared to assume, for the purpose of argument, that the element of State control was present, but it held that Rolls-Royce did not provide a public service; there was no relevant statute or other measure adopted by the State; nor did it enjoy any special powers. The fact that it produced military equipment, much of which was sold to the State, was not enough: such sales were made at arm's length on a commercial basis.

In *NUT v. St Mary's School*,[124] on the other hand, the Court of Appeal held that the governing body of a voluntary aided school *was* an emanation of the State, thus enabling teachers who had lost their jobs at the school to rely on an EC directive in proceedings against it. St Mary's was a Church of England school which voluntarily decided to join the State system and to accept financial aid from the local education authority. Once it did this, it became an emanation of the State for the purpose of direct effect, since it was providing a public service on behalf of the State.

The granting of direct effect to directives is not the only purpose in Community law for which it is necessary to determine exactly what constitutes the State. Similar

118 This is indicated by the phrase 'in any event' in the quotation. In *Doughty v. Rolls-Royce* (below), the Court of Appeal held that the test was not intended to provide the answer to every category of case; nevertheless, it said that, in a case of the same general type as *Foster*, the formula must always be the starting point and would usually be the finishing point: if every element was present, it would require something very unusual to produce the result that the body was not an emanation of the State; conversely, if one element was not present, it would need the addition of something else not contemplated by the formula before it could be so regarded.

119 [1991] 2 AC 306.

120 Gas Act 1972, s. 2(1).

121 *Ibid.* ss. 4 and 7. The fact that the government did not have day-to-day control over British Gas was held by the House of Lords to be irrelevant.

122 *Ibid.*, s. 29 prohibited any person other than British Gas from supplying gas to any premises.

123 [1992] ICR 538; [1992] IRLR 126; *The Times*, 14 January 1992.

124 [1997] 3 CMLR 630; [1997] ICR 334, CA.

problems arise when Article 39(4) [48(4)] EC is invoked. Article 39 [48] is concerned with the rights of migrant workers. Article 39(2) [48(2)] prohibits all discrimination based on nationality against workers from another Member State, but Article 39(4) [48(4)] lays down an exception: it provides that the provisions of Article 39 [48] do not apply to 'employment in the public service'. Clearly, employment in the public service is a similar concept to employment by the State, though possibly wider. The European Court, however, has given it a narrower definition. It seems to cover only those officials who exercise governmental powers or policy-making functions. Nurses in public hospitals are excluded;[125] nor can there be much doubt that most – if not all – employees of nationalized industries are also excluded. Thus neither Ms Foster nor Ms Doughty would have been regarded as employed in the public service for the purpose of Article 39(4) [48(4)] EC. This shows that, in the hands of the European Court, the meaning of concepts such as 'the State' changes to fit the purpose for which they are employed. Where a narrow meaning enhances the effectiveness of Community law, such a meaning will be adopted; where the opposite is the case, a broad meaning will be given.[126]

The European Court's acceptance of the principle that directives cannot impose obligations on individuals may be viewed as a tactical retreat occasioned by the adverse reaction in certain quarters to the whole concept of granting direct effect to directives.[127] In view of the Court's deep commitment to the policy of promoting the effectiveness of Community law, it was inevitable that it would seek other means of recovering the lost ground. The wide meaning given to the concept of the State is part of this strategy. Two other developments, which make the distinction between vertical and horizontal direct effect of less practical importance, are what is sometimes called 'indirect effect', and the possibility of an action for damages against the government of a Member State for failure to implement a directive. These will now be considered.

## INDIRECT EFFECT

The term 'indirect effect', though not used by the European Court, is a handy label for the doctrine that Community provisions, even if not directly effective, must be taken into account by national courts when interpreting national legislation. It is also called the doctrine of 'consistent interpretation'. It is applied mainly (though not exclusively)[128] to directives, which, as we have seen, cannot always impose obligations directly on individuals.

[125] *Commission v. Belgium*, Case 149/79, [1980] ECR 3881 and [1982] ECR 1845.

[126] Cf. *per* Advocate General van Gerven in *Foster* (above) at I-3334–6.

[127] See, for example, the decision of the French *Conseil d'Etat* in the *Cohn-Bendit* case and the decision of the German *Bundesfinanzhof* in the *Kloppenburg* case (both discussed in Chap. 8).

[128] In *Grimaldi*, Case C-322/88, [1989] ECR 4407, the European Court held that recommendations (which have no binding force) must be taken into account by national courts when interpreting national or Community legislation. There is no doubt that the same would apply with regard to any Community instrument that is not directly effective. Thus, a directive can have indirect effect even if it is not vertically directly effective: *R v. Ministry of Agriculture, ex parte Hedley Lomas*, Case C-5/94, [1996] ECR I-2553, *per* Advocate General Léger at para. 64 of his Opinion; *Dekker*, Case C-177/88, [1990] ECR I-3941, *per* Advocate General Darmon at para. 15 of his Opinion.

It thus provides a back-door route by which something approaching the same result may be attained under the guise of interpretation.[129]

The doctrine originated in *Von Colson and Kamann v. Land Nordrhein-Westfalen*,[130] a case concerning a directive on sex discrimination. In the course of its judgment, the Court said, 'It is for the national court to interpret and apply the legislation adopted for the implementation of the directive in conformity with the requirements of Community law, in so far as it is given discretion to do so under national law'.[131]

This is an entirely reasonable requirement. If legislation is passed to implement a directive, it may be assumed that the national legislature intended the legislation to give full effect to the directive and it is right that it should be interpreted with this in mind.[132] Moreover, the European Court made clear that national courts were not being asked to go beyond what was permitted under national law.

Subsequently, the same doctrine was applied to national legislation not adopted to implement the directive,[133] indeed which was passed *before* the directive. This was in *Marleasing*,[134] a case which arose out of proceedings in a Spanish court. The Spanish Civil Code provides that contracts have no legal effect if they are without a cause or have an illegal cause,[135] and it was argued, on the basis of this provision, that a contract leading to the incorporation of a Spanish company was void, since it lacked cause, was a sham transaction, and was entered into in order to defraud the creditors of another

[129] In *R v. Ministry of Agriculture, ex parte Hedley Lomas*, Case C-5/94, [1996] ECR I-2553, Advocate General Léger said at para. 64 of his Opinion, that a directive can have indirect effect even before the time limit for implementation has expired, a proposition which he claimed was supported by para. 15 of the judgment in *Kolpinghuis Nijmegen*, Case 80/86, [1987] ECR 3969. This, however, is a misreading of the judgment. *Kolpinghuis Nijmegen* was a reference from a Dutch court in which the European Court was asked to answer four questions. In the first two, the Court was asked whether a directive could be horizontally directly effective: the Court replied that it could not. The third was whether a directive could have indirect effect in a criminal case: the Court replied that it could not have indirect effect where this would be against the interests of the accused (by making him liable or by aggravating his liability). The fourth question was whether the answers to the first three questions would be any different if the time limit for implementation of the directive had not yet expired: the Court answered this (in para. 15) by saying, first, that the answers to the first two questions would not be affected, and, secondly, by saying: 'As regards the third question concerning the limits which Community law might impose on the obligation or power of the national court to interpret the rules of its national law in the light of the directive, it makes no difference whether or not the period prescribed for implementation has expired.' Since the Court had said in its answer to the third question that indirect effect can never operate against the interests of the accused, it is obvious that this limit on indirect effect would apply *a fortiori* if the deadline had not expired. The Court's statement cannot, therefore, be taken as authority for the proposition that, in other situations, indirect effect operates even before expiry of the deadline.

[130] Case 14/83, [1984] ECR 1891.

[131] Para. 28 of the judgment, reproduced in the final sentence of para. 3 of the Ruling.

[132] This principle is applied in English law with regard to legislation passed to give effect, not only to a Community obligation, but also to obligations under other international treaties: see, e.g., *per* Lord Diplock in *Garland v. British Rail Engineering* [1983] 2 AC 751 at 771.

[133] There is a hint to this effect in para. 26 of the judgment in the *Von Colson* case (above) and in para. 12 of the judgment in *Kolpinghuis Nijmegen*, Case 80/86, [1987] ECR 3969; but see the opinion of Advocate General Slynn in the *Marshall* case, in which he said (at 733) that he was not satisfied that Community law obliged national courts to construe prior legislation in conformity with a directive.

[134] Case C-106/89, [1990] ECR I-4135.

[135] The concept of 'cause' (*causa* in Latin) has played an important role in the history of civilian legal systems and is found in several modern codes. It is not an easy concept to explain in a few words, but it is to some extent analogous to the purpose or object of the contract.

company. It was therefore claimed that the incorporation of the company was a nullity. A Community directive, however, gives an exhaustive list of the grounds on which the incorporation of a company may be declared void, and the lack of a legal cause is not one of them. There was thus a potential conflict between the provisions of the Spanish Civil Code and those of the directive, which had not been implemented in Spain. The Spanish court asked the European Court whether the directive was directly effective. As the parties to the case were all private, this raised the question of horizontal direct effect.

In answer to the question, the European Court reaffirmed the ruling in *Marshall*, that a directive cannot directly impose obligations on a private party. However, it then went on to consider the doctrine of indirect effect. It extended the principle in the *Von Colson* case to apply to national legislation passed before the directive, thus making it possible for the doctrine to apply to the relevant provisions of the Spanish Civil Code. Moreover, it said that the national law had to be interpreted so as to preclude the declaration of nullity of a company other than on the grounds permitted by the directive, thus implying that the national court had no option but to reach that result.

This suggests that the result envisaged by the directive must be attained irrespective of whether or not there is any doubt as to the meaning of the national provision and irrespective of whether or not the words of that provision could reasonably bear the meaning required by the directive. This, however, would no longer constitute interpretation – it would create horizontal direct effect under another name – and in *Webb v. EMO Air Cargo*[136] the House of Lords made clear that it did not accept such a reading of *Marleasing*. It said:[137]

> It is to be observed that the provision of Spanish law in issue in that case was of a general character capable of being construed either widely or narrowly. It did not refer specifically to the grounds upon which the nullity of a public limited company might be ordered. If it had done so, and had included among such grounds the case where the company had been formed with the purpose of defrauding creditors of one of the corporations, the Spanish court would have been entitled and bound to give effect to it notwithstanding the terms of the Directive. As the European Court of Justice said, a national court must construe a domestic law to accord with the terms of a Directive in the same field only if it is possible to do so.[138] That means that the domestic law must be open to an interpretation consistent with the Directive whether or not it is also open to an interpretation inconsistent with it.

The House of Lords then made a reference to the European Court under Article 234 [177] EC for a preliminary ruling on the interpretation of the directive in issue. The European Court gave the ruling without commenting on the passage quoted.[139] By that time, however, the European Court, sitting as a thirteen-judge Full Court, had already

136 [1993] 1 WLR 49, HL.

137 At 60, *per* Lord Keith of Kinkel, with whom Lords Griffiths, Browne-Wilkinson, Mustill, and Slynn of Hadley agreed. Lord Slynn, it should be remembered, had until recently himself been a judge on the European Court.

138 The phrase 'as far as possible' occurs in para. 8 of the judgment in *Marleasing*. It is not, however, repeated in later paragraphs nor is it to be found in the actual Ruling.

139 *Webb v. EMO Air Cargo*, Case C-32/93, [1994] ECR 3567.

ruled (in a case decided after the House of Lords had made the reference) that the obligation to interpret national legislation in accordance with Community law applies only in so far as such an interpretation is possible.[140] The wide reading of the judgment in *Marleasing* is, therefore, wrong. Whether this was a misunderstanding all along,[141] or whether the Court was testing the waters and decided to pull back, is not known.[142]

Even in its restrained form, the doctrine of indirect effect is a powerful tool for bringing national law into line. It nevertheless generates great uncertainty since it is hard to know how unclear national law must be for indirect effect to operate. Reasonably enough, English courts seem more willing to interpret a national provision in accordance with Community law when it was passed to give effect to Community law than when it was not.[143]

For some years, there has been speculation as to whether indirect effect can apply to a directive before the expiry of the deadline for its implementation. This controversy has now been settled by the decision of a Grand Chamber of the European Court in *Adeneler*,[144] in which it said that indirect effect in its full sense applies only after the expiry of the deadline. Before this date, national courts are required only to interpret national legislation (as far as possible) in accordance with the doctrine in *Inter-Environnement Wallonie v. Région Wallonne*.[145] This case was discussed above: it will be remembered that it held that, in the period between the adoption of the directive and the expiry of the deadline, Member States must not enact any legislation that could

[140] *Faccini Dori v. Recreb*, Case C-91/92, [1994] ECR I-3325 at para. 26 of the judgment.

[141] It appears from the opinion of Advocate General van Gerven that Spanish law was in fact far from clear on the point. The Spanish statute on company law did not state the grounds on which the incorporation of a company could be declared void, and it was on the basis of legal literature that it was contended that the contract provisions of the Code should be applied by analogy. If this was so, the statements by the Court could perhaps be justified by the facts of the case. For further analysis of *Marleasing*, see De Búrca, 'Giving Effect to European Community Directives' (1992) 55 MLR 215; Mead, 'The Obligation to Apply European Law: Is *Duke* Dead?' (1991) 16 ELRev. 490; Greenwood, 'Effect of EC Directives in National Law' [1992] CLJ 3 at 4–5; Maltby, '*Marleasing*: What is All the Fuss About?' (1993) 109 LQR 301.

[142] In recent years, the European Court seems to be doing everything within its power to emphasize the importance of indirect effect, though it never forgets to include the words 'so far as possible' in its rulings. See, for example, *Pfeiffer*, Cases C-397–403/01, 5 October 2004 (discussed above), at paras 110–119 of the judgment.

[143] In *Duke v. Reliance Systems* [1988] AC 618, a case decided before *Marleasing*, Lord Templeman refused to 'distort the meaning of a domestic statute so as to conform with Community law which is not directly applicable' (at 641); see also *Finnegan v. Clowney Youth Training Programme* [1990] 2 AC 407. In *Litster v. Forth Dry Dock & Engineering Co.* [1990] 1 AC 546, on the other hand, the House of Lords was prepared to imply words into British legislation passed to implement a Directive in order to make it conform to the Directive. After the European Court had given its ruling on the interpretation of the Directive in *Webb v. Emo Air Cargo*, the House of Lords interpreted the British legislation in conformity with the Directive, even though, had it not been for the Directive, it would have interpreted it differently: see *Webb v. EMO Air Cargo (No. 2)* [1995] 1 WLR 1454, HL. For a discussion of these cases, see Craig, 'Directives: Direct Effect, Indirect Effect and the Construction of National Legislation' (1997) 22 ELRev. 519 at 530–3. For a Scottish case in which the Inner House of the Court of Session said that the interpretation of national regulations enacted to implement a Directive can be affected by the Directive only to the extent that there is an ambiguity in the regulations which can be resolved by reference to the Directive, see *Stirling District Council v. Allan*, 1995 SC 420 at 424; [1995] IRLR 301 at 303 (para. 10). The European Court has also stated that the duty to interpret national legislation so as to be consistent with a directive arises *a fortiori* where the legislation in question was passed to give effect to the directive: *Pfeiffer*, Cases C-397–403/01, 5 October 2004 (discussed above), at para. 112 of the judgment.

[144] *Adeneler*, Case C-212/04, 4 July 2006.

[145] Case C-129/96, [1997] ECR I-7411.

seriously compromise the attainment of the result required by the directive. During this period, therefore, national legislation must (as far as possible) be interpreted so as to avoid this.[146]

Finally, a word should be said about criminal proceedings. If a directive is capable of direct effect, it can be invoked by the accused: this would constitute vertical direct effect;[147] on the other hand, it cannot be invoked by the prosecution against the accused: this would constitute horizontal direct effect.[148] Moreover, the European Court has held that a directive cannot have indirect effect in criminal proceedings in so far as this would make the accused guilty where he would otherwise have been acquitted, or where it would aggravate his guilt;[149] however, there is no reason why a directive which does not have (vertical) direct effect should not have indirect effect where this would benefit the accused.

### GOVERNMENTAL LIABILITY FOR NON-IMPLEMENTATION

Another way in which the European Court has tried to regain the ground lost in *Marshall* has been to develop the doctrine that a person who has suffered loss as a result of the failure of a national government to implement a directive may bring proceedings in tort in the national courts against the Government. However, as this is a general doctrine, applying to other infringements of Community law as well, it will be considered separately at the end of this chapter.

## DECISIONS

The next question is whether an EC or Euratom decision can have direct effect. It might be thought that this question was of only limited importance, since it was said previously that a decision was an executive act: the rights created by such an act would only rarely be invoked in the national courts. In fact, however, the Community institutions have not felt themselves precluded from adopting decisions of a legislative character: some of these are similar to directives and require Member States to take action in order to achieve a stated objective; others lay down general rules rather like regulations.

[146] *Adeneler*, at paras 107–24 (especially para. 123) of the judgment. Though *Mangold* was cited, there was no suggestion that it had widened the principle laid down in *Inter-Environnement Wallonie v. Région Wallonne*: see para. 121 of the judgment. For further discussion, see Klamert, 'Judicial Implementation of Directives and Anticipatory Indirect Effect: Connecting the Dots' (2006) 43 CMLRev. 1251.

[147] This occurred in *Ratti*, Case 148/78, [1979] ECR 1629 (with regard to the Directive for which the deadline had already expired).

[148] *Pretore di Salò v. X.*, Case 14/86, [1987] ECR 2545; *Kolpinghuis Nijmegen*, Case 80/86, [1987] ECR 3969 (the first two questions); *Arcaro*, Case C-168/95, [1996] ECR I-4705 (the second question).

[149] *Kolpinghuis Nijmegen* (above) (the third question); *Arcaro* (above) (the third question, especially para. 42 of the judgment). For the possibility that this paragraph might impose limitations on indirect effect even outside the criminal area, see Craig, 'Directives: Direct Effect, Indirect Effect and the Construction of National Legislation' (1997) 22 ELRev. 519 at 526–8.

In view of the Court's rulings in the case of directives, it would have been surprising if it had not also declared that decisions can be directly effective. In fact, this occurred first: the *Grad* case,[150] in which the European Court decided that decisions can be directly effective, was decided some four years before the *Van Duyn* case.[151] The reasons given were the same.

Most of the comments made previously with regard to directives apply also to decisions. Of course, a decision is different from a directive, in that it can be addressed to an individual as well as a Member State. However, in view of what the Court said in the *Marshall* case,[152] it would seem that a decision can impose a directly effective obligation only on the addressee.[153] Where the decision is addressed to a Member State, it cannot be horizontally directly effective.[154]

## GENERAL PRINCIPLES OF LAW

Until the decision of the European Court in *Mangold*, it was assumed by everyone that general principles of law, being inherently amorphous and uncertain, can have no direct effect. However, as was indicated above, the alternative line of reasoning pursued by the Court[155] in *Mangold* was that non-discrimination on grounds of age is a general principle of Community law.[156] As such, the Court said, its observance cannot be dependent on whether or not the deadline for implementing a directive giving effect to it has expired. If the Court meant – as its words appeared to mean – that general principles of law have horizontal direct effect – or any direct effect at all, for that matter – the implications for legal certainty are immense. *Mangold* was a case between two private individuals: the effect of the Court's ruling was to deprive one of them of the rights he would otherwise have had, on the basis of a principle, the details of which were completely uncertain. It is hard to believe that a mere general principle can do this. It may well be that non-discrimination on grounds of age is in some sense a general principle of law; however, it is subject to numerous qualifications and exceptions. Until it has been clarified and given a clear form, it comes nowhere near satisfying the test for direct effect, one of the requirements for which is a reasonable degree of clarity and precision.[157] Perhaps what the Court meant in *Mangold* is that where such clarity and precision are provided by a directive, the principle has direct effect, even in proceedings between two individuals and even if the deadline for implementation has not yet expired.[158] In view of the defective reasoning in *Mangold*, however, even this is doubtful. Further confirmation will be required.

150 Case 9/70, [1970] ECR 825. 151 See above. 152 See above.

153 According to Art. 249 [189] EC, a decision is binding only on the person (or persons) to whom it is addressed.

154 But see *per* Advocate General Reischl in *Unil-It*, Case 30/75, [1975] ECR 1419 at 1434.

155 The Court prefaced this part of its judgment with the words 'In the second place and above all', thus implying that this was its preferred ground for reaching its conclusion: para.74 of the judgment.

156 Para. 75 of the judgment. 157 See the section entitled 'Clear and Unambiguous', above.

158 To give direct effect – whether horizontal or vertical – to a directive before the deadline has expired is objectionable because it deprives the Member State in question of the right given by the Treaty to choose the 'form and methods' of implementation. It cannot be accused of being in default until the deadline has expired.

## AGREEMENTS WITH THIRD COUNTRIES

Agreements with non-Member States are obviously in a different category from the Community Treaties and Community legislation. In particular, it might be thought that there would be a lack of balance and reciprocity if they were directly effective in the Community countries but not in the other countries. This argument appears originally to have had some influence,[159] but it was subsequently rejected by the European Court, at least with regard to association agreements and bilateral trade agreements.[160] The position now is that such agreements – whether they are intended to establish a special regime giving greater rights to the third country than to the Community,[161] or are intended to be reciprocal[162] – can be directly effective in the courts of the Member States of the Community, even if they are not directly effective in the non-Member State. The test appears to be the same as for the Community Treaties.

This is the case, irrespective of whether the agreement is concluded (on the Community side) by the Community alone, as occurred in *Kupferberg*,[163] or by the Community and the Member States acting together (mixed agreement), as occurred in *Bresciani*.[164] In the latter case, however, national law will determine the effect of those parts of the agreement that are outside the treaty-making competence of the Community.[165] With regard to agreements concluded by the Member States alone which become binding on the Community by succession (such as the old GATT), the European Court appears to accept the possibility of direct effect in principle, though in practice it has always ruled against it.[166]

In *Kupferberg*,[167] it was argued that a German tax on wine could not apply to imports from Portugal (before Portugal joined the Community) because it conflicted with a provision in the Free Trade Agreement between the Community and Portugal. This raised the question whether the relevant provision of the Free Trade Agreement was directly effective in Germany. The European Court held that this question could not be left to the national law of each Member State because a uniform solution throughout the Community was desirable. So Community law had to decide,[168] and the Court held, after examining the provision, that it was directly effective. The fact that it was probably not directly effective in Portugal was regarded as irrelevant.[169]

[159] *Bresciani*, Case 87/75, [1976] ECR 129 at 148–9 (*per* Advocate General Trabucchi) and para. 22 of the judgment; *Polydor*, Case 270/80, [1982] ECR 329 at 355 (*per* Advocate General Rozès).

[160] *Kupferberg* (discussed below). [161] *Bresciani* (above). [162] *Kupferberg* (discussed below).

[163] Below. [164] Above.

[165] *Dior v. Tuk Consultancy*, Cases C-300, 392/98, 14 December 2000 (discussed in Chap. 6).

[166] See *International Fruit Company*, Cases 21–4/72, [1972] ECR 1219; *Schlüter*, Case 9/73, [1973] ECR 1135; *SPI*, Cases 267–9/81, [1983] ECR 801.

[167] Case 104/81, [1982] ECR 3641. See also *Sevince*, Case C-192/89, [1990] ECR I-3461; *Demirel*, Case 12/86, [1987] ECR 3719; *Kziber*, Case C-18/90, [1991] ECR I-199.

[168] But the European Court said, at para. 17 of its judgment, that if the agreement itself provides whether or not it is to be directly effective, that will be decisive. Such provisions are not, however, normal, and there was no such provision in the agreement with Portugal. In the absence of such a provision, the European Court will decide the question according to its own criteria.

[169] See para. 18 of the judgment.

The result is that non-Community businessmen selling in the Community could have a more effective means of enforcing the agreement than Community businessmen exporting to the foreign country. However, the European Court has also made clear that provisions in agreements with non-Member States are not necessarily to be given the same wide and policy-oriented interpretation that is given to the Community Treaties. This is so even if, as is often the case, the agreement reproduces almost exactly the wording of a provision in the EC Treaty.[170]

The reason the European Court has adopted this strategy appears to be as follows. When the Community enters into an agreement with a non-Member State, it is under an obligation to ensure that the agreement is carried out. Frequently, however, the implementation of the agreement on the Community side will depend on the Member States. The Community could, therefore, be embarrassed in its relations with the non-Member State, if the Member States failed to give effect to the agreement.

Agreements between the Community and a non-Member State are, of course, binding on the Member States,[171] and an action under Article 226 [169] EC[172] could be brought against any Member State which failed to abide by it. But this is a cumbersome remedy. By making such agreements directly effective, the European Court has established an easy means of enforcement. At the same time, by refusing to apply its normal method of interpretation to such agreements, it has ensured that non-Community countries will not be given too great an advantage.

Different considerations have prevailed in the case of the GATT, now part of the WTO Agreement.[173] The old GATT was held not to be directly effective on the ground that its provisions were too flexible.[174] It seems to have been thought that parties to GATT had the option either of obeying GATT rules or of accepting that other parties could take countervailing action.[175] The fact that other parties did not regard the Agreement as directly effective was also relevant.[176] It appears to have been thought that if the Agreement were held to be directly effective in the Community, this would put the Community at a disadvantage since the Community could not take unilateral action when other parties violated it.[177]

Whatever justification there might have been for this attitude under the old GATT, it might have been thought that the position would be different under the WTO Agreement, which has a much stronger enforcement system. Nevertheless, in *Portugal v. Council*,[178] the European Court held that the position had not altered. In particular, the Court seemed to be unwilling to 'deprive the legislative or executive organs of the Community of the scope for manœuvre enjoyed by their counterparts in the

[170] *Polydor*, Case 270/80, [1982] ECR 329; *Kupferberg* (above) at paras 28–31 of the judgment. This means that the same words can mean one thing in the EC Treaty and another in an agreement with a third country.

[171] Art. 300(7) [228(7)] EC. [172] See Chap. 10.

[173] *Portugal v. Council*, Case C-149/96, [1999] ECR I-8395, para. 42 of the judgment.

[174] See *International Fruit Company*, Cases 21–4/72, [1972] ECR 1219; Schlüter, Case 9/73, [1973] ECR 1135; *SPI*, Cases 267–9/81, [1983] ECR 801.

[175] See *per* Advocate General Reischl in *SPI*, Cases 267–9/81, [1983] ECR 801 at 790.

[176] *Ibid.* at 791. See also *Portugal v. Council* (above) at paras 43–45 of the judgment.

[177] See *per* Advocate General Reischl in *SPI* at 791. [178] Case C-149/96, [1999] ECR I-8395.

Community's trading partners'.[179] This ruling has attracted criticism;[180] however, though hardly consistent with the Court's claim to uphold the rule of law, it is nevertheless understandable from the political point of view.[181] Subsequently, the Court has held that it makes no difference if there has been a ruling of the Dispute Settlement Body of the WTO holding the Community measure contrary to the GATT;[182] nor is it possible for an importer to sue the Community in tort for damages: this too has been blocked by the Court.[183] The same political arguments apply in all these cases.

## ACTS OF INSTITUTIONS ESTABLISHED BY AGREEMENTS WITH THIRD COUNTRIES

Agreements with third countries sometimes establish institutions, such as councils of association under association agreements. In *Sevince*,[184] the European Court held that acts (decisions) adopted by such institutions can be directly effective in the Community if they comply with the same requirements as apply to agreements between the Community and non-Member States.

## THE SUPREMACY OF COMMUNITY LAW AND THE RESTRICTION OF NATIONAL POWERS

It is a basic rule of Community law that (subject to one exception)[185] a directly effective provision of Community law always prevails over a provision of national law. This rule, which is not found in any of the Treaties but has been proclaimed with great emphasis by the Court, applies irrespective of the nature of the Community provision (constitutive Treaty, Community act, or agreement with a non-Member State) or that of the national provision (constitution, statute, or subordinate legislation); it also applies irrespective of whether the Community provision came before, or after, the national provision: in all cases the national provision must give way to Community law.[186]

[179] At para. 46 of the judgment.

[180] See, for example, Griller, 'Judicial Enforceability of WTO Law in the European Union' (2000) 3 Journal of International Economic Law 441. See also Petersmann, 'European and International Constitutional Law: Time for Promoting "Cosmopolitan Democracy" in the WTO' in Gráinne de Búrca and Joanne Scott (eds), *The EU and the WTO: Legal and Constitutional Issues* (2001) 81.

[181] See Peers, 'Fundamental Right or Political Whim? WTO Law and the European Court of Justice' in Gráinne de Búrca and Joanne Scott (eds), *The EU and the WTO: Legal and Constitutional Issues* (2001) 111.

[182] *Van Parys*, Case C-377/02, 1 March 2005 (Grand Chamber).

[183] *Biret International v. Council*, Case C-93/02 P, [2003] ECR I-10497. For a comment, see Thies (2004) 41 CMLRev.1661.

[184] Case C-192/89, [1990] ECR I-3461.

[185] The only exception is where the national provision is necessary to give effect to obligations under an international agreement entered into by the Member State before it became a party to the relevant Community Treaty: see *Levy*, Case C-158/91, [1993] ECR I-4287 (discussed in Chap. 6, above).

[186] For a succinct survey of the relevant case law, see the opinion of Advocate General Reischl in the *Simmenthal* case, Case 106/77, [1978] ECR 629 at 651–2.

The second *Simmenthal* case[187] provides a good example. The facts were simple: Simmenthal imported some beef from France into Italy and was made to pay a fee for a public health inspection when the meat crossed the frontier. This was laid down by an Italian law passed in 1970; it was, however, contrary to the EC Treaty and two Community regulations passed in 1964 and 1968 respectively. The case began in an Italian court where two points were raised by the Italian authorities: first, that the Italian law must prevail because it was passed *after* the two Community regulations; and, secondly, that even if the Italian law conflicted with Italy's treaty obligations, it had to be applied by the Italian courts until such time as it had been declared unconstitutional by the Italian Constitutional Court. This latter contention was based on a principle of Italian constitutional law according to which questions concerning the constitutionality of Italian laws had to be determined by the Constitutional Court. A reference was made to the European Court to obtain a ruling on these issues.

The European Court held that it was the duty of a national court to give full effect to the Community provisions and not to apply any conflicting provision of national legislation, even if it had been adopted subsequently. It also held that it should not wait for the national law to be set aside either by a constitutional court or by the legislature. The key passages in the judgment deserve to be quoted in full:[188]

> Furthermore, in accordance with the principle of the precedence of Community law, the relationship between provisions of the Treaty and directly applicable measures of the institutions on the one hand and the national law of the Member States on the other is such that those provisions and measures not only by their entry into force render automatically inapplicable any conflicting provision of current national law but – in so far as they are an integral part of, and take precedence in, the legal order applicable in the territory of each of the Member States – also preclude the valid adoption of new national legislative measures to the extent to which they would be incompatible with Community provisions.
>
> Indeed any recognition that national legislative measures which encroach upon the field within which the Community exercises its legislative power or which are otherwise incompatible with the provisions of Community law had any legal effect would amount to a corresponding denial of the effectiveness of obligations undertaken unconditionally and irrevocably by Member States pursuant to the Treaty and would thus imperil the very foundations of the Community.

Three points about this should be noted: the Court's statement is limited to Treaty provisions and 'directly applicable measures of the institutions'; secondly, it does not state that conflicting national provisions are void, but merely that they are 'inapplicable'; and, thirdly, the second paragraph is concerned not only with national legislation which conflicts directly with a Community provision, but also with national laws which 'encroach upon the field within which the Community exercises its legislative power'.

As regards the first point, it is obvious that a Community provision will prevail over national legislation only if the Community provision is directly effective. The use by the Court of the term 'directly applicable' does not indicate that the principle of supremacy is limited to regulations: to the extent that they are directly effective, directives and

[187] Case 106/77, [1978] ECR 629. [188] Paras 17 and 18 of the judgment.

decisions will also prevail over inconsistent national legislation. The *Ratti*[189] and *Marshall*[190] cases are both examples of the supremacy of directives over national legislation – provided the right contained in the directive is invoked against the State. It is equally clear from the cases discussed above[191] that a directly effective provision in an international agreement will prevail over inconsistent national legislation.

The significance of the second point mentioned above is that there is, according to the European Court, a positive obligation on Member States to repeal conflicting national legislation, even though it is inapplicable. This was laid down in the *French Merchant Seamen* case,[192] which concerned a French law which provided that a certain proportion of the crew on French merchant ships had to be of French nationality. This was plainly in conflict with Community law and enforcement proceedings under Article 226 [169] EC were brought against France. The French Government argued that the French law was not in fact applied and that, since under Community law it was inapplicable, the continued existence of the law did not constitute a violation of the Treaty. The European Court held, however, that the failure to repeal the law created 'an ambiguous state of affairs' which would make Community seamen uncertain 'as to the possibilities available to them of relying on Community law'.[193] Judgment was therefore given against France.

The discussion so far has been concerned with the situation where there is a direct conflict between Community and national law; however, the significance of the third point is that the powers of Member States can be limited even where the conflict is only indirect or potential. Although the position is not entirely clear, it seems that this can occur in certain situations. For example, in the field of agriculture, if the Community has introduced a common organization of the market for a given product, the Member States are precluded from adopting any measures which 'might undermine or create exceptions to it'.[194]

## REMEDIES AND PROCEDURE IN NATIONAL COURTS

As a general rule, Community law does not provide remedies for the infringement of rights it confers: this is left to national law.[195] Although Member States do not necessarily have to create new remedies for Community purposes, all remedies normally available

[189] Case 148/78, [1979] ECR 1629, discussed above.

[190] Case 152/84, [1986] ECR 723, discussed above.

[191] See, e.g., *Bresciani*, Case 87/75, [1976] ECR 129.

[192] *Commission v. France*, Case 167/73, [1974] ECR 359.

[193] See para. 41 of the judgment.

[194] See *Pigs Marketing Board v. Redmond*, Case 83/78, [1978] ECR 2347 at para. 56 of the judgment. For a detailed discussion of the cases in this area, see Baumann, 'Common Organizations of the Market and National Law' (1977) 14 CMLRev. 303 and Usher, 'The Effects of Common Organizations and Policies on the Powers of a Member State' (1977) 2 ELRev. 428.

[195] National law also normally governs questions of evidence and procedure. These include such matters as the appropriate court or tribunal to hear the case, time limits for commencing proceedings, and the burden of proof: *Rewe-Zentralfinanz*, Case 33/76, [1976] ECR 1989; *Comet v. Produktschap voor Siergewassen*, Case 45/76, [1976] ECR 2043; *Deutsche Milchkontor v. Germany*, Cases 205–15/82, [1983] ECR 2633.

under national law must be open to litigants seeking to enforce claims under Community law. Such litigants must be able to enjoy these remedies on terms that are no less favourable than those that apply to litigants with claims under national law: there must be no discrimination.[196]

This has been made clear by the European Court in numerous cases. For example, in *Rewe v. Hauptzollamt Kiel*[197] it said:

> [I]t was not intended to create new remedies in the national courts to ensure the observance of Community law other than those already laid down by national law. On the other hand the system of legal protection established by the Treaty, as set out in Article 234 [177] in particular, implies that it must be possible for every type of action provided for by national law to be available for the purpose of ensuring observance of Community provisions having direct effect, on the same conditions concerning the admissibility and procedure as would apply were it a question of ensuring observance of national law.[198]

The principle of equal availability of national remedies is, however, subject to the overriding principle that Member States must ensure that there is an *effective* remedy for the enforcement of Community rights. In particular, if the application of the normal national remedies would mean that it was impossible, or excessively difficult, in practice to enforce the Community right, the Member State is obliged to create special remedies.[199] Thus in *Von Colson and Kamann v. Land Nordrhein-Westfalen*,[200] a case concerning a directive on sex discrimination, the European Court said:[201]

> Although . . . full implementation of the directive does not require any specific form of sanction for unlawful discrimination, it does entail that that sanction be such as to guarantee real and effective judicial protection. Moreover, it must also have a real deterrent effect on the employer. It follows that where a Member State chooses to penalize the breach of the prohibition of discrimination by the award of compensation, that compensation must in any event be adequate in relation to the damage sustained.[202]

[196] *Comet v. Produktschap voor Siergewassen* (above) (para. 13 of the judgment); *Deutsche Milchkontor v. Germany* (above) (para. 23 of the judgment); *BP Supergas*, Case C-62/93, [1995] ECR I-1883.

[197] Case 158/80, [1981] ECR 1805. [198] Para. 44 of the judgment.

[199] In *Emmott*, Case C-208/90, [1991] ECR I-4269, the European Court held that, until a directive has been properly implemented, the defaulting Member State cannot rely on national time limits for bringing legal proceedings to claim rights arising under it. However, two later cases, *Steenhorst-Neerings*, Case C-338/91, [1993] ECR I-5475 and *Johnson v. Chief Adjudication Officer*, Case C-410/92, [1994] ECR I-5483 held the opposite. In *Steenhorst-Neerings* the Court purported to distinguish *Emmott* on the facts, though in *Johnson* Advocate General Gulmann had some difficulty 'at first glance' in understanding what the difference was (at 5498–9). It seems that the *Emmott* rule will now apply only where the time-bar has the result of depriving the claimant of *any* opportunity of relying on the directive: para. 26 of the judgment in *Johnson*; *Ansaldo Energia*, Cases C-279–281/96, [1998] ECR I-5025 (paras 19–21 of the judgment).This could be regarded as an application of the general rule that it must not be impossible in practice to obtain a remedy (but see Hoskins, 'Tilting the Balance: Supremacy and National Procedural Rules' (1996) 21 ELRev. 365 at 371–2, where it is suggested that *Emmott* should be overruled). See, further, *Biggs v. Somerset County Council* [1966] ICR 364 (CA).

[200] Case 14/83, [1984] ECR 1891. [201] Para. 23 of the judgment.

[202] On the extent to which national procedural rules may be applied to prevent parties in proceedings before appellate courts from raising new issues based on Community law, see, *Van Schijndel*, Cases C-430, 431/93, [1995] ECR I-4705 and *Peterbroeck v. Belgium*, Case C-312/93, [1995] ECR I-4599, two cases in which the European Court gave seemingly conflicting judgments on the same day. For trenchant criticism of the judgment

There are some situations – at present, still rare – in which the European Court will itself take action to ensure that there is an appropriate remedy. Four examples will be given. The first is *UNECTEF v. Heylens*,[203] where the European Court laid down the rule that a decision by a national authority rejecting a claim under Community law must be reasoned and subject to judicial review in the national courts even, it seems, if this is not normally the case under the relevant national legal system.

The second example is *R v. Secretary of State for Transport, ex parte Factortame (No. 2)*.[204] The origin of the series of cases that goes under the name 'Factortame' was a decision by the Community to adopt fish conservation measures. To achieve this objective, limits were laid down to the total number of fish of various species that could be caught in a given period. Quotas were allotted to each Member State. Certain Spanish fishermen, however, thought that they could obtain a share of the British quota by the expedient of registering companies in the United Kingdom and transferring the ownership of their boats to those companies. They claimed that, since their boats were owned by British companies, they were entitled to fly the British flag and therefore take fish from the British quota, rather than the Spanish quota. British fishermen objected to this manœuvre, and the British Government passed legislation to prevent it.[205] The Spaniards immediately challenged the legislation in the British courts and a reference was made to the European Court to determine whether it was contrary to Community law.

At the time, the European Court normally took between one and two years to decide such cases; so this would have meant that the fishing boats would have been idle for a significant period. The Spaniards therefore applied for an interim injunction to preclude the Government from enforcing the British statute until the European Court had given its ruling. This was granted by the Divisional Court, but rescinded by the Court of Appeal, a decision upheld by the House of Lords, which ruled that, under United Kingdom law, there was no power to grant an injunction against the Crown to suspend the application of an Act of Parliament.[206] The House of Lords itself then made a reference to the European Court on the question of remedies: did Community law require that interim injunctions against the Crown should be available to litigants claiming rights under Community law?

The questions referred by the House of Lords were actually decided by the European Court before those referred by the Divisional Court.[207] The European Court ruled that where, in a case involving Community law, a national court considers that the sole obstacle to the granting of interim relief is a rule of national law, Community law requires it to set aside that rule.

that the Court was about to deliver in *Peterbroeck*, see the Opinion of Advocate General Jacobs in that case. These two cases are discussed in the 5th edition of this book at pp. 230–2.

[203] Case 222/86, [1987] ECR 4097. [204] Case C-213/89, [1990] ECR I-2433; [1990] 3 WLR 818.

[205] The Merchant Shipping Act 1988, Part II; the Merchant Shipping (Registration of Fishing Vessels) Regulations 1988 (S.I. 1988 No. 1926). The purpose of this legislation was to ensure that boats could not fly the British flag unless they had a genuine link with the United Kingdom. This was to be achieved by laying down new requirements for registration – for example, that boats owned by a company could not be registered unless 75 per cent of the shares in the company were held by British citizens resident and domiciled in the United Kingdom. [206] *R v. Secretary of State for Transport, ex parte Factortame* [1990] 2 AC 85.

[207] These were decided soon afterwards: *R v. Secretary of State for Transport, ex parte Factortame (No. 3)*, Case C-221/89, [1991] ECR I-3905.

The House of Lords had asked the European Court whether, in the situation before it, Community law either required or empowered a national court to grant interim relief. The European Court did not directly answer this question, but it seems implicit in its ruling that national courts are not required to grant interim relief in all cases where the validity of national legislation is subject to challenge on the basis of Community law. Rather, the position seems to be that the same criteria must be applied as would apply under national law if there was no question of suspending national legislation: the normal rules for interim injunctions must be extended to apply against the Crown.[208]

The third example is the second *Marshall* case.[209] This was a sequel to the case in which the European Court held that directives do not have horizontal direct effect. Ms Marshall was a woman employed by the National Health Service in England, who had been forced to retire shortly after reaching the age of sixty, when, if she had been a man, she could have continued working until the age of sixty-five. Her action had originally been brought in an industrial tribunal and when the case was remitted to the industrial tribunal after the European Court's judgment, the question of compensation arose. The industrial tribunal considered that the appropriate sum was £19,405, an amount which included interest. This gave rise to two difficulties: first, there was an upper limit under English law to the amount of compensation that could be awarded in such proceedings (at the relevant time, this stood at £6,250); secondly, it was uncertain whether industrial tribunals had the power to grant interest. In a second reference to the European Court, the latter ruled that neither restriction could apply where Community law formed the basis of the claim. Thus, there can be no *a priori* limit to the amount of damages recoverable in such a case, and the national court or tribunal must be free to award interest according to the normal national rules.

The fourth example concerns the liability in tort of national governments for failure to obey Community law. But this is so important a topic, that it requires a separate section to itself.

[208] See *R v. Secretary of State for Transport, ex parte Factortame (No. 2)* [1990] 3 WLR 856, where, after a careful consideration of the matter, the House of Lords decided to grant the injunction. See, further, *R v. HM Treasury, ex parte British Telecommunications, The Times*, 2 December 1993, CA. It is interesting to note that, shortly after the *Factortame* decision, the European Court laid down rules for the granting of interim relief by national courts where the validity of a national measure implementing Community law is challenged on the ground that the Community provision it implements is invalid (*Zuckerfabrik Süderdithmarschen*, Cases C-143/88, 92/89, [1991] ECR I-415). These rules, which concern the temporary suspension of the national measure while a decision by the European Court is pending on the validity of the Community provision, are not dissimilar to the normal English rules for interim relief, which were applied by the House of Lords in the *Factortame* case (above) when it granted the interim injunction. In both cases, there must be a serious doubt as to the validity of the measure (Community or English, as the case may be), damages must not be an adequate remedy, and the balance between the public interest and the interest of the applicant must come down in favour of the latter. See, further, *Giloy*, Case C-130/95, [1997] ECR I-4291. For the suspension of a Community measure by a national court pending a reference to the European Court, see *Atlanta Fruchthandelsgesellschaft* (*Bananas* case), Case C-465/93, [1995] ECR I-3761. National courts cannot, however, grant interim measures where the Community *fails* to act, since in such cases they cannot make a reference to the European Court under Art. 234 [177] EC: *Port*, Case C-68/95, [1996] ECR I-6065.

[209] *Marshall v. Southampton and South West Hampshire Area Health Authority (Teaching) (No. 2)*, Case C-271/91, [1993] ECR I-4367.

## GOVERNMENTAL LIABILITY IN TORT

The *Francovich*[210] case opened a new chapter in the European Court's campaign to make Community law more effective. The case concerned an EC directive intended to ensure that full payment of salary arrears is received by employees if their employer becomes insolvent. This was to be achieved through the establishment in each Member State of 'guarantee institutions', which had to be financed by the employers but had to be independent of them, and not subject to claims by their creditors. The directive should have been implemented by 23 October 1983. Italy failed to adopt the necessary legislation and the Commission brought a successful action against it under Article 226 [169] EC.[211] In spite of this, there was still no action to implement the directive.

A group of employees, who had been unable to obtain arrears of pay from their employers, then sued the Italian Government, claiming either the sums payable under the directive or damages for its non-implementation. The Italian court hearing the case referred the matter to the European Court, which ruled that the directive was not directly effective, since the guarantee institutions were not established by the directive but were to be set up by the Member States: the Italian Government could not itself be regarded as the guarantee institution merely because it had not implemented the directive. The first argument put forward by the employees therefore failed.

The European Court, however, ruled in their favour on the second argument. It held that there is a general principle inherent in the Treaty that a Member State is liable to compensate individuals for loss caused to them as a result of a violation of Community law for which the Member State is responsible. It based this holding on the same policy argument as was used to justify the doctrine of direct effect: the effectiveness of Community law would be prejudiced and the protection of the rights of individuals weakened if such a rule did not exist.[212] In other words, the principle exists because it is in the interests of the Community that it should exist.[213]

Having established the existence of the principle, the Court next laid down the requirements for its application. In the case of non-implementation of a directive, three requirements must be satisfied. First, the result to be achieved under the directive must involve the conferring of rights on individuals; secondly, those rights must be identifiable from the provisions of the directive; and thirdly, there must be a causal link between the violation of Community law by the Member State and the loss suffered by the applicant. National law determines the procedural details, but the national rules must not be less favourable to the applicant than those applicable to similar claims under national law, nor must they make it impossible (or excessively difficult) in practice for a remedy to be obtained.

210 *Francovich v. Italy*, Cases C-6, 9/90, [1991] ECR I-5357.

211 *Commission v. Italy*, Case 22/87, [1989] ECR 143.

212 It also invoked Art. 10 [5] EC, which requires the Member States to take all appropriate measures to ensure the fulfilment of Community obligations. This provision too has been used to justify the principle of direct effect.

213 For further discussion, see Trevor C Hartley, *Constitutional Problems of the European Union* (1999), pp. 59–65.

The failure of the Italian Government to implement the directive had already been established by the judgment of the European Court in the earlier case; the result to be achieved under the Directive involved the conferring of rights on individuals and the nature of these rights could be determined from the provisions of the directive.[214] Therefore, all the requirements were fulfilled. The case was sent back to the Italian court for it to provide an appropriate remedy.[215]

The principle laid down was potentially of great significance, but just how significant was not appreciated until its full scope was revealed in later cases. The first of these were two cases based on different facts which were joined for the purpose of proceedings before the European Court, *Brasserie du Pêcheur v. Germany* and *R v. Secretary for Transport, ex parte Factortame*,[216] the former being a reference from Germany and the latter from England.

The facts in the *Factortame* case were set out above: it will be remembered that an Act of Parliament had been passed to prevent Spanish fishermen from registering their boats as British. The European Court subsequently held that this was contrary to Community law.[217] Because it took some time for the European Court to give this ruling (and for it to decide that an interim injunction should be granted), the Spaniards incurred considerable losses for which they claimed compensation from the British Government. They argued that, since the passing of the Act of Parliament was an infringement of Community law, the British Government was liable in tort for any harm that resulted. The Government replied that the legislation had been passed in good faith to meet what it regarded as a problem: the legislation had been suspended when the European Court ruled that it had to be suspended, and repealed when the Court ruled that it had to be repealed.

Unlike the situation in *Francovich*, the provision which Britain had violated was not a directive, but Article 43 [52] of the EC Treaty, which was directly effective. This, the Court ruled, did not prevent liability from arising.[218] It was argued that there could be no liability where the wrongful act – the passing of the statute – had been committed by a national legislature: the Court rejected this.[219] It also held that a prior ruling by the European Court was not a necessary precondition for liability.[220]

The general principles concerning national remedies – equal availability and effectiveness – are still applicable,[221] but Community law now goes much further than

[214] This had been established by the Court in an earlier part of its judgment when it was considering the question of direct effect: it had found that in this respect the Directive was sufficiently clear and precise to be directly effective.

[215] For at least some of the claimants, this was not immediately forthcoming: see *Bonifaci v. INPS*, Cases C-94/95 and 95/95, [1997] ECR I-3969; *Palmisani v. INPS*, Case C-261/95, [1997] ECR I-4025; *Maso v. INPS and Italy*, Case C-373/95, [1997] ECR I-4051.

[216] Cases C-46/93 and 48/93, [1996] ECR I-1029; [1996] 2 WLR 506.

[217] *R v. Secretary of State for Transport, ex parte Factortame (No. 3)*, Case C-221/89, [1991] ECR I-3905.

[218] Paras 18–23 of the judgment.

[219] Para. 36 of the judgment and para. 1 of the Ruling.

[220] Para. 95 of the judgment and para. 5 of the Ruling. It will be remembered that in *Francovich* the European Court had previously ruled that Italy was in default, but the Italian Government had taken no steps to comply with the judgment.

[221] The Court said, for example, that the English remedy of exemplary damages must be available for a violation of Community law in the same circumstances in which it would apply to a violation of English law.

national law – certainly than English law – in providing a remedy in tort. This could be regarded as an application of the principle of effectiveness,[222] but what is really involved is the creation of a new remedy.

As regards the circumstances in which Member States incur liability, the European Court said that the principles to be applied cannot, in the absence of special justification, differ from those governing the liability of the Community.[223] The latter will be discussed in Chapter 16, but their most remarkable feature is that it is extremely difficult in practice for an applicant ever to obtain damages. According to Advocate General Tesauro, speaking in 1995, only eight awards had ever been made.[224] However, the European Court clearly does not intend to interpret the law in the same way when it is applied to the Member States: in five of the first six cases to come before it, it indicated that the Member State should be liable.[225]

In principle, all that has to be done to establish liability is to show that the Member State has violated Community law: it is not necessary to prove deliberate wrongdoing or even negligence.[226] However, one of the rules applied to the Community is that, in a legislative context characterized by the exercise of a wide discretion, the Community cannot incur liability unless the institution concerned has manifestly and gravely disregarded the limits on the exercise of its powers.[227] Where they enjoy a similar discretion, the same principle applies to Member States.[228] In establishing whether a national government manifestly and gravely disregarded the limits to its discretion, the factors which must be taken into consideration include the following: 'the clarity and precision of the rule breached, the measure of discretion left by that rule to the national or Community authorities, whether the infringement and the damage caused was intentional or involuntary, whether any error of law was excusable or inexcusable, the fact that the position taken by a Community institution may have contributed towards the omission, and the adoption or retention of national measures or practices contrary to Community law'.[229]

The European Court said that the national courts have sole jurisdiction to apply these principles and to characterize the breaches of Community law at issue.[230] In spite of this, however, it went on to indicate what it thought the result should be in each of

[222] The European Court seems to take this view: see paras 39 and 52 of the judgment.

[223] Para. 42 of the judgment.

[224] See his Opinion in *Brasserie du Pêcheur* and *Factortame*, [1996] ECR at 1101, n. 65.

[225] Although the final outcome rests with the national courts, the European Court indicated in all the cases in question what it thought the result should be. The five cases in which it considered that the State should be liable are: *Francovich v. Italy*, Cases C-6/90 and C-9/90, [1991] ECR I-5357; *Brasserie du Pêcheur v. Germany*, Case C-46/93 (in part) and *R v. Secretary for Transport, ex parte Factortame*, Case C-48/93 (joined cases) [1996] ECR 1209; *R v. Ministry of Agriculture, ex parte Hedley Lomas*, Case C-5/94, [1996] ECR I-2553; and *Dillenkofer v. Germany*, Cases C-178, 179, 188–190/94, [1996] ECR I-4845. The case in which it considered that there should be no liability was *R v. HM Treasury, ex parte British Telecommunications*, Case C-392/93, [1996] ECR I-1631. For a more recent case in which the European Court did not indicate whether it thought there should be liability, see *R v. Secretary of State for Social Security, ex parte Sutton*, Case C-66/95, [1997] ECR I-2163.

[226] See paras 75–80 of the judgment and para. 3 of the Ruling.

[227] See Chap. 16, below.

[228] Para. 47 of the judgment.

[229] Para. 56 of the judgment. The Court went on to say (para. 57) that, on any view, the breach of Community law will be sufficiently serious if it has persisted despite a judgment finding the infringement in question to be established.

[230] Para. 58.

the two cases. It considered that both cases fell into the 'wide discretion' category; so the test outlined above had to be applied. In *Brasserie du Pêcheur*, there were two separate violations of Community law: the Court indicated that one was difficult to regard as an excusable error, but the position was less clear with regard to the other.[231] The violation of Community law that had occurred in *Factortame* was, in the Court's view, sufficiently serious for the British Government to incur liability.[232]

While the question of liability now depends on Community law, the other aspects of the tort – for example, causation and damages – are governed by national law, provided that it is not impossible or excessively difficult for a remedy to be obtained.[233]

The next case to come before the Court was *R v. Ministry of Agriculture, ex parte Hedley Lomas*[234] which arose out of a ban imposed by the British Government in 1990 on the export of animals for slaughter in Spain. The reason for the ban was that it was believed that the animals would suffer unnecessarily in Spanish abattoirs. This problem had been around for some years and in 1974 the Community had adopted a directive[235] to deal with it. The directive, which was supposed to be the first step towards a general Community policy against cruelty, required Member States to ensure that animals were stunned before slaughter. In Spain, the Government gave effect to this by adopting legislation making stunning obligatory, but there was no provision for any penalty if stunning did not take place.

On the basis of information obtained from various sources – including an animal welfare organization in Spain – the British Ministry of Agriculture concluded that the directive and the Spanish legislation were being ignored in a significant number of abattoirs in Spain. Some abattoirs did not even possess stunning equipment. It was for this reason that the ban on live exports to Spain was adopted. The ban was based on Article 30 [36] EC, which permits Member States to restrict exports on grounds of, *inter alia*, public morality, public policy, and the protection of the health and life of animals – grounds that might have appeared wide enough to cover the case.

As a result of complaints addressed to it in 1990, the Commission had entered into discussions with the Spanish authorities on the lack of enforcement of the directive. The latter gave certain assurances; the Commission then dropped the matter. In July 1992, it informed the British Government that it considered that the export ban could not be justified under Article 30 [36] EC.

The British Government lifted the export ban as from 1 January 1993. This resulted from a meeting between the Chief Veterinary Officer of the United Kingdom and his opposite number in Spain to devise a procedure to ensure that all animals exported from the United Kingdom were sent only to abattoirs certified by the Spanish authorities as conforming to the provisions of the directive.

[231] In the end, the *Bundesgerichtshof* (German Supreme Court) held that the latter was the determinative one; so it ruled that Germany was not liable: BGH, EuZW 1996, 761.

[232] It was subsequently held that the Crown was liable to pay damages: *R v. Secretary for Transport, ex parte Factortame (No. 5)* [1999] 3 WLR 1062; [1999] 4 All ER 906; [1999] 3 CMLR 597 (HL).

[233] On these matters, see *Bonifaci v. INPS*, Cases C-94 and 95/95, [1997] ECR I-3969; *Palmisani v. INPS*, Case C-261/95, [1997] ECR I-4025; *Maso v. INPS and Italy*, Case C-373/95, [1997] ECR I-4051.

[234] Case C-5/94, [1996] ECR I-2553.

[235] Directive 74/557, OJ 1974 L316/10.

Shortly before the ban was lifted (in October 1992), Hedley Lomas applied for a licence for the live export of sheep destined for slaughter in a named abattoir in Spain. Hedley Lomas claimed that the abattoir in question conformed to the provisions of the directive and the British Government had no proof to the contrary. Nevertheless, the licence was refused. Hedley Lomas then brought proceedings in the English courts for a declaration that the refusal was contrary to Community law, and for damages. The English court made a reference to the European Court.

The European Court first considered whether the export ban was justified by virtue of Article 30 [36] EC. Although Britain had no proof that every abattoir in Spain was violating the directive, it considered that there was a significant risk that animals exported to Spain would suffer. It regarded the risk as sufficient to justify the ban. This might have seemed reasonable, since the prevention of unnecessary suffering during slaughter was one of the objectives of the directive. However, instead of making the export ban legitimate in Community eyes, the directive made it illegitimate. The reason, according to the European Court, was that when a problem is recognized by the Community and dealt with in a Community measure, it is taken out of the hands of the Member States and becomes a Community matter. Member State action is no longer permitted; only the Community can take action. The fact that the Community action is ineffective does not seem to make any difference. Britain had no right to act. Member States, said the Court, must trust each other. Although this general principle had been applied in previous cases and the British Government should perhaps have known about it, as applied to the facts of the case it led to the paradoxical result that the directive, which was supposed to benefit animals, actually made things worse. If it had not existed, the ban might have been upheld under Article 30 [36].

Having determined that the ban was contrary to Community law, the Court turned to the question of damages. It repeated the principles laid down previously and considered their application to the facts of the case. Though it reached no final conclusion – this was a matter for the English courts – it made clear that it thought the British Government should be liable. Although Article 30 [36] gave the Government a margin of discretion, this was considerably reduced, if it did not entirely disappear, once the Directive had been adopted. In such a situation, *any* violation of Community law would result in liability.

Two cases on the transposition of directives should be mentioned. These are *Dillenkofer v. Germany*,[236] and *R v. HM Treasury, ex parte British Telecommunications*.[237] In the former, the German Government had failed entirely to implement a directive by the deadline: the European Court held that this in itself was enough to produce liability.[238] In the latter, the British Government had implemented the directive, but had done so incorrectly because it had misunderstood what the directive required.

236 Cases C-178, 179, 188–190/94, [1996] ECR I-4845.

237 Case C-392/93, [1996] ECR I-1631; [1996] 3 WLR 203. See also *Denkavit Internationaal v. Bundesamt für Finanzen*, Cases C-283, 291and 292/94, [1996] ECR I-5063.

238 The directive was intended to protect travellers whose tour-provider had become bankrupt, and the German Government was obliged to compensate a large number of people as a result of the European Court's ruling.

The European Court held that this mistake was excusable, since the directive was reasonably capable of bearing the construction given to it by the British Government; so no liability arose.

In 2003, the European Court gave a judgment that produced a sense of shock in some quarters: it held that, in certain situations, an incorrect ruling by a national court on a point of Community law can give rise to liability in tort under the *Francovich* principle. The liability is not that of the judges as individuals, but of the State. Nevertheless, the ruling could be regarded as conflicting with the idea of judicial independence.[239]

The case was *Köbler v. Austria*, [240] and the facts were as follows. Under Austrian legislation, professors who had completed fifteen years' service were entitled to a special length-of-service increment. However, the service had to be in Austrian universities. Professor Köbler was a professor at an Austrian university. He had not completed fifteen years' service in Austrian universities, but he had done so if his combined service in universities in Austria and other Community countries was taken into account. He argued that it was contrary to Community law to make the increment dependent on service only at Austrian universities; so he brought proceedings for a ruling that he was entitled to the increment.

The case came on appeal before the *Verwaltungsgerichtshof*, the highest administrative court in Austria. That court initially took the view that the increment was not a loyalty bonus, but a normal component of salary. It made a reference to the European Court for a ruling whether such an increment was compatible with Community law if it distinguished between service in Austria and elsewhere in the Community. The Registrar of the European Court asked it whether it wished to maintain its request for a ruling in view of an earlier judgment of the European Court which appeared to cover the point.[241] This case held that such an increment was not compatible with Community law. The *Verwaltungsgerichtshof* then withdrew the request for a reference. However, at the same time it reversed its earlier ruling that the increment was not a loyalty bonus. It then decided that the earlier judgment of the European Court was not applicable and decided the case against Professor Köbler. There was no appeal against this judgment.

Professor Köbler next brought an action for damages against the Austrian Government in an ordinary civil court, the *Landesgericht für Zivilrechtssachen Wien* (Vienna Civil Court). He argued that the *Verwaltungsgerichtshof* had infringed Community law by giving judgment against him, and that Austria was liable in tort for this infringement of Community law. The Vienna Civil Court made a reference to the European Court.

The European Court held that the *Francovich* principle applies to all organs of the State, including the judiciary.[242] However, it sweetened the pill by saying that, in the latter

[239] The principle of *res judicata* is not affected: the original judgment, which may have been between two private individuals, still stands, but the Government has to pay compensation to the party who suffered loss.

[240] Case C-224/01, [2003] ECR I-10239

[241] *Schöning-Kougebetopoulou*, Case C-15/96, [1998] ECR I-47.

[242] It pointed out that such a principle also applies under international law – for example, under the European Convention on Human Rights.

case, liability would arise only 'in the exceptional case where the court has manifestly infringed the applicable law'.[243] It made clear, however, that a deliberate refusal to follow Community law would result in liability.[244] The European Court then applied these principles to the facts of the case. It held that the *Verwaltungsgerichtshof* had given a decision contrary to Community law, but that it was not sufficiently serious to result in liability. So Professor Köbler lost his case.

The European Court clearly hopes that the *Francovich* principle will make Community law more effective. However, those countries that show least respect for Community law in general are unlikely to show any greater respect for the new remedy, the application of which will always remain in the hands of the national courts.[245]

## FURTHER READING

DASHWOOD, 'The Principle of Direct Effect in European Community Law' (1978) 16 JCMS 229.

STEINER, 'Direct Applicability in EEC Law – A Chameleon Concept' (1982) 98 LQR 229.

BEBR, 'Agreements Concluded by the Community and Their Possible Direct Effect: From International Fruit Company to Kupferberg' (1983) 20 CMLRev. 35.

PESCATORE, 'The Doctrine of "Direct Effect": An Infant Disease in Community Law' (1983) 8 ELRev. 155.

GREEN, 'Directives, Equity and the Protection of Individual Rights' (1984) 9 ELRev. 295.

STEINER, 'How to Make the Action Suit the Case: Domestic Remedies for Breach of EEC Law' (1987) 12 ELRev. 102.

CURTIN, 'Directives: The Effectiveness of Judicial Protection of Individual Rights' (1990) 27 CMLRev. 709.

CURTIN, 'The Province of Government: Delimiting the Direct Effect of Directives in the Common Law Context' (1990) 15 ELRev. 195.

STEINER, 'Coming to Terms with EEC Directives' (1990) 106 LQR 144.

CRAIG, 'Once upon a Time in the West: Direct Effect and the Federalization of EEC Law' (1992) 12 OJLS 453.

MALTBY, '*Marleasing*: What is All the Fuss About?' (1993) 109 LQR 301.

STEINER, 'From Direct Effects to *Francovich*: Shifting Means of Enforcement of Community Law' (1993) 18 ELRev. 3.

[243] Para. 53 of the judgment. [244] Para. 55 of the judgment.

[245] A study published in 2001 (Tridimas, 'Liability for Breach of Community Law: Growing Up and Mellowing Down?' (2001) 38 CMLRev. 301) indicates that, except for *Francovich* itself, all the cases that had so far come before the European Court came from Germany, Austria, Sweden, Denmark, or the United Kingdom, countries with a fairly good record for respecting Community law: see, in addition to the cases mentioned in the text above, *Norbrook Laboratories v. Ministry of Agriculture*, Case C-127/95, [1998] ECR I-1531; *Brinkmann Tabakfabriken v. Skatteministeriet* (Denmark), Case C-319/96, [1998] ECR I-5255; *Konle v. Austria*, Case C-302/97, [1999] ECR I-3099; *Andersson v. Sweden*, Case C-321/97, [1999] ECR I-3551; *Rechberger v. Austria*, Case C-140/97, [1999] ECR I-3499; *Haim v. Kassenzahnärztliche Vereinigung Nordrhein* (Germany), Case C-424/97, [2000] ECR I-5123. This suggests that courts in some Member States are simply not sending cases to the European Court.

Coppel, 'Rights, Duties and the End of *Marshall*' (1994) 57 MLR 859.

Van Gerven, 'Non-Contractual Liability of Member States, Community Institutions and Individuals for Breaches of Community Law' (1994) 1 Maastricht Jo. of European and Comparative Law 6.

Plaza Martin, 'Furthering the Effectiveness of EC Directives and the Judicial Protection of Individual Rights Thereunder' (1994) 43 ICLQ 26.

Eleftheriadis, 'The Direct Effect of Community Law: Conceptual Issues' (1996) 16 YEL 205.

Van Gerven, 'Bridging the Unbridgeable: Community and National Tort Laws after *Francovich* and *Brasserie*' (1996) 45 ICLQ 507.

Harlow, '*Francovich* and the Problem of the Disobedient State' (1996) 2 ELJ 199.

Hoskins, 'Tilting the Balance: Supremacy and National Procedural Rules' (1996) 21 ELRev. 365.

Convery, 'State Liability in the United Kingdom after *Brasserie du Pêcheur*' (1997) 34 CMLRev. 603.

Craig, 'Directives: Direct Effect, Indirect Effect and the Construction of National Legislation' (1997) 22 ELRev. 519.

Craig, 'Once More unto the Breach; the Community, the State and Damages Liability' (1997) 113 LQR 67.

Downes, 'Trawling for a Remedy: State Liability under Community Law' (1997) 17 Legal Studies 286.

Eeckhout, 'The Domestic Legal Status of the WTO Agreement: Interconnecting Legal Systems' (1997) 34 CMLRev. 11.

Himsworth, 'Things Fall Apart: The Harmonization of Community Judicial Procedural Protection Revisited' (1997) 22 ELRev. 291.

Lackhoff and Nyssens, 'Direct Effect of Directives in Triangular Situations' (1998) 23 ELRev. 397.

Hilson and Downes, 'Making Sense of Rights: Community Rights in EC Law' (1999) 24 ELRev. 121.

Dougan, 'The "Disguised" Vertical Direct Effect of Directives?' [2000] CLJ 586.

Lenz, Tynes, and Young, 'Horizontal What? Back to Basics' (2000) 25 ELRev. 509.

Prechal, 'Does Direct Effect Still Matter?' (2000) 37 CMLRev. 1047.

Weatherill, 'A Case Study in Judicial Activism in the 1990s: The Status Before National Courts of Measures Wrongfully Unnotified to the Commission', *ibid.*, Chap. 31.

Tridimas, 'Enforcing Community Rights in National Courts: Some Recent Developments' in David O'Keeffe and Antonio Bavasso (eds), *Judicial Review in European Union Law: Liber Amicorum Gordon Slynn* (2000), p. 465.

Peers, 'Fundamental Right or Political Whim? WTO Law and the European Court of Justice' in Gráinne de Búrca and Joanne Scott (eds), *The EU and the WTO: Legal and Constitutional Issues* (2001).

Tridimas, 'Liability for Breach of Community Law: Growing Up and Mellowing Down?' (2001) 38 CMLRev. 301.

Weatherill, 'Breach of Directives and Breach of Contract' (2001) 26 ELRev. 177.

Anagnostaras, 'State Liability and Alternative Courses of Action: How Independent Can an Autonomous Remedy Be?' (2002) 21 YEL 355.

Davies, 'Bananas, Private Challenges, the Courts and the Legislature' (2002) 21 YEL 299.

Klabbers, 'International Law in Community Law: The Law and Politics of Direct Effect' (2002) 21 YEL 263.

TRIDIMAS, 'Black, White and Shades of Grey: Horizontality of Directives Revisited' (2002) 21 YEL 327.

KREMER, 'Liability for Breach of European Community Law: An Analysis of the New Remedy in the Light of English and German Law' (2003) 22 YEL 203.

WATTEL, '*Köbler, CILFIT* and *Welthgrove*: We Can't Go on Meeting Like This' (2004) 41 CMLRev. 177.

DRAKE, 'Twenty Years after *Von Colson*: the Impact of "Indirect Effect" on the Protection of the Individual's Community Rights' (2005) 30 ELRev. 329.

ANAGNOSTARAS, 'Erroneous Judgments and the Prospect of Damages: The Scope of the Principle of Governmental Liability for Judicial Breaches' (2006) 31 ELRev. 735.

DAVIS, 'Liability in Damages for a Breach of Community Law: Some Reflections on the Question of Who to Sue and the Concept of the "State"' (2006) 31 ELRev. 69.

KLAMERT, 'Judicial Implementation of Directives and Anticipatory Indirect Effect: Connecting the Dots' (2006) 43 CMLRev. 1251.

# 8

# THE NATIONAL RESPONSE

In the previous chapter the relationship between Community law and national law was discussed from the Community side. The rules we considered were what the European Court thinks the Member States accepted when they signed the Community Treaties. In this chapter, we will consider how the Member States have responded to these demands.

We saw in the Introduction to this Part that some countries (called 'monist' for convenience) have provisions in their legal systems (usually in their constitutions) permitting international agreements to have direct effect in certain cases. Where there is a conflict with national law, some monist countries – for example, the Netherlands – will recognize the supremacy of the treaty. Such countries have a ready-made mechanism for giving effect to Community law.

Another possibility is for the Member State to transfer powers to the Community. This solution can be adopted even by countries which apply the dualist approach to international law. Express provision for the transfer of powers to international organizations is found in Article 24(1) of the German Constitution and Article 20 of the Danish Constitution. There is a similar provision in Article 67 of the Dutch Constitution: the Netherlands can therefore apply the Treaties on the basis of the monist theory and give effect to Community legislation under the terms of Article 67. In Italy, the constitutional position appears at first sight to be less clear-cut, but Article 11 of the Constitution, which authorizes such limitations of sovereignty as may be necessary to ensure peace and justice between nations, has been pressed into service to provide the constitutional foundation for Italian membership of the Community.[1]

A further possibility is to amend the constitution to provide for Community membership. This was done in Ireland, where the Constitution was amended to provide that nothing in it would prevent Community measures from having the force of law in Ireland.[2] Germany and France have also amended their Constitutions, though this was not originally necessary.

Not being in a position to adopt a constitutional amendment, the United Kingdom passed a simple Act of Parliament, the European Communities Act 1972, which made provision for the direct effect and supremacy of Community law.

Thus each Member State has found its own way of giving effect to Community law. In all cases, however, Community law has effect in the state concerned only because the law of that state so provides. As a result, it can have effect only to the extent that the

[1] See the *Frontini* case, *Corte Costituzionale*, 27 December 1973, [1974] 2 CMLR 372 at 384–5 (para. 7 of the judgment).

[2] Third Amendment to the Constitution.

national constitution permits. Moreover, although the European Court likes to talk as if the transfer was irreversible,[3] the process can always be reversed, though in the case of some countries a constitutional amendment may be required.

We shall now consider selected countries in more detail. The discussion that follows will focus on only the most important issues.

## BELGIUM

The particular interest of Belgium lies in the fact that its constitution contained no statement that international treaties have direct effect and override national law, and it was originally unclear whether it adopted the monist or dualist theory of international law. The Belgian courts therefore had to face the challenge of Community law without the support of an appropriate constitutional provision.

The test came in *Minister for Economic Affairs v. Fromagerie Franco-Suisse 'Le Ski'*.[4] A number of royal decrees had imposed import duties on dairy products which the respondent had been obliged to pay. However, in enforcement proceedings brought by the Commission under Article 226 [169] EC against Belgium and Luxembourg, the European Court had declared these duties to be contrary to the EC Treaty.[5] They were then abolished, but the Belgian Parliament passed a statute providing that money already paid could not be recovered. The respondent objected to this and instituted legal proceedings in the Belgian courts to recover the duties it had paid. It won a judgment in its favour in the Brussels *Cour d'Appel* and the Minister appealed to the *Cour de Cassation*, the highest civil court in the country.

Two main arguments were put forward by the Minister. First, he referred to the fact that, when Belgium joined the EC, a statute was passed by the Belgian Parliament ratifying the Treaty. The effect of the Treaty in Belgium was, he argued, dependent on that statute: since the statute prohibiting recovery of the money was passed subsequent to it, the latter must prevail over the former and, therefore, over the Treaty as well: a later law always prevails over an earlier one.

The second argument put forward was that the judgment of the *Cour d'Appel* had violated a provision of the Belgian Constitution according to which only the Belgian Parliament may determine the constitutionality of a statute: the courts have no right to annul any Act of Parliament. It will be noticed that both these arguments are very pertinent to the British situation.

The *Cour de Cassation* dismissed the appeal and upheld the right of the respondent to reclaim the money. It met the first argument by declaring that when the Belgian Parliament passes a statute to ratify a treaty, that statute is merely the constitutionally prescribed method of giving assent to a treaty entered into by the Crown: the treaty

[3] See *Costa v. ENEL*, Case 6/64, [1964] ECR 585 at 594, where it said that the Member States had agreed to 'a permanent limitation of their sovereign rights'.

[4] *Cour de Cassation*, Belgium, 21 May 1971, [1972] CMLR 330.

[5] *Commission v. Luxembourg and Belgium*, Cases 90, 91/63, [1964] ECR 625.

does not take effect in Belgian law as part of the statute, but as a treaty. In other words, the Court declared in this case that Belgium was a monist country. Consequently, the conflict was not between two statutes, but between two instruments of a fundamentally different nature: a treaty and a statute. The Court then continued:[6]

> The rule that a statute repeals a previous statute in so far as there is a conflict between the two, does not apply in the case of a conflict between a treaty and a statute.
>
> In the event of a conflict between a norm of domestic law and a norm of international law which produces direct effects in the internal legal system, the rule established by the treaty shall prevail. The primacy of the treaty results from the very nature of international treaty law.
>
> This is a fortiori the case when a conflict exists, as in the present case, between a norm of internal law and a norm of Community law.
>
> The reason is that the treaties which have created Community law have instituted a new legal system in whose favour the Member States have restricted the exercise of their sovereign powers in the areas determined by those treaties.

It concluded that since the provision of Community law violated by the royal decrees, Article 25 [12] EC, was directly effective, it was the duty of the courts to uphold it, even when it was in conflict with a statute.

The second argument of the Minister was met by stating that the *Cour d'Appel* had not annulled the law prohibiting recovery but had merely declared its operation suspended to the extent of the conflict. This could be regarded as a distinction without any real difference: but once the monist position is accepted, it necessarily follows that the courts must have the power to disregard national legislation when it conflicts with a directly effective treaty provision. The truly innovative part of the judgment, therefore, was the acceptance of the monist doctrine as a part of Belgian law.

This judgment was satisfactory from the point of view of Community law. It would not, however, be of much assistance to the British courts if they had to face a similar problem, since it is quite firmly established that the United Kingdom is a dualist country: when the British Parliament passes a statute to give effect to a treaty, the courts apply the treaty only because they are required to do so by the statute: in the United Kingdom the conflict *is* between two statutes.

## GERMANY

Germany and Italy, the two former Axis Powers, emerged from defeat in the Second World War with constitutions giving significantly more protection to fundamental human rights than those of the other Member States. This has created special problems with regard to Community law: can Community measures override national constitutional provisions and take effect in Germany and Italy even if they are contrary to fundamental human rights as understood in those countries?

[6] [1972] CMLR at 373.

In Germany, the best-known case is the decision of the Constitutional Court in *Internationale Handelsgesellschaft v. EVGF*.[7] The background to this case was considered in Chapter 5, above: it will be remembered that the plaintiff had asked a German administrative court to annul a decision of the EVGF based on two Community regulations; it argued that the regulations should not to be applied in Germany on the ground that they were contrary to the fundamental human rights provisions of the German Constitution. The administrative court first made a reference to the European Court, which ruled that the validity of Community provisions should be determined according to Community law, not national constitutional law, and that the provisions in question did not violate the Community concept of human rights.[8]

This was not, however, the end of the matter: the administrative court next made a reference to the Federal Constitutional Court (*Bundesverfassungsgericht*) for a ruling on whether the regulations were contrary to the fundamental human rights provisions of the German Constitution. Before considering this question, the Constitutional Court had to decide whether the reference was admissible: in other words, whether Community measures are subject to the German Constitution.

The first question considered by the Constitutional Court was the relationship between German constitutional law and Community law. It took the view that Community law 'is neither a component part of the national legal system nor international law, but forms an independent system of law flowing from an autonomous legal source'[9] and concluded from this that the two legal systems were independent of each other.

The Constitutional Court next pointed out that the Community lacked a directly elected parliament[10] to which the Community organs with legislative powers were responsible on a political level and that it also lacked a 'codified catalogue of fundamental rights' comparable to that in the German Constitution. It concluded that until such time as Community protection for fundamental rights measured up to that in the German Constitution, Community measures would be subject to the fundamental rights provisions of the German Constitution.

Having thus decided the question of its own jurisdiction, the Constitutional Court next considered the substantive issue: it ruled that the Community measures in issue were not contrary to the German Constitution.

This case therefore represented a potential, rather than an actual, rebellion. In fact the Constitutional Court never found any Community measure to be contrary to the German Constitution and, after hinting at a new approach in 1979,[11] it finally ruled in 1986 that the protection of human rights in the Community had developed sufficiently to meet the requirements of the German Constitution. This occurred in the *Wünsche Handelsgesellschaft* case,[12] where the Constitutional Court stated that, provided the

[7] *Bundesverfassungsgericht*, 29 May 1974, [1974] 2 CMLR 540.

[8] Case 11/70, [1970] ECR 1125. [9] [1974] 2 CMLR at 549 (para. 19 of the judgment).

[10] At the time when the case was decided the European Parliament was not directly elected.

[11] *Steinike & Weinlig*, 25 July 1979, [1980] 2 CMLR 531 at 537 (para. 12).

[12] Decision of 22 October 1986, [1987] 3 CMLR 225. The most important developments, in the eyes of the Constitutional Court, were the further elaboration by the European Court of its doctrine of fundamental

general level of protection of human rights under Community law remained adequate by German standards, it would no longer entertain proceedings to test Community measures against the human rights provisions of the *Grundgesetz*. Later cases have made clear, however, that the application of Community law in Germany is still subject to the *Grundgesetz*. If the European Court failed to give sufficient protection to human rights as defined in it, the Constitutional Court would itself have to take up the task again.[13]

This also follows from the amendment to the Constitution made in 1992 to make better provision for Germany's membership of the EU. The amended Article 23(1) permits the transfer of sovereign powers to the Union, but this is subject to certain basic principles of the German Constitution, including fundamental rights.[14]

Problems have also been caused by the refusal of the Federal Tax Court (*Bundesfinanzhof*) to accept the direct effect of directives. It should be explained that in Germany there are no fewer than five separate court systems: in addition to the ordinary courts, there are specialized courts dealing with tax, labour, social security, and administrative matters. Each of these court systems is headed by a federal supreme court, the Federal Tax Court being at the top of the tax court system. Each system is independent of the others, so that the Federal Tax Court is not bound by the rulings of, for example, the Federal Administrative Court and *vice versa*. On constitutional matters, however, all courts are subject to the rulings of the Federal Constitutional Court.

The problem regarding the direct effect of directives arose when Germany was tardy in implementing a Community Directive dealing with VAT. Certain provisions of this Directive gave tax exemptions which were not recognized by the relevant German law. Could a tax-payer claim an exemption on the basis of the Directive, even though it conflicted with German legislation?[15] In two cases, decided in 1981[16] and 1985[17] respectively, the Federal Tax Court held that this was not possible. The two cases were similar, but the second was more interesting since the judgment of the Federal Tax Court directly contradicted a ruling given by the European Court at an earlier stage of the proceedings in the case.[18] This was the *Kloppenburg* case, in which a lower tax court, the *Niedersächsisches Finanzgericht*, had referred the question to the European Court and been told that the relevant provision of the Directive was directly effective. The lower tax court then ruled in favour of the tax-payer. The tax authorities appealed, and the Federal

rights, especially the significance now attached to the constitutions of the Member States, and the Joint Declaration of 5 April 1977 of the Parliament, the Council, and the Commission.

[13] See, for example, the decision of the Constitutional Court of 12 May 1989 in the *Tobacco Advertising* case, Case 2 BvQ 3/89, [1990] 1 CMLR 570, in which the Constitutional Court pointed out that a directive infringing fundamental human rights as understood in Community law could be brought before the European Court. It added, however, that if this proved inadequate to protect the constitutional standards considered unconditional by the German Constitution, recourse could be had to the Constitutional Court. It also said that German legislation to implement a directive would be subject to constitutional review. See also the *Brunner* case (German *Maastricht* case), discussed below.

[14] Art. 23(1) of the *Grundgesetz*, referring to Art. 79(3).

[15] Since the defendant was the State, the issue was one of vertical direct effect only.

[16] *Bundesfinanzhof*, decision of 16 July 1981, [1982] 1 CMLR 527.

[17] *Bundesfinanzhof*, decision of 25 April 1985 (VR 123/84), *Entscheidungen des Bundesfinanzhofes* 143, p. 383 (noted by Crossland, (1986) 11 ELRev. 473 at 476–9).

[18] *Kloppenburg*, Case 70/83, [1984] ECR 1075.

Tax Court reversed the lower court's judgment. Its reasoning started from the premise that Community law could have effect in Germany only to the extent that Germany had transferred legislative powers to the Community. This transfer, permitted by Article 24(1) of the German Constitution, was limited by the terms of the EC Treaty, which in the case of tax matters gave the Community the power to adopt only directives. According to Article 249 [189] EC, directives leave the Member States free to choose the form and methods of giving effect to them; so national implementing legislation is necessary for the provisions of a directive to have the force of law in the Member States. From this the Federal Tax Court concluded that directives can never have direct effect, an argument not lacking in legal logic. It supported this conclusion with references to both the *travaux préparatoires* to the EC Treaty (in which the German Government had said that a directive cannot directly bind an individual in the absence of national legislation) and the decision of the French *Conseil d'Etat* in the *Cohn-Bendit* case (discussed below). The Federal Tax Court did not allow itself to be deflected by the European Court's ruling: it said that the latter's jurisdiction under Article 234 [177] was limited to Community law and that it did not have the power to determine which law should be applied by national courts. It also stated that the preliminary reference procedure could not be used to extend the legislative jurisdiction of the Community beyond that laid down in the Treaties.

The matter did not rest there, however, because the tax-payer, Ms Kloppenburg, then brought proceedings before the Federal Constitutional Court, which ruled that the Federal Tax Court had acted unconstitutionally: it should either have followed the ruling of the European Court or made a second reference. The third paragraph of Article 234 [177] EC states that a court 'against whose decision there is no judicial remedy' is obliged to make a reference when its judgment depends on a question of Community law. The Federal Tax Court was such a court; therefore its failure to make the reference (or follow the ruling in the earlier reference) was a violation of Article 234 [177]. The reason this violation of the EC Treaty also constituted a violation of the German Constitution was that Article 101(1) of the latter guarantees that no one shall be deprived of his 'lawful judge'. This provision, which protects the right of the citizen to have his case heard by the lawfully constituted court having jurisdiction in the matter, was intended to prevent the establishment of special courts, which might be less impartial than the ordinary courts. The Constitutional Court had already held in the *Wünsche Handelsgesellschaft* case (above) that the European Court is a 'lawful judge' in terms of Article 101(1). By deliberately refusing to make a reference to the European Court, the Federal Tax Court had deprived Ms Kloppenburg of her 'lawful judge'. Its judgment was therefore annulled.[19]

Another challenge to the Community arose in 1993 when a group of Germans headed by Manfred Brunner, a former official at the Commission, asked the Constitutional Court to rule on the constitutionality of Germany's ratification of the Maastricht Agreement (Treaty on European Union). The Constitutional Court held the application admissible, but eventually dismissed it.[20] Reported in English as *Brunner v. European*

[19] *Bundesverfassungsgericht*, decision of 8 April 1987 (2 BvR 687/85), [1987] RIW 878; [1988] 3 CMLR 1.

[20] The delay meant, however, that Germany was the last Member State to ratify.

*Union Treaty*,[21] this judgment is of great importance for some of the statements it contains.

First, the Constitutional Court said it will continue to guarantee the effective protection of basic rights, as against the Community, for the inhabitants of Germany. It said, however, that it will do this in co-operation with the European Court, a statement which appears to mean that the latter will have the task of reviewing Community measures on a case-by-case basis and the former will restrict itself to a more general role.[22]

The Constitutional Court next considered the legal nature of the Community and classified it as a 'union (or federation) of states' (*Staatenbund*), not a federal state (*Bundesstaat*). The Community, it said, is intended to provide for an ever closer union of the peoples of Europe (the latter being organized through states); it is not a state based on a single European nation.[23] As such, the Community derives its authority from the Member States and can have no greater powers than those conferred on it. The Member States, in a memorable phrase, are the 'masters of the Treaties' ('*Herren der Verträge*'). Germany, it said, remains a sovereign state.[24]

It follows from the above that the Community cannot take for itself greater powers than those granted by the Treaties. If it did so, the resulting legislation would be legally invalid in Germany, and the German Government would be constitutionally prohibited from applying it. The Constitutional Court reserved to itself the power of reviewing Community legislation to ensure that it stays within the bounds of the powers conferred on the Community.[25] It also made clear that there are limits to the extent to which the European Court can extend the powers of the Community through its judgments.[26]

This last statement is perhaps the most important because it asserts the right of the *Bundesverfassungsgericht*, rather than the European Court, to act as ultimate arbiter on the division of power between the Community and the Member States. The courts of the other Member States no doubt take the same view, but the *Bundesverfassungsgericht* was the first to express it so clearly.

In a more recent decision (18 July 2005), the *Bundesverfassungsgericht* held that the German legislation giving effect to the EU third-pillar framework decision on the European Arrest Warrant[27] was invalid because it was contrary to the constitutional provision forbidding the extradition of German citizens.[28] This provision is contained in Article 16(2) of the *Grundgesetz*. Originally, it was stated in absolute terms,

[21] *Bundesverfassungsgericht*, decision of 12 October 1993, [1994] 1 CMLR 57. For the German text, see 2 BvR 2134/92 and 2 BvR 2159/92. The background and significance of the case are explained in Foster, 'The German Constitution and EC Membership' [1994] PL 392.

[22] Para. B(2)(b) of the judgment; para. [13], p. 79 of the CMLR.

[23] Para. C II of the judgment; para. [51], p. 89 of the CMLR.

[24] Para. C II(1) of the judgment; para. [55], p. 91 of the CMLR.

[25] Para. C I(3) of the judgment; para. [49], p. 89 of the CMLR.

[26] Para. C II(3)(b) of the judgment; para. [99], p. 105 of the CMLR. The Constitutional Court said the same thing (though less assertively) in the *Kloppenburg* case (above), [1988] 3 CMLR 1, para. [6], p. 13; para. [19], p. 18; and para. [21], p. 19. Some of the other statements in *Brunner* were also first made in *Kloppenburg*.

[27] Council Framework Decision 2002/584/JHA, OJ 2002, L190/1.

[28] 2 BvR 2236/04: see *http://www.bundesverfassungsgericht.de/en/decisions/rs20050718_2bvr223604en.html* (English translation). For a comment, see Hinarejos Parga, (2006) 43 CMLRev. 583.

but an amendment adopted in 2000[29] made provision for exceptions in the case of extradition to other EU states or international tribunals, provided the principles of the rule of law (*rechtsstaatliche Grundsätze*) were guaranteed. The Constitutional Court held, however, that any such exception was subject to the constitutional principle of proportionality. The German legislation had not complied with this principle; so it had to be struck down.[30] It is, however, clear from the judgment that effect could be given to the EU framework decision in Germany if this was done in the appropriate manner. Consequently, the case does not constitute a rejection of the Community decision itself.

## DENMARK

The Danish *Maastricht* decision, *Carlsen v. Rasmussen*,[31] in many ways covers the same ground as the German one; however, the relative brevity of the Court's reasoning and the less abstract language in which it is expressed mean that the judgment is easier for foreign lawyers to understand. The case also began with a legal action by a group of citizens to challenge ratification of the Maastricht Agreement (Treaty on European Union).

The provision of the Danish Constitution permitting Denmark's membership of the Community is section 20, which states that powers may be delegated to an authority 'to an extent specified by statute', a requirement that precludes the delegation of unlimited or undefined powers. The appellants argued that the powers delegated to the Community under the Treaty on European Union were too ill-defined to satisfy the requirements of section 20. In particular, they referred to the open-ended nature of the Council's legislative power under Article 308 [235] EC and the law-making activities of the European Court.

The Danish Supreme Court rejected these arguments and held that Denmark could ratify the Treaty on European Union. It began its reasoning by stating that section 20 does not permit an international organization (such as the Community) to be given power to adopt legal acts or to make decisions that are contrary to the provisions of the Danish Constitution.[32] Secondly, it made clear that an international organization cannot be permitted to determine for itself what its powers are.[33]

[29] This was the 47th Amendment to the Constitution.

[30] An additional ground was that a decision of the German Government granting an extradition order was not subject to judicial review. Unlike the Polish Constitutional Court in its decision on the constitutionality of implementing legislation for the same EU framework decision (discussed below in the section on 'Poland'), the German Constitutional Court did not suspend the effect of its decision to enable the necessary amendments to be made.

[31] Danish Supreme Court, judgment of 6 April 1998, Case I 361/1997, [1999] 3 CMLR 854 (English translation).

[32] Section 9.2 of the judgment.

[33] *Ibid.* It is not, however, necessary that the powers should be specified so precisely that there is no room left for discretion or interpretation.

Having specified the requirements of the Constitution, the Supreme Court next considered whether they had been met. It first noted that the EC Treaty is based on the principle of conferred powers, the principle that the Community possesses only those powers given to it by the Treaties.[34] It then turned its attention to Article 308 [235]. This provision was discussed in Chapter 4: it will be remembered that it states that if, in the course of the operation of the common market, action by the Community is necessary to attain its objectives and the Treaty has *not* provided the necessary powers, the Council can take the appropriate measures anyway. The Supreme Court gave a fairly restrictive interpretation to the provision,[35] partly on the basis of a passage from the European Court's judgment in the *ECHR* case.[36] It concluded that if Article 308 [235] was applied no more widely than this, the requirements of section 20 of the Danish Constitution would be satisfied. If an attempt were made to apply it on a wider basis, the Danish Government would be obliged to veto it.[37]

The Supreme Court next dealt with the argument that the European Court's methods of 'interpreting' Community law are contrary to section 20 of the Constitution. It indicated that it was prepared to allow the European Court a great deal of latitude: it was in fact prepared to accept the European Court's law-making activities, provided these remained within the scope of the EC Treaty.[38] The Supreme Court recognized that the European Court had been given jurisdiction to rule on the validity of Community acts; as a consequence, it said, Danish courts cannot declare Community acts inapplicable in Denmark without first referring the question of their validity to the European Court. The European Court's ruling on such questions should, in general, be accepted by Danish courts. However, the Supreme Court held that the requirement of specificity in section 20 of the Danish Constitution meant that Danish courts cannot be deprived of their right to judge for themselves whether EC acts go beyond the powers conferred on the Community. Consequently, if the European Court held the act valid, the Danish courts could in exceptional situations nevertheless hold it inapplicable in Denmark. The same applies, said the Supreme Court, to legal principles derived from the case law of the European Court.[39]

On these grounds, the Supreme Court ruled that neither the open-ended nature of Article 308 [235] nor the law-making activities of the European Court rendered Danish ratification of the Treaty on European Union unconstitutional.[40] This judgment allows Denmark to give effect to Community law, but nevertheless makes clear that the Danish courts retain their power to ensure that the Community does not go beyond the Treaties.

[34] See Arts 5, first paragraph [3b, first paragraph] and 7(1) [4(1)] EC.

[35] It noted that Art. 308 [235] applies only 'in the course of the operation of the common market'. The precise meaning of this restriction has been subject to much speculation, but the Supreme Court seems to consider that it precludes the application of Art. 308 [235] with regard to economic and monetary union or the implementation of common policies and actions.

[36] Opinion 2/94, [1996] ECR I-1759 (para. 30 of the Opinion).

[37] Measures may be adopted under Art. 308 [235] only if the members of the Council are unanimous.

[38] See the last paragraph of section 9.5 of the judgment.

[39] Section 9.6 of the judgment.

[40] Section 9.7 of the judgment.

## FRANCE

In France, the courts cannot review statutes (*lois*) after promulgation in order to determine their constitutionality.[41] Moreover, since it is provided in Article 55 of the French Constitution that international treaties have authority superior to that of any national law, one might have assumed that the application of Community law raised no problems in France. However, this has not always been entirely true.

It should be explained at the outset that there are two separate court systems in France: the ordinary (judicial) courts, which deal with civil and criminal matters, and the administrative courts, which hear cases where action on the part of the administration is subject to challenge.[42] The administrative courts may also annul legislative measures enacted by the executive. The highest court in the judicial order is the *Cour de Cassation*; while the *Conseil d'Etat* is the supreme administrative court. These two court systems have very different traditions, and one of the most notable features of the French response to Community law has been the difference in attitude displayed by the judicial and administrative courts, especially by the *Cour de Cassation* and the *Conseil d'Etat*, the former being more willing to meet the demands of the European Court than the latter.

What obstacles have there been to the application of Community law in France? The most important has been the traditional reluctance of all French courts to question the validity of a statute and of the judicial courts to query actions of the administration, whether legislative or executive. In particular, this has made it difficult for them to refuse to apply a French law when it conflicts with Community law. A second obstacle has been that Article 55 of the Constitution makes the supremacy of treaties over national legislation subject to a proviso: the treaty in question must be applied by the other party. This could be regarded as making the application of Community law in France contingent on its application in other Member States.

The leading case in the *Cour de Cassation* is *Directeur Général des Douanes v. Société Vabre & Société Weigel*,[43] decided in 1975. The facts of the case were that Vabre had imported soluble coffee extract into France from Holland and was required to pay customs duties under a French statute passed in 1966. Since coffee extract produced in France was subject to tax at a lower rate, it claimed that it had been discriminated against contrary to Article 90 [95] EC. Vabre, and its agent Weigel, claimed repayment of the duties, and damages: the Paris *Cour d'Appel* upheld their claim on the ground that the EC Treaty prevailed even over a subsequent statute;[44] a further appeal was then taken to the *Cour de Cassation*.

[41] Draft legislation may, however, be reviewed by the *Conseil Constitutionnel* before enactment to determine whether it is in accordance with the Constitution.

[42] The division of jurisdiction between the two sets of courts is actually much more complicated than this. Conflicts of jurisdiction are settled by the *Tribunal des Conflits*, which is composed of an equal number of judges from the *Cour de Cassation* and the *Conseil d'Etat*; the Minister of Justice, who may preside, has a casting vote.

[43] *Cour de Cassation*, 24 May 1975, [1975] 2 CMLR 336.

[44] 7 July 1973, [1975] 2 CMLR 336.

It was argued by the Director-General of Customs that the Paris *Cour d'Appel* had arrogated to itself the right to determine the constitutionality of a statute and this it could not do. He also pointed out that under Article 55 of the French Constitution a treaty is applicable in France only if the other country also applies it: no attempt had been made to ascertain whether the Netherlands, the country from which the coffee extract had been imported, met this condition of reciprocity. He therefore concluded that Article 55 could not be invoked to provide a basis for the application of the EC Treaty in the case.

The *Cour de Cassation* rejected these arguments and upheld the judgment of the Paris *Cour d'Appel*. In reply to the first argument of the Director-General, the *Cour de Cassation* stated that the Community Treaties had created a separate legal order which was binding on the national courts. The second argument was rejected on the ground that Article 227 [170] EC grants each Member State the right to bring legal proceedings in the European Court against any other Member State which fails to apply the Treaty. Since there is thus a legal procedure to remedy any lack of reciprocity, this could not constitute a ground for not applying the Treaty.

This judgment did a great deal to put Community law on a secure footing in France. It should also be mentioned that the case was heard by a 'mixed chamber' of the Court, which means that the decision has special authority in the French judicial court system.[45] Shortly afterwards, moreover, the *Cour de Cassation* held in the case of *Von Kempis v. Geldof*[46] that the Treaty also prevails over earlier French legislation. These rulings, therefore, firmly established the supremacy of Community law as far as the judicial courts of France are concerned.

In the administrative courts, on the other hand, the story has been rather different. Over a considerable period, the *Conseil d'Etat* and the *tribunaux administratifs* had been less willing to find acceptable solutions. Then, in the *Semoules* case,[47] decided in 1968, the *Conseil* refused to accept the supremacy of a Community regulation over a French statute passed subsequent to the regulation, a position maintained in several later cases.[48] It was only in 1989 that the *Conseil d'Etat* abandoned this position, though it did so by implication rather than by an express declaration of principle. This was in the *Nicolo*

[45] The *Cour de Cassation* is divided into a number of chambers and cases are normally allocated to one or other of these. Specially important cases are, however, heard by a mixed chamber: this is presided over by the First President and normally includes the Presidents of several other chambers.

[46] *Cour de Cassation*, 15 December 1975, [1976] 2 CMLR 152.

[47] *Conseil d'Etat*, 1 March 1968, [1970] CMLR 395. In this case the *Conseil* appeared to accept the view of the *Commissaire du gouvernement* (analogous to an advocate general in the European Court) that French courts cannot refuse to apply a statute because it conflicts with a treaty. For a fuller discussion of the attitude of the French administrative courts towards Community law at this time, see Weiss, 'Self-Executing Treaties and Directly Applicable EEC Law in French Courts' (1979) 1 LIEI 51 at 69–71 and 73–4.

[48] See, e.g., *Conseil d'Etat*, 22 October 1979, [1980] AJDA 39, a case concerning a conflict between the EC Treaty and a subsequent French statute. In view of the long-standing general rule, in both the judicial and the administrative courts, that international treaties to which France is a party prevail over prior statutes, it is doubtful whether there would have been any problem with regard to statutes passed before the EC Treaty: see Manin, 'The *Nicolo* Case of the *Conseil d'Etat*: French Constitutional Law and the Supreme Administrative Court's Acceptance of the Primacy of Community Law over Subsequent National Statute Law' (1991) 28 CMLRev. 499 at 501–2.

case,[49] in which the French statute providing for elections to the European Parliament was challenged on the ground that it was contrary to the EC Treaty. The *Conseil d'Etat*'s judgment was terse in the extreme: it considered whether a conflict existed and ruled that the statute was compatible with the Treaty. In doing so, however, it implicitly accepted the supremacy of the Treaty; otherwise, it could have rejected the application on the simpler ground that such a conflict, even if it existed, was no reason for not applying the statute.[50] This decision therefore constituted an important advance for Community law in France.[51]

Directives have caused even greater difficulties. The starting point for any discussion must be the *Cohn-Bendit* case.[52] Cohn-Bendit was a German citizen who was permanently resident in France. He was a student of sociology at Paris–Nanterre University and became one of the leaders of the student revolt of May 1968. On 24 May 1968, the French Minister of the Interior (equivalent to the Home Secretary) issued a deportation order against him on the ground that his presence in France was contrary to the public good (*ordre public*). He therefore had to leave. Some years later, in 1975, Cohn-Bendit wanted to return to France in order to take up an offer of employment which had been made to him. He requested the Minister to rescind the deportation order, but this was refused, without any proper reason being given, by a decision of 2 February 1976.

Cohn-Bendit challenged this refusal in proceedings brought before the Paris *Tribunal Administratif*: he argued that the Minister's refusal was contrary to Article 39 [48] EC and infringed, in particular, Article 6 of Directive 64/221.[53] Article 39 [48] gives Community citizens a right to enter another Community country in order to take up employment but makes this right subject to limitations 'justified on grounds of public policy, public security, or public health'. Directive 64/221, however, gives Community citizens various rights when the public policy proviso is invoked; one of these, laid down in Article 6, states that the immigrant must be given the reasons for the decision, unless this would be contrary to the interests of state security. The *Tribunal Administratif* made a reference to the European Court for the interpretation of these provisions and stayed the proceedings until an answer was received.

By making this order, the *Tribunal Administratif* implicitly recognized that the Directive could be invoked by Cohn-Bendit. The Minister refused to accept this and appealed to the *Conseil d'Etat* against the order of reference. Shortly before judgment was given, however, the Minister revoked the deportation order. One might have thought that this would have been the end of the matter, but the *Conseil d'Etat* went ahead and delivered a very surprising judgment: it allowed the appeal on the ground that, under the EC Treaty, directives cannot be invoked by individuals in the national courts in order to challenge an individual administrative decision; Cohn-Bendit could not, therefore, invoke Directive 64/221 before the court. The interpretation of the Directive was consequently irrelevant to the proceedings.

[49] *Conseil d'Etat*, 20 October 1989, [1990] 1 CMLR 173.

[50] For a full and informative discussion of the case, see Manin, 'The *Nicolo* Case of the *Conseil d'Etat*: French Constitutional Law and the Supreme Administrative Court's Acceptance of the Primacy of Community Law over Subsequent National Statute Law' (1991) 28 CMLRev. 499.

[51] See also *Conseil d'Etat*, 24 September 1990 (*Boisdet*) [1991] 1 CMLR 3, which concerned an EC regulation.

[52] *Conseil d'Etat*, 22 December 1978, Dalloz, 1979, 155.

[53] OJ (Spec. Ed.) 1963/64, p. 17.

It is, of course, true that there are good reasons for thinking that the authors of the Treaty did not intend directives to have direct effect: in this respect, there is a great deal to be said in favour of the *Conseil d'Etat*'s interpretation of the Treaty. However, the doctrine of the direct effect of directives had been firmly established by the date of the *Cohn-Bendit* judgment[54] and the *Conseil* was perfectly well aware of it. This judgment was a clear and deliberate act of defiance: by rejecting the authority of the European Court – even where it could be said to have gone beyond the Treaty – the *Conseil d'Etat* struck a blow at the foundations of the Community.

As a result of the *Cohn-Bendit* case, the validity of an individual administrative act (a decision by an administrative authority dealing with a particular case) could not be challenged on the ground that it was contrary to a directive.[55] However, the *Conseil d'Etat* subsequently began to soften its position and held that legislation adopted by the French Executive (as distinct from statutes passed by the French Legislature) could be annulled if it conflicted with the result to be achieved under a directive. This ruling was fully consistent with the *Conseil d'Etat*'s interpretation of Article 249 [189] EC: it considered that a directive could not be directly effective since it could not confer rights directly on individuals; but since it was binding on the Member States as to the result to be achieved, it could constitute the foundation for an action to annul a decree, or other administrative measure of a legislative nature.[56] Thus in one case a ministerial order permitting the hunting of turtle doves was annulled because it conflicted with the objective of a directive on the protection of birds.[57]

These decisions were followed by the *Rothmans* and *Arizona Tobacco* cases,[58] which arose out of the special regime for the sale of tobacco in France. For a long time, the importation and sale of tobacco products had been a state monopoly in France. In order to meet the requirements of Community law, a statute, the Law of 24 May 1976, abolished this monopoly in so far as it related to the importation of tobacco products from other Community countries (though the retail sale of all tobacco products continued to be in State hands). Section 6 of this Law, together with Article 10 of a Decree of 11 December 1976, which was adopted on the basis of the Law, provided that the retail price of any tobacco product could be fixed by the Minister of Finance.

[54] It had also been clearly laid down that Directive 64/221 was directly effective: see, e.g., *Van Duyn v. Home Office*, Case 41/74, [1974] ECR 1337; *Bonsignore*, Case 67/74, [1975] ECR 297; *Rutili*, Case 36/75, [1975] ECR 1219; *Royer*, Case 48/75, [1976] ECR 497; and *Watson and Belmann*, Case 118/75, [1976] ECR 1185.

[55] See *Tribunal Administratif*, Paris, 2 December 1980, Dr. Fisc. 1981, No. 2384; *Conseil d'Etat*, 28 November 1980, Dr. Fisc. 1980, No. 21 comm. 1121; *Conseil d'Etat*, 25 February 1981, [1981] Recueil Dalloz Sirey (Informations Rapides) 331; *Conseil d'Etat*, 13 December 1985, [1985] Recueil des Décisions du Conseil d'Etat 515.

[56] For further details, see Tatham, 'Effect of European Community Directives in France: The Development of the *Cohn-Bendit* Jurisprudence' (1991) 40 ICLQ 907.

[57] *Conseil d'Etat*, 7 December 1984, [1985] RTDE 187. The proceedings were brought by various conservationist groups, including an organization for the protection of birds. See also *Conseil d'Etat*, 28 September 1984, (*Confédération Nationale des Sociétés de Protection des Animaux*) [1984] RTDE 759; *Conseil d'Etat*, 6 March 1987, (*Fédération Française des Sociétés de Protection de la Nature*) [1985] Revue Française de Droit Administratif 303; *Conseil d'Etat*, 3 February 1989 (*Compagnie Alitalia*) [1990] 1 CMLR 248.

[58] *Conseil d'Etat*, 28 February 1992, [1993] 1 CMLR 253.

The companies in question, which were importers of tobacco products into France from other Community countries, asked the Minister to permit an increase in the price of their products. When this was not granted, they brought proceedings for judicial review of the decisions of refusal which, under French administrative law, were deemed to have been taken by the Minister. They argued that the fixing by the French Government of the selling price of tobacco products imported from other Member States was contrary to a Community directive adopted in 1972.

The *Conseil d'Etat* held in favour of the applicants. It ruled that section 6 of the Law, being contrary to the Directive, could not be applied; Article 10 of the decree therefore lacked a legal foundation and was void; consequently, the decisions of refusal were void. The decisions of refusal were therefore annulled and the applicants in the *Arizona Tobacco* case were awarded damages.

These decisions are remarkable for a number of reasons. First, they show that the *Conseil d'Etat* accepts the primacy of a directive over a statute, even one adopted subsequent to the directive. Secondly, they could be regarded as marking the end of the *Cohn-Bendit* doctrine, since the implied decision of refusal was certainly an individual act (though it might be argued that the effect of the directive operated *via* the Law and the Decree, rather than directly on the decision of refusal). Thirdly, they show that the *Conseil d'Etat* is willing to award damages to applicants who have suffered loss as a result of governmental action that conflicts with Community law. In this respect, it is consonant with the decision of the European court in *Francovich v. Italy*,[59] decided some two months previously. However, the lack of any clear statement of principle in the decisions means that doubts still remain regarding the attitude of the *Conseil d'Etat* towards Community law in general and directives in particular.[60]

The judgments in which the contrast in attitudes between the *Conseil d'Etat* and the *Cour de Cassation* has been most strikingly reflected were given in a group of cases concerning monetary compensatory amounts ('MCAs'). The details of the cases were complicated but the essential facts were simple. In the circumstances of the cases, MCAs took the form of levies payable on exports of agricultural products. They were imposed by Community regulations but were collected by the national governments. In France, MCAs on exports to other Community countries were payable to the French Customs, while MCAs on exports to non-Member States were collected by a French governmental agency called ONIC. This difference had one important consequence: disputes regarding the amount payable fell within the jurisdiction of the administrative courts when ONIC was involved but, by virtue of a special provision of French law, came within the jurisdiction of the judicial courts when the Customs were the collecting agency. In the end, this difference turned out to be crucial.

The first group of cases concerned three exporters, Roquette, Maïseries de Beauce, and Providence Agricole. Roquette had exported within the Community and had been obliged to pay MCAs to the French Customs. It then brought proceedings before a

[59] Cases C-6, 9/90, [1991] ECR I-5357.

[60] For a full discussion, see Simon, 'Le Conseil d'Etat et les directives communautaires: Du gallicanisme à l'orthodoxie' [1992] RTDE 265.

judicial court, the *Tribunal d'Instance* of Lille, to recover the payments, claiming that the relevant regulations were invalid. The other two exporters had similar claims against ONIC, and they sued in the administrative courts (in Orléans and Châlons-sur-Marne, respectively). All three courts made preliminary references to the European Court asking for a ruling on the validity of the regulations in question. The European Court gave similar judgments in all three cases: it held that the regulations were invalid, but went on to declare that this would not enable the charging of MCAs to be challenged with regard to the period prior to the date of the judgment.[61] This meant that money already paid could not be recovered.[62]

This judgment was controversial because, though Article 234 [177] EC gives the European Court the power to declare a Community act invalid, there is no express power to rule on the consequences of such invalidity, or to declare a regulation invalid for the future but valid for the past. Article 231 [174], second paragraph, does give such a power, but it applies only to annulment actions under Article 230 [173]. The European Court, however, said that Article 231 [174], second paragraph, applies 'by analogy' to rulings under Article 234 [177].

When proceedings recommenced in France, the result was the same in each case: the three courts each ruled that the jurisdiction of the European Court was limited to answering the questions asked by the French courts. They had asked whether the regulations were invalid; they had not asked what the consequences of invalidity were. In answering a question which had not been asked, the European Court had gone beyond its jurisdiction and its ruling on this point was not binding on the French courts. They each ruled that the MCAs had to be repaid.[63]

These judgments went on appeal. In the case of Roquette, the appeal went first to the *Cour d'Appel* of Douai (which upheld the lower court's judgment)[64] and then to the *Cour de Cassation.* In the other two cases the appeal went to the *Conseil d'Etat.*

The *Conseil d'Etat* upheld the judgments of the lower courts.[65] It said that the European Court's ruling on the consequences of invalidity, being outside the scope of the questions asked, was not binding on the French court. The *Cour de Cassation*, on the other hand, reached the opposite conclusion. It said that the European Court's ruling on the consequences of invalidity should have been followed.[66]

These cases had an interesting sequel. Another French exporter, which (before the European Court's judgments in the earlier cases) had paid MCAs to both ONIC and the French Customs, decided to bring proceedings to recover them. It sued ONIC in

[61] *Roquette v. French Customs*, Case 145/79, [1980] ECR 2917; *Maïseries de Beauce v. ONIC*, Case 109/79, [1980] ECR 2883; *Providence Agricole v. ONIC*, Case 4/79, [1980] ECR 2823.

[62] In *Fragd*, Case 33/84, [1985] ECR 1605, an identical ruling was given by the European Court in a reference from an Italian court. This, too, caused problems: see the decision of the Italian Constitutional Court in the *Fragd* case, decision 232 of 21 April 1989, (1989) 72 RDI 103.

[63] *Tribunal d'Instance*, Lille, 15 July 1981, (*Roquette*) [1982] Recueil Dalloz Sirey (Jurisprudence) 9; *Tribunal Administratif*, Orléans, 23 February 1982, (*Maïseries de Beauce*) [1982] Recueil des Décisions du Conseil d'Etat 471.

[64] *Cour d'Appel*, Douai, 19 January 1983, [1983] Gazette du Palais 292.

[65] *Conseil d'Etat*, 26 July 1985, (*Maïseries de Beauce*) [1985] Recueil des Décisions du Conseil d'Etat 233; [1985] AJDA 615, [1986] RTDE 158; *Conseil d'Etat*, 13 November 1985 (*Providence Agricole*) (not reported).

[66] *Cour de Cassation*, 10 December 1986, [1986] RTDE 195.

the Paris *Tribunal Administratif* and the Customs in the Paris *Tribunal d'Instance*. The latter made a reference to the European Court, asking expressly whether the invalidity of the regulations entitled the exporter to claim a refund. The European Court gave the same answer as in the previous cases but this time there could be no objection that it had gone beyond the questions asked.[67] The *Tribunal d'Instance* therefore ruled that the exporter was not entitled to a refund.[68]

The *Tribunal Administratif*, on the other hand, made no reference to the European Court. It held that ONIC was obliged to repay the money.[69] This judgment went on appeal to the *Conseil d'Etat*, where it was argued that the European Court's ruling on the reference from the Paris *Tribunal d'Instance*, as well as similar rulings on references from courts in other Member States, should be followed. The *Conseil d'Etat* rejected this with the curt statement that the European Court's rulings, having been made in the course of proceedings in other courts between different parties, were not binding on the Paris *Tribunal Administratif*. The appeal was dismissed.[70]

Even if one accepts the view that the earlier judgments of the European Court were not binding, it could still be argued that the *Conseil d'Etat* should itself have referred the question to the European Court: under Article 234 [177] EC a court from which there is no appeal is obliged to refer any question on the interpretation of the EC Treaty, or on the validity or interpretation of a Community act. It is possible that the *Conseil d'Etat* considered that Article 234 [177] does not cover a question concerning the consequences of the invalidity of a Community act. Opinions may differ as to whether a power to rule on the validity of an act includes the power to rule on the consequences of its invalidity; but since this involves the interpretation of Article 234 [177], and therefore raises a question on the interpretation of the EC Treaty, it is itself covered by Article 234 [177]. The *Conseil d'Etat* should, if it had entertained doubts on the matter, have made a preliminary reference to the European Court asking whether the obligation under Article 234 [177] to refer questions on the validity of Community acts includes an obligation to refer a question on the consequences of the invalidity of such an act.[71] The *Conseil d'Etat*'s failure to do this is indicative of its determination to prevent the European Court from using its power as the supreme authority on the interpretation of the Treaty as a means of extending its own jurisdiction.

The position of Community law in France has been put in a new perspective by amendments[72] to the French Constitution adopted in order to permit France to ratify the Treaty on European Union.[73] They were necessitated by a judgment of the *Conseil*

[67] *Société des Produits de Maïs v. French Customs*, Case 112/83, [1985] ECR 719.

[68] *Tribunal d'Instance*, First Arrondissement, Paris, 11 July 1986 (not reported). The *Tribunal d'Instance*, which was differently constituted when it gave this judgment from the way it had been when it made the reference, was nevertheless unable to resist criticizing the European Court's ruling for lack of legal logic, and almost seemed to regret that the European Court had been asked the questions on the consequences of the invalidity of the regulations.

[69] *Tribunal Administratif*, Paris, 17 May 1983 (not reported).

[70] *Conseil d'Etat*, 13 June 1986, [1986] RTDE 533.

[71] The *Conseil d'Etat* would probably justify its attitude on the basis of the *acte clair* doctrine (discussed in Chap. 9) but it is doubtful whether this doctrine can legitimately be applied in such a case.

[72] No referendum was needed for these amendments; instead, a joint sitting of both Houses of Parliament was held to adopt them. This had to be done by a three-fifths majority.

[73] See Oliver, 'The French Constitution and the Treaty of Maastricht' (1994) 43 ICLQ 1.

*Constitutionnel*,[74] which declared certain provisions of the Treaty on European Union[75] to be incompatible with the French Constitution.[76] The most important amendment was the addition to the Constitution of Title XIV,[77] which makes provision for French membership of the European Communities and the European Union.[78] Previously the Constitution had made no mention of the Community.

Once the Constitution had been amended, the Treaty on European Union could have been ratified by statute; instead, however, President Mitterrand decided to call a referendum. As is well known, this almost resulted in disaster for him. In the end, however, there was a narrow majority in favour of ratification, which duly took place.[79]

In more recent times, there have been a number of decisions of the *Conseil Constitutionnel* concerned with Community law, and two further Community Treaties were held to require constitutional amendments.[80] These decisions make clear that the *Conseil Constitutionnel* considers that the French Constitution is supreme law in France and that Community law takes effect in France subject to its provisions.[81]

## POLAND

Poland is a former Soviet-bloc country that now has a democratic Constitution. The Constitution provides for a Constitutional Court, which has the power to rule on the

[74] Decision of 9 April 1992, [1993] 3 CMLR 345.

[75] These were Art. 19(1) [8b(1)] EC, which would permit European Union citizens resident in France to vote in municipal elections; the provisions on economic and monetary union; and Art. [100c(3)] EC, which provided for qualified majority voting in the Council from 1 January 1996 when decisions were taken on the non-Member States whose citizens had to be in possession of a visa when entering a Member State from outside the Community.

[76] Decisions of the *Conseil Constitutionnel* (in French) may be found on *http://www.conseil-constitutionnel.fr/*.

[77] For the full text in French, see Oliver, 'The French Constitution and the Treaty of Maastricht' (1994) 43 ICLQ 1 at 24–5.

[78] It dealt expressly with the provisions of the Treaty on European Union which had been ruled incompatible with the French Constitution.

[79] Further attempts to block ratification were rejected by the *Conseil Constitutionnel*: decision of 2 September 1992 (Case 92–312, [1992] JORF 12095) and decision of 23 September 1992 (Case 92–313, [1992] JORF 13337).

[80] See the decision of 13 September 1997 (Treaty of Amsterdam) and the decision of 19 November 2004 (the proposed European Constitution).

[81] Thus in its decision of 19 November 2004 on the constitutionality of the proposed European Constitution, it said that the European Constitution 'is without effect on the existence of the French Constitution and its place at the summit of the internal legal order' ('*est sans incidence sur l'existence de la Constitution française et sa place au sommet de l'ordre juridique interne*') (para. 10). See also the decision of 10 June 2004 on the e-commerce directive, in which it said 'the transposition into internal law of a Community directive results from a constitutional requirement which cannot be obstructed except by reason of an express provision to the contrary in the Constitution' ('*la transposition en droit interne d'une directive communautaire résulte d'une exigence constitutionnelle à laquelle il ne pourrait être fait obstacle qu'en raison d'une disposition expresse contraire de la Constitution*') (para. 7). The constitutional basis for the transposition of directives referred to by the *Conseil* was Art. 88–1 of the French Constitution, which provides for French membership of the EC and EU.

constitutionality of Polish legislation and Government decisions. Acting under this power, it has given a number of rulings of relevance to the European Union.[82]

The fullest analysis of the relationship between Community law and Polish law is to be found in the decision of 11 May 2005 on the constitutionality of Poland's membership of the European Union.[83] Although it held Poland's membership constitutional, the Constitutional Court made clear that the Polish Constitution is supreme law in Poland. Community law has effect in Poland only by virtue of, and to the extent permitted by, the Polish Constitution.[84] However, the Constitution requires Poland to respect provisions of international law binding on Poland.[85] If a conflict arose between Community law and the Polish Constitution, it could not be solved by giving Community law precedence over the Polish Constitution. Possible solutions would be for Poland to amend the Constitution, for the Community to amend the relevant Community provision, or for Poland to withdraw from the Community. The Constitutional Court also said that the Member States retain the right to decide whether, when Community organs adopt legal acts, they are acting within the powers conferred on them by the Treaties and in accordance with the principles of subsidiarity and proportionality. If they are not, Community law would not have precedence over Polish law in Poland.

In a judgment given a few weeks earlier, that of 27 April 2005,[86] the Constitutional Court held that Polish legislation enacted to give effect to the EC third-pillar framework decision on the European Arrest Warrant was invalid. It ruled that the legislation was contrary to the constitutional provision prohibiting the extradition of Polish citizens. However, it suspended the effect of its decision for eighteen months to give the Government the opportunity to amend the Constitution. This shows that the Constitutional Court is sensitive to the needs of the EU and will do what it can, within the limits of what is constitutionally possible, to ensure that Poland meets her Community obligations.

## THE UNITED KINGDOM

Since the United Kingdom has a largely unwritten constitution, provision for membership could not be made by means of a constitutional amendment (as was done in the Republic

[82] These include Cases K 11/03, K 33/03, K 15/04, K 18/04, K 24/04, and P 1/05. English translations and summaries of decisions of the Polish Constitutional Court may be found on *http://www.trybunal.gov.pl/eng/summaries/wstep_gb.htm.*

[83] Case K 18/04 (Internet citation above). Para. 6–16 of the English language summary contain the most important points.

[84] The Constitutional Court said that Poland could denounce the Community Treaties under the conditions laid down by international law as expressed in the 1969 Vienna Convention on the Law of Treaties.

[85] This means that Polish courts should interpret Polish law, as far as possible, so as not to conflict with Community law. The Constitutional Court said that a reciprocal duty rested on the European Court to be sympathetically disposed towards national legal systems.

[86] Case P 1/05 (Internet citation above). For a comment, see Leczykiewicz, (2006) 43 CMLRev. 1181. The decision of the German Constitutional Court on the same issue is discussed above in the section on 'Germany'.

of Ireland). Moreover, the attitude of the United Kingdom towards international law is strictly dualist: there is no general rule of law allowing treaties to take effect in the internal legal system. So this route could not be used to give effect to the Community Treaties. These problems could be, and were, overcome by means of a special Act of Parliament. However, none of this could affect the principle of Sovereignty of Parliament, the fundamental doctrine of the British Constitution.

## THE EUROPEAN COMMUNITIES ACT 1972

The European Communities Act 1972 was passed by Parliament to make provision for Britain's membership of the Community. An Act of Parliament was necessary for a number of purposes, but above all to make Community law applicable in the national legal system: without the European Communities Act, the Community Treaties and Community legislation – though binding on the United Kingdom at the international level – would have been of no effect internally. This was made clear by Lord Denning MR in the following *dictum* from *McWhirter v. Attorney-General*,[87] a case decided before the Act had been passed: 'Even though the Treaty of Rome has been signed, it has no effect, so far as these Courts are concerned, until it is made an Act of Parliament. Once it is implemented by an Act of Parliament, these Courts must go by the Act of Parliament.'

This shows that the doctrine adopted by the Belgian *Cour de Cassation* in the *Fromagerie 'Le Ski'* case[88] does not apply in the United Kingdom: the European Communities Act is not merely the means by which Parliament gave assent to the Treaties (something which is not strictly necessary in British constitutional law),[89] it also provides the legal foundation for the direct effect of Community law in the United Kingdom. Because of this, the provisions of the Act are of special importance.

## THE COMMUNITY TREATIES

Section 1(2) of the Act defines what is meant by the 'Community Treaties' (usually referred to in the Act as 'the Treaties'), the main ones being listed by name. This list is similar to the list of constitutive Treaties given in Chapter 3, above, but it includes instruments, such as certain Council decisions of a constitutional nature, which are not, strictly speaking, treaties. Treaties entered into *by* the Communities (with or without the participation of the Member States) are included. The EEA Treaty is expressly mentioned. Treaties entered into by the Member States which are ancillary to any of the other Community Treaties are also covered. It is provided by section 1(3) that an Order in Council may declare a treaty to be a 'Community Treaty', and such a declaration is conclusive. An Order in Council is not, however, necessary: an agreement which falls

[87] [1972] CMLR 882 at 886. [88] See above.

[89] It is, however, normal practice (and possibly a constitutional convention) for treaties requiring ratification by the Crown to be laid before Parliament 21 days before they are ratified (the 'Ponsonby Rule'): see (1924) 171 H.C. Debates, cols 2001–4.

within the definition of a 'Community Treaty' will be so regarded, even without a declaration. There is, however, one exception: a post-accession treaty *entered into by the United Kingdom* (other than a pre-accession treaty to which the United Kingdom accedes on terms settled on or before 22 January 1972)[90] will not be regarded as a 'Community Treaty' unless it is so specified in an Order in Council of which a draft has been approved by resolution of each House of Parliament.[91]

This provision gives Parliament control over three classes of agreement:[92] first, it covers agreements concluded by the Member States between themselves – new constitutive Treaties (including treaties amending or supplementing existing constitutive Treaties), subsidiary conventions, and acts of the representatives of the Governments of the Member States meeting in the Council (in so far as these constitute international agreements); secondly, it applies to so-called 'mixed agreements' (agreements between, on the one side, the Community and the Member States, and, on the other side, third countries); and thirdly, it could apply to agreements between the Member States and third countries which are binding on the Community and consequently part of Community law (assuming this is possible). In all these cases, parliamentary approval will normally be required in the other Member States as well.

## DIRECT EFFECT

Section 2(1) of the Act makes provision for the direct effect of Community law in the United Kingdom. It reads as follows:

> All such rights, powers, liabilities, obligations and restrictions from time to time created or arising by or under the Treaties, and all such remedies and procedures from time to time provided for by or under the Treaties, as in accordance with the Treaties are without further enactment to be given legal effect or used in the United Kingdom shall be recognised and available in law, and be enforced, allowed and followed accordingly; and the expression 'enforceable Community right' and similar expressions shall be read as referring to one to which this subsection applies.

Three comments may be made about this: first, it provides for the direct effect of both the Community Treaties (as previously defined) and Community legislation ('rights . . . created or arising . . . *under*[93] the Treaties'); secondly, it includes future Community law ('from time to time created'); and thirdly, it makes clear that

[90] See Art. 3(1) of the Act of Accession: agreements falling within Art. 3(2) would not come within this exception as the terms had to be agreed to at a later date. Thus the United Kingdom's accession to the Convention on Jurisdiction and the Enforcement of Judgments in Civil and Commercial Matters (now replaced by a Community regulation except as regards Denmark) required a Convention of Accession, signed in 1978, which amended the original Convention: see OJ 1978, L304.

[91] For an (unsuccessful) attempt by a private citizen to prevent an agreement between the Member States from being so specified, see *R v. HM Treasury, ex parte Smedley* [1985] QB 657, CA.

[92] In one special case, Parliament must give its approval by statute: under the European Assembly Elections Act 1978, s. 6(1), it is stated that no treaty providing for any increase in the powers of the European Parliament may be ratified by the United Kingdom unless it has been approved by Act of Parliament. For an example of such approval, see the European Communities (Amendment) Act 1986, s. 3(4), which concerned the increases in the powers of the European Parliament contained in the Single European Act.

[93] Emphasis added.

Community law determines whether a particular provision is directly effective ('as *in accordance with the Treaties*[94] are without further enactment to be given legal effect').

In view of the wide definition given to 'Community Treaties', section 2(1) covers all forms of written Community law. The only provisions of Community law which might not be covered are the general principles of law; but these only rarely apply in the national courts and could probably be brought within the terms of section 2(1) on the ground that they are impliedly based on the Treaties and therefore arise 'under' the Treaties.[95]

## IMPLEMENTATION

Section 2(2) makes provision for the implementation of Community law by means of subordinate legislation. This may be done either by Order in Council or by regulation made by a Minister or department designated for this purpose by Order in Council.[96] In both cases the measure must be in the form of a statutory instrument[97] and must be approved by Parliament.[98]

This power may be used for the following purposes:

1 implementing any Community obligation of the United Kingdom;
2 enabling any such obligation to be implemented;
3 enabling any rights enjoyed, or to be enjoyed, by the United Kingdom under, or by virtue of, the Treaties to be exercised;
4 dealing with matters arising out of, or related to, any such obligation or rights, or the coming into force, or the operation from time to time, of the above.

'Community obligation' means an obligation 'created or arising by or under the Treaties'.[99] It follows from this that the power is dependent on the existence of a right or obligation under the Community Treaties (as previously defined) or under Community legislation,[100] and can be used only for purposes subordinate to such right or obligation. Consequently, if the British Government uses this power to implement a Community provision but misconstrues that provision so that the implementing measure goes substantially beyond the provision, the implementing measure may be ruled *ultra vires* by the British courts. Where the Community provision turns out to be invalid, there will of course be no Community obligation to implement; therefore, the implementing measure will be even more clearly invalid.[101] It follows from this that, in order to determine the validity of the implementing measure under British law, the British court may have

94 Emphasis added. 95 See Chap. 5.

96 See the European Communities (Designation) Order 1973 (SI 1973/1889).

97 Statutory Instruments Act 1946, s.1(1), Sch. 2, para. 2(1).

98 If the instrument has not been approved in draft by each House of Parliament, it will be subject to annulment by negative resolution of either House: European Communities Act 1972, Sch. 2, para. 2(2).

99 Sch. 1, Part II.

100 A right or obligation under Community legislation would constitute a right or obligation arising 'under' the Treaties.

101 *R v. Minister of Agriculture, ex parte Fédération Européenne de la Santé Animale* [1988] 3 CMLR 661, English High Court.

to make a reference to the European Court under Article 234 [177] EC in order to obtain a ruling on the interpretation or validity of the Community provision. This will be the case even where the Community provision is not directly effective.

It is provided by section 2(4) of the Act that implementing measures made under section 2(2) may include 'any such provision (of any such extent) as might be made by Act of Parliament'.[102] There are, however, four things which are expressly prohibited. These are specified in Schedule 2, paragraph 1, which provides that the power may not be used:

(a) to impose or increase taxation;

(b) to enact retroactive legislation;

(c) to sub-delegate legislative power (except to make rules of procedure for any court or tribunal);

(d) to create any new criminal offence punishable with imprisonment for more than two years or punishable on summary conviction with imprisonment for more than three months or with a fine of more than £400 (if not calculated on a daily basis) or with a fine of more than £5 per day.

If it is necessary to do any of these things to implement Community law, an Act of Parliament will have to be passed.

## ENFORCEMENT OF JUDGMENTS

The European Communities (Enforcement of Community Judgments) Order 1972,[103] which was made under section 2(4) of the Act, makes provision for the enforcement in the United Kingdom of judgments of the European Court, and of decisions of the Council or Commission imposing fines or penalties. The judgment or decision must be registered by the High Court (after the Secretary of State has appended an enforcement order) and is then enforced in the same way as an ordinary High Court judgment.

## SUPREMACY OF COMMUNITY LAW[104]

Section 2(4) of the European Communities Act 1972 also provides that 'any enactment passed or to be passed, other than one contained in this Part of this Act, shall be construed and have effect subject to the foregoing provisions of this section'. Now, the foregoing provisions of section 2 include section 2(1), which states that directly

[102] It is not entirely clear what the purpose of this provision is, but it is possible that it was intended to exclude the common law presumptions applicable to delegated legislation (other than those given statutory force in Sch. 2, para. 1). For a general discussion of these presumptions, see TC Hartley and JAG Griffith, *Government and Law*, 2nd edn (1981), pp. 360–2. On the effect of measures under s. 2(2), see *Thoburn* v. *Sunderland City Council* [2002] EWHC 195; [2002] 3 WLR 247; [2002] 1 CMLR 50 (DC), discussed below.

[103] SI 1972/1590 (as amended).

[104] For a more detailed discussion of this topic, see the article by Clarke and Sufrin listed below under 'Further Reading'.

effective Community law must be recognized and enforced in the United Kingdom; consequently, it seems that Parliament intended that all Acts of Parliament, both past and future, should be subordinated to Community law. This view is strengthened by section 3(1), which states that any question as to the 'effect' of any of the Treaties or of Community legislation must be decided 'in accordance with the principles of any relevant decision of the European Court'. One such principle is, of course, that of the supremacy of Community law.

There is no doubt that these provisions are effective as regards United Kingdom legislation passed prior to the European Communities Act: Parliament can obviously state that all previous legislation is subject to the provisions of a new statute. The same applies to delegated legislation made under a statute passed prior to the European Communities Act, even if the delegated legislation itself was adopted after the European Communities Act: the force and effect of delegated legislation can never be greater than that of the empowering statute itself.

The real problem concerns statutes passed after the European Communities Act. It is true that, under section 2(4), these are also subject to Community law; however, the principle of Sovereignty of Parliament intrudes at this point and limits the effectiveness of this provision. The doctrine of the Sovereignty of Parliament is the fundamental principle of the British Constitution: it states that there are no legal limits to the legislative power of Parliament, except that Parliament cannot limit its own powers for the future. It follows from this that section 2(4) must be ineffective if it was intended to deprive Parliament of the power to pass legislation which would override Community law: Parliament is constitutionally unable to deprive itself of this power.

This does not, however, mean that post-accession Acts of Parliament prevail over Community law in the absence of express words to this effect. Section 2(4) could be regarded as laying down a rule of interpretation – and in view of the United Kingdom's membership of the Community, it is a very strong rule – that Parliament is to be presumed not to intend any future statute to override Community law. Thus in *R v. Secretary of State for Transport, ex parte Factortame*,[105] the House of Lords said that section 2(4) of the European Communities Act has the same effect as if a section were incorporated in every subsequent Act of Parliament, expressly stating that the provisions of the latter were to be without prejudice to directly effective Community law.[106] Consequently, Community law will always prevail unless Parliament clearly and expressly states in a future Act that the latter is to override Community law. This, of course, would constitute a repudiation of the Treaty and would lay the United Kingdom open to proceedings in the European Court for violation of a Treaty obligation. Responsibility would then rest with Parliament, not with the courts. The position was clearly expressed by Lord Denning MR in *Macarthys Ltd v. Smith*[107] where he said:

[105] [1990] 2 AC 85. [106] *Per* Lord Bridge at 140.

[107] [1979] 3 All ER 325 at 329. See also *per* Lawton LJ at 334. In subsequent proceedings in the same case, Lord Denning made the point even more forcefully: see [1981] 1 All ER 111 at 120. For an earlier statement by Lord Denning, see *Shields v. E. Coomes (Holdings) Ltd* [1979] 1 All ER 456 at 461–2, [1978] 1 WLR 1408 at 1414, CA.

> If the time should come when Parliament deliberately passes an Act with the intention of repudiating the Treaty or any provision in it or intentionally of acting inconsistently with it and says so in express terms then I should have thought that it would be the duty of our courts to follow the statute of our Parliament. I do not however envisage any such situation... Unless there is such an intentional and express repudiation of the Treaty, it is our duty to give priority to the Treaty.[108]

This means that ultimate sovereignty still rests with Parliament: Community law prevails only because Parliament wants it to prevail. Parliament could always repeal the European Communities Act and then Community law would cease to have effect in the United Kingdom.

This same result was reached by a slightly different route in the judgment of the Divisional Court in *Thoburn v. Sunderland City Council.*[109] The issue was whether subordinate legislation adopted in 1994 under section 2(2) of the European Communities Act to implement a directive could repeal the Weights and Measures Act 1985, an Act of Parliament passed after the European Communities Act. The Divisional Court held that it could. It rejected the argument that the 1985 Act had impliedly repealed the European Communities Act to the extent that the latter permitted the adoption of subordinate legislation that was inconsistent with it. It did so, however, on the ground that the European Communities Act was a constitutional statute and that, as such, it could be repealed only by express words. This is by virtue of the common law, not by virtue of European Community law.

In the course of his judgment, Laws LJ, made the following comment about the relationship between Community law and British law:

> Thus there is nothing in the [European Communities Act] which allows the [European Court], or any other institutions of the EU, to touch or qualify the conditions of Parliament's legislative supremacy in the United Kingdom. Not because the legislature chose not to allow it; because by our law it could not allow it. That being so, the legislative and judicial institutions of the EU cannot intrude upon those conditions. The British Parliament has not the authority to authorise any such thing. Being sovereign, it cannot abandon its sovereignty. Accordingly there are no circumstances in which the jurisprudence of the [European Court] can elevate Community law to a status within the corpus of English domestic law to which it could not aspire by any route of English law itself. This is, of course, the traditional doctrine of sovereignty. If it is to be modified, it certainly cannot be done by the incorporation of external texts. The conditions of Parliament's legislative supremacy in the United Kingdom necessarily remain in the United Kingdom's hands.

He went on to make clear that the relationship between the United Kingdom and the European Union depends on United Kingdom law, not European Union law.[110]

[108] In *Garland v. British Rail Engineering Ltd* [1983] 2 AC 751; [1982] 2 All ER 402; [1982] 2 WLR 918, the House of Lords expressly refrained from considering the correctness of this approach. It was sufficient for the purposes of that case to affirm that post-accession statutes should, if reasonably capable of bearing such a meaning, be construed so as to be consistent with Community law. See also *National Smokeless Fuels Ltd v. IRC* [1986] 3 CMLR 227; but see *Duke v. GEC Reliance* [1988] 1 All ER 626, HL.

[109] [2002] EWHC 195; [2002] 3 WLR 247; [2002] 1 CMLR 50 (DC).

[110] Para. 69, proposition 4.

## FURTHER READING

MITCHELL, KUIPERS, AND GALL, 'Constitutional Aspects of the Treaty and Legislation Relating to British Membership' (1972) 9 CMLRev. 134.

TRINDADE, 'Parliamentary Sovereignty and the Primacy of Community Law' (1972) 35 MLR 375.

WADE, 'Sovereignty and the European Communities' (1972) 88 LQR 1.

BOULOUIS, 'L'applicabilité directe des directives. A propos d'un arrêt Cohn-Bendit du Conseil d'Etat' [1979] RMC 104.

MARESCEAU, 'The Effect of Community Agreements in the UK under the European Communities Act 1972' (1979) 28 ICLQ 241.

SIMON AND DOWRICK, 'Effect of EEC Directives in France: The Views of the Conseil d'Etat' (1979) 95 LQR 376.

WEISSV, 'Self-Executing Treaties and Directly Applicable EEC Law in French Courts' (1979) 1 LIEI 51.

CLARKE AND SUFRIN, 'Constitutional Conundrums: The Impact of the United Kingdom's Membership of the Communities on Constitutional Theory' in Furmston *et al.* (eds), *The Effect on English Domestic Law of Membership of the European Communities and of Ratification of the European Convention on Human Rights* (1983), p. 32.

GANSHOF VAN DER MEERSCH, 'Community Law and the Belgian Constitution' in St John Bates *et al.* (eds), *In Memoriam J. D. B. Mitchell* (1983), p. 74.

KOOPMANS, 'Receptivity and its Limits: The Dutch Case', *ibid.*, p. 91.

LA PERGOLA AND DEL DUCA, 'Community Law and the Italian Constitution' (1985) 79 Am. J. Int. L. 598.

PETRICCIONE, 'Italy: Supremacy of Community Law over National Law' (1986) 11 ELRev. 320.

SIMON, 'L'effet dans le temps des arrêts préjudiciels de la CEE: enjeu ou prétexte d'une nouvelle guerre des juges?' in *Liber Amicorum P. Pescatore* (1987).

GAJA, 'New Developments in a Continuing Story: The Relationship between EEC Law and Italian Law' (1990) 27 CMLRev. 83.

SCHERMERS, 'The Scales in Balance: National Constitutional Court v. Court of Justice' (1990) 27 CMLRev. 97.

MANIN, 'The *Nicolo* Case of the *Conseil d'Etat*: French Constitutional Law and the Supreme Administrative Court's Acceptance of the Primacy of Community Law over Subsequent National Statute Law' (1991) 28 CMLRev. 499.

ROTH, 'The Application of Community Law in West Germany: 1980–1990' (1991) 28 CMLRev. 137 (especially at 137–45).

TATHAM, 'Effect of European Community Directives in France: The Development of the *Cohn-Bendit* Jurisprudence' (1991) 40 ICLQ 907.

DANIELE, 'Après l'arrêt *Granital*: droit communautaire et droit national dans la jurisprudence récente de la Cour constitutionnelle italienne' [1992] CDE 3.

GENEVOIS, 'Le Traité sur l'Union européenne et la Constitution' (1992) 8(3) Revue Française de Droit Administratif 374.

SIMON, 'Le Conseil d'Etat et les directives communautaires: Du gallicanisme à l'orthodoxie' [1992] RTDE 265.

FOSTER, 'The German Constitution and EC Membership' [1994] PL 392.

HERDEGEN, 'Maastricht and the German Constitutional Court: Constitutional Restraints for an "Ever Closer Union"' (1994) 31 CMLRev. 233.

OLIVER, 'The French Constitution and the Treaty of Maastricht' (1994) 43 ICLQ 1.

ROSEREN, 'The Application of Community Law by French Courts from 1982 to 1993' (1994) 31 CMLRev. 315.

TOMLINSON, 'Reception of Community Law in France' (1995) 1 CJEL 183.

MOUTHAAN, 'France: Amending the Amended Constitution' (1998) 23 ELRev. 592.

MAGANARIS, 'The Principle of Supremacy of Community Law – The Greek Challenge' (1998) 23 ELRev. 179.

HØEGH, 'The Danish Maastricht Judgment' (1999) 24 ELRev. 80.

MAGANARIS, 'The Principle of Supremacy of Community Law in Greece – From Direct Challenge to Non-Application' (1999) 24 ELRev. 426.

SCHILLING, 'The Court of Justice's Revolution: Its Effects and the Conditions for its Consummation. What Europe Can Learn from Fiji' (2002) 27 ELRev. 445.

ALBI AND VAN ELSUWEGE, 'The EU Constitution, National Constitutions and Sovereignty: An Assessment of a "European Constitutional Order"' (2004) 29 ELRev. 741.

BECK, 'The Problem of *Kompetenz Kompetenz*: A Conflict between Right and Right in which There Is No *Praetor*' (2005) 30 ELRev. 42.

CLAES, 'Constitutionalising Europe at its Source. The "European Clauses" in the National Constitutions: Evolution and Typology' (2005) 24 YEL 81.

# 9

# PRELIMINARY REFERENCES

The preliminary reference procedure is one of the most original features of the Community system. Although the idea of giving an international court jurisdiction of this kind had been around for a long time,[1] the European Court seems to have been the first international court actually to be granted it. Subsequently, jurisdiction of a similar kind has been conferred on the Benelux Court, the Andean Court of Justice, and the EFTA Court, the last having jurisdiction only to give advisory opinions.[2]

There are two major differences between an appeal and a reference. First, in the case of an appeal the initiative lies with the parties: the party who is dissatisfied with the court's judgment decides whether to appeal and then takes the necessary procedural steps. The court *a quo* normally has no further say in the matter and cannot prevent the appeal from being lodged.[3] Secondly, the appeal court decides the *case*, even though the appeal may be on limited grounds only, and it has the power to set aside the decision of the court *a quo*; normally it can then substitute its own decision for that of the lower court.[4] These features are not found in the procedure for a preliminary reference: the court *a quo* decides whether the reference should be made, and only specific issues are referred to the European Court. Once it has decided these, the European Court remits the case to the national court for a final decision.

This procedure puts the European Court in a weaker position than would be normal for the supreme court in a federation. It suggests that the national courts are not subordinate to the European Court, but co-equal: the relationship is not one of hierarchy, but of co-operation.

The relevant provisions are Articles 234 [177] EC and 150 Euratom, which are virtually identical. Article 234 [177] EC reads:[5]

[1] Plender, 'The European Court as an International Tribunal' [1983] CLJ 279 at 284. See also H Lauterpacht, 'Decisions of Municipal Courts as a Source of International Law' (1929) 10 BYIL 65 at 94–5, where it was suggested that the Permanent Court of International Justice might one day be given jurisdiction to hear references from national courts.

[2] On the Benelux Court, see Art. 6 of the Treaty establishing the Benelux Court, 1965 (in force on 1 January 1974); on the Andean Court, see Arts 28–31 of the Treaty creating the Court of Justice of the Cartagena Agreement, 1979, (1979) 18 ILM 1203; on the EFTA Court, see Art. 34 of the Agreement between the EFTA States on the establishment of a Surveillance Authority and a Court of Justice, OJ 1994, L344.

[3] In some cases, however, the parties may appeal only with the leave of the court *a quo* or the appeal court.

[4] In some Continental countries, e.g., France, the position is different in the case of an appeal in cassation: if the Court of Cassation allows the appeal, it quashes the lower court's judgment and then sends the case to an other *Cour d'Appel* – not the one from which the appeal came – for a new decision.

[5] In Art. 150 Euratom, the words 'save where those statutes provide otherwise' replace 'where those statutes so provide'; and the reference to the ECB (inserted into Art. 234 [177] EC by the Maastricht Agreement (TEU)) is absent.

> The Court of Justice shall have jurisdiction to give preliminary rulings concerning:
>
> (a) the interpretation of this Treaty;
>
> (b) the validity and interpretation of acts of the institutions of the Community and of the ECB;
>
> (c) the interpretation of the statutes of bodies established by an act of the Council, where those statutes so provide.
>
> Where such a question is raised before any court or tribunal of a Member State, that court or tribunal may, if it considers that a decision on the question is necessary to enable it to give judgment, request the Court of Justice to give a ruling thereon.
>
> Where any such question is raised in a case pending before a court or tribunal of a Member State against whose decisions there is no judicial remedy under national law, that court or tribunal shall bring the matter before the Court of Justice.

It will be seen from this that questions both of interpretation and validity may be referred to the European Court: references for interpretation may be made with regard to both the Treaty and Community acts, but references for a ruling on validity may be made only in the case of the latter. Since the Treaties are, in a sense, the constitution of the Community, it is understandable that their validity cannot be challenged in terms of the Community legal order.

One of the most important issues that may be referred to the European Court is that of the *effect* of a Community provision. The direct effect of Community provisions is treated by the European Court as a matter of interpretation, since the Member States are regarded as having agreed to it when they signed the Treaties. The result is that three issues may be referred for a ruling – interpretation, effect, and validity – though the latter applies only in certain cases. Questions of fact and of national law may not be referred, nor may the European Court rule on the *application* of the law to the particular case – though the exact borderline between interpretation and application is at the best of times uncertain.

## WHICH PROVISIONS MAY BE REFERRED?

Articles 234 [177] EC and 150 Euratom cover three kinds of provision: (a) the Treaty; (b) acts of Community institutions and of the ECB; and (c) statutes of bodies established by an act of the Council. The first two items will be discussed below, but a word should be said here about the third. What is meant by this? In Community law the word 'statute' normally refers to the instrument governing the working of some body or institution: the statute of the European Court, for example, provides for various procedural matters; the statute of the European Investment Bank provides for the setting up of the Bank, the powers of the Board of Governors, etc. If, therefore, the word 'statute' in sub-paragraph (c) of Articles 234 [177] EC and 150 Euratom refers to the instrument setting up the body, it will by definition be an act of the Council.

The significance of this is that acts of the Council are already covered by sub-paragraph (b). Therefore, the effect of sub-paragraph (c) is not to add to the jurisdiction of the European Court, but to restrict it: all that sub-paragraph (c) does is to limit the scope of sub-paragraph (b). First of all, under sub-paragraph (c) a preliminary ruling may be given regarding a statute *only* if that statute *so provides*, while under sub-paragraph (b) acts of the Council may in all cases be referred; therefore, sub-paragraph (c) prevents a reference regarding a statute which does not so provide. (Under sub-paragraph (c) of Article 150 Euratom the position is slightly different: a preliminary ruling may be made *except where the statute provides otherwise*; consequently, its effect is that a prohibition in such a statute would deprive the European Court of jurisdiction, even though a similar prohibition in any other act of the Council would be ineffective.)

The second consequence of sub-paragraph (c) is that it prevents the Court from ruling on the *validity* of such a statute: under sub-paragraph (b) the validity of a Community act may normally be decided on a preliminary reference, but this is not possible where the act constitutes the statute of a body.

In practice, the important provisions of the first paragraph of Articles 234 [177] EC and 150 Euratom are sub-paragraphs (a) and (b). The effect of these can best be considered by looking in turn at each of the sources of Community law.

## TREATIES

The words 'this Treaty' in sub-paragraph (a) of Article 234 [177] EC cover the EC Treaty and all Treaties amending or supplementing it.[6] The Euratom Treaty, and all Treaties amending or supplementing it, are covered by sub-paragraph (a) of Article 150 Euratom.

The European Court's jurisdiction with regard to the Treaty on European Union is limited, however, though it was slightly increased by the Treaty of Amsterdam and again by the Treaty of Nice.[7] Apart from its final provisions, and those provisions that amend the other Treaties, the Court may give preliminary rulings only with regard to Title VI (police and judicial co-operation in criminal matters), Title VII (enhanced co-operation), Article 6(2) [F(2)] TEU (fundamental rights), and, under the Treaty of Nice, the purely procedural stipulations of Article 7 (serious breach of democracy and fundamental rights by a Member State). In the case of Title VI, however, the Court's jurisdiction applies only to certain instruments[8] and only to those Member States that make a declaration that they want the Court to have jurisdiction;[9] and in the case of Title VII, it is subject to Articles 11 and 11a EC and Article 40 TEU.[10] The Court has no jurisdiction with regard to the common foreign and security policy (Title V).

[6] With regard to the instruments by which new Member States accede to the Community, see, e.g., Art. 1(3) of the Treaty of Accession 1972, which brings that Treaty and the Act of Accession annexed to it within the scope of Art. 234 [177] EC.

[7] Art. 46 [L] TEU, as amended.

[8] It may give rulings on the validity and interpretation of framework decisions and decisions on the interpretation of conventions, and on the validity and interpretation of measures implementing conventions: Art. 35(1) TEU.

[9] Art. 35(3) TEU.

[10] Art. 46(c) TEU, as amended by the Treaty of Nice.

## SUBSIDIARY CONVENTIONS

Even if adopted to attain objectives set out in the EC Treaty (as was the case with the Convention on Jurisdiction and the Enforcement of Judgments in Civil and Commercial Matters, 27 September 1968), subsidiary conventions cannot be regarded as forming part of the EC Treaty; therefore, they are not covered by the words 'this Treaty' in sub-paragraph (a) of Article 234 [177].[11] However, the convention might itself make provision for preliminary references to the European Court.

## ACTS OF THE REPRESENTATIVES OF THE MEMBER STATES

By definition, these are not acts of a Community institution and are therefore excluded from sub-paragraph (b); nor are they part of the EC or Euratom Treaties. Consequently, they fall outside Articles 234 [177] EC and 150 Euratom, and cannot be referred to the European Court. This is not very significant, however, because national courts would not normally have occasion to consider them.

## COMMUNITY ACTS

These are covered by sub-paragraph (b) of Articles 234 [177] EC and 150 Euratom,[12] which refer simply to acts of 'the institutions of the Community'. In practice, most Community acts are adopted by either the Commission or the Council, but there is no doubt that acts of the European Parliament, the Court of Auditors, and even of the Court itself, are also covered by sub-paragraph (b). In addition, sub-paragraph (b) of Article 234 [177] EC also applies to acts of the European Central Bank.

It should be noted that all the provisions mentioned above refer simply to 'acts': it is not necessary that the act be directly effective. As was explained in Chapter 8, a national court might have good reason for referring an act that was not directly effective for a ruling on its validity or interpretation.[13] It follows from this that all binding acts are covered, including acts *sui generis*.[14]

[11] See *Hurd v. Jones*, Case 44/84, [1986] ECR 29, in which the European Court held that the agreements between the Member States setting up European Schools in various Community countries were not covered by Art. 234 [177].

[12] But Art. 234 [177] EC does not cover international agreements concluded by national organizations to give effect to a directive: *Demouche*, Case 152/83, [1987] ECR 3833, a case concerning an agreement between national motor insurance bureaux on the 'green card' system.

[13] In *Haaga*, Case 32/74, [1974] ECR 1201, a German court asked for a reference on a directive which was not directly effective in order to elucidate the meaning of a national implementing measure; the European Court had no hesitation in giving the ruling. See also *Mazzalai*, Case 111/75, [1976] ECR 657 at 665.

[14] It was held in the *ERTA* case (*Commission v. Council*, Case 22/70, [1971] ECR 263) that an act *sui generis* is an 'act' for the purpose of Art. 230 [173] EC (see Chap. 4); consequently, it must also be an 'act' for the purpose of Art. 234 [177].

Non-binding acts, such as EC recommendations or opinions, are none the less 'acts'[15] and may also be referred:[16] national courts must take them into account when interpreting national and Community measures.[17]

## GENERAL PRINCIPLES OF LAW

According to the Treaty, these cannot form the subject matter of a reference, as they are neither part of the Treaties nor Community acts. However, if a national court referred a provision of one of the Treaties or a Community act, the European Court would also interpret any general principle of law that was relevant to the provision referred.

## AGREEMENTS WITH NON-MEMBER STATES

Since these are clearly not part of the EC or Euratom Treaties, they will be covered only if they are regarded as acts of Community institutions. As has already been explained, agreements between the Community and non-Member States are normally concluded by the Council:[18] in the *Haegeman* case[19] the European Court seized on this as a ground for regarding such agreements as Community acts. The Court therefore ruled that the Association Agreement between the Community and Greece (before Greece joined the Community) was covered by sub-paragraph (b) of Article 234 [177].

Is this view justified? First, it should be pointed out that there is a distinction between an international agreement and a national measure passed by one of the Contracting Parties to conclude or ratify the agreement: the latter is simply the constitutionally required method of giving assent to the agreement. In the *Haegeman* case the Court mentioned that the Association Agreement had been concluded by means of a Council decision. However, it was not the Council decision that the Court interpreted, but the Agreement itself. The two should not be confused.[20]

It should also be noted that the party to the agreement on the Community side is the Community itself – the EC or Euratom, as the case may be – not the Council.[21] Such agreements, therefore, do not constitute acts of an *institution* of the Community, as required by sub-paragraph (b) of Article 234 [177]: they are acts of the Community. Even if one takes the view that one cannot distinguish the Community from its institutions,

[15] This follows by implication from Arts 230 [173] EC and 146 Euratom, which speak of 'acts . . . other than recommendations or opinions'.

[16] *Grimaldi*, Case C-322/88, [1989] ECR 4407, a case dealing with EC recommendations.

[17] *Ibid.*

[18] See Chap. 6. Under Art. 101(3) Euratom, agreements may in certain cases be concluded by the Commission.

[19] Case 181/73, [1974] ECR 449.

[20] See *France v. Commission*, Case C-327/91, [1994] ECR I-3641 at paras 13–17 of the judgment, where the Court held that the appropriate subject matter of an action under Art. 230 [173] EC – a provision which gives the Court jurisdiction to annul acts of the Council and Commission – is the decision to conclude the agreement, not the agreement itself.

[21] *France v. Commission* (above) at para. 24 of the judgment.

moreover, it is still doubtful whether agreements are covered by sub-paragraph (b) of Article 234 [177]: this provision was surely intended to apply to unilateral acts, not bilateral acts such as international agreements.[22]

Whatever view one takes of the *Haegeman* case, there can be no doubt that its reasoning can apply only if the Community formally becomes a party to the agreement by means of an act of one of its institutions. This would seem to exclude the possibility that the European Court could take jurisdiction under Article 234 [177] to interpret an international agreement such as the original General Agreement on Tariffs and Trade (old GATT), to which the Community did not formally adhere, even though the European Court has held that the Community became bound by it because it succeeded to the rights and obligations under it of the Member States.[23] Yet the European Court, in one of the most blatantly policy-based judgments it has ever given, has ruled that the GATT *is* covered by Article 234 [177].

This occurred in the *SPI* case,[24] where the Italian *Corte Suprema di Cassazione* expressly asked the European Court whether the old GATT fell within the scope of Article 234 [177].[25] The European Court's answer was not based on the wording of Article 234 [177], which it did not even quote, but on pure policy.[26] It started with the proposition that the GATT, like all agreements binding on the Community, should receive a uniform interpretation throughout the Community: any divergence in its application in the different Member States would compromise the unity of the Community's common commercial policy and create distortions in trade within the Community. The Court then characterized its jurisdiction under Article 234 [177] on a functional basis: it referred to it as 'the jurisdiction conferred upon the Court in order to ensure the uniform interpretation of Community law'.[27] It was then able to conclude that Article 234 [177] must cover the GATT.[28]

The Court's rhetoric in this case was beguiling, but it should not be allowed to obscure the nature of the Court's reasoning. The Court was saying, quite simply, that

[22] This is the view of Advocate General Trabucchi, who said in *Bresciani*, Case 87/75, [1976] ECR 129 at 147, that a convention is of necessity a bilateral or multilateral legal instrument, and, as such, 'does not lend itself to identification with the acts of the Community executive, which are inherently unilateral'. Advocate General Trabucchi concluded that the *Haegeman* judgment therefore means that, in Community law, international agreements are not binding on private individuals as such, but only by virtue of an act of a Community institution (i.e., the decision or regulation formally concluding the agreement). It appears from this that the Advocate General regards the Community as adopting an essentially dualist approach to international law. This seems to be the only way in which the European Court's judgment in *Haegeman* can be justified; but the view that the Community adopts a dualist approach to international law does not seem consistent with the general tenor of the Court's judgments, especially its decision in the *SPI* case (below), nor does it seem to be borne out by the wording of the decisions or regulations themselves.

[23] See Chap. 6, above.

[24] Cases 267–9/81, [1983] ECR 801. See also *Singer and Geigy*, Cases 290–1/81, [1983] ECR 847.

[25] This was in a reference under Art. 234 [177]. Since it involved the interpretation of the EC Treaty, this question was itself covered by Art. 234 [177].

[26] The relevant passages are contained in paras 14–19 of the judgment.

[27] Para. 15.

[28] The Court stated that this was the case only from 1 July 1968, the date on which the Common Customs Tariff came into force in the Community. (It was on this date that, according to the Court, the Community took the place of the Member States with regard to the GATT.) Prior to this date, only the national courts could interpret the GATT.

because it would be desirable for the GATT to be covered by Article 234 [177], therefore it *is* covered. This is the reasoning of politics, not law.[29]

It should be noted that the Court stated in the *Haegeman* case that it had jurisdiction to interpret the agreement *within the framework of Community law*;[30] it also said that the agreement constituted an act of a Community institution *in so far as it concerned the Community*.[31] These phrases indicate that the Court was interpreting the agreement only in so far as it applied as part of Community law, and was not claiming that its interpretation was binding on the other party to the agreement. This is clearly right: if the other Contracting State felt that the European Court had misinterpreted the agreement and that as a result it was not being properly applied on the Community side, it would be entitled to complain that the Community was failing in its obligations under the agreement and, if this produced no results, to resort to the remedies available under international law.

The Association Agreement with Greece, which featured in the *Haegeman* case, was concluded jointly by the Community and the Member States on the one side, and by Greece on the other (mixed agreement). This was because it was considered to fall partly within the treaty-making competence of the Community and partly within that of the Member States. Later cases show that the European Court has jurisdiction to interpret a mixed agreement only with regard to those provisions falling within Community competence, unless there is some special reason for going beyond this.[32] In the absence of such a reason, provisions falling within the exclusive competence of the Member States cannot be considered by the European Court.

Where the international agreement as a whole is not binding on the Community, the European Court has no jurisdiction to interpret it, even if one of the Member States is a party to it and it conflicts with one of the Community Treaties. Thus in *Levy*[33] it was argued that France could not give effect to a directive on sex equality[34] which required the repeal of French legislation prohibiting women from working at night, because the legislation had been passed to implement an international convention[35] to which France was a party. Since the convention had been entered into by France before it became a party to the EC Treaty, the provisions of the convention prevailed over those of the EC Treaty to the extent to which they were incompatible.[36] The correct interpretation of the convention was, therefore, central to the proceedings; nevertheless, the European Court held that only the national court could decide this.[37]

[29] For an acknowledgment that criticism of the case is justified, see *R v. Secretary of State for the Home Department, ex parte Evans Medical* (*Generics* case), Case C-324/93, [1995] ECR I-563 *per* Advocate General Lenz at 581 (para. 40 of his Opinion).

[30] Para. 6 of the judgment.

[31] Para. 4 of the judgment.

[32] See *Hermès v. FHT*, Case C-53/96, [1998] ECR I-3603; *Dior v. Tuk Consultancy*, Cases C-300, 392/98, 14 December 2000, both discussed in Chap. 6.

[33] Case C-158/91, [1993] ECR I-4287. The case was a criminal prosecution against an employer for having employed twenty-three women on night work contrary to Art. L 213–1 of the French Labour Code. See also *R v. Secretary of State for the Home Department, ex parte Evans Medical* (*Generics* case), Case C-324/93, [1995] ECR I-563 (paras 27–30 of the judgment).

[34] Directive 76/207.

[35] ILO Convention No. 89, prohibiting night work for women.

[36] Art. 307 [234] EC.

[37] It was also necessary to consider whether the convention was repealed or modified by subsequent conventions between the same parties. This, too, had to be determined by the national court.

## ACTS OF INSTITUTIONS ESTABLISHED BY AGREEMENTS WITH NON-MEMBER STATES

The Association Agreement with Turkey provides for the setting up of a Council of Association, which has the power to adopt decisions. In *Sevince*,[38] the European Court held that it has jurisdiction to give preliminary rulings on the interpretation of such decisions: its argument appears to be that its jurisdiction to interpret agreements with non-Member States in some way extends to the acts of institutions set up by such agreements. This nicely illustrates the hollowness of the Court's reasoning: even if agreements with non-Member States were regarded as acts of an institution of the Community, how can acts of institutions set up by such agreements be acts of a Community institution?

## NATIONAL PROVISIONS BASED ON COMMUNITY LAW

It sometimes happens that a provision of national law refers to a provision of Community law or is in some way based on it. In such a case, Community law may, by reason of national law, apply beyond its intended scope. When the national court applies the national provision, it may, therefore, need to know the correct interpretation of the Community provision. Does the European Court have jurisdiction to interpret the Community provision in such a case?

An example is provided by the *Dzodzi* case,[39] which concerned a woman of Togolese nationality, Mrs Dzodzi, who married a Belgian citizen. Since the husband had never exercised his right under Community law to migrate to another Community country, Community law did not apply to the case and Mrs Dzodzi could claim no right under it to reside in Belgium. If, on the other hand, she had been married to a citizen of another Community country who had availed himself of his Community right to reside in Belgium, Community law would have given her the right to reside there.

It seems that the Belgians thought it wrong that the wife of a citizen of another Community country should have more rights in Belgium than the wife of a Belgian citizen; consequently, legislation was passed to extend to the wives of Belgian citizens the rights given by Community law to the wives of citizens of other Community countries. As a result, Mrs Dzodzi was, under Belgian law, entitled to reside in Belgium if, under Community law, she would have had such a right if she had been married to a citizen of another Community country. The Belgian court therefore asked the European Court, in a reference under Article 234 [177], whether she would have had a right of residence in Belgium if she had been married to a citizen of another Member State. The European Court decided that it had jurisdiction to interpret the relevant Community provisions in order to answer the question.[40]

[38] Case C-192/89, [1990] ECR I-3461. See also *Deutsche Shell*, Case C-188/91, [1993] ECR I-363, where the European Court held that it had jurisdiction to decide on the interpretation of 'arrangements' adopted by the Joint Committee set up under the Convention on a Common Transit Procedure, even though the 'arrangements' were not legally binding.

[39] *Dzodzi*, Cases C-297/88, 197/89, [1990] ECR I-3763.

[40] See also *Gmurzynska-Bscher*, Case C-231/89, [1990] ECR I-4003, in which rights under German tax law depended on provisions of the EC Common Customs Tariff. In both cases, Advocate General Darmon took the view that the European Court had no jurisdiction.

Similar rulings were given in a number of later cases,[41] but a different approach was adopted in *Kleinwort Benson v. City of Glasgow District Council*,[42] a reference by the English Court of Appeal. The case concerned a subsidiary convention, the Brussels Convention of 1968 on Jurisdiction and the Enforcement of Judgments in Civil and Commercial Matters, which laid down rules as to when a court in one Member State could take jurisdiction over a defendant domiciled in another. References to the European Court to interpret the Convention were governed by a Protocol of 3 June 1971, which was similar to Article 234 [177] EC.

The case concerned jurisdiction as between England and Scotland. Since this was internal to a Member State, it was not covered by the Convention. However, the British legislation which gave effect to the Convention, the Civil Jurisdiction and Judgments Act 1982, contained a slightly modified version (contained in Schedule 4) which applied as between different parts of the United Kingdom.[43] The provisions before the Court of Appeal were Article 5(1) and Article 5(3) of Schedule 4, the wording of which was substantially the same as the equivalent provisions in the Convention. Under section 16(3) of the Act, United Kingdom courts were obliged, when interpreting Schedule 4, to have regard to decisions of the European Court as to the meaning of the equivalent provisions of the Convention. The Court of Appeal, therefore, asked the European Court to give a ruling on the interpretation of Articles 5(1) and 5(3) of the Convention.

The European Court held that it had no jurisdiction to do this. The reason it gave was that the Convention did not apply *as such* to the facts of the case, since the national legislation had not made a direct and unconditional reference to it and United Kingdom courts were not absolutely bound by the European Court's rulings. This the Court regarded as unacceptable; so it refused to rule.[44]

In subsequent cases, in which the Community provision did apply as such, the Court has returned to its previous practice of giving a ruling.[45]

## WHICH COURTS ARE COVERED?

Article 234 [177] EC draws a distinction between courts which *may* make a reference and those which *must* do so: the former are covered by the second paragraph and the latter by the third.

[41] *Tomatis*, Case C-384/89, [1991] ECR I-127; *Federconsorzi*, Case C-88/91, [1992] ECR I-4035; *Fournier*, Case C-73/89, [1992] ECR I-5621. In *Federconsorzi*, the Community provision applied, not by virtue of national legislation, but by virtue of a contract, and in *Fournier*, the Court was asked to interpret a term of an agreement which reproduced the provisions of a directive. In both cases, the European Court nevertheless interpreted the provision in question.

[42] Case C-346/93, [1995] ECR I-615.

[43] Schedule 4 is printed in such a way that it is possible to tell at a glance where it differs from the Convention.

[44] The Court seems to be extremely sensitive about giving rulings which are not absolutely binding: see the first *EEA* case, Opinion 1/91, [1991] ECR I-6079 (para. 61 of the judgment).

[45] *Giloy*, Case C-130/95, [1997] ECR I-4291; *Leur-Bloem*, Case C-28/95, [1997] ECR I-4161. The Court did this despite a vigorous plea to the contrary by Advocate General Jacobs. See, further, *Adam*, Case C-267/99, [2001] ECR I-7467; *Kofisca Italia*, Case C-1/99, [2001] ECR I-207.

## POWER TO REFER

The second paragraph of Article 234 [177] EC states that 'any court or tribunal of a Member State' may request a ruling. This, therefore, lays down two requirements: the body making the request must be a court or tribunal and it must be 'of a Member State'.[46]

What are the essential characteristics of a court or tribunal? It is generally recognized that this is a question which must be decided by Community law: it is not decisive whether the body is recognized as a court under national law.[47] It does not matter what the body is called: according to the European Court, the important question is whether it performs judicial functions.[48] The concept of a 'judicial function' is notoriously difficult to pin down, but one would normally regard a body as being judicial if it had power to give binding determinations of legal rights and obligations. Thus, it should be established by law; it should be permanent; its jurisdiction should be compulsory; its procedure should be *inter partes* (though this is not always required[49]); it should apply rules of law; and it should be independent.[50]

The requirement of independence has given rise to seemingly conflicting decisions. The problem arises where an administrative body hears disputes between the citizen and the government. If the decision-making body is part of the relevant government department, it might be thought that it is not independent, especially if its members are appointed by the relevant minister and can be dismissed by him. In some cases, the European Court has held that such a body cannot make a reference: for example, it has held that if a tax-payer is in dispute with the revenue service, the director of that service cannot be make a reference, even if he has the power to hear appeals from decisions of subordinate officials.[51]

[46] The view has been put forward that a body may be entitled to make a reference even if it is not covered by the second paragraph of Art. 234 [177]. The argument is that the second paragraph of Art. 234 [177] is not an exhaustive statement of the power to refer: the first paragraph of Art. 234 [177] should, according to this view, be regarded as independently conferring a power to make a reference: see Mok, 'Should the "First Paragraph" of Art. 177 of the EEC Treaty be Read as a Separate Clause?' (1967–68) 5 CMLRev. 458, where this theory is considered but ultimately rejected. There seems little doubt in fact that the drafters of the Treaty intended that the second and third paragraphs should define the scope of the general principle laid down in the first: a body that is not a court or tribunal would not, therefore, be covered by Art. 234 [177].

[47] *Corbiau v. Administration des Contributions*, Case C-24/92, [1993] ECR I-1277 (para. 15 of the judgment); see also *per* Advocate General Gand in *Vaassen*, Case 61/65, [1966] ECR 261 at 281. It follows from this that the question whether a body is a court or tribunal for the purposes of Art. 234 [177] may itself be referred to the European Court, either by the body in question or by another body, for example a court hearing an appeal against the first body's decision to refer or not to refer.

[48] *Politi v. Italy*, Case 43/71, [1971] ECR 1039 at para. 5; *Simmenthal*, Case 70/77, [1978] ECR 1453 at para. 9.

[49] See *Job Centre*, Case C-111/94, [1995] ECR I-3361 (para. 9 of the judgment); *Corsica Ferries*, Case C-18/93, [1994] ECR I-1783 (at para. 12 of the judgment); *Birra Dreher v. Italian Finance Administration*, Case 162/73, [1974] ECR 201 (at paras 2 and 3 of the judgment); *Politi v. Italy*, Case 43/71, [1971] ECR 1039; and *Hoffmann-La Roche v. Centrafarm*, Case 107/76, [1977] ECR 957 at para. 4 of the judgment. In *Dorsch Consult*, Case C-54/96, [1997] ECR I-4961 the European Court said that an adversarial procedure is not an absolute requirement (para. 31 of the judgment).

[50] *Garofalo*, Cases C-69–79/96, [1997] ECR I-5603; *Dorsch Consult*, Case C-54/96, [1997] ECR I-4961. The latter judgment contains a detailed discussion of these requirements. See also *Gabalfrisa*, Cases C-110–147/98, [2000] ECR I-1577 (paras 33–41 of the judgment).

[51] *Corbiau v. Administration des Contributions*, Case C-24/92, [1993] ECR I-1277. See also *Criminal proceedings against X*, Cases C-74 and 129/95, [1996] ECR I-6609; *Almelo and Others*, Case C-393/92, [1994] ECR I-1477, para. 21.

In other cases, however, such a body *has* been allowed to make a reference.[52] The inconsistency of some of these decisions came under attack from Advocate General Colomer in *De Coster v. Collège des bourgmestre et échevins de Watermael-Boitsfort*,[53] who put forward a more structured and systematic approach based on the case law of the European Court of Human Rights.[54] His proposal was not followed by the Court, though since then the Court has seemed to place more emphasis on independence.[55]

In addition to this, one would normally expect to find a procedure under which the determination was made on the basis of evidence and legal argument. However, although courts are normally concerned with declaring the rights of parties, they do have discretionary powers and to that extent exercise functions which might not be regarded as strictly judicial. Moreover, courts also hear non-contentious proceedings and do not always operate under normal adversarial procedure: the European Court has, in fact, held that a reference can be made in *ex parte* and interlocutory proceedings.[56] On the other hand, one would not usually regard a body as judicial if its functions were purely advisory, investigatory, or conciliatory, nor if they were legislative or executive.[57] In addition to these requirements, the body should enjoy some measure of official recognition: it should in some sense be part of the state machinery.

In *Nederlandse Spoorwegen*,[58] the European Court had to decide whether a body whose decisions were in theory only advisory came within the terms of the second paragraph of Article 234 [177]. This was the Dutch *Raad van State* (Council of State) which is in effect the supreme administrative court in the Netherlands. In strict law, however, the application for review is made to the Crown, which is advised by the *Raad van State*. Like the Privy Council, the *Raad van State* has a judicial committee which functions as a court and operates according to normal judicial procedure. The European Court had no difficulty in accepting the *Raad van State* as a court for the purpose of Article 234 [177], thus showing that the reality of the matter is more important than the theory. This does not, however, mean that a body whose decisions were in fact, as well as in theory, only advisory could make references to the European Court.[59]

[52] *Gabalfrisa*, Cases C-110–147/98, [2000] ECR I-1577; *Köllensperger and Atzwanger*, Case C-103/97, [1999] ECR I-551; *Dorsch Consult*, Case C-54/96, [1997] ECR I-4961.

[53] Case C-17/00, [2001] ECR I-9445.

[54] See paras 11–118 of his Opinion.

[55] See *Schmid*, Case C-516/99, [2002] ECR I-4573.

[56] See *Politi v. Italy*, Case 43/71, [1971] ECR 1039; *Birra Dreher v. Italian Finance Administration*, Case 162/73, [1974] ECR 201.

[57] If the proceedings are non-contentious, a reference will normally be inadmissible: *Lutz GmbH*, Case C-182/00, [2002] ECR I-547; *HSB-Wohnbau GmbH*, Case C-86/00, [2001] ECR I-5353; *Salzmann*, Case C-178/99, [2001] ECR I-4421; *Victoria Film*, Case C-134/97, [1998] ECR I-7023; *Job Centre*, Case C-111/94, [1995] ECR I-3361.

[58] Case 36/73, [1973] ECR 1299. The jurisdictional problem was discussed by Advocate General Mayras at 1317–20. An interesting possibility raised by this case is whether the Parliamentary Commissioner for Administration in Britain could make a reference.

[59] However, in *Garofalo* (above), the European Court held that the Italian *Consiglio di Stato* (Council of State) is a court for this purpose, even when it is giving an opinion on an 'extraordinary petition'. Under this procedure, the final decision is that of the President of the Italian Republic. It seems that the opinion of the *Consiglio di Stato* is not absolutely binding; if the President departs from it, however, the matter must first be considered by the Council of Ministers. Moreover, the President must state the reasons why he did not follow the opinion.

The requirement of official authority has been considered by the European Court in several cases. The first is *Vaassen*,[60] which concerned a reference from a body in the Netherlands, officially described as an 'arbitration tribunal' (*scheidsgerecht*), which settled disputes regarding the pension fund for the mining industry. Although the pension scheme was set up privately by organizations representing employers and workers in the industry, it was approved both by the minister responsible for mining and the minister responsible for social security, the latter's approval being necessary for the purpose of obtaining exemption from the national social insurance scheme. This meant that any subsequent changes in the rules of the scheme also required ministerial approval. The members of the arbitration tribunal were appointed by the minister, and it operated according to adversarial procedure of the normal judicial type. By virtue of a regulation of the Council of the Mining Industry – a public body – all eligible persons were obliged to be members of the scheme, and any disputes concerning rights under the scheme had to be taken to the arbitration tribunal for decision. These features indicate that the *scheidsgerecht* was not really an arbitral body: as was pointed out by Advocate General Gand, it was 'a judicial body duly representing the power of the state, and settling as a matter of law disputes concerning the application of the insurance scheme'.[61] In these circumstances, it is hardly surprising that the European Court held that it was a court or tribunal within the meaning of Article 234 [177].

The *Broekmeulen* case[62] involved similar issues. It concerned a body in the Netherlands called the Appeals Committee for General Medicine. This body heard appeals from the General Practitioners Registration Committee, which registered GPs wishing to practise in the Netherlands. Both bodies were set up by the Royal Netherlands Society for the Promotion of Medicine. Though a private association of doctors, the Society had a large degree of control over the practice of medicine in the Netherlands and GPs were not recognized for the purposes of Dutch social security legislation unless they were registered with the society; so, from a practical point of view, it was impossible to practise without registration.

The Appeals Committee was constituted as follows: one-third of its members were appointed by the medical faculties of the Dutch universities, one-third by the Society, and one-third by the Dutch Government. It followed adversarial procedure and legal representation was allowed.[63] It was not, however, a court or tribunal under Dutch law; nevertheless the European Court held that it could make a reference under Article 234 [177].

Both these cases concerned bodies which enjoyed a significant degree of official recognition and to some extent carried out a public function. Where this is not the case, the situation will be different. Thus, the European Court has held that a private arbitrator, deriving his powers from an arbitration clause in a contract freely entered into by private parties, cannot make a reference under Article 234 [177], even though he is obliged to decide the case according to the law and his awards are enforceable through the judicial system.[64] It is also doubtful whether a purely domestic tribunal, operating

[60] Case 61/65, [1966] ECR 261. [61] At 282. [62] Case 246/80, [1981] ECR 2311.

[63] In some circumstances there might have been a right of appeal to the courts from its decisions, but no such appeal had ever been made.

[64] *Nordsee v. Reederei Mond*, Case 102/81, [1982] ECR 1095. The result of this ruling is that the only way in which a point of Community law raised in an arbitration can be referred to the European Court is through an

under the rules of a private association, could make a reference unless some measure of official recognition was accorded to it.

The second requirement of the second paragraph of Article 234 [177] is that the court or tribunal must be 'of a Member State', which suggests not only that the body should have official standing, but also that it should be *in* a Member State, or at least part of the judicial system of a Member State. This raises questions with regard to courts in dependencies of Member States. There can be little doubt that Article 234 [177] applies to the courts of territories to which the EC Treaty applies in full, even if such territories are not an integral part of any Member State.[65] It also applies to the courts of territories to which the general institutional provisions of the EC Treaty apply, even if other parts of the Treaty do not apply.[66] Thus the courts of the Isle of Man are covered.[67] Advocate General Jacobs has gone further and suggested that Article 234 [177] applies to the courts of territories to which any part of the EC Treaty applies, since such courts will need to obtain rulings from the European Court on those provisions.[68] It is likely that the Court will accept this, since it would otherwise be impossible to ensure the uniform interpretation and application of the Treaty, something to which the Court attaches great importance.[69]

Foreign (non-Community) courts are clearly excluded, even if they are parties to an association agreement with the Community, such as the Lomé Convention;[70] it is also doubtful whether international courts, such as the European Court of Human Rights, come within the terms of the provision, though some may take a different view. On the other hand, there is a ruling by the European Court that a court, such as the Benelux Court,[71] that is common to a number of Member States may make a reference when it has to decide a point of Community law.[72] Such a court could perhaps be regarded as a joint court of the Member States in question since certain points of law that would otherwise have been decided by their courts are decided by it.

Where a body has the right to make a reference under Community law, it cannot be deprived of that right by national law. This is illustrated by the *Rheinmühlen* cases,[73]

appeal to a court, which can then make the reference. For a case in which this occurred, see *Bulk Oil v. Sun International* [1984] 1 WLR 147, CA. On the duties under Community law of a national court in such a situation, see *Eco Swiss v. Benetton International*, Case C-126/97, [1999] ECR I-3055.

[65] See, e.g., territories to which the Treaty applies by virtue of Art. 299(4) [227(4)] EC.

[66] *Barr and Montrose Holdings*, Case C-355/89, [1991] ECR I-3479 (paras 6–10 of the judgment).

[67] *Ibid.* [68] *Ibid.* at 3493. [69] *Ibid.*, para. 9 of the judgment.

[70] See *per* Advocate General Mischo in *Kaefer and Procacci*, Cases C-100, 101/89, [1990] ECR I-4647 at 4658. In this case, the European Court held that the *Tribunal Administratif* of Papeete, French Polynesia, was covered by Art. 234 [177], since it was an integral part of the French judicial system.

[71] It was established under a Treaty of 1965 between Belgium, the Netherlands, and Luxembourg. It is composed of judges of the supreme courts of these three states. In certain cases, courts in the Benelux countries have to refer questions to it under a procedure similar to that for preliminary references to the European Court.

[72] *Parfums Christian Dior v. Evora*, Case C-337/95, [1997] ECR I-6013 (paras 15–31 of the judgment). What the European Court must have meant by this ruling is that, when they concluded the agreement setting up the Benelux Court, the Member States were obliged under the EC Treaty to require it to make references to the European Court on questions of Community law. If the point arose before it, the Benelux Court would have to interpret the agreement that created it in order to see whether, under *that* agreement, it did have such a power. It might well conclude that, since all the parties to the agreement were parties to the EC Treaty, they must have intended that their obligations under that Treaty would not be prejudiced by the agreement.

[73] Cases 166/73, [1974] ECR 33 and 146/73, [1974] ECR 139.

which concerned an attempt by a German cereal exporter to obtain an export rebate under Community law. The *Hessisches Finanzgericht* (Hessian Tax Court) ruled against Rheinmühlen, which then appealed to the highest German court in these matters, the *Bundesfinanzhof* (Federal Tax Court). The *Bundesfinanzhof* quashed the judgment and held that Rheinmühlen was entitled at least to a rebate at a lesser rate. The case was then sent back to the *Hessisches Finanzgericht* for a decision on certain questions of fact.

Under German law, the Hessian court was bound by rulings of the Federal court on points of law. The *Hessisches Finanzgericht* was not, however, prepared to accept the ruling in this case, as questions of Community law were involved. It therefore made a reference to the European Court for an interpretation of the relevant provision; it also asked the European Court for a ruling on the question whether it is permissible for a lower court to make a reference when the case has been sent back to it by a higher court after an earlier judgment has been set aside.

Rheinmühlen then appealed to the *Bundesfinanzhof* against the Hessian court's order referring the case to the European Court and the *Bundesfinanzhof* itself made a reference to the European Court: it asked whether Article 234 [177] gives lower courts an unfettered right to refer, or whether it is subject to national provisions under which lower courts are bound by the judgments of superior courts. This was of course substantially the same as the second question referred by the Hessian court.

The European Court held that the power of a lower court to make a reference cannot be abrogated by a provision of national law: it stated that the lower court must be free to make a reference if it considers that the superior court's ruling could lead it to give judgment contrary to Community law. This means that national rules of *res judicata* do not apply to Community law. On all questions of Community law, including the question of supremacy, the European Court must be the final authority.

It is interesting to note that the Advocate General, Mr Warner, went even further: he suggested that there ought not even to be a right of appeal against an order for reference. In his view, such a right of appeal itself fettered the power of the lower court to make a reference. On this point, however, the European Court did not follow him. The position is, therefore, that national law cannot take away the right given in the second paragraph of Article 234 [177], but this does not prevent the lower court's order for reference from being quashed on appeal. The consequences of this are considered below.

## OBLIGATION TO REFER

The third paragraph of Article 234 [177] EC provides that a court or tribunal of a Member State 'against whose decisions there is no judicial remedy under national law' *must* make a reference. Two points of view exist as to the meaning of this phrase: according to the 'abstract theory', the only courts within the scope of the provision are those whose decisions are *as a general rule* not subject to appeal; according to the 'concrete theory', on the other hand, the important question is whether the court's decision *in the case in question* is subject to appeal. This distinction can be important where, for example, there is a right of appeal only if the sum of money in issue is more than a certain amount.

The wording of the third paragraph of Article 234 [177] itself favours the abstract theory: if the authors of the Treaty had intended the decisive point to be whether there was a right of appeal in the particular case in question, they would not have put the word 'decisions' into the plural. The use of the plural suggests that the general position regarding appeals is the criterion. Another argument may be derived from considerations of legal policy: the reason rights of appeal are limited in certain cases is to prevent proceedings from becoming too drawn out and to keep costs within reasonable bounds. These objectives would be jeopardized if national courts were obliged to make a reference to Luxembourg even where the sum in issue was small or the case was generally of limited importance.

The policy of Community law, on the other hand, places great importance on maintaining uniformity of interpretation of Community provisions: this could be undermined if it were possible for a case involving Community law to run its course without a reference being made. Some of the most important judgments of the European Court have in fact been handed down in cases involving very small sums of money.[74]

There is an *obiter dictum* of the European Court supporting the concrete theory: this was in *Costa v. ENEL*,[75] a reference from a *giudice conciliatore* (magistrate) in Italy. Although the decisions of a *giudice conciliatore* are appealable in some cases, there was no right of appeal against the decision in the proceedings in question because the sum of money involved was so small. In the course of its judgment, the European Court said, with reference to Article 234 [177]:[76] 'By the terms of this Article, however, national courts against whose decisions, *as in the present case*, there is no judicial remedy, must refer the matter to the Court of Justice.' This suggests that the European Court considered that the third paragraph of Article 234 [177] refers to the highest court in the case, rather than the highest court in the country.

On the other hand, the European Court's ruling in *Parfums Christian Dior v. Evora*[77] (discussed below) makes sense only if the abstract theory is correct. According to this judgment, the highest court of a Member State is obliged to refer questions of Community law to the European Court even if, in the particular case before it, it is required under national law to refer the same point to an international court, such as the Benelux Court (which, the European Court ruled, is also bound by the third paragraph of Article 234 [177]).[78] In such a situation, the highest court in the Member State is not the highest court in the case; so this judgment presupposes that the abstract theory is correct. However, since the case was not argued in these terms, it would be dangerous to place too much weight on this inference.[79]

Special difficulties arise with regard to the English Court of Appeal. If the abstract theory is correct, it is never bound to refer; but what if the concrete theory is correct?

[74] In *Costa v. ENEL* (below), for example, the sum in dispute was less than £2.

[75] Case 6/64, [1964] ECR 585.

[76] At 592 (emphasis added).

[77] Case C-337/95, [1997] ECR I-6013.

[78] The European Court did, however, say that neither court was obliged to refer a point if the same point had already been referred by the other.

[79] See, further, *per* Advocate General Capotorti in *Hoffmann-La Roche v. Centrafarm*, Case 107/76, [1977] ECR 957 at 979–80.

Decisions of the Court of Appeal may be taken on appeal to the House of Lords only if the leave of either the Court of Appeal or the House of Lords is obtained. Clearly, if the Court of Appeal is prepared to grant leave to appeal in a particular case, it would not be under an obligation to make a reference to the European Court: it would, on any theory, be outside the third paragraph of Article 234 [177]. But what if it refuses leave to appeal?

Assuming that the concrete theory is correct, there are two possible solutions: on the one hand, it could be argued that, if a reference is appropriate and the Court of Appeal does not make it, it *must* grant leave to appeal to the House of Lords.[80] If it does not, it would be in breach of the third paragraph of Article 234 [177]. On the other hand, the position could be saved if the House of Lords itself granted leave. In other words, if the Court of Appeal does not make a reference and refuses leave, the House of Lords would be obliged – if the concrete theory is correct – to grant leave to appeal.[81]

The decision of the European Court in *Lyckeskog*,[82] a reference from a court of appeal in Sweden, answers these questions. In Sweden, there is a right of appeal from a court of appeal to the Supreme Court (*Högsta Domstolen*) only if the latter gives leave. The European Court held that a Swedish court of appeal is never obliged to make a reference: it seems that the right to petition the Supreme Court for leave is itself a judicial remedy. However, the Supreme Court must make a reference, either when considering whether to grant leave or (if it grants leave) when deciding the appeal. This implies that the English Court of Appeal is not obliged to make a reference, but the House of Lords must do so, either when hearing the petition for leave to appeal[83] or when hearing the appeal.

Up to now it has been assumed that the question is simply one of appeal; but it will be remembered that the phrase in the Treaty is 'judicial remedy'. This clearly does not cover a non-judicial remedy, such as the prerogative of mercy, but would it cover judicial review? If the decision of a tribunal, though not subject to appeal, may be quashed in proceedings for judicial review, this should be regarded as constituting a 'judicial remedy'?[84]

What is the position where the judgment may be reconsidered in other proceedings? This occurs if an interim order is given in interlocutory proceedings: the order may not be subject to appeal in the interlocutory proceedings, but will be subject to review in the main action.

The point arose in *Hoffmann-La Roche v. Centrafarm*,[85] in which the plaintiff had applied to the German courts for an interim order to prohibit the defendant from

[80] See Jacobs and Durand, *References to the European Court* (1975), p. 163; and Jacobs, 'Which Courts and Tribunals are Bound to Refer to the European Court?' (1977) 2 ELRev. 119 at 121.

[81] See Jacobs (1977) 2 ELRev. 119 at 121.

[82] Case C-99/00, [2002] ECR I-4839; [2003] 1 WLR 9.

[83] It might be objected that, when the appellants are petitioning for leave to appeal, the case is not 'pending' before the House of Lords, as required by the third paragraph of Article 234 [177]. Perhaps, however, the 'case' is not the appeal itself but the application for leave to appeal: this certainly would be pending before the House of Lords. Since the House of Lords would grant leave if it considered that the Community point had been wrongly decided by the Court of Appeal, the decision to grant leave would depend on the point of Community law.

[84] *Re a Holiday in Italy* [1975] 1 CMLR 184. See also *R v. National Insurance Commissioner, ex parte Warry*, Case 41/77, [1977] ECR 2085. For a detailed discussion of this question, see Jacobs, 'Which Courts and Tribunals Are Bound to Refer to the European Court?' (1977) 2 ELRev. 119.

[85] Case 107/76, [1977] ECR 957. For an enlightening comment, see Jacobs (1977) 2 ELRev. 354.

marketing pharmaceutical products with a particular trade mark. Centrafarm maintained that it had a right under Community law to market the products, but the court of first instance granted the order. On appeal, Centrafarm asked the *Oberlandesgericht* Karlsruhe to refer the relevant provisions of Community law to the European Court. The *Oberlandesgericht* was apparently unwilling to make the reference unless it was obliged to do so; it therefore referred three questions to the European Court: the first concerned the interpretation of the third paragraph of Article 234 [177] itself and was aimed at discovering whether it applied in interlocutory proceedings; the other two related to the substantive issues in the case, but the *Oberlandesgericht* stated that these were to be answered only if the ruling on the first question meant that a reference was obligatory. This rather unusual procedure could have caused the European Court some embarrassment; however, it dealt with the matter by confining the proceedings in the first instance to the question relating to Article 234 [177], the other two questions being left over for later consideration.

The judgment of the *Oberlandesgericht* was not subject to appeal within the context of the interlocutory proceedings, but was subject to review in the main proceedings. In other words, any ruling on a point of Community law made by the *Oberlandesgericht* could be challenged subsequently in the main proceedings. Under German law, the defendant could, moreover, compel the plaintiff to institute the main action. In view of this, it was fair to say that the judgment of the *Oberlandesgericht* was not final, except in a temporary sense.

The European Court began its judgment by expressly affirming that interlocutory proceedings are covered by the second paragraph of Article 234 [177]: the summary and urgent character of these proceedings does not deprive the court of the *power* to make a reference. This is clear enough (though it had been doubted by the German court); but what about the third paragraph of Article 234 [177]: does the possibility of review in the main action constitute a 'judicial remedy'?

In deciding this question, the Court started from the premise that the function of the third paragraph of Article 234 [177] 'is to prevent a body of national case law not in accord with the rules of Community law from coming into existence in any Member State'. This suggests that the important thing is that, *at some stage in the course of the national proceedings*, there should be an obligation to refer. In accordance with this, the Court therefore held that there is no obligation to make a reference in interlocutory proceedings for an interim order, even if there is no appeal against that decision in the context of those proceedings, provided the decision is subject to review in subsequent proceedings which may be instituted by, or at the request of, either party.

This last point is, of course, crucial: if the ruling cannot be reconsidered in the main proceedings, or if each party is not given the right to insist that those proceedings take place, the judgment in the interlocutory proceedings will not be subject to a 'judicial remedy'. It is of course true that in practice interlocutory orders are often allowed to stand. But this is because the losing party does not consider it worthwhile to contest the order further. The same thing happens in ordinary proceedings: a court gives a judgment which is subject to appeal, but the unsuccessful party decides not to appeal. In both cases, however, the party against whom judgment is given has the right to take the matter further.

What is the position where there is a remedy in an international court? This point arose in *Parfums Christian Dior v. Evora*[86] (discussed above). The case was referred to the European Court by the *Hoge Raad*, the highest court in the Netherlands, which wanted to know whether the highest court in a Member State is still obliged to refer questions to the European Court if it is also obliged to refer the same question to a court such as the Benelux Court. The European Court answered this by saying that *both* courts were obliged to refer questions of Community law to it. Since there is no appeal from the judgments of the Benelux Court, and those judgments are binding on the courts of the Benelux countries, it falls under the third paragraph of Article 234 [177] EC and is, therefore, obliged to refer. However, the European Court went on to hold that since the *Hoge Raad* is the highest court in the Netherlands, it is also covered by the third paragraph of Article 234 [177]. It seems, therefore, that a judicial remedy to a court outside the Member State in question does not absolve the highest court in that Member State from the obligation to refer.

### PRELIMINARY RULINGS ON VALIDITY

Under Article 41 of the ECSC Treaty (now expired), it was provided that the European Court had *exclusive* jurisdiction to rule on the validity of an act of the Commission or Council. This means that no national court could declare an ECSC act invalid. There is no equivalent provision under the EC or Euratom Treaties, but the European Court has achieved the same result by judicial decision. This was in the *Foto-Frost*[87] case, where it said that, while national courts may declare a Community act valid, they have no power to declare it invalid.[88] The decision was justified on the basis of policy considerations, the desirability of safeguarding the uniform application of Community law being the most important.[89]

## HYPOTHETICAL QUESTIONS AND CONTRIVED PROCEEDINGS

The European Court has no jurisdiction to give rulings on hypothetical questions, even if the reference comes from a court or tribunal. The issues referred to the Court must be in controversy in judicial proceedings. For this to be the case, three conditions should be fulfilled: there must be a dispute; that dispute must be the subject of proceedings before a body which has the power to resolve it in a legally binding way; and the questions put to the European Court must be in issue in those proceedings.

[86] Case C-337/95, [1997] ECR I-6013. [87] Case 314/85, [1987] ECR 4199.

[88] The case was decided under Art. 234 [177] EC, but the ruling would also apply to the Euratom Treaty.

[89] It is interesting to note that some years ago the European Court proposed that the Treaties should be amended to incorporate such a rule: see *Suggestions of the Court of Justice on European Union*, EC Bull., Supp. 9/75, p.17 at p. 21. This proposal was not put into effect, and the Court apparently decided to take the necessary action itself.

In the *Borker*[90] case, a member of the Paris Bar had been refused permission by a German court to appear before it. He considered that this was contrary to Community law and complained to the Paris Bar Council, which made a reference to the European Court. Since the Paris Bar Council has no jurisdiction to decide who can appear before a German court, the proceedings before it could not lead to a 'decision of a judicial nature'. The European Court therefore ruled that it could not accept the reference.[91]

The question of the nature of the proceedings sometimes also involves that of the appropriate point at which to make the reference, since the nature of the proceedings may undergo a change at a certain point – for example, from investigatory (administrative) to judicial. This can happen in criminal proceedings, where one might regard the judicial phase as commencing when a suspect is arrested, or perhaps when he is charged.

These issues arose in an Italian case known, revealingly, as *Pretore di Salò v. Persons Unknown.*[92] The proceedings began when Italian anglers, concerned at the high level of pollution in a river, complained to the local *Pretore*, who instituted criminal proceedings under Italian anti-pollution legislation against a person or persons unknown. (According to the European Court, a *Pretore* is a judge who combines the duties of public prosecutor and investigating judge.) The *Pretore* made a reference to the European Court on the interpretation of a directive that was relevant to the case.

Since no one had so far been charged, it could have been (and was) argued that the reference was premature: the proceedings had not yet assumed a judicial character. The European Court, however, accepted the reference, saying that it is for the national court to decide when the reference should be made.[93]

The most controversial case on this issue is *Foglia v. Novello.*[94] This was a reference by an Italian court in an action between two Italians who had entered into a contract of sale requiring delivery of the goods in France. The contract provided that the buyer would not be responsible for the payment of any taxes imposed in contravention of Community law. The goods were duly delivered. The seller was required to pay a consumption tax in France and claimed reimbursement from the buyer. The latter refused on the ground that the tax was contrary to Community law. Thus the Italian courts were required to decide whether the French tax was in accordance with Community law.

There were in fact grounds for believing that the whole transaction was contrived in order to raise a test case. For this reason, the European Court refused to accept the

[90] Case 138/80, [1980] ECR 1975. See also *Victoria Film*, Case C-134/97, [1998] ECR I-7023; *Job Centre*, Case C-111/94, [1995] ECR I-3361; *Greis Unterweger*, Case 318/85, [1985] ECR 955.

[91] The position would have been different if the Paris Bar Council had been dealing with a matter over which it did have jurisdiction. The right to appear before the Paris courts may well be such an issue.

[92] Case 14/86, [1987] ECR 2545. See also *Pretore of Cento v. A Person or Persons Unknown*, Case 110/76, [1977] ECR 851.

[93] This was in spite of the fact that, as the European Court recognized, some of the *Pretore*'s duties were not of a strictly judicial nature.

[94] Case 104/79, [1980] ECR 745. See also the earlier case of *Mattheus v. Doego*, Case 93/78, [1978] ECR 2203, where the parties to a private contract tried to make the European Court give a ruling on the admission of Spain and Portugal to the Community.

reference, stating that there was no genuine dispute between the parties. The Italian court, which had to give judgment in the case, was unwilling to accept this and made a second reference; but the European Court remained adamant.[95]

This ruling could be criticized because, whatever the motives of the parties, the Italian court was faced with what, on the surface at least, was a genuine dispute. Moreover, the bringing of a test case is a recognized device for obtaining a ruling on a disputed question of law. For these reasons, the European Court has accepted references in several later cases, even though the proceedings appear to have been contrived specifically for the purpose of obtaining a ruling.[96]

In between the two rulings in *Foglia v. Novello*, two other references were made to the European Court by courts in Italy. In both these cases, *Chemial v. DAF*[97] and *Vinal v. Orbat*,[98] the facts were similar to those in *Foglia v. Novello*, except that the disputed tax was Italian, not French. In the first case, the Advocate General (Mr Mayras) regarded the case as covered by the decision in *Foglia v. Novello (No. 1)*, and urged the Court to refuse to give a ruling. In *Vinal v. Orbat*, however, a different Advocate General (Mr Reischl) said that the Court should accept the reference, first, because the action was not *manifestly* bogus and, secondly, because it was an *Italian* tax that was in issue. In both the cases, the Court accepted the reference, thus suggesting that it agreed with Advocate General Reischl's opinion. In fact it seems likely that the real reason for its decision in *Foglia v. Novello* was one of policy: it did not wish to offend France by allowing the lawfulness of its taxes to be challenged by such roundabout means, rather than by the more normal route of an enforcement action under Article 226 [169] EC.[99] This view is supported by the fact that in *Foglia v. Novello (No. 2)* the Court said that special vigilance was required where the legislation of one Member State is subject to challenge in the courts of another Member State.[100]

Even if there is a genuine dispute, and genuinely judicial proceedings, the European Court may be asked to rule on questions which, though they are of great general interest, are not actually relevant to those proceedings. This may occur either because one of the parties manipulates the procedure in order to obtain a ruling on some general issue or because the national court wants to obtain a general clarification of the law. Since the early 1990s, the European Court has often refused to answer such questions.[101] It will

[95] Case 244/80, [1981] ECR 3045.

[96] See, for example, *Mangold*, Case C-144/04, 25 November 2005; *PreussenElektra*, Case C-379/98, [2001] ECR I-2099. The *Mangold* case was discussed in Chap. 7.

[97] Case 140/79, [1981] ECR 1.

[98] Case 46/80, [1981] ECR 77.

[99] Or by means of a reference from a *French* court.

[100] Para. 30 of the judgment in Case 244/80; see, however, Anderson, 'The Admissibility of Preliminary References' [1994] YEL 179 at 194–5, where it is pointed out that there are other cases in which the European Court has accepted a reference in such circumstances.

[101] See *Meilicke*, Case C-83/91, [1992] ECR I-4871; *Dias*, Case C-343/90, [1992] ECR I-4673. The judgment in the first of these cases was given by the Full Court, and that in the second by the Fifth Chamber; yet identical words were used in both cases to explain the Court's position, thus sending a clear signal to national courts (compare paras 21–5 of the judgment in the *Meilicke* case with paras 13–17 of the judgment in the *Dias* case). See also *Legros*, Case C-163/90, [1992] ECR I-4625, in which (despite the contrary view of the Advocate General) the Court refused to rule on a matter of great general importance, which was not strictly relevant to the issue before the national court, but which had been fully argued in the proceedings before the European Court.

also refuse to give a ruling if the referring court fails to provide it with sufficient information regarding the factual and legal background of the case.[102] Such information is needed by the Court to give an appropriate interpretation; it is also necessary to enable it to ascertain whether the question is genuinely relevant to the proceedings.[103]

## WHEN SHOULD A REFERENCE BE MADE?

Two separate, but related, questions must now be considered. First of all, in what circumstances does the power, or obligation, to refer come into existence? Secondly, where the court has the power to refer, but is not obliged to do so, how should it exercise its discretion? The first question concerns the law; the second relates to judicial policy.[104]

### THE LAW

The first paragraph of Article 234 [177] states which questions may be referred to the European Court; this has already been discussed. The second paragraph then provides that where 'such a question' is raised, the court may make a reference 'if it considers that a decision on the question is necessary to enable it to give judgment'. Here the phrase 'such a question' refers back to the first paragraph and means those questions of Community law covered by that provision. Consequently, there are two requisites which must be fulfilled before the second paragraph comes into operation: an appropriate question of Community law must be *raised* before the court; and a decision on that question must be *necessary* to enable it to give judgment.

At first sight it appears that, under the third paragraph of Article 234 [177], only the first requisite need be met: the third paragraph states merely that where 'any such question is raised', the court must refer the matter to the European Court. Here the phrase 'any such question' could be read as meaning the same thing as 'such a question' in the second paragraph and therefore referring back to the first paragraph. However, it would be absurd if a court were obliged to refer a question which was quite irrelevant to the proceedings; therefore, 'any such question' must refer back to the second paragraph and mean any question which falls within that provision, i.e., a question of Community law

[102] *Telemarsicabruzzo v. Circostel*, Cases C-320–2/90, [1993] ECR I-393; *Pretore di Genova v. Banchero*, Case C-157/92, [1993] ECR I-1085. Both these rulings were given by a Full Court (thirteen judges). See also *Laguillaumie*, Case C-116/00, [2000] ECR I-4979; *Lehtonen and Castors Braine*, Case C-176/96, [2000] ECR I-2681.

[103] For a general discussion of these questions, see Kennedy, 'First Steps towards a European Certiorari?' (1993) 18 ELRev. 121; Anderson, 'The Admissibility of Preliminary References' [1994] YEL 179; Barnard and Sharpston, 'The Changing Face of Article 177 References' (1997) 34 CMLRev. 1113, especially at 1127–57. For a full list of cases in which the new policy has been applied, see Barnard and Sharpston, 1126, n. 67. For criticism of the European Court, see O'Keeffe, 'Is the Spirit of Article 177 under Attack? Preliminary References and Admissibility' (1998) 23 ELRev. 509. For more recent developments, see Tridimas, 'Knocking on Heaven's Door: Fragmentation, Efficiency and Defiance in the Preliminary Reference Procedure' (2003) 40 CMLRev. 9 at pp. 21–6.

[104] On both these questions, see Jacobs, 'When to Refer to the European Court' (1974) 90 LQR 486.

on which a decision is necessary to enable the court to give judgment.[105] It follows from this that the same two requisites apply under the third paragraph.

What is the meaning of these two requisites? The first could suggest that a reference cannot be made unless one or other of the parties has raised a point of Community law: the phrase 'raised *before* any court' could be read as precluding the court itself from raising the point of its own motion. This, however, seems an unduly restrictive interpretation and has been rejected by the European Court, which has ruled that a reference may be made by the national court of its own motion.[106]

The second requisite is that the national court must consider that a decision on the question is necessary to enable it to give judgment. Two points should be noted at the outset: it is not a *reference* to the European Court which must be necessary, but a *decision* on the question; secondly, the Treaty makes clear that this is a question for the national court to decide and, unless Community law is clearly inapplicable to the case[107] or the questions asked are clearly irrelevant to the issues before the national court,[108] the European Court will not question whether the reference is necessary.

When is a decision necessary in order to give judgment? Clearly, the outcome of the case must be dependent on the decision: as Lord Denning has said,[109] if the Community point is decided in one way, judgment for one party must result; if it is decided in another way, judgment must be given for the other party. This does not, however, mean that everything must hinge on the Community point: it would be sufficient if the final judgment were in any way different, even if it were a question only of the measure of damages or terms of the order. If, on the other hand, the judgment would be exactly the same however the Community point was decided, a decision on it would not be necessary for the judgment.

What if the Community point would be conclusive only in certain circumstances? Two examples may be given of such a situation. Assume that one party bases his case exclusively on a provision of Community law, but that provision would be applicable only if certain contested facts are established. Before those facts have been established, the court cannot be certain whether a decision on the Community point is necessary or not: if the facts cannot be established, the outcome of the case would be the same irrespective of how the Community point was decided. Until evidence has been heard, therefore, the Community point is only potentially decisive.

The second example is a case where one party puts forward two quite separate grounds, each of which, if established, would make good his claim. If one ground is based on Community law and one on national law, the court cannot tell whether the Community point is decisive until it has decided the other point: if the party can win on that, it would not matter which way the Community point was decided; only if the national point goes against him, would the Community point become decisive.

[105] See *Bulmer v. Bollinger* [1974] Ch 401 at 421; [1974] 3 WLR 202 at 211–12; [1974] 2 All ER 1226, at 1234, *per* Lord Denning MR, and the decision of the Dutch *Hoge Raad* (the highest civil court in the Netherlands) in the *Reinvoorde* case, 7 April 1970, [1973] CMLR 175 (para. 20).

[106] *Salonia*, Case 126/80, [1981] ECR 1563 (para. 7 of the judgment); see also CPR 68.2(1)(a).

[107] See *Rijksdienst voor Werknemerspensioenen v. Vlaeminck*, Case 132/81, [1982] ECR 2953.

[108] *Meilicke*, Case C-83/91, [1992] ECR I-4871; *Dias*, Case C-343/90, [1992] ECR I-4673.

[109] In *Bulmer v. Bollinger* [1974] Ch 401 at 422; [1974] 3 WLR 202 at 212; [1974] 2 All ER 1226 at 1234; but see *Foglia v. Novello*, discussed above.

The problem in both these situations is that, until the other matters have been decided, the Community point would dispose of the case only if it was decided in one particular way. In the first example, it would dispose of the case if it were decided against the person relying on Community law: in such a case, he would lose even if he succeeded in establishing his contentions of fact. In the second example, on the other hand, the Community point would dispose of the case only if it were decided in favour of the person relying on it: he would then win even if the other point went against him.

What should a court do in such a situation? It could be argued that the court cannot make a reference until the other matters have been decided: unless it does this, it cannot be certain that a decision on the Community point is really necessary.[110] This, however, is too restrictive an interpretation.[111] From a practical point of view, it might be much better in some cases to decide the Community point first. If it is fairly simple, but the other matters are complex, it could be less expensive and more expeditious to make an immediate reference to the European Court. It is suggested, therefore, that 'necessary' should be interpreted to mean that the point *could* be decisive. In other words, it should be sufficient if a decision on the point is potentially decisive: it should not have to be proved that it would be decisive in all possible eventualities. If this interpretation is accepted, the national court would then be able to decide for itself when to make the reference.[112]

What is the position where the point has already been decided by the European Court in a previous case? The European Court has ruled that in such a case the national court is not obliged to make a reference even if it is a court against whose decisions there is no judicial remedy under national law.[113] In such a situation the point can be regarded as settled and the case would be exempted from the third paragraph of Article 234 [177]: according to the European Court, the authority of the previous ruling would deprive the obligation under the third paragraph of Article 234 [177] of its purpose 'and thus empty it of its substance'.[114] However, the European Court is not bound by its own previous decisions, and if the national court thought that the previous judgment was wrong and wanted the European Court to reconsider the matter, it would be entitled to make the reference.[115] The existence of a previous ruling, therefore, removes the obligation to refer, but does not affect the power to refer.

Some lawyers push this argument further and apply the same rule where the Community provision is regarded as clear, even if the European Court has not ruled on it. This is the so-called '*acte clair*' doctrine, according to which a clear provision (*acte clair*) does not require 'interpretation' and therefore falls entirely outside the scope of Article 234 [177] as a whole. If there is no doubt as to the meaning of the provision, it is

110 *Per* Lord Denning MR in *Bulmer v. Bollinger* [1974] Ch 401 at 423; [1974] 3 WLR 202 at 213; [1974] 2 All ER 1226 at 1235. In Lord Denning's view, the court should decide the facts before making the reference.

111 Lord Denning's view to the contrary (above) has been subject to widespread criticism and was not in *R v. Plymouth Justices, ex parte Rogers* [1982] 3 WLR 1; [1982] 2 All ER 175; [1982] 3 CMLR 221; see also *Polydor v. Harlequin Record Shops* [1980] 2 CMLR 413, CA.

112 As far as the English High Court is concerned, it is expressly stated in CPR 68.2(1)(a) that the order may be made at any stage in the proceedings.

113 *Da Costa*, Cases 28–30/62, [1963] ECR 31 at 38; *CILFIT*, Case 283/81, [1982] ECR 3415 (paras 13–15).

114 *Da Costa*, (above). 115 *Ibid.*

argued, there can be no 'question' on which a decision is necessary: all the court has to do is to apply the provision.

This doctrine has something to recommend it from a common-sense point of view and has attracted the support of some eminent jurists.[116] However, it is a well-known fact that what is clear to one set of lawyers can be extremely doubtful to another set of lawyers. This is especially true where the two groups belong to different legal traditions or look at the law from different points of view. In the case of Community law in particular, the policy-oriented approach of the European Court can produce very different results from the more traditional methods of an English judge.

This controversy is important only with regard to the third paragraph of Article 234 [177]: since a lower court is not in any case obliged to make a reference, it would be entitled to refrain from doing so on the ground that the provision is sufficiently clear. In the case of a court against whose decisions there is no judicial remedy, however, the question is crucial: is such a court exempted from the obligation to refer if it considers that the provision does not require interpretation?

In spite of its dangers, the *acte clair* doctrine has been fairly widely accepted by national courts in the Community,[117] and in 1982 it gained the approval of the European Court, though this approval was subject to so many conditions that one might think the Court was really trying to kill the idea.[118] The case in question was *CILFIT*,[119] where the European Court said that even a court covered by the third paragraph of Article 234 [177] is not obliged to make a reference where the answer is 'so obvious as to leave no scope for any reasonable doubt'.[120] It qualified this, however, by saying that the national court must be convinced that the answer would be equally obvious to a court in another Member State and to the European Court. In deciding whether the answer is obvious, the national court must compare the different versions of the text in the various Community languages. It must also bear in mind that legal concepts and terminology do not necessarily have the same meaning in Community law as in national law. The European Court concluded by saying that 'every provision of Community law must be placed in its context and interpreted in the light of the provisions of Community law as a whole, regard being had to the objectives thereof and to its state of evolution at the date on which the provision in question is to be applied'.[121] Put more simply, the national court must remember the European Court's habit of giving great weight to policy.

[116] See, e.g., Lagrange, 'The Theory of the *Acte Clair*: A Bone of Contention or a Source of Unity?' (1971) 8 CMLRev. 313.

[117] The Commission has also expressed its acceptance of the doctrine: see European Parliament, Question 608/78, 31 January 1979, OJ 1979, C28/9. Lord Denning gave the doctrine his approval in *Bulmer v. Bollinger* [1974] Ch 401 at 423; [1974] 3 WLR 202 at 213; [1974] 2 All ER 1226 at 1235, and it was applied in *SA Magnavision NV v. General Optical Council (No. 1)* [1987] 1 CMLR 887 and *(No. 2)* [1987] 2 CMLR 262; see also *R v. Secretary of State for Social Services, ex parte Bomore Medical Supplies* [1986] 1 CMLR 228, CA. However, in *R v. Henn* [1980] 2 WLR 597 at 636–7; [1980] 2 All ER 166 at 196–7, the House of Lords went no further than to say that a reference need not be made where the point is covered by an 'established body of case law' of the European Court. It also stressed the pitfalls of applying English canons of statutory interpretation to Community law.

[118] See Rasmussen, 'The European Court's *Acte Clair* Strategy in *CILFIT*' (1984) 9 ELRev. 242.

[119] Case 283/81, [1982] ECR 3415.

[120] At para. 16 of the judgment.

[121] Para. 20 of the judgment.

It is not hard to see that full compliance with these requirements is virtually impossible. In particular, the obligation to compare the text in its different linguistic versions could cause great difficulties. In the absence of expert evidence, an English court could not compare, for example, the Greek and Danish texts. The importance of this is, however, beyond doubt since it can often happen that a text which appears straightforward in one language may be ambiguous (or mean something different) in another. An example in point is *Koschniske*,[122] in which a Dutch social security tribunal had to interpret a Community regulation which contained, in the Dutch text, the word '*echtgenote*'. The English version of the regulation uses the word 'spouse' and all the other texts use a word which can apply to both a husband or a wife; the Dutch word, however, can apply only to a woman: it means 'wife'. (The masculine form is '*echtgenoot*'.) The question before the Dutch tribunal was whether the term could cover a husband. On the basis of the Dutch text alone, it might have seemed clear that it could not. Fortunately, the tribunal made a reference to the European Court which ruled, after considering all the versions of the provision, that it covered both a husband and a wife. If the tribunal had interpreted the provision for itself without considering the other versions of the text, it would have made a serious mistake.

## DISCRETION

A court has a discretion only if its decisions are subject to an appeal or other judicial remedy. Assuming this to be the case, how should the discretion be exercised?[123] This is, of course, a question for the national courts themselves, but among the factors which they may wish to take into consideration are the following. Should the facts be decided first? In many cases this will be desirable,[124] but in some it may be better to obtain a ruling from the European Court right at the outset: until that has been obtained, it might not be clear what facts *are* relevant.

Referring a case to Luxembourg will involve a considerable delay in the proceedings. In some cases a lower court might feel that the time factor is so important that it would be justified in deciding the point itself. However, if the case is taken on appeal, a reference may well be made in the end and the result might be that a final judgment takes even longer to obtain. In some interlocutory cases – for example, an application for an injunction pending trial – the best course might be for the court to grant the order and at the same time make the reference. This will protect the plaintiff's position while the Luxembourg proceedings are taking place.

[122] Case 9/79, [1979] ECR 2717.

[123] For a general discussion, see *Bulmer v. Bollinger* [1974] Ch 401 at 423–4; [1974] 3 WLR 202 at 213–15; [1974] 2 All E.R. 1226 at 1235–6, CA; *Church of Scientology of California v. Customs and Excise Commissioners* [1981] 1 All ER 1035, CA; *R v. Plymouth Justices, ex parte Rogers* [1982] 3 WLR 1; [1982] 2 All ER 175; [1982] 3 CMLR 221; *Customs and Excise Commissioners v. Samex* [1983] 1 All ER 1042; [1983] 3 CMLR 194; *R v. International Stock Exchange, ex parte Else* [1993] QB 534; [1993] 2 WLR 70; [1993] 1 All ER 420, CA; see also Jacobs, 'When to Refer to the European Court' (1974) 90 LQR 486. In *R v. Henn* [1980] 2 WLR 597 at 635; [1980] 2 All ER 166 at 196, the House of Lords said that in a criminal trial on indictment it will rarely be proper for the trial court to make a reference.

[124] See *Irish Creamery Milk Suppliers Association v. Ireland*, Cases 36, 71/80, [1981] ECR 735, where, however, the European Court stressed that it was for the national court to decide when to make the reference. See also the English cases cited in the previous note.

The difficulty and importance of the point, as well as the expense of a reference in comparison to the amount at stake, will also be considered, though there have been cases where points of great public importance have been decided in actions involving only very small sums of money. The wishes of the parties will not be ignored, but it must be remembered that the decision to refer is that of the court, not the parties.

In *R v. International Stock Exchange, ex parte Else*,[125] Sir Thomas Bingham MR said that if the facts have been found, and the Community law issue is critical to the court's final decision, the appropriate course is ordinarily to refer the issue to the European Court unless the English court can with complete confidence resolve the issue itself.[126] This probably expresses the gist of the matter.[127]

## PROCEDURE

### ENGLISH COURTS

In England, provision for preliminary references has been made in the rules of procedure of the most important courts.[128] However, even where this is not the case, any court or tribunal covered by Article 234 [177] may make a reference: its power to do so derives from the Treaty and section 2(1) of the European Communities Act 1972; the procedural details may be fixed by the court itself under its inherent power to regulate such matters.[129] The discussion which follows is based on the Civil Procedure Rules Part 68,[130] which applies to the High Court and the Court of Appeal; similar provisions are applicable in the other courts for which special provision has been made, and CPR Part 68 would no doubt furnish a model for those courts and tribunals for which no special provision has been made.

It is expressly provided that an order for reference may be made by the court on application by either party, or of the court's own motion.[131] It is also expressly stated that it may be made at any stage of the proceedings;[132] thus there is no requirement in the Rules that the evidence must be heard before a reference may be made.

If the court decides to make the reference, the order will contain a schedule in which the request for a ruling and the questions asked will be set out. The proceedings will then be stayed (unless the court orders otherwise) until the European Court has given

[125] [1993] QB 534; [1993] 2 WLR 70; [1993] 1 All ER 420, CA. [126] [1993] 2 WLR at 76.

[127] For a suggestion that this way of putting it represents a change from the previous approach (in favour of a greater willingness to refer), see Walsh, 'The Appeal of an Article 177 EEC Referral' (1993) 56 MLR 881.

[128] For the High Court and Court of Appeal, see CPR Part 68.

[129] Jacobs and Durand, *References to the European Court* (1975), pp. 164 and 167.

[130] See also Practice Direction 68 and the European Court's 'Guidance on References by National Courts for Preliminary Rulings' included therein. The latter is also published in OJ 2005, C143/1 and maybe found on the Court's website. [131] CPR 68.2(1).

[132] *Ibid.* A reference cannot, however, be made after delivery of judgment, even if the order of the court has not yet been drawn up: *SA Magnavision NV v. General Optical Council (No. 2)* [1987] 2 CMLR 262.

its ruling.[133] The Senior Master of the Supreme Court (Queen's Bench Division) will transmit the order to the European Court.[134]

If the point at issue is whether a British statute is incompatible with Community law, the court can suspend the operation of the statute while the reference is pending.[135] If the reference concerns the validity of a Community measure, the court can also suspend the operation of any British measure that is dependent on it.[136]

## THE REFERENCE

The form and content of the reference are not covered by the rules of procedure of either the English courts or the European Court. However, certain general practices have grown up. Normally the order for reference will contain a brief summary of the facts of the case (in so far as these have already been established), an account of the procedure followed prior to the reference, the order sought by the claimant, the matters raised in defence, the main arguments of the parties on the Community point and the reasons of the court for making the reference. Where national law is relevant, the national court should give a clear statement of the provisions in question: the European Court has no power to rule on national law, but a knowledge of the relevant national provisions may be useful in order to define the exact issues at stake.[137] It is important that the background of the reference should be fully explained: if insufficient detail is given, the European Court may refuse to entertain the proceedings.[138]

In proceedings for a preliminary reference, the European Court has no jurisdiction to rule on the *application* of Community law to the facts of the case: all it can do is to interpret Community law and, in the case of Community acts, rule on their validity. For this reason, the questions put to the European Court should be phrased in an abstract way: the Court should, for example, be asked whether a particular provision of Community law is to be interpreted as having a particular meaning, rather than asked whether it provides a defence to the charge in the case. The European Court, however, adopts a flexible approach and will not refuse to give a ruling on the ground that questions are improperly phrased: it will simply decide what questions should have been asked and then proceed on the basis that those are the questions referred. In this way it can get to the substance of the matter with the minimum of formality and delay.

## APPEALS AGAINST AN ORDER FOR REFERENCE

Is it legitimate for national law to provide for a right of appeal against an order for reference? It has already been mentioned that in the *Rheinmühlen* case[139] Advocate

[133] CPR 68.4. [134] CPR 68.3(1).

[135] *R v. Secretary of State for Transport, ex parte Factortame (No. 2)*, Case C-213/89, [1990] ECR I-2433; [1990] 3 WLR 818 (discussed in Chap. 7).

[136] *Zuckerfabrik Süderdithmarschen*, Cases C-143/88, 92/89, [1991] ECR I-415.

[137] See the European Court's *Guidance on References by National Courts for Preliminary Rulings*, para. 6 [1999] 1 WLR 261.

[138] *Telemarsicabruzzo v. Circostel*, Cases C-320–2/90, [1993] ECR I-393; *Pretore di Genova v. Banchero*, Case C-157/92, [1993] ECR I-1085. [139] Cases 146, 166/73, [1974] ECR 33 at 43–7.

General Warner suggested that the existence of a right of appeal constituted an improper fetter on the power of a national court to make a reference. This was rejected by the European Court, which ruled that the order for reference remains 'subject to the remedies normally available under national law'.[140] The mere fact that an appeal has been lodged will not, however, deter the European Court from going ahead with the reference: only if the order for reference is withdrawn by the court which made it, or is set aside by a higher court, will the European Court decline to give a ruling.[141]

As was pointed out by Advocate General Warner in the *Rheinmühlen* case, this rule could mean that the European Court would give unnecessary rulings: if the appeal is allowed after the ruling has been made, the ruling will not be applied by the national court. This is not, however, likely to occur very often, as the time needed for a ruling by the European Court will normally be greater than that for an appeal against the order for reference; moreover, the most likely reason for the appeal to be allowed is that the appellate court might think that the Community point is not relevant to the proceedings: if this is the case, the European Court's ruling will not be applied anyway. Normally, the appeal will be decided before the case is heard by the European Court and the existence of a right of appeal is therefore more likely to prevent the European Court from giving unnecessary judgments.

In England, unless the court orders otherwise, a copy of the order for reference will not be sent to the European Court until the time for appealing against the order has expired, or any application for permission to appeal has been refused, or any appeal has been determined;[142] consequently, most of the questions discussed in the previous paragraphs are unlikely to arise in the case of references from English courts.

It should also be said that, in England, the court which made the order has the power to withdraw it; however, it will not normally do so unless it is manifest that the reference would serve no useful purpose.[143]

[140] [1974] ECR at 147, para. 3. It is interesting to note that Advocate General Warner's view seems to have found favour in Ireland, where the Irish Supreme Court held in *Campus Oil v. Minister of Industry and Energy* [1984] 1 CMLR 479 that Art. 234 [177] is part of domestic Irish law, and *under Irish law* precludes any appeal against an order for reference. Irish law made no express provision for an appeal and the Supreme Court said that the Irish Parliament lacks the power to make such provision. The Supreme Court was aware of the *Rheinmühlen* case, but considered it irrelevant since it was deciding the matter under Irish law. See, further, O'Keeffe, 'Appeals against an Order to Refer under Art. 177 of the EEC Treaty' (1984) 9 ELRev. 87.

[141] [1974] ECR at 147, para. 3. See also *BRT v. SABAM*, Case 127/73, [1974] ECR 51 at para. 9 of the judgment and *Simmenthal*, Case 106/77, [1978] ECR 629 at para. 10 of the judgment. See also *De Geus v. Bosch*, Case 13/61, [1962] ECR 45, where the Court held that the mere fact that one of the parties had appealed against the order for reference did not preclude it from hearing the case. In *Chanel v. Cepeha*, Case 31/68, [1970] ECR 403, however, the court which made the reference informed the European Court that an appeal had been lodged and stated that the effect of this under national law was to suspend the order for reference. The European Court thereupon stayed the proceedings. Subsequently, the parties agreed to a settlement and the appeal was allowed; the European Court then removed the case from the register.

[142] CPR 68.3(3).

[143] *Royscot Leasing v. Commissioners of Customs and Excise* [1999] 1 CMLR 903; *The Times*, 23 November 1998 (CA). The judgment of the European Court in the *Rheinmühlen* case (above) makes clear that it is perfectly in order for a court to withdraw a reference.

### THE EUROPEAN COURT

The procedure in the European Court was discussed in Chapter 2. The parties – together with the Member State, the Commission, and, where one of its acts forms the subject matter of the proceedings, the Council – have the right to submit written observations and make oral submissions. However, the issues before the Court are determined by the order for reference, and the role of the parties in this regard is limited to making suggestions to the Court as to how the reference should be interpreted. As was mentioned previously, the Court does not pay excessive regard to the exact wording of the questions submitted by the national court but tries rather to get to the heart of the matter. If the case can be disposed of without answering all the questions posed by the national court, the European Court will do this: for example, if the European Court is asked questions concerning the validity and interpretation of a Community measure, it will not concern itself with the interpretation if it holds the measure invalid.

The European Court has no jurisdiction to give rulings which bind the national court on questions of fact. It often cannot decide the relevant points of law without some basis of fact, but it normally relies on the national court to supply this. For these reasons, the European Court is not normally required to make findings of fact in preliminary references. There are, however, exceptions: for example, if the validity of a Community act is in issue, the Court may have to decide a question of fact in order to determine whether the Community act is valid. In this situation the Court will decide the question of fact according to its normal procedure, if necessary hearing witnesses, and then rule on the validity of the measure.[144] The national court is bound by the ruling on the point of validity, though not (presumably) on the findings of fact on which it was based.

In its judgment, the European Court will, after setting out the facts and background to the case, discuss the questions posed and give the reasons for its rulings on the various issues. At the end of its judgment, it will give formal rulings on the questions asked, or state that certain questions do not require an answer.[145] As was mentioned above, if the questions are put in an improper form, the Court will answer them as if they had been properly put. Sometimes two or more questions will be answered together. Occasionally the Court will answer more than was asked.

## INTERPRETATION AND APPLICATION

It has already been pointed out that the European Court has power to interpret Community law, but not to apply it to the facts of the case. The precise distinction

[144] See *per* Advocate General Warner in *EMI*, Case 51/75, [1976] ECR 811 at 854. A case in which such questions of fact had to be decided was *Milac*, Case 131/77, [1978] ECR 1041.

[145] The formal rulings must be interpreted in the light of the reasons: *Bosch*, Case 135/77, [1978] ECR 855 (para. 4).

between interpretation and application is, however, very elastic and the European Court appears to make use of this elasticity for its own purposes. Thus, if it is asked to interpret a Community provision, it may satisfy itself with a general indication of the provision's meaning and then state that it is a question of fact, to be decided by the national court, whether a particular case comes within its scope: in such a situation, the effective determination of the case rests with the national court. On the other hand, however, it might give such a precise and specific interpretation that the national court is left with nothing more to do, other than to give a formal judgment. Its choice between these two approaches seems to depend on policy (though one might surmise that the Court would incline towards the first alternative if its members were unable to agree among themselves on the precise interpretation of the provision).

The distinction between these approaches may be made clear by two examples. The first is *Walrave and Koch v. Union Cycliste Internationale*,[146] which concerned motor-paced cycle racing. In this sport, one person rides ahead on a motorcycle and is followed by another on a racing bicycle, the former being called the 'pacer', and the latter the 'stayer'. The idea is that the pacer creates a slipstream and if the stayer remains within it he can achieve considerable speeds. The case arose because the body controlling the sport made a rule that pacer and stayer had to be of the same nationality. The two plaintiffs, who were both professional pacers, felt that the rule would make it difficult for them to obtain work. They therefore brought proceedings in a national court for a declaration that the rule was contrary to Community law. The EC Treaty prohibits discrimination against workers, self-employed persons, and providers of services, and the European Court, to which a reference was made under Article 234 [177] EC, had no difficulty in finding that professional sportsmen were covered by the relevant provisions. However, they took the view that, notwithstanding the prohibition against discrimination, national teams could be selected on the basis of nationality. The question, therefore, was whether pacer and stayer constituted a team or whether the stayer was the only competitor and the pacer a mere auxiliary, like a trainer or coach. Instead of giving a clear answer, however, the European Court merely stated:[147] 'it is for the national court . . . to decide in particular whether in the sport in question the pacemaker and stayer do or do not constitute a team'. This left everything to the national court.

This may be contrasted with another case also concerning the rights of Community immigrants, *Cristini v. SNCF*.[148] Under Article 7(2) of Regulation 1612/68 it is provided that a Community national working in another Member State is entitled to the same 'social advantages' as national workers in the country of immigration. A French court asked the European Court whether a French provision entitling large families[149] to a special card giving them the right to reduced fares on the French railways was a 'social advantage' within the meaning of the Regulation.

The European Court might have given some vague definition of a 'social advantage' and left it to the French court to decide whether this covered the French provision.

[146] Case 36/74, [1974] ECR 1405.

[147] At para. 10 of the judgment.

[148] Case 32/75, [1975] ECR 1085.

[149] Families with three or more children under the age of eighteen.

Instead it went right to the point. After first disclaiming any power to 'apply the Community rule to a specific case', it stated:[150] 'Article 7(2) of Regulation (EEC) No. 1612/68 of the Council must be interpreted as meaning that the social advantages referred to by that provision include fares reduction cards issued by a national railway authority to large families.' This clearly left nothing more to be decided by the national court.

## EFFECTS OF PRELIMINARY RULINGS

After the European Court has given judgment, the case is sent back to the national court which made the reference. The proceedings will then continue in the national court from the point at which they were suspended. The national court is not obliged to apply Community law – it may eventually decide the case on other grounds – but if it does apply it, it is bound by the European Court's ruling. [151]

What is the effect of the ruling in *subsequent* cases? As was mentioned above, if the same issue arises again in a later case in the courts of the Member State from which the reference was made, or in the courts of another Member State, the ruling may be applied again without its being necessary to make a new reference. This is so even if the court concerned is one from which there is no appeal. On the other hand, the court is not *precluded* from making a reference if it wishes. It might do this if it considers the previous ruling mistaken and would like the European Court to reconsider the matter. As no strict doctrine of precedent operates in Community law, the European Court could in theory overrule its previous decision; in practice, however, it would be very unlikely to do so, since individuals and courts in the Member States might have relied on it.

Are all courts and tribunals in Member States *bound* by the ruling unless and until it is overruled in a later judgment? It is suggested that this is the case: even if the court in question is not covered by the third paragraph of Article 234 [177], it should be obliged either to follow the ruling or to make a new reference.[152] It would be improper for it simply to depart from the ruling because it thought that it was wrong. This is certainly the position in the United Kingdom, where it is provided by section 3(1) of the European Communities Act 1972 that any question as to the meaning or effect of any of the Treaties, or as to the validity, meaning, or effect of any Community instrument, must, if not referred to the European Court for a ruling, be decided in accordance with the principles laid down by any relevant decision of the European Court.[153]

150 At para. 19 of the judgment; see also the formal ruling.

151 *Milch- Fett- und Eierkontor*, Case 29/68, [1969] ECR 165 (para. 3 of the judgment).

152 For a general discussion of this question, see Trabucchi, 'L'effet "erga omnes" des décisions préjudicielles rendues par la Cour de justice des Communautés européennes' [1974] RTDE 56.

153 The position regarding preliminary rulings on the validity of a Community act is discussed further in Chap. 14, below.

## FURTHER READING


LAGRANGE, 'The Theory of the *Acte Clair*: A Bone of Contention or a Source of Unity?' (1971) 8 CMLRev. 313.

JACOBS, 'When to Refer to the European Court' (1974) 90 LQR 486.

JACOBS AND DURAND, *References to the European Court* (1975).

BARAV, 'Some Aspects of the Preliminary Rulings Procedure in EEC Law' (1977) 2 ELRev. 3.

BEBR, 'Article 177 of the EEC Treaty in the Practice of National Courts' (1977) 26 ICLQ 241.

BARAV, 'Preliminary Censorship? The Judgment of the European Court in *Foglia v. Novello*' (1980) 5 ELRev. 443.

ALEXANDER AND GRABANDT, 'National Courts Entitled to Ask Preliminary Rulings under Article 177 of the EEC Treaty: The Case Law of the Court of Justice' (1982) 19 CMLRev. 413.

BARAV, 'Imbroglio préjudiciel' [1982] RTDE 431.

BEBR, 'The Possible Implications of *Foglia v. Novello II*' (1982) 9 CMLRev. 421.

GRAY, 'Advisory Opinions and the European Court of Justice' (1983) 8 ELRev. 24.

DASHWOOD AND ARNULL, 'English Courts and Article 177 of the EEC Treaty' (1984) 4 YEL 255.

O'KEEFFE, 'Appeals against an Order to Refer under Article 177 of the EEC Treaty' (1984) 9 ELRev. 87.

RASMUSSEN, 'The European Court's *Acte Clair* Strategy in *CILFIT*' (1984) 9 ELRev. 242.

BEBR, 'Arbitration Tribunals and Article 177 of the EEC Treaty' (1985) 22 CMLRev. 489.

HENRY G SCHERMERS *et al.* (eds), *Article 177 EEC: Experiences and Problems* (1987).

ARNULL, 'The Use and Abuse of Article 177 EEC' (1989) 52 MLR 622.

LAWRENCE COLLINS, *European Community Law in the United Kingdom*, 4th edn (1990), Chap. 3.

ARNULL, 'The Evolution of the Court's Jurisdiction under Article 177 EEC' (1993) 18 ELRev. 129.

ANDERSON, 'The Admissibility of Preliminary References' [1994] YEL 179.

STRASSER, 'Evolution and Effort: Docket Control and Preliminary References in the European Court of Justice' (1995/96) 2 Columbia JEL 49.

BARNARD and SHARPSTON, 'The Changing Face of Article 177 References' (1997) 34 CMLRev. 1113.

O'KEEFFE, 'Is the Spirit of Article 177 under Attack? Preliminary References and Admissibility' (1998) 23 ELRev. 509.

DAVID ANDERSON AND MARIE DEMETRIOU, *References to the European Court*, 2nd edn (2002).

TRIDIMAS, 'Knocking on Heaven's Door: Fragmentation, Efficiency and Defiance in the Preliminary Reference Procedure' (2003) 40 CMLRev. 9.

WATTEL, 'KÖBLER, *CILFIT* and *Welthgrove*: We Can't Go on Meeting Like This' (2004) 41 CMLRev. 177.

LEFEVRE, 'The Interpretation of Community Law by the Court of Justice in Areas of National Competence' (2004) 29 ELRev. 501.

ANAGNOSTARAS, 'Preliminary Problems and Jurisdiction Uncertainties: The Admissibility of Questions Referred by Bodies Performing Quasi-Judicial Functions' (2005) 30 ELRev. 878.

# 10

# ENFORCEMENT ACTIONS

There are two ways in which Community law can be enforced against national governments. The first is through action taken by private individuals in the national courts. This is possible only through the application of the doctrine of direct effect; but as long as that doctrine is accepted by the national courts, it provides an effective means of enforcing Community law: its particular advantages are that it puts no strain on Community manpower, and national governments are not likely to disobey the rulings of their own courts. Its main limitations are that it applies only with regard to directly effective provisions – though the European Court is now prepared to hold most provisions directly effective – and then only if an individual or company whose interests are affected is prepared to take legal action. So far the Commission has not itself brought proceedings in national courts in order to secure compliance with Community law, nor does it appear to be prepared to give financial assistance to would-be litigants for this purpose.

One situation in which national proceedings are appropriate is where a national government purports to restrict the freedom of action of its citizens in a way which is contrary to Community law. It may do this by making it a criminal offence to do something which is covered by a Community right: in such a case the accused can plead Community law as a defence and a preliminary reference will normally be made to the European Court to determine whether the provision should be interpreted in the way suggested by the accused; if the European Court decides that it should, he will be acquitted. Thus, for example, when the Irish Government imposed restrictions on fishing in Irish waters which were contrary to Community law, a Dutch fisherman was able to invoke Community law as a defence to a charge of illegal fishing.[1]

Another possibility is that the national government will take administrative action contrary to some provision of Community law. For example, in 1977 the Ministry of Agriculture in Britain imposed a ban on the importation of main-crop potatoes. A Dutch potato exporter challenged this by applying for a declaration in the High Court that the ban was contrary to Community law. A reference was made to the European Court, which held that this was indeed the case.[2] The ban was then lifted.

[1] *Minister for Fisheries v. Schoenenberg*, Case 88/77, [1978] ECR 473. Parallel proceedings under Art. 226 [169] EC were also brought: see *Commission v. Ireland*, Case 61/77, [1978] ECR 417.

[2] *Meijer v. Department of Trade*, Case 118/78, [1979] ECR 1387. A parallel action under Art. 226 [169] was brought in this case as well: *Commission v. United Kingdom*, Case 231/78, [1979] ECR 1447. In both this and the Irish fisheries case, the proceedings under Art. 226 [169] were, as things turned out, unnecessary.

A third possibility is that the national authorities will refuse to grant an individual a benefit to which he is entitled under Community law. The *Cristini* case, discussed in the previous chapter, provides an example of the way in which national proceedings and a reference under Article 234 [177] EC can be used by the person concerned to vindicate his rights.

This way of proceeding is of great importance and will be very valuable to the individual concerned; it is not, however, sufficient in itself to ensure the effectiveness of Community law in all cases. The second way in which Community law can be enforced against national governments is by direct proceedings against the Member State concerned. Special provision is made for this in the Treaties and it was originally thought by many to be the only way in which Community law could be enforced.[3]

The relevant provisions are Articles 226–228 [169–171] EC and 141–143 Euratom. In addition, there are certain special procedures which apply only in the case of violations of particular rules of Community law. The main examples are found in Articles 88 [93], 95(4) [100a(4)], 237 [180], and 298 [225] EC and Articles 38 and 82 Euratom. These provisions lay down variants of the normal procedure, which replace the latter in the circumstances indicated. There is also a special procedure under Article 7 [F.1] TEU, which applies when a Member State is accused of a serious and persistent breach of the principles of liberty, democracy, respect for human rights and fundamental freedoms, and the rule of law. This may result in the suspension of some of the rights of that Member State under the Treaty, including its right to vote in the Council.

The bulk of this chapter will be taken up with a discussion of the normal enforcement procedure against Member States – that is to say, the procedure initiated by the Commission under the general enforcement provisions mentioned previously: the rights of Member States, and of private individuals, to take action will be dealt with separately; the special enforcement procedures will be considered only incidentally.

## WHAT CONSTITUTES A VIOLATION?

### PROVISIONS COVERED

What constitutes a violation of Community law for the purpose of an enforcement action? According to the Treaty, proceedings may be brought only if a Member State has failed 'to fulfil an obligation under this Treaty': only a violation of such an obligation will provide the foundation for an enforcement action. What does this cover? Clearly, a violation of a provision in one of the constitutive Treaties (the EC and Euratom Treaties, together with any amending and supplementing Treaties) would be included. On the other hand, certain provisions of the Treaty on European Union are not covered: this is laid down by Article 46 [L] TEU.[4]

[3] See, e.g., the arguments advanced by the Dutch and Belgian Governments in *Van Gend en Loos*, Case 26/62, [1963] ECR 1.

[4] Art. 46 [L] provides that the European Court has no jurisdiction with regard to the Treaty on European Union except for certain specified matters. These include Title VI (police and judicial co-operation in criminal

A violation of an obligation contained in Community legislation enacted under one of the constitutive Treaties would be covered: violation of the legislation would constitute a violation of the Treaty provision empowering its enactment. The same would apply to a violation of a provision in an agreement between the Community and a non-Member State: this would be a violation of the constitutive Treaty under which the Community was empowered (expressly or impliedly) to conclude the agreement.[5] This is particularly clear in the case of the EC in view of Article 300(7) [228(7)], which states that international agreements concluded under the procedure laid down in Article 300 [228] are binding on the Member States.[6] Though more difficult to justify, it is probable that the European Court would also regard an obligation as covered if it arose under an act of an institution set up by such an international agreement.[7]

It is hard to see how international agreements between the Member States (without the Community) and third countries could be covered, even if, as in the case of the GATT, they are binding on the Community.[8] Article 300 [228] EC would not apply in such a case, as it covers only 'agreements between the Community and one or more States'. However, in view of the disregard for the words of the Treaty displayed by the European Court in the *SPI*[9] case, one cannot rule out the possibility that it would hold these agreements to be covered by Article 226 [169].

What is the position with regard to an agreement concluded jointly by the Community and the Member States, on the one side, and one or more non-Member States on the other side? It will be remembered that these 'mixed agreements' are normally entered into where the matters dealt with are thought to fall partly within the jurisdiction of the Community and partly within that of the Member States.[10] If this is so, a breach by a Member State of an obligation under a mixed agreement could form the subject matter of an enforcement action if the obligation fell within the jurisdiction of the Community, but should not do so otherwise.[11]

Agreements between the Member States themselves (other than the constitutive Treaties) pose similar problems. A decision of the representatives of the Governments of the Member States meeting in the Council cannot constitute an obligation under the EC or Euratom Treaties if, on its true construction, it is no more than an international agreement in simplified form.[12] The same is true of subsidiary conventions.[13]

matters); Title VII (enhanced co-operation); and Art. 6(2) [F(2)] (human rights). An amendment introduced by the Treaty of Nice adds the purely procedural stipulations in Art. 7. However, actions against Member States for a violation of Title VI are possible only in the limited circumstances laid down by Art. 35(7) TEU. Art. 6(2) [F(2)] (human rights) does not apply to Member States. The most important matter over which the European Court has no jurisdiction is the common foreign and security policy.

[5] First *EEA* case, Opinion 1/91, [1991] ECR I-6079 (para. 38).

[6] It is true that Art. 300(1) [228(1)] commences with the words 'Where this Treaty provides for the conclusion of agreements between the Community and one or more states', but this could be regarded as including implied provision for the conclusion of an international agreement; there is little doubt that the European Court would take this view.

[7] The European Court has already held that such acts are part of the Community legal system and are covered by Art. 234 [177] EC: *Greece v. Commission*, Case 30/88, [1989] ECR 3711 (para. 13 of the judgment); the first *EEA* case (above) (para. 37); *Sevince*, Case C-192/89, [1990] ECR I-3461.

[8] See Chap. 6.

[9] Cases 267–9/81, [1983] ECR 801.

[10] See Chap. 6, above.

[11] *Commission v. France*, Case C-239/03, 7 October 2004, paras 23–31 of the judgment.

[12] See Chap. 3.

[13] Conventions entered into under Art. 293 [220] EC may constitute an exception.

Difficulties also arise with regard to obligations derived from general principles of law: unless they can be regarded as in some way inherent in the constitutive Treaties, they would not fall within the scope of an enforcement action.[14] This problem is not likely to arise very often. What could easily happen, however, is that a Member State might be bound by an express provision of Community law and the European Court might have recourse to a general principle of law in order to interpret the provision: in this situation the general principle would be indirectly applicable to the Member State and a breach of it would also constitute a violation of the express provision. In such a case, of course, no difficulties would arise.

## VIOLATIONS BY THE LEGISLATURE OR JUDICIARY OF A MEMBER STATE

What is the position where the violation of Community law is the result of action (or failure to act) on the part of the national legislature or courts? For example, the national parliament may fail to pass legislation introduced by the government to give effect to a Community obligation, or it may insist on enacting legislation contrary to Community law. A violation by the courts could take a number of forms: they could refuse to give direct effect to a provision of Community law; they could refuse to make a reference to the European Court even where bound to do so under the third paragraph of Article 234 [177] EC; or they could refuse to accept that Community law overrides national law in the event of conflict. Is the national government responsible for these violations?

The short answer to this question is that, although the national government appears before the European Court in enforcement actions, the actual defendant is the State, not the government.[15] Since the legislature and judiciary are organs of the State just as much as the government is, there is no reason in principle why a violation of Community law by the legislature or courts should not engage the responsibility of the State in the same way as a violation by the executive. There have, in fact, been cases in which national legislation was required in order to comply with Community law and the national government introduced a bill and did all in its power to secure its enactment, but the national legislature failed to pass it: in these cases the national government argued before the European Court that it was absolved from responsibility for the violation of Community law as it had done everything it could to get the measure approved. The Court, however, rejected these arguments on the ground given above.[16]

[14] It should, however, be noted that both Mertens de Wilmars and Verougstraete, 'Proceedings against Member States for Failure to Fulfil Their Obligations' (1970) 7 CMLRev. 385 at 388 (para. 5) and Barav, 'Failure of Member States to Fulfil Their Obligations under Community Law' (1975) 12 CMLRev. 368 at 377 consider that general principles of law are covered by Art. 226 [169], though neither gives any satisfactory reasons to support this opinion.

[15] See *per* Advocate General Warner in *Cremonini*, Case 815/79, [1980] ECR 3583 at 3621–2, and in *R v. Bouchereau*, Case 30/77, [1977] ECR 1999 at 2020. There appears to be one exception to this, *Commission v. Government of the Italian Republic*, Case 16/69, [1969] ECR 377, but this is probably a mistake. The Court itself gave judgment against the 'Italian Republic', not the Italian Government.

[16] See *Commission v. Belgium*, Case 77/69, [1970] ECR 237 and *Commission v. Italy*, Case 8/70, [1970] ECR 961. In the former case the Court said that a Member State is responsible even for the actions of 'a constitutionally independent institution' (para. 15 of the judgment): this phrase could cover the courts as well as the legislature.

Similar arguments can be used in the case of the judiciary, but so far no enforcement action has been brought for a violation of Community law by national courts, though – as was shown in Chapter 8 – there have been several occasions on which such violations occurred.[17] In practice, the Commission has shown itself loath to institute proceedings in such cases.[18] It seems that this is partly because the independence of the judiciary might appear to be undermined by such proceedings and partly because the effective application of Community law depends to a great extent on the co-operation of the national courts. This is normally given, but if relations between the European Court and the national courts were soured by proceedings in which the former appeared to sit in judgment over the latter, the national judges might change their attitude.

The European Court has also ruled that constitutional difficulties are no excuse for a failure to fulfil an obligation under the Treaty.[19] If the defendant Member State is a federation, it will not constitute a defence to show that the violation was due to the action of a constituent State, such as a German *Land*.[20] The same rule would apply with regard to a violation by the legislature, executive, or judiciary of a dependency of a Member State, provided it was covered by the Treaty. Thus the United Kingdom would be liable for a violation by Gibraltar, the Channel Islands, or the Isle of Man.

## THE ADMINISTRATIVE STAGE

The proceedings in enforcement actions consist of two stages: an administrative stage and a judicial stage. The administrative stage is covered by the first paragraph of Articles 226 [169] EC and 141 Euratom. These state:

> If the Commission considers that a Member State has failed to fulfil an obligation under this Treaty, it shall deliver a reasoned opinion on the matter after giving the State concerned the opportunity to submit its observations.

[17] Notably by the French *Conseil d'Etat*.

[18] Proceedings against Germany were apparently commenced after the decision of the *Bundesverfassungsgericht* in the *Internationale Handelsgesellschaft* case but they were not pursued: *Europe*, 27 December 1974, No. 1657, p. 9. When the French *Conseil d'Etat* refused to make a reference to the European Court in the *Semoules* case (1 March 1968, [1970] CMLR 395), the Commission evidently considered whether action under Art. 226 [169] should be taken against France: see the Commission's replies to Parliamentary Questions 28/68 (OJ 1968, C71/1) and 349/69 (OJ 1970, C20/4). In *Meyer-Burckhardt v. Commission*, Case 9/75, [1975] ECR 1171 at 1187, Advocate General Warner said that proceedings can be brought under Art. 226 [169] where a national court covered by the third paragraph of Art. 234 [177] fails to make a preliminary reference when required to do so by that provision; but he made clear that the Commission has a discretion whether or not to initiate the procedure and said that proceedings should 'not lightly be undertaken'. For references to the views of writers on this question, see Barav, 'Failure of Member States to Fulfil Their Obligations Under Community Law' (1975) 12 CMLRev. 369 at 379–80.

[19] See *Commission v. Italy*, Case 100/77, [1978] ECR 879 (para. 21 of the judgment).

[20] See *Casagrande v. Munich*, Case 9/74, [1974] ECR 773: this was a reference under Art. 234 [177], but the European Court made clear that Community law is binding at all levels in a Member State. The position would be the same in the case of a violation by a local authority.

The use of the word 'shall' in these provisions suggests that the Commission is under an obligation to deliver the opinion or take the decision. (This contrasts with the second paragraph, where it is stated that, if the Member State does not comply with the opinion, the Commission 'may' bring the matter before the European Court.) However, this obligation can arise only if two conditions are fulfilled: the Commission must consider that a breach has taken place and the Member State must have been given an opportunity to submit its observations.

The structure of the Treaty provision suggests that the normal order of events will be: first, the Commission concludes that a violation has taken place; then it allows observations to be submitted; and finally it delivers the opinion. However, no reasonable administrative authority would reach a definite conclusion on a matter as important as this until *after* it had considered the Member State's observations: it is an essential part of the *audi alteram partem* doctrine that the hearing must precede the decision. Therefore, the correct order of events should be: first the observations; then the conclusion that there has been a violation; and finally the delivery of the opinion. However, the Commission would not ask the Member State for its observations unless it had reason to believe that a breach might have taken place. Therefore, the formal request for observations must itself be preceded by a preliminary determination that a violation appears to have occurred.

In fact, the whole administrative stage can be subdivided into two distinct phases: the informal phase and the formal phase. In the informal phase the Commission investigates a possible breach and considers whether there is sufficient evidence to justify the commencement of formal proceedings.[21] This informal investigation will be conducted with discretion, and the Commission will try to avoid press publicity. Informal discussions with the Member State will be held in an attempt to ascertain the facts and to reach a settlement. Only when the Commission feels that the factual and legal issues have been fully investigated will it consider whether to move on to the formal phase. It will then decide either that further proceedings are not warranted, in which case the matter will be at an end, or it will decide that sufficient evidence of a violation exists to justify the commencement of the formal phase.

The formal phase will begin with a formal request to the Member State to submit its observations (originally called an 'Article-169 letter', now known as a 'letter of formal notice'). This formal communication specifies what the Member State is alleged to have done wrong and which rule of Community law has been infringed;[22] it will also lay down a time-limit for the submission of observations.[23] Further discussions may take

[21] Member States are obliged (under Art. 10 [5] EC) to co-operate with the Commission in its investigations. Failure to do so may itself result in proceedings under Art. 226 [169]: *Commission v. Greece*, Case 240/86, [1988] ECR 1835. Any information requested must, therefore, be handed over within a reasonable time.

[22] The Member State must be told in clear terms, either in the formal communication or at an earlier stage, exactly what the allegations against it are; otherwise the whole proceedings could be nullified: see *Commission v. Denmark*, Case 211/81, [1982] ECR 4547 (paras 5–12 of the judgment); see also *Commission v. Italy*, Case 309/84, [1986] ECR 599; *Commission v. Denmark*, Case C-52/90, [1992] ECR I-2187. The formal notice must refer to an existing violation of Community law, not a possible future one: *Commission v. Netherlands*, Case C-341/97, [2000] ECR I-6611.

[23] This time-limit must be reasonable; otherwise, subsequent court proceedings will be dismissed as inadmissible: *Commission v. Belgium*, Case 293/85, [1988] ECR 305. What is reasonable depends on the facts of the case.

place after the Member State's observations have been received: the Commission is always anxious to reach an amicable settlement, if this is possible. Only when it becomes clear that the Member State is not prepared voluntarily to accept the Commission position will the Commission issue the reasoned opinion formally recording the violation.

## COMMISSION DISCRETION

Must the Commission issue a formal opinion to record every failure to observe the Treaty that comes to its notice? Or does it have a discretion as to which cases it will pursue? As was shown above, the Treaty suggests that the Commission has no discretion once it has concluded that a violation has taken place. However, it was also shown that the Commission will normally reach such a conclusion only after a fairly complex procedure of investigation and consultation has taken place. Before this has happened, the Commission will not be in a position to reach a definite conclusion; and before such a conclusion is reached, the obligation to deliver the opinion or take the decision will not arise.

The important question, therefore, is whether there is any obligation on the Commission to set the investigatory procedure in motion whenever it appears, either on the basis of information arising in the course of the Commission's normal operations or as a result of representations made by some outside person or body, that there are reasonable grounds for believing that a violation might have occurred. Articles 226 [169] EC and 141 Euratom contain no direct statement that such an obligation exists. It would not, however, be unreasonable to take the view that an implied obligation exists to consider with an open mind whether investigations should begin. This view is supported by Articles 211 [155] EC and 124 Euratom, which provide that the Commission 'shall ensure that the provisions of this Treaty and the measures taken by the institutions pursuant thereto are applied'.

Before considering the existence and limits of any obligation that may exist regarding the setting in motion of the enforcement procedure, however, it would be desirable to turn for a moment from legal principle to practicalities. First, it should be noted that a large number of contraventions of Community law takes place. Many directives are implemented by the Member States only after the time-limit has expired.[24] When implementation does take place, it is not always wholly satisfactory. The scope for enforcement actions is therefore very large: since the Commission has only limited staff available, it is not possible for it to investigate every suspected violation.

Secondly, there is a tendency for national governments to resent the initiation of enforcement proceedings against them. As was once said by Advocate General Roemer,[25] this procedure puts the Member State's prestige in issue: no one likes to be accused of having broken the law. Since the Community mechanism functions only if there is mutual trust and goodwill between the Member States and Community institutions, excessive resort to enforcement actions might do more harm than good.

[24] See the various reports submitted by the Commission to the European Parliament on the implementation of Community law.

[25] *Commission v. France*, Case 7/71, [1971] ECR 1003 at 1026.

In view of these considerations, it would be unreasonable to hold that there is an absolute obligation on the Commission to commence enforcement proceedings in every case where a violation may have occurred. On the other hand, however, it would be wrong to assume that there is no obligation at all. The true position seems to be that the Commission has a discretion but is also subject to a duty. The duty is to take the most appropriate action to ensure that Community law is obeyed; the discretion concerns the determination of what is most appropriate in the circumstances.[26] This discretion must, however, be exercised according to the correct criteria.

In *Commission v. France*[27] (*Euratom* case) Advocate General Roemer indicated some of the situations in which the Commission might be justified in not initiating the enforcement procedure: where there is a possibility that an amicable settlement may be achieved if formal proceedings are delayed; where the effects of the violation are only minor; where there is a major political crisis which could be aggravated if proceedings are commenced with regard to matters of secondary importance; and where there is a possibility that the Community provision in issue might be altered in the near future. These are only examples: the basic principle is that the Commission must balance the harm caused by non-compliance with the law against the embarrassment and inconvenience that could result from bringing proceedings.

## RECORDING THE VIOLATION

After it has considered any observations submitted by the Member State within the time-limit laid down in the request, the Commission must decide whether a violation has occurred. If it considers that it has, it will record this infringement in a reasoned opinion. The main function of the opinion is to specify exactly what the Member State has done wrong. If the matter subsequently goes to the European Court, the opinion serves as a definition of the issues before the Court: the Commission cannot raise any violations which are not set out in it.[28] The reasons given by the Commission will help the Member State to prepare its case before the Court. They should be sufficient to enable the Member State to know precisely why the Commission thinks it has infringed the Treaty.

The Commission has to set a time-limit within which the Member State must end the violation,[29] and it cannot bring legal proceedings until it has expired.[30] The time-limit thus gives the Member State a period of grace within which it is protected from the threat of legal proceedings.[31]

[26] *Commission v. France* (above) at para. 5 of the judgment. [27] [1971] ECR at 1025.

[28] *Commission v. Belgium*, Case 298/86, [1988] ECR 4343 (paras 9–11 of the judgment).

[29] This must be reasonable. If it is too short, the subsequent application to the Court will be dismissed as inadmissible: *Commission v. Belgium*, Case 293/85, [1988] ECR 305. What is reasonable depends on all the circumstances.

[30] Arts 226(2) [169(2)] EC and 141(2) Euratom. If legal proceedings are brought, the onus is on the Commission to prove that the violation was not rectified before the expiry of the time-limit: *Commission v. Belgium*, Case 298/86, [1988] ECR 4343 (para. 15 of the judgment).

[31] The reasoned opinion cannot, however, affect the rights of third parties. A finding that no violation occurred does not preclude proceedings in the national courts by private individuals, nor does it prevent the

The reasoned opinion also specifies what action may be taken by the Member State to end its infringement. However, as the opinion is merely declaratory – it simply records a violation – the Commission cannot impose any new obligation on the Member State:[32] the Member State can therefore choose what measures it takes, so long as the infringement is in fact terminated.

## TIME-LIMIT FOR COMMISSION ACTION

There is no time-limit for the initiation of proceedings or for the delivery of the reasoned opinion: it falls within the Commission's discretion to decide when to act. This is illustrated by a case under Article 141 Euratom, *Commission v. France*.[33] The case concerned Title II, Chapter VI of the Euratom Treaty, which contained various provisions designed to ensure that all users of nuclear fuels in the Community could obtain reasonable supplies. A special Supply Agency was set up to control the supply of nuclear materials. The French Government, however, took the view that these provisions lapsed after seven years, as they had not been confirmed by the Council under Article 76(2) Euratom. In 1965, it informed French undertakings that the provisions of Chapter VI were no longer applicable: the French Government itself ceased to comply with them. In particular, it did not inform the Supply Agency of contracts it had concluded for the procurement and supply of nuclear materials. The Commission considered, however, that Chapter VI was still in force, and in 1970 it commenced proceedings under Article 141: France was invited to submit observations; a reasoned opinion was given declaring France guilty of a violation of the Treaty; and, after France had failed to comply with it within the period laid down, an action was instituted before the European Court.

One argument put forward by the French Government was that the proceedings had been started too late. It maintained that it had made its views known in 1965 and that it was not open to the Commission to wait so long before bringing the action. The Court rejected this contention. It held:[34]

> The action for a declaration that a State has failed to fulfil an obligation provided for by Article 141 of the Treaty, does not have to be brought within a predetermined period, since, by reason of its nature and purpose, this procedure involves a power on the part of the Commission to consider the most appropriate means and time-limits for the purposes of putting an end to any contraventions of the Treaty.

The action was therefore declared admissible;[35] the Court went on to hold that Chapter VI had not lapsed: it gave judgment against France.

European Court from ruling against the Member State in a reference from a national court under Art. 234 [177] EC: see *Essevi*, Cases 142–3/80, [1981] ECR 1413 at paras 13–18 of the judgment.

[32] See *Netherlands v. High Authority*, Case 25/59, [1960] ECR 355 at 373–5. This case concerned the ECSC Treaty; the position is even clearer under the EC and Euratom Treaties, since the reasoned opinion is not legally binding.

[33] Case 7/71, [1971] ECR 1003.

[34] Para. 5 of the judgment.

[35] The Court's ruling that no time-limit exists with regard to proceedings by the Commission against a Member State contrasts with its decision to create such a time-limit in the case of proceedings by a Member State against the Commission: see *Netherlands v. Commission*, Case 59/70, [1971] ECR 639, discussed below.

### CONSEQUENCES OF PROCEDURAL DEFECTS

It will be seen from what has been said that there are a number of procedural requirements which must be complied with by the Commission: the Member State must be given a fair opportunity to submit its observations (this involves both giving it sufficient information regarding the case it must meet and allowing a reasonable time for the observations to be communicated); the opinion must be properly reasoned; and the Member State must be given a reasonable period to end its violation. If the Commission violates one of these requirements, the Member State may raise the procedural infringement in any subsequent proceedings before the Court. If it is sufficiently serious, it would constitute a bar to the action, since the procedural requirements laid down in the Treaty are essential preconditions for the admissibility of an enforcement action.[36]

## THE JUDICIAL STAGE

The delivery of the reasoned opinion marks the end of the administrative stage. Next comes the judicial stage, where the matter is put before the European Court for a final ruling. There is no deadline for the commencement of the action, but, as we have seen, the Commission must wait until the expiry of the time-limit in its reasoned opinion.[37]

The Court has full jurisdiction to consider all the issues. The proceedings are not a review of the opinion: the Court considers *de novo* whether the violation has occurred. As will be seen in Chapter 15, the powers of the Court in review proceedings are restricted: it may annul the measure in question on limited grounds only; its power to review the Commission's evaluation of a situation is restricted; and the only remedy it can grant is a declaration of invalidity: it cannot substitute its decision for that of the Commission. These restrictions do not apply when the Court exercises plenary jurisdiction. However, the scope of the proceedings is limited to the infringements specified in the reasoned opinion: the Commission cannot raise new allegations before the Court.[38]

[36] In *Commission v. Italy*, Case 7/61, [1961] ECR 317, the Court appeared to consider an allegation that the opinion did not contain sufficient reasons as going to the admissibility of the enforcement action; and in *Commission v. Italy*, Case 31/69, [1970] ECR 25, the Court said that the opportunity to submit observations was 'an essential procedural requirement' (para. 13 of the judgment); see also *Commission v. Germany*, Case 325/82, [1984] ECR 777 (para. 8 of the judgment); *Commission v. Belgium*, Case 293/85, [1988] ECR 305; *Commission v. Denmark*, Case C-52/90, [1992] ECR I-2187. In *Commission v. Netherlands*, Case C-341/97, [2000] 6611 the Court held the proceedings inadmissible because the formal notice was defective, since, at the time when it was issued, the Member State had not committed the violation.

[37] The European Court cannot extend or reduce the time-limit set by the Commission: *Commission v. Italy*, Case 28/81, [1981] ECR 2577.

[38] See, e.g., *Commission v. Italy*, Case 166/82, [1984] ECR 459 (para. 16 of the judgment). However, if the Commission is seeking to establish that the Member State is guilty of a general and persistent failure to abide by Community law (a concept discussed below), it can introduce evidence of further specific violations (in addition

Proceedings cannot be brought if the breach is terminated before the deadline laid down in the reasoned opinion,[39] but what happens if it is terminated after the deadline but before judgment is given? This occurred in *Commission v. Italy*[40] (*Pork Imports* case) where the Court ruled that it did not constitute a bar to the action.[41] Proceedings cannot, on the other hand, be brought regarding a violation which had not occurred when the Commission invited the Member State to submit its observations, even though the Commission may have had reason to believe that it was contemplated.[42]

It is no defence to argue that the Commission or Council is also in breach of the Treaty with regard to the same subject matter, or that the act complained of was in retaliation for a comparable violation by another Member State.[43] Nor may a Member State complain that other Member States were doing exactly the same thing and no proceedings were brought against them.[44] In general, the Court, though willing to consider policy issues, is not impressed by technical, legalistic defences.

If the Court finds the allegations proved, it will give judgment against the Member State. This takes the form of a declaration that the Member State has failed to fulfil an obligation under the Treaty. The Court will, of course, specify what act or omission is the source of the violation. The Court has no power specifically to order the Member State to do, or not to do, something;[45] nor, if the violation takes the form of national legislation contrary to Community law, can it declare the legislation invalid.[46] This does not, however, mean that the Member State is not obliged to comply with the judgment.

to those given in the reasoned opinion) in order to show that the failure is general and persistent: see *Commission v. Ireland*, Case C-494/01, 26 April 2005 (Grand Chamber) at paras 37–8 of the judgment. These further allegations will not lead to a judgment that the Member State is guilty of further specific violations, but may lead to a judgment that it is guilty of a general and persistent failure to comply with Community law. This latter allegation must, of course, be made in the reasoned opinion.

[39] However, there is an exception if, in addition to alleging various specific violations, the Commission also claims that the Member State is guilty of a general and persistent failure to abide by Community law (see previous note). Here, a specific violation that ended before the deadline may still be used as evidence of a general and persistent failure, even though it can no longer lead directly to a judgment against the Member State: see *Commission v. Ireland*, Case C-494/01, 26 April 2005 (Grand Chamber) at paras 29–32 of the judgment.

[40] Case 7/61, [1961] ECR 317 at 326.

[41] There are various reasons why the Commission might wish to continue with the action: e.g., it might want to obtain a ruling to clarify the matter in case the violation is repeated at a later stage. In practice, however, it will usually drop the proceedings once the breach has been remedied.

[42] See *Commission v. Italy*, Case 31/69, [1970] ECR 25 (paras 11–14 of the judgment); see also *Commission v. Italy*, Case 309/84, [1986] ECR 599.

[43] See *Commission v. Luxembourg and Belgium*, Cases 90, 91/63, [1964] ECR 625 at 631, where it was held that failure by the Community to carry out its obligations does not justify the Member States' taking the law into their own hands, and *Steinike und Weinlig*, Case 78/76, [1977] ECR 595, where the Court held that a breach by a Member State of an obligation under the Treaty cannot be justified by the fact that other Member States have also failed to fulfil the obligation in question (para. 24 of the judgment). *Commission v. France*, Case 26/69, [1970] ECR 565, suggests, however, that a Member State might be excused if it was not engaged in an act of retaliation but, through no fault of its own, was forced into violating the Treaty by a wrongful act on the part of the Community.

[44] See *Germany v. Commission*, Cases 52, 55/65, [1966] ECR 159 at 170–2.

[45] This does not apply in the case of interim orders (discussed below). The Court might, of course, try to help the Member State by suggesting ways in which it could bring the violation to an end.

[46] In *Commission v. Italy* (second *Art Treasures* case), Case 48/71, [1972] ECR 527 (paras 7–9 of the judgment) the Court emphasized that national authorities should not apply national legislation that is incompatible with

The first paragraph of Articles 228 [171] EC and 143 Euratom states:

> If the Court of Justice finds that a Member State has failed to fulfil an obligation under this Treaty, the State shall be required to take the necessary measures to comply with the judgment of the Court of Justice.

This makes clear that the judgment, though declaratory in nature, is binding: the Member State is obliged to terminate the violation found by the Court, though it can choose the way in which this will be done.

## REMEDIES WHERE THE COMMISSION FAILS TO ACT

It was said previously that the Commission has a discretion whether to set the enforcement procedure in motion, but there is a duty to exercise that discretion properly. What remedies exist if the Commission fails in that duty?

Under the ECSC Treaty it was possible for either another Member State or a private party with sufficient standing to bring an action for failure to act under Article 33 ECSC.[47] This was because, instead of giving a reasoned opinion, the Commission adopted a reasoned decision, which constituted a reviewable act[48] for the purpose of Article 35. This remedy is not available under the EC and Euratom Treaties, because a reasoned opinion, unlike a reasoned decision under the ECSC Treaty, is not legally binding and hence not a reviewable act. Even if it were, a private individual could not challenge it because he would lack standing:[49] if given, the opinion would not be addressed to him, nor would it concern him directly and individually; consequently, an omission or refusal to give an opinion (or to take any of the preceding steps) cannot be challenged under Article 230 [173] or 232 [175] EC or under Article 146 or 148 Euratom.[50] This is not important as far as Member States are concerned, since Articles 227 [170] EC and 142 Euratom give Member States the right to bring proceedings themselves. Private individuals, on the other hand, are in a much less advantageous position than they were under the ECSC Treaty.

Community law: this, of course, is a simple reiteration of the doctrines of direct effect and the supremacy of Community law discussed in Chap. 7.

[47] *De Gezamenlijke Steenkolenmijnen in Limburg v. High Authority*, Case 17/57, [1959] ECR 1; *Groupement des Industries Sidérurgiques Luxembourgeoises v. High Authority*, Cases 7, 9/54, [1956] ECR 175.

[48] This concept is discussed in Chap. 11.

[49] The rules for standing were less strict under the ECSC Treaty than they are under the EC and Euratom Treaties.

[50] *Lütticke v. Commission*, Case 48/65, [1966] ECR 19; *Commission v. France*, Cases 6, 11/69, [1969] ECR 523 (paras 35–7 of the judgment); *Star Fruit v. Commission*, Case 247/87, [1989] ECR 291 (para. 13 of the judgment); *Emrich v. Commission*, Case C-371/89, [1990] ECR I-1555; *Sonito v. Commission*, Case C-87/89, [1990] ECR I-1981 (paras 5–7 of the judgment); *Asia Motor France v. Commission*, Case C-72/90, [1990] ECR I-2181; *Asia Motor France v. Commission*, Case C-29/92, [1992] ECR I-3935; *Bundesverband der Bilanzbuchhalter v. Commission*, Case C-107/95 P, [1997] ECR I-947. For the possibility that there might be exceptional situations in which an individual may be able to bring proceedings against a refusal by the Commission to adopt a decision under the special procedure laid down in Art. 86 [90] EC, see *Bundesverband der Bilanzbuchhalter v. Commission* (above) at para. 25 of the judgment.

Are any other remedies available? In *Vloeberghs v. High Authority*,[51] a case under the ECSC Treaty, Vloeberghs, a Belgian coal dealer, suffered loss because the French Government refused to allow the entry into France of a consignment of coal which Vloeberghs had imported into Belgium from outside the Community. He maintained that the French had violated the Treaty and asked the Commission to take action under Article 88 ECSC, the equivalent of Article 226 [169] EC. The Commission refused. Vloeberghs then brought an action for damages against the Commission and claimed compensation for the loss he had suffered through not being able to export the coal to France.[52] He lost the action in the end, but there was no suggestion in the case that such actions are not available in principle.

Can actions in tort (or 'non-contractual liability', as it is called in Community terminology) be brought under the EC and Euratom Treaties? In principle, there seems to be no reason why the position should be any different from that under the ECSC Treaty: the distinction between an opinion and a decision is not relevant in actions for damages. In *Denkavit v. Commission*,[53] a private firm sued the Commission for damages for loss caused by the fact that deliveries of feeding-stuffs had been stopped at the Italian frontier. The Italian authorities had done this on the ground that the potassium nitrate content of the feeding-stuffs was higher than that permitted under an 'urgent note' which had been issued by the Italian Minister of Health a year previously. Denkavit claimed that the 'urgent note' violated the Treaty and that the Commission was partly to blame for the situation, as it had acted too slowly in taking measures to require Italy to revoke the note.

The Advocate General, Mr Mayras, was unsympathetic to this claim.[54] The Court, however, did not dismiss it out of hand but considered it on its merits: it eventually concluded that the Commission's tardiness – it did eventually take action – was excused by the legal uncertainties and scientific doubts which existed at the time. The Court said, however, that the 'urgent note' constituted an obstacle to trade between Member States and that it was 'necessary to consider whether the Commission, by conduct for which there was no justification, did not improperly contribute to the maintenance of that obstacle and thereby incur liability'.[55] This suggests that in principle such an action can be brought. Subsequently, however, the Court seems to have turned against the idea: in *Asia Motor France v. Commission*,[56] it declared the action inadmissible on the ground that the Commission is not under a duty to commence proceedings under Article 226 [169] EC.[57]

[51] Cases 9, 12/60, [1961] ECR 197.

[52] He was unable to use the procedure under Art. 35 ECSC because, as a coal dealer and not a coal producer, he lacked standing under Arts 33 and 35 ECSC.

[53] Case 14/78, [1978] ECR 2497.

[54] See [1978] ECR at 2515–16.

[55] Para. 8 of the judgment. See also *Lütticke v. Commission*, Case 4/69, [1971] ECR 325, which concerned the special procedure under Art. 97(2) EC. See further *Société d'Initiatives et de Coopération Agricoles v. Commission*, Case 114/83, [1984] ECR 2589; *GAARM v. Commission*, Case 289/83, [1984] ECR 4295.

[56] Case C-72/90, [1990] ECR I-2181.

[57] Para. 13 of the judgment. In an earlier case, *Meyer-Burckhardt v. Commission*, Case 9/75, [1975] ECR 1171 at 1190, Advocate General Warner came down against the possibility of such an action on the ground that it would be wrong for the Court to decide whether a Member State had infringed the Treaty if that State was not a party to the proceedings and did not enjoy the safeguards provided for in Article 226 [169].

## ACTIONS BY MEMBER STATES

Articles 227 [170] EC and 142 Euratom permit enforcement actions to be brought by a Member State. These provisions, which are identical, read as follows:

> A Member State which considers that another Member State has failed to fulfil an obligation under this Treaty may bring the matter before the Court of Justice.
>
> Before a Member State brings an action against another Member State for an alleged infringement of an obligation under this Treaty, it shall bring the matter before the Commission.
>
> The Commission shall deliver a reasoned opinion after each of the States concerned has been given the opportunity to submit its own case and its observations on the other party's case both orally and in writing.
>
> If the Commission has not delivered an opinion within three months of the date on which the matter was brought before it, the absence of such opinion shall not prevent the matter from being brought before the Court of Justice.

The first steps under this procedure are clear enough. The applicant requests the Commission to deliver a reasoned opinion on the alleged infringement. The Commission must comply with this request within three months; otherwise the applicant may commence proceedings before the Court without waiting for the opinion. The procedure before the Commission is similar to that under Article 226 [169] EC but the rights of the Member States are more extensive: each party is entitled both to present its own case and to comment on that of the other party; moreover these proceedings are both written and oral.[58]

It is less clear exactly what happens after the opinion has been given – assuming that it is duly given within the three-month period. There are several possibilities. Assume, first, that the opinion is to the effect that there has been no infringement: is this the end of the matter or may the applicant persist in its claim and bring the case before the Court? It would seem that it can:[59] the first paragraph of Article 227 [170] EC gives Member States a general right to bring proceedings. This is qualified by the second paragraph, which lays down a procedural condition, but this condition is satisfied once the matter has been 'brought before the Commission' and the latter has been given an opportunity (three months) to deliver its opinion: there is no requirement that the opinion must be favourable to the applicant's case. Once the opinion has been given, the procedural conditions are satisfied and the general right in the first paragraph then has full application.[60]

[58] The English text is ambiguous as to whether the words 'both orally and in writing' in the third para. of Art. 227 [170] EC apply only to the observations on the other party's case or also to the submission of the Member State's own case. The French text, however, makes clear that it applies to both. It reads: '*La Commission émet un avis motivé après que les Etats intéressés aient été mis en mesure de présenter contradictoirement leurs observations écrites et orales.*'

[59] Mertens de Wilmars and Verougstraete (1970) 7 CMLRev. 385 at 393.

[60] There is no time-limit for bringing the action.

What happens if the opinion is that the defendant has committed a breach? There is no statement in the Treaties that the opinion must set a time-limit within which the defendant must cease the violation. Could this be implied by analogy with Articles 226 [169] EC and 141 Euratom? Some writers consider this to be so,[61] but it is hard to see what function such a time-limit would serve, since the applicant would not be obliged to wait for the expiration of the period before going to the Court.

Further difficulties could arise if the Commission upholds the applicant's claim only in part. Say the applicant alleges that the defendant has broken the Treaty in three ways but the Commission rejects two of these complaints and upholds only the third: if the defendant then complies with the opinion, can the applicant nevertheless go to the Court with regard to the first two complaints? If the applicant can go to the Court when the opinion is wholly against it – as was suggested above – it would be strange if it could not do the same when the opinion is partly in its favour and partly against it. It seems, therefore, that the defendant cannot necessarily obtain immunity from legal action by complying with the opinion, as it can under Article 226 [169]. This means that the opinion has little significance under Article 227 [170], except as an indication to the Court of how the Commission views the matter.[62]

As was mentioned previously, the procedure under Article 227 [170] is little used. The first case under it to go to judgment was an action brought by France against the United Kingdom in which it was claimed that certain fish conservation measures adopted by Britain were contrary to the Treaty. The Commission was asked by France to give an opinion and, after the parties had put forward their views in writing, it held a hearing at which the parties could present their cases orally. It then gave an opinion which stated that the United Kingdom had infringed the Treaty. (No time-limit was set for ending the infringement nor were any suggestions made as to what action would be sufficient to bring this about.) France then took the matter before the Court and the Commission applied for leave to intervene in support of France. This was granted. The hearing then proceeded in the normal way; judgment was given against the United Kingdom.[63]

## INTERIM MEASURES

When Member States break the Treaty – as they sometimes do quite consciously – they usually intend their action to be only temporary: they know they will have to come into line eventually but try to put it off as long as possible. They therefore play for time in their negotiations with the Commission, and the Commission tries to hurry the procedure along. In such a situation, the ability to apply for an interim order from the Court is a useful weapon.

[61] Mertens de Wilmars and Verougstraete, (above) at 393.

[62] It is possible, however, that the Commission might feel obliged to intervene in the Court proceedings in support of its opinion, as it did in *France v. United Kingdom* (below).

[63] *France v. United Kingdom*, Case 141/78, [1979] ECR 2923.

The relevant provisions are Articles 243 [186] EC and 158 Euratom. They provide: 'The Court of Justice may in any case before it prescribe any necessary interim measures.' This rather uninformative provision gives no indication of what kinds of interim measures may be prescribed, but it has come to be accepted that something in the nature of an English interlocutory injunction can be granted.

Despite initial doubts,[64] it was established in *Commission v. United Kingdom* (*Pig Producers*)[65] that such a remedy is available against a Member State. There are three main considerations which the Court will take into account when deciding whether to grant it.[66] First, it will consider the likelihood of the proceedings being successful: no order will be made if the claim in the main action is manifestly unfounded. Secondly, it must be shown that the need for the order is urgent.[67] Thirdly, the Commission will normally be required to demonstrate that irreparable damage to the Community interest will occur if the order is not given, but the defendant may attempt to show that irreparable damage to its interests will ensue if the order is granted.[68]

*Commission v. Germany*[69] (*Road Tax* case) illustrates the application of these principles. Germany had introduced a tax on heavy goods vehicles using German roads which, it was alleged, applied in a way that was unfair to carriers from other Member States. The Commission brought enforcement proceedings against Germany under Article 226 [169] and applied for an interim order suspending application of the tax until the Court had given judgment. Five other Member States intervened in support of the Commission. As he was entitled to do under Article 84(2) of the Court's Rules of Procedure, the President of the Court granted the application on a temporary basis even before Germany had been able to put its case. He then referred the matter to the Court,[70] which, under Article 85 of the Rules of Procedure, was obliged to give it priority over all other cases.[71]

In its judgment, the Court first examined the substantive claim and concluded that the Commission had established a *prima facie* case of sufficient strength to justify an

[64] In enforcement actions, the judgment takes the form of a declaration that the Member State has failed to fulfil an obligation under the Treaty: the Court does not expressly order the Member State to do anything, though Article 228 [171] EC requires the Member State to take the 'necessary measures' to comply with the judgment. If the final judgment is only declaratory, it might be asked, can the Court grant an interim order specifically requiring the Member State to do something?

[65] Cases 31, 53/77 R, [1977] ECR 921. See also *Commission v. Ireland*, Case 61/77 R, [1977] ECR 937; *Commission v. Italy*, Case 154/85 R, [1985] ECR 1753; *Commission v. Belgium*, Case 293/85 R, [1985] ECR 3521.

[66] See *per* Advocate General Mayras in *Commission v. United Kingdom*, Cases 31, 53/77 R, [1977] ECR 921 at 931–5 and *per* Advocate General Reischl in *Commission v. Ireland*, Case 61/77 R, [1977] ECR 937, at 953–4.

[67] In *Commission v. Ireland*, however, Advocate General Reischl took the view that the mere fact that the Irish measures were actually being applied was sufficient to establish the requisite degree of urgency (at 954).

[68] For the application of these principles to the special procedure under Art. 298 [225] EC, see *Commission v. Greece* (*Macedonia* case), Case 120/94 R, [1994] ECR I-3037.

[69] Case C-195/90 R, [1990] ECR I-3351.

[70] It seems rather strange that the President should both make an order himself – in effect, an 'interim' interim order, since it applied only until the Court made a 'final' interim order – *and* refer it to the Court. The Rules of Procedure made no provision for this: the first para. of Art. 85 stated simply that the President 'shall *either* decide on the application himself *or* refer it to the Court' (emphasis added). The reason, presumably, was that the matter was thought too urgent to be delayed until the Court could deal with it, but too politically delicate for the President to decide it alone.

[71] The Court acted fast: its order was made exactly two weeks after that of the President.

interim order. It next considered whether there was a risk that a subsequent award of damages would not constitute sufficient compensation for the harm suffered by carriers from other Member States. It concluded that such a risk existed, since some of the carriers might be driven into bankruptcy. Germany argued that it would suffer irreparable damage if the tax *were* suspended, since there would be no way in which it could recover the lost revenue. The Court, however, rejected this argument on the ground that the interim order would only restore the *status quo* before the tax was introduced, a ground that raises a number of unanswered questions. It also rejected Germany's demand that the Commission should lodge security for half a billion Deutschmarks to provide it with compensation, should the final judgment be in Germany's favour: the Court held that the lodging of security, for which there is provision in the Rules of Procedure,[72] is not to be required unless there is a risk of non-payment as a result of insolvency, an unlikely contingency in the case of the Community. An interim order was therefore made in virtually the same terms as those of the President.[73]

## RESTITUTION AND DAMAGES

If the delinquent Member State could be forced to undo its action, delaying tactics would serve no purpose. In some situations this might be impossible, but if the violation consisted of an illegal subsidy or an unlawful tax, restitution might be feasible. This could occur under national law simply as a result of the Court's judgment in the enforcement action: for example, the European Court's decision in *Commission v. Luxembourg and Belgium*[74] that import duties imposed by the Belgian Government on dairy products were in violation of Community law was followed by a successful action by importers to reclaim money already paid.[75] (Such actions are, of course, based on the doctrine of direct effect and could succeed even without enforcement proceedings having been brought; where this is the position, a reference will normally be made to the European Court under Article 234 [177].)

In some cases, however, national law will make no provision for restitution. Where this is so, can the Member State be forced to repay or reclaim the money by means of the procedure under Articles 226–228 [169–171]? The difficulty here is that a judgment under Article 226 [169] EC does no more than declare that the defendant Member State has failed to fulfil an obligation under the Treaty: as was mentioned previously it does not (except in the case of interim measures) order the Member State to take any specific action. Article 228 [171] EC requires the Member State to take 'the necessary measures

72 Art. 86(2).

73 See also *Commission v. Austria*, Case C-320/03 R, [2003] ECR I-7929, [2003] ECR I-11665, [2004] ECR I-3593.

74 Cases 90, 91/63, [1964] ECR 625.

75 *Minister for Economic Affairs v. Fromagerie Franco-Suisse 'Le Ski', Cour de Cassation*, Belgium, 21 May 1971, [1972] CMLR 330.

to comply with the judgment of the Court of Justice', but it is generally assumed that it is for the Member State itself to decide what these are. Although it must end its infringement, it is not clear to what extent Article 228 [171] obliges the Member State to attempt to undo its past misconduct.

One possibility would be for the Commission to request the Member State to repay or reclaim the money. If it refused, new enforcement proceedings could be commenced for a breach of Article 228 [171]: in this way, the Court could be asked to rule on the matter. So far, however, the Commission has not resorted to this procedure.

The only cases in which the Commission has required restitution concern illegal state aid, which is not covered by Articles 226–228 [169–171] but falls under a special procedure laid down by Articles 88 [93] and 89 [94] EC. The first case in which this occurred was *Commission v. Germany*[76] (*Kohlegesetz*). The German Government had made provision for certain investment grants which the Commission regarded as contrary to Article 87 [92] EC. On 17 February 1971 the Commission adopted a decision requiring Germany to cease paying the grants: the German Government complied, but only after a certain period of time. The Commission regarded this delay as unacceptable and brought proceedings under Article 88 [93]: it asked the Court not only for a declaration that Germany had failed to comply with the decision of 17 February 1971, but also for a ruling that it was obliged to obtain repayment of grants made after the promulgation of the decision.

The German Government objected to the admissibility of this second claim but the Court overruled the objection. The Court pointed out that the Commission has the power, when it rules that an aid is contrary to the Treaty, to require the Member State to abolish or alter it: this is specifically stated by Article 88(2) [93(2)]. It then said: 'To be of practical effect, this abolition or modification may include an obligation to require repayment of aid granted in breach of the Treaty, so that in the absence of measures for recovery, the Commission may bring the matter before the Court.'[77]

It might be thought that this applied only under the special procedure laid down by Article 88 [93] EC, but the Court went out of its way to dispel any such idea: it expressly said that in an action under Articles 226–228 [169–171], the Commission can apply for a declaration that 'in omitting to take specific measures' the Member State has failed to fulfil an obligation under the Treaty. It then continued:[78]

> Since the aim of the Treaty is to achieve the practical elimination of infringements and the consequences thereof, past and future, it is a matter for the Community authorities whose task it is to ensure that the requirements of the Treaty are observed to determine the extent to which the obligation of the Member State concerned may be specified in the reasoned opinions or decisions delivered under Articles 226 [169] and 88(2) [93(2)] respectively and in applications addressed to the Court.

This suggests that in its decision (under Article 88 [93]) or reasoned opinion (under Article 226 [169]) the Commission may specify what remedial measures are required: failure to carry these out would itself be a breach of the Treaty. For example, the

[76] Case 70/72, [1973] ECR 813. [77] At para. 13 of the judgment. [78] *Ibid.*

Commission could say in its reasoned opinion that the Member State had violated the Treaty (i) by applying an illegal tax and (ii) by not repaying money already collected. If the Member State refused to comply, the Court could grant a declaration in similar terms.

In *Commission v. Germany* the Court decided in the end that the Commission had failed to establish its case; so the order sought by the Commission was not granted. Nevertheless, the judgment clearly establishes the principle. In spite of this, however, the Commission for many years made no further attempt to obtain restitution. Then in 1980 it announced a change of policy regarding state aid to industry: it said that in future it would require repayment of aid granted in violation of Community law.[79] After a somewhat shaky start,[80] this new policy has now become firmly established.[81] It has, however, been applied only to state aid: the Commission has never accepted the Court's invitation to adopt a similar policy in proceedings under Article 226 [169].

Where the Treaty violation consists of, say, an import ban, there can be no question of restitution. Could the procedure under Articles 226–228 [169–171] be used to make a Member State pay damages? In the course of the dispute over the French Government's refusal to obey the Court's judgment in the *Sheepmeat* case (discussed below), the British Government spoke of the possibility of obtaining damages. It could perhaps be argued that failure to compensate British exporters was itself a violation of the Treaty, either because there is an independent obligation to compensate the victims of illegal acts, or because of Article 228 [171]. When the dispute was settled, however, the claim for damages was dropped.[82] It is uncertain, therefore, whether damages can be obtained in this way. On the other hand, as we saw in Chapter 7, it is open to claimants who have suffered loss as a result of a Member State's violation of Community law to bring proceedings for damages in the national courts. The case in which this was established, *Francovich v. Italy*,[83] did in fact arise following a judgment against Italy under Article 226 [169], but, as we saw, the right to bring proceedings is not dependent on such a judgment.[84]

[79] See OJ 1983, C318/3.

[80] The first time the policy was put to the test, something rather strange occurred: a Commission decision was adopted requiring Belgium to reclaim illegal aid granted to a factory making wall coverings (Decision 82/312, OJ 1982, L138/18); some months later, however, a 'corrigendum' was published deleting the provisions requiring repayment (OJ 1982, L289/35). So Belgium did not have to reclaim the aid.

[81] See the line of cases beginning with *Commission v. Belgium*, Case 52/84, [1986] ECR 89. For a discussion of the rules laid down by these cases, see Priess, 'Recovery of Illegal State Aid: An Overview of Recent Developments in the Case Law' (1996) 33 CMLRev. 69. See now Art. 14 of Reg. 659/1999, OJ 1999 L83.

[82] The request for damages was made to the Commission. The idea was that the Commission would ask the Court to make a declaration that France's failure to pay compensation was a violation of the Treaty. The sum claimed was approximately £20 million: see *The Times*, 11 January 1980.

[83] Cases C-6, 9/90, [1991] ECR I-5357.

[84] If the national courts persistently failed to grant a remedy, proceedings could be brought in the European Court under Art. 226 [169] EC; however, as was mentioned above, the Commission is reluctant to bring proceedings for a violation of Community law by national courts and one would not expect it to do so unless the failure was blatant.

## THE NORTH–SOUTH GRADIENT

The Commission, which has the task of monitoring the application of Community law by the Member States, issues annual reports on its activities in this connection. From them, it is possible to discover where particular Member States rank as regards their willingness to observe Community law. These rankings are remarkably consistent over the years, showing that underlying factors (probably of a cultural nature) are responsible. The most striking feature is that there is a discernible North–South gradient. Denmark, Sweden, and Finland are almost always at the top, being the States showing the highest level of respect for Community law, and Greece, Italy, and France usually come at the bottom.[85]

## ENFORCEMENT

In the past, Member States have sometimes taken a considerable period – occasionally as long as several years – to comply with the judgment.[86] Where compliance is unduly delayed the Commission may bring a second action, claiming that the failure to obey the first judgment is itself a violation of the Treaty.[87] This tactic was used against France in the notorious *Sheepmeat* case, which began when France (with some justification on legal and social grounds) refused to admit imports of lamb and mutton from other Member States, principally Britain. The Commission brought proceedings and in due course the Court gave judgment against France.[88] The French Government, however, made clear that it would not comply with the judgment until the Council agreed to a Community support system which would protect French farmers, a measure blocked by Britain.

The Commission then brought new proceedings and applied for an interim order requiring France to admit British lamb without restrictions. Surprisingly, this was refused by the Court on the ground that it would substantially duplicate the previous judgment and would not, therefore, be 'necessary', as required by Article 243 [186] EC.[89] In fact, one suspects that the Court, knowing that any order it gave would be ignored, decided that it would be better to save what was left of its tattered authority by refusing the order. In the end, the case never went to a final judgment: Britain agreed to a Community regime for lamb and mutton in exchange for concessions on its budgetary claims; France then lifted the ban on imports. This case must be regarded as a victory

[85] See Trevor C Hartley, *Constitutional Problems of the European Union* (1999), Chap. 6. Spain and Portugal rank higher than their geographical position would suggest. France ranks lower. It is too early to comment on the Member States that joined in 2004 and in 2007.

[86] In one case, *Commission v. Italy*, Case 79/72, [1973] ECR 667, the judgment had still not been obeyed after ten years: HAH Audretsch, *Supervision in European Community Law*, 2nd edn (1986), pp. 395–6.

[87] Art. 228 [171] EC requires a Member State to comply with a judgment under Arts 226 [169] and 227 [170]. Failure to comply is, therefore, a violation of Art. 228 [171].

[88] *Commission v. France*, Case 232/78, [1979] ECR 2729.

[89] Cases 24, 97/80R, [1980] ECR 1319.

for France and shows that, for a powerful and determined Member State, defiance of the Court can sometimes pay off.

What can be done if a Member State fails to obey a judgment? Under Article 88 ECSC there was provision for the imposition of sanctions: money payable to the delinquent Member State could be withheld, or other Member States permitted to take action 'to correct the effects of the infringement'. The Commission authorized these sanctions but the assent of the Council (acting by a two-thirds majority) had to be obtained. In fact, no sanctions were ever imposed during the fifty years in which the ECSC Treaty was in operation.

Until the Treaty on European Union came into force, there was no provision for sanctions under the EC or Euratom Treaties. Now, however, the Court can impose fines on Member States if they fail to obey a judgment. This is under an amendment to Article 228 [171] EC (and an identical amendment to Article 143 Euratom).[90] The procedure is the same as that for bringing a new action under Article 226 [169]. If the Commission considers that a Member State has not complied with a judgment of the Court, it issues a reasoned opinion after giving the Member State the opportunity to submit its observations. The opinion must specify the points on which the Member State has not complied with the judgment and must lay down a time-limit for compliance. If the Member State does not fall into line within the time-limit, the Commission may bring the case before the Court. When it does so, the Commission may specify the amount of the lump-sum fine or penalty payment that it considers appropriate. (A penalty payment is a payment of a specified amount for each day (or other period of time) that elapses[91] until compliance takes place.) The Court is not obliged to follow the Commission's proposal, though it takes it into account.

On 6 July 1996, the Commission issued a memorandum setting out the criteria it intended to apply in asking the Court to impose monetary penalties.[92] In this it said that, as the purpose of the procedure is to ensure compliance, a periodic penalty payment would normally be more appropriate than a lump sum.[93] In calculating the amount of the penalty to be proposed, the Commission takes three factors into account: the seriousness of the infringement, its duration, and the need to deter future infringements. The seriousness of the infringement is determined on the basis of the importance of the Community rule infringed, and the effect of the infringement on the interests of the Community and of individuals. To ensure a deterrent effect, the penalty is higher if there is a risk of a repetition, or if there has been a repetition.

On 8 January 1997, the Commission announced the method it would use to calculate penalties.[94] It starts with the sum of €500 per day. This is multiplied by two coefficients, the first (on a scale of 1 to 20) reflecting the seriousness of the infringement, and the second (on a scale of 1 to 3) reflecting its duration. To achieve deterrence, the result will be multiplied by a factor reflecting the ability of the Member State to pay (based on its

[90] It has been said that these amendments were adopted at the suggestion of the United Kingdom: *Financial Times*, 6 February 1991.

[91] According to the Commission, time runs from the date on which the judgment was originally served on the recalcitrant Member State: see the Commission's *Fourteenth Annual Report* (above), p. 19.

[92] OJ 1996, C242/6. [93] *Ibid.*, para. 4. [94] OJ 1997, C63/2.

GDP) and the number of votes it commands in the Council. The Commission communication said that this ranges from 1 for Luxembourg to 26.4 for Germany. As a result, a daily penalty payment at the top of the scale for both seriousness and duration would range from €30,000 for Luxembourg to €791,293 for Germany.[95]

Almost seven years after the system was first introduced, a fine was imposed for the first time. The country concerned was Greece. In 1992, the Court gave judgment against Greece for failure to implement a directive on environmental pollution.[96] Greece did nothing to comply and further proceedings were commenced in 1995. The Court gave judgment in July 2000.[97] It imposed a fine of €20,000 per day, somewhat less than the €24,600 proposed by the Commission.[98]

Since this case, the Commission has been sparing in the use of its power to bring applications before the Court under this procedure. In 2003, the Court imposed an annual penalty on Spain in a case concerning pollution of the sea,[99] and in 2005 it imposed a lump-sum fine *and* a periodic penalty payment on France in a case concerning conservation of fish.[100] The imposition of both kinds of penalty in the same case was controversial in view of the fact that Article 228 [171] EC speaks of 'a lump sum *or* penalty payment'.[101] The Court's judgment is lacking in clarity, but it seems that the lump sum may have been intended to punish France for past behaviour; the periodic penalty was to ensure future compliance.[102]

Another development occurred in 2005, when the European Court gave judgment in *Commission v. Ireland*.[103] This concerned illegal dumping of waste (rubbish) by private individuals in Ireland. The Irish Government was accused of violating Community law by failing to take adequate steps to prevent it. The innovative features of the case were, first, that the Commission brought proceedings for a whole lot of specific instances in one action; and, secondly, that it asked the Court to find not only that Ireland had violated Community law in those specific instances, but also that it was guilty of a general and persistent failure to comply with Community law. This latter claim was based on the contention that the Irish Government had failed to put adequate legal and administrative mechanisms in place to ensure that illegal dumping did not occur. The Court agreed with the Commission. It held that Ireland had failed to take the measures necessary to ensure the correct implementation of the relevant Directive. The significance of this is that it will not be enough for Ireland to rectify the various

[95] *Fourteenth Annual Report* (above), p. 20. These figures do not work out quite right: 30,000 multiplied by 26.4 is 792,000. Presumably, the coefficient for Germany is not exactly 26.4.

[96] *Commission v. Greece*, Case C-45/91, [1992] ECR I-2509.

[97] *Commission v. Greece*, Case C-387/97, [2000] ECR I-5047.

[98] Greece paid this fine until the Commission concluded, in July 2001, that it had complied with the judgment. This means that it took almost exactly a year from the date of the second judgment (almost nine years from the date of the original judgment) for Greece to comply.

[99] *Commission v. Spain*, Case 278/01, [2003] ECR I-14141. The fine was fixed at an annual amount of €624,150 for each 1 *per cent* of the total area that remained polluted.

[100] *Commission v. France*, Case C-304/02, 12 July 2005 (Grand Chamber).

[101] Italics added.

[102] The lump sum was only €20 million. The periodic penalty was €57,761,250 for every six months during which France had not complied.

[103] Case C-494/01, 26 April 2005 (Grand Chamber).

specific instances of illegal dumping in order to comply with the judgment; it will also be necessary for it to show that it has taken the necessary steps to ensure that the Directive is enforced in general.[104]

Violation of Community law by popular action is a problem of a somewhat different nature. This has occurred mainly in France, where farmers have blocked imports of agricultural produce from other Member States by ambushing the trucks bringing it. The French police are notoriously reluctant to intervene in such cases, so that the drivers are almost entirely at the mercy of their attackers. For many years, nothing was done about this. In 1985, the Commission wrote a formal letter to the French Government. In August 1995, it brought proceedings before the Court, claiming that France's failure to take effective measures to prevent such occurrences was a violation of the Treaty.

In December 1997, the Full Court (thirteen judges) ruled against France.[105] It held that France had violated Article 28 [30] EC coupled with Article 10 [5] EC. The former prohibits restrictions on imports of goods; the latter requires Member States to take all appropriate measures to ensure the fulfilment of their Treaty obligations. Although the Court was prepared to accept that, in specific instances, inaction might be excused if there was a threat to public order of such magnitude that the Member State could not cope with its consequences, France had failed to establish that this was the case in any of the instances in question.

This judgment is to be welcomed. As the Court pointed out, the mere threat of such attacks could be enough to deter producers in other Member States from exporting to France. Compensation for those actually attacked is not, therefore, enough.

## FURTHER READING

MERTENS DE WILMARS AND VEROUGSTRAETE, 'Proceedings against Member States for Failure to Fulfil their Obligations' (1970) 7 CMLRev. 385.

BARAV, 'Failure of Member States to Fulfil Their Obligations under Community Law' (1975) 12 CMLRev. 369.

EVANS, 'The Enforcement Procedure of Article 169 EEC: Commission Discretion' (1979) 4 ELRev. 442.

GRAY, 'Interim Measures of Protection in the European Court' (1979) 4 ELRev. 80.

EBKE, 'Enforcement Techniques within the European Communities' (1985) 50 Journal of Air Law and Commerce 685.

HAH AUDRETSCH, *Supervision in European Community Law*, 2nd edn (1986).

OLIVER, 'Enforcing Community Rights in the English Courts' (1987) 50 MLR 881.

[104] For a general discussion of this case, see Wennerås, 'A New Dawn for Commission Enforcement under Articles 226 and 228 EC: General and Persistent (GAP) Infringements, Lump Sums and Penalty Payments' (2006) 43 CMLRev. 31 at pp. 33–50.

[105] *Commission v. France*, Case C-265/95, [1997] ECR I-6959.

STEINER, 'How to Make the Action Suit the Case: Domestic Remedies for Breach of EEC Law' (1987) 12 ELRev. 102.

DASHWOOD AND WHITE, 'Enforcement Actions under Articles 169 and 170 EEC' (1989) 14 ELRev. 388.

BONNIE, 'Commission Discretion under Article 171(2) EC' (1998) 23 ELRev. 537.

ALBERTO GIL IBAÑEZ, *The Administrative Supervision and Enforcement of EC Law: Powers, Procedures and Limits* (1999).

THEODOSSIOU, 'An Analysis of the Recent Response of the Community to Non-Compliance with Court of Justice Judgments' (2002) 27 ELRev. 25.

WENNERÅS, 'A New Dawn for Commission Enforcement under Articles 226 and 228 EC: General and Persistent (GAP) Infringements, Lump Sums and Penalty Payments' (2006) 43 CMLRev. 31

# PART IV

# ADMINISTRATIVE LAW

# INTRODUCTION

The Rule of Law is fundamental to all systems of constitutional law. It is so fundamental, in fact, that if it does not exist in at least its most basic form – that governmental authorities not only enforce the law but are also bound by it themselves – there can be no constitutional law. Constitutional law is, after all, the system of legal rules regulating governmental authority and the relations between citizens and the State.

The Rule of Law in this basic sense is, of course, a principle of the Community. However, if the concept is to attain its full realization, more is required than this. In addition, the legality of governmental action should be subject to determination by an independent, impartial adjudicatory body – in short, by a court. In the Community, the appropriate body is the European Court. How far may the Court pass judgment on the actions of the Community authorities? This raises the question whether the Community possesses a system of administrative law to provide the citizen with a remedy in the event of a legal dispute with the Community. This involves three main issues: whether the European Court may review (and, if necessary, quash) Community measures, whether it may require the Community to act where its failure to act is a violation of the law, and, finally, whether it is possible to enforce obligations in contract, quasi-contract, and tort against the Community.

With regard to the first issue, a distinction must be made between a direct challenge and an indirect challenge to a Community act. The object in the former is to obtain a declaration of invalidity. The object of the latter, on the other hand, is something quite different, and the validity of the act arises for decision only because the main question before the court depends on it: the challenge to the act is merely a preliminary step in a procedure leading to a decision on a different issue.

This distinction is important as regards the way the proceedings are instituted. As might be expected, a declaration of invalidity can be obtained only in proceedings specially instituted for this purpose under the relevant provision in the Treaty. In the case of an indirect challenge, on the other hand, the direct object of the proceedings is, and must be, something other than the determination of the validity of the act. In other words, an indirect challenge is made when the act in question is applicable to, or otherwise relevant in, proceedings concerned with something else, and it is argued that the act should not be applied on the ground that it is invalid. The court will then consider its validity. If it finds it invalid, it will refuse to apply it. The purpose of making an indirect challenge, then, is to induce the court not to apply the act to the proceedings.

An important point to note is that, while a direct challenge can be made only before the European Court, an indirect challenge may be made both before a national court and before the European Court. If it is made before a national court, the question of the validity of the act will be referred to the European Court for a preliminary ruling.

It will be seen from this that there are three procedural mechanisms or 'avenues of review' by which the question of validity can be brought before a court: a direct challenge before the European Court; an indirect challenge before the European Court; and an indirect challenge before a national court. However, an essential principle is that, whatever avenue of review is used, the *substantive* question before the Court is always the same: the validity of the act.

If proceedings are brought to quash a Community act (direct challenge) the first question that must be considered is jurisdiction. Closely related to this is the concept of *locus standi* (standing). Jurisdiction is concerned with the power of the Court to hear the case. Looked at from the point of view of the applicant, *locus standi* relates to his right to bring the proceedings, his right to appear before the Court and put his case to it. In other words, if there is an admittedly unlawful act, the question still arises who has the right to ask the Court to quash it.

However, if one looks at it from the point of view of the Court it appears as an aspect of jurisdiction: does the Court have the power to hear proceedings brought by *this* applicant? Thus, from the Court's point of view one can distinguish two kinds of jurisdiction. The first is concerned with the Court's power to hear a case concerning a particular subject matter. This is jurisdiction *ratione materiae* (regarding the subject matter). The second, otherwise known as *locus standi*, is jurisdiction *ratione personae* (regarding the person who is bringing the proceedings). There is also a third kind of jurisdiction: jurisdiction *ratione temporis* (regarding the time of the proceedings). This is concerned with the question: can the Court hear proceedings brought *at this time*? The importance of this is that there are strict time-limits for bringing proceedings: if the application is too late, the Court will not be able to hear it. The time-limit in annulment actions is two months under Article 230 [173] EC.

The second issue mentioned above concerns an unlawful failure to act. In one sense a remedy for failure to act is simply the reverse of an annulment action. In fact, however, the matter is more complicated. If an annulment action is successful, the Court will declare the act void; but if proceedings for failure to adopt an act are successful, the Court merely declares that the defendant's failure is contrary to the Treaty: it cannot itself adopt the act. For this reason, an indirect challenge is not possible in the case of inaction: in collateral proceedings the Court cannot be asked to decide the case on the basis that the act in question has been adopted. This means that the remedies open to the individual are more restricted in the case of a failure to act.

The third issue concerns the enforcement of Community obligations, in particular the right to obtain damages from the Community.

These are the matters that will be considered in this final part of the book.

## FURTHER READING

Carol Harlow, *Accountability in the European Union* (2002).

Paul Craig, *EU Administrative Law* (2006).

Jürgen Schwarze, *European Administrative Law*, rev. edn (2006).

Angela Ward, *Judicial Review and the Rights of Private Parties in EU Law*, 2nd edn (2006).

# 11

# REVIEWABLE ACTS

The first question concerns jurisdiction *ratione materiae*: over what matters does the Court have jurisdiction? Review proceedings are brought for a particular purpose: to have the Court *declare a Community act void*. This is laid down in Articles 230 [173] and 231 [174] EC.[1] The first paragraph of Article 230 [173] provides:

> The Court of Justice shall review the legality of acts adopted jointly by the European Parliament and the Council, of acts of the Council, of the Commission and of the ECB, other than recommendations and opinions, and of acts of the European Parliament intended to produce legal effects *vis-à-vis* third parties.

And Article 231 [174] states: 'If the action is well founded, the Court of Justice shall declare the act concerned to be void.'

It should be noted that in Community law there is no procedure equivalent to the English action for a declaration (or injunction). The Court cannot consider the legal position of the applicant in the abstract. If the action is brought under Article 230 [173], the applicant must find some 'act' to be the subject matter of the proceedings: he can then ask the Court to declare it void. Without this, the Court lacks jurisdiction *ratione materiae*. The first question therefore is concerned with the concept of an 'act'.

Except in the case of the European Parliament acting alone, Article 230 [173] EC applies only to 'acts . . . other than recommendations or opinions'.[2] It will be remembered that Article 249 [189] EC[3] lists five kinds of act that the European Parliament acting jointly with the Council, the Council, and Commission are empowered to pass. These are:

1 regulations;
2 directives;
3 decisions;
4 recommendations;
5 opinions.

[1] Equivalent provisions are contained in Arts 146 and 147 Euratom. These are the same except that there is no reference to acts adopted jointly by the European Parliament and the Council or to acts of the ECB.

[2] It is interesting to speculate why the authors of the EC Treaty defined reviewable acts by means of a negative definition. Did they consider that the list in Art. 249 [189] EC was not exhaustive? This is unlikely since, until the decision of the European Court in the *ERTA* case, it was generally believed that the list *was* exhaustive. Perhaps it was merely thought to be a more elegant style of drafting, and the authors of the Treaty did not intend to widen the scope of the Court's jurisdiction. If this is so, the decision of the European Court in *Commission v. Council* (*ERTA* case), Case 22/70, [1971] ECR 263, brought about an effective modification of the Treaty.

[3] Identical provisions are contained in Art. 161 Euratom.

The European Court has, however, held that this list is not exhaustive. There is also an innominate class of acts *sui generis*. These acts, since they are 'acts other than recommendations or opinions', are subject to review under Article 230 [173] EC.[4]

What are the essential characteristics of reviewable acts under Article 230 [173]? This can be discovered by looking at recommendations and opinions, the two classes of acts that are expressly excluded, except in the case of the Parliament acting alone. It is stated in Article 249 [189] EC that these 'shall have no binding force'. Regulations, directives, and decisions, on the other hand, are all stated to have binding force. It is a reasonable inference, therefore, from the provisions of the Treaty – and this has, in fact, been affirmed by the European Court on numerous occasions – that, except where the European Parliament is acting alone, the essential characteristic of a reviewable act under the EC Treaty is that it must have binding force or, to put it another way, it must have *legal effects*.[5] Moreover, where the European Parliament is acting alone, it is expressly stated in Article 230 [173] that proceedings may be brought only with regard to acts intended to 'produce legal effects *vis-à-vis* third parties.' In all cases under the EC Treaty, therefore, an act cannot be subject to review unless it has legal effects. The same is true under Article 146 Euratom. The result is that an act cannot be subject to review under either of the Treaties unless it has legal effects.[6]

What does 'having legal effects' mean? One might say that an act has legal effects if it alters the legal position of some person. A person's legal position is the sum total of his legal rights and obligations (in a broad sense). In other words, to have legal effects, an act must produce a change in somebody's rights and obligations.[7]

## THE NOORDWIJKS CEMENT ACCOORD CASE

A good illustration of the way this principle applies is the *Noordwijks Cement Accoord* case.[8] In order to grasp the issues in this case it is necessary to have some understanding of the Community law relating to competition. The relevant provision in the EC Treaty is Article 81 [85]. Paragraph 1 of this prohibits agreements between undertakings which restrict competition in the common market. In order to put teeth into this, the Council (acting under a power granted by Article 83 [87] EC) made Regulation 17, which imposed fines on undertakings guilty of violating Article 81(1) [85(1)]. It was, however, realized by the authors of the Treaty that not all restrictive agreements are bad; so provision was made in Article 81(3) [85(3)] for exemptions to be granted to

[4] *Commission v. Council* (*ERTA* case), Case 22/70, [1971] ECR 263, discussed in Chap. 4, above.

[5] See, e.g., *Italy v. Commission*, Case 151/88, [1989] ECR 1255.

[6] It is not necessary, however, that it should be adopted pursuant to provisions of one of the Treaties: *Parliament v. Council*, Case C-316/91, [1994] ECR I-625 (para. 9 of the judgment).

[7] Art. 230 [173] expressly provides that, where the Parliament acts alone, the legal effects must apply *vis-à-vis* third parties. This is no doubt true in the other cases as well: the act must produce a change in the legal rights and obligations of some person other than the author of the act.

[8] Cases 8–11/66, [1967] ECR 75.

agreements that are economically beneficial. Such exemptions are granted by the Commission after an examination of the agreement in question.

Under the procedure established by Regulation 17, a restrictive agreement must be notified to the Commission, which then has the task of deciding whether it violates the provisions of Article 81(1) [85(1)]. If it does not, there is no problem. If it does, the Commission must decide whether an exemption under Article 81(3) [85(3)] should be granted. It is only if the Commission refuses to grant an exemption that the firms concerned are liable to be fined.

The problem with this procedure is that it may take a considerable time for the Commission to reach a decision on these two points. What are the firms to do in the meantime? If they decide not to operate the agreement, which may eventually be held lawful, they will suffer commercially. But if they carry out the agreement and it is finally held unlawful, they might be subject to heavy fines. This difficulty was understood by the authors of Regulation 17, and it is therefore provided in Article 15(5) of the Regulation that undertakings will enjoy an immunity from fines from the time when the agreement is notified until the Commission reaches its decision. This, of course, gives the firms full protection; but it appears to have been thought too favourable to them. So it was provided in Article 15(6) of the Regulation that the immunity will cease to apply once the Commission has informed the firms, *after a preliminary examination*, that the agreement appears to violate Article 81(1) [85(1)] and that there appear to be no grounds to justify an exemption under Article 81(3) [85(3)]. Once the firms receive this communication, they continue to operate the agreement at their own risk: if eventually it is held to be lawful, well and good; otherwise they will be subject to fines.

In the *Noordwijks Cement Accoord* case the companies concerned had notified their agreement to the Commission. In due course they received a letter under Article 15(6) of Regulation 17. It stated:

> The Commission subjected the agreement in question to a provisional examination. It reached the conclusion that the conditions of the application of Article 81(1) [85(1)] of the Treaty were met and that application of Article 81(3) [85(3)] to the said agreement, in the form in which it was notified, was not justified.

The letter then went on to inform the companies that the immunity from fines would cease as from the receipt of the letter. The companies concerned brought proceedings under Article 230 [173] EC to quash the decision contained in the letter.

The Commission argued that the proceedings were inadmissible because the Court had no jurisdiction *ratione materiae*: no 'act' was in existence which could be quashed. The letter, they said, contained a mere *opinion* by the Commission, which would be subject to reconsideration and which was not legally binding. It was not, therefore, a reviewable act.

The Court rejected this contention. After pointing out that the effect of the decision was to remove the immunity provided by Article 15(5), it stated:[9]

> This measure deprived them of the advantages of a legal situation which Article 15(5) attached to the notification of the agreement, and exposed them to a grave financial risk.

[9] *Ibid.* at 91.

> Thus the said measure affected the interests of the undertakings by bringing about a distinct change in their legal position. It is unequivocally a measure which produces legal effects touching the interest of the undertakings concerned and which is binding on them. It thus constitutes not a mere opinion but a decision.

The proceedings were therefore held to be admissible.

This judgment shows that it is sufficient if the act has only a contingent effect on the legal position of those concerned.[10] The immunity taken away by the decision was in the nature of an insurance policy: if in the end the agreement was held not to infringe Article 81 [85], the immunity would – with hindsight – turn out to have been unnecessary. Only if this was not the case would the applicant's legal rights have been affected by the decision.

## PROBLEM CASES

In most cases it will be fairly obvious whether or not an act of a Community institution has legal effects. Some examples have already been given. However, there are a number of difficult cases that have been brought to light in judgments of the European Court. This section is devoted to a discussion of them.

First, if a legal act merely confirms a previous act, it does not change anyone's legal position. It has no legal effects.[11] This does not apply, however, if the later act goes beyond the first one and creates new rights or obligations,[12] or if after the adoption of the first act there has been a fundamental change in the circumstances such that the legal effects of the first act are modified.[13] In particular, this will be the case where the judgment of a court obliges the authority to reconsider the first act.[14] It should also be said that, where the Council confirms a decision taken by COREPER, the definitive act is that of the Council, since COREPER is not a Community institution. Therefore, the Council's decision is a reviewable act.[15]

Secondly, the European Court has said that an act is not reviewable if it has only internal effects.[16] By this it means that if the act affects only the internal organization or

[10] See also *Deshormes v. Commission*, Case 17/78, [1979] ECR 189 (at paras 8–17 of the judgment).

[11] See *SNUPAT v. High Authority*, Cases 42, 49/59, [1961] ECR 53 at 75–6.

[12] See, e.g., *France v. Commission*, Case C-325/91, [1993] ECR I-3283; *France v. Commission*, Case C-303/90, [1991] ECR I-5315. In the first of these cases a 'communication' and in the second a 'code of practice' were held to be reviewable acts, since they sought to impose rights and obligations beyond those contained in the principal measure to which they applied. See also *France v. Commission*, Case C-57/95, [1997] ECR I-1627.

[13] See *ERTA*, Case 22/70, [1971] ECR 263 at para. 66 of the judgment and *per* Advocate General de Lamothe at 286.

[14] *SNUPAT v. High Authority* (above).

[15] *Commission v. Council* (*FAO* case), Case C-25/94, [1996] ECR I-1469 (paras 22–8).

[16] *Group of the European Right v. Parliament*, Case 78/85, [1988] ECR 1753; *Les Verts v. Parliament*, Case 190/84, [1988] ECR 1017; *France v. Parliament*, Cases 358/85, 51/86, [1988] ECR 4821 (para. 17 of the judgment). These cases concerned, respectively, a decision that a motion to set up an inquiry into Fascism was admissible, decisions implementing the budget, and a decision to hold an urgent debate on a particular topic.

operation of the institution which adopted it, third parties cannot challenge it.[17] The principle has been applied mainly to acts of the European Parliament[18] and is now expressly set out in Article 230 [173] EC with regard to those cases where the Parliament does not act jointly with the Council.[19] It is not always easy, however, to draw the line between a purely internal act and one that affects third parties.[20]

Difficult problems arise where an authority adopts an act which binds it as to how it will act in the future. Since this may deprive it of a power – the power to act differently – it can affect the legal position of those who would benefit from the exercise of the power. The matter is difficult, however, because the authority may be able to revoke the act. Nevertheless, if the authority is bound by the act until it is revoked, it should probably be regarded as reviewable.

An example of this is the case of *Lassalle v. European Parliament.*[21] In this case a Community official on the staff of the European Parliament brought proceedings[22] to annul a notice of vacancy for the post of Head of Division in the division in which he worked. The notice specified that one of the qualifications for the post was a 'perfect knowledge of Italian'. There was no actual reason why the holder of the post had to have a perfect knowledge of Italian and this was, in fact, a disguised way of saying the job was reserved for an Italian national. This requirement would have precluded Lassalle from being a candidate and he therefore wished to have the notice quashed. The admissibility of the application was not in fact contested by the defendant and was not therefore discussed in detail by the Court. However, the Advocate General stated:[23]

> ... the notice of vacancy in this instance contains various conditions which limit the choice which the administration will have eventually to make. In short, it is limiting its choice in advance and, in so doing, is taking a decision which, when published, has an immediate adverse effect on servants who, like the applicant, do not fulfil one or other of the required conditions ...

The notice was, therefore, a reviewable act.

Though theoretically different, cases in which an authority merely makes a statement as to how it will exercise its powers in future are often hard to distinguish in practice

[17] This does not prevent a member of the staff of the institution from challenging the act if it affects his legal rights.

[18] It may to some extent be based on the concept of parliamentary sovereignty or autonomy.

[19] Art. 230 [173] states that such acts can be challenged only if they are 'intended to produce legal effects *vis-à-vis* third parties'. This provision, which was added by the Treaty on European Union, incorporates into the Treaty a principle first laid down by the European Court in *Les Verts v. Parliament*, Case 294/83, [1986] ECR 1339 (para. 25 of the judgment).

[20] See, e.g., *France v. Commission*, Case C-366/88, [1990] ECR I-3571, a case concerning internal instructions by the Commission to its officials as to how they should exercise certain powers. The Court held that the instructions were reviewable because they affected the rights of third parties.

[21] Case 15/63, [1964] ECR 31. See also *Küster v. European Parliament*, Case 79/74, [1975] ECR 725 (at paras 4–8 of the judgment) and *De Roubaix v. Commission*, Case 25/77, [1978] ECR 1081 (at paras 6–9 of the judgment).

[22] The proceedings were brought under Art. 91 of the Staff Regulations (Regulation 31/1962, JO 1962, p. 1385): see Art. 236 [179] EC. The issue, however, was the same as under Art. 230 [173] EC.

[23] At 41.

from those in which it adopts an act which binds it in this regard. As was pointed out earlier, one of the defects of Community law is that it has no equivalent to the English action for a declaration. The European Court has, however, tried to alleviate this by ruling that a statement of future intention can be a reviewable act. Strictly speaking, this would be the case only if the authority was bound by its statement; however, this could have undesirable consequences, as the persons concerned might be deprived of a remedy.

The case of *Fédération Charbonnière de Belgique v. High Authority*[24] provides an example. In this case, the Commission wrote to the Belgian Government and told it that continued grants of equalization aid for the Belgian coalfields would be conditional on the Belgian Government's taking certain steps. This obviously meant that the subsidies would be withdrawn if the steps were not taken. Strictly speaking, nobody's legal rights were affected because the Commission was not (presumably) bound by its statement. Yet it was obviously desirable that the mining companies should be allowed to obtain a ruling on the validity of the Commission's decision as soon as it was made, rather than making them wait to see what action the Commission took if the Belgian Government refused to comply. A declaration would have been the appropriate remedy. In the absence of such a remedy the Court had to characterize the Commission's letter as a reviewable act. This is what it did. It justified its ruling as follows:[25]

> In its letter of 28 May 1955 the High Authority accepted that equalization aid must be accompanied by a series of measures to be adopted by the Belgian Government. Furthermore, it considers that the Belgian Government ought to apply four measures, indicated at points (a), (b), (c) and (d). The action referred to under (d) is, therefore, one of the series of measures which the Belgian Government would be obliged to take if the circumstances so required. The High Authority has thus unequivocally determined the attitude which it has decided to take henceforth should the circumstances mentioned under point 2(d) of the letter arise. In other words, it has laid down a rule to be applied if necessary. It must therefore be seen as a decision within the meaning of Article 14 of the Treaty.

Another example is the case of *Algera v. Common Assembly*.[26] The applicants were all officials of the Common Assembly of the ECSC who had been appointed on fixed-term contracts. When the Staff Regulations for Community employees were adopted, the applicants were offered permanent appointments under them. They were, however, unwilling to accept the gradings they were offered. A letter was written to them on behalf of the Assembly noting their rejection of their gradings and stating that if they continued in this attitude they would be regarded as only temporary employees and would lose various benefits. The Court held that this letter constituted a reviewable act because it specified with all necessary precision what action the Common Assembly intended to take if the applicants continued to refuse the grading offered.[27]

The European Court has in fact adopted a general doctrine that any statement by a Community institution as to the action it intends to take in given circumstances is a

[24] Case 8/55, [1956] ECR 245. [25] [1956] ECR at 257.
[26] Cases 7/56, 3–7/57, [1957] ECR 39. [27] [1957] ECR at 54.

reviewable act provided it is definite and unequivocal. The fact that such a statement does not legally bind the institution appears to be immaterial. It is obviously desirable that the persons affected should be able to test the legality of the action proposed and they are entitled to assume that the authority means what it says. Thus, though such a statement of intention may not strictly speaking be a legal act, it is desirable on policy grounds that it should be treated as such in the absence of provision for an action to obtain a declaration.

In view of these earlier cases, it is hard to understand the judgment of the European Court in *United Kingdom v. Commission*,[28] a case concerning the awarding of contracts to companies to provide services to Third World countries under an EC aid programme.[29] Companies bidding for contracts were required to submit applications to the Commission, which drew up a short-list. The problem arose when the Commission announced that in doing this it would take into account the nationality of the company concerned. The idea was that contracts should, as far as possible, be shared out among companies in each Member State according to the money contributed to the aid programme by the Member State in question: it seems that a company could be excluded from the short-list if too many other companies from the same Member State had already been awarded contracts.

The Commission partly abandoned this policy, and then took a decision to apply it fully again. This decision was challenged by the United Kingdom,[30] which argued that it had legal effects, since it could lead to the exclusion of a company from the short-list. The Court, however, rejected this on the ground that the legal effects were produced, not by the decision itself, but by the drawing up of the short-lists.[31] The United Kingdom's challenge was therefore inadmissible.

This ruling seems unfortunate. Even if the Commission's policy could be challenged in the course of proceedings to annul the decision to exclude a particular company from the short-list, it would be difficult in practice to prove that a company had been excluded for this reason. Moreover, such proceedings would provide an effective remedy only if the selection process were frozen until the Court had given its ruling. This could result in a two-year delay in the provision of aid. It would have been far more sensible for the Court to have decided the question of principle as soon as the Commission announced its new policy.[32]

Another problem arises where the procedure laid down for taking a decision involves a number of steps, each step being itself a sort of preliminary decision. It might, for

[28] Case 114/86, [1988] ECR 5289. [29] The Second ACP–EEC Convention of Lomé, 1979.

[30] The United Kingdom was supported by the Netherlands; Italy intervened in support of the Commission.

[31] The Court sought to reinforce its conclusion by pointing out that the lists were not always settled entirely in conformity with the criteria adopted by the Commission. It is hard to see how this is relevant: even if the criteria were applied on only some occasions, they could still affect the rights of applicants.

[32] See the Opinion of Advocate General Lenz, who took the view that the proceedings were admissible and that the decision should be annulled. It is possible that the Court deliberately declared the application inadmissible so that it could avoid having to give a ruling on the substance. It is likely that the Commission's policy was supported by the majority of the Member States; so if the Court had declared it unlawful, it would have offended those States. On the other hand, if it had upheld it, it would have created a precedent which could have caused problems in cases where Member States were accused of discriminating on grounds of nationality.

example, be required that, before the final decision is taken, the opinion of certain bodies should be obtained. The question is whether each of these preliminary decisions should be regarded as a reviewable act or whether they should be regarded as being subsumed in the final decision. From an analytical point of view, the correct answer to this question might depend on the exact requirements of the law. If it is provided merely that the opinion of a certain body must be *taken into account* by the authority making the final decision, it might seem that the preliminary decision does not affect anyone's legal position and is not, therefore, a reviewable act. If, on the other hand, the law states that the authority making the final decision cannot decide in a certain way unless some other body gives a favourable opinion, the preliminary decision will restrict the power of the body giving the final decision. In such a case the preliminary decision should be regarded as a reviewable act.

This, however, is not the view which has been taken by the Court. In the case of *Huber v. Commission*[33] the Court had to consider a problem concerned with the establishment of a Community official. Under the Staff Regulations the opinion of the Establishment Board had first to be obtained. It was moreover provided that the decision-making authority, the Committee of Chairmen, could not establish an official unless the report of the Establishment Board was favourable. In *Huber v. Commission* the report was unfavourable and the Advocate General stated that, since the appointing authority was legally precluded from establishing an official if the report of the Establishment Board was unfavourable, this report was a reviewable act.[34] It took away the power to establish from the Committee of Chairmen and thus put an end to the official's chances of establishment. The Court, however, rejected this opinion and held that the report was not a reviewable act, on the ground that it was not separable from the final decision.[35]

This ruling is questionable from the legal point of view but it probably did little harm on the facts of the case since the Court made clear that the report could be challenged in the course of proceedings to annul the final decision. Moreover, the applicant would benefit in one respect, since the time-limit for bringing the proceedings would begin only on the date of the final decision. The result of this and subsequent cases is that preliminary decisions of this kind are not reviewable in their own right.[36] To come within this rule, the preliminary decision must not affect the applicant's rights independently of the final decision. Its only legal consequences must be its effects on the final decision.[37]

The leading case is now *IBM v. Commission*,[38] another decision under EC competition law. The Commission decided to open proceedings against IBM for abuse of a

[33] Case 78/63, [1964] ECR 367. This was also a case under the Staff Regulations. The issue, however, was the same as under Art. 230 [173] EC.

[34] *Ibid.* at 383.

[35] At 375–6.

[36] See also *Weighardt v. Euratom Commission*, Case 11/64, [1965] ECR 285 at 298; *Bossi v. Commission*, Case 346/87, [1989] ECR 303 (para. 23 of the judgment); *Marcopoulos v. European Court of Justice*, Cases T-32, 39/89, [1990] ECR II-281 (paras 20–3 of the judgment).

[37] In the *Noordwijks Cement Accoord* case (above) the Commission argued that the decision in its letter was a mere preliminary decision, but the Court rejected this because the decision had immediate legal consequences which were independent of the final decision.

[38] Case 60/81, [1981] ECR 2639.

dominant position and it wrote IBM a letter informing it of this and inviting it to put its case. A statement of objections, specifying what IBM was alleged to have done, was enclosed. This communication was a necessary preliminary to any decision against a defendant in such proceedings. IBM, however, objected to the proceedings on a number of grounds extrinsic to the substance of the case. In particular, it alleged that the statement of objections lacked clarity (it said that it had no clear idea what it was alleged to have done), that the decision to bring proceedings had not been taken by the Commissioners themselves but by an official and that the proceedings were contrary to international law because the Commission was attempting to apply Community law extraterritorially. There were obviously great advantages in obtaining a decision on these points before the substance of the action was dealt with; so IBM brought an annulment action against the decision to commence proceedings and against the statement of objections.

The Court, however, held that these were not reviewable acts: they were mere preliminary decisions which could be challenged only in the course of a review of the final decision. The Court justified this on the ground that the consequences of the decision to bring proceedings were either wholly favourable to IBM (for example, it precluded proceedings by the national authorities) or merely paved the way for later steps in the procedure.[39]

This judgment may have been correct in terms of the previous case law of the Court, but it had unfortunate consequences for IBM because it meant that IBM had to incur the great expense of fighting the case on the merits before it could raise its preliminary objections.[40]

Another case in which the Commission raised the 'preliminary decision' argument was *AKZO Chemie v. Commission*.[41] This was also a competition case, in which the Commission decided to show certain documents to the complainant. The company against which the proceedings had been brought, AKZO, claimed that the documents contained confidential information which it did not want business rivals to see; it therefore brought an annulment action against the Commission's decision to show the

[39] On the other hand, a decision *not* to continue with an investigation initiated at the request of a complainant is a reviewable act since it is the final step in the procedure: it will not be followed by any other decision amenable to annulment proceedings by the complainant. See *SFEI v. Commission*, Case C-39/93P, [1994] ECR I-2681 (appeal from Case T-36/92, [1992] ECR II-2479), paras 27–8 of the judgment. See also *AKZO Chemie v. Commission*, Case 5/85, [1986] ECR 2585. On whether a notification under Art. 6 of Regulation 99/63 is a reviewable act, see *Guérin Automobiles v. Commission*, Case C-282/95, [1997] ECR I-1503 (appeal from Case T-186/94, [1995] ECR II-1753): the previous case law is summarized by Advocate General Tesauro at paras 10–17 of his Opinion.

[40] For two other decisions along the same lines, see *Nashua Corporation v. Commission and Council*, Cases C-133, 150/87, [1990] ECR I-719 and *Gestetner Holdings v. Commission and Council*, Case C-156/87, [1990] ECR I-781, both of which concerned anti-dumping proceedings. The actions were brought to annul the refusal by the Commission to accept undertakings offered by the companies concerned: the Court held that this refusal was not a reviewable act, because the Commission plays only a preliminary role in the proceedings, the final decision being taken by the Council, which was not bound to adopt any proposal that might be put forward by the Commission. If the Council imposed an antidumping duty, the companies concerned could challenge the Commission's refusal in the context of a challenge to the regulation introducing the duty.

[41] Case 53/85, [1986] ECR 1965.

documents to the complainant. This time the Court held the proceedings admissible: the decision directly affected AKZO's right to confidentiality, independently of the final decision. Moreover, a right to challenge the decision on the documents in the course of a review of the final decision would not constitute an adequate remedy because by then the damage would already have been done.

The position was similar in *Italy v. Commission*,[42] a case on state aid to industry. Under Article 87 [92] EC, such aid is deemed incompatible with the Common Market if it distorts competition, though there are a number of exceptions. Article 88 [93] EC draws a distinction between existing aid and new aid. The latter must be notified to the Commission before it is put into effect. If, after a preliminary examination, the Commission considers that it is not compatible with the Common Market, it sets in motion the procedure laid down under Article 88(2) [93(2)] EC to determine whether the aid is compatible with the Common Market. In such a case, the Member State is not permitted to give the aid until a final decision has been taken. Aid granted contrary to this rule must be recovered from the recipient, even if the final decision declares the aid compatible with the Common Market.[43] In the case of existing aid, on the other hand, a decision by the Commission to open the procedure does not entail the suspension of the aid.

The case concerned aid which the Italian Government regarded as existing aid. The Commission, however, considered it to be new aid and took a decision to open the procedure under Article 88(2) [93(2)]. Since this affected the right of the recipient to receive the aid while the procedure was pending, the Court held, despite the protests of the Commission, that it was a reviewable act. It made clear, however, that the review would be limited to the question whether the aid was new, rather than existing: the question of its compatibility with the Common Market would have to wait until the Commission had taken a final decision.

Finally, a word should be said about *NBV and NVB v. Commission*,[44] a case decided by the Court of First Instance. This was a competition case in which the applicants had applied to the Commission for negative clearance of an agreement.[45] This was granted. The decision which granted it stated that, although the agreement was inherently restrictive of competition, it was not contrary to Community law because it did not affect trade between Member States.[46] The applicants then brought proceedings to annul the part of the decision which said that the agreement was inherently restrictive of competition. Since they wanted to annul only that part, the question was whether *that part* had legal effects, and since it did not – any effects it might have had were negatived by the finding that the agreement did not affect trade between Member States – it was not a reviewable act. The application was therefore inadmissible.[47]

[42] Case C-47/91, [1992] ECR I-4145.

[43] *Fédération Nationale du Commerce Extérieur v. France*, Case C-354/90, [1991] ECR I-5505.

[44] Case T-138/89, [1992] ECR II-2181.

[45] Negative clearance is a decision that an agreement does not infringe Community law.

[46] Under Art. 81 [85] EC, agreements are within the scope of Community law only if there is a possibility that they will affect trade between Member States.

[47] For further cases on legal effect, see *Assicurazioni Generali v. Commission*, Case T-87/96. [1999] ECR II-203; *Coca-Cola v. Commission*, Cases T-125, 127/97, [2000] ECR II-1733; *Geotronics v. Commission*, Case C-395/95 P, [1997] ECR I-2271; *Ca'Pasta v. Commission*, Case C-359/98, [2000] ECR I-3977.

## VOID AND VOIDABLE ACTS

Up to now nothing has been said about the validity of acts. This is obviously important because it might be thought that an invalid act could have no legal effects. However, in Community law the general rule is that invalid acts are voidable, not void. In other words, they have legal effects unless and until the European Court sets them aside.[48] Since the question of jurisdiction is decided at the beginning of the hearing, it is clearly proper, in the case of a voidable act, to assume its validity for the purpose of deciding whether it has legal effects.

The rule that invalid acts are normally voidable and not void is important for another reason as well. It will be remembered that there is a very short time period for bringing proceedings to quash an act. Once this has gone by, the act can no longer be annulled. An invalid act which is immune from review for this reason is not, however, the same as a valid act, since it may be subject to indirect challenge.[49] However, this right is limited; so for some purposes a voidable act which has not been annulled within the time-limit has the same effect as a valid one.

The reason for the rule that invalid acts are merely voidable, and also for the very short period within which a challenge may be brought, is said to be a desire to protect legal certainty. If an act of a public authority has the appearance of being valid, it is desirable that it should be treated as such unless and until it is annulled; and the period of uncertainty is restricted as much as possible by having a short time-limit. However, if the act is quite patently and obviously invalid – for example, if it is made by an authority which could not possibly have the power to make it – legal certainty is no longer in issue. In such a case the act may be regarded as being void: 'non-existent' in Community terminology.[50]

This has two important consequences. First, paradoxical as it may seem, the European Court will have no jurisdiction to quash it. Since it is non-existent, it can have no legal effects; therefore it is not a reviewable act. If proceedings are brought to annul such an 'act', the Court will declare them inadmissible: it will lack jurisdiction *ratione materiae*. This is quite logical, though it may seem strange to the Anglo-Saxon mind that an act which is vitiated by a significant but not obvious fault may, being merely voidable, be quashed by the Court; but that an 'act' which is patently invalid, being absolutely void, cannot be annulled. In practice, however, this is not as serious a drawback as it might appear since, if the Court gives a judgment stating that the case is inadmissible because the 'act' is non-existent, the practical effect will be the same as a declaration of invalidity (and costs may even be granted to the applicant – who is technically the losing party – if he can show that the defendant was at fault in leading him to believe that the 'act' was in fact legally effective).[51]

[48] *Commission v. BASF*, Case C-137/92P, [1994] ECR I-2555 (appeal from Cases T-79/89 (etc.), [1992] ECR II-315) at para. 48 of the judgment of the European Court.

[49] See Chap. 14.

[50] *Commission v. BASF* (above), para. 49 of the judgment of the European Court.

[51] See *Lemmerz-Werke v. High Authority*, Cases 53–4/63, [1963] ECR 239 at 249. In this case the applicant had to pay a quarter of the costs and the defendant had to pay three-quarters. In the *Tubes de la Sarre* case

The second consequence of the 'act' being non-existent is that the expiry of the time-limit cannot give it even the shadow of validity. It is open to indirect challenge in all circumstances since, once it is shown to be non-existent, no court is entitled to take cognizance of it.[52] The passage of time can never confer validity on such an act.[53]

It is not easy to say precisely in what circumstances an act will be non-existent, but the European Court has said that the defects of the act must be particularly serious and obvious.[54] Normally, the invalidity of the act must be apparent on its face. In *Société des Usines à Tubes de la Sarre v. High Authority*[55] the European Court held that the absence of reasons renders an act non-existent. However, this has not been followed in later cases[56] and cannot now be regarded as good law. The two cases in which an act probably would be non-existent are where it is clearly and obviously *ultra vires*, for example if it deals with a subject-matter completely outside the scope of the Treaties,[57] or if there are such major procedural defects in its enactment that it could not be said to have been adopted by the authority.

The latter situation was considered by the European Court in *Lemmerz-Werke v. High Authority*,[58] in which the Court had to decide whether certain letters constituted reviewable acts under Article 33 ECSC. The Commission (High Authority) had previously issued a general decision[59] (Decision 22/60) prescribing the form that decisions had to take.[60] One of these requirements was that the decision had to be signed by a member of the Commission on its behalf. The letters, which were signed merely by an official of the Commission, did not comply with these requirements and the Court held that they did not constitute decisions and were not, therefore, reviewable. It gave its reasons as follows:[61]

> According to Article 14, decisions shall be taken by the High Authority, that is to say by its members sitting as a body. As such decisions are 'binding in their entirety' however, they must show that they are intended to have legal effects upon those to whom they are addressed.

(below), the applicant had to pay all the costs; but in *Commission v. BASF* (above), the Court of First Instance ordered the defendant (Commission) to pay all the costs. On appeal, the European Court held that the decision was not non-existent, but it annulled it. It ordered the Commission to pay all the costs both in the Court of First Instance and on appeal.

[52] In *Commission v. BASF* (above), the Court of First Instance said that a plea that an act is non-existent, being a matter of public interest, may be relied upon by the parties at any time during the proceedings and must be raised by the Court of its own motion (para. 68 of its judgment). This passage was quoted without comment by the European Court in the appeal (para. 16 of the judgment of the European Court).

[53] *Consorzio Cooperative d'Abruzzo v. Commission*, Case 15/85, [1987] ECR 1005 (para. 10 of the judgment).

[54] *Commission v. BASF* (above), para. 50 of the judgment of the European Court; *Consorzio Cooperative d'Abruzzo v. Commission* (above), para. 10 of the judgment. See further *Algera v. Common Assembly*, Cases 7/56, 3–7/57, [1957] ECR 39 at 60–1.

[55] Cases 1, 14/57, [1957] ECR 105.

[56] See, e.g., *Nold v. High Authority*, Case 18/57, [1957] ECR 121, and the *Noordwijks Cement Accoord* case, Cases 8–11/66, [1967] ECR 75.

[57] *Commission v. France* (*Rediscount Rate*), Cases 6, 11/69, [1969] ECR 523.

[58] Cases 53, 54/63, [1963] ECR 239.

[59] Equivalent to a regulation under the EC Treaty.

[60] On this, see *Krupp v. Commission*, Cases 275/80, 24/81, [1981] ECR 2489; see also *National Carbonising v. Commission*, Cases 109, 114/75, [1977] ECR 381 at 388 *per* Advocate General Mayras.

[61] [1963] ECR at 248.

> It follows from the natural meaning of the word that a decision marks the culmination of procedure within the High Authority, and is thus the definitive expression of its intentions.
>
> Finally, it is necessary for the legal protection of all those affected that they should be able to identify by its very form a decision which involves such serious legal consequences, in particular a compulsory time-limit for exercising the right of instituting proceedings against it. In particular, for a measure to amount to a decision, those to whom it is addressed must be enabled clearly to recognize that they are dealing with such a measure.
>
> It follows therefore from all these considerations that a decision must appear as a measure taken by the High Authority, acting as a body, intended to produce legal effects and constituting the culmination of a procedure within the High Authority, whereby the High Authority gives its final ruling in a form from which its nature can be identified.
>
> Any measure, therefore, which in particular, does not appear to have been debated and adopted by the High Authority and authenticated by the signature of one of its members, cannot be regarded as a decision.

It is not easy to know to what extent the principles laid down in this passage are based on Decision 22/60 as distinct from the Treaty itself. The judgment was not expressly based on Decision 22/60, and the Court was careful to point out that the absence of a non-essential requirement of form will not prove fatal as long as the 'fundamental conditions underlying the concept of a decision within the meaning of the Treaty' are satisfied. This suggests that the judgment was, at least in part, independent of Decision 22/60. If this is so, it must now be regarded as a doubtful authority if it is to be understood as requiring the signature of a member of the Commission in all cases:[62] it would be unreasonable if the Commission could not delegate less important decision-making powers to its staff, and there have been a number of cases in which the Court has recognized that letters signed by Commission officials can constitute reviewable acts.[63]

The leading case on this question is now *Commission v. BASF*.[64] This concerned a Commission decision which declared that a number of companies had infringed Article 81 [85] EC by participating in a price-fixing arrangement. The companies, which had been fined by the Commission, brought proceedings before the Court of First Instance to annul the decision. In the course of the hearing the Commission admitted it was unable to produce an original copy of the decision, signed and duly authenticated as required by its Rules of Procedure. In fact, it seems likely that the Commissioners themselves did not agree on a precise text but only on the substance

[62] The third para. of the quotation suggests that the Court may have intended the principle to apply only to decisions which involve 'serious legal consequences'.

[63] For instance, in the *Noordwijks Cement Accoord* case, Cases 8–11/66, [1967] ECR 75; see further Usher (1984) 9 ELRev. 261 at 262. It is interesting to note that in *Kohler v. Court of Auditors*, Cases 316/82, 40/83, [1984] ECR 641, a case under the Staff Regulations, the European Court held that an oral decision can be a reviewable act (see Usher, above); and in *Air France v. Commission*, Case T-3/93, [1994] ECR II-121 the Court of First Instance reached a similar conclusion in proceedings under Art. 230 [173] EC (paras 55–60 of the judgment). In *AKZO Chemie v. Commission*, Case 5/85, [1986] ECR 2585 the Court held that measures of management or administration may be delegated by the Commission to a single Commissioner (paras 28–40 of the judgment); see also *VBVB v. Commission*, Cases 43, 63/82, [1984] ECR 19.

[64] Case C-137/92P, [1994] ECR I-2555 (appeal from Cases T-79/89 (etc.), [1992] ECR II-315).

of the decision. In any event, the text had been significantly altered after the date on which it was supposed to have been adopted; moreover, the Dutch and Italian versions had been adopted by only a single Commissioner, who had acted after he had ceased to hold office.

The Court of First Instance began its judgment by stressing the importance of the rule that decisions cannot be altered after they have been adopted,[65] a rule it considered essential for legal certainty. It found that it was impossible to ascertain the precise content of the decision because the Commission had completely disregarded the authentication procedure laid down in the its Rules of Procedure.[66] It was also impossible to know exactly when and by whom it had been adopted. For these reasons, the 'decision' was declared non-existent. The case went on appeal to the European Court, where it was held that the defects were not serious enough to render the decision non-existent; nevertheless, they were serious enough to render it voidable and it was duly annulled.

## THE AUTHOR OF THE ACT

In addition to the requirement of legal effects, an act is reviewable only if it has been adopted by the appropriate Community institution or body. The position is different under each of the two Treaties. Article 230 [173] EC permits review of the following:

1 acts adopted jointly by the European Parliament and the Council;
2 acts of the Council;
3 acts of the Commission;
4 acts of the European Central Bank (ECB);
5 acts of the European Parliament.

Prior to the Treaty on European Union, Article 230 [173] applied only to the Council and Commission. The European Court had, however, decided that acts of the European Parliament were also covered (provided they have legal effects *vis-à-vis* third parties)[67] and Article 230 [173] was amended by the Treaty on European Union to give formal effect to this. The European Court has also held that acts of the Court of Auditors may be challenged,[68] but the Treaty has not been amended to give formal effect to this. Acts adopted jointly by the European Parliament and the Council became possible for the

[65] This does not mean that they cannot be amended by a later decision: it just means that the text cannot be surreptitiously changed by an official (or even a Commissioner) without going though the procedure for adopting a new decision.

[66] Under Art. 12 of these Rules, the text of acts adopted by the Commission, authenticated by the signatures of the President and Secretary-General of the Commission, must be annexed to the minutes recording their adoption.

[67] *Parti Ecologiste – 'Les Verts' v. European Parliament*, Case 294/83, [1986] ECR 1339.

[68] *Maurissen v. Commission*, Cases 193 and 194/87, [1989] ECR 1045. The remarkable thing about this decision is that the Court did not discuss the issue, though the Advocate General did: see his Opinion at 1063–5.

first time as a result of the Treaty on European Union,[69] which also provided for the creation of the ECB. Article 230 [173] therefore had to be extended to apply to these two categories of acts as well.[70]

Article 146 Euratom was extended by the Treaty on European Union to cover acts of the Parliament (not acting jointly with the Council) in the same terms as Article 230 [173] EC. Acts adopted jointly by the European Parliament and the Council are not covered, nor are acts of the ECB.

If the author of the act is not one of the bodies listed above, the act will not be reviewable. Thus, for example, an act of the representatives of the Governments of the Member States is not reviewable under Article 230 [173] EC, even if the representatives were meeting in the Council.[71] The Court will not, however, look simply at the designation of the act: it will verify whether or not it was adopted by the body in question by considering its content and the circumstances in which it was adopted.[72]

The existence of different provisions in the two Treaties could cause difficulties. There is, of course, no problem if the measure is passed under one Treaty only. But what if a single measure is passed simultaneously under both Treaties? This question arose in *Luxembourg v. European Parliament*,[73] where the act subject to review was adopted under the EC, ECSC, and Euratom Treaties. The act was a resolution by the European Parliament that it would hold its future sessions in Strasbourg. Since it had previously held some of its sessions in Luxembourg, the Luxembourg Government wished to challenge the resolution. The case arose before the Treaty on European Union came into force and before the European Court had 'rewritten' Article 230 [173] EC so as to cover the Parliament; so the apparent position was that acts of the European Parliament could be reviewed only under the ECSC Treaty, Article 38 of which allowed acts of the Parliament to be challenged at the suit of a Member State or the Commission.

There was only one Parliament for all three Communities and the future sessions would concern all three. Could the resolution be reviewed on the basis of one Treaty only? The Parliament maintained that it could not. It argued that in passing the resolution it had made a single and indivisible use of its powers under all three Treaties. The Court, however, held that the resolution could be annulled on the basis of Article 38 ECSC alone. It therefore appears that, where an institution's activities are not confined to one Treaty alone, the remedies given by any relevant Treaty can be used to challenge the measure.[74] It seems that if an act is annulled under one Treaty, it is annulled for all relevant Treaties: it cannot be regarded as annulled for the one but still operative for the others.[75]

69 See now Art. 251 [189b] EC.

70 Art. 237 [180] EC allows acts of the Board of Governors and the Board of Directors of the European Investment Bank to be challenged in certain circumstances.

71 *European Parliament v. Council*, Cases C-181, 248/91, [1993] ECR I-3685.

72 *Ibid.*

73 Case 230/81, [1983] ECR 255.

74 See also *Municipality of Differdange v. Commission*, Case 222/83, [1984] ECR 2889 (para. 6 of the judgment).

75 In *Luxembourg v. European Parliament* the resolution was not annulled, but in a similar case decided the following year, *Luxembourg v. European Parliament*, Case 108/83, [1984] ECR 1945, a later resolution of the Parliament was annulled.

What happens if a Community institution, the acts of which are reviewable, delegates power to some other body? Will the acts of this other body be reviewable? There will, of course, be no problem if the power is delegated to another Community institution whose acts are also reviewable. For example, if the Council delegates power to the Commission, the European Court will have jurisdiction to review any act adopted under the delegated power.[76]

A more difficult problem arises where power is delegated to a body specially set up by a Community institution. An example of this occurred under the ECSC Treaty where the Commission set up two subordinate bodies, the *Office commun des consommateurs de ferrailles* and the *Caisse de péréquation de ferrailles importés* (CPFI). The function of these organizations, which were both established as co-operatives under Belgian law, was to administer the subsidy system for steel scrap. This was financed by a levy[77] on all steel-making enterprises and it was the job of the CPFI to determine how much each enterprise had to pay.

In the case of *SNUPAT v. High Authority*,[78] a steel-making firm, SNUPAT, was in dispute with the CPFI as to the amount it owed under the levy. On 12 May 1958 the CPFI wrote to SNUPAT rejecting its contentions and stating that it owed a certain sum. The CPFI was empowered to do this under the Commission's Decision 2/57, Article 12(2), which authorized it to collect payments under the levy. In the event of an enterprise failing to pay, the CPFI would ask the Commission to take a decision which would be enforceable against the enterprise by virtue of Article 92 ECSC.

One of the issues in the case was whether the CPFI's letter was a reviewable act in view of the fact that it originated, not from the Commission, but from the CPFI. After deciding that a notification of this kind created an obligation on the enterprise (and thus had legal effects) the Court said:[79]

> Article 33 of the ECSC Treaty only provides for actions against decisions of the High Authority [Commission]. It is therefore necessary to examine whether decisions adopted by the CPFI are equivalent to decisions of the High Authority.
>
> In this regard there must be taken into consideration the fact that the CPFI was an organ of a financial arrangement set up by the High Authority and that it held its powers from the latter.
>
> Moreover, as has been found above, notifications from the CPFI in fact constituted the final administrative decision, which the High Authority could have avoided if it had made provision for administrative appeals against the deliberations of the Brussels agencies under clearly defined conditions.
>
> Therefore, it must be accepted – and to do otherwise would be to deprive the undertakings of the protection afforded them by Article 33 of the ECSC Treaty – that the decisions adopted by the CPFI under Article 12(2) of Decision No 2/57 rank as decisions of the High

[76] Nor will there be any problem if an institution, such as the Commission, delegates power to one of its members, since the decision will have been adopted in the name of the institution: *AKZO Chemie v. Commission*, Case 5/85, [1986] ECR 2585 (para. 36 of the judgment).

[77] The authority to impose levies was granted by Art. 49 ECSC. See also Art. 50(2) ECSC.

[78] Cases 32–3/58, [1959] ECR 127.

[79] [1959] ECR at 137–8.

Authority and, as such, are open to applications for annulment under the conditions laid down in Article 33.

The principle laid down in this judgment would probably apply to other cases where the Commission set up a body in order to delegate powers to it, but it is not clear whether it would apply in other cases, especially if powers were delegated to a Member State.

Up to now it has been assumed that the act is a unilateral one, but what is the position if it is bilateral? For example, can an international agreement be a reviewable act? In *France v. Commission*,[80] the French Government brought proceedings under Article 230 [173] EC to challenge an international agreement on competition law concluded by the Commission with the United States. The Commission argued that an international agreement is not a reviewable act under Article 230 [173], since it is bilateral. France argued that a bilateral act can be reviewable; alternatively, it maintained that the proceedings should be regarded as directed against the Commission decision authorizing the conclusion of the agreement. Advocate General Tesauro, after pointing out that an *obiter dictum* of the Court states that an international agreement can be a reviewable act,[81] said that it was of little importance whether the agreement itself or the decision to conclude it was the subject matter of the proceedings. The Court held that, since the agreement was intended to produce legal effects, 'the act whereby the Commission sought to conclude the Agreement' must be regarded as reviewable.[82] It ruled that France's action should be regarded as directed against that act.[83] This could be seen as implicitly accepting that only a unilateral act can be reviewable.

## FURTHER READING

R. H. LAUWAARS, pp. 256–61.

WAELBROECK, 'La notion d'acte susceptible de recours dans la jurisprudence de la Cour de Justice des Communautés européennes' [1965] CDE 225.

[80] Case C-327/91, [1994] ECR I-3641.

[81] *Local Cost Standard* case, Opinion 1/75, [1975] ECR 1355 at 1361.

[82] Para. 15 of the judgment.

[83] Para. 17 of the judgment.

# 12

# *LOCUS STANDI*

## PRIVILEGED APPLICANTS

Under the second paragraph of Article 230 [173] EC,[1] as amended by the Treaty of Nice, the European Court has jurisdiction in actions for judicial review brought by a Member State, the European Parliament, the Council, or the Commission. Parties covered by this provision will be referred to as 'privileged applicants': they always have *locus standi* (standing) to challenge any reviewable act, even a decision addressed to someone else.[2]

Originally, the European Parliament had no *locus standi* under Article 230 [173]. In the *Comitology* case,[3] the Parliament claimed that it should benefit from the unlimited standing conferred on privileged applicants, but the Court rejected this. The Court also said that the Parliament was not a 'legal person' within the meaning of what is now the fourth paragraph of Article 230 [173],[4] which meant that it could not bring any proceedings at all under Article 230 [173]. Subsequently, the Court had a change of heart and ruled in the *Chernobyl* case[5] that the Parliament did have *locus standi* but on a limited basis: it could bring proceedings only to safeguard its prerogatives, and such proceedings could be founded only on submissions alleging the infringement of those prerogatives. This ruling, which might be regarded as a compromise between the provisions of the Treaty and the claims of the Parliament,[6] was embodied in the EC Treaty by the Treaty on European Union, which extended it to cover the European Central Bank as well. It then constituted the third paragraph of Article 230 [173]. It was amended by the Treaty of Amsterdam to add the Court of Auditors.

The Treaty of Nice made a further change: it removed the Parliament from the third paragraph and put it into the second paragraph, along with Member States, the Council, and the Commission.[7] The position under the Treaty of Nice is, therefore, that the Member States, the Parliament, the Council, and the Commission have full 'privileged' status (second paragraph); while the Court of Auditors and the ECB have

[1] The second paragraph of Art. 146 Euratom is identical.

[2] See, e.g., *Commission v. Council*, Case 45/86, [1987] ECR 1493 (para. 3 of the judgment); *United Kingdom v. Council*, Case 131/86, [1988] ECR 905 (para. 6 of the judgment).

[3] *European Parliament v. Council*, Case 302/87, [1988] ECR 5615.

[4] At the time of the case, it constituted the second paragraph.

[5] *European Parliament v. Council*, Case C-70/88, [1990] ECR I-2041. This case actually concerned Art. 146 Euratom, but the two provisions were identical.

[6] On these aspects of the judgment, see Chap. 2.

[7] It made a similar change to Art. 146 Euratom. This provision is thus identical to Art. 230 [173] EC, except that the ECB is not covered by the third paragraph.

'semi-privileged' status (third paragraph): they can bring proceedings only to protect their prerogatives.[8]

The justification for giving privileged applicants unlimited *locus standi* is that *every* Community act concerns them. In this respect, a parallel may be drawn with the Crown (represented by the Attorney-General) in English administrative law. This idea of universal interest is justified in the case of the three 'privileged' Community institutions by reason of their wide responsibilities; while the Member States, as the creators of the whole system, may equally be regarded as interested in everything it does. This explains why privileged status attaches only to the parties to the Treaties – the Member States as such – and not to political sub-divisions of a Member State.[9] Scotland or Wales, for example, would not constitute privileged applicants, even if the subject matter of the measure under review was something within their jurisdiction.[10]

## NON-PRIVILEGED APPLICANTS: BASIC REQUIREMENTS UNDER THE EC TREATY

Applicants who do not fall into the 'privileged' or 'semi-privileged' categories are dealt with in what is now the fourth paragraph[11] of Article 230 [173] EC. This reads:

> Any natural or legal person may... institute proceedings against a decision addressed to that person or against a decision which, although in the form of a regulation or a decision addressed to another person, is of direct and individual concern to the former.

It will be immediately apparent from this that the rights of ordinary persons to bring proceedings are restricted. The first point to note is that they may bring proceedings against only one kind of legal act: a decision. This is clearly stated in the provision.

It is obvious that this provision – especially the phrase, 'a decision... in the form of a regulation' – would not make sense unless it was understood that there is a distinction between the form of an act and its essential nature. This is in fact the case, as has been stressed many times by the European Court: neither the form in which an act is adopted nor the designation which it gives itself is conclusive as to its essential nature.[12]

This distinction between form and substance can give rise to ambiguity. When the Treaty uses the word 'decision', one might not be sure whether it means 'an act in the

[8] The case law on what constituted an infringement of the Parliament's prerogatives will continue to apply to the Court of Auditors and the ECB. On this, see *European Parliament v. Council*, Case C-316/91, [1994] ECR I-625 (paras 10–19 of the judgment); *European Parliament v. Commission*, Case C-156/93, [1995] ECR I-2019 (paras 10–13 of the judgment).

[9] *Région Wallonne v. Commission*, Case C-95/97, [1997] ECR I-1787 (para. 6 of the judgment). See also *Regione Toscana v. Commission*, Case C-180/97, [1997] ECR I-5245.

[10] They could, however, constitute non-privileged applicants under the fourth paragraph of Art. 230 [173]: see *Regione Autonoma Friuli-Venezia v. Commission*, Case T-288/97, [1999] ECR II-1871.

[11] Prior to the Treaty on European Union, it was the second paragraph.

[12] See, e.g., *Confédération Nationale des Producteurs de Fruits et Légumes v. Council*, Cases 16–17/62, [1962] ECR 471 at 478–9.

form of a decision' (a decision in the formal sense) or 'an act which is in substance a decision' (a decision in the material sense). One assumes, of course, that in normal circumstances these two will be the same thing: normally the author of the act will adopt it in its correct form and give it its correct designation. Nevertheless, there can be exceptional cases in which this is not so.

It is stated in the fourth paragraph of Article 230 [173] that there are three situations in which non-privileged applicants may bring review proceedings. These are where the challenged act is:

1 a decision addressed to the applicant;
2 a decision in the form of a regulation;
3 a decision addressed to another person.

It is clear that in the second case the word 'decision' means an act which is in substance a decision. What about cases 1 and 3? The decision in the *Noordwijks Cement Accoord* case[13] shows that case 1 is also concerned with a decision in the material sense. In this case, it will be remembered, the challenged act was a letter addressed to the applicants which withdrew the immunity from fines which they had hitherto enjoyed. The letter was not a decision in the formal sense and the Commission argued that it was not a reviewable act at all. The Court, however, found that it was a decision in the material sense and ruled that the proceedings were therefore admissible.

It is hard to doubt that case 3 also refers to a decision in the material sense.[14] If this is so, any act, irrespective of its form, that is addressed to either the applicant or any other person (including, it has been held,[15] a Member State) may be the subject of proceedings brought by a private person, provided it is in substance a decision and the other requirements of the fourth paragraph of Article 230 [173] are met.[16] The only possible exception is an act in the form of a directive. Although there are cases in which the European Court has been prepared to consider whether an act in the form of a directive was in substance a decision,[17] it has always concluded that it was not. It has not, therefore, had to rule on the point of principle.[18] The Court of First Instance has, however, said that an applicant should not be deprived of his right of review just because the act was adopted in the form of a directive.[19] This must surely be right.

What is the position where the act, being a decision in the material, but not the formal, sense, is not addressed to anyone? If it is in the form of a regulation, there is,

[13] Cases 8–11/66, [1967] ECR 75, discussed in Chap. 11.

[14] See *Air France v. Commission* (below).

[15] *Plaumann v. Commission*, Case 25/62, [1963] ECR 95.

[16] However, though the Court has been prepared to hold that an act which is not in the form of a decision is in substance a decision, it has not so far applied the process in reverse and ruled that an act in the form of a decision is in substance some other kind of act.

[17] *Fédération Européenne de la Santé Animale v. Council*, Case 160/88R, [1988] ECR 4121; *Gibraltar v. Council*, Case C-298/89, [1993] ECR I-3605; *Asocarne v. Council*, Case C-10/95 P, [1995] ECR 4149 (appeal from Case T-99/94).

[18] See *Asocarne v. Council* (above) at para. 32 of the judgment, where it expressly left the point open.

[19] *UEAPME v. Council*, Case T-135/96, [1998] ECR II-2335 (paras 62 *et seq.*); *Salamander v. Parliament and Council*, Case T-172/98, [2000] ECR II-2487. In both these cases the Court of First Instance ruled in the end that the applicants lacked standing.

of course, no problem. It comes under case 2. If this is not the case – for example, if the act is not in any recognized legal form – it might seem at first sight that it could not be challenged by a private person. However, in *Air France v. Commission*,[20] the Court of First Instance allowed Air France to challenge an oral statement made by a Commission spokesman at a press conference. Apparently no written text existed.[21] Though a decision in substance, it was not in the form of a decision, neither was it addressed to anyone in particular; nevertheless, the Court of First Instance held that Air France, a non-privileged applicant, had *locus standi* to challenge it under Article 230 [173] EC. Though this interpretation is not consistent with the wording of Article 230 [173], it is hard to believe that the authors of the Treaty would have intended otherwise: it would be wrong if the Commission could deprive an applicant of the right to challenge a decision by the simple expedient of not formally addressing it to anyone. Thus it seems that the form of the measure does not matter as long as it is in substance a decision. If it is, a private applicant can challenge it, provided the other requirements of the fourth paragraph of Article 230 [173] are met.

What are these other requirements? In the case of a decision addressed to the applicant, there are none. In all other cases, however, it must in addition be shown that the decision is of direct and individual concern to the applicant, in which case he might be regarded as a sort of *de facto* addressee.[22] One can, therefore, summarize the position by saying that a private person may challenge an act that is in essence a decision, provided it is either addressed to him or is of direct and individual concern to him.

It has just been said that a person directly and individually concerned by an act may be regarded as a *de facto* addressee. If the act is in fact addressed to another person (case 3), must the applicant prove that the other person is an addressee in form only and not an addressee in substance at all? The wording of paragraph 4 of Article 230 [173] might suggest this: 'a decision which, although in the form of a regulation or a decision addressed to another person . . . ' In spite of this, however, the European Court has never required an applicant under case 3 to show that the actual addressee is not genuinely affected by the act.[23] It is, of course, quite possible that two people might be directly and individually concerned by an act, possibly in different ways, and if this is the case there is no reason why both should not have *locus standi* to challenge it: it should not be necessary for the applicant to prove an *exclusive* interest.

In any proceedings brought by an ordinary litigant, it is an essential requirement that the challenged act be shown to be a decision in the material sense. How is this to be done? What *is* the essential nature of a decision? These are not easy questions to answer, but one can start off by pointing out that a decision is a reviewable act. It can, therefore, be distinguished from opinions and other non-reviewable acts by the test of legal effect (discussed in Chapter 11). This is what occurred in the *Noordwijks Cement Accoord* case,[24] where the Commission argued that the act in question was an opinion. Once this

[20] Case T-3/93, [1994] ECR II-121. [21] *Ibid.*, para. 58 of the judgment.

[22] See *Municipality of Differdange v. Commission*, Case 222/83, [1984] ECR 2889 (para. 9 of the judgment).

[23] *Plaumann v. Commission*, Case 25/62, [1963] ECR 95 at 113, *per* Advocate General Roemer; *Eridania v. Commission*, Cases 10, 18/68, [1969] ECR 459 at 490, *per* Advocate General Roemer.

[24] Cases 8–11/66, [1967] ECR 75.

possibility was ruled out on the ground that it had legal effects, the Court assumed that it was a decision.

The problem can, therefore, be reduced to one of distinguishing a decision from the other kinds of reviewable act: a regulation, directive, or act *sui generis*. The normal sort of case is one in which the alternative classification is a regulation, and for this reason the tests formulated by the Court have all been adopted with this purpose in mind; however, the same tests are applied where the act is in some other form.[25]

The European Court has held that the word 'decision' in Article 230 [173] has the same meaning as in Article 249 [189] EC.[26] No doubt the same applies to the word 'regulation'. It is useful, therefore, to compare the two provisions in Article 249 [189].[27] The provision concerning decisions states: 'A decision shall be binding in its entirety upon those to whom it is addressed.' It should be noted that the phrase 'those to whom it is addressed' in this provision must include what were previously termed '*de facto* addressees' as well as actual ones; otherwise it would be impossible to have a decision in the form of a regulation.

Article 249 [189] also provides: 'A regulation shall have general application. It shall be binding in its entirety and directly applicable in all Member States.' These two statements, which are not very satisfactory as definitions, nevertheless suggest a distinction: a decision is binding only on its addressee (actual or *de facto*); a regulation is binding generally.

The European Court has used this distinction as the foundation for its pronouncements on the subject. Thus, in *Confédération Nationale des Producteurs de Fruits et Légumes v. Commission*,[28] the first major case on this question, the Court expressed itself as follows:[29]

> Under the terms of Article 249 [189] of the EEC Treaty, a regulation shall have general application and shall be directly applicable in all Member States, whereas a decision shall be binding only upon those to whom it is addressed. The criterion for the distinction must be sought in the general 'application' or otherwise of the measure in question.
>
> The essential characteristics of a decision arise from the limitation of the persons to whom it is addressed, whereas a regulation, being essentially of a legislative nature, is applicable not to a limited number of persons, defined or identifiable, but to categories of persons viewed abstractly and in their entirety. Consequently, in order to determine in doubtful cases whether one is concerned with a decision or a regulation, it is necessary to ascertain whether the measure in question is of individual concern to specific individuals.
>
> In these circumstances, if a measure entitled by its author a regulation contains provisions which are capable of being not only of direct but also of individual concern to certain natural or legal persons, it must be admitted, without prejudice to the question whether that measure considered in its entirety can be correctly called a regulation, that in any case those provisions do not have the character of a regulation and may therefore be impugned by those persons under the terms of the second[30] paragraph of Article 230 [173].

[25] See *Fédération Européenne de la Santé Animale v. Council*, Case 160/88R, [1988] ECR 4121; *Gibraltar v. Council*, Case C-298/89, [1993] ECR I-3605; *Air France v. Commission*, Case T-3/93, [1994] ECR II-121.

[26] *Confédération Nationale des Producteurs de Fruits et Légumes v. Council*, Cases 16–17/62, [1962] ECR 471 at 478–9.

[27] The relevant provisions in Art. 161 Euratom are identical.

[28] Cases 16–17/62, [1962] ECR 471.

[29] At 478–9.

[30] Now the fourth paragraph.

Putting the matter in very crude and general terms, one might say that a regulation lays down general rules; a decision is concerned with individual cases. This basic distinction is well known to administrative lawyers and acts falling into the former category are variously known as 'legislative', 'normative', or 'general' acts; those in the latter category are usually called 'individual', 'executive', or 'administrative' acts.[31] A regulation, therefore, is a normative act; a decision is an individual one.

The next requirement is that of individual concern. Article 230 [173] states that, if the applicant is not the addressee of the decision, the proceedings will be inadmissible unless he is *individually concerned* by it. The meaning of this was explained by the Court in *Plaumann v. Commission* as follows:[32]

> Persons other than those to whom a decision is addressed may only claim to be individually concerned if that decision affects them by reason of certain attributes which are peculiar to them or by reason of circumstances in which they are differentiated from all other persons and by virtue of these factors distinguishes them individually just as in the case of the person addressed. In the present case the applicant is affected by the disputed decision as an importer of clementines, that is to say, by reason of a commercial activity which may at any time be practised by any person and is not therefore such as to distinguish the applicant in relation to the contested decision as in the case of the addressee.

In this case, the act in question was a decision of the Commission addressed to the German Government refusing permission to lower the duty on imported clementines. The applicant was an importer of clementines. He was affected by the decision, but only as a member of a general class: any other importer of clementines would be affected in the same way. He was not, therefore, individually concerned and consequently lacked *locus standi* to bring the proceedings.

## THE RELATIONSHIP BETWEEN THE REQUIREMENTS

The structure of Article 230 [173], fourth paragraph, indicates that, except in the case of a decision addressed to the applicant, there are three separate requirements for *locus standi*: first, the act must be a decision in the material sense; secondly, the applicant must be individually concerned by it; and thirdly, he must be directly concerned by it. There is no doubt that direct concern (discussed below) raises quite separate issues, but it will be apparent from what has already been said that the test for deciding whether an act is a decision, and the test for establishing individual concern, could be the same.[33]

[31] Some of these terms are, unfortunately, ambiguous. For example, an 'administrative act' can mean either an act of an administrative nature (as in the text) or an act (of whatever nature) adopted by an administrative authority.

[32] Case 25/62, [1963] ECR 95 at 107.

[33] In *Greek Canners v. Commission*, Case 250/81, [1982] ECR 3535 at 3544–5, Advocate General Slynn said that the two tests were 'analogous'. On the other hand, Advocate General Warner had said earlier, in the *Japanese Ball-Bearing* cases, Cases 113/77, etc. [1979] ECR 1185 at 1243, that the tests were separate and independent, a view repeated in *Calpak v. Commission*, Cases 789–90/79, [1980] ECR 1949, at 1970–1; see, further, Usher

Thus, in the passage from the *Confédération Nationale* case quoted above, the Court said that the criterion for determining whether a measure is a decision or a regulation is whether or not it is of individual concern to specific individuals.

This is a problem that has dogged the Court for over forty years. If the applicant can establish individual concern, does it automatically follow that the measure is (in substance) a decision? If it does, does it mean that the measure is a decision as regards all applicants, or can it be a decision for some but a regulation for others? If it does not, what is the test for a true decision?

Secondly, exactly what did the Court mean in the *Plaumann* case when it said that to establish individual concern the applicant must show that the measure affects him by reason of certain attributes peculiar to him or by reason of circumstances that differentiate him from all other persons? The answer given in some cases is that the applicant can establish individual concern if he can show that he was affected by the measure as a member of a closed category.[34] A closed category is a class of persons the membership of which is fixed when the measure comes into force. It is distinguished from an open category, which is a class the membership of which is not fixed when the measure comes into force. Thus if the measure applies only to persons who held an import licence during some period prior to the coming into force of the measure, the persons in question will be members of a closed category. If, on the other hand, it applies to anyone who wants to import fruit in the future, it will apply to an open category of persons, since, when the measure comes into force, it will not be possible to know who will want to import fruit. Anybody could decide to do so.

There have been some cases in which the Court has held that a determination of individual concern automatically means that the measure is in substance a decision, even if it is in the form of a regulation. In other cases, however, the Court has treated the question whether the act is in substance a decision as distinct from the question whether the applicant is individually concerned by it. It then usually says that the character of an act as a regulation is not called into question by reason of the fact that it is possible to determine the identity of the persons to whom it applies, as long as it applies to them by virtue of an objective legal or factual situation defined by the measure in relation to its purpose. This latter approach focuses on the terminology of the measure rather than on the persons affected by it. If it is couched in abstract terminology, the measure will be regarded as a true regulation even if it applies to a closed category of persons.

Prior to the early 1990s, the Court, when faced with a measure in the form of a regulation, applied these approaches in a seemingly arbitrary and unpredictable manner. Sometimes, it decided to consider first whether the measure was a true regulation. When it did this, it almost always applied the abstract terminology test, and almost invariably found that the measure was in substance a regulation. The application was

(1984) 9 ELRev. 263 at 264. For a detailed review of the Court's rulings on the subject, see the Opinion of Advocate General Jacobs in *Extramet Industrie v. Commission*, Case C-358/89, [1991] ECR I-2501 at 2515–19.

[34] On who is affected by a measure, see *CIDA v. Commission*, Case 297/86, [1988] ECR 3531 (an unsuccessful candidate is affected by a decision appointing the successful candidates); see also *Apesco v. Commission*, Case 207/86, [1988] ECR 2151.

then declared inadmissible on *locus standi* grounds without the Court having to consider individual concern.[35]

In other cases, however, it skipped over the question whether the measure was a true regulation, and proceeded directly to the question of individual concern. It then applied either the *Plaumann* test or the closed category test, and quite often found it satisfied. When this occurred, it did not consider whether the act was really a decision. It simply declared the application admissible (provided direct concern was also established).[36]

## INDIVIDUAL CONCERN AND THE NATURE OF A DECISION

In the pages that follow, an attempt will be made to analyse some of the decisions of the European Court. Since the reasons given by the Court are often scanty and sometimes conflicting, a distinction will be introduced which has not been adopted by the Court itself. This is between proceedings to annul acts of a quasi-judicial nature and proceedings to annul acts based purely on policy and discretion. Cases falling into the former category are those in which the Community institution adopting the act is bound by clear rules, and the final determination depends largely on questions of fact. A semi-judicial procedure is followed. The main cases falling into this category concern competition, dumping, and state aids; they will be given separate treatment in the section entitled 'Quasi-Judicial Determinations'. The preceding subsections will deal only with acts based on policy and discretion; most of these concern agriculture.

In addition to this distinction, it is also necessary to take into consideration the form of the act. Although in theory this is irrelevant for determining *locus standi*, in practice the European Court has been more willing to grant standing where the act is in the form of a decision. In such a case, it has never applied the abstract terminology test, nor has it ever held that the act is in substance a regulation.[37] For this reason, when we discuss open and closed categories, we will deal separately with acts in the form of a decision and those in the form of a regulation.

### SMALL GROUPS

The first situation to consider is where the measure is drafted in general terms but the persons affected, though members of a theoretically open category, in fact consist of a

[35] See, e.g., *Compagnie Française Commerciale et Financière v. Commission*, Case 64/69, [1970] ECR 221.

[36] See *CAM v. Council and Commission*, Case 100/74, [1975] ECR 1393; *Roquette v. Council*, Case 138/79, [1980] ECR 3333; *Agricola Commerciale Olio v. Commission*, Case 232/81, [1984] ECR 3881.

[37] In *Piraiki-Patraiki*, Case 11/82, [1985] ECR 207, the Court expressly said that it was not necessary to go into the legal nature of the decision (para. 5 of the judgment). In *Plaumann*, Case 25/62, [1963] ECR 95, the Commission argued that its decision was in substance a normative act but the Court held that it was an individual act. The nearest the Court seems to have come to reclassifying a decision was in *Spijker v. Commission*,

small and easily identifiable group. This situation arises quite frequently and the Court almost always denies *locus standi*. *KSH v. Council and Commission*[38] is an example. This concerned an act in the form of a regulation which applied to isoglucose, a form of sugar made from starch. The persons concerned were the producers of isoglucose. They were in theory a general class but in fact there were only very few of them. Their number was unlikely to increase, since heavy capital investment was necessary and some of the technology involved was protected by patents. It was probable that the relevant Community officials were aware of their identity. Nevertheless, the Court ruled that the measures were true regulations; so the producers had no *locus standi*.

*Spijker v. Commission*[39] shows that the Court adopts the same approach where the act is in the form of a decision (addressed to someone other than the applicant). The case arose when the Commission adopted a decision addressed to the three Benelux countries, banning imports into those countries of brushes manufactured in China. The persons concerned – brush importers in the Benelux countries – were an open category, but the applicant was in fact the only person in the three countries who imported Chinese brushes. Moreover, there was evidence indicating that the decision was passed expressly to deal with him (he was suspected by the Dutch Government of having previously committed a major fraud by making a false declaration regarding the origin of the product). For these reasons, Advocate General Rozès considered that the applicant had *locus standi*; but the Court held that he was not individually concerned.

*Binderer v. Commission*[40] also appears rather unfair. Binderer, a firm of wine merchants, had asked the Commission whether Community law prohibited the use of certain German words to describe wines produced in Hungary and Yugoslavia. The Commission replied that it did not. Binderer then took steps to import the wines, but the Commission subsequently passed a regulation prohibiting the use of the terms in question. Binderer brought proceedings to annul the regulation but the Court held that it lacked *locus standi*. It is true that Binderer was affected by the regulation only as a member of an open category – wine importers – but in view of the fact that Binderer had previously consulted the Commission and apparently relied on its reply, the Court might have found that it had been sufficiently singled out to be given *locus standi*.[41]

## OPEN AND CLOSED CATEGORIES: DECISIONS

We will now consider cases in which the measure, though drafted in abstract terms, applies (in whole or in part) to a closed category of persons. We will first take acts in the

Case 231/82, [1983] ECR 2559, where it said, in para. 9 of its judgment, that, with regard to importers, the decision was a 'measure of general application'.

[38] Case 101/76, [1977] ECR 797. See also *Buralux v. Council*, Case C-209/94 P, [1996] ECR I-615 (para. 29 of the judgment); *Campo Ebro v. Council*, Case T-472/93, [1995] ECR II-421 (paras 33–6 of the judgment) (Court of First Instance).

[39] Case 231/82, [1983] ECR 2559. But for a more liberal decision, see *Control Data Belgium v. Commission*, Case 294/81, [1983] ECR 911.

[40] Case 147/83, [1985] ECR 257.

[41] For more recent authorities on the position of members of small groups, see *Antillean Rice Mills v. Council*, Case C-451/98, [2001] ECR I-8949 (para. 52 of the judgment) and the cases cited therein.

form of a decision. In such cases, the Court has never considered whether it might be a disguised regulation: it has always taken for granted that it is correctly designated, and examined only whether the applicant is directly and individually concerned.

*Toepfer v. Commission*,[42] decided in 1965, is an example. The applicants in this case were a group of German grain dealers who, on 1 October 1963, applied to the relevant German authority for import licences. There was a variable levy on imports and the applicable rate (in the circumstances of the case) was that prevailing when the application was made. On 1 October 1963 the rate was zero. The German authority realized, however, that because of a change in market conditions, the importers were liable to make large profits; so it decided to reject all applications until the levy rate had been increased. It therefore told the importers that their applications would be refused, and asked the Commission to confirm this decision. On the same day, the Commission raised the levy rate as from 2 October. On 3 October, the Commission took a decision, addressed to Germany, confirming the ban with regard to applications made on 1–4 October, inclusive. The dealers brought proceedings to annul this decision.

The position here was that the category of persons affected by the decision was partly closed (those who had already applied) and partly open (those who would apply during the remainder of the period covered by the ban). The Court held that the dealers who had applied on 1 October were affected differently from the others because, if they resubmitted their applications when the ban expired, they would have to pay an increased levy. From this the Court concluded that the 1 October applicants were individually concerned. This case is interesting because it shows that if a measure in the form of a decision affects an open category of persons, but contained within that open category there is a closed category the members of which are affected in a significantly different way, the latter will be individually concerned.

A similar result was reached in *Bock v. Commission*.[43] Bock applied to the relevant German authority for a permit to import Chinese mushrooms. The German authority told him that this would be refused as soon as authorization had been obtained from the Commission. The Commission then took a decision authorizing the refusal of import permits, including those for which applications had already been made. Bock asked the Court to annul only the provision applying the decision to such applications. Since the persons affected by this provision were a closed category, the Court held that Bock was individually concerned, though it was less clear than in the previous case that such persons were affected differently from later applicants.

The same point arose in *Piraiki-Patraiki v. Commission*,[44] decided in 1985. This concerned a Commission decision (based on Article 130 of the Greek Act of Accession) permitting France to impose restrictions on imports of cotton yarn from Greece. The decision was challenged by a number of Greek manufacturers, some of whom had entered into contracts to export cotton to France which had not been carried out when the decision was taken. The Court held that these exporters were individually concerned. It said that Article 130 imposed an obligation on the Commission to take

[42] Cases 106–7/63, [1965] ECR 405.
[43] Case 62/70, [1971] ECR 897.
[44] Case 11/82, [1985] ECR 207.

the interests of such exporters into account and, since the Commission had not done so, it annulled the decision to the extent to which it applied to them.[45] If this obligation had not been imposed on the Commission, however, the fact that the decision applied to existing contracts would not have been enough to establish that the parties to those contracts were individually concerned.[46]

## OPEN AND CLOSED CATEGORIES: REGULATIONS

We will now consider cases involving closed categories where the measure is in the form of a regulation. The earliest such case was *Compagnie Française Commerciale et Financière v. Commission*,[47] which was decided in 1970. Most of the provisions of the regulation in issue applied to open categories of persons, but one provision, which was of a transitional nature, only affected French exporters who had entered into contracts before 11 August 1969, had registered them with the French authorities by 18 August, but had not carried them out when the regulation was made on 22 August. Such persons were a closed category and their identity could have been ascertained by the Commission when it adopted the regulation. For this reason, Advocate General Roemer considered that the exporters had *locus standi* to challenge the provision in question, but the Court held that the measure, including the provision subject to challenge, was a true regulation, which could not be challenged by a private applicant.

The next case, *International Fruit Company v. Commission*,[48] concerned the procedure for importing apples from non-member states. Under this, importers had to apply in advance to the national authorities for an import licence. Each week the national authorities would collate the applications made during the previous week and pass the details to the Commission. The Commission would then enact a measure in the form of a regulation laying down rules for deciding the applications in question. These measures concerned only a closed category of persons: those who had made applications during the preceding week. One such applicant brought annulment proceedings and the Court held that the relevant provision was in reality a bundle of decisions. The application was held admissible. In this case the measure as a whole concerned a closed category, unlike in the previous case. It is also worth noting that once the Court had decided that the measure was really a decision, it affirmed individual concern without further discussion.

Four years later, in 1975, the Court decided *CAM v. Commission*,[49] in which the facts were almost indistinguishable from those in the *Compagnie Française* case. Advocate General Warner considered that the Court should follow its earlier ruling and therefore concluded that the application was inadmissible. The Court, however, decided to consider first the question of individual concern. It applied the closed category test and, on finding this satisfied, held the application admissible. There was no express finding that

[45] See, further, *Antillean Rice Mills v. Council*, Case C-451/98, [2001] ECR I-8949 (para. 57 of the judgment); *Antillean Rice Mills v. Commission*, Case C-390/95 P, [1999] ECR I-769 (para. 25 of the judgment).

[46] *Buralux v. Council*, Case C-209/94 P, [1996] ECR I-615 (paras 30–4 of the judgment).

[47] Case 64/69, [1970] ECR 221.

[48] Cases 41–4/70, [1971] ECR 411.

[49] Case 100/74, [1975] ECR 1393.

the measure was a decision; the Court must have assumed that this followed from its finding on individual concern. The same approach was adopted in *Exportation des Sucres v. Commission*,[50] decided in 1977, and in *UNICME v. Council*,[51] decided in 1978. (In the latter case the regulation applied to an open category, and the application was consequently inadmissible, but the Court said that if direct and individual concern can be established, it is unnecessary to consider whether the measure is in substance a decision or a regulation.)[52]

At this point it might have seemed that the law was settled: the *Compagnie Française* case could have been dismissed as an early aberration and one could have concluded that the closed category test had triumphed. In succeeding cases, however, the Court swung back to the approach in the *Compagnie Française* case. The first such case was *Beauport v. Council and Commission*,[53] decided in 1979. Here, the entire regulation applied to a closed category, sugar refineries which had previously been allocated a sugar quota. Advocate General Warner considered that the measure was a disguised decision, but the Court ruled that it was a true regulation. Subject to a small number of exceptions, a similar approach was adopted throughout the 1980s: during this period, where the measure was in the form of a regulation and did not fall into the quasi-judicial category discussed below, the Court normally applied the abstract terminology test and did not concern itself with the question of individual concern.[54]

The most important exceptions were *Roquette v. Council*[55] and *Agricola Commerciale Olio v. Commission*.[56] Both these cases involved rather special circumstances. The facts in *Roquette* were similar to those in *Beauport* in that the measure concerned a closed category of persons, isoglucose producers who had previously been awarded a quota. On the basis of the more recent cases, this would not in itself have been enough to ensure *locus standi*. However, there was an annex to the regulation, which was an integral part of it, which listed the producers by name and stated exactly what their quotas would be under the new rules laid down by the regulation. The Court therefore concluded that the producers were directly and individually concerned by the regulation; the application was consequently admissible. (It is interesting to note that *Roquette* challenged the regulation only in so far as it fixed its quota, but the Court went on to annul the whole regulation, on the ground that the Parliament had not been consulted.)

[50] Case 88/76, [1977] ECR 709.

[51] Case 123/77, [1978] ECR 845.

[52] See para. 7 of the judgment.

[53] Cases 103–9/78, [1979] ECR 17.

[54] See *Wagner v. Commission*, Case 162/78, [1979] ECR 3467; *Calpak v. Commission*, Cases 789–90/79, [1980] ECR 1949; *Moksel v. Commission*, Case 45/81, [1982] ECR 1129; *Deutz und Geldermann v. Council*, Case 26/86, [1987] ECR 941; *Asteris v. Commission*, Cases 97, 99, 193, 215/86, [1988] ECR 2181; *Abertal v. Commission*, Case C-213/91, [1993] ECR I-3265; *UCDV v. Commission*, Case C-244/88, [1989] ECR 3811; *Fédération Européenne de la Santé Animale v. Council*, Case 160/88R, [1988] ECR 4121; *Gibraltar v. Council*, Case C-298/89, [1993] ECR I-3605 (the last two cases concerned directives, but the Court's approach seemed to be the same). For further discussion, see Rosa Greaves, 'Locus Standi under Art. 173 EEC when Seeking Annulment of a Regulation' (1986) 11 ELRev. 119.

[55] Case 138/79, [1980] ECR 3333. Other aspects of this case were discussed in Chap. 1.

[56] Case 232/81, [1984] ECR 3881. See also *Salerno v. Commission and Council*, Cases 87, 130/77, 22/83, 9–10/84, [1985] ECR 2523 at paras 26–32 of the judgment (Case 22/83). This was a staff case concerning the re-employment of officials of an organization which was about to be dissolved.

It could be argued that in *Roquette* the measure was in substance a decision even under the abstract terminology test, though the Court did not expressly decide it on that ground. In *Olio*, however, it is hard to see how the test could have been satisfied. The case concerned the procedure for disposing of surplus stocks of olive oil held by the intervention authorities. A Commission regulation was passed providing for the sale of the oil by tender. This duly took place and, as the sale was greatly oversubscribed, lots were drawn. Then the Commission realized that, due to a change in market conditions, the successful tenderers stood to make large profits. So two further regulations were passed cancelling the sale. These were challenged before the Court by the successful tenderers. The Court declared that, though the letters of allocation (which declared the successful tenderers owners of the oil) had not yet been sent, there was nothing further to negotiate and both sides were committed to going through with the transaction: 'the situation between the parties to the sale was determined',[57] a phrase which suggests that the successful tenderers could be regarded to some extent as having vested rights. For these reasons, said the Court, the measures were of direct and individual concern to the applicants. The applications were ruled admissible without any express finding that the measures were really decisions.

In the 1990s, a more liberal approach became the norm again. The first case was *Sofrimport v. Commission*,[58] which concerned Commission regulations imposing a temporary ban on imports of Chilean apples into the Community. The applicant was a French importer which had a consignment of apples in transit to Europe and had applied for an import licence on the day the ban was imposed. The Advocate General took the view that, on the basis of prior decisions of the Court,[59] the measures subject to challenge were true regulations; he therefore considered the application inadmissible. The Court, however, passed over the question whether the measures were true regulations and went straight to the question of individual concern. It applied the closed category test and held that importers whose goods were in transit when the ban was adopted were sufficiently well defined in relation to other importers – by reason of the fact that a prior Council regulation required the Commission to take special account of their position – for them to be individually concerned,[60] though only to the extent to which they challenged the measure with regard to its effect on products in transit. Sofrimport, the applicant in the case, fell into this category and the application was consequently admissible. The regulations were annulled in so far as they concerned products in transit.

This was followed by *Weddel v. Commission*,[61] a case on all fours with *International Fruit Company v. Commission*. It concerned importation of meat into the Community and the system was the same as that in *International Fruit*: importers lodged applications for permits and the Commission then adopted a regulation specifying to what extent they would be granted. On the facts of the case, a regulation adopted on

[57] Para. 11 of the judgment. [58] Case C-152/88, [1990] ECR I-2477.

[59] *Moksel v. Commission*, Case 45/81, [1982] ECR 1129; *UCDV v. Commission*, Case C-244/88, [1989] ECR 3811.

[60] If the regulation had not required the Commission to take special account of their position, they would not have been individually concerned: *Unifruit Hellas v. Commission*, Case T-489/93, [1994] ECR II-1201 (paras 24–8 of the judgment). [61] Case C-354/87, [1990] ECR I-3847.

18 September 1987 applied to applications made on 1–10 September. Since it granted the applications only as to a very small percentage of the quantity requested, one applicant brought proceedings to annul it. The Court held the application admissible on the basis of the decision in *International Fruit*.[62]

In 1994, the Court decided *Codorniu v. Council*,[63] a decision of the Full Court that, until 2002, constituted the leading case. It concerned a Spanish company, Codorniu, which since 1924 had marketed one of its quality sparkling wines under the trademark '*Gran Cremant de Codorniu*'. However, in 1989 the Council passed a regulation which provided that the French word '*Crémant*', and its translations into other languages, could be used only for quality sparkling wines produced in France and Luxembourg. This would have meant that Codorniu would have been precluded from using the term. It therefore brought proceedings to annul the relevant provision of the regulation.

The Court ruled that the measure was a true regulation, but nevertheless held the application admissible on the basis that the applicant was individually concerned.[64] It might be thought that Codorniu, who was not the only Spanish producer who marketed quality sparkling wine under the designation '*Cremant*' might not have satisfied the *Plaumann* test. The Court held, however, that Codorniu was sufficiently singled out by virtue of the fact that, long before the regulation was adopted, it had registered a trade mark incorporating the word '*Cremant*'.

This case establishes that if the applicant can demonstrate individual concern, it is not necessary to show that the measure is a true decision. It seems to suggest, however, that individual concern does not automatically mean that the measure is a decision; rather it has been taken to mean that a non-privileged applicant may challenge a true regulation provided he can satisfy the *Plaumann* test.[65]

This was the last case decided by the European Court before jurisdiction in actions by non-privileged parties was transferred to the Court of First Instance: since then, such cases have normally come before it only on appeal. After *Codorniu*, there were many cases,[66] but no major developments until 2002, when the Court decided *Unión de*

[62] The Court did not apply the abstract terminology test, but went straight to the question of direct and individual concern: see para. 18 of the judgment. See also *Emerald Meats v. Commission*, Cases C-106, 317/90, C-129/91, [1993] ECR II-209, in which the situation was similar and the admissibility of the proceedings was not contested.

[63] Case C-309/89, [1994] ECR I-1853.

[64] Paras 19–22 of the judgment.

[65] *Antillean Rice Mills v. Council*, Case C-451/98, [2001] ECR I-8949 (paras 43–46 of the judgment). See, further, Arnull, 'Private Applicants and the Action for Annulment since *Codorniu*' (2001) 38 CMLRev. 7 at pp. 20–21 and the decisions of the Court of First Instance cited therein.

[66] See, for example, *Greenpeace v. Council*, Case C-321/95 P, [1998] ECR I-1651 (affirming Case T-585/93, [1985] ECR II-2205); *CNPAAP v. Council*, Case C-87/95 P, [1996] ECR I-2003 (affirming Case T-116/94, [1995] ECR II-1); *Buralux v. Council*, Case C-209/94 P, [1996] ECR I-615 (affirming Case T-475/93, 17 May 1994, not published in the ECR); *Exporteurs in Levende Varkens v. Commission*, Cases T-481 and 484/93, [1995] ECR II-2941; *Terres Rouges v. Commission*, Case T-47/95, [1997] ECR II-481 (para. 43 of the judgment); *Antillean Rice Mills v. Commission*, Case C-390/95 P, [1999] ECR I-769 (affirming Cases T-480 and 483/93, [1995] ECR II-2305); *Antillean Rice Mills v. Council*, Case C-451/98, [2001] ECR I-8949. For cases in which the Court of First Instance has specifically rejected the closed category test, see *Roquette v. Council*, Case T-298/94, [1996] ECR II-1531; *Michailidis v. Commission*, Case T-100/94, [1998] ECR II-3115. See, further, Arnull, 'Private Applicants and the Action for Annulment since *Codorniu*' (2001) 38 CMLRev. 7 at pp. 32 *et seq.*

*Pequeños Agricultores v. Council* (the *UPA*case),[67] a decision in which considerations of fundamental human rights played an important role.

It is generally accepted that, in order to comply with the requirements of human rights, the Community must provide everyone with an effective means of legal redress when his interests are affected by a Community provision alleged to be invalid.[68] Since, as we have seen, the standing of non-privileged applicants to bring annulment actions is severely restricted, this raises the question whether the other avenues of redress – proceedings in national courts followed by a reference to the European Court or actions in tort in the European Court – provide a satisfactory alternative.

In the *UPA* case, UPA, a Spanish organization representing small agricultural businesses, challenged a Council regulation withdrawing subsidies and other benefits from olive oil producers. UPA admitted that the measure was a true regulation, but argued that since it did not require implementation at national level, there was no way in which an action to challenge it could be brought before the national courts. It claimed that it would be denied a remedy if it was not allowed to being a direct action.[69]

The Court of First Instance held that UPA had no *locus standi.* UPA appealed to the European Court. The appeal was heard by a Full Court, thus indicating the Court's willingness to reconsider its case law. In a lengthy and closely argued Opinion that was remarkable for focusing almost entirely on policy, Advocate General Jacobs concluded that the Court's existing case law on *locus standi* was incompatible with the principle of effective judicial protection. He therefore proposed a radical revision of the law. He suggested that a non-privileged applicant should be regarded as individually concerned where, by reason of his particular circumstances, the measure has, or is liable to have, a substantial adverse effect on his interests.

The European Court rejected these arguments and upheld the interpretation of individual concern originally put forward in the *Plaumann* case. It accepted that the Rule of Law requires individuals to have an effective means of redress, but said that this should be achieved through the national courts. If this was not possible, the fault lay with the Member States. It rejected the contention put forward by UPA that an applicant should be given standing to bring a direct action whenever he can demonstrate that a remedy does not exist in the national courts. This would require the European Court to decide difficult questions of national law, something on which it has no jurisdiction to give an authoritative ruling.

It is of interest that in 1995 the Court proposed to the Member States that the Treaty should be amended to increase the rights of non-privileged applicants.[70] The Member

67 Case C-50/00 P, [2002] ECR I-6677.

68 See Arts 6 and 13 of the European Convention on Human Rights and Art. 47 of the Charter of Fundamental Rights of the European Union.

69 For earlier cases in which the Court alluded to the question of alternative remedies, see *Alusuisse v. Council and Commission*, Case 307/81, [1982] ECR 3463 (para. 13 of the judgment); *Spijker v. Commission*, Case 231/82, [1983] ECR 2559 (para. 11 of the judgment); *Allied Corporation v. Commission*, Cases 239, 275/82, [1984] ECR 1005 (para. 15 of the judgment); *Union Deutsche Lebensmittelwerke v. Commission*, Case 97/85, [1987] ECR 2265 (para. 12 of the judgment).

70 *Report of the Court of Justice on Certain Aspects of the Application of the Treaty on European Union*, Luxembourg, May 1995.

States did not, however, act on this suggestion. This is probably why the Court said in its judgment that if change is needed, it is for the Member States to effect it by amending the Treaty.[71]

The European Court did, however, clarify the law in one respect. It made clear that a non-privileged applicant cannot challenge an act that is in substance a regulation.[72] However, it explained the decision in *Codorniu* by saying that a true regulation can, in certain circumstances, be of individual concern to certain non-privileged applicants and thus be 'in the nature of a decision in their regard'.[73] It therefore seems that the fact that the measure is of individual concern to the applicant (judged by the *Plaumann* test) automatically means that it is a decision. However, it is a decision only with regard to those who are individually concerned by it; otherwise, it retains its character as a regulation. Thus it seems that a measure *can* at the same time be both a true decision and a true regulation. This is not unreasonable, since a measure might well apply to most people as members of a general category, but to some on an individual basis. There is, however, a hint that the test for individual concern might be applied more strictly in the case of such 'hybrid' measures, since the Court said that if the *Plaumann* test is not satisfied, a non-privileged applicant 'does not, under any circumstances, have standing to bring an action for the annulment of a regulation'.[74]

After Advocate General Jacobs had given his Opinion in the *UPA* case but before the Court gave judgment, the Court of First Instance decided *Jégo-Quéré v. Commission.*[75] This was a challenge against a Commission regulation which prohibited the use in specified waters of fishing nets with mesh below a certain size. The applicant was a fishing company that regularly fished in the waters in question using nets with a mesh below the minimum size. The Commission claimed that it had no standing. The Court of First Instance accepted that this was so under the existing case law. The applicant, however, argued that if it was denied standing, it would be left without a remedy.

Drawing inspiration from the Opinion of Advocate General Jacobs in the *UPA* case, the Court considered whether an action in the national courts would afford an adequate remedy. The only way this could be done appears to have been for the applicant deliberately to break the law and, when prosecuted, to plead the invalidity of the regulation as a defence. The Court considered that it was not acceptable that a person should have to break the law in order to obtain a remedy. It also regarded an action in tort as unsatisfactory. For these reasons, it held that an applicant should be regarded as having standing if the measure affects his legal position in a manner that is both definite and immediate, by restricting his rights or imposing obligations on him, a rule similar to that put forward by Advocate General Jacobs in the *UPA* case. It therefore held the application admissible. The case then went on appeal, and the European Court reversed it.[76]

[71] Para. 47 of the judgment. [72] Para. 35 of the judgment. [73] Para. 36 of the judgment.
[74] Para. 37 of the judgment. [75] Case T-177/01, [2002] ECR II-2365.
[76] Case C-263/02 P, [2004] ECR I-3425. In the appeal, the European Court stated that the interpretation given to the fourth paragraph of Art. 230 [173] EC had the effect of 'removing all meaning' from the requirement of individual concern set out in it (para. 28 of the judgment).

Finally it should be mentioned that there is an earlier case in which a very generous decision by the Court on the issue of standing seems to be explicable only on the basis that the applicant would otherwise have been left without a remedy. This is *Parti Ecologiste – 'Les Verts' v. European Parliament.*[77] The facts of this case were outlined above,[78] where it was explained that the European Parliament had adopted a decision to use public money to subsidize the election expenses of the parties fighting the forthcoming elections. The decision, however, discriminated against parties which were not already represented in the Parliament. In other words, the parties already in the Parliament awarded the bulk of the money to themselves. Clearly they would have no interest in challenging the decision. On the other hand, parties not already represented were affected by the decision only as members of an open category. According to the normal rules, such parties would not be individually concerned. However, since there was no adequate alternative remedy, the Court granted standing to one such party, the Parti Ecologiste. It pointed out that if standing were restricted to parties already represented (a closed category), the result would be unequal protection for parties competing in the same election. After surmounting other obstacles, the Court held the application admissible, and went on to annul the decision.

## QUASI-JUDICIAL DETERMINATIONS

The concept of a quasi-judicial determination is not one recognized by the European Court; nevertheless, special considerations apply in such a case. An attempt was made earlier to explain what was meant by it. The core idea is that the determination is to a large extent made on the basis of objective considerations and is the culmination of a procedure which has judicial features. Such determinations are predominantly decisions of fact and law, rather than discretionary decisions. There are, moreover, persons who could be regarded as being, in some sense, parties to the proceedings. Once one acknowledges that someone is a 'party' to the proceedings which resulted in the determination, it is easy to conclude that he should have *locus standi* to challenge it.

### COMPETITION PROCEEDINGS

The first example is a decision whether a firm has violated Community competition law. Articles 81 [85] and 82 [86] EC prohibit certain activities and the Commission has the task of ensuring compliance. The essence of the procedure is that the Commission first conducts an investigation and then holds a hearing at which the firm whose conduct is under consideration is invited to appear and present its case. Such a firm could therefore be regarded as the defendant. The determination takes the form of a decision addressed to the defendant. It may exonerate the defendant or find that it has violated the law. In the latter case a fine may be imposed. Since the decision is addressed to the defendant, it can clearly challenge it before the Court under Article 230 [173].

[77] Case 294/83, [1986] ECR 1339. [78] See Chap. 2.

What about the victim of the alleged malpractice? Community law allows anyone with a 'legitimate interest' to lodge a complaint with the Commission. Such a complainant is granted various procedural rights and may be entitled to participate in the hearing.[79] Can a complainant bring proceedings under Article 230 [173] to challenge the final determination, especially if it exonerates the defendant?

This question came before the Court in 1977 in *Metro v. Commission.*[80] Metro was a self-service wholesaler dealing in electronic goods, which complained that another firm, SABA, was acting in violation of Article 81 [85] because its conditions of sale, which applied to all its dealers, had the effect of precluding self-service wholesalers from distributing its products. The Commission investigated this complaint and took a decision exonerating SABA.

Metro wished to have this decision annulled. Since it was not the addressee of the decision (though it had been informed of it), it had to show that it was directly and individually concerned. One might have thought that it was not individually concerned since it was affected by the decision simply as a self-service wholesaler in electronic goods, a commercial activity which – in the words of the judgment in the *Plaumann* case – may at any time be practised by any person. The Court, however, held the proceedings admissible. It pointed out that the decision had been adopted as a result of Metro's complaint and said that it was in the interests of a 'satisfactory administration of justice' that anyone entitled to make a complaint should be allowed to institute proceedings against a decision dismissing the complaint. This case therefore establishes that in competition proceedings a complainant is regarded as individually concerned by the final decision even if it is affected by it in the same way as other members of an open category.[81]

## ANTI-DUMPING PROCEEDINGS

The second example concerns measures adopted in the course of anti-dumping proceedings. (Dumping is a form of unfair competition in international trade, usually involving selling in different markets at different prices, particularly exporting at a lower price than that applicable on the home market.) A special difficulty arises here because the normal remedy for dumping is an anti-dumping duty, which under Community law has to be imposed by regulation. This raises the question, discussed previously, whether a non-privileged applicant may challenge a true regulation. In *Alusuisse v. Commission*[82] (decided in 1982), the Court implied that a measure can be

[79] See Regulation 17, OJ (Spec. Edition) 1959–62, p. 87, Art. 3(2)(b) and Art. 19(2); see also Regulation 99/63, OJ (Spec. Edition) 1963–64, p. 47, Art. 5 and Art. 7. Regulation 99/63 has now been replaced by Regulation 2842/98, OJ 1998 L354, p. 18, of which see Arts 6–8.

[80] Case 26/76, [1977] ECR 1875.

[81] See further *GEMA v. Commission*, Case 125/78, [1979] ECR 3173; *Demo-Studio Schmidt v. Commission*, Case 210/81, [1983] ECR 3045 (paras 10–16 of the judgment); *Metro v. Commission (No. 2)*, Case 75/84, [1986] ECR 3021; *BAT and Reynolds v. Commission*, Cases 142 and 156/84, [1987] ECR 4487 (paras 11–13 of the judgment and pp. 4546–9 of Advocate General Mancini's Opinion); *SFEI v. Commission*, Case C-39/93P, [1994] ECR I-2681; *Lord Bethell v. Commission*, Case 246/81, [1982] ECR 2277.

[82] Case 307/81, [1982] ECR 3463 (para. 9 of the judgment).

simultaneously both a regulation and a decision (even though a previous case had expressly said that this is impossible),[83] while in *Allied Corporation v. Commission*[84] (decided in 1984), it described the anti-dumping regulation in issue as having a 'legislative character',[85] but nevertheless allowed a private applicant to challenge it. This is in line with its decision in the *Codorniu* case (1994), though for the ten years between the two cases it was unclear whether the principle applied outside the special field of quasi-judicial measures. One assumes that the *UPA* principle that a measure can be a decision with regard to certain particular individuals while remaining a regulation otherwise now applies also in the anti-dumping field.

The procedure in anti-dumping cases is analogous to that in competition cases. The status of complainant is fully recognized and proceedings are not normally initiated without a complaint. The role of defendant is more ambiguous because anti-dumping duties are usually imposed on all goods of the relevant kind from the country in question. This means that all exporters of such goods in the foreign country, as well as importers in the Community, could be regarded as having an interest in the proceedings. Public notice is given of the initiation of proceedings, and all exporters and importers known to be concerned are informed individually by the Commission. They have the right to make representations in writing and are normally entitled to make oral representations as well. The Commission usually invites them to give evidence and Commission inspectors may visit their plants. Firms that participate in the procedure in this way could be regarded as parties.

The first judgment to consider is that in the *Japanese Ball-Bearing* cases.[86] This concerned a challenge to a Council regulation imposing an anti-dumping duty on all ball-bearings manufactured in Japan. The duty was, however, suspended for as long as the four major producers (who were named in the regulation) carried out an undertaking to raise their prices. Did the four producers have *locus standi* to challenge the regulation? According to the normal principle, they were not individually concerned because they were affected by the regulation only as exporters of ball-bearings from Japan, an activity that could be practised by anyone. The Court nevertheless held that they had *locus standi* since they were named in the regulation, the purpose of which was to ensure that they carried out their undertakings.

The *Japanese Ball-Bearing* cases were concerned with a rather unusual situation, but *Allied Corporation v. Commission*[87] clarified and broadened the law. It established that exporters could challenge a regulation laying down an anti-dumping duty either if they

[83] *Moksel v. Commission*, Case 45/81, [1982] ECR 1129 (para. 18 of the judgment). This discrepancy is all the more surprising in view of the fact that both these cases were decided by the Third Chamber, with the same judges sitting on each occasion.

[84] Cases 239, 275/82 [1984] ECR 1005 (para. 11 of the judgment). This was a judgment of the Full Court.

[85] Para. 11 of the judgment.

[86] *NTN v. Council*, Case 113/77, [1979] ECR 1185; *ISO v. Council*, Case 118/77, [1979] ECR 1277; *Nippon Seiko v. Council and Commission*, Case 119/77, [1979] ECR 1303; *Koyo Seiko v. Council and Commission*, Case 120/77, [1979] ECR 1337; and *Nachi Fujikoshi v. Council*, Case 121/77, [1979] ECR 1363.

[87] Cases 239, 275/82, [1984] ECR 1005. See also *Toyo v. Council*, Case 240/84, [1987] ECR 1809 (another case involving Japanese ball-bearings).

were identified in the measure *or* if they were 'concerned by the preliminary investigations',[88] that is, took part in the Commission investigation.[89]

Importers were originally in a less favourable position (possibly because they are normally the persons who pay the import duty and therefore have a remedy in the national courts): for a long time they were not normally accorded *locus standi* unless they were named in the regulation, the Commission used their retail prices as a basis for constructing the export price,[90] or they were associated with exporters on whose products duties were imposed (though possibly only if the export price had been calculated on the basis of their selling prices in the Community).[91] In their case, participation in the investigation was not sufficient.[92] In the 1990s, the Court seemed to be moving towards a more liberal approach,[93] though it now seems that, outside the situations mentioned above, importers will be granted standing only in exceptional cases.[94]

Complainants have been treated more generously[95] (like exporters, they have no alternative remedies). *Timex v. Council and Commission*[96] concerned a regulation imposing an anti-dumping duty on mechanical watches from the Soviet Union. The proceedings had been initiated after a complaint by a British trade association on behalf of Timex, the only British manufacturer. Timex participated in the investigation and the duty was fixed in the light of the effect of the dumping on Timex, which was named in the preamble to the regulation. Timex, however, thought that the duty was too low and brought proceedings to annul the regulation. It was argued by the defendants that Timex was not individually concerned because it was affected only as a manufacturer of mechanical watches, an activity that may be carried on by anyone. However, the Court held that Timex had *locus standi*: the regulation was 'a decision which is of direct and individual concern to Timex'.[97]

[88] Para. 12 of the judgment.

[89] It is interesting that in the *Allied Corporation* case the Commission informed the Court that it was in favour of the exporters' actions being held admissible because otherwise Community exporters to the United States might not be allowed to challenge anti-dumping measures against their goods: see para. 9 of the judgment.

[90] Para. 15 of the judgment in the *Allied Corporation* case; *Sermes v. Commission*, Case 279/86, [1987] ECR 3109; *Frimodt Pedersen v. Commission*, Case 301/86, [1987] ECR 3123; *Nachi Europe*, Case C-239/99, [2001] ECR I-1197 (para. 21 of the judgment). For a fuller discussion of the law, see the Opinion of Advocate General Jacobs in *Extramet Industrie v. Commission*, Case C-358/89, [1991] ECR I-2501.

[91] *Canon v. Council*, Case 300/85, [1988] ECR 5731 (paragraph 8 of the judgment).

[92] *Nuova Ceam v. Commission*, Case 205/87, [1987] ECR 4427. See also *Alusuisse v. Council and Commission*, Case 307/81, [1982] ECR 3463, paras 12 and 13 of the judgment.

[93] *Extramet Industrie v. Commission*, Case C-358/89, [1991] ECR I-2501 (a decision of the Full Court). The Opinion of Advocate General Jacobs in this case puts the issues with great clarity. Unfortunately, the Court, though it followed his conclusions, was not prepared to accept his invitation to reassess its previous case law. Further evidence of flexibility is to be found in the earlier case of *Nashua Corporation v. Commission and Council*, Cases C-133, 150/87, [1990] ECR I-719 (paras 12–21 of the judgment) (also a decision of the Full Court). For a discussion of the whole question following the *Extramet* case, see Arnull, 'Challenging EC Anti-Dumping Regulations: The Problem of Admissibility' [1992] 2 ECLR 73.

[94] See *British Shoe Corporation Footwear Supplies v. Council*, Case T-598/97, [2002] ECR II-1155.

[95] *FEDIOL v. Commission*, Case 191/82, [1983] ECR 2913, establishes that a complainant has a remedy where the Commission fails to initiate proceedings.

[96] Case 264/82, [1985] ECR 849.

[97] Para. 16 of the judgment. In para. 12, however, the Court said that anti-dumping regulations are 'legislative in nature and scope, inasmuch as they apply to traders in general'.

## STATE AID

State aid which distorts competition is (generally speaking) contrary to Community law and Article 88(2) [93(2)] EC lays down a procedure for determining when a violation has occurred. This involves an investigation by the Commission, followed by a decision addressed to the Member State alleged to have granted the aid. That Member State can clearly challenge the decision under Article 230 [173],[98] but what are the rights of a complainant? The status of complainant is not given formal recognition in the same way as in the case of competition and anti-dumping proceedings, but in practice competitors of the firms receiving the aid are allowed to participate in the investigations.

In *COFAZ v. Commission*,[99] COFAZ and three other French fertilizer producers complained through their trade association to the Commission that their Dutch competitors were receiving aid from the Dutch Government. The Commission initiated the procedure under Article 88(2) [93(2)] EC and the French firms played some part in the proceedings. Eventually, the Commission concluded that no aid was involved and it took a decision, addressed to the Dutch Government, terminating the proceedings. COFAZ challenged this decision, but the Commission argued that it was not individually concerned because it was affected only in its capacity as a fertilizer producer. The Court, however, held the application admissible. It said that firms playing a part in the procedure comparable to that of a complainant should have *locus standi*, provided their position in the market was significantly affected by the aid. Subsequent cases have established that complainants also have standing where the decision was taken by the Commission without commencing the procedure under Article 88(2) [93(2)].[100]

## CONCLUSIONS

The cases discussed show that where a quasi-judicial determination is challenged, the Court has adopted a more liberal attitude than in the case of a discretionary act. Not only did it accept ten years earlier that a non-privileged applicant can challenge a true regulation, but complainants and other persons who have played a part in the proceedings have been granted standing even though they have been affected by the measure only as members of an open category.

[98] But firms receiving the aid and bodies involved in its distribution cannot, in the absence of special circumstances, challenge the decision: *DEFI v. Commission*, Case 282/85, [1986] ECR 2469 (where the statutory body administering the aid was held not to have *locus standi*); *Van der Kooy v. Commission*, Cases 67, 68, 70/85, [1988] ECR 219 (where it was held that individual recipients had no *locus standi*, but an organization representing them could challenge the decision since it had played a part in the proceedings under Art. 88(2) [93(2)] and other special circumstances applied).

[99] Case 169/84, [1986] ECR 391. See also *ASPEC v. Commission*, Case T-435/93, [1995] ECR II-1281; *Ducros v. Commission*, Case T-149/95, [1997] ECR II-2031; *Gestevisión Telecinco v. Commission*, Case T-95/96, [1998] ECR II-3407.

[100] *Cook v. Commission*, Case C-198/91, [1993] ECR I-2487; *Matra v. Commission*, Case C-225/91, [1993] ECR I-3203; see also *CIRFS v. Commission*, Case C-313/90, [1993] ECR I-1125. For further cases and a detailed discussion of standing in state aid cases, see Winter, 'The Rights of Complainants in State Aid Cases: Judicial Review of Commission Decisions Adopted under Article 88 (ex 93) EC' (1999) 36 CMLRev. 521.

## DIRECT CONCERN

As explained above, direct concern raises issues of cause and effect. The main situation in which it is important is where the effect of the decision on the applicant depends on the discretion of another person.[101] Thus if a Community institution grants a discretionary power to another authority (e.g., a Member State), the mere fact that the power would, if exercised, affect the applicant does not mean that he has *locus standi* to challenge the decision granting it: the interposition of an autonomous will between the decision and its effect on the applicant means that he is not *directly* concerned. Moreover, since a negative act is treated in the same way as a positive act for the purpose of jurisdiction, a decision by a Community institution refusing to grant a discretionary power cannot be challenged by those who would have been affected by its exercise, had it been granted.

The best case to illustrate these principles is *Alcan v. Commission.*[102] The facts in the *Alcan* case were that, under the relevant provisions, Member States could apply to the Commission for a quota of unwrought aluminium imports at a reduced rate of duty. In October 1968 the Belgian Government made a request for such a quota for the year 1968 and a request for an increased quota was made in December 1968. In May 1969, the Commission took a decision addressed to the Belgian Government rejecting the request. The question was whether the applicants, Alcan and two other aluminium-refining companies in Belgium, could challenge this decision.

Two points about the situation should be noted: first, that if the quota had been granted, the Belgian Government would not have been obliged to allow the quantity of unwrought aluminium in question to be imported at the reduced rate. In other words, the Commission would merely have given an authorization: the Belgian Government would have had a discretion whether or not to make use of it. Secondly, since the Commission's decision was not made until May 1969, and the quota was for the year 1968, the effect of the authorization (if it had been given by the Commission and put into effect by the Belgian Government) would merely have been that companies which had imported aluminium in 1968 would have been able to claim a refund on duty paid by them. In view of this latter fact, Advocate General Gand considered that the applicants were individually concerned; but both he and the Court took the view that they were not directly concerned because, even if the authorization had been granted, the Belgian Government might have decided not to use it. It was probably unlikely, in the circumstances, that this would have happened – why would the Belgian Government have made the request if it had not intended making use of it? – but the possibility was enough to eliminate *locus standi.*

[101] Problems can also arise where the contested act is one giving aid to a competitor (*Eridania v. Commission*, Cases 10, 18/68, [1969] ECR 459) or refusing to prevent a Member State from doing so (*COFAZ v. Commission*, Case 169/84, [1986] ECR 391). This in turn raises the question whether there must be an effect on the applicant's *rights*, or whether an effect on his *interests* is sufficient. Community law has not yet come to terms with this problem.

[102] Case 69/69, [1970] ECR 385. See also *Mannesmann-Röhrenwerke v. Commission*, Case 333/85, [1987] ECR 1381; *L'Etoile Commerciale v. Commission*, Cases 89, 91/86, [1987] ECR 3005; *Arposol v. Council*, Case 55/86, [1988] ECR 13.

If, however, the power is not discretionary, or if it is exercised first and confirmed afterwards, those affected by its exercise will be directly concerned by the act conferring or confirming it. An example of the first situation is the *International Fruit Company* case (discussed above). It will be remembered that, under the provisions then in force, persons wishing to import table apples were required to obtain an import permit from the national authorities. Each week the national authorities would inform the Commission of the number of applications for permits made to them during the preceding week. The Commission would then adopt an act (which the Court held to be a bundle of decisions, though it was in the form of a regulation) which laid down a formula for deciding how the applications should be dealt with. The national authorities then granted import permits on the basis of the formula. The Court held that, since the formula left no discretion to the national authorities, an applicant for a permit was directly concerned by the Commission's decision.

An example of the second situation is the *Toepfer* case (discussed above), which also concerned import permits but the system in operation was different. Normally all applications had to be granted by the national authorities; but on this occasion the national authorities had decided to apply 'safeguard measures' and this entitled them to refuse applications, provided that their decision to apply the 'safeguard measures' was confirmed by the Commission. The applicant applied for a permit; the German authorities declared that safeguard measures were to be applied; the Commission confirmed this; and the applicant was then informed that his application was rejected. Since the Commission's decision confirming the measures was taken after the German authorities' decision to apply them, the applicant was, the Court held, directly concerned by the Commission's decision: at the time when it was taken, an independent will no longer stood between the decision and its effect on the applicant.[103]

A more difficult case relating to this problem is *Bock v. Commission*,[104] which concerned import permits for mushrooms. At the time in question, the German Government had a policy of excluding imports of mushrooms that originated in the People's Republic of China. It was not, however, easy to give effect to this policy when the mushrooms were already in free circulation in another Member State. For, although such imports could not be made without an import permit, the German authorities were obliged to grant such a permit within a reasonable time (normally four days) after the application, unless they first obtained authorization from the Commission to suspend the issue of permits.

In the case, Bock lodged his application for a permit on 4 September 1970. On 11 September, the German authorities told the Commission that they had received an application for an import permit for Chinese mushrooms, and they requested authorization to exclude imports of such mushrooms 'including the import envisaged by the import application in question'. On the same day the German authorities informed

[103] The position might be different in the case of someone who applied for a permit *after* the Commission's decision was taken. Even if the Commission authorized the continuance of the 'safeguard measures' for a certain period of time subsequent to its decision, the national authorities would, presumably, retain the discretion to revoke them sooner.

[104] Case 62/70, [1971] ECR 897.

Bock that his application would be rejected as soon as the Commission had given its authorization. On 15 September, the Commission made a decision addressed to the German Government authorizing the excluding of Chinese mushrooms, including those for which applications for import permits were pending.[105] Bock's application was then formally rejected. He brought proceedings to quash the decision in so far as it applied to applications already pending.

The Commission objected to the admissibility of the case on the ground that Bock was neither individually nor directly concerned. The Court, however, held the application was admissible. It considered Bock individually concerned because his application was lodged before the decision was made. In so far as the decision applied to such applications (and it was challenged only to the extent that it did), the persons affected were ascertainable when the decision was made. The Court also considered that Bock was directly concerned: the German authorities had already informed him that his application would be rejected as soon as authorization had been obtained and the authorization had been requested for precisely this purpose.

One might criticize this decision on the ground that the German authorities were, nevertheless, still legally entitled not to make use of the authorization. They had been given a discretionary power. It is true that they would not have asked for the power if they had not intended using it, and they clearly did intend using it with regard to Bock's application. But they could have changed their minds. After all, in the *Alcan* case one could have argued that the Belgian Government would not have asked for the authorization unless they had intended using it. Yet the Court held, in that case, that the applicant was not directly concerned.

These two cases are obviously very similar. However, there are two important differences between them. The first was that the German authorities had expressly told Bock that, if they obtained the authorization, it would be used to reject his application. There was no evidence that this was so in the *Alcan* case. The second difference was that in the *Alcan* case the Belgian Government had been acting in the interest of Alcan and the other importers in making the application. One might almost say that it had been acting on their behalf. Since the importers and the Member State were 'on the same side', so to speak, it would not have been unreasonable to regard the interests of the importers as sufficiently protected by the right of the Belgian Government to bring proceedings to set aside the decision. As it was a privileged applicant, there could have been no objections to the Belgian Government's *locus standi*. The fact that the Belgian Government did not bring an application suggests either that it did not consider it would meet with success or that it had changed its mind about the desirability of making use of the authorization. In the *Bock* case, on the other hand, the German Government was obviously acting against the interests of the importer. Bock could not look to his Government to bring an application to quash the decision. So if he had been refused *locus standi* there would have been no possibility that the legality of the decision would have been challenged (except in the somewhat unlikely circumstance of an application

[105] There was some dispute as to the correct interpretation of this part of the decision but the Court held that this is what it meant.

by another Member State, perhaps Holland, the country from which the import was to have been made).

The first distinguishing fact was recognized by the Court itself and is obviously relevant. The second was not alluded to by the Court, but it may have been influenced by it. It is obviously a factor of great practical importance, though it is hardly something that could have been expressly stated by the Court.

A later case, which is similar to *Bock* but goes further, is *Piraiki-Patraiki v. Commission*.[106] The facts of this case were outlined earlier: it will be remembered that the Commission took a decision authorizing France to exclude Greek cotton yarn. Since France was not legally obliged to exercise the power, it could be argued that the Greek exporters who challenged the decision were not directly concerned by it. However, France was already exercising a very restrictive system of licences for such imports and the Court said that the possibility that France might decide not to make use of the authorization was 'entirely theoretical';[107] so the applicants were held to be directly concerned.[108] This is probably the Court's most liberal decision on the subject.[109]

## NON-PRIVILEGED APPLICANTS: THE ECSC TREATY

Although the ECSC Treaty has now expired, it is still of interest in this regard because of the light it sheds on the EC Treaty. Paragraph 2 of Article 33 of the ECSC Treaty provided:

> Undertakings or the associations referred to in Article 48 may... institute proceedings against decisions or recommendations concerning them which are individual in character or against general decisions or recommendations which they consider to involve a misuse of powers affecting them.

Although narrower in some respects than the fourth paragraph of Article 230 [173] EC,[110] it was more liberal with regard to the kinds of act that could be challenged. Article 33 allowed non-privileged applicants to bring proceedings to quash two categories of acts: 'decisions and recommendations... which are individual in character' and 'general decisions and recommendations'. Individual decisions under the ECSC were equivalent to EC decisions. Recommendations under the ECSC were different from EC recommendations: they were legally binding and were analogous to EC directives.

[106] Case 11/82, [1985] ECR 207. See also *ASPEC v. Commission*, Case T-435/93, [1995] ECR II-1281 (paras 60–61 of the judgment).

[107] Para. 9 of the judgment.

[108] See also *AIUFFASS v. Commission*, Case T-380/94, [1996] ECR II-2169 (paras 46 and 47 of the judgment).

[109] For later decisions of the Court of First Instance which display a restrictive attitude, see Arnull, 'Private Applicants and the Action for Annulment since *Codorniu*' (2001) 38 CMLRev. 7 at pp. 25–30.

[110] It applied only to undertakings engaged in production in the coal or the steel industry and their trade associations: see Art. 80 ECSC. It also applied only to acts of the Commission (but see Art. 38 ECSC).

General decisions were normative acts, equivalent to EC regulations. These general acts could be challenged by non-privileged applicants under the ECSC Treaty, but only on one ground: a misuse of powers affecting the applicant. Although this ground was difficult to establish, the fact that the Treaty allowed non-privileged applicants to proceed at all against normative acts was a significant difference compared with the wording of the EC Treaty.

Article 33 was also wider in scope with regard to *locus standi*. In the case of individual acts, all that Article 33 required was that the challenged act should concern the applicant. That concern did not have to be individual or direct. This was an important difference. Where the challenged act was general, it had to be shown that the misuse of powers affected the applicant: it did not have to affect him individually or directly.

Two of the decisions on these points throw valuable light on the EC Treaty, because the authors of Article 230 [173] had them in mind when they drafted the latter Article. The first is *Groupement des Industries Sidérurgiques Luxembourgeoises v. High Authority*.[111] This case, which was decided in 1956, concerned a decree enacted by the Luxembourg Government establishing two official bodies called the *Office Commercial* and the *Caisse*. The decree provided that the former would have the sole right of importing coal into Luxembourg, and that a levy on all sales of coal to industrial enterprises in Luxembourg had to be paid to the latter. The applicants in the case were a group of Luxembourg steel producers. They wrote to the Commission requesting it to adopt a decision declaring that the *Office*'s monopoly of coal imports and the levy were both illegal. No action was taken by the Commission during the two months following receipt of this request; consequently, under the provisions of Article 35 ECSC, they were deemed to have passed a decision refusing to comply with it. The applicants, therefore, brought proceedings in the Court to have this implied decision set aside.

Since the applicants did not allege a misuse of power, they had to prove, in order to establish the admissibility of the proceedings, that the decision was individual and that it concerned them.

In order to discover whether these conditions were met, it is necessary to see what the decision would have been if it had been expressed. It would have stated that the monopoly enjoyed by the *Office Commercial* and the levy payable to the *Caisse* were not contrary to Community law. Such a decision would obviously have affected the legal position of these two bodies by confirming their powers. From their point of view, it would have been an individual act. But the decision would also have affected the legal position of coal importers and coal users: it would have confirmed that they were not legally entitled to import coal and that they were obliged to pay the levy. Since they would have been affected as members of an open category, the decision would, from their point of view, have been normative (general).

The Advocate General (Mr Roemer) stated that, in his opinion, the implied decision was individual but that, in so far as it concerned the legality of the *Office Commercial*'s import monopoly, the applicants lacked *locus standi* because their interest in the matter was not peculiar to them: it was shared with all other users of coal and coal dealers.

[111] Cases 7, 9/54, [1956] ECR 175.

What the Advocate General was saying – if one might use the terminology of the EC Treaty – was that the applicants were not individually concerned.[112]

The Court rejected the Advocate General's opinion. It held that the applicants had *locus standi*. It is sufficient, it said, if the decision possesses the characteristics of an individual decision and it is 'not necessary for the decision to manifest this character in relation to the applicant'.[113] In other words, the Court confirmed that individual concern is not necessary under the ECSC Treaty.

The other case is *Fédération Charbonnière de Belgique v. High Authority*[114] (discussed in Chapter 11). One of the issues in this case was the right of a non-privileged applicant to challenge a general decision (normative act). It was argued by the defendant that this could not be done unless the decision was general in form only, that is, if it was an individual decision disguised as a general decision. This contention was rejected by the Court. It said:

> A disguised individual decision remains an individual decision, since its nature depends on its scope rather than on its form... The Court considers that Article 33 clearly states that associations and undertakings may contest not only individual decisions but also general decisions in the true sense of the term.[115]

The interesting point about these two cases is that when the authors of the EC Treaty drafted Article 230 [173], they incorporated into the text of that Article precisely those ideas which had been rejected by the Court in its interpretation of the ECSC Treaty. It is not enough, under the EC Treaty, that the act is individual, it must also be of individual concern to the applicant. (It might be mentioned that the idea of direct concern was also mooted by Advocate General Roemer in the *Groupement des Industries Sidérurgiques Luxembourgeoises* case, though he considered that this requirement was met on the facts of the case.)[116] Moreover, under Article 230 [173] EC only an act *in the form of* a regulation may be challenged by a non-privileged applicant: the unsuccessful contention of the Commission in the *Fédération Charbonnière* case was adopted in the text of the EC Treaty.

It is clear, therefore, that the authors of the EC Treaty made a deliberate choice in favour of a more restrictive system.[117] They apparently thought that Article 33 ECSC, as interpreted by the Court, was too liberal. The reasons for this are not altogether clear, but they are probably related to the general weakening of the supranational elements in the EC as compared with the ECSC. It is possible, moreover, that the authors of the EC Treaty (representatives of the national governments) thought it unnecessary to provide

[112] See [1956] ECR 175 at 215. The Advocate General's opinion, which seems hard to sustain on the basis of the English text of Art. 33, was probably inspired by the German text. There was, unfortunately, a discrepancy between the French, Italian, and, subsequently, the English texts, on the one hand, and the German and Dutch, on the other. The former all spoke of individual decisions or recommendations concerning the applicant; the latter, however, referred to decisions or recommendations concerning the applicant individually – a more restrictive formulation. This divergence would have been troublesome had it not been for the fact that under the ECSC Treaty the French text alone was authentic.

[113] [1956] ECR at 192.

[114] Case 8/55, [1956] ECR 245.

[115] [1956] ECR at 257–8.

[116] [1956] ECR at 214–15.

[117] Advocate General Jacobs rejected this contention in the *UPA* case (see paras 76–77 of the Opinion), but the Court did not follow his Opinion.

for such extensive judicial control of the Commission (since its powers were less) and undesirable to have too much judicial control of the Council (since it represented the Member States). It is also possible that the Court interpreted the ECSC Treaty more liberally than had been intended by its authors, though this is doubtful.

## FURTHER READING

FROMONT, 'L'influence du droit français et du droit allemand sur les conditions de recevabilité du recours en annulation devant la Cour de Justice des Communautés européennes' (1966) 2 RTDE 47.

HARDING, 'Decisions Addressed to Member States and Article 173 of the Treaty of Rome' (1976) 25 ICLQ 15.

KOVAR AND BARAV, 'Le recours individuel en annulation' (1976) 12 CDE 68.

STEIN AND VINING, 'Citizen Access to Judicial Review of Administrative Action in a Transnational and Federal Context' (1976) 70 Am. J. Int. L. 219.

DINNAGE, 'Locus Standi and Article 173 EEC' (1979) 4 ELRev. 15.

P VAN DIJK, *Judicial Review of Governmental Action and the Requirement of an Interest to Sue* (1980), Chap. 7.

HARDING, 'The Private Interest in Challenging Community Action' (1980) 5 ELRev. 354.

RASMUSSEN, 'Why is Article 173 Interpreted against Private Plaintiffs?' (1980) 5 ELRev. 112.

G BEBR, *Development of Judicial Control of the European Communities* (1981).

GREAVES, 'Locus Standi under Article 173 EEC when Seeking Annulment of a Regulation' (1986) 11 ELRev. 119.

ARNULL, 'Challenging EC Anti-Dumping Regulations: The Problem of Admissibility' [1992] 2 ECLR 73.

HARLOW, 'Towards a Theory of Access for the European Court of Justice' (1992) 12 YEL 213.

CRAIG, 'Legality, Standing and Substantive Review in Community Law' (1994) 14 OJLS 507.

ARNULL, 'Private Applicants and the Action for Annulment under Article 173 of the EC Treaty' (1995) 32 CMLRev. 7.

GREAVES, 'The Nature and Binding Effect of Decisions under Article 189 EC' (1996) 21 ELRev. 3.

NEUWAHL, 'Article 173, Paragraph 4 EC: Past, Present and Possible Future' (1996) 21 ELRev. 17.

ARNULL, 'Private Applicants and the Action for Annulment since *Codorniu*' (2001) 38 CMLRev. 7.

USHER, 'Direct and Individual Concern – An Effective Remedy or a Conventional Solution?' (2003) 28 ELRev. 575.

WARD, 'Locus Standi under Article 230(4) of the EC Treaty: Crafting a Coherent Test for a "Wobbly Polity"' (2003) 22 YEL 45.

ENCHELMAIER, 'No-One Slips through the Net? Latest Developments, and Non-Developments, in the European Court of Justice's Jurisprudence on Art. 230(4) EC' (2005) 24 YEL 173.

KOCH, '*Locus Standi* of Private Applicants under the EU Constitution: Preserving Gaps in the Protection of Individuals' Right to an Effective Remedy' (2005) 30 ELRev. 511.

ANGELA WARD, *Judicial Review and the Rights of Private Parties in EU Law*, 2nd edn (2006).

# 13

# FAILURE TO ACT

A remedy for a wrongful failure to act is provided by Article 232 [175] EC,[1] which reads as follows:

> Should the European Parliament, the Council or the Commission, in infringement of this Treaty, fail to act, the Member States and the other institutions of the Community may bring an action before the Court of Justice to have the infringement established.
>
> The action shall be admissible only if the institution concerned has first been called upon to act. If, within two months of being so called upon, the institution concerned has not defined its position the action may be brought within a further period of two months.
>
> Any natural or legal person may, under the conditions laid down in the preceding paragraphs, complain to the Court of Justice that an institution of the Community has failed to address to that person any act other than a recommendation or an opinion.
>
> The Court of Justice shall have jurisdiction, under the same conditions, in actions or proceedings brought by the ECB in the areas falling within the latter's field of competence and in actions or proceedings brought by the latter.

It will be noticed that this provision bears a fairly strong resemblance to Article 230 [173] EC. The first paragraph in both Articles is concerned with the rights of so-called 'privileged applicants'. The second paragraph of Article 232 [175], which deals with procedure and time-limits, corresponds to the fifth paragraph of Article 230 [173]; the third paragraph of Article 232 [175] deals with the rights of non-privileged applicants, and this parallels the fourth paragraph of Article 230 [173].

The most obvious difference between the two Articles is that proceedings cannot be brought under Article 232 [175] unless the applicant has first addressed a request for action to the defendant. The defendant must be given two months to comply and the action may then be brought within the following two months. Another difference is that only one ground of review is laid down by Article 232 [175], while under Article 230 [173] there are four. (The grounds of review under both Articles are discussed in Chapter 15.)

From a theoretical viewpoint, it is quite clear that proceedings to quash a legal act, and proceedings to require a public authority to take action, are two aspects of the same legal remedy. The similarities between the two sets of provisions in each of the Treaties

[1] Art. 148 Euratom is the same as Art. 232 [175] EC, except that two additions to the latter made by the Treaty on European Union do not apply to the former. The first allows proceedings to be brought against the European Parliament and the second, which now constitutes the final paragraph of Art. 232 [175] EC, allows proceedings to be brought by and against the European Central Bank.

indicate that the authors of the Treaties were well aware of this. It is no surprise, therefore, that the European Court has adopted this doctrine as a general principle. Thus in *Chevalley v. Commission*[2] it was not clear whether the application should have been under Article 232 [175] or under Article 230 [173]. The action had originally been brought under Article 232 [175] but, in the course of the hearing, the applicant had requested the Court to consider it as an application under either Article 232 [175] or Article 230 [173], depending on which the Court considered appropriate. In its judgment, however, the Court did not regard it as necessary to characterize the proceedings as being under either one or the other, since the two Articles 'merely prescribe one and the same method of recourse'.[3]

The principle that the two Articles are concerned with essentially the same remedy, which for the sake of brevity will henceforth be referred to as the 'unity principle', is not of merely theoretical interest but has a very important practical consequence. It implies that the conditions and limitations applicable to the remedy should be the same under the two procedures, except to the extent that different rules are a necessary consequence of the inherent differences between an act and a failure to act, between commission and omission. Subject to this exception, one would expect the applicant to have the same rights in proceedings under Article 232 [175] as he has in proceedings under Article 230 [173]. Generally speaking, this is indeed the case, though, as we shall see below, there are some anomalies.

## NEGATIVE DECISIONS

A 'negative decision' is a decision of a public authority in which it decides not to act in a particular way. A rejection of a request is the most common example. From a strictly theoretical viewpoint, a negative decision would be a reviewable act – an act having legal effects – only if it was binding on the authority, in the sense that it precluded the authority, at least for a period, from changing its mind and taking the action in question. In such a situation the authority will have lost the power to take the action in question. Where this is not the case, however, the decision will have no legal effects: in law the legal position of the authority and of the person making the request will be the same as before. Normally, of course, a negative decision is not binding on the authority making it.

It will, however, be remembered that the European Court has departed from strict theory by ruling that a statement by a Community institution on how it intends to act in

[2] Case 15/70, [1970] ECR 975.

[3] Para. 6 of the judgment. For similar statements by advocates general, see: *Mackprang v. Commission*, Case 15/71, [1971] ECR 797 at 802 (*per* Advocate General Dutheillet de Lamothe); *Nordgetreide v. Commission*, Case 42/71, [1972] ECR 105 at 116 (*per* Advocate General Roemer); *Compagnie d'Approvisionnement v. Commission*, Cases 9, 11/71, [1972] ECR 391 at 414 (*per* Advocate General Dutheillet de Lamothe); and *Holtz & Willemsen v. Council*, Case 134/73, [1974] ECR 1 at 14 (*per* Advocate General Reischl). However, in *European Parliament v. Council* (*Comitology* case), Case 302/87, [1988] ECR 5615 (para. 16 of the judgment), the Court said that there is 'no necessary link between the action for annulment and the action for failure to act'. For the special context in which this was said, see below.

the future, even if it is not legally binding on the institution, is to be regarded as a reviewable act if it is definite and unequivocal.[4] As was explained above, this was necessitated by the absence in Community law of anything corresponding to the English action for a declaration. Were it not for this doctrine, it would be impossible for the legality of a proposed course of action to be challenged until it had actually been carried out.

Since a negative act is no more than a (negative) statement of future intention, it is not surprising that the European Court has adopted a general doctrine that a negative act which is sufficiently clear and precise constitutes a reviewable act, provided the act which the Community institution has refused to adopt would itself have been reviewable.[5] If, for example, the Commission informs a citizen that it will not address a decision to him, the citizen would be able to challenge the refusal in annulment proceedings, since the decision, if it had been taken, would have been reviewable.

A negative act is, moreover, classified for the purpose of *locus standi* in the same way as the positive act. Thus if a private individual requests the Commission to pass a regulation and the Commission refuses, the negative decision containing the refusal is regarded for review purposes as a general (normative) act, even though the refusal is addressed solely to the person concerned. He cannot, therefore, challenge it in review proceedings, since, as was pointed out in Chapter 12, non-privileged applicants have (in principle) no *locus standi* under the EC Treaty to challenge a general act.[6]

This attitude makes sense if one realizes that a challenge to a negative act is in reality an application for a remedy for a failure to act; consequently, it is really directed at the defendant's failure to adopt the requested act and it is therefore right that questions of *locus standi*, as well as questions of reviewability, should be determined with reference to that act. This may be demonstrated by considering the effect of a judgment in favour of the applicant. A declaration by the Court that a negative act is invalid would be meaningless, were it not for the fact that the defendant must then adopt the act which it had previously refused to adopt. This follows from the first paragraph of Article 233 [176] EC, which states:

> The institution whose act has been declared void or whose failure to act has been declared contrary to this Treaty shall be required to take the necessary measures to comply with the judgment of the Court of Justice.

If the negative act has been quashed because the defendant had no right to refuse to take the action required, the 'necessary measures' would clearly be the adoption of the act in question.

[4] See *Fédération Charbonnière de Belgique v. High Authority*, Case 8/55, [1956] ECR 245, discussed in Chap. 11.

[5] *De Gezamenlijke Steenkolenmijnen in Limburg v. High Authority*, Case 30/59, [1961] ECR 1 at 15; *Lütticke v. Commission*, Case 48/65, [1966] ECR 19 at 31, *per* Advocate General Gand; *Irish Cement v. Commission*, Cases 166, 220/86, [1988] ECR 6473 at 6495–6, *per* Advocate General Darmon. See also *Buckl*, Cases C-15, 108/91, [1992] ECR I-6061 (paras 22 and 23 of the judgment); *Zunis Holding*, Case T-83/92, [1993] ECR II-1169 (para. 31 of the judgment).

[6] *Nordgetreide v. Commission*, Case 42/71, [1972] ECR 105; *Asteris v. Commission*, Cases 97, 99, 193, 215/86, [1988] ECR 2181 (para. 17 of the judgment); *Sonito v. Commission*, Case C-87/89, [1990] ECR I-1981 (para. 8 of the judgment); *Buckl*, Cases C-15, 108/91, [1992] ECR I-6061 (paras 19–31 of the judgment); *Zunis Holding*, Case T-83/92, [1993] ECR II-1169 (para. 31 of the judgment).

An action to annul a negative decision is, therefore, a remedy for failure to act; nevertheless in form it is still an action to annul, and it is governed by Article 230 [173] EC and not by Article 232 [175]. The latter Article comes into play only when the defendant has not 'defined its position'. The meaning of this phrase must now be considered.

## DEFINITION OF POSITION

One would have thought that any clear and definite answer to the request for action, including a total or partial refusal, would constitute a definition of position. Though it might seem strange that a remedy under Article 232 [175] could be barred by an outright refusal, no problems will be caused as long as the refusal constitutes a negative decision which the applicant can challenge under Article 230 [173]. This should normally be the case. Where it is not, however, serious difficulties could arise, since the applicant might be deprived of any remedy.

An example of a refusal to act that cannot be challenged under Article 230 [173] concerns the European Parliament. The Parliament has always had standing as a privileged applicant under Article 232 [175],[7] but, prior to the *Chernobyl* case,[8] it had no standing to bring an annulment action.[9] This meant that if the Parliament brought proceedings under Article 232 [175] and was met with a flat refusal, it could not challenge the refusal as a negative act. Consequently, if such a refusal were regarded as a definition of position for the purpose of Article 232 [175], the Parliament's right to bring proceedings under that Article would be largely illusory.

The first time the question arose was in the *Transport* case,[10] in which the Parliament brought proceedings against the Council because the latter had failed to establish a common transport policy for the Community. The Court, however, avoided the issue by ruling that the somewhat equivocal reply given by the Council was not sufficiently clear to constitute a definition of position.[11]

The issue arose again in the *Comitology* case.[12] This, it will be remembered, was the case in which the Parliament argued that, in spite of the wording of Article 230 [173], it *was* entitled to bring proceedings under that provision. One of the most powerful arguments in favour of its position was that if it were not entitled to bring proceedings under Article 230 [173], its admitted right of action under Article 232 [175] could be rendered nugatory by the simple expedient of an outright refusal.

[7] It is covered by the phrase 'the other institutions of the Community' in the first para. of Art. 232 [175]: *European Parliament v. Council* (*Transport*), Case 13/83, [1985] ECR 1513.

[8] *European Parliament v. Council*, Case C-70/88, [1990] ECR I-2041. See now the amendment to Art. 230 [173] brought in by the Treaty of Nice.

[9] It was not listed among the privileged applicants in the first para. of Art. 230 [173] and the Court held in the *Comitology* case (*European Parliament v. Council*, Case 302/87, [1988] ECR 5615) that it could not bring proceedings as a non-privileged applicant under what is now the fourth para. of Art. 230 [173].

[10] *European Parliament v. Council*, Case 13/83, [1985] ECR 1513.

[11] *Ibid.*, para. 25 of the judgment.

[12] *European Parliament v. Council*, Case 302/87, [1988] ECR 5615.

Since the Court intended to deny the Parliament's claim, it had to meet this argument. It did so by rejecting the premise on which it was based. It stated: 'A refusal to act, however explicit it may be, can be brought before the Court under Article 232 [175] since it does not put an end to the failure to act.'[13]

This must mean that even an explicit refusal does not constitute a definition of position. If this were accepted as a general proposition, however, two serious problems would arise. The first is that it would be hard to see what *could* constitute a definition of position if a clear and explicit refusal does not do so. It could hardly have been the intention of the authors of the Treaty that the only way a defendant under Article 232 [175] could define its position would be to agree to whatever was requested.

The second difficulty is that there have been several cases in which a statement by the defendant that it would not meet the request *has* been held by the Court to constitute a definition of position.[14] In none of them, however, was the applicant thereby deprived of a remedy which he would otherwise have had.[15] Perhaps it is only where this would be the case that a refusal will not be regarded as a definition of position.

As was explained in Chapter 12, the European Court subsequently modified its position on the Parliament's right of action under Article 230 [173] by ruling, in the *Chernobyl* case, that the Parliament *can* bring proceedings, though only for the purpose of protecting its prerogatives,[16] a rule subsequently embodied in the text of Article 230 [173] by an amendment under the Treaty on European Union. The problem is now fully solved by the Treaty of Nice, which gives the Parliament the full rights of a privileged applicant.

## PARTIES TO THE PROCEEDINGS

The first paragraph of Article 232 [175] EC makes provision for proceedings against the Parliament, the Council, and the Commission. The fourth paragraph (inserted by the Treaty on European Union) adds the European Central Bank. There are thus four potential defendants.

As far as potential applicants are concerned, the first paragraph of Article 232 [175] provides that the Member States and 'the other institutions of the Community' may bring proceedings. This latter phrase covers the Council, the Commission, and the Parliament.[17] The Court is probably also covered, though it is not likely to commence proceedings. In addition, the fourth paragraph of Article 232 [175] provides that the ECB can bring proceedings in the areas falling within its field of competence. These are all privileged applicants.

13 Para. 17 of the judgment.

14 See, e.g., *Lütticke v. Commission*, Case 48/65, [1966] ECR 19; *Nordgetreide v. Commission*, Case 42/71, [1972] ECR 105; *Irish Cement v. Commission*, Cases 166, 220/86, [1988] ECR 6473; *Buckl*, Cases C-15, 108/91, [1992] ECR I-6061; *Guérin Automobiles v. Commission*, Case C-282/95, [1997] ECR I-1503 (appeal from Case T-186/94, [1995] ECR II-1753).

15 See below, where this is explained.

16 *European Parliament v. Council*, Case C-70/88, [1990] ECR I-2041.

17 *European Parliament v. Council (Transport)*, Case 13/83, [1985] ECR 1513.

The third paragraph of Article 232 [175] grants a limited right of action to non-privileged applicants. 'Any natural or legal person' may bring proceedings on this basis, subject to the rules on *locus standi*, which are discussed below.

## REVIEWABLE OMISSIONS

What kind of act may the Commission or Council be required to perform by means of proceedings under Article 232 [175]? In other words, what kind of omission is reviewable? This question is, of course, the negative equivalent of the question discussed in Chapter 11: what acts are reviewable? From the point of view of theory (unity principle), one would expect the answer to be that only an omission to adopt a reviewable act – an act having legal effects – would be reviewable under Article 232 [175]. In order to facilitate discussion, this view will henceforth be referred to as the 'narrow interpretation' while the view that other kinds of omissions are also reviewable will be called the 'wide interpretation'.

Article 232 [175] EC refers in its first paragraph simply to a failure 'to act'. This contrasts with the first paragraph of Article 230 [173] which applies to 'acts . . . other than recommendations or opinions'. Does the fact that non-binding acts (recommendations and opinions) are not expressly excluded in Article 232 [175] mean that a failure to adopt such an act may be challenged by proceedings under Article 232 [175]? It could, of course, be argued that 'act' in Article 232 [175] is impliedly limited to a reviewable act; but this could be countered by reference to the third paragraph of Article 232 [175]. This provision, which is concerned with proceedings by non-privileged applicants, refers to 'any act other than a recommendation or an opinion': if the word 'act' in the first paragraph is impliedly limited to a reviewable act, it would be unnecessary expressly to exclude a recommendation or an opinion in the third paragraph. It seems, therefore, that an analysis of the text lends support to the wide interpretation.

The objection to such a conclusion is that it conflicts with the unity principle: if the action to annul and the action for a remedy for failure to act are, as the European Court has confirmed, merely different aspects of the same remedy, how can the subject-matter of the second be wider than that of the first?

In the *Draft Budget* case,[18] Advocate General Mischo came out explicitly in favour of the narrow interpretation. He said:[19]

> The decisive criterion is therefore that of the legal effects. Thus, a 'failure to act' within the meaning of Article 232 [175] may be constituted by the non-adoption by the Council or by the Commission of an act or measure, of whatever nature, form or description, which is capable of producing legal effects *vis-à-vis* third parties.

The case was an action brought under Article 232 [175] by the Parliament against the Council because the latter had failed to place the draft budget before the Parliament by

[18] *European Parliament v. Council*, Case 377/87, [1988] ECR 4017; see also *Commission v. Council*, Case 383/87, [1988] ECR 4051. [19] *European Parliament v. Council*, Case 377/87 at 4029 (para. 30).

the due date. The Council argued that the action was inadmissible because the draft budget was not a reviewable act – in its opinion, only the final budget would be reviewable – and consequently its failure to adopt it was not a reviewable omission in terms of Article 232 [175]. This argument was of course based on the narrow interpretation. In his Opinion, Advocate General Mischo accepted that the narrow interpretation was correct, but maintained that the draft budget *was* a reviewable act because it had legal effects. The Court did not decide the point. The Council had in fact adopted the draft budget within two months of being called on to act, and the Court therefore concluded that the subject matter of the action (the failure to act) had ceased to exist. The final ruling was, 'The Court declares that there is no need for it to give a decision.'

This was not the end of the matter, however, because in the *Comitology* case[20] the Court stated that, as was 'shown' by its judgment in the *Draft Budget* case, an action for failure to act can be brought by the Parliament if the Council fails to adopt a draft budget. This, the Court said, establishes that an action under Article 232 [175] can be brought by the Parliament for failure to adopt a measure that is not itself a reviewable act. It seems, therefore, that the Court now rejects the narrow interpretation, though its decision in the *Draft Budget* case is not an authority for this.

It should be said that the Court's statement in the *Comitology* case was made very much with a particular purpose in mind. The *Comitology* case, it will be remembered, was the case in which the Parliament argued that, in spite of the clear wording of the first paragraph of Article 230 [173] as it then stood, it should nevertheless be entitled to bring proceedings as a privileged applicant. One of the arguments it put forward was that, since it had standing under Article 232 [175], it would be illogical to deny it standing under Article 230 [173]. The Court replied to this by saying that there is 'no necessary link' between the two actions, and supported this assertion by saying that a non-reviewable act can constitute a reviewable omission. Since the Court was about to rule against the Parliament, it is possible that it was trying to sweeten the pill by expressly confirming the Parliament's right to bring proceedings under Article 232 [175] in the case of a preliminary act such as a draft budget, a right which was actually left uncertain by the *Draft Budget* case. If this is correct, it is possible that the Court's adoption of the wide interpretation will apply only in the case of preliminary acts (discussed below).

## PRELIMINARY ACTS

A 'preliminary act' is the first step in the adoption of some other act. The concept was discussed in Chapter 11, where it was suggested that the reviewability of a preliminary act should depend on whether or not it has legal effects. For example, if the law provides that the final act cannot be adopted until some other body has been consulted, it would be wrong to regard the opinion of this other body as a reviewable act, since it is not binding on the authority empowered to adopt the final act. If, on the other hand, the final act can be adopted only if the other body gives its consent, then the 'opinion' of

[20] *European Parliament v. Council*, Case 302/87, [1988] ECR 5615.

that other body would have legal effects and ought to be regarded as reviewable. However, as was pointed out in Chapter 11, the European Court has taken the view that, even in this case, such a preliminary act will not necessarily be a reviewable act. This does not normally have serious consequences, however, because the preliminary act may be reviewed in the context of proceedings to annul the final act.

Unfortunately, this will not always be possible in the case of a failure to act, particularly where the preliminary act is the responsibility of a different body from that empowered to adopt the final act: if proceedings are brought against the body responsible for the final act, it can raise the defence that it cannot adopt it until the preliminary act has been adopted; since the latter is not its responsibility, it could not be held to blame for the failure to act.

The draft budget has already been mentioned as an example of this problem. The Community's budget is adopted by the Parliament, but it can act only if the Council first adopts a draft budget. If the Council fails to make such a proposal, the Parliament is powerless to act. If Article 232 [175] did not apply in such a case because (as was argued by the Council in the *Draft Budget* case) a draft budget is only a preliminary act, there would be no remedy open to the Parliament. It could not bring proceedings against the Council for failure to adopt a final budget, since the Parliament itself does this. It should also be noted that the Council cannot adopt the draft budget until the Commission draws up the preliminary draft budget. The same problem would arise if the Commission failed to do this. Moreover, the problem is not limited to the budget since most of the legal acts which the Council is empowered to adopt may be enacted only on the basis of a proposal from the Commission.

As was pointed out above, there are strong theoretical grounds for saying that drafts and proposals of this kind *are* reviewable acts. By adopting a draft budget, for example, the Council confers a power on the Parliament to adopt the final budget. This was the view of Advocate General Mischo in the *Draft Budget* case.[21] The same is true of a Commission proposal for a measure to be adopted by the Council. However, since the Court regards preliminary acts as non-reviewable under Article 230 [173], it probably felt that it could not say they were reviewable for the purpose of Article 232 [175]. This, it is suggested, is why it ruled instead that a failure to act can include a failure to adopt a non-reviewable act.

A situation in which the preliminary and the final act are both adopted by the same authority occurs in Community competition procedure. As was mentioned in Chapter 12, a person with a legitimate interest may submit a complaint to the Commission that another person has violated Community competition law.[22] This does not, however, mean that the complainant has an absolute right to require the Commission to investigate the complaint.[23] The Commission must have the necessary flexibility to use its

[21] See above. [22] Regulation 17, OJ (Spec. Edition) 1959–62, p. 87, Art. 3(2)(b); see also Art. 19(2).

[23] See *GEMA v. Commission*, Case 125/78, [1979] ECR 3173; *Automec v. Commission (No. 2)*, Case T-24/90, [1992] ECR II-2223 (paras 71–82 of the judgment). For a helpful summary of the position, see the Opinion of Advocate General Tesauro in *Guérin Automobiles v. Commission*, Case C-282/95, [1997] ECR I-1503 (appeal from Case T-186/94, [1995] ECR II-1753), paras 10–17.

limited resources to the best advantage. It is, however, obliged to examine carefully the particulars brought to its notice by the complainant before deciding whether or not to commence an investigation.[24] Moreover, the complainant does have a procedural right: if the Commission intends to take no action, it must inform him of that fact and give him an opportunity to make any final submissions before taking a definitive decision.[25] This is done by means of a letter pursuant to Article 6 of Regulation 2842/98[26] (formerly, Article 6 of Regulation 99/63[27]), the provision which grants the right in question. Since it is not the final step in the procedure, however, such a letter is not a reviewable act under Article 230 [173] EC:[28] the complainant must wait until the definitive decision has been taken by the Commission (after hearing any representations the complainant may make in response to the letter) and then challenge that.

What is the position if the Commission fails to send a letter under Article 6: can the complainant bring proceedings under Article 232 [175]? If such a possibility were rejected on the ground that this does not constitute a reviewable omission, the complainant might be without a remedy, since the Commission could argue, if proceedings were brought for failure to adopt the definitive decision, that it cannot adopt the latter unless it has first sent the letter. For this reason, it must be possible to bring an action under Article 232 [175] for failure to send the letter, even though the letter is not itself a reviewable act.[29] If the letter is not followed by the definitive decision within a reasonable time, a second action may be brought under Article 232 [175].[30] A definitive decision refusing to take action *would* be a reviewable act under Article 230 [173].[31] Consequently, the complainant would always have a remedy whatever happened.

## FAILURE TO REPEAL AN ACT

Assume that a Community institution adopts a legal act and, after the time limit for challenging it in annulment proceedings has passed, the applicant requests the institution to repeal it on the ground that it violates Community law. If the Community institution does not comply with this request, may the applicant bring proceedings for a remedy for failure to act? In support of such an application it could be argued that, since all Community institutions are obliged to respect the law, there is a legal obligation to repeal any act which is inconsistent with Community law, even if the time limit for an annulment action has expired. Moreover, since the repealing act would clearly have legal effects, the controversy over the wide and the narrow interpretations would not affect the matter.

24 *Automec v. Commission (No. 2)*, (above) at para. 79 of the judgment.

25 This applies both where the Commission decides not to open an investigation and where it opens one, but decides to close the file without taking any proceedings against the person alleged to have committed the violation.

26 OJ 1998 L354, p. 18. 27 OJ (Spec. Edn) 1963–64, p. 47.

28 *Guérin Automobiles v. Commission*, (above) at paras 33–5 of the judgment of the European Court; *Automec v. Commission (No. 1)*, Case T-64/89, [1990] ECR II-367 at paras 45–6 of the judgment.

29 *Guérin Automobiles v. Commission*, (above), *per* Advocate General Tesauro at para. 16 of his Opinion (p. 1514).

30 *Guérin Automobiles v. Commission* (above) at paras 36–8 of the judgment of the European Court.

31 *Demo-Studio Schmidt v. Commission*, Case 210/81, [1983] ECR 3045 (paras 10–16 of the judgment); *BAT and Reynolds v. Commission*, Cases 142 and 156/84, [1987] ECR 4487 (paras 11–13 of the judgment);

The European Court has, however, ruled that this cannot be done. The leading case is *Eridania v. Commission*,[32] in which an Italian sugar-refining concern brought proceedings to challenge three Commission decisions granting aid to its competitors. The applicant claimed that these decisions were illegal and requested the Commission to revoke them. When this request was not met, it brought two actions: first, proceedings under Article 230 [173] to annul the decisions (Case 10/68); secondly, proceedings under Article 232 [175] for a remedy for the Commission's failure to revoke the decisions (Case 18/68). These two actions were joined and the Court decided them both in a single judgment. Case 10/68 was declared inadmissible because the applicant lacked *locus standi*: the decisions were not addressed to the applicant and the applicant was not, in the opinion of the Court, directly and individually concerned by them. Case 18/68 was also declared inadmissible. The reasoning of the Court was as follows:

> This application concerns the annulment of the implied decision of rejection resulting from the silence maintained by the Commission in respect of the request addressed to it by the applicants seeking the annulment or revocation of the three disputed decisions for illegality or otherwise because they are inappropriate.
>
> The action provided for in Article 232 [175] is intended to establish an illegal omission as appears from that article, which refers to a failure to act 'in infringement of this Treaty' and from Article 233 [176] which refers to a failure to act declared to be 'contrary to this Treaty'.
>
> Without stating under which provision of Community law the Commission was required to annul or to revoke the said decisions, the applicants have confined themselves to alleging that those decisions were adopted in infringement of the Treaty and that this fact alone would thus suffice to make the Commission's failure to act subject to the provisions of Article 232 [175].
>
> The Treaty provides, however, particularly in Article 230 [173], other methods of recourse by which an allegedly illegal Community measure may be disputed and if necessary annulled on the application of a duly qualified party.
>
> To admit, as the applicants wish to do, that the parties concerned could ask the institution from which the measure came to revoke it and, in the event of the Commission's failing to act, refer such failure to the Court as an illegal omission to deal with the matter would amount to providing them with a method of recourse parallel to that of Article 230 [173], which would not be subject to the conditions laid down by the Treaty.
>
> This application does not therefore satisfy the requirements of Article 232 [175] of the Treaty and must thus be held to be inadmissible.

This does not mean that there is no obligation on Community institutions to repeal an invalid act: all the Court decided was that it had no jurisdiction to consider the question in proceedings brought under Article 232 [175]. The ruling was procedural, not substantive. This is also clear from the ruling in an earlier case under the ECSC Treaty, *Meroni v. High Authority*[33] (fifth *Meroni* case), in which the Court stated that 'an

*SFEI v. Commission*, Case C-39/93 P, [1994] ECR I-2681 (appeal from Case T-36/92, [1992] ECR II-2479) (paras 27–33 of the judgment of the European Court). The challenge will, however, be successful only if the complainant can show that the decision to close the file was vitiated by some illegality.

[32] Cases 10, 18/68, [1969] ECR 459 at 482–3.

[33] Cases 21–6/61, [1962] ECR 73 at 78.

applicant cannot be permitted, by using the procedural artifice of an action for failure to act, to ask for the annulment of decisions which might have been declared void if proceedings had been instituted within the time-limit laid down in the third paragraph of Article 33.'

The Court's objection to the use, for this purpose, of proceedings for a remedy for failure to act is that it would allow a decision to be challenged after the expiry of the time limit for annulment actions. This is what the Court meant in the *Eridania* case when it said that, if this procedure were allowed, applicants would be provided with a method of recourse 'which would not be subject to the conditions laid down by the Treaty'. This cannot refer to the *locus standi* provisions, since these are the same in actions for a remedy for failure to act as in annulment actions (see below).

It is interesting to note in this connection that the *Eridania* case (Case 18/68) could in fact have been decided on the ground of *locus standi.* This was the ground on which the annulment action (Case 10/68) was decided; but the same reasoning could have been applied to the action for a remedy for failure to act. The third paragraph of Article 232 [175] EC allows a non-privileged applicant to bring proceedings only where the defendant has failed to address an act *to him.* The applicant's request in the *Eridania* case was for the revocation of the three decisions and this could have been done only by passing three further decisions revoking the earlier ones. These latter decisions would have been addressed to the same persons as the earlier ones, namely the recipients of the aid (the rival firms) and the Italian Government. Eridania was not, therefore, asking the Commission to address an act to it; moreover, since the original decisions were not – in the Court's view – of direct and individual concern to Eridania, the repealing decisions would also not have been of direct and individual concern to it. Consequently, it had no greater *locus standi* in the Article 232 [175] proceedings than it had in the Article 230 [173] proceedings.

It should also be pointed out that the rationale given by the Court is not entirely sound. The purpose of the short time-limit in annulment actions is the protection of persons who have relied on the act in question – the principle of legal certainty – and it is to uphold this principle that the Court does not allow acts to be challenged by means of proceedings for a remedy for failure to act. However, where the act is repealed, the interests of these persons could, in some cases at least, be protected by means of transitional provisions in the repealing measure. Moreover, it should be remembered that the repeal of an act need not be retroactive, while the annulment of an act normally has the effect of rendering it void *ab initio.* Consequently, repeal does not pose the same threat to legal certainty as annulment.

Whatever view one takes of this, there are some special situations in which it seems the Court *will* allow the action. One is where the act in question is originally quite valid, but subsequently becomes incompatible with Community law as a result of a later development. If this development takes place more than two months after the publication, or notification, of the act, it will not be possible to bring proceedings under Article 230 [173]. In such a case, an action under Article 232 [175] will be the only possibility, and it would be a particularly appropriate remedy since an act which was validly passed, but which subsequently became illegal, ought more properly to be repealed than annulled. A *dictum* by Advocate General Roemer in the *Eridania* case suggests that an exception might exist in such a case.[34]

A second such situation is where a judgment by the European Court annulling one act also requires the amendment or repeal of another. This was the situation in *Asteris v. Commission*,[35] which concerned aid to producers of tomato concentrates in Greece. In a judgment given in 1985,[36] the Court had annulled a regulation granting the aid for the marketing year 1983/84 on the ground that it was too little. The Commission then adopted a new regulation increasing the aid. This applied only to 1983/84, even though the reasoning of the judgment was equally applicable to other years. The measure dealing with the three years subsequent to 1983/84 had been adopted in 1984, over a year prior to the judgment. By the time the judgment was given, therefore, it was too late for Greece to commence proceedings to annul it under Article 230 [173]. Instead it initiated the procedure under Article 232 [175] by asking the Commission to amend the regulation to bring it into line with the judgment. When the Commission refused, Greece brought proceedings to annul the refusal. The Court held the proceedings admissible and ruled that the refusal was void.

## THE REQUEST FOR ACTION

The most important procedural difference between actions for a remedy for failure to act and annulment actions is that in the former case there is a special preliminary procedure which must be gone through before the application may be made to the European Court. This procedure consists of a formal request to the defendant to take action. The request must state clearly what action is required.[37] This is important since, when the case goes before the Court, the applicant can complain only that the defendant failed to take the action previously requested.

It must also be made clear that the request is being made in terms of Article 232 [175] EC, and that the applicant considers the defendant legally obliged to take the action required.[38] For this reason, 'request' is probably too mild a term to use: 'demand' might be more appropriate. It would be desirable, therefore, for the applicant to refer expressly to the Treaty or to state that legal proceedings will be taken if the required action is not forthcoming.

After the request for action has been made, the defendant institution has a period of two months to comply. Only if this period expires without action by the defendant may the application be made to the Court.[39] There is, however, a time-limit for this

34 [1969] ECR at 494.

35 Cases 97, 99, 193, 215/86, [1988] ECR 2181.

36 *Greece v. Commission*, Case 192/83, [1985] ECR 2791.

37 *Nuovo Campsider v. Commission*, Case 25/85, [1986] ECR 1531.

38 *Ibid.*

39 Moreover, the European Court has held that a definition of position – in the case in question, an outright refusal – which takes place *after* the expiry of the two-month period, but before judgment, also puts an end to the action under Art. 232 [175] EC (though it may open up an action under Art. 230 [173]): *Buckl*, Cases C-15, 108/91, [1992] ECR I-6061 (paras 13–18 of the judgment).

application: it must be brought within two months. This time-limit (which runs from the end of the initial two-month period) is very short, and the action will be declared inadmissible if it is brought either too early or too late. This could cause difficulties for the applicant if he is uncertain whether a particular communication constitutes a formal request for action or not: if he goes to Court and it transpires that it does not, his application will be declared inadmissible and he will have to pay costs; but if he fails to institute proceedings within the time-limit and it is subsequently established that the communication did constitute a request for action, he will have lost the right to bring proceedings. (It is not clear whether he could start the procedure all over again with a new request for exactly the same action; the Court might hold his right of action had been time-barred.)

What is the purpose of this special procedure? In answering this question it must be remembered that an important difference between an act and an omission is that, while one can say exactly what the contents of an act are and when it came into existence, this is not always so easy in the case of an omission. The function of the special procedure is to make good this deficiency: the omission is deemed to have taken place at the end of the first two-month period and its contents are defined by the terms of the request. The purpose of the procedure is, therefore, formally to put the defendant in default.[40] It is interesting to note that there is a similar preliminary procedure where the Commission brings proceeding against a Member State for a failure to comply with an obligation under Community law: see Chapter 10, above.

## TIME-LIMIT FOR MAKING REQUEST

It will be noticed that the Treaties lay down no time-limit within which the request for action must be made. This is quite logical if one accepts that the failure to act is established only when the preliminary procedure has been completed. In spite of this, however, the European Court has stated, in *Netherlands v. Commission*[41] (a case under the ECSC Treaty), that the preliminary procedure must be initiated within a 'reasonable time'. The case arose in the following circumstances. The French Government had drawn up a plan for restructuring the iron and steel industry, which entailed low-interest Government loans to iron and steel producers. The French Government informed the Commission of this in September 1966 and the Commission had to consider whether the plan contravened the ECSC Treaty, especially Article 4(c), which prohibits state subsidies and aids. The Commission reached a provisional conclusion that the plan was not contrary to the Treaty and informed the other Member States of this in June 1967. The Dutch Government immediately expressed its reservations, and in April 1968 it requested the Commission to define its position further. After further consideration, the Commission reached a final conclusion that the plan did not violate Community law and it informed the Dutch Government of this on 9 December 1968. A year and a

[40] There are, of course, some cases in which this is not necessary, for example where the law lays down both the content of the action and the date by which it must be performed. In these cases the only function of the procedure will be to give the defendant the opportunity to comply with the request before legal proceedings are brought.

[41] Case 59/70, [1971] ECR 639.

half later, on 24 June 1970, the Dutch Government made a formal request in terms of Article 35 ECSC (the equivalent of Article 232 [175] EC) that the Commission take a decision under Article 88 ECSC to the effect that the French plan involved violations of Community law; the Commission did not comply and the Netherlands then brought the action.[42]

The Court, however, held that the application was inadmissible because the period of eighteen months between the communication of 9 December 1968 and the request for action of 24 June 1970 was too great.[43] The Court began its reasoning by mentioning that Article 35 ECSC lays down no time-limit for bringing the request for action. It then continued:[44]

> It follows, however, from the common purpose of Articles 33 and 35 that the requirements of legal certainty and of the continuity of Community action underlying the time-limits laid down for bringing proceedings under Article 33 must also be taken into account – having regard to the special difficulties which the silence of the competent authorities may involve for the interested parties – in the exercise of the rights conferred by Article 35.
>
> These requirements may not lead to such contradictory consequences as the duty to act within a short period in the first case and the absence of any limitation in time in the second.
>
> This view finds support in the system of time-limits in Article 35, which allows the Commission two months in which to define its position, and the interested party one month in which to institute proceedings before the Court.
>
> Thus it is implicit in the system of Articles 33 and 35 that the exercise of the right to raise the matter with the Commission may not be delayed indefinitely.
>
> If the interested parties are thus bound to observe a reasonable time-limit where the Commission remains silent, this is so *a fortiori* once it is clear that the Commission has decided to take no action.

It will be noticed that the Court purports to base its argument on the unity principle: if there is a time-limit under Article 33 ECSC (the equivalent of Article 230 [173] EC), there should also be such a limit under Article 35. However, there *is* a time-limit under Article 35: this is the period within which the action must be brought (one month under the ECSC Treaty). This runs, of course, from the end of the two-month period, that is from the date on which the defendant is formally deemed to be in default. The

[42] It might be thought that the Commission decision that the plan did not contravene Community law (communicated to the Dutch Government on 9 December 1968) constituted a reviewable act since it was a refusal to take a decision under Art. 88. However, in an earlier case, *De Gezamenlijke Steenkolenmijnen in Limburg v. High Authority*, Case 17/57, [1959] ECR 1, the European Court had ruled that a determination of this kind does not constitute a reviewable act because Art. 88 gives the power only to take a decision that a violation *has* occurred: there is no power to take a decision that a Member State has *not* violated the Treaty. This judgment, which is hardly in conformity with the general doctrine of the Court on negative acts, seems to have established a special rule that a decision by the Commission not to act under Art. 88 cannot be challenged in annulment proceedings. Consequently, the communication of 9 December 1968 could not impair the right of the Dutch Government to bring the proceedings for failure to act.

[43] It is interesting to compare this with the decision in *Commission v. France (Euratom)*, Case 7/71, [1971] ECR 1003, decided a few months later, in which the Court refused to lay down a time limit where a *Member State* fails to comply with the Treaty: see para. 5 of the judgment and *per* Advocate General Roemer at 1026.

[44] [1971] ECR at 653.

proposition that there must be a time-limit for making the *request* can be deduced from the unity principle only if one accepts that the cause of action arises at some earlier date; but this cuts away the justification for the preliminary procedure.

The proposition accepted by the Court was considered by Advocate General Roemer. He rejected it on the ground that the adoption of a period of limitation of no specific length – that the request must be made within a reasonable time – was contrary to the principle of legal certainty.[45] How can the parties know where they stand if they cannot be sure how long the period of limitation is?

The principle of legal certainty was, of course, one of the principles invoked by the Court in support of its ruling. This was because the justification usually given for the short time-limit under Article 33 is that, by annulling an apparently valid legal act, the Court could upset the legitimate expectations of persons who relied on it; therefore, in order to limit as much as possible the uncertainty caused by annulment actions, the period within which they may be brought should be as short as possible. However, as was pointed out above, the analogy between Articles 33 and 35 does not hold good at this point, since proceedings under Article 35 do not result in any *retrospective* change in the legal rights of the persons concerned: the annulment of a legal act invalidates it from the moment when it was adopted; but an order under Article 35 merely requires the defendant to adopt an act in the future. Such an act need not be retrospective.

It is true that in the special case of a decision under Article 88 ECSC legal expectations could be upset if the Commission is required to take action. Such a decision could oblige a Member State to modify or abandon a scheme which might have been in operation for some time. There is no time-limit within which the Commission must commence proceedings under Article 88; but if the Commission has informed the Member State that it considers its action to involve no violation of Community law, it would not be unreasonable for the persons concerned to believe that the matter had finally been settled.[46] However, even if the imposition of a time-limit for an action for a remedy for failure to act is justified in the case of proceedings under Article 88, there is no reason why it should apply to all proceedings under Article 35 ECSC or Article 232 [175] EC. Yet the extract from the judgment quoted above clearly shows that it was the Court's intention to lay down a general rule.[47]

A final difficulty raised by the judgment, in so far as it applies outside the context of Article 88, concerns the moment when the 'reasonable period' begins to run. In *Netherlands v. Commission* it began when the Dutch Government was informed that the Commission had reached a final decision not to take action. Paragraph 19 of the judgment (quoted above) makes clear, however, that the time-limit can apply even where no such decision is taken. But the Court gave no indication when it would begin to run in such a case. Uncertainty on this point, coupled with uncertainty as to the length of the

45 [1971] ECR at 658.

46 In *Netherlands v. Commission* this point was considered by Advocate General Roemer but rejected on the ground that the French Government had put their plan into operation before the Commission decision had been made. It could not, therefore, be said that they had relied on the decision: see *ibid.*, at 658–9.

47 For a case in which the principle was raised by the Commission in proceedings under the Euratom Treaty, but rejected on the facts, see *ENU v. Commission*, Case C-107/91, [1993] ECR I-599.

'reasonable period', could create intolerable difficulties for an applicant. It could, moreover, have the undesirable consequence that applicants would feel obliged to commence the procedure at the earliest possible moment, thus forcing the defendant institution to take a decision before they were ready to do so. For these reasons, it is unfortunate that the Court did not restrict its ruling to cases involving Article 88 ECSC.[48]

## *LOCUS STANDI*

It will be remembered from Chapter 12, above, that, in proceedings under Article 230 [173] EC, privileged applicants always have *locus standi*; non-privileged applicants, on the other hand, may challenge an act only if it is addressed to them or if it is of direct and individual concern to them. The position under Article 232 [175] EC is similar: privileged applicants always have *locus standi*; but non-privileged applicants have *locus standi* only where the defendant institution has 'failed to address' to them 'any act other than a recommendation or an opinion'.

In theory, the word 'act' in this provision should mean an act that is reviewable under Article 230 [173]: this would seem to follow from the unity principle laid down in the *Chevalley* case.[49] As we have seen, however, there is at least one situation in which this is not so: this is in the case of an act that is not regarded by the Court as reviewable because it is merely a step in the procedure and is not the definitive decision. Under Community competition law, for example, a complainant can use Article 232 [175] to require the Commission to send him a letter under Article 6 of Regulation 2842/98[50] (formerly, Article 6 of Regulation 99/63[51]), even though such a letter, being a mere step in the procedure, is not itself a reviewable act under Article 230 [173].[52]

Under Article 232 [175], an applicant can only complain that the defendant has failed to address an act to him. What is meant by 'address'? Must the act be formally addressed to him or is it sufficient if he is directly and individually concerned by it? It will be remembered from the discussion in Chapter 12 that the latter is sufficient under Article 230 [173], and it was said that in such a case the person concerned was a '*de facto*' addressee. If one accepts the unity principle, the same rule should apply under Article 232 [175] and this would seem to follow from the *Chevalley* case. Moreover, although most of the texts of Article 232 [175] are the same as the English, the Dutch and Italian texts suggest that this wider interpretation is legitimate: these texts state that a non-privileged applicant may bring proceedings where the defendant institution has failed to adopt an act other than a recommendation or opinion 'with respect to him'.

[48] The problem cannot arise in the case of Art. 226 [169] EC because proceedings under Art. 232 [175] cannot be used with regard to Art. 226 [169]: see *Lütticke v. Commission*, Case 48/65, [1966] ECR 19 (discussed below).

[49] Above.

[50] OJ 1998 L354, p. 18.

[51] OJ (Spec. Edn) 1963–64, p. 47.

[52] See *Guérin Automobiles v. Commission*, Case C-282/95, [1997] ECR I-1503, *per* Advocate General Tesauro at para. 16 of his Opinion (p. 1514) (discussed above).

This wider view was strongly supported by Advocate General Dutheillet de Lamothe in *Mackprang v. Commission.*[53] In that case, the Commission had argued in favour of the narrow interpretation, that is, that the act requested must be one which would be *formally addressed* to the applicant. Advocate General de Lamothe replied to this contention as follows:

> The Commission's argument on this point comes up against a very strong objection. If the concept of a measure against which individuals could bring proceedings were different in scope with regard to the application of Article 230 [173] from that with regard to the application of Article 232 [175] the result would be that, in certain cases, the existence or absence of a judicial remedy would depend on the actions of the Community authorities to which the request was submitted.
>
> If those authorities replied to the request either by accepting it or by rejecting it, the author of the request would be entitled to proceed under Article 230 [173], even if he is not the addressee of the measure adopted or requested, provided that this measure is of direct and individual concern to him.
>
> On the other hand, if the Community authorities did not reply to the person concerned he would, according to the Commission's argument, be deprived of any method of recourse if he is not the addressee of the measure requested, *even if the latter is of direct and individual concern to him.*[54]
>
> It is obviously difficult to justify making the existence or absence of a judicial remedy depend on the action or inaction of the administrative body to which a request is submitted.

The Court did not rule on the question in *Mackprang v. Commission* and more than twenty years were to elapse before the matter was finally settled.[55] This was in *ENU v. Commission,*[56] a case under the Euratom Treaty.[57] ENU, a company producing a form of uranium, had asked the Commission to adopt a decision under Article 53 Euratom. When the Commission failed to do so, ENU brought proceedings under Article 148 Euratom (the equivalent of Article 232 [175] EC). The Commission argued that ENU lacked standing because the decision would have been addressed to the Euratom supply agency, not to ENU. The Court, however, held that ENU would have been directly and individually concerned by the decision and that this was sufficient to give it standing. The application was admissible (and ultimately successful).

It follows, therefore, that a non-privileged applicant under Article 232 [175] EC has *locus standi* either if the act requested would have been formally addressed to him or if he would have been the '*de facto*' addressee, i.e., if it would have concerned him directly and individually. This makes the position the same as under Article 230 [173].

[53] Case 15/71, [1971] ECR 797 at 807–8. But see *per* Advocate General Slynn in *Lord Bethell v. Commission*, Case 246/81, [1982] ECR 2277 at 2295–6 (and the statements by other advocates general there cited).

[54] Emphasis in the original.

[55] But hints as to how the Court viewed the matter may be found in *Star Fruit v. Commission*, Case 247/87, [1989] ECR 291 (para. 13 of the judgment), and in *Lord Bethell v. Commission*, Case 246/81, [1982] ECR 2277, where the Court four times used phraseology suggesting acceptance of this wider view: it referred to the adoption of an act 'in relation to' the applicant (para. 13 of the judgment), 'in respect of' him (paras 15 and 16), and 'with regard to' him (para. 16).

[56] Case C-107/91, [1993] ECR I-599.

[57] For the EC Treaty, see *Port*, Case C-68/95, [1996] ECR I-6065 at paras 58–9 of the judgment; *Gestevisión Telecinco v. Commission*, Case T-95/96, [1998] ECR II-3407, at paras 58 *et seq.* of the judgment.

It was said above that it would be wrong if the applicant's right to obtain a remedy were affected by the fact that proceedings which began as an action under Article 232 [175] were switched to an action under Article 230 [173] because the defendant defined its position by refusing to comply with the request. So far at least, this does not seem to have occurred.[58]

Two cases which are sometimes thought to indicate that this could happen are *Lütticke v. Commission*[59] and *Nordgetreide v. Commission.*[60] The first concerned a private firm which considered that Germany had violated the EC Treaty. It requested the Commission to commence the procedure under Article 226 [169]; but the Commission took the view that Germany had not infringed the Treaty and therefore refused to comply. The applicant then brought proceedings before the Court under Article 230 [173] to quash the negative decision of refusal; alternatively it asked for a remedy under Article 232 [175].

The Court held the application inadmissible. In so far as it was based on Article 230 [173], it was inadmissible because the refusal to act was not a reviewable act. The reason for this was that no measure taken by the Commission during the preliminary procedure under Article 226 [169] – neither the request to the Member State to submit its observations, nor the reasoned opinion – has any binding force. In other words, the acts which the applicant requested the Commission to perform were not reviewable acts; therefore, the Commission's refusal to perform them could not be a reviewable act. The application was also inadmissible in so far as it was based on Article 232 [175], because the refusal constituted a definition of position.

This does not reveal a gap in the law, however, because the result would have been exactly the same if the Commission had remained silent instead of giving an express refusal. As we have seen, a private applicant, as was Lütticke, may bring proceedings under Article 232 [175] EC only with regard to a failure by a Community institution to adopt an act which would have been addressed to it or which would have concerned it directly and individually. Since Lütticke had not asked the Commission to adopt such an act, its application would have been inadmissible irrespective of whether the Commission had defined its position or not.

In *Nordgetreide v. Commission* the applicant had requested the Commission to amend a regulation dealing with monetary compensatory amounts. The Commission refused to make the amendment and the applicant brought proceedings under Article 230 [173] to quash the refusal; alternatively, it asked for a remedy under Article 232 [175]. The Court stated that, since the measure to be amended was a regulation, the amending measure would also have to be a regulation. Such an amending measure would not have concerned the applicant directly and individually. Since it would have had no *locus standi* to challenge the act requested, it likewise had no *locus standi* to

[58] At one time it was thought that *GEMA v. Commission*, Case 125/78, [1979] ECR 3173, revealed that this could occur in the field of competition law, but more recent cases show that this is not the case: see, in particular, *Guérin Automobiles v. Commission*, Case C-282/95, [1997] ECR I-1503 (appeal from Case T-186/94, [1995] ECR II-1753), discussed above.

[59] Case 48/65, [1966] ECR 19. See also *Star Fruit v. Commission*, Case 247/87, [1989] ECR 291.

[60] Case 42/71, [1972] ECR 105.

challenge the negative decision refusing to adopt it. The application was, therefore, declared inadmissible in so far as it was based on Article 230 [173]; in so far as it was based on Article 232 [175], it was inadmissible because the Commission's refusal constituted a definition of position.

Here too, the position would have been exactly the same if the Commission had remained silent. *Nordgetreide* would still have lacked *locus standi* since it had not asked the Commission to adopt an act which would have been addressed to it or which would have concerned it directly and individually.

## FORM OF JUDGMENT

Under Article 230 [173] the consequence of a successful action is that the provision in question is declared void by the Court. In proceedings under Article 232 [175], however, the Court has no power itself to adopt the act which the defendant wrongfully failed to pass: all it can do is to declare that the failure to act was contrary to the Treaty. However, Article 233 [176] EC provides that the defendant institution 'shall be required to take the necessary measures to comply with the judgment of the Court of Justice'. This obliges the defendant to take action; but it still retains such measure of discretion as to the form and content of the act as is granted to it under the provision requiring the act to be performed.

## FURTHER READING

Barav, 'Considérations sur la spécificité du recours en carence en droit communautaire' [1975] RTDE 53.

Toth, 'The Law as it Stands on the Appeal for Failure to Act' (1975) 2 LIEI 65.

Angela Ward, *Judicial Review and the Rights of Private Parties in EU Law*, 2nd edn (2006).

# 14

# INDIRECT CHALLENGE

An indirect challenge to the validity of an act is a challenge made in the course of proceedings not instituted for that purpose. The object of the proceedings must, therefore, be something other than the annulment of the act and the court must have jurisdiction on some ground independent of the indirect challenge. The purpose of an indirect challenge is to require the court to decide the case on the basis that the act in question is invalid; consequently the challenge may be made only if the act is *relevant* to the proceedings.[1] It follows as a matter of theory, therefore, that an act is susceptible to indirect challenge whenever it is relevant to the proceedings, but is not itself the subject matter of the proceedings.

Another name for an indirect challenge, often used by writers on Community law, is 'plea of illegality'. This indicates that a party to proceedings has contended that an act is illegal and therefore invalid.[2] It is a translation of the French term, *exception d'illégalité* (sometimes mistranslated as 'exception of illegality'). It does not, however, convey the idea quite as well as 'indirect challenge', which expresses both the fact that the validity of the act is under attack and that the challenge is incidental to the primary object of the proceedings.

Since Community law is applied at the national level as well as at the Community level, an indirect challenge to a Community act may be brought in a national court as well as in the European Court. When this occurs, the question of the validity of the act is referred to the European Court under sub-paragraph (b) of the first paragraph of Article 234 [177] EC or of Article 155 Euratom. Once the European Court has made a ruling, the case goes back to the national court, which will give judgment on the basis of the decision of the European Court.

Some writers take the view that the issues involved where the European Court makes a decision under this procedure are fundamentally different from those where the indirect challenge is made in proceedings brought initially in the European Court.[3] This view derives some justification from the fact that different Treaty provisions are applicable and also from the fact that the relationship between Community law and

[1] See *Italy v. Commission*, Case 32/65, [1966] ECR 389.

[2] Most writers, however, use this term only where the challenge is made in proceedings brought in the European Court and not where it is made in a national court.

[3] See Bebr, 'Examen en validité au titre de l'article 177 du traité CEE et cohésion juridique de la Communauté' [1975] CDE 379 at 417–20. Many writers, however, accept the basic identity between the two cases: see Arendt, 'La procédure selon l'article 177 dutraité instituant la Communauté Economique Européenne' (1965) 13 SEW 383 at 409; Mertens de Wilmars, 'La procédure suivant l'article 177 CEE' (1965) 13 SEW 437 at 444; for further references, see Bebr, (above), 417, n. 110.

national law is involved. However, at a more fundamental level the issues are identical, since the legal nature of an indirect challenge is the same, irrespective of the court in which it is brought. For this reason, the general principles of indirect challenge will be discussed in this chapter in the context of both kinds of procedure.

The theoretical possibility of an indirect challenge (which may, of course, be brought by either applicant or defendant) could arise in almost any proceedings in the European Court. Thus, in an annulment action under Article 230 [173] EC, the validity of the act subject to direct challenge could depend on the validity of another act, and an indirect challenge could be made against this. For example, the former act might have been adopted on the basis of powers delegated by the latter. Other questions which could in theory depend on the validity of an act which is not itself the subject matter of the proceedings are: in an action under Article 232 [175] EC for a remedy for failure to act, the obligation to act; in actions arising out of a contract (Article 238 [181] EC), the validity of the contract; in actions in tort (Articles 235 [178] and 288(2) [215(2)] EC), the lawfulness of the allegedly wrongful act; in enforcement actions against a Member State under Article 226 [169] EC, the existence of the obligation which the Member State is alleged not to have fulfilled; and in appeals against penalties under Article 229 [172] EC, the validity of the measure that the appellant is alleged to have violated. In a national court the question could arise whenever Community law was relevant to the proceedings, for example when a party claims a right based on a directly effective Community measure or when a national measure is enacted in implementation of a Community measure.

Theoretically, the potential scope for indirect challenge is wide. The question to be considered in this chapter is whether it may be invoked whenever appropriate, or whether there are restrictions on its use. In particular, there is the question whether it should be regarded as available in all cases where it is not excluded by express enactment (as is the case in English law) or whether it may be invoked only where there is express authorization in the Treaties.

## TREATY PROVISIONS

The EC Treaty contains two provisions dealing with indirect challenge.[4] The first is Article 241 [184], which reads:

> Notwithstanding the expiry of the period laid down in the fifth paragraph of Article 230 [173], any party may, in proceedings in which a regulation adopted jointly by the European Parliament and the Council, or a regulation of the Council, of the Commission, or of the ECB is at issue, plead the grounds specified in the second paragraph of Article 230 [173] in order to invoke before the Court of Justice the inapplicability of that regulation.

[4] Before the Treaty on European Union came into force, Arts 156 and 150 Euratom were identical to Arts 241 [184] and 234 [177] EC. Now both the latter have been amended so that under the EC Treaty acts of the ECB can be challenged to the same extent as acts of the Council or Commission; in addition, Art. 241 [184] EC now contains an express reference to regulations adopted jointly by the European Parliament and the Council (under Art. 234 [177], they are included in the phrase 'acts of the institutions').

This is a classic description of an indirect challenge. The grounds of invalidity are, as in English law, exactly the same as in the case of a direct challenge. If successful, the effect of the challenge is that the act is not applied in the case in question.

Although Article 241 [184] is expressed in general terms, it nevertheless contains two limitations: first – and most important – it applies only to regulations; secondly, it applies only where the challenge is made in the course of proceedings in the European Court (this is not clear from the wording of Article 241 [184] but was laid down by the European Court in *Wöhrmann v. Commission*[5]). The first of these restrictions raises fundamental issues which will be discussed below; the second, however, is easily explained by virtue of Article 234 [177].

Sub-paragraph (b) of the first paragraph of Article 234 [177] EC is the second Treaty provision dealing with indirect challenge. It makes provision for national courts to refer to the European Court questions concerning 'the validity . . . of acts of the institutions of the Community and of the ECB'. Since the national courts have no power to hear a direct challenge to the validity of Community acts, this must refer to an indirect challenge; it therefore implicitly accepts that an indirect challenge may be made before a national court. It should be noted that this provision does not lay down any limitations as to the kind of act that may be challenged, provided it is a Community act.

Cases decided under the ECSC Treaty establish that, as in English law, the right to make an indirect challenge is not dependent on an express Treaty provision: it is a general principle of law.[6] However, unlike in English law, this general principle does not apply in all cases. The next question to consider is the scope of the principle and the restrictions to which it is subject.

## WHAT ACTS MAY BE CHALLENGED?

Here the crucial distinction is between normative (general) acts and individual acts. This distinction was discussed in Chapter 12: regulations are normative acts; decisions are individual acts. However, it is not the form of the act which is decisive but its substance; therefore an act in the form of a regulation may turn out to be, in substance, a decision (individual act). This same distinction applies with regard to indirect challenge: in *Simmenthal v. Commission*[7] the European Court held that an act which was not in the form of a regulation, but was normative in substance, should be treated as a regulation for the purpose of an indirect challenge under Article 241 [184] EC.

There are no problems as far as normative acts are concerned. The right to make an indirect challenge to a normative act in proceedings before the European Court is laid down by Article 241 [184] EC. There has never been any doubt that a normative act is

[5] Cases 31, 33/62, [1962] ECR 501.

[6] *Meroni v. High Authority*, Case 9/56, [1958] ECR 133 (discussed further in Chap. 4); *Meroni v. High Authority*, Case 10/56, [1958] ECR 157; *Compagnie des Hauts Fourneaux de Chasse v. High Authority*, Case 15/57, [1958] ECR 211.

[7] Case 92/78, [1979] ECR 777 (paras 39–41 of the judgment).

subject to indirect challenge in the national courts. This means that normative acts are open to indirect challenge in all courts.

In the case of individual acts, on the other hand, the position is more complex. In cases under the ECSC Treaty it has been held that the addressee of an individual act may not challenge it indirectly in the European Court.[8] This applies just as much under the EC Treaty. Thus, for example, if a decision is addressed to a Member State under Article 86 [90] EC (public undertakings)[9] or Article 88 [93] EC (state aid)[10] and the Member State neither complies with it nor brings proceedings to annul it within the time limit laid down by Article 230 [173] EC, it cannot thereafter challenge it indirectly in the course of an action against it under Article 226 [169] EC or Article 88(2) [93(2)] EC.[11]

It is also clear that a person who is *not* the addressee of an individual act and does not have *locus standi* to challenge it directly may challenge it indirectly in a national court: thus, for example, if the Commission addresses a decision to a Member State empowering it to take certain action, and the Member State takes that action, a person affected by it may make an indirect challenge to the Commission decision in the course of proceedings brought in the national courts to challenge the validity of the action of the Member State.[12]

Until the beginning of 1994, this also appeared to be true if the person making the indirect challenge was directly and individually concerned by the Community act and, as a result, could have challenged it directly in the European Court under Article 230 [173] EC. There were two authorities. The first was the *Universität Hamburg*[13] case, in which the Court allowed the University of Hamburg to make an indirect challenge in the German courts against a decision which (though addressed to the German Government) concerned the University directly and individually and which could, therefore, have been challenged directly by it under Article 230 [173] EC.[14] The reason the Court gave was that the University might not have been aware of the decision before the expiry of the time limit under Article 230 [173] because the Commission was not obliged to inform the University or even to publish the decision; consequently, the University might not have been able to exercise its right to challenge the decision directly. This would be true in most cases where the decision was not addressed to the person concerned.

The second authority was *Rau v. BALM*,[15] in which the European Court made the following statement:[16]

> It must be emphasised that there is nothing in Community law to prevent an action from being brought before a national court against a measure implementing a decision adopted by

[8] *Dalmas v. High Authority*, Case 21/64, [1965] ECR 175; *Sideradria v. Commission*, Case 41/85, [1986] ECR 3917.

[9] *Commission v. Greece*, Case 226/87, [1988] ECR 3611.

[10] *Commission v. Belgium*, Case 156/77, [1978] ECR 1881; *Commission v. Greece*, Case C-183/91, [1993] ECR I-3131.

[11] The same is true where the proceedings are under Art. 88 ECSC: *Germany v. High Authority (Railway Tariffs)*, Case 3/59, [1960] ECR 53.

[12] See, e.g., *Gesellschaft für Getreidehandel v. EVGF*, Case 55/72, [1973] ECR 15. See also *Handelsvereniging Rotterdam*, Cases 73–4/63, [1964] ECR 1, especially *per* Advocate General Roemer at 20–2.

[13] Case 216/82, [1983] ECR 2771.

[14] This was established in the earlier case of *Control Data Belgium v. Commission*, Case 294/81, [1983] ECR 911.

[15] Cases 133–6/85, [1987] ECR 2289.

[16] Para. 11 of the judgment.

> a Community institution where the conditions laid down by national law are satisfied. When such an action is brought, if the outcome of the dispute depends on the validity of that decision the national court may submit questions to the Court of Justice by way of a reference for a preliminary ruling, without there being any need to ascertain whether or not the plaintiff in the main proceedings has the possibility of challenging the decision directly before the Court.

In 1994, however, the European Court decided the *TWD* case.[17] This concerned a German company which had been given aid by the German authorities. The Commission subsequently took a decision addressed to Germany, which declared the aid incompatible with the Common Market and required the German Government to obtain its repayment. The German Government informed the company of the decision and told the company that it could challenge the decision in the European Court under Article 230 [173] EC. The company did not do so.

Acting on the basis of the decision, the German Government then adopted a measure which would have had the effect of requiring the repayment of the aid. The company challenged this measure in the German courts, partly on the ground that the Commission decision on which it was based was invalid. The German court made a preliminary reference to the European Court asking, first, whether an indirect challenge is possible in such a situation and, secondly, whether the Commission decision was invalid. By the time the indirect challenge was made in the German court, the time limit for a direct challenge had expired.

Following the lead of Advocate General Jacobs, the European Court held that no indirect challenge could be made, since the company had been informed of the Commission decision by the German Government and could 'without any doubt'[18] have challenged it directly under Article 230 [173] EC.[19]

The law now appears to be that a party with *locus standi* to make a direct challenge to a decision may challenge it indirectly only if either its *locus standi* is not beyond doubt – a far from unlikely possibility in view of the inconsistent case law of the European Court on this point – or if it is not officially informed of the decision in sufficient time to make the direct challenge.[20] The European Court also stated that there is a general principle of Community law that a party can always make an indirect challenge against a Community act if it lacks *locus standi* to challenge it directly.[21] This principle seems to apply both in the European Court and the national courts. On the other hand, it follows *a fortiori* from the *TWD* case that the addressee of an individual act can never challenge it indirectly, either in the European Court or in the national courts.[22]

[17] Case C-188/92, [1994] ECR I-833.

[18] Para. 24 of the judgment.

[19] It distinguished *Rau v. BALM* on the ground that in that case a direct challenge under Art. 230 [173] was in fact pending when the reference was made.

[20] For later cases, see *R v. Intervention Board for Agricultural Produce, ex parte Accrington Beef*, Case C-241/95, [1996] ECR I-6699 (paras 14–16 of the judgment); *Eurotunnel v. SeaFrance*, Case C-408/95, [1997] ECR I-6315 paras 26–30 of the judgment); *Nachi Europe*, Case C-239/99, [2001] ECR I-1197.

[21] This was previously laid down in *Simmenthal v. Commission*, Case 92/78, [1979] ECR 777.

[22] *Wiljo v. Belgium*, Case C-178/95, [1997] ECR I-585. For earlier (inconclusive) cases on this point, see *De Bloos v. Bouyer*, Case 59/77, [1977] ECR 2359; *Commission v. Belgium*, Case 156/77, [1978] ECR 1881. For further discussion, see Wyatt, 'The Relationship between Actions for Annulment and References on Validity after *TWD Deggendorf*' in J Lonbay and A Biondi (eds), *Remedies for Breach of EC Law* (1997).

## WHO MAY MAKE THE CHALLENGE?

Are privileged applicants (the Commission, the Council, and the Member States) ever entitled to make an indirect challenge, or are they precluded from doing so by virtue of their status, irrespective of the nature of the act involved? Since they have *locus standi* to challenge *any* reviewable act, it could be argued that they can never make an indirect challenge.

The question arose in *Italy v. Commission.*[23] Here, Italy brought proceedings under Article 230 [173] to quash a Council regulation, and also made an indirect challenge against two other regulations. The Commission questioned whether a Member State is entitled to make an indirect challenge, but Advocate General Roemer stated that a Member State should have the same rights as other applicants. He based his opinion on two arguments: first, Article 241 [184] is expressed in general terms and provides that 'any' party may make the challenge; and secondly, he said that the Member State might not have exercised its right to make a direct challenge because the defects in the regulation might not have been fully apparent until it was applied in a particular case.[24] The European Court did not deal with the point; it rejected the challenge on the ground that the regulations in question were not relevant to the issue before the Court.[25] The matter therefore remains unresolved.

## IN WHAT PROCEEDINGS MAY THE CHALLENGE BE MADE?

It was shown above that the theoretical conditions for an indirect challenge could occur in proceedings of almost any kind. Are there in fact any limitations on the proceedings in which the challenge may be made? So far, the European Court has allowed the challenge to be made in annulment actions, actions under Article 35 ECSC for a remedy for failure to act,[26] staff actions under Article 236 [179] EC,[27] enforcement actions under Article 226 [169] EC,[28] and proceedings in a national court. There is no doubt that it may also be made in an appeal against a penalty: under the ECSC Treaty this was expressly covered by the third paragraph of Article 36. It appears, therefore, that an indirect challenge is not ruled out in any kind of proceedings.

[23] Case 32/65, [1966] ECR 389. [24] [1966] ECR at 414.

[25] The Court did, however, repeat the words of Art. 241 [184] EC ('any party may . . .') and some writers have taken this as an indication that the Court accepted the Advocate General's Opinion: see Barav, 'The Exception of Illegality in Community Law: A Critical Analysis' (1974) 11 CMLRev. 366 at 372. This view, however, may involve reading too much into the judgment.

[26] *SNUPAT v. High Authority*, Cases 32–3/58, [1959] ECR 127 at 139.

[27] *Sabbatini v. European Parliament*, Case 20/71, [1972] ECR 345.

[28] See *Commission v. Germany*, Case 116/82, [1986] ECR 2519, where Germany was allowed without objection to make an indirect challenge to a regulation as a defence to an action against it under Art. 226 [169] EC. A Member State cannot, of course, make an indirect challenge to an individual act addressed to it.

## ON WHAT GROUNDS MAY THE CHALLENGE BE MADE?

Article 241 [184] EC makes clear that where the challenge is made in the European Court the grounds of review are exactly the same as in the case of a direct challenge under Article 230 [173]. At one time there was some doubt whether this was also true in the case of a challenge in the national courts in view of the fact that Article 234 [177] EC speaks of the 'validity' of an act, while Article 230 [173] EC uses the word 'legality'. Is there any difference between validity and legality? In the *Handelsvereniging Rotterdam* case[29] it was suggested by the German Government in its observations that 'validity' had a much more restricted meaning than 'legality' and that in proceedings under Article 234 [177] the Court could consider only whether or not the act was non-existent (void) and not whether it might be merely voidable. (It will be remembered from the discussion in Chapter 11, that invalid Community acts are normally voidable and not void: the latter is the case only in very special circumstances where the act lacks any semblance of validity.)

This argument was rejected by Advocate General Roemer who took the view that the same grounds of review apply as in the case of a direct challenge.[30] The Court did not specifically consider the problem but it has never given any indication that narrower grounds should be applied under Article 234 [177], and in the third *International Fruit Company* case[31] it expressly stated that the grounds of review under Article 234 [177] cannot be restricted. One can conclude, therefore, that the grounds of review are identical in all cases.[32]

## THE EFFECT OF A SUCCESSFUL CHALLENGE

Since the purpose of an indirect challenge is to persuade the Court to decide the case before it on the basis that the act subject to the indirect challenge is invalid, it might be thought that a successful challenge could have no consequences beyond the case in question: unlike a ruling in an annulment action, it would have no *erga omnes* effect. In practice, however, it appears to have much the same effect, since the European Court has held that when an act has been declared invalid on a reference from a national court, though that ruling is binding only on the court which made the reference, 'it is sufficient

[29] Cases 73–74/63, [1964] ECR 1. [30] [1964] ECR at 19–20.

[31] Cases 21–4/72, [1972] ECR 1219 (para. 5 of the judgment). See also *Racke*, Case C-162/96, [1998] ECR I-3655 (paras 25–28 of the judgment).

[32] At one time it was thought that there might be an exception where the Community act is contrary to an international agreement which is not directly effective. In the third *International Fruit Company* case (above) the European Court held that this could not be a ground of review under Art. 234(1)(b) [177(1)(b)] (see also *Schlüter*, Case 9/73, [1973] ECR 1135 (paras 24–31 of the judgment) and *Bresciani*, Case 87/75, [1976] ECR 129 (paras 15–26 of the judgment)). Some commentators took the view that this would be a ground of review under Art. 230 [173]. However, this has been rejected by the European Court in *Germany v. Council* (*Bananas* case),

reason for any other national court to regard that act as void'[33] (though such court may, if it wishes, refer the matter to the European Court again).[34] The strong implication of this judgment is that a ruling of invalidity is binding on other national courts, unless the European Court rescinds it on a subsequent reference – an unlikely occurrence. Moreover, the European Court has also ruled, on a reference from a national court, that an act may be invalid for the future but valid for the past.[35] Such a ruling would be pointless if it was not applicable in later cases.

## NON-EXISTENT ACTS

In the above discussion it has been assumed that the act subject to challenge, though invalid, is not non-existent (not void *ab initio*). If the act is non-existent, on the other hand, it is treated for all purposes as if it had never been adopted. As we saw in Chapter 11, it is not necessary for such an act to be annulled under Article 230 [173]; indeed, it *cannot* be annulled because such proceedings would be inadmissible: the Court would lack jurisdiction *ratione materiae*, as there would be no reviewable act. As a result, it can be challenged indirectly – it might be more proper to say that its non-existence can be asserted – in *any* proceedings. Even the 'addressee' of a non-existent act can assert its non-existence, and it does not matter if the time limit under Article 230 [173] has expired.[36]

## FURTHER READING

ANGELA WARD, *Judicial Review and the Rights of Private Parties in EU Law*, 2nd edn (2006).

BARAV, 'The Exception of Illegality in Community Law: A Critical Analysis' (1974) 11 CMLRev. 366.

BEBR, 'Judicial Remedy of Private Parties against Normative Acts of the European Communities: The Role of the Exception of Illegality' (1966) 4 CMLRev. 7.

BEBR, 'Examen en validité au titre de l'article 177 du traité CEE et cohésion juridique de la Communauté' [1975] CDE 379.

BEBR, 'Preliminary Rulings of the Court of Justice: Their Authority and Temporal Effect' (1981) 18 CMLRev. 475 (especially 475–83).

Case C-280/93, [1994] ECR I-4973, where it was confirmed that the position is the same under Art. 230 [173] as under Art. 234(1)(b) [177(1)(b)]: see paras 103–12 of the judgment).

[33] *International Chemical Corporation*, Case 66/80, [1981] ECR 1191 (first para. of the ruling).

[34] This could be to ask the European Court to reconsider its previous ruling; a more likely reason would be to request clarification on the temporal effect of the ruling (whether it applies only to the future or also to the past).

[35] *Providence Agricole de la Champagne*, Case 4/79, [1980] ECR 2823; *Maïseries de Beauce*, Case 109/79, [1980] ECR 2883; *Roquette*, Case 145/79, [1980] ECR 2917. See also *Roquette*, Case C-228/92, [1994] ECR I-1445.

[36] *Commission v. Greece*, Case 226/87, [1988] ECR 3611 (para. 16 of the judgment).

Harding, 'The Impact of Article 177 of the EEC Treaty on the Review of Community Action' (1981) 1 YEL 93.

Trabucchi, 'L'effet "erga omnes" des décisions préjudicielles rendues par la Cour de Justice des Communautés européennes' [1974] RTDE 56.

Vogt, 'Indirect Judicial Protection in EC Law – The Case of the Plea of Illegality' (2006) 31 ELRev. 364.

# 15

# REVIEW AND ANNULMENT

## GROUNDS OF REVIEW

When the applicant has overcome all jurisdictional hurdles and problems of admissibility, he must convince the Court that the measure ought to be annulled. To do this, he must establish one or other of the grounds of review set out, in identical terms, in Articles 230 [173] EC, and 146 Euratom. These grounds apply not only in direct actions for annulment, but also in the case of an indirect challenge.[1] The grounds of review are four in number:

1 lack of competence;

2 infringement of an essential procedural requirement;

3 infringement of the Treaty or any rule of law relating to its application;

4 misuse of powers.

These grounds are derived from French administrative law; this does not, however, mean that they will necessarily be applied in the same way in Community law as in French law: the legal traditions of all the Member States, as well as the special circumstances of the Community, will be taken into account by the European Court.

It will be noticed that these grounds are broad and cover almost every possible illegality. They also overlap to a considerable extent. In fact, if the third ground were given a sufficiently extensive interpretation, it could cover all the other three. Special considerations apply where a measure is attacked on procedural grounds or where a misuse of powers is claimed;[2] beyond this, it does not matter very much which formal ground is applicable. For this reason, the European Court does not normally state which of the four formal grounds is involved when it annuls a measure. Nevertheless, a word should be said about each of them.

### LACK OF COMPETENCE

Here 'competence' means legal power to adopt an act. The principle of the Treaties is that institutions have no power to adopt an act unless they are authorized to do so by a Treaty provision: the Community has no inherent legislative or executive power.

[1] See Chap. 14.

[2] This ground stands apart from the others because it involves subjective factors.

For every act, therefore, it must be possible to point to a Treaty provision (or to another legal act in turn based on a Treaty provision) which provides its legal basis. If there is no such basis, the act will be annulled for lack of competence.[3] The equivalent concept in English law is *ultra vires*.

Although it raises fundamental issues, this ground is rarely invoked because it is difficult – except, perhaps, in cases of delegation – to establish that the enacting authority lacked competence. It will be remembered from the discussion in Chapter 4, that the European Court gives a wide interpretation to empowering provisions in the Treaties; the theory of implied powers also extends the competence of the Council and Commission. On top of this, Article 308 [235] EC (and its equivalents) are of such wide scope that, except in the case of matters wholly outside the ambit of the Treaty, it is almost always possible to find a legal basis for a Council act.[4]

A more common complaint is that the act was adopted under the wrong empowering provision, that is to say that the Council or Commission had the power to adopt it under one provision, but acted under another.[5] This was discussed in Chapter 4, and it will be remembered that the Court will annul the measure if resort to the wrong empowering provision had significant consequences – for example, if the provision required unanimity while the correct provision provided for qualified majority voting. If there are no such consequences, the measure will not be annulled. In cases of this kind, the formal ground of review would appear not to be lack of competence – since the institution in question admittedly has the power to adopt the measure – but rather an infringement of an essential procedural requirement. It is, however, curious that the adoption of a measure by unanimity, instead of by a qualified majority, should constitute such an infringement, since a unanimous vote necessarily constitutes a majority.[6]

## INFRINGEMENT OF AN ESSENTIAL PROCEDURAL REQUIREMENT

This ground of invalidity includes requirements which may be regarded as procedural in the strict sense, such as a requirement to consult another authority, and also requirements concerning the form of the measure – for example, the requirement to give reasons.

The requirement may be laid down either in the Treaty or in secondary legislation (for example, in the case of delegation, a requirement to consult); it may also be prescribed by a general principle of law. An example of the latter is the principle of *audi alteram partem*, which was held in the *Transocean Marine Paint* case[7] to be binding on the Commission even in the absence of an express legislative provision.[8]

[3] See the first para. of Art. 5 [3b] EC.

[4] But for cases in which a Commission measure was annulled for lack of competence, see *France v. Commission*, Case C-327/91, [1994] ECR I-3641; *Germany v. European Parliament and Council* (*Tobacco Advertising* case), Case C-376/98, [2000] ECR I-8419.

[5] Such arguments are facilitated by the fact that regulations, directives, and decisions adopted by the Council or Commission must specify the empowering provision under which they were adopted: see below.

[6] For a bizarre incident in which the Council changed the legal basis of a measure *ex post facto* by means of another measure, see Regulation 2746/72, JO 1972, L291/148, amending Regulation 947/71, JO 1971, L106/1.

[7] Case 17/74, [1974] ECR 1063. [8] See Chap. 5.

It will be noticed that only an 'essential' procedural requirement is a ground of annulment. The distinction between essential and non-essential requirements, which was adopted from French administrative law,[9] is similar to the English distinction between procedural provisions that are mandatory and those that are merely directory. The philosophy behind this distinction is the same in all three systems: to invalidate an act for an insignificant procedural defect would unduly hamper administrative activity and would encourage excessive formalism and 'red tape', which in turn would stifle initiative and slow down the administrative process; on the other hand, not to annul for any formal defect at all would be detrimental to good administration and would prejudice the rights of individuals. The law therefore tries to achieve a compromise by restricting the sanction of invalidity to those cases where an important provision has been violated.

This compromise has many advantages; but it has the disadvantage of uncertainty: how does one tell whether a requirement is to be regarded as essential or not? Community provisions laying down procedural requirements do not normally state whether their infringement will lead to invalidity. Therefore, one must look to the function of the provision and to the likely consequences if it is not observed. Thus, if failure to observe it could affect the final content of the act, one would be justified in concluding that it was an essential requirement. For example, a requirement to consult another body, or to grant the person concerned a hearing, is classifiable as essential on the basis of this test: the facts and arguments that would be brought to the notice of the enacting authority through this procedure could induce it to alter the content of the measure.

It would be a mistake, however, to conclude that this is the sole test: procedural requirements which have no possible effects on the content of the act can also be classified as essential. For example, the most important objectives of the requirement to give reasons are, according to the European Court, to help the persons concerned defend their rights, to help the Court exercise its supervisory functions, and to enable third parties to appreciate the way in which the enacting authorities use their powers.[10] None of these considerations relates to the content of the measure;[11] yet the requirement to give reasons can certainly constitute an essential procedural requirement.

Article 253 [190] EC provides that regulations, directives, and decisions of the Council and Commission must state the reasons on which they are based. This includes a requirement to specify the legal provision under which they were adopted (legal basis). In the *Tariff Preferences* case,[12] however, the Court held that failure to refer to a precise provision of the Treaty is not necessarily an infringement of an essential

[9] The term used in French law for an essential procedural requirement is '*une forme substantielle*'; this is also the term used in the French version of the Treaties.

[10] See Chap. 4.

[11] It is, of course, true that another function of the requirement to give reasons is to clarify the enacting authority's objectives in adopting the measure; thus the discipline of formulating the reasons could induce it to reconsider the content of the measure. To this extent, the classification of this requirement as essential could be justified on the basis of the first test. This function has not, however, been mentioned by the European Court and it must be regarded as secondary.

[12] *Commission v. Council*, Case 45/86, [1987] ECR 1493.

procedural requirement if it is possible to determine from other parts of the measure what its legal basis is. Where, however, the parties and the Court would otherwise be uncertain as to its precise legal basis, an explicit reference is, it held, 'indispensable'.[13] It would appear that in the former case there would be an infringement of a non-essential procedural requirement and in the latter of an essential one.[14] This shows that the terminology of the Treaty is misleading: what is important is not the nature of the procedural requirement infringed, but the consequences, in the particular circumstances of the case, of the infringement.

Requirements so far held to be essential include the requirement to give reasons, the requirement to grant a hearing (*audi alteram partem*),[15] the requirement to attain assent,[16] the requirement to consult,[17] and the requirement that a Council measure be based on a proposal from the Commission.[18]

The case of *United Kingdom v. Council*[19] establishes that the Council's Rules of Procedure can contain essential procedural requirements. Article 6(1) of the Rules of Procedure[20] permitted measures to be adopted by the written procedure (without an actual meeting) provided no Member State objected. At a meeting of the Council held on 19 December 1985 it was decided, despite the contrary votes of the United Kingdom and Denmark, to adopt a particular directive by means of the written procedure before 31 December 1985. On 23 December, the Secretary General of the Council telexed the British Minister for Agriculture asking for his vote, which he was required to give by 30 December. In a letter dated 31 December, the Minister replied that the United Kingdom objected to the use of the written procedure and also to the directive itself. On the same day the Council notified the United Kingdom that the directive had been adopted.

The United Kingdom brought proceedings to annul the directive on the ground that resort to the written procedure violated Article 6(1) of the Council's Rules of Procedure. This raised the question whether the requirement of unanimity in that provision constituted an essential procedural requirement.[21] The Court held it did, and therefore annulled the directive.

[13] Para. 9 of the judgment.

[14] It is not entirely clear whether, even here, the measure would be invalid if it had in fact been adopted under the correct empowering provision, or if resort to an incorrect empowering provision had not affected the procedure followed: see *per* Advocate General Lenz [1987] ECR at 1514–15 (paras 91–5).

[15] *Transocean Marine Paint v. Commission*, Case 17/74, [1974] ECR 1063.

[16] *Klöckner-Werke v. Commission*, Case 119/81, [1982] ECR 2627 (para. 6 of the judgment). This case concerned the duty to attain the assent of the Council under Art. 58(1) ECSC.

[17] *Italy v. High Authority*, Case 2/54, [1954] ECR 37 at 51–2 (duty under Art. 60(1) ECSC to consult the Consultative Committee); *Netherlands v. High Authority*, Case 6/54, [1955] ECR 103 at 112; *Roquette v. Council*, Case 138/79, [1980] ECR 3333; and *Maizena v. Council*, Case 139/79, [1980] ECR 3393 (duty to consult the European Parliament).

[18] In *United Kingdom v. Council*, Case 68/86, [1988] ECR 855 (para. 32 of the judgment), it was held that failure to identify the Commission proposal on which a measure is based is not an infringement of an essential procedural requirement, provided the measure is in fact based on a Commission proposal.

[19] Case 68/86, [1988] ECR 855. [20] OJ 1979, L268/1.

[21] The requirement of unanimity for the adoption of the written procedure is separate from the question whether unanimity is required for the adoption of the directive itself: see para. 47 of the judgment.

## INFRINGEMENT OF THE TREATY OR OF ANY RULE OF LAW RELATING TO ITS APPLICATION

If narrowly interpreted, this ground applies only to those cases where the act subject to challenge violates an express prohibition (in this respect, it contrasts with lack of competence, which applies in the absence of any relevant provision), but if given a wide interpretation it overlaps with virtually every other ground of annulment, since each could be said to involve an infringement of some rule of Community law. For this reason, it is almost always pleaded by litigants in addition to any other ground they might think appropriate.

What does it cover? First, it covers all provisions in the relevant Treaty – EC or Euratom – and all other Treaties amending or supplementing it; consequently it covers all the constitutive Treaties.[22] Secondly, it covers 'any rule of law' relating to the application of any of those Treaties. At first sight, the meaning of this phrase may give rise to doubt. The Dutch version of the Treaty uses the phrase *enige uitvoeringsregeling daarvan*, which means 'any rule executing it'. This suggests that the phrase applies only to implementing provisions, but this is too narrow an interpretation: the European Court has made clear that it applies to all rules of Community law other than those found in the constitutive Treaties.

Each of the following is a possible source of rules of law relating to the application of the Treaty:[23]

1 Community acts (including acts *sui generis*);
2 subsidiary conventions (provided they are part of the Community legal system);
3 acts of the representatives of the Member States (in so far as they are legally binding);
4 treaties with third countries binding on the Community (whether entered into by the Community or by the Member States);
5 the general principles of Community law;
6 international law.

Each of these will be considered in turn.

Violation of another Community act will be a ground of annulment if that other act was binding on the author of the act subject to challenge. This will occur where the latter is delegated legislation and also in those cases where the principle of legal certainty (protection of legitimate expectations) requires that the author of the act subject to challenge abide by some previous act adopted by it. The *Staff Salaries* case[24] (discussed above)[25] furnishes an example of this: the Court there annulled a measure of the Council providing salary increases for Community staff because it violated a previous Council decision laying down the formula on the basis of which future salary increases were to be calculated. The Court held that the principle of legitimate expectations required the Council to adhere to its previous decision.

[22] See Chap. 3. [23] See Vandersanden and Barav, pp. 188–201.
[24] *Commission v. Council*, Case 81/72, [1973] ECR 575. [25] See Chap. 5.

The question whether a subsidiary convention prevails over a Community act has already been discussed; the matter is not free from doubt but it was suggested that it probably does not.[26] If this is correct, violation of such a convention will not be a ground of annulment; but if the European Court takes the opposite view, there is no doubt that it would annul the act in question for violation of a rule of law relating to the application of the Treaty. It will also be remembered that acts of the representatives of the Member States are in some cases a species of international agreement between the Member States.[27] In such cases they will be of a similar status to the subsidiary conventions.

International agreements with non-Member States concluded by the Community, or otherwise binding on it, are also covered; so any Community act contrary to such an agreement would be annulled by the Court, provided that the agreement was directly effective.[28]

The general principles of Community law play an important part in annulment actions.[29] An infringement of such a principle is a ground of invalidity except in those cases where the principle is merely interpretative or intended only to fill gaps in Community legislation.

In the *Racke* case,[30] the European Court held that the principles of customary international law may be applied to determine the validity of a Community regulation. The regulation in question had suspended a trade agreement between the Community and Yugoslavia, and it was argued by someone who claimed directly-effective rights under the agreement that the suspension was contrary to international law. The European Court held that customary international law is applicable as part of the Community legal system, but that a measure should be declared invalid for infringement of international law only when the Community institution adopting it made 'manifest errors of assessment' concerning the conditions for applying the relevant rules.[31]

## MISUSE OF POWERS

Though of great theoretical interest, this ground is only rarely established in practice. It is derived from French administrative law – where it is known as *détournement de pouvoir* – but is also found, in one form or another, in the legal systems of most Western countries. A misuse of powers has been defined by the Court as the adoption by a Community institution of a measure with the exclusive or main purpose of achieving an end other than that stated, or evading a procedure specifically prescribed by the Treaty for dealing with the circumstances of the case.[32] Put more simply, it is the

[26] See Chap. 3. [27] See Chap. 3.

[28] *International Fruit Company*, Cases 21–4/72, [1972] ECR 1219 (para. 5 of the judgment); *Schlüter*, Case 9/73, [1973] ECR 1135 (paras 24–31 of the judgment); *Bresciani*, Case 87/75, [1976] ECR 129 (paras 15–26 of the judgment); *Germany v. Council* (*Bananas* case), Case C-280/93, [1994] ECR I-4973 (paras 103–12 of the judgment). [29] See Chap. 5.

[30] Case C-162/96, [1998] ECR I-3655. [31] Para. 52 of the judgment.

[32] See, e.g., *European Parliament v. Commission*, Case C-156/93, [1995] ECR I-2019 at para. 31 of the judgment.

exercise of a power for a purpose other than that for which it was granted.[33] It is a well-established ground of invalidity in English administrative law, where it is usually referred to, more informatively, as 'improper purpose'.

Unlike the other grounds of invalidity, which are objective in character, misuse of powers is subjective: in order to establish it, one has to discover what the subjective purpose – the motive or intention – was of the authority exercising the power.[34] For this reason, misuse of powers is more difficult to prove than other grounds: in the absence of a document emanating from the authority which indicates its purpose in adopting the measure, the applicant may have to rely on inference from the content of the measure and the general circumstances prevailing when it was enacted.[35] It is not, however, necessary to prove bad faith: an authority may quite innocently misuse its powers if it fails to appreciate the purpose for which they were given.

It will be apparent that misuse of powers is closely related to the doctrine of proportionality. This is one of the general principles of Community law (discussed in Chapter 5); it requires that burdens imposed on the citizen be proportionate to the objective pursued: the means chosen must be reasonably likely to attain the objective and the detriment inflicted on those concerned must not be disproportionate to the general benefit. The difference between proportionality and misuse of powers is that proportionality is purely objective: the terms of the measure are balanced against the objective of the provision under which it was adopted; in the case of misuse of powers, on the other hand, the subjective intention of the author of the act is the relevant factor. If the authority is genuinely pursuing the proper objective, but uses inappropriate means, the measure will be annulled for lack of proportionality; if the objective is improper, misuse of powers will be the correct ground of review. However, though the two doctrines are quite distinct in theory, they can easily merge in practice, since the fact that the measure is inappropriate for the attainment of its ostensible objective will suggest that this was not the objective which its author was trying to attain.

In what circumstance will misuse of powers apply? French writers sometimes divide it into two categories, primary *détournement de pouvoir* and secondary *détournement de pouvoir*. The former comprises those cases where the power is not used in the public

[33] See *Netherlands v. High Authority*, Case 6/54, [1955] ECR 103 at 116; *Compagnie des Hauts Fourneaux de Chasse v. High Authority*, Case 15/57, [1958] ECR 211 at 230.

[34] In some of its earlier judgments, however, the European Court seems to have veered away from the pure doctrine of misuse of powers and allowed an objective element to enter its reasoning. Thus in *Hauts Fourneaux et Aciéries Belges v. High Authority*, Case 8/57, [1958] ECR 245 at 256, the Court said that violation of the principle of equality could constitute misuse of power; while in other cases there is a suggestion that lack of foresight could lead to misuse of power: see *Fédéchar v. High Authority*, Case 8/55, [1956] ECR 292 at 303, and *Chambre Syndicale de la Sidérurgie Française v. High Authority*, Cases 3–4/64, [1965] ECR 441 at 454–5; see further, Vandersanden and Barav at pp. 207–8. This extended concept of misuse of powers (which appears to have been derived from German law: see Dickschat, 'Problèmes d'interprétation des traités européens résultant de leur plurilinguisme' [1968] Revue Belge de Droit International 40 at 47) was probably adopted by the Court because of the special role played by misuse of powers in the ECSC Treaty, particularly with regard to the right of non-privileged applicants to challenge normative measures. By applying the wider concept, the Court could extend the right of non-privileged applicants to obtain judicial review under Art. 33 ECSC.

[35] The Court has said that the misuse of powers must be established 'on the basis of objective, relevant and consistent facts': see *Gutmann v. Commission*, Cases 18, 35/65, [1966] ECR 103 at 117 and *Lux v. Court of Auditors*, Case 69/83, [1984] ECR 2447 (para. 30 of the judgment).

interest at all, but is used for some private objective of its author, perhaps to advance his own interests or to spite someone he dislikes. For example, if an official were refused a particular post because the decision-maker wished to appoint his girlfriend, one would have a case of primary misuse of powers.[36]

Secondary misuse of powers occurs where the objective pursued is in the public interest but it is not one which the author of the act is entitled to pursue. The case of *Gutmann v. Commission*[37] furnishes a good example. The applicant in this case was a Euratom official who was transferred from the Research Centre at Ispra to Brussels on the basis of a provision authorizing the transfer of an official 'in the interests of the service'. The Court held, however, that this was not the real reason for the decision to transfer him: it was actually taken for disciplinary purposes. The decision was, therefore, annulled for misuse of powers.

Another case in which the plea was successfully invoked was *Giuffrida v. Council*.[38] This concerned an official called Signor Martino, who held an appointment at a particular grade, even though for many years he had performed duties appropriate to an official of a higher grade. In an attempt to remedy this anomalous situation, the Council organized a competition for a post at the higher grade. The sole object of this was, by the Council's own admission, to allow Signor Martino to be appointed to a post corresponding to his duties. Two officials applied, Signor Martino and the applicant in the case, Signor Giuffrida; Signor Martino was appointed and Signor Giuffrida brought proceedings to annul the appointment. The Court held that the objective of any recruitment procedure, including an internal competition, should be to appoint the best person for the job; by deciding in advance whom they would appoint, the Council was guilty of a misuse of powers. The appointment was therefore quashed.

A misuse of powers may also occur if an authority, for an improper reason, adopts a measure under one provision when another provision would have been more appropriate. This was recognized by the Court in *Compagnie des Hauts Fourneaux de Chasse v. High Authority* where it said:[39]

> In this connexion it must be recognized that there might have been a misuse of powers if the High Authority had been faced with a situation covered by the procedure in Article 59 and, in order to evade the safeguards provided for in Article 59, had nevertheless deliberately decided to make use of Article 53(b) and of the financial arrangements provided for therein.

This rule would not, of course apply if both provisions were appropriate and the authority's choice was not made on improper grounds.

It is important to note that a measure will not be annulled for misuse of powers if the improper purpose had no effect on its substance. After all, why should a measure be quashed if it would have been enacted in exactly the same terms even if its author had

[36] *Cf. Mirossevich v. High Authority*, Case 10/55, [1956] ECR 333. Here similar allegations were made but were not proved.

[37] Cases 18, 35/65, [1966] ECR 103.

[38] Case 105/75, [1976] ECR 1395. See also *Fabrique de Fer de Charleroi v. Commission*, Cases 351, 360/85, [1987] ECR 3639, a case involving steel quotas in which the Commission adopted criteria designed to help a particular Member State rather than to spread the burden fairly among all steel enterprises.

[39] Case 15/57, [1958] ECR 211 at 231. The Court actually found that misuse of powers had not been proved.

not been pursuing an illegitimate objective? Consequently, it will be valid if pursuit of the proper purpose would inevitably have led to the same result.[40]

It follows from the above rule that if the authority has two objectives, one proper and one improper, the measure will not be annulled if the proper objective was the decisive one. In such a case, the improper objective will have no influence on the outcome. In *Fédéchar v. High Authority*[41] the Court said:

> Even if one unjustified reason were included among those which justify the action of the High Authority, the decision would not for that reason involve a misuse of powers, in so far as it does not adversely affect the basic aim of [the provision under which it was taken].

This statement suggests that, so long as the legitimate aim is attained, the presence of an improper purpose will be of no consequence. It seems to extend the rule slightly, since the improper purpose may have had some effect on the terms of the measure, even if it did not prevent the fulfilment of the legitimate objective. In other cases, there are suggestions that, where several motives are present, the applicant must prove that the improper motive was the sole, or at least the dominant, one.[42]

## THE TIME FACTOR

In all annulment actions, the validity of the act must be determined on the basis of the situation existing at the time when it was adopted. A measure cannot, therefore, be annulled because of a subsequent event. This is logical in view of the fact that annulment is normally retroactive: the Court declares the act to have been invalid *ab initio*.[43] It follows from this that an act cannot be annulled on the ground that it is in conflict with a superior rule of law contained in a measure enacted at a subsequent date. The superior measure will, of course, prevail and the first act will be inapplicable to the extent of the conflict; but the Court will not annul it.

These principles can be illustrated from the case law of the European Court. *Schroeder v. Germany*,[44] for example, concerned a Community measure passed in order to limit imports of tomato concentrate from Greece. It was argued that the measure was not appropriate to achieve its objective – it was enacted under a power to pass 'appropriate' measures – because it could easily be circumvented. In dealing with this point, the Court said that the matter had to be approached on the basis of what was known when the measure was introduced: 'retrospective considerations of its efficacy' could not be taken into account.[45]

[40] *Fédéchar v. High Authority*, Case 8/55, [1956] ECR 292 at 300–1.

[41] Case 8/55, [1956] ECR 245 at 301. See also *France v. High Authority*, Case 1/54, [1954] ECR 1 at 16.

[42] See the *Fédéchar* case, Case 8/55, [1956] ECR 292 at 303; and *Hauts Fourneaux de Chasse v. High Authority*, Case 2/57, [1958] ECR 199 at 232. Compare the English decision of *R v. Brixton Prison Governor, ex parte Soblen* [1963] 2 QB 243 (Lord Denning's judgment).

[43] See below.

[44] Case 40/72, [1973] ECR 125.

[45] At para. 14 of the judgment.

In the *Compagnie d'Approvisionnement* case,[46] the measure in issue was intended to counteract the effects of the devaluation of the French franc and it did this, in part, by granting subsidies to French exporters of agricultural produce. The applicant, which was a French exporter, maintained, however, that the subsidies were not high enough. One of its objections to the measure was that it infringed the principle of equality, since it was less generous than another regulation passed at a later date granting subsidies to German and Dutch importers consequent on a revaluation of the German and Dutch currencies. It alleged that this constituted discrimination against French exporters. The Court, however, ruled that the validity of the first regulation could not be called into question on the basis of subsequent events; consequently a comparison with the later measure could not be used to establish discrimination.[47]

This latter case raises some interesting issues: if two measures are passed dealing with situations which are sufficiently similar to bring the principle of equality into play, the possibilities of annulment might depend on which is passed first. If the less favourable measure is passed after the more favourable, it could be annulled for violation of the principle of equality. If, on the other hand, the less favourable measure is passed first, it is doubtful whether either could be annulled on this ground: the less favourable measure could not be annulled because of the time factor; the more favourable would not be quashed because the persons benefiting from it would not wish to challenge it and those covered by the less favourable measure would normally lack *locus standi.*

Is there no remedy in the latter case? One possibility is that those covered by the less favourable measure might request the enacting institution to amend it to bring it into line with the other measure; if this request were not met, proceedings could be brought for a remedy for failure to act. It will be remembered that in *Eridania v. Commission*[48] the Court ruled that an action for failure to act cannot be used for the purpose of obliging a Community institution to repeal an invalid act. It was, however, suggested above[49] that there should be an exception to this rule where the act was initially valid but subsequently became incompatible with Community law as a result of a later development. If such an exception exists, the case where the less favourable measure is passed first would be precisely the situation in which it should be applied.

## INTEREST

The (rather strict) rules of *locus standi* applicable in Community law were discussed in Chapter 12, above: is it sufficient if these are satisfied and it is thus established that the applicant has a legally-recognized interest in the annulment of the act; or must he also prove an interest in each ground of annulment pleaded? In the national systems of the Community countries there is a sharp divergence on this point:[50] in French, Belgian,

[46] Cases 9, 11/71, [1972] ECR 391.

[47] At para. 39 of the judgment.

[48] Cases 10, 18/68, [1969] ECR 459.

[49] See Chap. 13.

[50] See the Opinion of Advocate General Warner in *Deboeck v. Commission*, Case 90/74, [1975] ECR 1123 at 1140–1.

and Italian law the view is taken that it is enough that the applicant has an interest in the annulment of the measure itself. If this is the case, he is entitled to put forward any ground recognized by law. In England, Scotland, Denmark, the Netherlands, and Germany, on the other hand, the applicant must, in at least some cases, show that he has an interest in the ground pleaded. This latter view has prevailed in Community law, at least with regard to staff cases.

In *Marcato v. Commission*[51] a Commission official, who had been unsuccessful in his application for a more senior post, brought proceedings to annul the competition for the appointment. One of his objections was that the notice of competition did not lay down an age limit for candidates, as was required by the Staff Regulations. The applicant was, in fact, the second oldest of the candidates and, as the Commission pointed out, an age limit of fifty or sixty would not have eliminated any of the candidates, while a limit of forty would have eliminated the applicant himself. The Commission therefore argued that he could not object to the absence of an age limit, since his interests were not affected. This argument was fiercely rejected by Advocate General Mayras (a Frenchman) on the basis of the standard French doctrine. The Court, however, accepted it. The relevant passage of the judgment reads:[52]

> The setting of an age limit could only have resulted either in eliminating the applicant himself from the competition, which would have been directly contrary to his interest, or else in eliminating other, possibly qualified, candidates, which in the circumstances cannot be regarded as a legitimate interest of his.

The interesting point to note is that it is not enough for the applicant to have an actual interest in the ground pleaded; his interest must also be regarded as *legitimate.* Presumably the Court considered that the rule regarding age limits had been enacted solely in the interests of the service and not in order to benefit rival candidates.[53]

Two other examples may briefly be mentioned.[54] In *De Dapper v. Parliament*[55] another unsuccessful candidate complained that the persons who were appointed to the post had remained in the same grade: the Court held that only *they* could complain about this. In *Deboeck v. Commission*[56] an unsuccessful candidate objected to the fact that the notice of competition had not been preceded by a notice of vacancy. The function of a notice of vacancy is to allow the appointing authority to consider whether the post might not be filled by transfer or promotion instead of by competition. The applicant, however, was not eligible for transfer or promotion to the post: her only chance of appointment lay in a competition; therefore, she was not entitled to object.[57]

[51] Case 37/72, [1973] ECR 361. [52] Para. 6 of the judgment.

[53] A similar argument has been adopted in a number of English decisions: see, e.g., *R v. Commissioners of Customs and Excise, ex parte Cooke and Stevenson* [1970] 1 All ER 1068.

[54] See also *Alfieri v. Parliament*, Case 35/64, [1965] ECR 261 at 267; *Serio* v. *Commission*, Case 115/73, [1974] ECR 341 at 349; and *De Vleeschauwer v. Commission*, Case 144/73, [1974] ECR 957 at 986.

[55] Case 29/74, [1975] ECR 35 at 40. [56] Case 90/74, [1975] ECR 1123.

[57] Another possible objection to the omission was that it might have meant that certain potential candidates would not have known of the competition; but this did not affect the applicant: she *did* know of it.

It is not entirely clear exactly when an applicant will be regarded as not having an interest in a particular ground, but it is probably legitimate to formulate the rule as follows: where the complaint is that the author of the act failed to do something, the applicant will not be entitled to object if he would have been no better off if the omission had not occurred; where, on the other hand, something was done which ought not to have been done, the applicant will be able to rely on the irregularity only if his interests were prejudiced. An applicant will not, moreover, be regarded as affected unless he has a *legitimate* interest: an interest would probably be regarded as legitimate only if it was one which the rule of law violated might reasonably be supposed to have been intended to protect.

The cases do not indicate the scope of the rule. It will apply most often to procedural irregularities, but it appears also applicable to defects of substance: the allegations in *Marcato*, and even more so in *De Dapper*, go beyond what could be regarded as procedure. It will not of course apply to serious violations of the law: the Court usually investigates these of its own motion; so it will be irrelevant whether or not the applicant has an interest.

## MISTAKE OF FACT

A decision of fact is a determination whether or not a particular state of fact exists. It is quite different from a decision to act, though the two kinds of decision are frequently linked: the power to adopt a measure may be dependent on the prior existence of a situation of fact. The enacting authority must then determine the question of fact before it can exercise the discretionary power. If, however, it makes a wrong decision of fact, it may enact a measure when it has no power to do so: such a measure will be invalid and will be quashed by the European Court if appropriate proceedings are brought. The formal ground of annulment will usually be infringement of the Treaty or of a rule of law relating to its application.

A good example is provided by *Barge v. High Authority*.[58] This was another of the many cases under the ECSC Treaty concerning the scrap iron equalization scheme. It will be remembered that under this scheme imported scrap was subsidized and the subsidy paid for by a levy on all users of scrap, both imported and home-produced.[59] Since the levy was based on the quantity of scrap used, the Commission had to determine this before it could decide how much was owed by any given firm. Where the firm failed to provide the relevant figures, the Commission was obliged to make an estimate of scrap used. This was what occurred in the *Barge* case, where the estimate was based on the amount of electricity used by the steel foundry in question. The Commission

[58] Case 18/62, [1963] ECR 259. See also *Milac*, Case 131/77, [1978] ECR 1041 (where the question of fact on which the validity of the measure depended was whether the price of one product was dependent on that of another) and *per* Advocate General Mayras in *Westzucker*, Case 57/72, [1973] ECR 321 at 351.

[59] See Chap. 4.

then passed two decisions; one set out the estimated quantities of scrap used and the other fixed the amount due by way of the levy. These decisions were challenged by Barge which succeeded in proving that the assessment of scrap consumed was inaccurate. The Court thereupon quashed both decisions.

Where a Community institution makes a mistake concerning a purely factual question of this kind, the Court will always quash the measure if its validity is dependent on the decision of fact. However, in many cases the relevant question is not one of 'pure' fact, but is rather an evaluation or judgment based on facts. For example, there are a number of provisions giving the Commission power to adopt measures if a given situation has produced 'economic difficulties' in a particular Member State or if there is a threat of 'serious disturbances' to the market in a given product. Clearly, a determination by the Commission that economic difficulties exist or that serious disturbances are threatened is a decision of a somewhat different nature from a determination that a particular firm has consumed X tons of ferrous scrap.

A decision of this kind is a complex determination containing, first, a number of purely factual decisions – for example, on the level of imports, exports, prices, profits, etc. – and, secondly, an evaluation of the situation thus revealed in which it is decided that these 'primary' facts either establish, or do not establish, the existence of economic difficulties or a threat of serious disturbances, as the case may be. Though factual in one sense, this evaluation depends on the Commission's judgment, exercised on the basis of its experience. Though it does not, strictly speaking, involve a discretion,[60] it does contain a subjective element. Since the European Court lacks the political and economic expertise of the Commission and Council, it would be inappropriate if it were too ready to review it.

In view of these considerations, it is not surprising that the ECSC Treaty contained a provision in Article 33 imposing restraints on the Court. This precluded the Court from examining the evaluation of the situation in the light of which the Commission adopted the act, unless it was alleged to have misused its powers or to have manifestly failed to observe the provisions of the Treaty or any rule of law relating to its application.[61]

The EC Treaty contains no equivalent provision, and at first the Court was prepared to consider the relevant economic data in some detail. One case in which this occurred was *Italy v. Commission*,[62] which concerned the problems caused by the increasing numbers of Italian refrigerators imported into France after 1961. The French invoked Article [226] EC and asked the Commission for permission to take protective measures.

[60] See *per* Advocate General Gand in *Germany v. Commission*, Case 50/69R, [1969] ECR 449 at 458.

[61] On the application of this provision, see *Kergall v. Common Assembly*, Case 1/55, [1955] ECR 151 at 157 (the assessment of professional competence is normally a matter for the administration); *Mirossevich v. High Authority*, Case 10/55, [1956] ECR 333 at 342 (it is within the discretion of the competent authority to assess the aptitude of candidates for their duties but the Court may review the methods by which such assessment is made); *Bourgaux v. Common Assembly*, Case 1/56, [1956] ECR 361 at 368 (the question as to which of five officials whose posts had been abolished were to be given three new posts was within the discretion of the Assembly, but it could be challenged on the ground of misuse of powers); *Leroy v. High Authority*, Cases 35/62, 16/63, [1963] ECR 197 (complex value judgments contained in a report assessing the professional competence of an official cannot be reviewed by the Court).

[62] Case 13/63, [1963] ECR 165.

The Commission then took a decision allowing France to impose a special duty on Italian imports. Under Article [226], the Commission was entitled to authorize protective measures only where 'difficulties arise which are serious and liable to persist in any sector of the economy'. The Italian Government brought proceedings for the annulment of the Commission's decision, and in the course of these proceedings challenged the Commission's finding that this requirement had been satisfied. In dealing with this question, the Court gave quite detailed consideration to the relevant economic factors; however, it did so only in order to discover whether the Commission had misinterpreted the concept of serious difficulties.

In *Toepfer v. Commission*[63] the Court appeared to go further. The facts of this case have already been discussed;[64] here it will be sufficient to recall that the Commission had been slow to increase the levy on maize imports into Germany when the new French harvest came on to the market. Certain German grain importers were quick to take advantage of this and put in applications for import permits for fairly large quantities of maize (in all, approximately 125,000 metric tons, about 8–10 per cent of annual imports). The German intervention agency tried to block this by immediately asking the Commission for authorization to suspend all maize imports. This was granted.

Toepfer was one of the German importers who challenged the Commission decision granting the authorization. Under the relevant provision, the Commission could give authorization only if the imports in question threatened to cause 'serious disturbances' to the market. Toepfer claimed that this was not the case, and that the decision was consequently invalid for an infringement of the Treaty or a rule of law relating to its application. In ruling on this, the Court analysed the economic data and concluded that the quantity of maize in question was not sufficient to cause serious disturbances even if it were sold at low prices. The decision was therefore annulled.

In this case the Court seems to have come close to reviewing the Commission's evaluation of the situation, though it could be argued that the evidence showed that the Commission had misconceived the idea of 'serious disturbances'. In fact, though the Court did not decide the case on this basis, it could be maintained that there had really been a misuse of powers by the Commission: it had not actually been concerned with preventing a collapse of the market but rather with depriving the importers of the financial 'killing' they had expected. However, the evidence was probably insufficient to establish this.

The first express reference in an EC case to the doctrine of restraint is probably a statement by Advocate General Dutheillet de Lamothe in 1971 in *Rewe- Zentrale.*[65] This case was concerned with Article [226] EC, and it is desirable to say a little more about this provision in order to appreciate the remarks of the Advocate General. Article [226] was applicable only during the transitional period before the Common Market was fully established, and was intended as a safeguard provision to deal with emergencies. Where it was established to the satisfaction of the Commission that such a situation had arisen, it was for the Commission to decide what measures were necessary. In deciding

[63] Cases 106–7/63, [1965] ECR 405. [64] See Chap. 12. [65] Case 37/70, [1971] ECR 23.

this, the Commission was obliged by Article [226(3)] to give priority to 'such measures as will least disturb the functioning of the common market'. Advocate General de Lamothe began his discussion by commenting that, though Article [226] does not confer a discretion on the Commission, it grants it a wide power of appraisal, which is, however, subject to review by the Court.[66] He then continued:[67]

> I consider that it follows from this that, apart from a major infringement of a procedural requirement or a misuse of powers, decisions taken by the Commission in implementation of Article [226] are unlawful only in the following cases: first, where the Commission's appraisal is based on substantially incorrect facts. The illegality is thus established. Secondly: where, although the Commission's appraisal is based on substantially correct facts, it is nevertheless *clearly* wrong. Thirdly: where a measure derogating less substantially from the rules of the common market would *clearly* have sufficed to remedy the situation which called for the employment of Article [226].

The Court itself made no direct reference to the doctrine in *Rewe-Zentrale.* Two years later, however, such a reference was made in *Westzucker.*[68] This case concerned a Commission decision suspending payment of a grant. In reviewing the validity of this decision, the Court said that the Commission enjoyed a 'significant freedom of evaluation' in fixing the level of the grant. It then continued:[69]

> When examining the lawfulness of the exercise of such freedom, the courts cannot substitute their own evaluation of the matter for that of the competent authority but must restrict themselves to examining whether the evaluation of the competent authority contains a patent error or constitutes a misuse of power.

This formula has been repeated in later cases.[70] In *Racke,*[71] however, the Court expanded on it by adding to the two grounds of review already established – patent error and misuse of power – a third ground: that the competent authority had clearly exceeded the limits of its power of evaluation.[72] One can conclude from this that the position under the EC Treaty is now the same as it was under the ECSC Treaty: the absence of an express provision in Article 230 [173] is irrelevant.

## FAILURE TO ACT

Special considerations apply where the action is for a remedy for failure to act. First, it is necessary to draw a distinction between a negative decision (a decision refusing to act) and failure even to reply to a request for action. Since the former is technically an act, and the proceedings technically an action for annulment, the grounds of review will

[66] See also *per* Advocate General Gand in *Germany v. Commission,* Case 50/69R, [1969] ECR 449 at 458.
[67] [1971] ECR at 42. [68] Case 57/72, [1973] ECR 321. [69] Para. 14 of the judgment.
[70] See *Deuka,* Case 78/74, [1975] ECR 421 at para. 9 of the judgment.
[71] Case 136/77, [1978] ECR 1245 at para. 4 of the judgment.
[72] The English text of the judgment mistranslates the French word *appréciation* as 'discretion'; it should, of course, be 'evaluation': compare the French and English texts of Art. 33 ECSC.

in theory be those set out in Articles 230 [173] EC and 146 Euratom. However, since the proceedings are in reality designed to require the defendant to act, certain grounds will be inappropriate. For example, an applicant would hardly plead lack of competence: if the defendant has no competence in the matter, it would not be able to perform the act in question even if it wanted to; so any proceedings would be in vain. A negative decision may, on the other hand, be attacked on procedural grounds (including natural justice) or for defects of form (including lack of reasoning); however, if it is annulled on one of these grounds the applicant may find that he has won a hollow victory: the defendant may simply take the same decision over again after complying with the relevant requirements.

Where the defendant fails even to reply to the request for action, there can obviously be no question of pleading lack of form or failure to comply with the appropriate procedure: non-action, by its very nature, has no form, and no procedure applies to it. As in the case of a negative act, lack of competence is also inappropriate. This leaves only two possible grounds: infringement of the Treaty or any rule of law relating to its application, and misuse of powers.

When will these grounds apply? Article 232 [175] EC states:[73]

> Should the European Parliament, the Council or the Commission, in infringement of this Treaty, fail to act, the Member States and the other institutions of the Community may bring an action before the Court of Justice to have the infringement established.

This suggests that infringement of the Treaty is the only ground that may be pleaded. However, the matter is more complicated than this. In order to analyse it, we must make a distinction between a requirement to act and a power to act.

## REQUIREMENT TO ACT

Here there must be an obligation on the defendant to adopt a legal act. The main problem concerns the source of the obligation. Obviously an obligation contained in one of the constitutive Treaties will be sufficient: the phrase 'this Treaty' in Articles 232 [175] EC and 148 Euratom covers each of those Treaties, together with any amending or supplementing Treaties. Obligations contained in secondary legislation (Community acts) are not expressly mentioned; there can be little doubt, however, that the phrase 'in infringement of this Treaty' covers them as well, since an infringement of a measure passed under a Treaty is also an infringement of the Treaty itself: if a Treaty empowers a Community institution to enact legislation, it impliedly provides that it must be obeyed by other institutions – the essence of legislation is, after all, that it is legally binding. The same is probably true of an obligation contained in an international agreement binding on the Community.

Will an obligation derived from a general principle of law be sufficient? Though the position is not free from doubt, the European Court might hold that the obligation to respect the general principles of law is inherent in the Treaties. Articles 220 [164] EC and 136 Euratom could perhaps be invoked for this purpose.

[73] Art. 148 Euratom is similar except that there is no reference to the European Parliament.

### POWER TO ACT

It might be thought that no remedy for failure to act could be obtained where there is merely a discretionary power to act. For various reasons, however, this is not the case. First of all, a power is almost always coupled with a duty, even if this duty is no more than to consider, with an open mind, whether the power should be exercised. Public authorities are not given powers to be exercised according to whim: a public authority must exercise its powers for the public good; and it must ascertain the public good according to the criteria laid down by law. Consequently, whenever granted a power, it must be willing to consider – in appropriate cases – whether to exercise it or not. This obligation applies to Community institutions as much as to any other public authorities. Therefore, if the power is granted by the Treaty or a provision of Community legislation, the institution will be guilty of an infringement of the Treaty if it fails to give the matter proper consideration.

Secondly, if the authority does apply its mind to the matter, but decides not to act, it will violate the law if it reaches its decision improperly. If it acts for the wrong motive, or takes improper considerations into account, or fails to take proper considerations into account, it will be guilty of a misuse of powers. This will be impliedly covered by the phrase 'infringement of this Treaty'. If the Treaty (or Community legislation passed under the Treaty) gives a discretionary power, there is an implied obligation to exercise that power according to the proper criteria. A misuse of that power is therefore an infringement of the empowering provision in the same way that a failure to consider whether it should be exercised is an infringement of it.[74]

## ANNULMENT

If the applicant establishes that one of the grounds of review exists, the Court will annul the measure. Annulment is not, however, a simple matter. We shall now consider some of the problems.

### RETROACTIVITY

The basic principle of Community law is that invalid acts are voidable, but annulment is retroactive. This means, first, that invalid acts which are not annulled are valid to the extent that they cannot be challenged indirectly; and secondly, that if they *are* annulled, they are deemed never to have existed. Moreover, since an annulment operates *erga omnes*, its effects apply equally to persons who were not parties to the annulment proceedings.[75] These principles are, however, subject to exceptions. The first is that in

[74] See Vandersanden and Barav, pp. 242–3.

[75] It follows logically from these principles that once an act has been annulled, any subsequent action to annul it, even if brought by another party, should be declared inadmissible for lack of jurisdiction *ratione materiae*: there is no longer anything left to annul. However, the Court has not been consistent on this

certain rare cases an act will be absolutely void – in Community terminology, 'non-existent' – in which case annulment is neither necessary nor, indeed, possible, since the act is treated for all purposes as if it had never been adopted.[76]

Secondly, the principle that annulments are retroactive does not apply in certain cases. This is because retroactivity could have unfortunate consequences, especially in the case of a normative measure (regulation), since persons might have relied on it in good faith; moreover, other measures may have been taken under it, and, if the validity of these other measures depends on that of the annulled measure, they will be invalid too.

Since this could conflict with the principle of legal certainty, one aspect of which is non-retroactivity, there is a provision in the EC Treaty[77] which enables the Court to avoid such a consequence in the case of a regulation. This is the second paragraph of Article 231 [174] EC which, after providing that an act against which a successful challenge has been made will be declared void, states:

> In the case of a regulation, however, the Court of Justice shall, if it considers this necessary, state which of the effects of the regulation which it has declared void shall be considered as definitive.

This provision allows the Court to limit the retroactive effect of the annulment in appropriate cases.[78] It could apply where the Commission acted under the regulation, for example by conferring benefits on particular individuals: the Court could then declare that benefits already conferred would not be affected by the annulment of the regulation.

In the *Staff Salaries* case[79] the Court made a much more striking use of Article 231 [174]. This was a case brought by the Commission against the Council to establish whether the annual salary increase granted to Community officials was large enough. The case was discussed above,[80] and it will be remembered that the Council had decided, after discussions with the Commission and the staff associations, that future salary increases would be based on an agreed formula. However, when the next increase was made, it was – in the opinion of the Commission – below the minimum permissible under the formula. Now, the only way in which the Commission could bring the issue before the Court was to institute an action for the annulment of the Council regulation setting out the new salary scales. The action was successful: the Court ruled that the formula was binding on the Council and the new scales were indeed too low. However, the Court was then faced with a problem: if it annulled the regulation, the staff would not be entitled to *any* increases until such time as a new regulation was adopted. To avoid this, the Court resorted to Article 231 [174] and ruled that the

point: compare *Italy v. High Authority*, Case 2/54, [1954] ECR 37; *Assider v. High Authority*, Case 3/54, [1955] ECR 63; *ISA v. High Authority*, Case 4/54, [1955] ECR 91; *Italy v. High Authority* Case 20/59, [1960] ECR 325; *Netherlands v. High Authority*, Case 25/59, [1960] ECR 355. See, further, Liliane Plouvier, *Les décisions de la Cour de Justice des Communautés Européennes et leurs Effets Juridiques* (1975), pp. 96–100.

[76] See Chap. 11. [77] There is an identical provision in the Euratom Treaty, Art. 147(2).

[78] See *per* Advocate General Dutheillet de Lamothe in *Compagnie d'Approvisionnement v. Commission*, Cases 9, 11/71, [1972] ECR 391 at 411.

[79] *Commission v. Council*, Case 81/72, [1973] ECR 575. For another example, see *European Parliament v. Council*, Case C-360/93, [1996] ECR 1195. [80] In Chap. 5.

annulment would be projected into the future so that the regulation would continue in force until such time as a new measure was adopted; only then would it take effect.

According to its terms, Article 231 [174] is limited to regulations; nevertheless, the Court has also applied it to a directive. This was in the *Student Right of Residence* case,[81] where the European Parliament brought proceedings to annul a directive on the ground that it had been adopted on the wrong legal basis.[82] The Court annulled the directive; but, since it had already been implemented by the Member States, the Court ruled that the annulment would not take effect until a new directive had been adopted on the correct legal basis.

In *Portugal v. Commission*,[83] the Commission tried to pre-empt the Court's power to apply Article 231 [174]. It had adopted a regulation, parts of which admittedly went beyond its powers. When Portugal brought proceedings to annul the relevant parts, the Commission withdrew them with retroactive effect. However, the regulation withdrawing them stated that the withdrawal would not affect rights already acquired. It then asked the Court to declare that there was no need to adjudicate on the application brought by Portugal because it would serve no purpose. The Court rejected this. It annulled the relevant parts of the original regulation, and refused to apply Article 231 [174].

## COMPLIANCE WITH THE JUDGMENT

Article 233 [176] EC states:[84]

> The institution or institutions whose act has been declared void . . . shall be required to take the necessary measures to comply with the judgment of the Court of Justice.[85]

What are these steps (or measures) likely to be? Besides the obvious fact that the Commission or Council will no longer operate or enforce the annulled act, positive action may have to be taken to undo the effects of past enforcement. In addition to the payment of damages (discussed in Chapter 16, below) it may be necessary to withdraw or amend other acts, perhaps because the reasoning in the judgment applies just as much to them.[86]

This provision was invoked in *AssiDomän Kraft Products v. Commission*,[87] a case in which the Commission had taken a decision imposing fines on a number of companies for breach of Community competition law. Some companies appealed to the European Court. The appeal was partly successful. The Court annulled parts of the Commission decision, in which it was held that certain offences had taken place. As a consequence,

[81] *European Parliament v. Council*, Case C-295/90, [1992] ECR I-4193.

[82] It had been adopted under Art. 308 [235] EC; the Parliament thought it should have been adopted under the second paragraph of what was then Art. 7 EC and became, first Art. 6 and then Art 12. It concerned the right of students from one Member State to reside in another Member State while attending a course of study there.

[83] Case C-89/96, [1999] ECR I-8377.

[84] Art. 149 Euratom contains an equivalent provision.

[85] This Article also applies to the ECB.

[86] *SNUPAT v. High Authority*, Cases 42, 49/59, [1961] ECR 53 (at pp. 86–8 of the judgment); *Asteris v. Commission*, Cases 97, 99, 193, 215/86, [1988] ECR 2181.

[87] Case C-310/97 P, [1999] ECR I-5363 (appeal against Case T-227/95, [1997] ECR II-1185).

it annulled the fines imposed on some of the companies that had brought the appeal, and reduced those imposed on the others. The companies that had not appealed then asked the Commission to reduce the fines imposed on them in accordance with the same principles. When the Commission took a decision refusing to do so, they brought proceedings before the Court of First Instance to annul that decision.

Two arguments were put forward. The first was that the Commission had infringed the principle that the annulment of a decision is retroactive and applies *erga omnes*. The Court of First Instance rejected this on the ground that the Commission's decision holding that the offences had occurred and imposing fines was not in reality one single decision, but rather a bundle of separate decisions, each addressed to a different defendant. So when the European Court annulled parts of it as a consequence of the appeal, what it really did was to annul parts of each of the decisions addressed to the appellants. The decisions addressed to the companies that had not appealed were not affected.

The second argument was based on Article 233 [176] EC. This argument was accepted by the Court of First Instance. It held that Article 233 [176] required the Commission to reconsider the decisions addressed to the companies that had not taken part in the appeal and to reduce the fines imposed on them to the extent that the findings of the European Court were also applicable to them.

The Commission appealed against this judgment to the European Court, which allowed the appeal. It held that Article 233 [176] applies only to the decisions annulled by the Court, not to other decisions addressed to other parties, even if they are similar.[88] It, therefore, held that the Commission had acted lawfully in refusing to reconsider the fines imposed on the companies that had not appealed, a ruling that could be regarded as putting formalism before justice.

It should finally be said that if the act was annulled on purely *formal* grounds – for example, for lack of natural justice or failure to give reasons – the enacting authority will not normally be precluded from re-enacting it according to the correct procedure. Subject to the principle of legal certainty, it could even be retroactive.[89] If, on the other hand, it was annulled for some reason of substance, such as lack of competence, infringement of the Treaty, or misuse of powers, re-enactment will not normally be permissible. It may, however, be necessary to replace it with a new measure containing different provisions.

## PARTIAL ANNULMENT

The Court is not bound always to annul the whole measure: where the invalidity affects only certain provisions, and these provisions are severable from the rest of the instrument, it may annul them only. A provision will not be severable if the rest of the instrument will not make sense without it; nor will it be severable if the purpose of the

[88] The Court distinguished the *SNUPAT* and *Asteris* cases, cited above.

[89] *Amylum v. Council*, Case 108/81, [1982] ECR 3107; *Roquette v. Council*, Case 110/81, [1982] ECR 3159; *Tunnel Refineries v. Council*, Case 114/81, [1982] ECR 3189.

instrument will be prejudiced to such an extent that the enacting institution would probably not have adopted it at all if it had known that the provision in question was illegal. *Transocean Marine Paint Association v. Commission*[90] is a good example of the problems which can arise where the application is for the annulment of only part of a decision. The applicant in this case had applied to the Commission for exemption from the provisions of Article 81 [85] EC and had been granted it subject to certain conditions, one of which was that the Commission had to be informed of any financial links between the members of the association and other firms. The association maintained that this condition was unjustifiable and brought proceedings to have it annulled. The Court decided that it should be annulled because the Commission had not given the association advance warning that it had the condition in mind. The association was thus precluded from putting its case to the Commission before the decision was made. The Court held that this infringed the rules of natural justice.

The difficulty then confronting the Court was that, if it merely annulled the condition, the association might be in too favourable a position: even the latter was prepared to concede that the Commission was entitled to be given *some* information. The solution put forward by Advocate General Warner was to interpret Article 233 [176] EC as allowing the Court to refer the matter back to the enacting authority. He, therefore, proposed that the condition should be annulled and referred back to the Commission, which could then reconsider the matter and possibly replace it with a less onerous requirement. This suggestion was followed by the Court.

### REJECTION OF APPLICATION

Finally, it should be mentioned that the *rejection* of an application to annul does not definitively establish the validity of the measure; in particular, it does not preclude a new application by another party based on different grounds of invalidity.[91]

## INDIRECT CHALLENGE

In theory, a declaration of invalidity resulting from an indirect challenge is applicable only to the case in question; in practice, however, its effects are much wider than this.[92] To this extent, it has been assimilated to an annulment. In addition, the Court has

[90] Case 17/74, [1974] ECR 1063; discussed in Chap. 5.

[91] In *Assider v. High Authority*, Case 3/54, [1955] ECR 63, the application was directed against various measures, all of which had been the subject of a previous application in which some had been annulled and others not. As regards the measures that had not been annulled, the Court merely referred to the previous judgment and stated that, as no new grounds of invalidity had been put forward, the application would be dismissed. It is not entirely clear whether the previous judgment operated as *res judicata*, in the sense that it precluded a reconsideration of the arguments previously advanced, or whether it would be open to the applicant in the new proceedings to attempt to make the Court change its mind, perhaps by bringing new evidence. The fact that the application was held *admissible* suggests that the latter alternative may be correct. There is, however, no doubt that a fresh application may be made on *different* grounds.

[92] See Chap. 14.

applied Articles 231 [174] and 233 [176] by analogy to declarations of invalidity under Article 234 [177], thus narrowing the differences between the two remedies even more.

In the *Quellmehl* and *Gritz* cases,[93] the Council had given a subsidy both to starch producers and to the producers of two competing products, quellmehl and gritz. It subsequently passed a regulation withdrawing the subsidy from quellmehl and gritz, but not from starch. The quellmehl and gritz producers brought proceedings in the national courts and a reference was made to the European Court, which held that it was contrary to the principle of equality to subsidize the one and not the other. It did not, however, hold the regulation invalid (which would have allowed the quellmehl and gritz producers to succeed in their claim for payment of the subsidies). Instead, the Court ruled that the Council had to pass a new regulation either restoring the subsidy to the quellmehl and gritz producers or withdrawing it from the starch producers. It subsequently justified this ruling on the basis of Article 233 [176].[94]

In the *Maize* cases,[95] the Commission had passed a regulation applying a system for calculating monetary compensatory amounts for maize products. In proceedings resulting from a reference under Article 234 [177] EC, the European Court held the regulation invalid. However, it applied the second paragraph of Article 231 [174] by analogy to enable it to hold that its ruling would not affect the payment of monetary compensatory amounts on transactions prior to its judgment. In effect, this meant that the regulation was annulled prospectively but not retrospectively.[96]

## FURTHER READING

AUBY, 'The Abuse of Power in French Administrative Law' (1970) 18 Am. Jo. Comp. L. 549.

WAELBROECK, 'Examen de Jurisprudence 1955 à 1971' [1971] Revue Critique de Jurisprudence Belge 513 at 540–6.

RIGAUX, 'Pouvoir d'appréciation de la Cour de Justice des Communautés Européennes à l'égard des faits', in *Miscellanea Ganshof van der Meersch* (1972), vol. II, 365.

BEBR, 'Preliminary Rulings of the Court of Justice: Their Authority and Temporal Effect' (1981) 18 CMLRev. 475.

BROWN, 'Agrimonetary Byzantinism and Prospective Overruling' (1981) 18 CMLRev. 509.

HARDING, 'The Impact of Article 177 of the EEC Treaty on the Review of Community Action' (1981) 1 YEL 93.

[93] *Ruckdeschel*, Cases 117/76, 16/77, [1977] ECR 1753; *Moulins de Pont-à-Mousson*, Cases 124/76, 20/77, [1977] ECR 1795.

[94] See the *Maize* cases (below).

[95] *Providence Agricole v. ONIC*, Case 4/79, [1980] ECR 2823 (paras 42–6 of the judgment); *Maïseries de Beauce v. ONIC*, Case 109/79, [1980] ECR 2883 (paras 42–6 of the judgment); *Roquette v. French Customs*, Case 145/79, [1980] ECR 2917 (paras 50–5 of the judgment).

[96] For the reaction to this in the French courts, see Chap. 8.

WAELBROECK, 'May the Court Limit the Retrospective Operation of its Judgments?' (1981) 1 YEL 115.

KPE LASOK, 'Judicial Review of Issues of Fact in Competition Cases' [1983] *European Competition Law Review* 85.

TOTH, 'The Authority of Judgments of the European Court of Justice: Binding Force and Legal Effects' (1984) 4 YEL 1.

PAUL CRAIG, *EU Administrative Law* (2006).

TAKIS TRIDIMAS, *The General Principles of EC Law*, 2nd edn (2006).

# 16

# COMMUNITY OBLIGATIONS

This chapter is concerned with the liability of the Community in contract, for restitution, and in tort.

## CONTRACT

The two main questions regarding contracts entered into by the Community are the jurisdiction of the European Court and the law to be applied.

### JURISDICTION OF THE EUROPEAN COURT

The jurisdiction of the European Court (cases are heard by the Court of First Instance, with a right of appeal on points of law to the European Court) with regard to Community contracts is laid down by Article 238 [181] EC:[1]

> The Court of Justice shall have jurisdiction to give judgment pursuant to any arbitration clause contained in a contract concluded by or on behalf of the Community, whether that contract be governed by public or private law.

It will be seen that this provision uses the phrase 'arbitration clause', thus suggesting that the European Court has jurisdiction only as an arbitrator. The significance of this is that in many countries the activities of arbitrators are subject to the supervision of the courts. There cannot, of course, be any question of this with regard to the European Court; so it would have been better if the Treaty had not used the terminology of arbitration. A preferable phrase would have been 'jurisdiction clause', which is used in private international law to describe a provision in a contract conferring jurisdiction on the courts of a particular country.[2]

It should also be noted that the provision does not state that the 'arbitration clause' must refer only to disputes arising out of the contract in which it is contained. A common clause would be of this type (for example, 'all disputes arising out of this contract shall be heard by the Court of Justice of the European Communities') but it may also be

[1] Art. 153 Euratom contains an identical provision; everything in the text regarding the EC applies equally to Euratom.

[2] Alternative terms are 'choice-of-court' clause and 'forum-selection' clause.

possible for the parties to enter into a contract conferring jurisdiction on the European Court to hear disputes arising out of *another* contract.

If the European Court does not have jurisdiction by virtue of such a clause, the national courts will be entitled to hear the case.[3] This follows from Articles 240 [183] EC and 155 Euratom.[4]

In determining whether it has jurisdiction under such a clause, the Court applies Community law alone: rules of national law on the validity of jurisdiction clauses cannot be taken into account.[5]

There is no indication in the Treaty as to the form which the clause should take, though the requirement in Article 38(6) of the Rules of Procedure of the European Court[6] that a copy of the clause must be submitted with the application implies that it should be in writing.[7] One solution would be for the Court to apply the rules laid down in Article 23 of Regulation 44/2001 on jurisdiction and the recognition and enforcement of judgments in civil and commercial matters.[8] This provides that an agreement conferring jurisdiction on the courts of a Member State must be 'either (a) in writing or evidenced in writing; or, (b) in a form which accords with practices which the parties have established between themselves; or (c) in international trade or commerce, in a form which accords with a usage of which the parties are or ought to have been aware and which in such trade or commerce is widely known to, and regularly observed by, parties to contracts of the type involved in the particular trade or commerce concerned'. These rules are binding only on national courts but the European Court might look to them as a source of inspiration. This is especially appropriate since the European Court has jurisdiction to interpret them on a reference from a national court for a preliminary ruling.

In *Commission v. Zoubek*,[9] the Court referred to the Brussels Convention, the forerunner of Regulation 44/2001, though for a different purpose. In that case the Commission brought proceedings against a journalist under a contract it had concluded with him. The Court had jurisdiction to hear this claim since the contract contained an 'arbitration clause'. The Commission claimed that Zoubek had not performed his side of the contract: it asked for a declaration that the contract had been terminated and for an order that Zoubek should return an advance payment that had been made to him under the contract. Zoubek replied by bringing a counterclaim: he said that, under a separate contract with the Commission, it had been agreed that he could discharge his obligation to repay the money by supplying the Commission with certain publications.

Could the Court hear this counterclaim, in view of the fact that Zoubek did not claim that the separate contract contained an 'arbitration clause' conferring jurisdiction on

[3] *Flemmer*, Cases C-80–82/99, [2001] ECR I-7211.

[4] These provisions state that national courts are entitled to hear actions against the Community except where the European Court has jurisdiction.

[5] *Commission v. Feilhauer*, Case C-209/90, [1992] ECR I-2613.

[6] See also Art. 44(5a) of the Rules of Procedure of the Court of First Instance.

[7] The Rules are published in OJ 2001 C34. For an updated version, see the Court's website, http://www.curia.eu.int/en.

[8] OJ 2000 L12/1. This replaces the Brussels Convention, except in the case of Denmark.

[9] Case 426/85, [1986] ECR 4057.

the Court?[10] In answering this question, the Court referred to Article 6(3) of the Brussels Convention, which provides that a national court with jurisdiction over one claim may also hear a counterclaim arising 'from the same contract or facts on which the original claim was based'. Although the Court did not purport to apply this provision directly, it reached the same conclusion: it held that it could consider a counterclaim only if it was 'directly connected' with the contract containing the 'arbitration clause'. On the facts of the case, it held that this requirement was met; it therefore had jurisdiction to hear the counterclaim.[11]

## CHOICE OF LAW

What law will be applied to a Community contract? The first paragraph of Article 288 [215] EC and of Article 188 Euratom purports to deal with this problem but does so in an unsatisfactory way. It reads: 'The contractual liability of the Community shall be governed by the law applicable to the contract in question.' In so far as it is more than a tautology, this means only that the liability of the Community is governed by the same law as governs the contract as a whole. This is, of course, what one would have assumed to be the case anyway. The provision does, however, have some value – though of a purely negative kind – in that it makes clear that the Community claims no special privileges or immunities.[12]

An inference may, perhaps, be drawn from what the first paragraph of Article 288 [215] does *not* say: it does not expressly empower the European Court to build up a Community law of contract. This omission is noteworthy in that the second paragraph of Article 288 [215], which deals with non-contractual liability, envisages the creation of a Community law of tort. It states that the non-contractual liability of the Community is to be governed by 'the general principles common to the laws of the Member States'. The contrast between these two paragraphs of Article 288 [215] indicates, therefore, that contractual liability is not in principle governed by Community law.

In the *Flemmer* case,[13] the European Court had to decide the law applicable to a contract concluded between a farmer, on the one hand, and the Council and Commission, on the other hand. The contract, which had been made through the agency of the relevant national authority, was to settle claims in tort arising out of the second *Mulder* case.[14] It contained no forum-selection clause or choice-of-law clause. Proceedings were brought before the German courts, which made a reference to the European Court. The European Court held that national law applied (it did not specify

[10] The Court held that this question had to be decided by Community law, even though the original contract was governed by Belgian law (para. 10 of the judgment). This was obviously correct, since questions of jurisdiction always depend on Community law.

[11] In the end, it held that the counterclaim had not been established. It therefore dismissed the counterclaim and gave judgment for the Commission on the original claim.

[12] See PJ Verdam, 'De privaatrechtelijke contractuele aansprakelijkheid der EEG' in *Volkenrechtelijke opstellen aan Prof. Dr Gesina H. J. van der Molen* (International Law Essays in Honour of Gesina HJ van der Molen), p. 169 at pp. 174–5.

[13] Cases C-80–82/99, [2001] ECR I-7211.

[14] *Mulder v. Commission and Council*, Cases C-104/89, 37/90, [1992] ECR I-3061 (discussed below).

which national law, but it was presumably German law) provided it did not prejudice the 'scope and effectiveness' of Community law.[15] One can conclude from this that national law will normally apply to Community contracts, but it will be subject to any overriding rule of Community law and to what may perhaps be called Community public policy.

The choice of the appropriate system of national law must be determined by the rules of private international law. There are in general no Community rules of conflict of laws; however, a subsidiary convention, the Convention on the Law Applicable to Contractual Obligations (1980), lays down uniform rules for choice of law in contracts in cases before national courts.[16] In proceedings before the European Court, it could be applied by analogy.

In practice the Commission normally insists on the insertion of a choice-of-law clause in its contracts. The validity and effect of such a clause has been disputed in only one case – on the ground that the contract was more closely connected with the law of another country and contained express references to the law of that country – but the Court upheld it, saying that an express choice of law prevails over all other considerations.[17]

When the European Court applies the law of a Member State, it decides questions of law on the basis of its own knowledge, after hearing argument, even if no judge from the country in question is sitting on the case.[18] It does not require expert evidence, as would an English court if it had to apply foreign law.[19]

Different principles apply in the case of contracts of employment of Community officials.[20] In two early cases the European Court classified these as public law contracts. In the first of these cases, *Kergall v. Common Assembly*,[21] the applicant was a senior administrative official working for the Common Assembly (European Parliament). The Court held that his contract of employment was a public law contract since he was required to perform 'public law functions' and his contract referred to the internal regulations of the Common Assembly. In *Von Lachmüller v. Commission*,[22] the applicants worked in the translation service of the Commission. After the Court had established that the Commission was a public authority (public law corporation), it continued:[23]

> Moreover, those contracts were concluded to enable the Language Service of the Commission to function properly. The work of that service, which is responsible for ensuring that the contents of the acts of the Commission shall be identical in the four official languages of the Community, constitutes an important element in the procedure

[15] Para. 2 of the Ruling.

[16] OJ 1980, C266. It is planned to replace this with a regulation.

[17] *Commission v. CO.DE.MI*, Case 318/81, [1985] ECR 3693 (see para. 21 of the judgment). This is in accordance with the Contractual Obligations Convention, though the Court made no reference to the Convention.

[18] See, e.g., *Commission v. CO.DE.MI* (above) and *Pellegrini v. Commission*, Case 23/76, [1976] ECR 1807 (decided under Art. 188(1) Euratom).

[19] On possible limits to the application of national law, see *Commission v. Tordeur*, Case 232/84, [1985] ECR 3223.

[20] Such cases are rare because Community officials do not normally hold office on a contractual basis.

[21] Case 1/55, [1955] ECR 151.

[22] Cases 43, 45, 48/59, [1960] ECR 463.

[23] At 473.

> which has as its purpose the formulation in each language of those acts; thus that service is of the same public nature as the Commission itself.
>
> Therefore the contracts at issue come under public law and are subject to the general rules of administrative law.

It appears from these extracts that it does not necessarily follow that all contracts of employment with Community institutions will automatically be classified as public law contracts. In both these judgments the Court went to some pains to establish that the work performed by the applicants was of a governmental nature. It might be legitimate to conclude that where this is not the case the contract will be governed by private law.[24] The consequence in these cases of the Court's characterization of the contract as public was that it was governed by administrative law. There was no suggestion that national administrative law was to be applied; so one must conclude that where public law is applicable, it will be *Community* public law. This was not expressly stated but, since the Court decided the cases on the basis of legal rules that were not stated to be those of any national system, one can reach no other conclusion. If this is correct, it means that the classification of a contract as public not only affects the kind of law applicable (public rather than private) but also the legal system – Community, rather than national, law.

## RESTITUTION

Most Western legal systems recognize a form of liability based on the principle of unjust enrichment. According to this principle, if the plaintiff can show that the defendant was unjustly enriched at his expense, the defendant is liable to make restitution to the extent that he has been enriched. This principle of liability is distinct from both contract and tort. In the past, some English authorities have based it on a fictitious promise to make restitution (hence the term 'quasi-contract'); but since the promise *is* fictitious, it cannot realistically be regarded as a form of contractual liability. It differs from tortious liability in two respects. First of all, the basis of a tort is usually thought to be a wrongful act – though liability without fault might seem an exception to this – and the liability to make restitution is independent of any wrongful act. Secondly, in tort the measure of liability is, as a basic rule, the extent of the loss suffered by the plaintiff; in unjust enrichment it is the extent to which the defendant was enriched.

Does this form of liability apply to the Community? This is obviously a matter of some practical importance, since a common situation in which liability might arise is where money is paid on the mistaken assumption that it is owed. It might happen that a person might pay a sum of money to a Community institution, thinking that he was legally obliged to pay it, and it might turn out later that there was no such obligation. Is the Community obliged to return it?

24 *Cf. Porta v. Commission*, Case 109/81, [1982] ECR 2469.

## SUBSTANTIVE LAW

There is no provision in the Treaties expressly dealing with restitution, but since this species of liability is generally recognized in the law of the Member States, it would be reasonable to expect that it would be accepted as one of the general principles of law applied by the European Court. This is, in fact, the case and there have been a number of decisions in which the European Court has given effect to the doctrine. Most of these are staff cases and a typical example is *Wollast v. EEC*,[25] in which a Community employee was illegally dismissed from her job. The Court annulled her dismissal with the result that she was entitled to receive pay for the period since the dismissal. She had not, however, done any work during this period and she had thus been able to avoid certain expenses that she would otherwise have incurred; for example, she had not had to employ domestic help for her three young children. The Court held that she had been unjustly enriched at the expense of the Community and ordered that a deduction of 15 per cent be made from her salary for the period in question.

A different situation arose in *Mannesmann v. High Authority*,[26] where a scrap iron subsidy had been wrongly paid and the Commission tried to recover it by taking a decision requiring Mannesmann, the user of the scrap, to refund it. Mannesmann brought proceedings under Article 33 ECSC to quash the decision. The European Court accepted that the Commission had the power to recover the money on the basis of restitution; nevertheless, it quashed the decision because the subsidy had been paid not to Mannesmann, but to his supplier.

## JURISDICTION

The cases in which the doctrine has been applied so far have all been ones in which the Court has had jurisdiction on some ground not specifically related to restitution: in the staff cases it was Article 236 [179] EC which gives the Court jurisdiction in disputes between the Community and its servants; in *Mannesmann* the issue arose incidentally in the course of review proceedings. The case where a private citizen has a claim against the Community for restitution is not covered by either of these provisions and the question arises whether there is any general ground of jurisdiction applicable to actions for restitution against the Community.

The only possibility under the EC Treaty is Article 235 [178]. This gives jurisdiction in disputes relating to 'compensation for damage' under Article 288 [215], second paragraph. The latter provision talks of non-contractual liability, rather than tortious liability, and might therefore be thought to cover restitution as well as tort. However, Article 235 [178] itself is concerned only with compensation for damage and Article 288 [215], second paragraph, requires the Community to 'make good any damage caused' by its institutions. This suggests that the basis of the liability covered by the

[25] Case 18/63, [1964] ECR 85. See also *Degreef v. Commission*, Case 80/63, [1964] ECR 391 and *Willame v. Commission*, Case 110/63, [1965] ECR 649. In *Danvin v. Commission*, Case 26/67, [1968] ECR 315, a Community servant claimed that the Community had been unjustly enriched at his expense but was unable to establish that he had suffered any loss.

[26] Cases 4–13/59, [1960] ECR 113.

provisions is the loss suffered by the applicant, rather than the enrichment of the defendant.

There is one possible way round these difficulties. One could argue as follows: it is true that the duty to make restitution is not based on fault and that the measure of liability is not the extent of the applicant's loss but the extent of the defendant's enrichment; but the failure of the defendant to make voluntary restitution once the true situation becomes known could be regarded as a fault and the loss suffered by the applicant as a result would be the amount which the defendant should have paid, that is the amount by which he was enriched.

It must be admitted that this argument is a strained one, and it seems probable that the authors of the Treaty did not have restitution in mind when they drafted these provisions.[27] It is nevertheless possible that the European Court may decide, for policy reasons, that it would be desirable for it to have jurisdiction to hear actions for restitution against the Community and if this were so it might consider that a wide interpretation of these provisions was the best way of achieving this.[28]

If the non-contractual liability provisions are eventually held not to cover restitution, there is another way in which an applicant might be able to bring his case before the European Court. This is by means of an indirect route: he would make a request to the Community institution in question to repay the money, and if it refused he would bring proceedings under Article 230 [173] EC to ask the Court to quash the decision rejecting his request. The ground of invalidity put forward would be the infringement of a rule of law relating to the application of the Treaty, which covers the infringement of general principles of law,[29] including the principle of unjust enrichment. If the Community institution failed to make a decision in response to the request for a refund, proceedings for a remedy for failure to act could be brought. Either way, the applicant could require the Court to consider whether his claim was well founded.[30] If he succeeded, the defendant institution would be 'required to take the necessary measures to comply with the judgment'.[31] This would include the payment of the sum.

The only objection that could be raised against this procedure is that a decision by a Community institution granting, or refusing to grant, repayment of a sum of money by which the Community was unjustly enriched might not be regarded as a reviewable act. The concept of a reviewable act was considered above,[32] and it will be remembered that the basic rule is that an act is not reviewable unless it has legal effects; in other words, it must cause some change in the legal rights and duties (using these terms in a wide sense)

[27] It is interesting to note that it was stated by counsel for the Commission in argument in *Roquette v. Commission*, Case 26/74, [1976] ECR 677 at 681, that quasi-contract was 'foreign to the action for compensation for damage under Art. 288 [215] of the EEC Treaty'.

[28] *Cf.* the decision in *Kalfelis v. Schröder*, Case 189/87, [1988] ECR 5565, where the Court ruled that the words 'matters relating to a tort, delict or quasi-delict' in Art. 5(3) of the Brussels Convention cover all forms of liability other than contract (para. 2(a) of the Ruling). This presumably includes unjust enrichment.

[29] See Chap. 15 above.

[30] This procedure was used by the applicant in *Haegeman v. Commission*, Case 96/71, [1972] ECR 1005, but the claim was held inadmissible on other grounds. For a discussion of the case, see below.

[31] Art. 233 [176] EC. [32] See Chap. 11.

of the applicant. It could be argued that, in the situation under consideration, a decision by the Community institution would not have legal effects since, if the applicant's claim were justified, he would be legally entitled to be paid anyway: a negative decision could not take away his right and a positive decision could not give him a greater right.

It is doubtful whether this argument is justified. From a practical point of view, a decision in the applicant's favour would be of the greatest value to him; even from a theoretical viewpoint it is not certain that his legal position would be unaltered, since a positive decision could be regarded as creating a new legal right and this could have consequences as regards the remedies open to him, including the time-limit for bringing proceedings. Moreover, the European Court has shown itself willing in the past to give more weight to practical considerations than theory in deciding what constitutes a reviewable act.

In conclusion, it should be mentioned that if it finally turns out that the European Court has no jurisdiction to hear claims for restitution, the way would then be open for proceedings against the Community in the national courts.[33]

## TORT

Community tort liability is dealt with in Articles 235 [178] and 288 [215], second paragraph, EC.[34] Article 235 [178] EC merely states that the European Court will have jurisdiction to decide disputes relating to compensation for damage as provided for in the second paragraph of Article 288 [215]. The latter reads as follows:

> In the case of non-contractual liability, the Community shall, in accordance with the general principles common to the laws of the Member States, make good any damage caused by its institutions or by its servants in the performance of their duties.

This contains the following elements. First, there must be an act or omission on the part of the Community; secondly, the applicant must have suffered damage; and thirdly, the act or omission must have caused the damage. The ECSC Treaty contained, in addition, the requirement of fault. The EC Treaty makes no mention of this. It does, however, provide that Community liability will arise in accordance with the general principles common to the laws of the Member States. These principles do, of course, depend to a large extent on fault; but liability without fault is not unknown.

Before discussing these elements in detail, it is worth considering some preliminary matters. First of all, it should be noted that there is no limitation on the persons who may sue. The restrictive provisions of judicial review are absent. Nor does the short time-limit within which review proceedings must be brought apply here. The period of limitation in tort actions is five years.[35]

[33] See Arts 240 [183] EC and 155 Euratom.

[34] Arts 151 and 188, second para., Euratom are the same as Arts 235 [178] and 288 [215], second para., EC.

[35] Prior to the Treaty of Nice, the relevant provisions were Art. 43 of the Statute of the Court of Justice of the EC and Art. 44 of the Statute of Euratom. Under the Treaty of Nice, the relevant provision is Art. 46 of the Statute. The last sentence of these provisions suggests that the period may be reduced if an application is made

The second question concerns the person against whom the action should be brought. Article 288 [215], second paragraph, EC says that 'the Community' must make good the damage. However, the Community can act only through its institutions. Which institution should represent the Community before the Court? In the case of *Werhahn v. Council and Commission*[36] it was argued (by the Commission) that the Commission should always fulfil this role. This contention was based on Article 282 [211] EC which provides that, in legal proceedings *in national courts*, the Community will be represented by the Commission. The Commission argued that this provision should be applied by analogy to proceedings in the European Court; but this was rejected by the Court, which held:[37]

> It is in the interests of a good administration of justice that where Community liability is involved by reason of the act of one of its institutions, it should be represented before the Court by the institution or institutions against which the matter giving rise to liability is alleged.

The case itself concerned a regulation enacted by the Council on the proposal of the Commission. Since both these institutions were responsible for the regulation which was the alleged wrongful act, the applicant had brought the action against both of them. The Court held that this was quite correct.

One can conclude from this that the action must be brought against the Community as represented by the institution which is responsible for the act or omission which forms the basis of the proceedings. Where there is joint responsibility, both institutions concerned must be named as defendants. If, therefore, the Council can adopt a legal act only on the proposal of the Commission (which is the normal situation), both are responsible.

In proceedings under Article 288 [215], second paragraph, the Court must give judgment in accordance with the 'general principles common to the laws of the Member States'. Since the Community is a public authority, it is to the law of *public* tort liability in the Member States that we must look.[38] In most Member States (including Britain) the liability of public authorities in tort is governed, in principle, by the same law as that of private individuals. But there are always a number of special rules which apply to

to the relevant institution of the Community, but this is not the case: the European Court held in *Kampffmeyer v. Commission*, Cases 5, 7, 13–24/66, [1967] ECR 245 at 259–60, that the period can never be less than five years. But an application to the institution can interrupt the running of time provided it is followed by the bringing of proceedings under Art. 230 [173]; the period is also interrupted by the institution of proceedings before the Court. See further *Giordano v. Commission*, Case 11/72, [1973] ECR 417. The expiry of the limitation period is not a bar to proceedings where the applicant only belatedly became aware of the event giving rise to the damage he suffered and did not have a reasonable time to commence proceedings before the limitation period expired: *Adams v. Commission*, Case 145/83, [1985] ECR 3539 (paras 48–51 of the judgment). See also *Birra Wührer v. Council and Commission*, Cases 256, 257, 265, 267/80, 5/81, [1982] ECR 85, which held that time cannot start to run before the damage has occurred, even if the defendant's action took place some time previously. If the defendant does not plead that the claim is time-barred, the Court cannot raise the issue of its own motion: *Roquette v. Commission*, Case 20/88, [1989] ECR 1553 (paras 11–13 of the judgment).

[36] Cases 63–9/72, [1973] ECR 1229.

[37] At para. 7 of the judgment.

[38] See *per* Advocate General Roemer in *Plaumann v. Commission*, Case 25/62, [1963] ECR 95 at 116–17, and *per* Advocate General Gand in *Kampffmeyer v. Commission*, Cases 5, 7, 13–24/66, [1967] ECR 245 at 352.

public authorities so that even in these countries there are significant differences between the law applied in the public and the private spheres. In France, on the other hand, there is a completely separate system of public (administrative) tort law.

It is important to note that the Treaty refers to 'general principles', not 'rules', of law. It is, in fact, widely recognized that the Court is not obliged to look for the lowest common denominator and find the Community liable only where liability would exist under the legal system of each of the Member States.[39] Such a solution would stunt the growth of Community law. What is required is that the Court should look to the very general principles which apply in all the Member States – such as causation, damage, fault, and risk – and build up from these principles a system of law suited to the needs of the Community. The particular rules applied at the Community level need not necessarily be found in a majority of national systems and, where the special character of the Community so requires, it may even be permissible to apply rules not found in any national system. This means that the national systems are no more than a starting point for the judges of the European Court. They must, of course, respect the general legal tradition common to the Member States, but they are not bound to adopt specific solutions. This gives the Court considerable scope for a creative approach.[40]

## ACTS IMPUTABLE TO THE COMMUNITY

The first basic requisite of Community liability in tort is that there should be an act imputable to the Community. The concept of an act in this context is very wide. It includes a physical act (e.g., driving a motor car), an act intended to have legal effects (e.g., a regulation), a verbal statement, and anything else that is capable of causing harm to others. It also includes a failure to act (omission), provided there was a duty to act. The special problems which arise in connection with acts intended to have legal effects are considered in a later section of this chapter.

Under the second paragraph of Article 288 [215] EC, an act is imputable to the Community either if it is an act of an institution of the Community ('damage caused by its institutions') or if it is an act of a servant of the Community and is performed in the course of his duties ('damage caused . . . by its servants in the performance of their duties').

The Treaties therefore recognize two categories of act for which the Community is responsible: acts performed by the Community itself (through its institutions) and acts performed by Community servants. Since Community institutions act through their servants (officials), it will be seen that there is a considerable overlap between these two categories. To an English lawyer, indeed, it might seem that the first category is entirely covered by the second and is therefore otiose. This is not entirely true, however, since there are certain acts which are more properly described as acts of the institution itself

[39] See *per* Advocate General Roemer in *Zuckerfabrik Schöppenstedt v. Council*, Case 5/71, [1971] ECR 975 at 989, and *per* Advocate General Gand in *Sayag v. Leduc*, Case 9/69, [1969] ECR 329 at 340.

[40] For a general discussion, see Usher, 'The Influence of National Concepts on Decisions of the European Court' (1976) 1 ELRev. 359.

rather than of its officials. The best example consists of formal (official) acts, that is, those performed by the official organ of the institution, such as decisions of the Commission or Council, or resolutions of the Parliament. The category would also include acts performed jointly by a number of officials over a period of time, for example monitoring of market conditions or supervision of subordinate authorities. The importance of the recognition by the Treaties of acts of the institutions themselves as a separate category is that an applicant in an action for damages does not have to name the official responsible; nor does it matter if no official was responsible. This is particularly important in the case of a failure to act: it is enough to show that there was a duty on the institution to act; it need not be shown that any individual official was responsible.

The term 'institutions' in the second paragraph of Article 288 [215] has a special meaning. It will be remembered that Article 7 [4] EC lists five bodies that qualify as institutions of the Community: the European Parliament, the Council, the Commission, the European Court, and the Court of Auditors. These all constitute 'institutions' for the purpose of Article 288 [215]. The third paragraph of Article 288 [215] provides that the ECB and its staff are also covered.[41] The ECB is therefore treated for this purpose as if it were an institution. In addition, the European Court held in *SGEEM v. European Investment Bank*,[42] that the term 'institutions' in Article 288 [215] also covers Community organs such as the European Investment Bank.[43] It is not clear what other bodies would constitute Community organs for this purpose, but it seems that any body established by the Treaty[44] and authorized to act in the name of the Community would be covered.[45]

In order to prove that an act of an official is imputable to the Community, it must be shown that the act was performed in the course of his duties. This concept will be familiar enough to English lawyers.[46] In *Sayag v. Leduc*[47] the European Court had to consider what is meant by an act performed in the course of an official's duties. Mr Sayag was an engineer employed by Euratom, who was instructed to take Mr Leduc and another person, who were both representatives of private undertakings, on a visit to the installations at Mol in Belgium. He decided to drive them there in his private car and was given a travel order for this purpose. (The significance of the travel order was that it meant that his expenses would be paid by the Community.) While he was driving them, he was involved in a traffic accident in which he and his passengers were injured. The passengers brought an action for damages in the Belgian courts against Sayag, but it was argued that he was acting in the performance of his duties when driving the car and that this meant that the action should have been brought against the Community instead.[48] The Belgian *Cour de Cassation* ordered that a preliminary reference be made to the European Court

[41] This applies only under the EC Treaty: there is no similar provision under the Euratom Treaty.

[42] Case C-370/89, [1992] ECR I-6211.

[43] *Ibid.*, para. 16 of the judgment.

[44] The EIB was established by Art. 129 EEC, now replaced by Art. 266 [198d] EC. Its statute is a Protocol annexed to the EC Treaty.

[45] See para. 15 of the judgment in the *SGEEM* case (above).

[46] In its original form, Article 40 ECSC was more restrictive. It provided for an action *against the official* in the European Court in those cases where he had caused damage by a personal wrong in the performance of his duties. Community liability existed only where the injured person was unable to obtain redress from the servant. Art. 40 ECSC was changed to its present form by Art. 26 of the Merger Treaty. This brought it into line with the EC Treaty.

[47] Case 9/69, [1969] ECR 329.

[48] This argument assumes that Community liability excludes individual liability, though this is by no means certain: see below.

to determine what is meant by the phrase 'in the performance of their duties' in the second paragraph of Article 188 Euratom (equivalent to Article 288 [215] EC).

The Court, following Advocate General Gand, gave a restrictive interpretation to the phrase. It ruled:[49]

> By referring at one and the same time to damage caused by the institutions and to that caused by the servants of the Community, Article 188 indicates that the Community is only liable for those acts of its servants which, by virtue of an internal and direct relationship, are the necessary extension of the tasks entrusted to the institutions.
>
> In the light of the special nature of this legal system, it would not therefore be lawful to extend it to categories of acts other than those referred to above.
>
> A servant's use of his private car for transport during the performance of his duties does not satisfy the conditions set out above.
>
> A reference to a servant's private car in a travel order does not bring the driving of such car within the performance of his duties, but is basically intended to enable any necessary reimbursement of the travel expenses involved in the use of this means of transport to be made in accordance with the standards laid down for this purpose.
>
> Only in the case of *force majeure* or in exceptional circumstances of such overriding importance that without the servant's using private means of transport the Community would have been unable to carry out the tasks entrusted to it, could such use be considered to form part of the servant's performance of his duties, within the meaning of the second paragraph of Article 188 of the Treaty.
>
> It follows from the above that the driving of a private car by a servant cannot in principle constitute the performance of his duties within the meaning of the second paragraph of Article 188 of the EAEC Treaty.

The result of this is that the liability of the Community for the acts of its servants is narrower than that of most Member States for the acts of their servants.[50] It is hard to see any justification for this.

Where the Community is not liable it is, of course, possible to sue the servant in his personal capacity. Such proceedings must be brought in the national courts and are governed by national law. Community officials enjoy immunity from suit in national courts in respect of 'acts performed in their official capacity',[51] but it is hard to see how this can apply where the Community is not itself liable.[52]

[49] [1969] ECR at 335–6.

[50] See the comparative survey made by Advocate General Gand, *ibid.* at 340–1, where it is shown that in most of the original six Member States liability for the acts of public servants is wide. The only exception appears to be Germany. In France there is authority relevant to the actual point at issue: it has been held that the state can be liable as a result of an accident caused by an official driving his private car on official business: *Bourrée, Conseil d'Etat*, 26 July 1944, Rec. Lebon, 217.

[51] Protocol on the Privileges and Immunities of the European Communities, Art. 12(a). It is provided in Art. 18 that the immunity must be waived by the Community whenever such waiver is not contrary to the interests of the Community.

[52] See *per* Advocate General Gand in an earlier case between the same parties, *Sayag v. Leduc*, Case 5/68, [1968] ECR 395 at 408. In this case the Court held that Sayag was not entitled to immunity, but it made clear (in the last paragraph of its judgment) that the immunity of the servant and the liability of the Community are separate questions. It is therefore possible, though unlikely, that in some cases they may both be liable.

Another problem concerns the extent to which the Community will be liable for the torts of other bodies to which it delegates powers. The Treaties say nothing about the liability of the Community for the acts of its agents. It will be remembered, however, that in the field of judicial review, the Court held, in *SNUPAT v. High Authority*,[53] that, where the Community set up a subordinate body and delegated powers to it, the acts of that body could be regarded as acts of the delegating institution for the purpose of review. Might not a similar rule apply in the case of tort liability?

In *SNUPAT v. High Authority*, the Commission had set up two subordinate bodies, the *Office commun des consommateurs de ferrailles* (OCCF) and the *Caisse de péréquation de ferrailles importés* (CPFI), which were both incorporated under Belgian law, to administer an equalization scheme for ferrous scrap. Under this scheme, imported scrap was subsidized and the cost was met by a levy on all scrap users. The CPFI had demanded that SNUPAT pay a certain sum of money under the levy and SNUPAT brought an action in the European Court under Article 33 ECSC to annul the demand. The Court ruled that decisions of the CPFI should be imputed to the Commission for the purpose of the admissibility of the action.

A later case, *Worms v. High Authority*,[54] raised the question of liability in tort. Mr Worms was a Dutch scrap dealer who claimed that he had suffered damage because the OCCF had refused to do business with him. He sued the Commission under Article 40 ECSC, and the Court had to decide whether the Community could be liable for the acts of the OCCF. In its judgment the Court pointed out that the CPFI and the OCCF had different functions: the former had executive functions concerning the equalization scheme while the latter's functions were normally of a commercial nature and were concerned with the purchase of scrap on the open market. The Court then stated:[55]

> When carrying on its strictly commercial activities, the OCCF, a Belgian company under private law, is governed by national law. It is only in cases where the OCCF's acts concern the functioning of the equalization scheme, and on that account have the character of a public duty, that they can be considered as directly giving rise to the liability of the High Authority.

The Court went on to hold that the buying of scrap was an activity of a purely commercial nature and any damage caused by the OCCF's refusal to do business with a particular dealer was not the responsibility of the Commission. Worms would have to sue the OCCF directly in the national courts.

From this it may be concluded that, where a Community institution delegates governmental powers to some other body, the acts of that body in the exercise of those powers may be imputed to the Community; but where such a body carries out functions which are not of a governmental nature, its acts will not be imputable to the Community. This distinction between governmental and non-governmental functions appears to be akin to that between public law and private law activities. Buying goods in

This would be the case only if it is possible for a Community official to be acting in the performance of his duties (the test for Community liability) without at the same time acting in his official capacity (the test for immunity).

[53] Cases 32–3/58, [1959] ECR 127. See Chap. 11.

[54] Case 18/60, [1962] ECR 195.

[55] *Ibid.* at 204.

the open market is a commercial (private law) activity; but collecting levies is a public law function and acts performed in this field would be imputable to the Community.

*Worms v. High Authority* appears to establish, therefore, that there are in fact *three* categories of acts which may be imputed to the Community: acts of Community institutions; acts of Community servants in the performance of their duties; and acts of other bodies performed in carrying out governmental (public) functions delegated to them by a Community institution.[56]

## DAMAGE AND CAUSATION

Once the existence of an act (or omission) imputable to the Community has been established, the next requisite is that it should have caused damage to the applicant. The European Court has never laid down any general principles as to the kinds of loss for which compensation may be claimed or the way in which damages will be calculated. Instead, it has proceeded on an *ad hoc* basis and tried to reach a result that was just in the circumstances. For this reason, and because there have not in fact been many awards of damages, it is impossible to do more than make a few brief comments.

The Court has shown itself willing to award compensation for financial losses. In *Kampffmeyer v. Commission*,[57] for example, it was held that where, as a result of unlawful Community action, a firm was forced to break a contract, the cancellation fees incurred might be recovered from the Community; and in *CNTA v. Commission*[58] it was held that a firm was entitled to compensation for losses caused by currency fluctuations where the Community was responsible for its having been exposed to this risk. It also seems probable, though it has not finally been decided, that compensation may be obtained for losses resulting from unlawful assistance given by Community institutions to competitors.[59]

In the *Kampffmeyer* case (above) the question also arose whether an applicant could claim for loss of profit. A number of German grain dealers had applied for permits to import maize from France into Germany at a time when, because of the zero rate of levy, it was possible to make substantial profits. The German authorities wrongfully refused to grant the permits and the Commission upheld this action. The Court ruled that the Community was liable in principle to compensate the dealers for their losses. The dealers who claimed for loss of profit fell into two categories: some had concluded contracts to buy grain in France and had cancelled them when import permits were refused; others had not concluded contracts before applying for permits. As regards the first category, the Court was prepared to award damages for loss of profit but it stated that, in view of the speculative nature of the transactions, it would award them only a

[56] The problems that arise when the Member States act on behalf of the Community are discussed below in the section on 'Concurrent Liability'.

[57] Cases 5, 7, 13–24/66, [1967] ECR 245. This decision is discussed further below.

[58] Case 74/74, decision of 14 May 1975, [1975] ECR 533; decision of 15 June 1976, [1976] ECR 797.

[59] There have been several cases in which damages have been claimed on this basis but they have been dismissed on other grounds. See, e.g., *Bertrand v. Commission*, Case 40/75, [1976] ECR 1; and *Roquette v. Commission*, Case 26/74, [1976] ECR 677. These cases show that proof of causation in this situation will be difficult.

sum equal to 10 per cent of what they would have had to pay by way of the levy if they had imported the maize after the levy rate had been raised to the normal level. Since their profits would probably have been at least equal to the normal levy rate, they were being awarded, in effect, only 10 per cent of the profits they could have made. Though it was reasonable to take into account the element of risk involved in transactions of this nature, this seems an excessively large reduction. The second category of applicants fared even worse: they were awarded no damages at all. The reason given by the Court was that their transactions lacked 'any substantial character'; but this does not seem entirely justifiable since they had taken a concrete step by applying for an import permit. Their decision not to conclude contracts until the permits had been obtained might be viewed as nothing more than normal business prudence. This case, therefore, shows a rather miserly attitude on the part of the Court; in later cases, however, it has been more generous.[60]

In staff cases the Court has been prepared to award damages for anxiety and hurt feelings in the case of Community employees who have been wrongfully dismissed or otherwise unfairly treated.[61] The sums granted under this head have usually been small. In cases of personal injury, damages for physical and mental suffering have been awarded.[62]

The duty to mitigate loss is, the Court has held, a general principle common to the legal systems of the Member States, which applies also in Community law.[63] Failure to mitigate leads to a reduction of damages. Damages will also be reduced if the applicant is partly to blame for his loss.[64]

It is possible to bring proceedings before the damage has actually occurred: in such a case the applicant can obtain a declaration that he is entitled in principle to compensation.[65] This is possible, however, only if the damage is imminent and there is a high degree of certainty that it will take place. This would normally mean that the cause of the damage (the Community action) must already have occurred even if its consequences have not yet been fully realized.[66] The importance of this ruling is that it enables persons affected by Community measures to challenge them as soon as they have taken place and thus obtain a ruling as to their legality. In other words, an action for a declaration under the second paragraph of Article 288 [215] EC could be used as a substitute for a review action under Article 230 [173] EC; this could be valuable in view of the limitations placed on the right of private individuals to bring review proceedings.[67]

60 *Mulder v. Council and Commission* (second *Mulder* case), Cases C-104/89, 37/90, [1992] ECR I-3061; *Stahlwerke Peine-Salzgitter v. Commission*, Case T-120/89, [1991] ECR II-279 (Court of First Instance); affirmed Case C-220/91 P, [1993] ECR I-2393 (ECJ).

61 See, e.g., *Algera v. Assembly*, Cases 7/56, 3–7/57, [1957] ECR 39 and *Willame v. Commission*, Case 110/63, [1965] ECR 649. However, time begins to run for limitation purposes only when the damage actually occurs: *Birra Wührer v. Council and Commission*, Cases 256, 257, 265, 267/80, 5/81, [1982] ECR 85.

62 *Grifoni v. Euratom*, Case C-308/87, [1994] ECR I-341 (paras 36–8 of the judgment).

63 *Mulder v. Council and Commission* (second *Mulder* case), Cases C-104/89, 37/90, [1992] ECR I-3061 (para. 33 of the judgment).

64 *Adams v. Commission*, Case 145/83, [1985] ECR 3539; *Grifoni v. Commission*, Case C-308/87, [1990] ECR I-1203.

65 *Kampffmeyer v. Council and Commission*, Cases 56–60/74, [1976] ECR 711.

66 See *per* Advocate General Reischl, *ibid.* at 753.

67 See Chap. 12.

Where damages are calculated in one currency (for example, euros) and awarded in another (for example, the national currency of the applicant, if that is different) the appropriate date for conversion is that of the judgment.[68] If, as is often the case, the Court first gives an interlocutory judgment on the question of liability and, if the parties are unable to reach agreement, fixes the amount of damages in a later judgment, the relevant date is that of the interlocutory judgment.[69] Interest is usually awarded from the date of the interlocutory judgment.[70]

The European Court has had little to say about the problem of causation. One situation which raises the question of remoteness is where a Member State acts in violation of the Treaty and thereby causes loss to the applicant. If the Commission was aware of the facts but failed to take enforcement proceedings against the Member State, can the applicant bring an action in tort against the Commission on the ground that its failure to act was the cause of its loss? There have been several cases in which such proceedings have been brought, but they have all been dismissed on other grounds.[71] In some of the earlier cases, the European Court appeared to accept that liability could arise in this way;[72] subsequently, however, it has adopted a more hostile attitude.[73]

## FAULT

Under the ECSC Treaty fault was an essential element of liability. There is no such requirement under the EC Treaty, but up to now the European Court has always required the proof of fault in actions under Article 288 [215], second paragraph (though a violation of Community law, even if unintentional, can be sufficient). It considered the possibility of non-fault liability in *Compagnie d'Approvisionnement v. Commission*,[74] which concerned the measures taken after the devaluation of the French franc in 1969. In order to minimize disruption to the Common Agricultural Policy, the

[68] *Dumortier v. Council*, Cases 64, 113/76, 167, 239/78, 27, 28, 45/79, [1982] ECR 1733. [69] *Ibid.*

[70] *Ibid.* See also *Mulder v. Council and Commission* (second *Mulder* case), Cases C-104/89, 37/90, [1992] ECR I-3061, para. 35 of the judgment. The European Court has never explained how it fixes the rate of interest, though it is normally between 6 and 8 per cent: Heukels (1993) 30 CMLRev. 368 at 385, n. 56. It will not be greater than the rate requested by the applicant; thus in the second *Mulder* case, only 7 per cent was awarded in one joined case (because this was all that was asked for) and 8 per cent in the other. The highest rate awarded seems to be 12 per cent: *Berti v. Commission*, Case 131/81, [1985] ECR 645. In this case, the applicant was resident in Belgium and the Court applied the rate set out in the relevant Belgian legislation. However, the Commission did not formally dispute the applicant's claim in this respect.

[71] See *Vloeberghs v. High Authority*, Cases 9, 12/60, [1961] ECR 197; *Lütticke v. Commission*, Case 4/69, [1971] ECR 325; *Bertrand v. Commission*, Case 40/75, [1976] ECR 1; *Denkavit v. Commission*, Case 14/78, [1978] ECR 2497; *Société d'Initiatives et de Coopération Agricoles v. Commission*, Case 114/83, [1984] ECR 2589; and *GAARM v. Commission*, Case 289/83, [1984] ECR 4295.

[72] See the *Vloeberghs* case, [1961] ECR at 216 (also *per* Advocate General Roemer at 240) and the *Denkavit* case, [1978] ECR 2497 at para. 8 of the judgment.

[73] In *Asia Motor France v. Commission*, Case C-72/90, [1990] ECR I-2181, the Court declared such an action inadmissible on the ground that the Commission is under no duty to take action under Art. 226 [169] EC (see para. 13 of the judgment). However, the possibility of an action might still arise if the Commission's decision not to act was taken on improper grounds.

[74] Cases 9, 11/71, [1972] ECR 391; see also *Biovilac v. EEC*, Case 59/83, [1984] ECR 4057 (paras 27–30 of the judgment), where reference was also made to the German concept of '*Sonderopfer*'; *Dorsch Consult v. Council and Commission*, Case T-184/95, [1998] ECR II-667; affirmed Case C-237/98 P [2000] ECR I-4549.

Council decided (among other things) that the French Government would grant subsidies on imports of cereal products. The amount of the subsidies was to be fixed by the Commission, and this was done by two Commission regulations. The applicants were cereal dealers who claimed to have suffered loss because the subsidies were fixed at too low a level to compensate for the devaluation of the franc. They put forward various arguments in order to establish the liability of the Community, including an argument based on the French doctrine of equal apportionment of public burdens (*l'égale répartition des charges publiques*) under which the state may be liable in certain circumstances in the absence of fault. To establish liability under this head in French law, it is necessary to show that measures taken by the state have placed an abnormal and unjustifiably severe burden on certain individuals who have thus suffered unusual and special damage and been required to make a disproportionate sacrifice in the general interest.

Advocate General Mayras considered this argument but decided that the applicants had not met the conditions imposed by French law.[75] The Court also rejected it without ruling on whether or not non-fault liability is part of Community law:[76]

> Any liability for a valid legislative measure is inconceivable in a situation like that in the present case since the measures adopted by the Commission were only intended to alleviate, in the general economic interest, the consequences which resulted in particular for all French importers from the national decision to devalue the franc.

In other words, the disputed measures did not impose a burden on the applicants; they gave them a benefit. Therefore no question of liability under this head could arise.

Non-fault liability continues to be a possibility, but the general tenor of the Court's judgments in cases under Article 288 [215], second paragraph, make clear that it will apply only in special circumstances: the normal rule is that fault must be established.[77] What is meant by fault? In broad terms, it means that the act or omission which forms the basis of the action must be wrongful. In the case of an omission this means that there must have been a duty (as distinct from a mere power) to act; in the case of a positive act it means either that the action was wrongful in itself or that it was carried out in a wrongful way.[78]

In general, any malfunctioning of the administrative system can constitute fault. One could perhaps say that there is a legal duty on Community institutions (and on other institutions to which Community functions are delegated and for whose acts the Community is responsible) to carry out their functions in a sensible and efficient manner – in other words, a duty of good administration. Consequently, any breach of this duty could constitute fault. Examples are: failure to adopt procedures necessary for the efficient functioning of the service, failure to supervise subordinate officials or outside

[75] At 422–3. [76] Para. 46 of the judgment.

[77] For further case law on the possibility of non-fault liability, see *Dorsch Consult v. Council and Commission*, Case T-184/95, [1998] ECR II-667 (paras 59 and 80 of the judgment); *Dorsch Consult v. Council and Commission*, Case C-237/98 P, [2000] ECR I-4549 at para. 6 of the Opinion of Advocate General La Pergola.

[78] On the possibility of obtaining damages for a violation by the Community of a rule of WTO law, see *Biret International v. Council*, Case C-93/02, [2003] ECT I-10497 (Full Court).

bodies to whom functions have been delegated, failure to obtain all the facts before making a decision, taking a decision on the basis of erroneous or irrelevant facts, giving misleading information to the public, failure to give necessary information to the public, delay, or lack of foresight – in short, everything which English lawyers sum up under the heading of 'maladministration'.[79] In addition, of course, a violation of any written or unwritten rule of law may also constitute fault, provided the rule in question is intended for the protection of individuals.[80]

It should not, however, be thought that *any* deviation from the standard of an ideal service constitutes fault. The concept, after all, carries a connotation of blameworthiness and it is therefore necessary to consider whether the shortcoming in question is excusable. For example, in the case of a decision of fact (that is, a judgment whether a certain state of facts exists) the institution concerned may be excused if it makes a mistake, provided it adopted the correct procedures and reached the conclusion which seemed indicated in the light of the information to hand.[81] A good example is to be found in the case of *Richez-Parise v. Commission*.[82] The applicants in this case were a number of officials of the EC who had been given incorrect information concerning their pensions and had thereafter resigned from the service and taken certain decisions regarding their financial rights. The information in question was based on an interpretation of the relevant legal provisions, and, at the time at which it was given, the Commission had no reason to believe that it was wrong. Subsequently the Commission discovered that its interpretation was of doubtful validity, but it took no immediate steps to inform the applicants of this. It was only some time later, after the applicants had committed themselves as regards the form in which they would take their accrued pension entitlements, that the position was rectified. The European Court held that the initial interpretation was not itself a wrongful act since the mistake was excusable, but the failure to correct it as soon as the Commission became aware of the true position did constitute fault.

In addition to administrative fault, there is also personal fault. This occurs where the individual officer acts wrongfully: where he fails to carry out instructions, or acts negligently, or illegally, or in bad faith – in other words, where the shortcoming is one of the individual rather than of the service.

*Adams v. Commission*[83] is one of the few cases in which an individual not employed by the Community has been awarded substantial damages. While working for a Swiss pharmaceutical company (Hoffmann-La Roche), Adams had, after requesting confidentiality, given the Commission documents which showed that the company was violating Community competition law. The Commission then brought proceedings against the company and as a result it was fined. Subsequently the company discovered, partly as a result of documents supplied by the Commission, that Adams was the informant.

[79] For an example, see *Fresh Marine Company v. Commission*, Case T-178/98, [2000] ECR II-3331; upheld on appeal, Case C-472/00 P, [2003] ECR I-7541.

[80] See below.

[81] See *per* Advocate General Gand in *Kampffmeyer v. Commission*, Cases 5, 7, 13–24/66, [1967] ECR 245 at 275–7.

[82] Cases 19, 20, 25, 30/69, [1970] ECR 325. For another case on misleading information, see *Compagnie Continentale France v. Council*, Case 169/73, [1975] ECR 117.

[83] Case 145/83, [1985] ECR 3539.

Under Swiss law Adams had committed a criminal offence by revealing the company's secrets to the Commission. By this time Adams had ceased to work for Hoffmann-La Roche and gone to live in Italy. However, he came to Switzerland on a visit and the company had him arrested. The Swiss police kept him in solitary confinement and did not allow him to communicate with his family. As a result, his wife, who had also been interrogated, committed suicide. After his release (he was convicted but given a suspended sentence) he sued the Commission for damages.

The Court held that the Commission was bound by a duty of confidentiality and that it had violated this, in particular by not warning Adams when it discovered that Hoffmann-La Roche was planning to have him prosecuted. However, it held that Adams was partly to blame for his own misfortune (for example, by returning to Switzerland) and it decided that liability should be apportioned equally between him and the Commission. The Commission was, therefore, ordered to compensate him to the extent of one half of the damage suffered.[84]

## LIABILITY FOR ACTS INTENDED TO HAVE LEGAL EFFECTS

Special considerations apply where the alleged wrongful act on the part of the Community is an act intended to have legal effects, that is, a reviewable act as defined in Chapter 11.

Under the ECSC Treaty there was a provision directly covering this situation, Article 34. This provided that where a Commission measure was annulled,[85] producers of coal or steel[86] that had suffered 'direct and special harm' could obtain redress if the Commission was guilty of a sufficient degree of fault. This provision applied only if the measure was first annulled;[87] however, this did not in itself establish that the requisite degree of fault existed.[88] The European Court refused to accept the view of the Court of First Instance[89] that the test applicable under Article 288 [215] EC for liability regarding a reviewable act should also be applied under Article 34,[90] though it is doubtful whether there was any marked difference in the requirements.

84 The amount of damages was settled in negotiations between the parties. According to *The Times*, 18 October 1986, Adams eventually accepted £200,000 (£100,000 for mental anguish and £100,000 for economic loss), plus £176,000 for costs.

85 It also applied where a failure to act was established: *Stahlwerke Peine-Salzgitter v. Commission*, Case T-120/89, [1991] ECR II-279; affirmed Case C-220/91 P, [1993] ECR I-2393 (ECJ).

86 See the definition of 'undertaking' in Art. 80 ECSC.

87 *Usinor v. Commission*, Cases 81, 119/85, [1986] ECR 1777.

88 *Finsider v. Commission*, Cases C-363–4/88, [1992] ECR I-359. See also *Stahlwerke Peine-Salzgitter v. Commission* (above).

89 *Stahlwerke Peine-Salzgitter v. Commission* (Court of First Instance) (above), para. 78 of the judgment.

90 *Stahlwerke Peine-Salzgitter v. Commission* (ECJ) (above), paras 27–30 of the judgment. The appeal was nevertheless dismissed.

In addition to fault, the applicant had to establish that it had suffered direct and special harm. According to the Court of First Instance, the concept of special harm involved, on the one hand, 'harm of a particular intensity' and, on the other, 'an impact on a limited and identifiable number of economic agents'.[91] Direct harm referred to causation.

Since Article 34 applied only to producers of coal and steel, other applicants could not rely on it. Could they bring an action under Article 40, the ECSC equivalent of Article 288 [215] EC? This question arose in *Vloeberghs v. High Authority*,[92] where a coal distributor (not producer) sued the Commission for damages under Article 40, because the latter had failed to take a decision requiring the French Government to allow its coal to enter France. The Commission claimed that the action was inadmissible, arguing that Article 34 provided the sole means of obtaining damages for loss caused by an act intended to have legal effects. It urged the Court not to allow Article 40 ECSC to be used as a means of circumventing the restrictions on judicial review imposed by Articles 33 and 35.

The Court rejected the Commission's argument. It pointed out that review actions and tort actions were quite separate remedies and that there was no reason why the restrictive conditions of the former should apply to the latter; it therefore concluded that it was not necessary for an applicant first to bring proceedings under Article 35. In the *Vloeberghs* case the Court left open whether the same applied where the basis of the action was a positive act rather than an omission, but the European Court subsequently held that it did.[93]

In the EC Treaty the nearest equivalent to Article 34 ECSC is Article 233 [176]. This reads:

> The institution whose act has been declared void or whose failure to act has been declared contrary to this Treaty shall be required to take the necessary measures to comply with the judgment of the Court of Justice.
>
> This obligation shall not affect any obligation which may result from the application of the second paragraph of Article 288 [215].

This gives no right to damages – unless the payment of damages were regarded as a 'necessary measure'[94] – but in view of its second paragraph it cannot hinder an action in tort.

## THE '*PLAUMANN* DOCTRINE'

The first case concerned with liability for a reviewable act under the EC Treaty was *Plaumann v. Commission*.[95] This case was discussed in Chapter 12. It will be remembered

[91] *Stahlwerke Peine-Salzgitter v. Commission* (Court of First Instance) (above), para. 131 of the judgment. On appeal, this was noted without comment by the European Court: Case C-220/91 P (ECJ), paras 53–8 of the judgment. As interpreted by the Court of First Instance, this concept bears a striking resemblance to the concept of a manifest and grave violation, which has been held by the European Court to apply under Art. 288 [215] EC.

[92] Cases 9, 12/60, [1961] ECR 197.

[93] *Finsider v. Commission* (above), para. 16 of the judgment; *Stahlwerke Peine-Salzgitter v. Commission* (ECJ) (above), para. 21 of the judgment.

[94] According to Advocate General Roemer in *Nordgetreide v. Commission*, Case 42/71, [1972] ECR 105 at 115, the Court does not have the power to specify what measures must be taken to comply with its judgments.

[95] Case 25/62, [1963] ECR 95.

that the German Government had applied to the Commission for permission to lower the duty on clementines from 13 per cent to 10 per cent. The Commission took a decision addressed to Germany refusing this request. Plaumann was a German importer of clementines who claimed that the Commission's refusal was illegal. He brought proceedings under Article 230 [173] EC for the annulment of the decision and also under Article 288 [215], second paragraph, for damages. The amount claimed in damages was a sum equal to the additional duty he had had to pay.

It will be remembered from the discussion in Chapter 12 that the review proceedings were declared inadmissible on the ground that Plaumann lacked *locus standi*. The Court declared the tort action admissible but dismissed it on the merits. It gave its reasons as follows:[96]

> The conclusions of the applicant ask for payment of compensation equivalent to the customs duties and turnover tax which the applicant had to pay in consequence of the Decision against which it has at the same time instituted proceedings for annulment. In these circumstances it must be declared that the damage allegedly suffered by the applicant issues from this Decision and that the action for compensation in fact seeks to set aside the legal effects on the applicant of the contested Decision.
>
> In the present case the contested Decision has not been annulled. An administrative measure which has not been annulled cannot of itself constitute a wrongful act on the part of the administration inflicting damage upon those whom it affects. The latter cannot therefore claim damages by reason of that measure. The Court cannot by way of an action for compensation take steps which would nullify the legal effects of a decision which, as stated, has not been annulled.
>
> The action brought by the applicant must therefore be dismissed as unfounded.

This reasoning will be familiar: exactly the same argument was put forward by the Commission in *Vloeberghs v. High Authority*. The argument rejected by the Court in that case was accepted in *Plaumann*. It is unclear why the Court changed its ground within so short a time (two years).[97] What should, however, be emphasized is that this restrictive approach was in no way required by the Treaty: there is nothing in the EC Treaty suggesting that a reviewable act which has not been quashed cannot form the basis of an action in tort; nor is this principle derived from the legal systems of the Member States.[98] As the Court said in the *Vloeberghs* case, actions for damages and applications for review are quite separate proceedings with different objectives.

This decision was subject to heavy criticism,[99] but it was almost eight years before the Court had an opportunity to reconsider it. This first occurred in *Lütticke v. Commission*,[100] in which a German company sued the Commission for damages

[96] [1963] ECR at 108.

[97] Plaumann could not have obtained a remedy in the national courts, since his complaint was that the Commission had failed to take a decision. There is no way a failure to act on the part of a Community institution can be challenged in the national courts. Consequently, the refusal by the Court to allow him to bring proceedings under Art. 288 [215] meant that he was left without any remedy at all.

[98] See *per* Advocate General Roemer in *Zuckerfabrik Schöppenstedt v. Council*, Case 5/71, [1971] ECR 975 at 990, and the authors there cited.

[99] *Ibid.* at 991.

[100] Case 4/69, [1971] ECR 325.

because it had failed to address a directive or decision to Germany requiring it to modify certain taxes which the company had been obliged to pay. The Commission contended that the action was inadmissible because it was intended to establish a failure to act on its part, and its effect would be to circumvent the limitations imposed by Article 232 [175] EC on the application for a remedy for failure to act. This, of course, was precisely the argument unsuccessfully put forward in *Vloeberghs* and adopted by the Court in *Plaumann*. This time the Court rejected it. Its words were:[101]

> The action for damages provided for by Article 235 [178] and the second paragraph of Article 288 [215] was established by the Treaty as an independent form of action with a particular purpose to fulfil within the system of actions and subject to conditions for its use, conceived with a view to its specific purpose. It would be contrary to the independent nature of this action as well as to the efficacy of the general system of forms of action created by the Treaty to regard as a ground of inadmissibility the fact that, in certain circumstances, an action for damages might lead to a result similar to that of an action for failure to act under Article 232 [175].

So the action was declared admissible (though it was dismissed on the merits on the ground that the Commission's failure to act was not wrongful).

The position was confirmed in *Zuckerfabrik Schöppenstedt v. Council*,[102] where the act in question was a Council regulation which provided for compensation for stockholders of sugar who had suffered loss as a result of the price changes that came about when a Community *régime* for sugar was introduced. The terms of this regulation did not, however, entitle the applicant, a German company, to any compensation. It claimed that this was wrong and sued the Council for damages. The Council contested the admissibility of the action on the ground that, in practical terms, its result would be the nullification of the legal effects of the regulation. This, it argued, would undermine the system of judicial review set up by Article 230 [173] EC under which private persons are not entitled to challenge the validity of regulations. The Court rejected this argument on the basis of the same reasoning as in the *Lütticke* case.[103]

[101] Para. 6 of the judgment. [102] Case 5/71, [1971] ECR 975.

[103] The argument was put again in a few subsequent cases but was always rejected by the Court. See, e.g., *Compagnie d'Approvisionnement v. Commission*, Cases 9, 11/71, [1972] ECR 391 (paras 3–7 of the judgment) and *Merkur v. Commission*, Case 43/72, [1973] ECR 1055 (paras 3 and 4 of the judgment). It appears, however, that the *Plaumann* doctrine still applies where the applicant claims not compensation for loss actually suffered, but the sum that would have been payable if the measure had not been adopted: see *Krohn v. Commission*, Case 175/84, [1986] ECR 753 (paras 30–4 of the judgment); *Birke v. Commission and Council*, Case 543/79, [1981] ECR 2669 (paras 23–8 of the judgment); *Bruckner v. Commission and Council*, Case 799/79, [1981] ECR 2697 (paras 14–20 of the judgment); *Cobrecaf v. Commission*, Case T-514/93, [1995] ECR 103 II-621 (paras 58–61 of the judgment); *AssiDomän Kraft Products v. Commission*, Case C-310/97 P, [1999] ECR I-5363 (appeal against Case T-227/95, [1997] ECR II-1185) (para. 59 of the judgment); *Fresh Marine Company v. Commission*, Case T-178/98, [2000] ECR II-3331 (paras 41–53); upheld on appeal, Case C-472/00 P, [2003] ECR I-7541. In *Cobrecaf v. Commission*, the applicants brought proceedings to annul a Commission decision refusing to grant them increased aid. These proceedings were held inadmissible because they were brought outside the time limit. In addition, they asked for damages under the second paragraph of Art. 288 [215], the sum claimed being the amount of the additional aid which the contested decision had refused to give. The Court of First Instance held that, as an exception to the principle in the *Lütticke* case, 'the fact that a claim for annulment is held to be inadmissible renders the claim for damages inadmissible where the action for damages is actually aimed at securing withdrawal of an individual decision which has become definitive and would, if upheld, have the effect

The significance of this should be emphasized. The rule in *Plaumann* was more than a procedural one. It has already been shown that the rules of admissibility for applications to annul and applications for a remedy for failure to act are extremely strict: the narrow concept of *locus standi* and the short time-limit impose stringent limitations on the right to bring these proceedings.[104] Therefore, if it had been accepted that such proceedings were a necessary precondition for an action for damages, the latter action would have been likewise restricted and Community liability would have been severely limited.

## THE '*SCHÖPPENSTEDT* FORMULA'

The *Schöppenstedt* case is important not only because it marked the final removal of the shackles imposed by *Plaumann*; it was also the first case in which the European Court made a general statement of the principles governing Community liability for an act intended to have legal effects. This statement, which will henceforth be referred to as the '*Schöppenstedt* formula', has been repeated, with small verbal differences, in most subsequent cases. In a later version it reads as follows: [105]

> The Court of Justice has consistently stated that the Community does not incur liability on account of a legislative measure which involves choices of economic policy unless a sufficiently serious breach of a superior rule of law for the protection of the individual has occurred.

We can analyse this as laying down three requirements for liability:

1. there must be a breach of a superior rule of law;
2. the breach must be sufficiently serious;
3. the superior rule of law must be one for the protection of the individual.

These requirements are intended to apply in addition to the general rules concerning damage and causation.

In *Bergaderm v. Commission*[106] (decided in 2000), the European Court held that the principles which it had previously laid down for the purpose of determining the liability of Member States under the *Francovich* doctrine (discussed in Chapter 7) should also apply to Community liability under Article 288 [215]. It said:[107]

> As regards Member State liability for damage caused to individuals, the Court has held that Community law confers a right to reparation where three conditions are met: the rule of law infringed must be intended to confer rights on individuals; the breach must be

of nullifying the legal effects of that decision . . .' (para. 59 of the judgment). It is not clear exactly what the scope of this exception is, in particular whether it applies only when the applicant could have obtained another remedy if he had acted in good time.

[104] See Chap. 12.

[105] *HNL v. Council and Commission*, Cases 83, 94/76, 4, 15, 40/77, [1978] ECR 1209 at para. 4 of the judgment.

[106] Case C-352/98 P, [2000] ECR I-5291 (appeal from Case T-199/96, [1998] ECR II-2805).

[107] At para. 42 of the judgment.

> sufficiently serious; and there must be a direct causal link between the breach of the obligation resting on the State and the damage sustained by the injured parties . . .

Although differently formulated, this seems substantially the same as the *Schöppenstedt* formula. Rule 1 and Rule 3 of *Schöppenstedt* have been conflated into a single rule (the first), and the requirement of causation has been taken from the general rules. The requirement of a sufficiently serious breach remains the same. We shall consider below whether the verbal differences are of any significance.

According to its terms, the *Schöppenstedt* formula applies where the source of liability is a legislative measure (normally a regulation) involving choices of economic policy. However, in *Bergaderm*, the Court held that what is important is not the nature of the measure but the degree of discretion enjoyed by its author. If it has little or no discretion, any infringement of Community law may be sufficient to incur liability.[108] In determining this, the general (legislative) or individual (administrative) nature of the measure is not the decisive criterion.[109]

The *Bergaderm* case arose when a directive adopted by the Commission prohibited a particular substance in suntan lotions.[110] Only one company used the substance, and it was driven into liquidation. It sued the Commission for damages, but lost in the Court of First Instance. On appeal to the European Court, one of its arguments was that the Court of First Instance had been wrong to regard the directive as a legislative measure in terms of the *Schöppenstedt* formula, since it affected the position of only one producer (itself). The European Court rejected this argument on the ground that it did not matter whether the measure was legislative or administrative.

One can conclude from this that the nature of the measure is important only as a pointer to the degree of discretion enjoyed. A legislative act will almost always involve a high degree of discretion. In some cases this will also be true of an administrative act – but not always. The test for determining whether there is discretion is whether the adoption of the act involves policy choices. It can hardly matter, however, whether these are economic, social, or political. The statement in the *Schöppenstedt* case that the formula applies only to liability on account of legislative measures that involve choices of economic policy must, therefore, be regarded as misconceived. The formula should rather be regarded as applying to any measure involving policy choices.

We shall now consider the three requisites laid down in the *Schöppenstedt* formula, as modified by *Bergaderm*.

## FIRST REQUISITE

The first requisite is that there must be a breach of a superior rule of law. *Bergaderm* requires merely that a rule of law must be infringed.[111] This change makes no difference.

[108] Para. 44 of the judgment. [109] Para. 46 of the judgment.

[110] It was thought by some scientists to cause cancer.

[111] For the possibility of liability resulting from an act that does not infringe any rule of law, see *Dorsch Consult v. Council and Commission*, Case T-184/95, [1998] ECR II-667; affirmed Case C-237/98 P, [2000] ECR I-4549.

Any rule of Community law could constitute a 'superior rule of law', provided it is binding on the author of the allegedly tortious act.

An example of a case in which the Court held that a general principle of law was sufficient for this purpose is *CNTA v. Commission.*[112] This case arose out of the system of monetary compensatory amounts (MCAs), which were intended to compensate for fluctuations in exchange rates. These payments had originally been granted on exports of colza seed from France, but on 26 January 1972 the Commission passed a regulation which abolished the system as from 1 February. The applicant was a French firm which had entered into a number of export contracts before the regulation was passed, and these were to be performed after the ending of the scheme. It claimed that it had entered into the contracts on the assumption that MCAs would be payable and had calculated its price on that basis. It argued that it had suffered loss by reason of the sudden ending of the scheme without warning and without any provision being made for transactions which were in the process of completion when it came into force. It therefore sued the Commission for damages.

In order to establish liability it had to prove that the Commission had been guilty of a wrongful act. It claimed that the regulation was such an act because it infringed the principle of legal certainty and in particular the principle of the protection of legitimate expectations.

The Court stated that, though the system of MCAs could not be regarded as furnishing a guarantee to exporters that they would not suffer loss as a result of fluctuations in the exchange rate, it nevertheless had the effect in practice of shielding them from such a risk. Consequently, even a prudent exporter might decide not to cover himself against it. The Court then continued:[113]

> In these circumstances, a trader may legitimately expect that for transactions irrevocably undertaken by him because he has obtained, subject to a deposit, export licences fixing the amount of the refund in advance, no unforeseeable alteration will occur which could have the effect of causing him inevitable loss, by re-exposing him to the exchange risk.
>
> The Community is therefore liable if, in the absence of an overriding matter of public interest, the Commission abolished with immediate effect and without warning the application of compensatory amounts in a specific sector without adopting transitional measures which would at least permit traders either to avoid the loss which would have been suffered in the performance of export contracts, the existence and irrevocability of which are established by the advance fixing of the refunds, or to be compensated for such loss.
>
> In the absence of an overriding matter of public interest, the Commission has violated a superior rule of law, thus rendering the Community liable, by failing to include in Regulation No. 189/72 transitional measures for the protection of the confidence which a trader might legitimately have had in the Community rules.

The Court went on to hold, however, that the Community was not liable to pay the full amount of the MCAs applicable to the transactions in question. The Community's obligation was solely to ensure that the exporter did not make an actual loss on the transaction as a result of a change in the exchange rate. In later proceedings[114] it was

[112] Case 74/74, [1975] ECR 533. [113] Paras 42–4 of the judgment. [114] [1976] ECR 797.

established that payment for the shipments had been made in French francs. Therefore CNTA had suffered no loss and it consequently obtained no damages.

It is important to note that the Court did not hold the regulation invalid. If it had done so, CNTA would have been entitled to the MCAs at the normal rate. The wrongful act was not the passing of the regulation but the failure either to give reasonable notice to interested parties that the system would soon be ended or, alternatively, to include transitional provisions to protect exporters who had already committed themselves. It was this omission which violated the principle of the protection of legitimate expectations, which, according to the Court, was a superior rule of law in the terms of the *Schöppenstedt* formula.

## SECOND REQUISITE

The second requisite is that the breach must be sufficiently serious. This is the same under the *Bergaderm* restatement. It is the most important aspect of the *Schöppenstedt* formula and it constitutes the most difficult hurdle for the applicant to surmount. The first decision to consider is *HNL v. Council and Commission*,[115] more commonly known as the second *Skimmed-Milk Powder* case. This arose out of the over-production of milk in the Community and the creation of a skimmed-milk powder 'mountain'. In an attempt to get rid of this, the Council passed a regulation obliging animal feed producers to purchase skimmed-milk powder from the intervention agencies. The idea was that skimmed-milk powder would replace soya as a source of protein in the animal feed. The drawback to this, however, was that skimmed-milk powder was much more expensive than soya and the consequence of the scheme was that farmers had to pay more for their animal feed.

The farmers objected and various actions were brought to contest the legality of the regulation. Some were brought in the national courts and referred to the European Court under Article 234 [177]; others were actions for damages brought in the European Court. Judgment was given first in the cases under Article 234 [177]: the Court ruled that the regulation was invalid because it obliged the producers to purchase skimmed-milk powder 'at such a disproportionate price that it was equivalent to a discriminatory distribution of the burden of costs between the various agricultural sectors' without being justifiable for the purpose of disposing of the stocks of skimmed-milk powder.[116] In other words, the regulation offended against the principles of equality and proportionality.[117]

The following year the Court gave judgment in the tort actions. Since the regulation had already been ruled invalid, there could be no dispute regarding the first requirement of the *Schöppenstedt* formula; nor did the Court have any difficulty in holding that the third requirement was satisfied. The difficulties centred around the second requirement: was the violation sufficiently serious?

[115] Cases 83, 94/76, 4, 15, 40/77, [1978] ECR 1209.

[116] See para. 3 of the judgment. See further *Bela-Mühle*, Case 114/76; *Granaria*, Case 116/76; and *Ölmühle Hamburg*, Cases 119–20/76, [1977] ECR 1211 *et seq.*

[117] These principles are discussed in Chap. 5.

It might have been thought that if the violation were serious enough to result in a ruling that the regulation was invalid, it would be serious enough to justify the award of damages; but the Court held that this was not the case. A ruling of invalidity merely satisfies the first requirement in the *Schöppenstedt* formula; it does not necessarily satisfy the second. The Court tried to justify this strict approach by pointing out that in national law it is only in exceptional cases that public authorities incur liability for legislative measures. It may be doubted, however, whether analogies with national law are very apposite in this regard, since the legislative process in the Community is so different from that in the Member States.

The Court then stated that, in a legislative field involving wide discretion, the Community will not be liable unless the institution concerned has 'manifestly and gravely disregarded the limits on the exercise of its powers', a requirement that was affirmed in *Bergaderm*, where the Court said that the decisive test for finding that a breach of Community law is sufficiently serious is whether the Community institution manifestly and gravely disregarded the limits on its discretion.[118]

The requirement of a serious violation has thus been enlarged: where the Community enjoys a wide measure of discretion, applicants must now establish a *manifest* and *grave* violation. The Court held that these requirements were not satisfied in the case. It gave four reasons: first, the regulation affected a wide category of persons, namely all buyers of protein animal feed; secondly, the price increase had only a limited effect on production costs; thirdly, the increase was slight in comparison with increases caused by fluctuations in world prices; and lastly, the effect of the regulation on profits did not exceed the normal level of risk inherent in activities in the agricultural sectors concerned.

One can conclude from this that liability will not result from measures of this kind unless the violation of the law has a serious impact on the interests of the applicants. The last three factors mentioned are all concerned with the degree of harm suffered by the victims. The first factor indicates that liability will be less likely to result where the loss is spread over a wide class of persons than where it is concentrated on a small number of victims.

The *HNL* case was followed a year later by a group of cases concerning two rather unusual products, quellmehl and gritz.[119] The former is made from maize or wheat and is used in bread production to keep the dough damp; the latter is also derived from maize and is used in brewing. The history of these cases began some years prior to the judgment when the Community decided to subsidize starch so it could compete with synthetic products. Starch is, however, to some extent interchangeable with quellmehl and gritz and the subsidy enabled it to undercut quellmehl in baking and gritz in brewing. To prevent this, the subsidies were granted to the latter products as well.

[118] Para. 43 of the judgment.

[119] *Dumortier v. Council*, Cases 64, 113/76, 167, 239/78, 27, 28, 45/79, [1979] ECR 3091; *Ireks-Arkady v. Council and Commission*, Case 238/78, [1979] ECR 2955; *DGV v. Council and Commission*, Cases 241, 242, 245–50/78, [1979] ECR 3017; *Interquell v. Council and Commission*, Cases 261–2/78, [1979] ECR 3045.

The trouble started when the Council passed a regulation withdrawing the subsidies for quellmehl and gritz but not for starch. The quellmehl and gritz producers objected and brought actions in the national courts. In references under Article 234 [177] EC the European Court ruled that the Council had been guilty of discrimination in treating quellmehl and gritz differently from starch.[120] The Council then restored the subsidies, but only from the date of the Court's judgment. The quellmehl and gritz producers claimed that they should have been backdated to when they were originally withdrawn and brought proceedings under Article 288 [215], second paragraph, for compensation for the loss they had suffered during the period when they were without subsidies.

There was again no difficulty in proving that the regulations which withdrew the subsidies violated a superior rule of law for the protection of the individual. Was the violation manifest and grave? The Court held that it was. Its reasons were not very clear, but it emphasized that the quellmehl and gritz producers were a small, clearly defined group, and stated that the loss they had suffered went beyond the risks normally inherent in their business. The Court therefore ruled that they were entitled to damages based on the amount of the subsidy they would have received if they had been treated on the same basis as the starch producers. However, this was to be reduced to the extent to which they had been able to pass on any part of the loss to their customers.[121]

This decision may be contrasted with the judgment given by the Court only two months later in the *Isoglucose* cases.[122] Isoglucose is a sweetener which competes with sugar in a certain sector of the market (soft drinks, jams, and similar products). It was first put on the market in 1976 and the Community authorities immediately took steps to meet the threat it posed to sugar, a product which was in surplus. The result was a regulation imposing on isoglucose a levy of such large proportions that, according to the producers, it would have made all production uneconomical. Two of the main factories were in England, and proceedings were brought in the English courts to challenge the validity of the regulation. The European Court held, on a reference under Article 234 [177], that the regulation infringed the principle of equality because it discriminated against isoglucose in comparison with sugar.[123] The levy was then withdrawn with retroactive effect.

This did not, however, end the troubles of the isoglucose manufacturers. They had been obliged to suspend production while the levy dispute was pending: if the levy had been upheld, their plants would have had to switch to other products or close entirely. They had therefore incurred heavy expenses from lost production and financial overheads. Hardest hit was the Dutch firm Koninklijke Scholten-Honig (KSH) which had been forced into liquidation. It had constructed a large plant at Tilbury which had been sold at a loss. It claimed that its total loss resulting from the imposition of the levy was

[120] *Ruckdeschel*, Cases 117/76, 16/77, [1977] ECR 1753 and *Moulins de Pont-à-Mousson*, Cases 124/76, 20/77, [1977] ECR 1795.

[121] The Court did not actually fix the amount of damages: this was left over for determination in later proceedings. See, further, [1982] ECR 3271 and 3293.

[122] *Amylum and Tunnel Refineries v. Council and Commission*, Cases 116, 124/77, [1979] ECR 3497; *KSH v. Council and Commission*, Case 143/77, [1979] ECR 3583 (second *Isoglucose* cases).

[123] *Royal Scholten-Honig*, Cases 103, 145/77, [1978] ECR 2037 (first *Isoglucose* cases).

over 147 million guilders (over £30 million). The other two producers, Amylum and Tunnel Refineries, had suffered less but their losses were quite considerable: Amylum claimed over 100 million Belgian francs and Tunnel Refineries over £1 million. No one could contend that these losses were within the normal risk of manufacturing even a new product.

The producers therefore brought actions for damages. There was again no problem with the first and third requisites under the *Schöppenstedt* formula, but was the violation manifest and grave? On the basis of the tests in the previous cases, one would have thought that it was. Isoglucose manufacturers were an even more restricted group than quellmehl and gritz producers: their numbers were limited by the heavy investment required and the fact that some of the technology involved was still under patent. Moreover, the impact of the regulation on their business was little short of catastrophic.

In spite of this, the Court held that they were entitled to no compensation. Its reasoning was sparse – suggesting that the judges were divided among themselves – and no consideration was given to the degree of harm suffered; instead, the Court concentrated on the extent to which the law had been violated. One would have thought that this was at least as great as in the previous case – the Court itself said that the charges borne by the isoglucose manufacturers were 'manifestly unequal' as compared to those imposed on sugar producers – but the Court ruled that the defendants' errors were not of such gravity that their conduct could be regarded as 'verging on the arbitrary' (a point on which opinions might differ).

It appears from these cases, which were all decided in the late 1970s, that the requirement that the violation be manifest and grave has two aspects to it: one is the degree of harm suffered and the extent to which it is concentrated on a small group of victims; the other is the extent to which the law has been violated. Moreover, the *Isoglucose* cases suggest that the Community will be liable only if the defendant's conduct verges on the arbitrary, a more stringent criterion than was applied in the earlier cases.

Evidence of a more liberal attitude became discernible in the 1990s. In *Stahlwerke Peine-Salzgitter v. Commission*[124] the European Court went out of its way to state that conduct verging on the arbitrary is *not* a requirement,[125] and in *Sofrimport v. Commission*[126] it awarded damages to an apple importer whose goods had been wrongfully excluded from the Community. Its most startling decision, however, was *Mulder v. Council and Commission*,[127] usually known as the second *Mulder* case. This again concerned measures taken by the Community to curb over-production of milk. Initially, the Community introduced a scheme under which dairy farmers were paid a premium for agreeing not to market milk during a five-year period. Over 100,000 farmers took advantage of this scheme. Some time later, the Community introduced a system of milk quotas, under which a special levy – a 'superlevy' – was payable by farmers who produced more than their quota of milk. The quotas were based on the quantity

[124] Case C-220/91 P, [1993] ECR I-2393 (ECJ), para. 51 of the judgment.

[125] The case was actually an action under Arts 34 and 40 ECSC, but the statement concerning arbitrariness was made with reference to Art. 288 [215], second para., EC.

[126] Case C-152/88, [1990] ECR I-2477.

[127] Cases C-104/89, C-37/90, [1992] ECR I-3061.

marketed during a year specified in the regulation. The problem was that the regulation did not take account of farmers who had produced no milk during the year in question because they had given an undertaking under the previous scheme. When this scheme ended, they had the worst of both worlds: they no longer received a premium, nor did they have a quota.

In proceedings under Article 234 [177] EC, the European Court held that the regulation introducing the quota system breached their legitimate expectations and was *pro tanto* invalid.[128] As a result, the Council adopted another regulation allowing the farmers in question a special quota of 60 per cent of the quantity marketed in the year immediately preceding that in which they had given their undertaking. In later proceedings under Article 234 [177], however, the Court held that a quota of only 60 per cent was too low.[129] So the Council introduced another regulation giving them a higher quota.

This put matters right for the future, but the question of compensation for past losses still remained. In the second *Mulder* case, some of the farmers brought an action for damages under Article 288 [215] EC. It had already been established in the earlier cases that the Community had violated the principle of legitimate expectations, a principle which the Court characterized as a superior rule of law for the protection of the individual; the case therefore hinged on the question whether the violation was sufficiently manifest and grave to entail the liability of the Community.

The Court held that, in the case of the regulation totally denying the farmers a milk quota, this requirement was met: the farmers in question were a clearly defined category and the risk of being permanently denied a milk quota was unforeseeable and went beyond the risks normally inherent in milk production. In the case of the regulation granting them a quota of 60 per cent, on the other hand, the violation was not sufficiently serious: the Council had made a choice of economic policy, which had involved balancing the need to avoid over-production of milk against the interests of the farmers who had previously entered into undertakings.[130] Though flawed, that choice did not constitute a sufficiently manifest and grave violation of the limits to its discretionary power. Consequently, the applicants were entitled to damages only until the entry into force of this latter regulation.

These damages were to compensate them for loss of profit based on the difference between what they might reasonably have been expected to earn if they had not been denied their rightful quotas and what they actually earned by selling milk outside the quota system together with what they actually earned, or could have earned,[131] by carrying on alternative activities.

The judgment in this case is remarkable because the number of producers affected was so large that it was impossible for the Council and the Commission to negotiate separately with each one; so the Council had to adopt a regulation setting out the

[128] *Mulder* (first *Mulder* case), Case 120/86, [1988] ECR 2321; *Von Deetzen*, Case 170/86, [1988] ECR 2355.

[129] *Spagl*, Case C-189/89, [1990] ECR I-4539; *Pastätter*, Case C-217/89, [1990] ECR I-4585; *Von Deetzen*, Case C-44/89, [1991] ECR I-5119.

[130] The Council evidently considered that if the farmers who had given undertakings were allowed a greater quota, over-production would result unless the other farmers had their quotas reduced.

[131] An application of the principle that there is a duty to mitigate loss.

compensation offered.[132] It seems clear, therefore, that the Court has abandoned the policy of restricting damage awards to cases where there are few potential claimants.

One can conclude, therefore, that the 'manifest and grave' requirement is now settled law, as is the requirement that the harm suffered must be outside the normal risks inherent in the activity in question.[133] It is not, however, necessary to prove that the conduct of the Community was verging on the arbitrary, nor is it any longer impossible to obtain damages where there are a large number of potential claimants.

## THIRD REQUISITE

The third requisite is that the rule of law infringed must be for the protection of the individual, or, in the words of *Bergaderm*, it must be intended to confer rights on individuals.[134] What this appears to mean is that the purpose of the violated rule must be to confer rights on individuals of the category to which the applicant belongs. If this is correct, the requirement is no more than a restatement of a principle which had been applied in cases decided before *Schöppenstedt*.

The principle was first laid down in *Vloeberghs v. High Authority*.[135] This case was discussed above and it will be remembered that it concerned a failure to take a decision under Article 88 ECSC. Vloeberghs was a Belgian coal dealer which had a number of customers in France to whom it wanted to sell coal which it had imported from the United States and which was in stock in Belgium. The French authorities refused to allow the coal to enter France. Vloeberghs regarded this as a violation of the Community principle of free circulation of goods which, it claimed, applied to coal originating outside the Community provided that it had been lawfully imported into a Member State. It therefore asked the Commission to institute enforcement proceedings against France under Article 88 ECSC. When the Commission failed to do so, Vloeberghs brought proceedings against it for damages on the ground that the Commission's failure to act was a violation of the Treaty, especially Article 8 ECSC which imposed a duty on the Commission to ensure that the objectives of the Treaty were attained.

The Court accepted that the principle of free circulation of goods applied to coal originating outside the Community provided it had been lawfully imported into a Member State. However, it stated that this principle had been established in the interests of Community production and, though it had been extended to coal produced outside the Community, it was not intended to benefit it and those dealing in it: the purpose of extending the principle to imported coal was merely to ensure that measures

[132] Regulation 2187/93, OJ 1993, L196/6. For further developments, see *Quiller v. Council and Commission*, Cases T-195 and 202/94, [1997] ECR II-2247; *Dethlefs v. Council and Commission*, Case T-112/95, [1998] ECR II-3819; *Flemmer*, Cases C-80–82/99, [2001] ECR I-7211.

[133] It seems that these risks must be assessed on the basis of the position as it existed when the applicant embarked on the venture which ultimately resulted in the loss incurred: see *Grands Moulins de Paris v. Council and Commission*, Case 50/86, [1987] ECR 4833, where the Court apparently considered that the risks are inherently greater in the case of a new product, and that loss is more easily foreseeable if there is a legislative trend in the direction of the measure which ultimately caused it.

[134] Para. 42 of the judgment.

[135] Cases 9, 12/60, [1961] ECR 197.

taken to restrict the movement of imported coal did not indirectly impede the circulation of Community coal. Consequently, though the Commission owed a duty to Community producers to enforce the principle of free circulation, it owed no such duty to dealers in non-Community coal. The action was therefore dismissed.

Another case in which the applicant failed to establish that the measure in question was intended to confer rights on persons in his position was *Vreugdenhil v. Commission.*[136] This concerned a Council regulation allowing goods which had been exported from the Community to be re-imported free of duty. The Commission, acting under a power delegated to it by the Council under another regulation, had provided that the right would not apply in certain cases. In earlier proceedings under Article 234 [177],[137] the Court had held that in doing this the Commission had gone outside the power delegated to it and had trespassed on the territory of the Council. The Commission measure was therefore declared invalid. In *Vreugdenhil v. Commission* the persons concerned claimed damages, but the Court held that the division of powers between the different Community institutions is intended to uphold institutional balance: it was not for the protection of individuals. The claim therefore failed.

*Kampffmeyer v. Commission*[138] contains the most illuminating discussion on this point. The case was discussed earlier in this chapter and will be considered again later; here it is sufficient to say that the applicants were German grain importers who had applied to the relevant German authority for licences to import maize from France. Under Article 22 of Regulation 19, the German authority could refuse such applications only if a serious disturbance of the market was threatened. Any such decision had to be confirmed by the Commission, which was under an obligation not to confirm it unless it considered that this condition was fulfilled. In the *Kampffmeyer* case, the German authority suspended imports and this decision was confirmed by the Commission. The applicants then sued the Community for damages.

The Court held that the condition laid down in Article 22 of Regulation 19 had not, in fact, been fulfilled and that the Commission decision confirming the German measures was consequently invalid. Was the rule of law violated (Article 22 of Regulation 19) intended to benefit the applicants? The Court held that it was. Its reasoning was as follows:[139]

> With regard to the argument that the rule of law which is infringed is not intended to protect the interests of the applicants, the said Article 22, together with the other provisions of Regulation No. 19, is directed, according to the wording of the fourth recital in the preamble to the regulation, to ensuring appropriate support for agricultural markets during the transitional period on the one hand, and to allowing the progressive establishment of a single market by making possible the development of the free movement of goods on the other. Furthermore, the interests of the producers in the Member States and of free trade between these States are expressly mentioned in the preamble to the said regulation. It appears in particular from Article 18 that the exercise of freedom of trade between States is subject only to the general requirements laid down by its own provisions and those of

[136] Case C-282/90, [1992] ECR-1937.

[137] *Vreugdenhil v. Minister van Landbouw en Visserij*, Case 22/88, [1989] ECR 2049.

[138] Cases 5, 7, 13–24/66, [1967] ECR 245. [139] [1967] ECR at 262–3.

> subsequent regulations. Article 22 constitutes an exception to these general rules and consequently an infringement of that article must be regarded as an infringement of those rules and of the interests which they are intended to protect. The fact that these interests are of a general nature does not prevent their including the interests of individual undertakings such as the applicants which as cereal importers are parties engaged in intra-Community trade. Although the application of the rules of law in question is not in general capable of being of direct and individual concern to the said undertakings, that does not prevent the possibility that the protection of their interests may be – as in the present case it is in fact – intended by those rules of law. The defendant's argument that the rule of law contained in Article 22 of Regulation No. 19 is not directed towards the protection of the interests of the applicants cannot therefore be accepted.

The task of determining the purpose of a legal rule often involves more than pure legal analysis, and for this reason it is impossible to lay down general rules. It is, however, interesting that the Court in the above passage expressly rejected two arguments. First, the fact that a provision has been enacted in the general interest does not mean that it cannot *also* have been intended to protect the interests of particular individuals. It is sufficient, therefore, if it is intended *in part* to protect their interests. Secondly, the fact that an individual would not have *locus standi* to challenge it in review proceedings, because it is not of direct and individual concern to him,[140] does not necessarily mean that the provision is not intended to protect his interests.

### CONCLUSIONS

It was said earlier that the advantage of a tort action is that it is not subject to the restrictive conditions applicable to actions for judicial review, especially the short time-limits and the strict rules for *locus standi*. This, however, is balanced by the fact that a more serious degree of misconduct has to be established on the part of the Community.

## CONCURRENT LIABILITY: THE COMMUNITY AND THE MEMBER STATES

The question to be considered here is the extent to which the liability of the Community is affected by the fact that there is concurrent liability on the part of a national authority. This often occurs, since it is normal practice for Community policies to be carried out by national authorities. Policy decisions are taken by Community institutions and the requisite legal acts are adopted; but the implementation of these policies is usually entrusted to agencies of the national governments acting on behalf of the Community. The citizen usually deals with the latter and if he suffers damage it is usually through the instrumentality of these authorities. If, therefore, he is forced to pay a sum of money that is not due, or refused a grant to which he is entitled,

[140] See Chap. 12.

it is the national authority which acts or fails to act. The root cause of the trouble may be some act or failure to act on the part of the Community but, since the matter is implemented by the national authority, the possibility arises of a right of action against the national authority as well as against the Community. The action against the national authority may be in tort, for restitution, or on the basis of a statutory obligation, and will have to be brought in the national courts, as there is no provision for a private person to sue a national government in the European Court.[141]

Will the existence of such a remedy affect any right of action the applicant may have against the Community in the European Court? Obviously he cannot be allowed to obtain compensation twice over. So any compensation already obtained in the national courts will have to be deducted from what he is awarded in the European Court. But what will happen if no compensation at the national level has yet been obtained either because no proceedings have been instituted or because they are still pending?

The first occasion on which the Court had to consider this problem was in *Kampffmeyer v. Commission.*[142] This case, which has already been discussed, concerned German grain dealers who had been refused permits to import maize from France into Germany. By the time the ban was lifted, the import levy had been increased; so those dealers who went through with their transactions were forced to pay a sum which would not otherwise have been payable. The decision to ban imports was taken by the German Government but it was approved, as required under Community law, by the Commission. In earlier proceedings[143] the Court annulled the Commission decision; now the importers brought proceedings against the Commission for damages. The Court held that by approving the German measures in circumstances in which they were not justified, the Commission had committed a wrongful act which could result in liability. The Court was prepared to consider compensation only for those importers who had concluded contracts to buy maize in France before the applications for import permits had been refused. The loss suffered fell into two categories: in some cases the grain bought had subsequently been imported and the levy paid; in others the contracts had been cancelled. In the former cases the loss suffered was equal to the levy paid; in the latter it was equal to the payments involved in cancellation plus loss of profit.[144]

As far as concurrent liability was concerned, there were two possible grounds on which a claim could be made against the German authorities. One was restitution. This applied only where the maize had been imported into Germany and the levy paid. The Court pointed out that the levy was paid into the German treasury and that it might be possible to recover it through proceedings in the German courts. It therefore ruled that this possibility must first be exhausted before it would consider awarding damages under this head against the Community.

The second possible cause of action against the German authority was in tort. The German decision to ban imports was illegal and the German authority was

[141] Actions against a Member State in the European Court may be brought only by the Commission or another Member State: Arts 226 [169] and 227 [170] EC, and 141 and 142 Euratom.

[142] Cases 5, 7, 13–24/66, [1967] ECR 245. See also *Becher v. Commission*, Case 30/66, [1967] ECR 285.

[143] *Toepfer v. Commission*, Cases 106–7/63, [1965] ECR 405 (discussed in Chap. 12).

[144] The question of damages was dealt with when the case was discussed earlier in this chapter.

consequently just as much at fault as the Commission: the Germans had imposed the ban; the Commission had confirmed it. Proceedings against the German Government had, in fact, already been instituted but the German court had stayed them to await the outcome of the Community proceedings. The European Court held that, before it could decide the extent of the Community's liability, the German courts should be given the opportunity to decide whether the German authority was liable. It therefore stayed the proceedings.

Was this decision justifiable? It seems clear that the basic premise of the judgment was that primary liability rested on the German authority and that Community liability was only subsidiary.[145] There was considerable justification for this view as regards the levy since, under the provisions applicable at that time, such levies were not handed over to the Community. If there was a right under German law to recover the levy, it was not unreasonable to regard this aspect of the claim as one where Community liability was subsidiary.

The ruling on the tort issue, however, is hard to justify. This was a case of joint liability, and there was no obvious reason why the liability of the Community should be subsidiary to that of the German authorities. The German proceedings had already been stayed to await the outcome of the Community action; now the European Court was staying the Community action to wait for the German court to give judgment. What if neither was prepared to act first? The European Court was sacrificing the interests of the applicants, who should have been permitted to sue whichever joint tortfeasor they chose, in order to shift the liability on to the German authority. The Court's justification for this was that it was necessary in order to 'avoid the applicants' being insufficiently or excessively compensated for the same damage by the different assessment of two different courts applying different rules of law'.[146] The German court could, of course, have given exactly the same reason for its ruling.

It is hard to know why the Court adopted this approach.[147] Perhaps it thought that if it were more liberal it would be swamped by actions for damages; perhaps it was afraid that the Commission would be outmanœuvred by the German authorities and the Community would end up having to meet the whole of the claim itself. Whatever the reasons, the decision produced totally unsatisfactory results for the applicants, who struggled for years to obtain a remedy.[148]

It was not until five years later that the problem again came before the European Court. This was in *Haegeman v. Commission*,[149] decided in 1972. Haegeman was a Belgian firm which imported wine from Greece (which was not then a Member State). A countervailing duty had been imposed on these imports by a Community regulation

[145] See *per* Advocate General Gand in *Becher v. Commission*, Case 30/66, [1967] ECR 285 at 305.

[146] [1967] ECR at 266.

[147] It should be noted that the solution adopted by the Court had been rejected by Advocate General Gand: see [1967] ECR at 278–9.

[148] See Schermers, 'The Law as It Stands on the Appeal for Damages' (1975) 1 LIEI 113 at 135 and Boulouis and Chevallier, *Grands arrêts de la cour de justice des communautés européennes*, Tome 1, 417, n. A1 (1974). After nine years the majority of the applicants did, in fact, obtain compensation in the German courts; but some had still not exhausted the remedies under national law: see Durand, 'Restitution or Damages: National or European Court?' (1976) 1 ELRev. 431 at 433.

[149] Case 96/71, [1972] ECR 1005.

and Haegeman claimed that this was illegal as it was contrary to the association agreement between the Community and Greece. It therefore wrote to the Commission and requested the return of the money it had paid. When this was refused it brought proceedings under Article 230 [173] EC to quash the decision refusing to refund the money.

It should be noted that the countervailing duty, though imposed by Community regulations, was collected by the Belgian authorities. In this respect it was similar to the levy in *Kampffmeyer*. There had, however, been an important development since that decision. The Council Decision of 21 April 1970 on the Replacement of Financial Contributions from Member States by the Communities' Own Resources[150] provided that as from 1 January 1971 the revenue from certain levies and duties would go to the Community. According to the Court, the countervailing duty in question came within the scope of this provision. In other words, while in *Kampffmeyer* the levies were paid into national funds, in *Haegeman* the money went into the Community treasury.[151]

One would have thought that this new factor would have greatly strengthened the case for holding that the Community was under an obligation to refund the money. The Court, however, ruled that because the collection of these funds was a matter for the national authorities, claims for refunds had to be made to them. Any ensuing litigation would then be brought in the national courts. The Commission was, therefore, not obliged to consider Haegeman's application and the annulment action was inadmissible.

This reasoning is hard to accept. The fact that the mechanics of collection are a matter for national provisions and the collection is carried out by national officials does not affect the question of who is liable to make repayment. The duties were imposed by Community provisions and collected on behalf of the Community. The national authorities were agents of the Community and the money was handed over to the Community. If the duties were illegal, it was the Community, not the national authorities, which was unjustly enriched. It was, therefore, unjustified to hold that the national authorities alone were liable to make restitution.[152]

Haegeman also claimed damages in tort for various losses it had suffered as a result of the imposition of the duty, but the Court held that, as the question of Community liability depended on the legality of the duty, this claim would be dismissed 'at the present stage'. It is not entirely clear what was meant by this, but it seems that the Court intended that Haegeman should first establish the illegality of the levy through proceedings in the Belgian courts with a reference to the European Court under Article 234 [177] EC. Then, if it were successful in this, it could return to the European Court with its tort action.

It is interesting that in a case decided only a few months before, *Compagnie d'Approvisionnement v. Commission (No. 2)*,[153] Advocate General Dutheillet de Lamothe had given careful consideration to just this possibility. In this case the applicants, which were French dealers in cereals, complained that a subsidy, granted

[150] Decision 70/243, JO 1970, L94.

[151] It is not clear from the case whether all the payments were made after 1 January 1971 but the Court assumed in its judgment that all the payments went into Community funds.

[152] But see Joliet, *Le contentieux*, p. 228.

[153] Cases 9, 11/71, [1972] ECR 391.

under a Council regulation, had been fixed by the Commission at too low a level. They therefore brought proceedings against the Commission under Article 288 [215], second paragraph. One argument put forward by the Commission was that the action was inadmissible because the applicants should first have brought proceedings in the French courts to establish that the Commission regulation fixing the level of the subsidy was illegal. This would have been referred under Article 234 [177] EC to the European Court and a ruling on the point would have been made. Only if this was successful, argued the Commission, could the applicants bring their action against the Community.

Advocate General Dutheillet de Lamothe rejected this argument. First, he pointed out that in view of the various levels of the national court system through which the case would have to pass, it might well be over five years before the matter was finally concluded. By this time the period of limitation for the action against the Community would have expired. (In his view there was no ground on which the running of time could be interrupted in these circumstances.) He also pointed out the extreme difficulties which similar doctrines had caused in France and other countries and suggested that the end result could be a denial of justice. Finally, he stated that there was nothing in the Treaty to justify such a procedure.

The Court declared the action admissible. Thus, though it did not explicitly deal with this particular point, it implicitly rejected the Commission's argument. One wonders why, so soon afterwards, it should have required Haegeman to make what Advocate General Dutheillet de Lamothe had referred to as the 'long march' through the national courts.

However, in a similar case decided a year after *Haegeman*, *Merkur v. Commission*,[154] the European Court held that the action was admissible. It said that, as it already had the case before it, it 'would not be in keeping with the proper administration of justice and the requirements of procedural efficiency to compel the applicant to have recourse to national remedies and thus to wait for a considerable length of time before a final decision on his claim is made'.[155] It is hard to regard this ruling as anything other than a rejection of the decision in *Haegeman*.[156]

For the next few years little was heard of the *Haegeman* ruling and one might possibly have thought that it had been quietly forgotten. In one case, *Holtz and Willemsen v. Council and Commission*,[157] it was argued by the Commission that the applicant's claim (for a subsidy) should have been brought in the national courts. This was rejected by Advocate General Reischl[158] and the Court, though it did not deal with the point, found the proceedings admissible. In *CNTA v. Commission*[159] the point was not even really argued.

In 1975, however, the Court again changed tack[160] and since then there have been many cases in which the applicant has been sent to the national courts. The case law

[154] Case 43/72, [1973] ECR 1055. [155] *Ibid.* at para. 6 of the judgment.

[156] See Van Gerven, 'De niet-contractuele aansprakelijkheid van de Gemeenschap wegens normatieve handelingen' [1976] SEW 2, at 7–8. [157] Case 153/73, [1974] ECR 675.

[158] [1974] ECR at 700–1. [159] Case 74/74, [1975] ECR 533 (discussed above).

[160] The doctrine was resurrected (somewhat ambiguously) in *Grands Moulins des Antilles v. Commission*, Case 99/74, [1975] ECR 1531 and (more emphatically) in *IBC v. Commission*, Case 46/75, [1976] ECR 65. For a

now seems to have stabilized itself sufficiently for it to be possible to give a statement of the legal position. To do this it is necessary to distinguish between three separate situations: first, where the applicant's loss lies in the fact that he was unlawfully obliged to pay a sum of money to the national authority; secondly, where his loss lies in the fact that the national authorities unlawfully refused to make a payment to him; thirdly, where his loss is of some other kind. In the first situation, his right of action against the national authority will be for restitution; in the second, it will be on the basis of a statutory obligation; in the third, it will be in tort. Each situation will be considered separately.

## RESTITUTION

Where the applicant's loss consists in the fact that he was unlawfully obliged to make a payment to the national authority, he will normally have a remedy for restitution against the national authority. In such a situation, he will not be entitled to bring proceedings against the Community even if the national authority acted as agent for the Community and handed the money over to it. In *Kampffmeyer*[161] the proceedings in the European Court were held admissible and the Community was held liable in principle; in the later cases the proceedings were held inadmissible. The latter is the rule today.[162]

## STATUTORY OBLIGATION

The second situation is where the national authority has wrongfully refused to make a payment to the applicant. In spite of the earlier cases discussed above, the general rule now is that such an action will be inadmissible, even if the basis of the obligation was a Community measure, and the national authority obtained its funds from the Community.[163]

## NO NATIONAL REMEDY

In both the situations discussed so far, the position is different where it is not possible for the applicant to obtain a remedy in the national courts. Since the alternative would be a denial of justice, the European Court has, after some hesitation,[164] held that

discussion of these, and later cases, see Hartley, 'Concurrent Liability in EEC Law: A Critical Review of the Cases' (1977) 2 ELRev. 249.

161 See above.

162 *Vreugdenhil v. Commission*, Case C-282/90, [1992] ECR I-1937 (para. 12 of the judgment).

163 *Asteris v. Greece*, Cases 106–20/87, [1988] ECR 5515, para. 25 of the judgment and the cases there cited.

164 *Roquette v. Commission*, Case 26/74, [1976] ECR 677. This case concerned an exporter who had been obliged to pay a levy under a provision of Community law. The levy was collected by the national authority and handed over to the Commission. The exporter considered that he had not been liable to make the payment and brought proceedings for its recovery, with interest, in both the national courts (against the national authority) and the European Court (against the Commission). The national court made a reference under Art. 234 [177] EC and the European Court gave a ruling in favour of the exporter (*Roquette v. France*, Case 34/74, [1974] ECR 1217). The national court then ordered the repayment of the sum in question, but refused to award interest,

proceedings can be brought directly before it against the appropriate Community institution.[165]

*Roquette v. Commission*[166] provides a good illustration. This was a sequel to an earlier case,[167] discussed in Chapter 8, above, in which a number of French grain exporters had been obliged to pay MCAs under Community regulations they claimed to be invalid. They brought proceedings in the French courts for the return of the sums paid (which had been collected by the French authorities on behalf of the Community). On a reference under Article 234 [177] EC, the European Court ruled that the regulations were indeed invalid, but nevertheless the applicants could not recover money already paid. Roquette then brought proceedings in the European Court under Article 288 [215] for damages to compensate it for the loss it had suffered. In these circumstances, as the European Court pointed out, Roquette could not obtain a remedy in the French courts because such a remedy had been barred by the European Court itself in the earlier case.[168] Despite the protestations of the Commission,[169] therefore, the proceedings were admissible.[170]

The circumstances in *Roquette* were unusual. A more common situation is where the sole cause of the problem is the failure of the Commission or Council to adopt a legal act. In such a case, the applicant cannot bring proceedings in the national court and ask it to decide the case on the basis that the measure has been enacted.[171] Not even the European Court can do this: in actions for a remedy for a failure to act, all it can do is to declare that the defendant's failure to act is contrary to the Treaty: it cannot itself adopt the measure.[172] In these circumstances there is, therefore, no procedure under which the applicant can bring his complaint before the national courts; consequently, he can bring proceedings before the European Court under Article 288 [215].[173]

This situation must be contrasted with another situation, superficially similar but in fact very different, in which the right in question already exists by virtue of a previous measure, but is wrongfully withdrawn by a later measure. Here a remedy would normally exist in the national courts since the applicant could argue that the later measure is invalid and of no effect. A reference could be made to the European Court and, if it held this was the case, the earlier measure could be applied as being still in force.[174]

partly on the ground that the Community had had the use of the money during the period in question. The exporter then continued his action against the Commission in the European Court in order to obtain the interest. The European Court, however, held this claim inadmissible on the ground that it was ancillary to the claim for the repayment of the levy, a claim which was within the exclusive jurisdiction of the national courts.

165 *Unifrex v. Commission and Council*, Case 281/82, [1984] ECR 1969 (paras 1–13 of the judgment); *Krohn v. Commission*, Case 175/84, [1986] ECR 753 (paras 24–9 of the judgment); see also *De Boer Buizen v. Council and Commission*, Case 81/86, [1987] ECR 3677 (paras 9–10 of the judgment) (claim in tort).

166 Case 20/88, [1989] ECR 1553.

167 *Roquette v. French Customs*, Case 145/79, [1980] ECR 2917.

168 See paras 14–17 of the judgment.

169 See para. 9 of the judgment.

170 The Court nevertheless held that the ruling in the earlier case required it to dismiss the claim on the merits.

171 *Port*, Case C-68/95, [1996] ECR I-6065, para. 53 of the judgment.

172 See Chap. 13, above.

173 *Unifrex v. Commission and Council*, Case 281/82, [1984] ECR 1969 (above).

174 *IBC v. Commission*, Case 46/75, [1976] ECR 65.

## TORT

In an action in tort the applicant is claiming not a specific sum of money, but compensation for loss suffered. It now appears to be settled that if this is the true nature of his claim, he can proceed directly against the Community in the European Court.[175]

This is shown by *Dietz v. Commission*.[176] Dietz was a German firm which entered into a contract to export sugar to Italy. After the contract was made but before it was performed, a levy was introduced on imports into Italy. The result was that Dietz made a loss on the transaction, and it brought an action against the Community in the European Court on the ground that the sudden imposition of the charge was a violation of the principle of the protection of legitimate expectations.

It will be remembered that in the *CNTA* case, which had been decided a couple of years previously, the Court had ruled that a claim of this nature is possible.[177] As that case made clear, however, an applicant in Dietz's position cannot claim a full refund of the levy; all it can claim is the amount of any actual loss – not loss of profit – that it suffered. For this reason, Dietz's claim was not for a fixed sum but was a true tort action; consequently it was admissible.

The *Quellmehl* and *Gritz* cases establish this even more firmly. It will be remembered[178] that the essence of the claim was that subsidies had been withdrawn from quellmehl and gritz but not from starch. Since starch was in competition with quellmehl and gritz, this constituted discrimination. The Court, however, held that the quellmehl and gritz producers did not have a claim to the subsidy as such; all they were entitled to was compensation for the loss they had suffered (though on the facts of the case it came to the same thing). This, too, was a true tort action and was therefore admissible.

It should finally be emphasized that no question of Community liability can arise unless the harm suffered was caused by an act of the Community; if it was caused by the national authorities acting independently, the Community cannot be held responsible: concurrent liability arises only where the national authorities are acting as agents of the Community or on the instructions of a Community institution.

[175] In addition to the cases discussed in the text, see *Zuckerfabrik Bedburg v. Council and Commission*, Case 281/84, [1987] ECR 49 (paras 10–12 of the judgment); *Vreugdenhil v. Commission*, Case C-282/90, [1992] ECR I-1937 (paras 9–15 of the judgment). In *Assurances du Crédit v. Council and Commission*, Case C-63/89, [1991] ECR I-1799, Advocate General Tesauro argued that, even in the case of a tort action, proceedings cannot be brought in the European Court if the applicant could have obtained an adequate remedy in the national courts. This contention, which was not considered by the Court, is, however, contrary to the judgment in *Zuckerfabrik Bedburg*, which drew a clear distinction between tort actions and actions for sums due; it is also contrary to the judgment in *Vreugdenhil*, which drew a similar distinction.

[176] Case 126/76, [1977] ECR 2431.

[177] See above.

[178] See above.

## FURTHER READING

R JOLIET, *Le contentieux*, pp. 243–71.

DURAND, 'Restitution or Damages: National Court or European Court?' (1976) 1 ELRev. 431.

HARDING, 'The Choice of Court Problem in Cases of Non-Contractual Liability under EEC Law' (1979) 16 CMLRev. 389.

LEWIS, 'Joint and Several Liability of the European Communities and National Authorities' [1980] Current Legal Problems 99.

BARAV, 'La répétition de l'indu' [1981] CDE 507.

BRIDGE, 'Procedural Aspects of the Enforcement of European Community Law through the Legal Systems of the Member States' (1984) 9 ELRev. 28.

OLIVER, 'Enforcing Community Rights in the English Courts' (1987) 50 MLR 881.

HENRY G SCHERMERS, TON HEUKELS, AND PHILIP MEAD (EDS), *Non-Contractual Liability of the European Communities* (1988).

SCHOCKWEILER, 'Le régime de la responsabilité extra-contractuelle du fait d'actes juridiques dans la Communauté européenne' [1990] RTDE 27.

WILS, 'Concurrent Liability of the Community and a Member State' (1992) 17 ELRev. 191.

CAPELLI AND MIGLIAZZA, 'Recours en Indemnité et Protection des Intérêts Individuels: Quelles sont les Changements Possibles et Souhaitables?' [1995] CDE 585.

TON HEUKELS AND ALISON MCDONNELL (EDS), *The Action for Damages in Community Law* (1997).

TRIDIMAS, 'Liability for Breach of Community Law: Growing Up and Mellowing Down?' (2001) 38 CMLRev. 301 (pp. 321–32).

# BIBLIOGRAPHY

Only general works are listed here; specialized materials are found in the 'Further Reading' after each chapter.


G Bebr, *Development of Judicial Control of the European Communities* (1981).

L Neville Brown and Tom Kennedy, *The Court of Justice of the European Communities*, 5th edn (2000).

Lawrence Collins, *European Community Law in the United Kingdom*, 4th edn (1990); 5th edn (2000).

Paul Craig, *EU Administrative Law* (2006).

Sionaidh Douglas-Scott, *Constitutional Law of the European Union* (2002).

Walter van Gerven, *The European Union, A Polity of States and Peoples* (2005).

Trevor C Hartley, *Constitutional Problems of the European Union* (1999).

René Joliet, *Le droit institutionnel des Communautés européennes: Le contentieux* (1981).

René Joliet, *Le droit institutionnel des Communautés européennes: Les institutions; Les sources; Les rapports entre ordres juridiques* (1983).

PJG Kapteyn and P VerLoren van Themaat, *Introduction to the Law of the European Communities*, 3rd edn (by Laurence W Gormley, 1998).

RH Lauwaars, *Lawfulness and Legal Force of Community Decisions* (1973).

Henry G Schermers and Denis F Waelbroeck, *Judicial Protection in the European Communities*, 6th edn (2001).

AG Toth, *Legal Protection of Individuals in the European Communities* (1978).

Takis Tridimas, *The General Principles of EC Law*, 2nd edn (2006).

G Vandersanden and A Barav, *Contentieux Communautaire* (1977).

Angela Ward, *Judicial Review and the Rights of Private Parties in EU Law*, 2nd edn (2006).


*These books are cited by name of author alone.*

# INDEX